School of American Research
Advanced Seminar Series

DOUGLAS W. SCHWARTZ, GENERAL EDITOR

SCHOOL OF AMERICAN RESEARCH BOOKS

The Pottery of Santo Domingo Pueblo
KENNETH CHAPMAN

The Pottery of San Ildefonso Pueblo
KENNETH CHAPMAN

A Colony on the Move: Gaspar
Castaño de Sosa's Journal, 1590–1591
ALBERT H. SCHROEDER AND DAN S. MATSON

Reconstructing Prehistoric Pueblo Societies
EDITED BY WILLIAM A. LONGACRE

New Perspectives on the Pueblos
EDITED BY ALFONSO ORTIZ

Structure and Process in Latin America
EDITED BY ARNOLD STRICKON AND SIDNEY M. GREENFIELD

The Classic Maya Collapse
EDITED BY T. PATRICK CULBERT

Methods and Theories of Anthropological Genetics
EDITED BY M. H. CRAWFORD AND P. L. WORKMAN

Methods and Theories
of Anthropological Genetics

METHODS AND THEORIES OF ANTHROPOLOGICAL GENETICS

EDITED BY
M. H. CRAWFORD
AND
P. L. WORKMAN

A SCHOOL OF AMERICAN RESEARCH BOOK

UNIVERSITY OF NEW MEXICO PRESS · Albuquerque

This book is dedicated to Professor
C. C. Li, an inspiration to us all

Preface

Most of the papers in this volume were presented in a symposium entitled "Methods in Anthropological Genetics," held in Santa Fe, New Mexico, on February 24–28, 1971, at the School of American Research. The idea of the conference was formulated jointly by C. C. Li and M. H. Crawford. The local arrangements were made by Douglas Schwartz, director of the School of American Research.

The primary function of this conference was to assemble geneticists and anthropologists for a discussion of the methods and theories that arise from a common concern with the study of variation within and among human populations. The result of this conference was a sharper definition of the theoretical problem areas and an assessment of the available methods and techniques of investigation. The discussion also revealed that certain theoretical areas and approaches were not represented, nor was the coverage adequate. As a result, the editors solicited several papers to fill the more obvious gaps. They were contributed by Russell M. Reid; Henry Harpending and Trefor Jenkins; Jean W. Mac-Cluer; Nancy Howell; Kenneth Morgan; N. E. Morton, J. N. Hurd, and G. F. Little; N. E. Morton; Richard H. Ward; and Solomon H. Katz.

Two of the papers, which were presented at the conference but which do not appear in this volume, are: "Current Directions in Behavior Genetics" by Steven G. Vandenberg, to be published in *Current Anthropology*, and "Applications of Dental Genetic Traits in Population Studies" by Christy G. Turner II.

During the past decade, research in anthropological genetics has been stimulated by developments in methodology and theory. Progress in computer science and technology permits the design of programs for estimation and prediction based on complex models, demographic and genetic simulation, and record storage, linkage, and retrieval; serology now provides a large number of genetic markers that can be used to characterize the gene pool of a population and that have revealed the richness of genetic variability within and between populations. The theoretical developments in population genetics and demography have found empirical expression in many studies. For example, Morton and his associates have successfully applied Malécot's treatment of kinship and isolation by distance to the analyses of population structure. The organizers of this conference had hoped to bring these advances in theories and methods together with the ever increasing richness of the recently collected field data.

Considering the breadth of the field of anthropological genetics, there is no attempt in this book to be exhaustive or definitive. The selection of the participants and the solicitation of papers were based on what we considered to be the most important and interesting research areas, mediated by the availability and willingness of researchers to participate. Because of space limitations, we were unable to include a number of contributions that logically fit in the volume.

We acknowledge the support of the School of American Research for sponsoring the conference and the International Center of the University of Pittsburgh for defraying the cost of travel of several participants. We thank Douglas Schwartz and his staff for making this symposium memorable, and Amy Ferrara for her aid in the compilation of this book.

M. H. Crawford
P. L. Workman

Contents

xi

Figures

Tables

Tables

Tables

1

Anthropological Genetics: Problems and Pitfalls

D. F. ROBERTS

Department of Human Genetics
University of Newcastle upon Tyne

When Hooton revised *Up from the Ape* in the 1940s, he wrote, "Human genetics is a thinly cultivated field, sporadically scratched." At that time, he was able to quote only four blood groups and red/green color blindness as simply inherited characters of anthropological relevance. Hooton could not have foreseen the dramatic growth of activity that was imminent—the prompt harvest of the serological field, yielding more and more blood group systems; the vigor that would stem from the fertilization of human genetics by the slowly accumulated pollen of the general theory of population genetics; the great flowering of technical advance that was to display undreamed-of richness of genetic variability in man; and the computer revolution that was to provide the power for (1) the cultivation of models of genetic structure and (2) the evolution of populations of previously unattainable complexity. For physical anthropology, the outcome was a great stimulus by human genetics.

1

Nor has the advantage been all in one direction. Many human geneticists have been quick to appreciate the profitability of investigating exotic communities. Some have made use of genetic variation, for example, for the elucidation of mode of inheritance of a character (rare in the home population) through studies in others where it is more frequent (Barnicot, Garlick, and Roberts 1960). And, since mode or degree of inheritance cannot be established in the absence of adequate variation, others have examined the genetic basis of interpopulation variability for the increased understanding of a little-varying character in the home population (Harrison and Owen 1964). Some investigations have made use of environmental variation, for example, to examine the dynamics of a particular polymorphism, as in the classic case of the abnormal hemoglobins. Most such investigations have concentrated on specific problems. The relative few that have embraced the anthropological concept of biologically rounded investigations of particular populations have proved very worthwhile. For example, the South American Indian studies of Neel and his collaborators resulted in a demonstration of a new type of genetic structure, quite different from the various models previously proposed, and much more in keeping with the fission-fusion situation long known in anthropological work.

Such is the field of this chapter—the terrain shared by human genetics and physical anthropology, the exploration of whose fertile soil will continue to be both adventurous and profitable. At the simplest level of return, how little do we know of interpopulation variation in the gene frequencies of the more recently discovered isoenzyme systems! For example, at the time of writing, there are in the world literature only some 50 samples giving the gene frequencies for adenylate kinase variants in different peoples; some 55 samples giving the frequencies at the phosphoglucomutase locus one; some 50 giving frequencies for 6-phosphogluconate-dehydrogenase types; more than 60 for the gene frequencies of acid phosphatase. Yet our knowledge here is rich in contrast to the little yet available for the exciting complex HLA antigens. There is still much to be done here in delineating the distribution of gene frequency of these acquisitions to the armamentarium of population genetics.

But for some time now, human population genetics has delved more deeply. No longer is it satisfied with counting genes in populations. Instead, being aware of differences in gene frequency between peoples (largely on account of the pioneer anthropological syntheses of Boyd

[1939] and Mourant [1954]), human population genetics has endeavored to understand the processes responsible for these differences and the mechanisms by which the observed frequencies are maintained and regulated. This type of problem is intimately linked with the one just mentioned, for it is necessary to know of the existence of variation before seeking to explain it, and highly useful clues as to the advantage or disadvantage of particular genes are to be derived from the environmental similarities common to peoples of higher or lower gene frequency respectively. A great deal of attention has been given to human polymorphisms over the last 20 years; yet, for none can we say that their balance is fully explained, and for the majority, we have not the faintest concept of their biological significance. But this has been said many times before and has prompted inquiry by many people of widely different interests. This chapter will explore some contributions to genetic knowledge that can profitably, or perhaps only, be made by anthropological cooperation. It is a theme that has been previously illustrated with reference to the use of demographic data (Roberts 1965); here, the focus is slightly wider and centers on applications of the detail in which a good anthropologist knows the structure and changing composition of his population and how this can be turned to genetic advantage.

THE USE OF VARYING SOCIAL PATTERNS

It is remarkable how little use has been made of the varying social structures and breeding systems in man for the elucidation of genetic problems. There has been little besides investigation of consanguinity effects in a limited number of different societies, investigation perhaps most fully developed in the studies in Japan (Schull and Neel 1965). The first topic here illustrates how profitably these may be exploited in genetic work.

The immunoglobulins are currently the focus of intense activity; their categorization, their molecular structure, their function are becoming better known almost daily. The problem addressed in this investigation was the extent to which the level of immunoglobulins is under genetic control. (The results have been fully presented elsewhere [Billewicz et al. 1970]. For this study, the home population of Great Britain, buffered as it is by the hygienic and public health measures expected in a sophisticated community, would be of little value. Some type of loading was required to make sure that immunoglobulin production was maximal and persistent. Families of Mohammedan Mandinko living in two villages in The Gambia, West Africa, provided the material. Exposed as they are to the constant assault of endemic and epidemic infection, there is ample environmental stimulus to immunoglobulin production. The villages had been the subject of detailed observations over a number of years by the Medical Research Council unit of Fajara, full and accurate data exist on the family relationships of the villagers, and these have, in the past, been checked for consistency against various genetic systems. High levels of gamma globulin have been reported for other West African populations (Fudenberg 1963), and a first study of the immunoglobulins in the present communities (Rowe et al. 1968) showed high levels of IgG, A, and M in adults.

A series of surveys was made of the levels of IgG, A, M, and D; these were standardized to eliminate the difficulties due to short-period fluctuations, variation in age and sex (to overcome the different sex composition of families), and the form of the distribution of the levels themselves. The family analysis consisted of calculation of correlation and regression coefficients between pairs of individuals of different relationships.

At this level of analysis, the correlation coefficients between parents were very low, quite compatible with zero correlations. There were positive correlations between parents and offspring, all positive but low, mostly statistically significant, and between full sibs. These were such as to suggest moderate genetic influence on immunoglobulin levels, and these allowed estimates of the upper limits of heritability. From the full-sib correlations, maximum heritabilities for levels of IgG, A, M, and D were, respectively, 0.37, 0.61, 0.38, and 0.50. From the regressions of offspring on father, the heritabilities were also calculated as 0.42, 0.60, 0.28, and 0.50, respectively, quite similar to those from the full-sib correlations. One would be justified in concluding that for at least three of the immunoglobulins, there was moderate heritability.

A major problem in genetic work is to isolate the effect of environment in promoting similarities between relatives. For instance, sibs share a common environment, they may share common maternal influence, and there will be further similarity for any dominance that may occur. Hence, these heritabilities must be regarded as upper limits. But this is as far as most investigations of quantitatively varying characters in man

4

manage to go, that is, the calculation of heritability from covariances between first degree relatives.

So far, all there is to distinguish this study from any family investigation is the fact that the African population was chosen because of the loading to be expected from the nature of its environment. There is, however, a further feature of direct relevance to this analysis, namely, its breeding system. In this community, polygny, both concurrent and sequential, is common, so that there are many paternal half sibs (that is, children of the same father by different mothers). These are particularly useful because offspring tend to be fed and generally cared for by the mother, so children of the same paternal genetic contribution are reared in different family environments. It is therefore possible to partition the variance in the total offspring into three components: a component attributable to differences between the children of different men; a component representing differences between children of different mothers by the same father; and a component attributable to differences among children by one mother and father. In these circumstances, it is possible to make a more accurate estimate of the heritability, because there are different causal components to the covariances (Table 1). The variance

TABLE 1

COMPONENTS OF PHENOTYPIC VARIATION

Observational Component	Causal Components
Between fathers	$\frac{1}{4}V_A$
Between mothers, within fathers	$\frac{1}{4}V_A + \frac{1}{4}V_D + V_{EC}$
Within full sibships	$\frac{1}{2}V_A + \frac{3}{4}V_D + V_{EW}$
Total (V_P)	$V_A + V_D + V_{EC} + V_{EW}$

components are estimated on the assumption that nonadditive genetic variance is negligible in amount. V_P represents the total phenotypic variance, V_A the component due to additive gene effect, V_{EW} the environmental variance within full sibships, and V_{EC} the variation due to the common environment shared by relatives. Interpretation of these estimates, like those from intrafamilial correlations, requires caution, for they strictly apply only to the sample investigated, with its own environmental experience, and, of course, only if the assumptions underlying the genetic model are met.

What a difference in the result! For IgD, the major contribution to the

5

variance is environmental and the heritabilities very low, 0.08 instead of 0.50. Similarly, for IgA, the additive genetic component appears slightly negative, presumably from chance factors, which may be taken to indicate a low or zero value for the heritability, zero instead of 0.6. IgM shows a heritability of 0.33, quite similar to the estimates from the parent/child and sib/sib correlations, appreciable but still showing that environment makes the predominant contribution to the variance. For IgG, the environmental variance within sibships remains moderately high, and the complication of an apparent negative value of the component deriving from common familial environment presumably is the result of chance factors, but heritability is probably moderate. This analysis suggests that for some of the immunoglobulins, the sib/sib and parent/offspring correlations owe much to common environment, by which they are inflated.

Here then, by using the breeding system to be found in this population, the final analysis puts into perspective heritabilities calculated from the simple correlations. Taken alone, the latter suggest moderate heritabilities. In the light of our half-sib analysis, these correlations are shown to be partly due to environmental similarities within families, and only two immunoglobulins appear to be of low or moderate heritability, IgM and IgG, respectively. In IgA and IgD levels, heritability appears to be negligible. There are many other similarly varying quantitative characters in man, and for relatively few has there been any analysis of their genetic basis. Existing analyses have tended to be essentially in terms of first degree relatives in sophisticated communities. The present analysis draws attention to one of the possible pitfalls, namely, that such correlations may be artificially inflated by environmental similarities, and hence, an exaggerated additive genetic component to the variance may result. In man, we cannot set up experiments to investigate inheritance. But from the variety of social practices that exists in different human communities, we can surely pick out those likely to further illuminate our immediate problem.

THE USE OF LONG-TERM STUDIES

Despite the interest of physical anthropology in human evolution, there have been relatively few studies of secular change in genetic constitution of populations. Some cultures are like our knowledge of genes; in both, there is little time depth. There are, however, a number of communities in which it is possible to trace the detailed history over a period of time, and so detect major episodes of gene frequency change. It is perhaps because almost all genetic studies of exotic populations have been by cross-sectional samples at a particular point in time that it has not been possible to do more than speculate on the processes responsible for gene frequency change. But it is worth remembering that even by a series of cross-sectional surveys, it would be very difficult to identify the genetic effects of, say, an epidemic or a population reduction. Certainly, the investigator would have to be extremely fortunate. He would have to know the gene frequencies in the population immediately before, and immediately after, the event occurred. He would require foresight to know that the size of the population was about to change and hindsight to know that it had finished changing.

The same results can be demonstrated, however, if the genetic constitution of the population is specified in a way other than by the usual array of gene and genotype frequencies: namely, in terms of the probable contribution that each of the founding ancestors makes to the gene pool at any given moment of time, or, if the founders are not known, then of the members of the population at some earlier period in time. The genetic constitution of a population can be regarded as comprising a pack of probable ancestral contributions. They are, of course, a reflection of the relative fertilities, survival, and migration of the ancestors concerned and their descendants, if no other mechanism of gene frequency change has operated. Hence, the calculation of these contributions at a series of points in time, tracing their secular variation, shows how the genetic constitution of the population so defined varies over the period. Here, then, is a starting point for the analysis of the genetic effect of any particular event. The calculations are simple, but, of course, due account has to be taken of multiple lines of descent where the population is in any way inbred.

This procedure has been applied to the population of Tristan da Cunha, which during the years from 1816 to 1961 passed through two periods of drastic population reduction—true bottlenecks, the number of people dropping in the first from 103 to 33, and in the second from 106 to 59 (Figure 1).

Immediately before the first bottleneck, 20 ancestors had contributed genes, their respective probable contributions to the gene pool varying

7

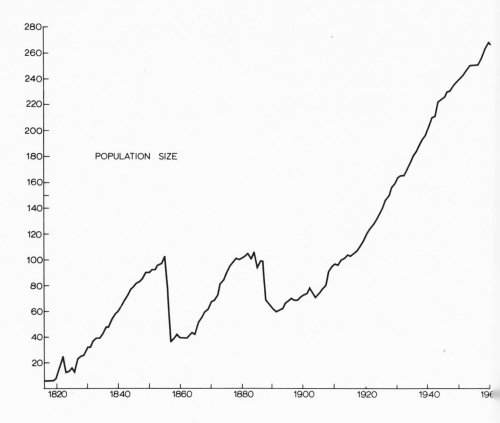

FIGURE 1. Population growth on Tristan da Cunha, 1816–1961.

from 0.005 to 0.137 (Figure 2); five individuals had contributed more than half the genes in the gene pool of the population at the end of 1855, the two greatest contributions being from the two original settlers (settlers 1 and 2). The effects of the bottleneck were twofold. A primary effect was the removal from the population of all the genes contributed by eight of its founder ancestors and a recent arrival, whose total contributions in 1855 had been more than one-third; genes from only 11 ancestors were to be found in the new gene pool. Second, there was a change in their relative contributions, as the genes from two of the principal contributors were among those that completely disappeared. The greatest contribution was now from ancestor 4 and the next three from ancestors 3, 9, and 10—the contributions from these individuals were each more

8

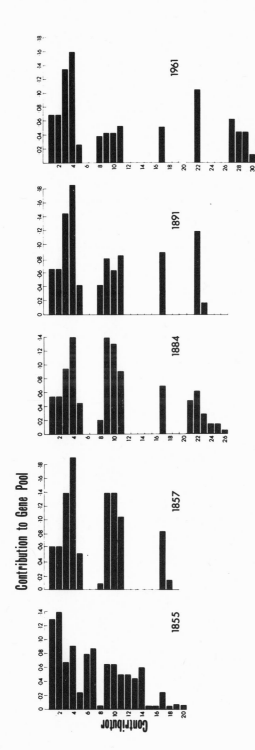

FIGURE 2. Ancestral contributions to the Tristan gene pool in 1855, 1857, 1884, 1891, and 1961.

than doubled, and between them, they now contributed 60 percent of the genes in the new population. The contributions of the first two settlers were halved, and that of a former minor contributor multiplied nearly threefold (ancestor 8).

In the phase of increase that followed this first reduction, the contribution of one further ancestor was lost, but new contributions to the island's gene pool came from six more arrivals. The relative contributions from the original ancestors correspondingly declined with the exception of one. By the end of 1884, the gene pool derived from 16 individuals. A boat disaster that initiated the next bottleneck had relatively little effect on the gene pool; the greatest changes were in the contribution of ancestor 22 (0.061 to 0.071) and of ancestors 1 and 2 (0.055 to 0.047), but many of the widows and offspring of the men who were drowned subsequently left the island, and this had a much more pronounced effect. In this phase of population reduction, again there was the loss of all the genes from several contributors, and again a rearrangement of the relative contributions of those remaining. The contributions completely lost (totaling some 8 percent) were from four relatively recent arrivals, so that the new gene pool derived from only 12 individuals. The greatest contribution was still that from ancestor 4, increasing from 0.139 to 0.186, the second largest from her husband, increasing from 0.109 to 0.144; those from two of the former principal contributors (ancestors 9 and 10) dropped to fifth and eighth places, respectively, from 0.138 to 0.081 and from 0.129 to 0.064.

In the period from 1891 to 1961 (the island was evacuated in 1961), all the genes from one earlier arrival had been lost, and eight new arrivals had contributed 22.4 percent of the gene pool, which thus derived from 19 ancestors. The principal changes were the diminution in the contributions of ancestors 9 and 17 by about half, but conspicuous are the great contributions made by two of the new arrivals (numbers 27 and 31), sixth and seventh in order of size. In 1961 as in 1891, the three greatest contributions were made by the same individuals. Indeed, there is a marked overall similarity between the figures for 1961 and those for 1891. This implies that apart from the contributions of the recent immigrants, the gene pool of the 1961 population derived its major features principally from the reduction in population that occurred in 1884–91, and the modification that occurred then acted on the gene pool whose features had been chiefly derived from the effects of the earlier exodus.

The genetic constitution defined as a pack of probable ancestral contributions is not, of course, the actual genetic constitution defined in terms of the array of gene frequencies, since it takes no account of (1) the random variation that occurs in the sampling process of transmitting gametes from one generation to the next, (2) nonrandom disturbances of segregation, or (3) differential mortality with respect to particular genes. But this difference itself is highly useful. Some genes can be traced back and the ancestor who introduced them identified. For example, there is no doubt that the Rhesus combination R' was introduced to Tristan by ancestor 29; out of 243 individuals whose blood groups were investigated by Mourant, only six heterozygotes showed this character instead of the number (10.6) expected on the basis of his contribution to the gene pool. Similarly, Harris et al. (1963) showed the C_5 serum cholinesterase phenotype to occur in 36 individuals out of 213 tested; all the pedigrees of these individuals converge on ancestor 4, and if the gene was introduced by only one ancestor, she was the person responsible. Her contribution to the 1961 population was 0.16, indicating an expected number of 34 heterozygote carriers in the population tested. There has been a slight loss of the R' combination and a slight gain of the C_5 gene, due perhaps to drift (gamete sampling), or perhaps to selection, other than through fertility.

The pack method has already been used to demonstrate the effect on genetic composition of population reduction (as here [Roberts 1968b]) and of differential fertility (Roberts 1968a). The latter analysis shows clearly that a succession of small changes through differential fertility may, accumulated, be responsible for pronounced changes in the genetic constitution—approximately 47 percent of the change in Tristan genetic constitution from 1827 to 1961 and considerably more in the stable periods. The pack concept has many other applications, still to be exploited. For instance, not only can the present genetic constitution of the population be specified, but also the relative contribution of each ancestor to any given individual in the present population. Therefore, one can estimate the contribution of each ancestor to variation in some quantitative character in the present population (for example, stature) by multiple regression analysis, and from this obtain an estimate of the number of genes responsible.

In these circumstances, it is worth looking more closely at the actual process of gene frequency change, which the pack method allows. As a

[handwritten margin note: does not consider selection]

result of our early acquaintance with the Hardy-Weinberg law (which, of course, only applies in an infinite population), we usually think of gene frequencies as being stable in a population. When we deal with finite populations, however, it is important to remember that gene frequency change perpetually occurs. Every time an individual dies, or moves away from or into the population or a new child is born, there is a slight re-adjustment of the gene frequencies. The complexity is illustrated quite clearly in the Tristan material (Figure 3). Obviously, if an individual in a population does not reproduce, his contribution to the gene pool will decline (for example, in Figure 3, G.P. 1827–36). However, once he starts to reproduce, there may occur a rapid rise in his contribution (for example, A.C. 1831–35). Whether this rise occurs—and if so, its extent and rapidity—depends on the rate at which his children are born, relative to the rate for other members of the community, either by their own reproduction or by immigration (compare A.C. 1831–35 with R.R. 1830–37). As the births of an individual's children become less frequent, decline occurs as the breeding of other members of the community increases their contributions (for example, W.G. 1834–47); thus, an [ancestor's contribution is cyclical in form. When emigration or death of an offspring occurs, that decline may become serious (for example, W.G. from 1847 onward). But if the ancestor's offspring themselves then begin to breed, his contribution may initiate a new cycle of increase, may maintain a plateau, or may continue to decline.] For this first, the reproduction of the offspring must be concentrated and rapid; if, because of their age differences, their initiation of reproduction is extended over a period, or the span of their children's arrival is very spread out, then the second or third is more likely. But differential fertility is not the only factor, as the initial period on Tristan shows. It is because M.L. had 16 children that her contribution amounted to one-seventh of the total gene pool in 1855; it is because T. R. fathered only one child that his contribution was only 0.5 percent. But if it were purely a matter of differential fertility, then one would expect the contribution of S.W., who contributed 13 offspring, to approach $13/16$ of M.L., who had 16 children, but instead the ratio is only $13/20$. One would expect A.C., who had 12 children, to have made some three-fourths of the contribution of W.G., who had 16 children, but instead the proportion is only half. Clearly, there are other factors to be considered.

From the ancestral contribution at the end of each year can be calcu-

depending on success of descendants

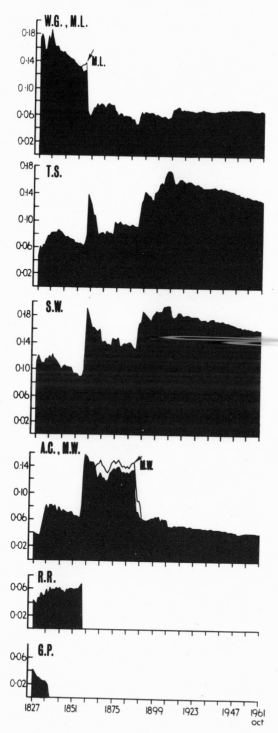

FIGURE 3. Contributions of 10 ancestors to the gene pool of the population at December 31 of each year, 1827–1960.

lated the year-to-year change in contribution (Figure 4). First, these data show that during the reproductive period, years of increment and years of slight decrement interdigitate, and then with the termination of their own reproduction, there follows a succession of years in which decrement preponderates, demonstrating the cyclical effect. Second, the magnitude of the annual change tends to diminish with the passage of time, and this suggests an effect of increase in population size. When the year-to-year change in contribution per ancestor is averaged regardless of sign, and this mean magnitude is plotted against the size of the population at the end of each year, there appears a strong curvilinear relationship (Figure 5). The same amount of reproductive effort has a greater effect on the gene pool in a small population than on a large one, and hence so does variation in reproductive effort; thus, population size has to be considered when discussing the genetic effects of differential fertility. Similarly, the magnitude of the change of the earliest reproducers tends to be greater than those in the corresponding phase of reproduction for the later reproducers; the first child of T.S., born in 1828, produced an increment in his contribution of 0.017, and that of G.L., born in 1895, 0.007, so the secular position in the population of each ancestor is of importance. Although this effect is related to population size, it is not entirely determined by it, for the final contribution of those who reproduced earlier tended to be greater, since their genes were passed on more rapidly by their children.

Envisaging the genetic constitution of the population as a pack of probable ancestral contributions instead of the usual array of gene and genotype frequencies allows the greater part of secular change in genetic constitution to be traced; thus, it is a useful tool for elucidating the effects of evolutionary processes. Genetic constitution is seen to be far from constant. Instead, the contributions of individual ancestors are seen, as it were, constantly jockeying for position, sometimes one in the lead, sometimes another. This effect is especially strong in small populations. These results are particularly important for their implications. First, they show that random unique events, which are almost completely indeterminate statistically and are therefore not adequately covered in any models so far applied, can be quantified and shown to have appreciable effect on genetic constitution. Second, they show that factors such as population size and rate of reproduction have to be taken into account when considering simple measurements of differential fertility. Third,

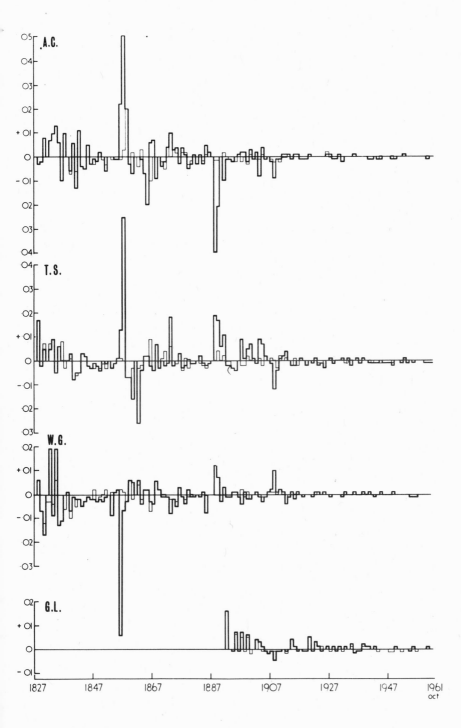

FIGURE 4. Year-to-year change in contribution to the gene pool.

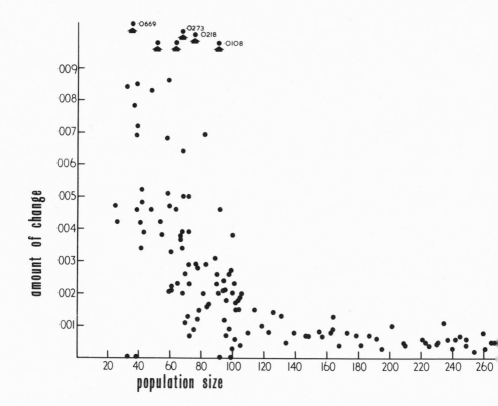

FIGURE 5. Relation between mean year-to-year change in ancestral contribution and population size.

they show that some caution needs to be exercised in the inter-pretation of changes in gene frequency that may be observed between successive cross-sectional studies.

CONCLUSION

The use of varying social patterns and the use of long-term studies have shown how, in anthropological genetics, anthropological detail of popu-

16

lations can be applied to resolve fundamental genetic problems and to avoid unsuspected pitfalls. There are, of course, many other investigations in which cooperation will be mutually profitable, ranging in complexity from simple gene frequency surveys to the formulation of genetic problems, for example, of peoples of ecological extremes. Rarely in the history of any discipline has there been a time of such opportunity as presently exists in our own.

The Use of Genetic Markers of the Blood in the Study of the Evolution of Human Populations

MICHAEL H. CRAWFORD

Department of Anthropology
University of Kansas

Since Landsteiner's discovery in 1900 of the ABO blood group system in man, there has been a rapid proliferation of new genetic markers[1] for use in population studies. At present, nearly 50 polymorphic gene systems with more than 140 common alleles, or chromosomal segments—each with a populational frequency greater than, or equal to, 0.01—have been discovered by the examination of human blood. These marker genes and their dates of discovery are summarized in Table 2.

The discussion in this chapter will be restricted to genetic markers of the blood that are available for population studies, and will describe their use in interpretations of evolutionary theory and the analyses of phylogenetic relations between populations. The question of how these genetic polymorphisms may be maintained will not be dealt with here. (See Chapter 3 for a discussion of several explanatory models.) The purpose of this chapter is (1) to review the technical and methodological innovations that have enabled the use of an increased number of genetic

TABLE 2
POLYMORPHIC LOCI OF HUMAN BLOOD

Genetic Marker System	Year of Discovery	Common Alleles
A. Blood groups		
1. ABO	1900	I^A, I^O, I^B
A_1A_2 subdivision	1911	I^{A1}, I^{A2}
2. MN	1927	L^M, L^N
MNS subdivision	1947	Ms, MS, Ns, NS
Uu	1953	U, u
3. P	1927	P_1, P_2
4. Rh	1940	$CDE, cde, CDe, cDE,$ C^WDe, Cde, cDe
5. Lutheran	1945	Lu^a, Lu^b
6. Lewis	1946	Le^a, Le^b
7. Kell	1946	K, k
Kp subdivision	1956	Kp^a, Kp^b
Sutter subdivision	1959	Js^a, Js^b
8. Duffy	1950	Fy^a, Fy^b, Fy
9. Kidd	1951	Jk^a, Jk^b
10. Vel	1952	Ve^a, Ve^b
11. Diego	1955	Di^a, Di^b
12. Cartwright	1956	Yt^a, Yt^b
13. Auberger	1961	Au, Au^a
14. Xg	1962	Xg, Xg^a
15. Dombrock	1965	Do^a, Do
16. Stoltzfus	1969	Sf^a, Sf
B. Red cell proteins		
1. Hemoglobin	1947	$Hb^A, Hb^S, Hb^C, Hb^D, Hb^E$
Thalassemia		T, t^t, t^o
2. Glucose-6-phosphate dehydrogenase (G6PD)		
Deficiency	1958	$Gd+, Gd-$
Structural	1962	Gd^A, Gd^B
3. Acetyl transferase	1958	Ac^S, Ac
4. Acid phosphatase	1963	P^a, P^b, P^c
5. 6-phosphogluconate dehydrogenase (6PGD)		
	1963	PGD^A, PGD^C
6. Phosphoglucomutase (PGM)	1964	$PGM_1{}^1, PGM_1{}^2$
7. Adenylate kinase	1966	AK^1, AK^2
8. Adenosine diaminase	1968	ADA^1, ADA^2
9. Phosphoglycerate kinase (PGK)	1970	PgK^1, PgK^2
10. Peptidase C	1970	$Pep\ C^1, C^2, C^0$
11. Glutamic—pyruvic transaminase	1971	Gpt^1, Gpt^2

TABLE 2, cont'd.

Genetic Marker System	Year of Discovery	Common Alleles
C. Serum proteins		
1. Haptoglobins	1955	Hp^1, Hp^2
Subdivision of Hp^1	1962	Hp^{1s}, Hp^{1f}
2. Gm groups	1956	1, 5, 13, 14;
		1, 5, 6, 14;
		1, 5, 6; 1, 13;
		1; 1, 5, 14; 1, 5;
		3, 5, 13, 14;
		1, 3, 5, 13, 14; 1, 2
3. Transferrins	1957	Tf^B, Tf^C, Tf^D
4. Pseudocholinesterase (E_1)	1957	$E_1{}^u, E_1{}^s, E_1{}^A, E_1{}^F$
(E_2)	1963	E_2+, E_2-
5. Albumin	1959	AL^A, AL^M
6. Group specific (G_c)	1959	Gc^1, Gc^2
7. Inv groups	1961	$Inv^1, Inv^{1,2}, Inv^3$
8. Beta lipoprotein allotypes	1961	Ag^x, Ag^y
Lp system	1963	Lp^a, Lp
9. Placental alkaline		
phosphatase	1961	PL^F, PL^S
10. Xm group	1966	Xm^a, Xm
D. White cells and platelets		
1. Ko platelet groups	1962	Ko^a, Ko^b
2. Zw platelet groups	1963	Zw^a, Zw^b
3. HLA		
LA series	1964	HL-A1, A2, A3, A9
		3002Q
4 series	1961	HL-A12, 4C, A7, A8

markers for population studies, (2) to indicate the extent of known genetic variability in man, (3) to examine the uses and limitations of data on gene frequency distributions, and (4) to suggest possible means by which marker genes may be used for future populational studies in genetics and physical anthropology.

METHODOLOGICAL INNOVATIONS

A number of methodological breakthroughs have contributed to the abundance of genetic markers presently available for use in the study of microevolution in human populations. The following are among the most significant recent developments.

(1) Zone electrophoresis permits the separation of proteins on the basis of molecular size, configuration, and charge. This teechnique has been applied primarily to the detection of genetic variants of red cell or serum proteins in human populations. Although electrophoresis has serious limitations (for example, in failing to distinguish the three types of hemoglobin that possess the same electrophoretic mobility as hemoglobin D), it is a valuable screening device for certain protein variants and has led to the recognition of a large number of polymorphic loci. It was this method that led to the recognition of sickle-cell anemia as a hemoglobinopathy resulting from a structural alteration.

(2) Some of the limitations of zone electrophoresis have been overcome by the development of chromatographic techniques and amino acid analysis. Used in conjunction with electrophoresis, these techniques permit the recognition of structural differences between proteins possessing similar or identical electrophoretic patterns. For example, several hemoglobins, on the basis of their electrophoretic patterns, were initially classified as hemoglobin D. However, amino acid analyses revealed that these hemoglobins differed structurally and resulted in their reclassification as $D\alpha$, $D\beta$, and $D\gamma$. These techniques are also sufficiently refined to establish that some proteins, formerly assumed to be different because of the distance of the populations in which they were found, are in fact identical. For example, two transferrin variants with similar electrophoretic patterns, Tf, D_1, one discovered in an Australian aborigine and the second found in an American Black, were regarded as different because of the geographic (and presumed genetic) distance between the two individuals. However, a comparison by enzyme digestion, followed by paper electrophoresis, chromatography, and amino acid analysis, suggested that the two variants were identical in structure as well as in mobility (Wang, Sutton, and Scott 1967). These findings have raised the question of the origin of the allele. Did the two variants result from two independent mutations, or are they the result of the common ancestry of Australian and African populations?

(3) Improvements in the methods of transport and storage of human blood have permitted the genetic description of geographically remote and isolated populations. Most striking among these is the use of liquid nitrogen for the storage of red blood cells for a number of years, with little loss of enzyme activity. It is now possible to store blood samples from several populations in liquid nitrogen tanks and to retrieve and analyze

the specimens whenever a new genetic polymorphism or variant is discovered. Thus, the investigator has access to a number of populations, from different geographical areas, in the laboratory. Although the preparation of the red blood cells for storage in liquid nitrogen is much more time-consuming and costly, this procedure is vastly superior to the citrated glycerol method of storing red blood cells. Storage in citrated glycerol results in considerable loss of enzyme activity, and a high percentage of erythrocytes are lost during the saline washing phase of cellular retrieval.

(4) Within the last decade, several rapid biochemical screening procedures have been developed for use in the field when dealing with blood enzymes that are unstable and subject to a rapid loss of activity or denaturation during prolonged periods in transit. The low cost and technical simplicity of these screening procedures are important considerations when compared with the logistics of shipping blood specimens in tanks of liquid nitrogen.

One of the most commonly used screening tests was developed by Motulsky and Campbell-Kraut (1960) for determining the presence of G6PD deficiency in red blood cells. This method is based on the decolorization of a brilliant cresyl blue dye in a prescribed period of time. It is sufficiently sensitive to reveal females who are heterozygous for the enzyme deficiency. This method does not require elaborate equipment and therefore can be used in the field for rapid identification of individuals who are G6PD deficient. Another factor in favor of such screening procedures is the small quantity of blood required, thus eliminating the need for venipuncture.

(5) Developments in computer technology have facilitated estimations of gene and chromosomal segment frequencies in loci with multiple alleles or segments. Maximum likelihood (ML) estimation computer programs, initially written by Balakrishnan and Sanghvi (1965), Kurczynski and Steinberg (1967), MacCluer et al. (1967), and Reed and Schull (1968), provide more accurate estimation of the *Rh* and *MNS* chromosomal segment frequencies in population studies. The computer program of Reed and Schull makes no prior assumptions concerning the presence or absence of alleles, or chromosomal segments, in contrast to the commonly employed method of Mourant (1954). Mourant's method assumes, in the absence of an appropriate indicator phenotype, that a particular gene is not present in the population. Gershowitz et al. (1970) compare the *Rh* gene frequencies for three Makiritare villages using five

different methods of estimating allelic frequencies, and only the eight-gene computer program of Reed and Schull assigns a frequency to the $r(cDe)$ gene. However, the other methods of calculation of the Rh gene frequencies (Mourant 1954; Schull's four-gene maximum likelihood program; Layrisse, Layrisse, and Wilbert 1963; and a gene counting method using pedigree analysis) are in much closer agreement with each other than with the method of Schull and Reed. These findings present a dilemma: "Which genes and which frequencies shall be accepted as a proper description of the population?" (Gershowitz et al. 1970). Basically, this question contrasts the goodness-of-fit of the observed phenotypic frequencies with those predicted by the derived gene frequencies. Although both approaches are adequate, the Reed and Schull method may be better, because it makes no assumptions about the presence or absence of any of the eight alleles theoretically possible and detectable with the five major Rh antisera commercially available. However, this theoretical question is probably of little relevance to field studies, because the differences between the various estimates are probably much less than the sampling error resulting from nonrandom selection of a sample population.

GENETIC VARIATION IN HUMAN POPULATIONS

On the basis of the number of the so-called private alleles, Lewontin (1967) has estimated that the proportion of polymorphic loci in man is 30 percent. This is probably an overestimate, since in the future, it may be shown that a great proportion of loci are familial (that is, less than 2 percent of the members of a population will be heterozygous for a given gene, a necessary prerequisite for classification as a polymorphism). However, this approximation was further supported by Harris (1966) who "randomly" selected 10 red cell enzyme loci and found that three of these loci maintained variants at polymorphic levels. Assuming that man has at least 120,000 loci encoding for protein structure (a conservative estimate made by Neel and Schull [1968] assumed the existence of 100,000), and further assuming that one locus controls the synthesis of one polypeptide chain and that an "average" protein possesses four polypeptide chains, man may possess up to 30,000 proteins, of which 10,000 would be structurally polymorphic. Those few polymorphic loci presently known provide only a small indication of the spectacular human diversity that must have been etched on the genome of man through time.

The proliferation of genetic markers in the last two decades has revealed great phenotypic variability both within and between populations. Giblett (1969) applied Race and Sanger's (1962) method of paternity exclusion to 17 genetic markers and showed that in western Europe or in the White portion of the United States population, less than one in 350,000 people would be expected to have the same combination of phenotypes. By considering not just 17 genetic markers, but 10,000, it is possible to account for all of the molecular genetic individuality of the ? hominids in existence for the last million years.

In a recent review article, Neel and Schull (1968:566) state that genetic polymorphisms "have now reached such numbers and new ones are being recognized at such a rate, that the understanding of the significance is unquestionably a focal problem in modern biomedicine." With this realization comes the necessity to explain how and why this genetic variation is maintained in human populations. As a result, it is not surprising to find that much of the research in physical anthropology and human genetics is presently directed to the elucidation of these questions. In the last decade, there has been much activity in the study of genetic markers and their frequencies in human populations, because the markers permit the description and quantification of the degree of genetic variation in a population. For analytical purposes, this variation can be viewed either on the intrapopulational or the interpopulational level, although these levels are interrelated.

INTRAPOPULATIONAL VARIATION

Populations are often divided into various subunits, such as bands, hordes, or villages. These may be either endogamous or exogamous, the latter being part of larger social units such as tribes, communities, or nations, which are usually the units of genetic analysis, or Mendelian populations, and are inclusive in terms of mate selection.

In several studies, new genetic markers have been used to study intrapopulation variability in man. Salzano (1968) compared the intratribal genetic variability of the Caingang and the Xavante Indians of Brazil with the intertribal variation among the South American Indians. Sixteen genetic markers were used for a comparison of seven Caingang settlements and three Xavante bands. Salzano found that the range of gene frequencies observed among the Caingang was larger than the range observed among the Xavante groupings (see Figure 6 and Table 3). Caution, however, must be exercised in interpreting these data, because of the disparity of sample numbers and the varying sizes of the subpopulations. The observed ranges of gene frequencies for six markers did not show overlapping ranges, suggesting that the two tribes can be distinguished genetically.

Moreover, there is great difficulty in interpreting results of genetic studies in terms of the demographic or social structure of a population. Workman and Niswander (1970) applied Wright's F statistics to the gene frequencies of the 10 subdivisions (districts) of the Papago Indian tribe of the southwestern United States. The degree of heterogeneity among the districts was expressed by means of one of the F statistics, F_{ST}, which is based on the ratio of the actual variance in gene frequencies among the groups to the product of the weighted mean gene frequencies. Thus, $F_{ST} = \sigma^2 p / (\bar{p}\bar{q})$, where $(\bar{p}\bar{q})$ are the weighted means and $\sigma^2 p$ is the variance of the gene frequencies.

A comparison of the degree of heterogeneity between the Papago and the Yanomama (of Venezuela) revealed that Yanomama villages were more heterogeneous genetically than the Papago districts. The comparison is based on the F ratio, made up of the sum of the χ^2 ($\Sigma\chi^2$) of the F_{ST} values for each of the bands. Further comparisons of the Papago with the Xavante and the Caingang Indians revealed that the Papago districts have significantly greater heterogeneity than either the Caingang or the Xavante. The F ratios permit comparisons of the degrees of differentiation of the subpopulations within a Mendelian population, as Workman and Niswander (1970:47) conclude: "These studies also show that demonstration of significant intra-population heterogeneity indicates nothing about the real structure of a population, past or present."

INTERPOPULATIONAL VARIATION

The evidence provided by marker genes of the high degree of interpopulational variability in man has raised more questions than it has answered. Salzano's (1968) compilation of the gene frequency distribu-

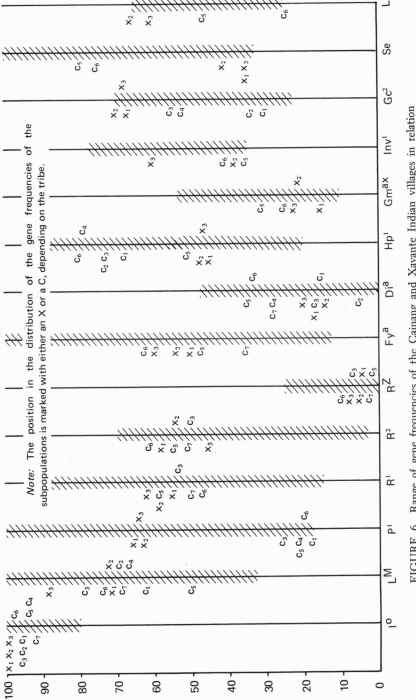

Note: The position in the distribution of the gene frequencies of the subpopulations is marked with either an X or a C, depending on the tribe.

FIGURE 6. Range of gene frequencies of the Cainang and Xavante Indian villages in relation to 14 genetic markers in South American Indians (the histograms). Source: F. M. Salzano, "Intra- and Inter-Tribal Genetic Variability in South American Indians," *American Journal of Physical Anthropology* 28 (1968): 183–90. Reprinted by permission.

TABLE 3

A COMPARISON OF THE GENETIC VARIABILITY FOUND IN FOUR AMERICAN INDIAN POPULATIONS WITH THE AVAILABLE GENE DISTRIBUTION OF THE SOUTH AMERICAN INDIANS

Alleles	Range of Gene Freq., 5 Caingang Communities*	Max. Deviation	Range of Gene Freq., 3 Xavante Communities*	Max. Deviation	Range of Gene Freq., 7 Makiritare Villages†	Max. Deviation	Range of Gene Freq., 10 Papago Districts‡	Max. Deviation	Range of Gene Freq., South American Indians*	Max. Deviation
I^o	0.93–1.00	0.07	1.00	0.00	1.00	0.00	0.86–1.00	0.14	0.80–1.00	0.20
L^M	0.50–0.78	0.28	0.71–0.87	0.16	—	—	—	—	0.32–1.00	0.68
P_1	0.16–0.27	0.11	0.63–0.66	0.03	0.30–0.52	0.22	0.37–0.59	0.22	0.16–1.00	0.84
R^1	0.47–0.57	0.10	0.54–0.62	0.08	0.27–0.44	0.17	0.54–0.71	0.17	0.12–0.96	0.84
R^2	0.28–0.40	0.12	0.24–0.39	0.15	0.47–0.62	0.15	0.27–0.40	0.13	0.02–0.73	0.71
R^z	0.00–0.10	0.10	0.03–0.08	0.05	0.00–0.10	0.10	0.00–0.04	0.04	0.00–0.25	0.25
Fy^a	0.36–0.63	0.27	0.50–0.59	0.09	0.64–0.80	0.16	0.76–1.00	0.24	0.13–1.00	0.87
Di^a	0.07–0.36	0.29	0.15–0.20	0.05	0.02–0.52	0.50	0.01–0.12	0.11	0.00–0.48	0.48
Hp^1	0.52–0.79	0.27	0.46–0.48	0.02	0.24–0.65	0.41	0.34–0.58	0.24	0.20–0.89	0.69
Gm^{ax}	0.26–0.32	0.06	0.16–0.23	0.07	—	—	—	—	0.10–0.54	0.44
Inv^1	0.33–0.40	0.07	0.37–0.63	0.26	—	—	—	—	0.33–0.76	0.43
Gc^2	0.28–0.56	0.28	0.67–0.70	0.03	0.11–0.36	0.25	0.09–0.27	0.17	0.22–0.70	0.48
Se	0.73–0.81	0.08	0.34–0.42	0.08	1.00	0.00	—	—	0.34–1.00	0.66
L	0.25–0.47	0.22	0.61–0.67	0.06	—	—	—	—	0.25–0.67	0.42

* Salzano (1968).

† Gershowitz et al. (1970) and Arends et al. (1970).

‡ Workman and Niswander (1970).

tions among aboriginal populations of South America demonstrates the existence of a high level of genetic variation between historically related human populations. The range of gene frequencies of South American Indians varies markedly from one locus to another. For example, the Duffy allele, Fy^a, has a range of 0.87 (gene frequencies of from 0.13 to 1.00 have been reported in various populations), while the I^o allele exhibits a range of 0.20, with a distribution of 0.80 to 1.00. Why do the frequencies of certain alleles vary only within narrow ranges, although the populations are widely dispersed, while those of other genetic loci, even in subdivisions of the same population, vary within broader ranges? There is no simple answer to this question. One must take into account the history of the population, many social and ecological factors, and the demographic structure, any or all of which may provide clues as to the relative actions of the forces of evolution. It is no longer acceptable to explain gene frequency differences, within or between populations, strictly on the basis of a single force of evolution, such as genetic drift; the exception is if the action of natural selection or gene flow can be shown to be minimal or unlikely through historical evidence or some peculiarity of the social structure or population size. All too often, investigators attribute genetic differentiation of populations to specific causes without adequate data. This is, to some extent, an artifact of the genetic models that were formulated with many assumptions and unfounded simplifications, and that only rarely considered the simultaneous action of more than one possible source of evolutionary change. However, the observable gene frequencies in human populations are the products of all the forces of evolution, acting not one at a time but simultaneously.

ANTHROPOLOGICAL USE OF GENE MARKERS

One of the major theoretical preoccupations of physical anthropologists in the 1930s and 1940s was the definition and classification of the races of man. Hooton (1946:448) defined *race* as "a great division of mankind, the members of which, though individually varying, are characterized as a group by a certain combination of morphological and metric features, principally non-adaptive,[2] which have been derived from their common descent." Racial classifications were based on various morphological criteria that were considered nonadaptive, and, therefore, similarities in these traits between populations denoted biological relationships. Thus, racial history, according to the early physical anthropologists, could be traced on a worldwide basis. The early students of race assumed they knew what characteristics of man were nonadaptive.

In the late 1940s and early 1950s, the so-called nonadaptive traits were being examined with suspicion. For example, Boyd (1952:18–19) stated, "it is doubtful if any hereditary characters are completely non-adaptive, and . . . probably we can deal only with different degrees of adaptive value." Hooton (1946), however, altered his opinion about the existence of nonadaptive traits in the second edition of his book: "the use of nonadaptive characters in human taxonomy now seems to me impractical and erroneous."

In the United States, with the demise of racial classification based on morphological, nonadaptive traits, came the use of blood group data for the same purposes. Boyd (1952:27), while discrediting morphologically based racial taxonomy, equivocally substituted blood groups in its place: "Among the racial characters which we would be tempted to pick out at the present time as non-adaptive, there are certain serological features of the blood, such as the genes O, A, B, M, N, etc."

Anthropologists in the 1940s, 1950s, and even into the late 1960s continued to classify races of the world, using allelic frequency distributions instead of the cephalic index or the bizygomatic breadth. Greater emphasis was placed on the process of racial differentiation than on the classification and taxonomy of man. Garn (1961) distinguished between three different kinds of races—geographical, local, and microraces—and thus "modernized" the age-old concept. However, even with these new frills and the acknowledgment of a genetic approach, Garn still attempted to define nine specific geographical races in his book.

Most anthropologists today prefer a genetic definition of *races* as "populations which differ in the frequency of some genes" (Livingstone 1964b); classification has, for the most part, ceased. Livingstone commented that the concept of race seemed to him to be of no use in describing or explaining human genetic variability, which is the central problem of physical anthropology today. It is for this reason that reference was made earlier only to intrapopulational and interpopulational variability, without invoking race or racial categories.

During the late 1950s and early 1960s, several scholars (Oschinsky

1959, Bielicki 1962, Wiercinski 1962) became highly critical of the use of the so-called genetical methods for the formulation of racial classification and for tracing phylogenetic relationships between populations. What initially appeared to be the panacea for racial classification in a mathematically precise manner later became bogged down in the contradictory and inconsistent schemes based on gene frequencies. Bielicki and Wiercinski advocated the return to conventional morphological and anthropometric criteria for racial classifications. Boyd (1963), in defense of the genetic method, reviewed what he considered its four most important contributions to anthropological theory. These contributions concerned theories of the ethnogenesis of the Gypsies, Lapps, American Blacks, and Pygmies of Equatorial Africa, and using these four groups, Boyd showed that some ethnologically derived theories may be tested biologically. Although most investigators shy away from tracing the ethnogenesis of various populations and races across the maps, cautious tests of possible relationships between populations with some suspected historical connections are possible through the use of marker gene distribution. The presence or absence of certain alleles may permit the testing of various ethnographic, linguistic, historical, and evolutionary hypotheses. For example, because of the linguistic similarities between the language of the Gypsies and Sanskrit, and because of the oral tradition of the Gypsies (which traces their origins to India), the ethnogenesis of these itinerants has been periodically questioned by various anthropologists. The blood group frequencies support the Gypsies' own claim of an Indian origin, at least for the Hungarian Gypsies (Boyd).

However, not all of the Gypsy populations are related to the Indian populations. The Irish itinerant populations (Tinkers)—sometimes referred to as Irish Gypsies—are genetically unrelated to the Romany Gypsies of the European mainland. The Irish itinerants are culturally distinct from the Irish people, speaking a language (Gammon) unintelligible to the Irish and moving about the countryside in caravans consisting of their nuclear or extended families.

A recent study (Crawford and Leyshon 1971) has shown that on the basis of 17 genetic loci, the Tinkers are more similar genetically to the Irish controls than they are to any of the Gypsy or Indian populations (Table 4). There are some differences between control and Tinker gene frequencies in the Lewis and Duffy systems, but these differences may be due to inbreeding or to sampling error. Even so, the frequencies peculiar

TABLE 4

A COMPARISON OF SOME BLOOD GROUP FREQUENCIES
BETWEEN AN IRISH CONTROL POPULATION,
AN INDIAN POPULATION, AND ·THE IRISH TINKERS

Blood Group	Alleles	Irish Controls (N = 97)	Indian Population* (N = 1168)	Irish Tinkers (N = 119)
ABO	A	0.1878	0.2244	0.2010
	B	0.1208	0.2183	0.1208
	O	0.6811	0.5573	0.6859
P	P	0.7216	0.32–0.50	0.7983
	p	0.2783	0.49–0.68	0.2016
MN	M	0.5979	0.6917	0.5466
	N	0.4020	0.3083	0.4533
Duffy	Fy^a+	0.4258	0.2886	0.3519
	Fy^a-	0.5742	0.7114	0.6481

* Mourant (1954).

to the Tinkers are much closer to those of the Irish than to the Indian populations.

Allelic frequencies can be utilized to estimate the degree of admixture and gene flow between populations. The study of Glass and Li (1953) of the American Blacks applied Bernstein's (1931) method to the frequencies of seven marker genes (R_o, R_1, T, r, B, A, and R_2) to estimate the amount of gene flow from the Caucasion population into the West African slave gene pool. This crude method of estimation revealed that approximately 30 percent of the American Black gene pool was of Caucasian origin. In the last decade, various estimates of the genetic makeup of the American Black populations have been made using more refined techniques. Both the estimates and the techniques are discussed by P. L. Workman in Chapter 6 of this book.

Most recently, Crawford, McClean, and Workman (1971) have attempted to reconstruct the amount of genetic admixture in Tlaxcala, Mexico, using the inhabitants of a Mestizo town (Tlaxcala) as the hybridized population and those of an Indian town (San Pablo), in the valley, as representative of one of the parental populations. Spanish gene frequencies were obtained from the literature for 23 different loci and are assumed to represent the second parental population. One of the investigators performed multiple regression analyses using three alternative models of the base populations for the Tlaxcala Mestizo. The first computer runs were based on San Pablo, representing the Indian parental population, and the European component was based on data from the largest available sample from Spain, or from other western European populations if the data from Spain could not be obtained. This method gives the composition of the Mestizo gene pool as 31.4 percent Spanish in origin with a standard deviation of 3.4 percent and a standard error of the slope of the regression line of 29.7.

Recognizing that the present population of San Pablo may imperfectly represent the Indian gene pool, a second run using estimated mean Nahua Indian gene frequencies for 16 loci and data from eight populations, including the San Pablo sample, was made. When the mean Nahua values were run in multiple regression, the estimate of the Mestizo composition was unchanged (31.6 percent of the gene pool was of Spanish origin), but the standard deviation more than doubled (to 7.0), and the standard error of the regression line increased to 53.5.

Because of the presence of the Rh_o factor (*cDe* chromosome segment present at a frequency of 0.09263 ± 0.0177) in the Mestizo population, suggestive of African admixture, a West African parental component was added for a triracial estimate of the Mestizo gene pool. In this model, the estimated contribution of West African genes is small (6.7 percent), with a standard deviation of 1.0, and appears to replace part of the Spanish component without affecting the estimated proportion of Indian genes. The estimate of Spanish contribution to the Mestizo gene pool decreases from 31.4 to 22.9 in the triracial fitting of the curve. The degree of fit is no better with a triracial estimate than that calculated for Spanish-Indian admixture alone. The diminution of the Spanish component as a result of the West African gene frequencies, together with demographic and historical documentation, is suggestive of an introduction of the African genes into the Mestizo gene pool through the Moorish elements in the Spanish army. It may be that this genetic survey has picked up African genes segregating in the Mestizo gene pool that were introduced into Europe through the Moorish invasion many centuries ago.

Although early writers such as Haddon (1925) and Deniker (1900) classified the Lapps with various Mongolian and proto-Mongolian groups, analysis of the blood group frequencies of the Lapps (Allison et al. 1956) revealed low gene frequencies of the *B* gene, a high frequency of the A_2 allele, and a low frequency of the *M* gene. These results contrast markedly with the high frequencies of blood group B, absence of A_2, and high frequencies of M, which would be expected from Mongoloid or related populations. From this evidence, it appears that the Lapps are distinctive European populations with no special affinity or relationship to the Mongoloids, despite their linguistic similarities. More recent investigations of the Lapp populations, based on haptoglobin types, Gc, and transferrins, also support the ethnographic conclusion that the Lapps are similar to their European neighbors, although heterogeneous genetically. Table 5 summarizes the gene frequencies at the haptoglobin locus among the Lapps and their neighbors.

TABLE 5

HAPTOGLOBINS IN LAPP AND NON-LAPP
SCANDINAVIAN POPULATIONS

Population	Sample Size	Gene Frequency Hp^1	Hp^2	Reference
Norwegian Lapps	301	0.311	0.689	Fleischer and Monn (1970)
Non-Lapp Norwegians	5,811	0.376	0.624	Fleischer and Mohr (1962)
Swedish Lapps	329	0.317	0.683	Beckman and Mellbin (1959)
Non-Lapp Swedes	1,272	0.393	0.607	Beckman, Heiken, and Hirschfeld (1961)
Finnish Skolt Lapps	300 (approx.)	0.434	0.566	Eriksson (1968)
Non-Lapp Finns	891	0.362	0.638	Makela, Eriksson, and Lehtovaara (1959)

The gene frequencies of the Gc^1 allele vary between 0.719 and 0.896 among the various Lapp populations, reaching the highest levels among the Swedish Lapps from the south (Reinskow and Kornstad 1965, Melartin 1965). There also appears to be a high frequency of the CD_1 variant of transferrin, but Melartin and Kaarsalo (1965) explain these in terms of possible consanguinity.

One of the most fascinating problems in physical anthropology is the origin and genetic affinities of the pygmy populations of the world. Populations of short stature, dark pigmentation, and Negrito morphological traits have been reported in a number of tropical forest regions of the world: the Philippine Islands, Malaya, Highland New Guinea, Central

34

Michael H. Crawford

Africa, and the Andaman Islands. A number of anthropologists have proposed an African genesis for these Negrito populations. Howells (1959: 339) concludes, "it is as plain as the nose on your face that the Negritos are intimately related to fully developed Negroes—a specialized kind of man—in skin, hair form, nose shape, and so on. The Negritos are really all similar and must have a common origin. And Negritos and Negroes cannot have appeared on separate continents; they too must have had a common origin." However, this example demonstrates the possible danger of misinterpretation when morphological traits such as skin color and hair form are used as criteria for establishing populational relationships. More recently, Howells has reinterpreted the question of the ethnogenesis of the Pygmies. Using multivariate analyses of cranial evidence, he postulates separate origins of the various populations of Negritos (see Chapter 8).

A comparison of the blood group frequencies of the African and Oceanic Negritos shows significant differences in the presence of certain marker genes in three populations compared by Boyd (1963). Table 6 illustrates the extent of variation between the three populations. The most significant differences between the Oceanic and African Pygmies were in the presence of the R_0 chromosomal segment and the relative frequency of the M and N antigens. The R_0 chromosomal segment is usually referred to as an African marker gene, because of its high frequency in Africa and its low frequency, or absence, in other parts of the world that had not experienced gene flow from African populations. The Pygmies of the Congo exhibit a frequency of the R_0 segment similar to frequencies found in other parts of Africa, in contrast to the low frequencies of this allele exhibited by Papuan Negritos and its total absence in the populations of the Andaman Islands. The highest frequency on earth of the M allele is found in New Guinea among the Papuan Pygmies. From these data, it apears that (1) the pygmy populations differ significantly among themselves, and (2) genetically, they resemble the surrounding populations more than these populations resemble each other. This is not surprising, considering the fact that in all cases, the Pygmies speak the language of their surrounding populations and apparently do not share a common language.

More recent genetic investigations have shown that, although the Pygmies are closer genetically to the Bantu than to the Bushman or Hottentots, they are also distinct populations differing from all others. For

35

TABLE 6
BLOCK...

BLOOD GROUP GENE FREQUENCIES IN PYGMY POPULATIONS

Population	Reference	Number Tested	Frequency of Gene								
			A	B	O	M	N	R_0	R_1	R_2	r
Pygmies Belgian Congo	Hubinot and Snoek (1949)	2,557	0.198	0.249	0.553	0.468	0.523	0.630	0.074	0.194	0.101
Papuan Pygmies	Graydon et al. (1958)	139	0.075	0.139	0.786	0.102	0.898	0.030	0.850	0.119	0.000
Andaman Negritos	Lehmann and Ikin (1954)	52	0.540	0.080	0.380	0.610	0.390	0.000	0.920	0.000	0.000

SOURCE: After Boyd (1963).

example, Benerecetti, Modiano, and Negri (1969) have demonstrated that a phosphoglucomutase (PGM) variant $PGM_2{}^{Pyg}$ is common only among the Babinga Pygmies of Africa, with a gene frequency of 7 percent. It has been suggested that this variant may be limited to the Pygmies and would therefore be a useful marker gene.

Another polymorphism that may be limited to the Pygmies was recently reported by Benerecetti and Negri (1970) at the red cell peptidase C locus. Although polymorphisms of other red cell peptidases have been reported (Lewis and Harris 1967, 1968, 1969), none have been detected for peptidase C until the report by Benerecetti and his colleagues. They describe a polymorphism controlled by three alleles at an autosomal locus, with Pep C^1 and Pep C^2 as co-dominant and Pep C^0 as a silent gene lacking a detectable electrophoretic component in the homozygous genotype.

Bodmer and Bodmer (1970) have described population differences in the HL-A system of leukocytic antigens in the Pygmies. The Pygmies differ from other populations on the basis of the total absence of the HL-A antigen and the very high incidence of the blank alleles for both the LA and 4 series. This suggests the existence of as yet unidentified antigens that have much higher frequencies in Pygmies than in Caucasians, and that may eventually serve as marker genes.

This concludes the review of the use of genetic markers for tracing phylogenetic relationships between human populations. Barnicot (1964), however, cautions against attempting to make historical inferences from gene distribution maps. He correctly argues that the presence of a common marker gene may not imply a phylogenetic relationship, but that each marker may have arisen independently in any population (Barnicot 1964:954): "To envisage human history as nothing but a series of migrations or intermixtures of peoples, each carrying its array of gene frequencies, like a convenient label to show its point of departure, may be an oversimplification."

Despite the contradictions and problems that have come to light through the use of genetic markers, a form of racial classification still persists. Although present statistical techniques are more sophisticated than those employed by the anthropologists of earlier decades, and although recent authors do not claim to be classifying races, the difference between earlier and present-day anthropologists is largely semantic—now they derive "trees of likely descent of populations" or "phylogenetic trees." Irrespective of the statistical trappings and the use of sophisticated computer programs, these exercises are basically as much a waste of time and money today as they were 50 years ago. Instead of attempting to classify the populations of the world on the basis of gene frequencies, basic research is needed to explain how and why the genetic variability is maintained at such high levels in human populations.

Two studies, Edmondson (1965) and Cavalli-Sforza, Barrai, and Edwards (1964), have proposed schemes of racial affinities based on gene frequency distributions. Edmondson, using 24 genetic traits from 124 populations, estimated the genetic distance between populations by averaging the differences in gene frequencies of all the populations of the sample. He then reconstructed the probable patterns of divergence of the major races of man. The Cavalli-Sforza study selected 15 populations and five blood group systems for estimating the most likely phylogenetic tree for the history of human racial separation. Surprisingly, although the methods used to calculate the phylogenetic affinities were different, the results were grossly similar. However, Cavalli-Sforza and his colleagues do not define the criteria used for selecting the genetic markers for their scheme. Moreover, neither of these methods assumes directional selection, nor does either control for gene flow and hybridization.

In conclusion, genetic markers can be cautiously employed in testing specific hypotheses of genetic relationship or affinity, as long as the limitations of the method are understood. Gene frequencies of simple Mendelian traits are the new materials for both population genetics and anthropological analyses. However, gene frequencies describe only a portion of the gene pool and permit a "glimpse" of the genetic structure of the population. Therefore, gene marker systems and their frequencies in human populations, when prudently used, can be a means to an end, but they are not an end in themselves.

NOTES

1. The term *genetic marker* will be restricted here to discrete, segregating, genetic traits which can be used to characterize populations by virtue of their presence, absence, or high frequency in some populations and low frequency in others.

2. By *non-adaptive*, Hooton means those traits not subject to the action of natural selection. He listed (1931) the following bodily characters as mainly nonadaptive variations: hair color and distribution, shape of lips, form of the incisors, the length of the forearm relative to the arm, and so forth.

Gene Frequency Differences in Human Populations: Some Problems of Analysis and Interpretation

FRANK B. LIVINGSTONE

Department of Anthropology
University of Michigan

$\mathbf{A}$s many others have pointed out, one of the major problems of biological science is the understanding, interpretation, or explanation of genetic variation. There are two aspects of this variation: the variation among individuals within a population, and the variation of gene frequencies among populations. These two aspects have both been the subject of recent controversy, but the last ten years have been a period of very significant advances in the genetic analysis of populations—perhaps as a result of this controversy. The interpretation of genetic variation within a population is now centered on the mutational load-neutral alleles-selective polymorphism controversy, while the race-cline-genetic drift question is concerned with the interpretation of genetic variation among populations. Obviously, these controversies are interrelated, and our attempts to deal with the latter will undoubtedly contribute to the former and vice versa. For example, if a particular locus is considered to have a "normal" or wild type allele with the other alleles as deleterious mutants, then the amount of allelic variation among the populations of the species should exhibit certain patterns; if it does not, other interpretations will have to be explored. Another recent controversy that centers on the distinction between variation within a population and among populations concerns the interpretaton of behavioral differences among individuals in different populations. There is an overwhelming amount of evidence that a genetic component is responsible for some of the differences among individuals within a population, but whether the differences among populations can be attributed to a genetic difference is another matter continually debated.

THE NATURE OF SCIENTIFIC MODELS

In comparison with other anthropological data, the theoretical basis of genetics data and the models that can be applied to them are far more advanced, quantitatively speaking. This chapter will examine the models of genetic processes, but first, it will make some generalizations about the nature of genetics—or any science—primarily because this seems to be an important part of the "methodology" of science and because there seems to be little concern with these basic questions of why we do things. The close fit of genetic models to data has been a detriment to such self-examination, and the models have tended to assume the character of "laws" or "truth." The Hardy-Weinberg "law" is a good example; no population or genetic locus in the world conforms to the assumptions of this law, but it is astonishing how close most gene frequencies are to those expected in a Hardy-Weinberg equilibrium. This close fit has also led to an emphasis on the descriptive nature of genetic models, and there is a tendency to think that genetic advances consist of simply more accurate descriptions of genetic processes occurring in human populations. With the great increase in the complexity of models made possible by the computer, exceedingly complicated and "accurate" simulations of population processes can be developed. But this approach has yet to contribute significantly to the major problem of genetic variation. For one reason, the necessary data are not and will not be available for many historical populations, and for another reason, the problems have tended to be obscured by this technological game playing.

As Kemeny (1961) and many others have stressed, mathematical or scientific models strive for simplicity and are only as complicated as is necessary for the problem. Thus, they strip away unessential details, and many details of genetic models have not been shown to be essential for most genetic problems. Any real phenomenon is complex, and physical phenomena no less so than biological or social ones; therefore, the old argument that the latter are different and more complex is just not true. It is rather our human perspective and the attitude of the social or biological scientist that makes them seem so. The current concern should thus be over what is essential to the model, not over what is more accurate or complex. Of course, what is unessential depends on the problem, but for the understanding of genetic variation among human populations, many genetic concepts do not seem particularly relevant. They may lend themselves to elegant mathematics, but these logical exercises seem to have contributed little to the understanding of evolution.

Kerner (1962:976) illustrates this view of science:

> Let us imagine that our knowledge of atomic phenomena had preceded that of celestial mechanics and that our empirical data in physics were wholly at what we now call the quantum level, our objects of study being atoms, molecules, and quanta. Things would be difficult. Such theories as might be attempted would likely deal directly in probabilities, that data being rather lawless and experiments being imperfectly reproducible. It would be at some stage, we may guess, a far-fetched speculation to suggest, for instance, that in a collision of two large molecules we forget the empirically visible complicated internal characteristics of each, forget the myriad electrons and nuclei and the massive data about them ever before our eyes, and treat the collision as a *two*-body collision, inventing a—to us—gross fiction of some kind of "billiard ball" representation of the molecules. Nevertheless, let us trust that the invention would be seen to be useful for explaining *some* things, although surely not everything. The further perception by a latter-day Newton of some simple limited kind of deterministic "laws" that could *for certain purposes* be used to help interpret the discreteness, discontinuities, and probabilities of our daily experimental fare would not be without merit. To be sure, we should not be fooled by such laws, knowing full well that reality was not so simple.

MODELS IN POPULATION GENETICS

Kerner is using this physical analogy with reference to ecology and the general Lotka-Volterra equations of species interaction, as opposed to the complexity of data on birth rates, age structure, breeding habits, and so forth, that constitute the science of ecology. The analogy is also particularly apt for population genetics. Simple deterministic models will probably explain many of the major gene frequency differences within the human species. Of course, population genetics following Fisher, Wright, and Haldane have already made significant advances in explaining the human genetic variation, and we have developed two "billiard ball" concepts, the gene and the population, that disregard the complexity of the data. The Mendelian concept of the gene as a bead on the chromosomal string is now known to be the most extreme of simplifications. But for most problems, it is still useful, and no one would deny the significant advances that have resulted from the model of a locus with two alleles, mutation rates between them, and fitnesses for the three genotypes—although this too is an extreme simplification for all genetically determined proteins. For example, thalassemia and the glucose-6-phosphate dehydrogenase deficiency are known to be due to many different alleles at their respective loci, and thalassemia itself is even due to different loci, but the problem of the high frequencies of these conditions can be handled without reference to this complexity. If, however, we were interested in why one allele and not another was present in a certain area of the world, then it would obviously be necessary to consider their dynamics separately. For the analysis of polygenic systems, another oversimplification, additive gene action, is added to the simple Mendelian model. To assume all loci are additive and their effects equal may be quite unrealistic in terms of gene action, but it seems that it will work even better than we might expect.

The other billiard ball concept, breeding population, is used at two or perhaps more different levels. At the most general level, the entire species is treated as a single population. Recent interpretations of the biochemical differences between man and the other primates and mammals (Wilson and Sarich 1969) and even the differences among all species (King and Jukes 1969) make this assumption. Wilson and Sarich's conclusion that molecular evolution occurs at a constant rate is based on the data of amino acid sequences in proteins and is comparable to the results of Kimura (1969) and many others, who have asserted that these genetic differences are due to non-Darwinian evolution or the fixation of neutral allelic substitutions. Obviously, the assumption of a constant rate of evolution disregards differences in the population structures of species and treats species as identical units. The theoretical model of Kimura (1968) and Kimura and Ohta (1969) has provided an estimate of the time required for the fixation of a neutral mutation. The average fixation time is $4N_e$, where N_e is the effective size of the population. Although the fixation time for a single mutant is proportional to the size of the population (since the number of mutants that occur in any population will also be proportional to its size), the rate of fixation or evolution thus turns out to be independent of population size and solely dependent on the mutation rate to neutral alleles. Nevertheless, these models assume that each species is a single population.

Perhaps in the early history of a species, a bottleneck or founder effect will result in a small effective population size, and then the later larger population size that occurs with the success of the species will simply have little influence on its gene frequencies. But this would still assume there was no equilibrium gene frequency. More recently, Maruyama (1970b) has shown that with subdivision of the population, the rate of fixation is not changed very much; his model, however, is quite restrictive. In another recent paper, Maruyama (1970c) has shown that the rate of decrease in genetic variation in a subdivided population is dependent on the number of subdivisions when that number is large. It would seem that the decay of heterozygosity and the fixation of alleles are the same stochastic process; thus, non-Darwinian evolution should be affected by the number of subdivisions. Maruyama (1970c) gives the rate of decay of heterozygosity as $m\pi^2/2n^2$, where m is the rate of migration between adjacent isolates and n the number of isolates. Since any successful widespread species, which man and his Australopithecine ancestors are and were, could contain thousands or tens of thousands of isolates, this formula seems to indicate that the rate of evolution would slow down considerably in such species. In any case, a constant rate of evolution would be a useful "evolutionary clock," but it remains to be seen how much the assumption of a single population for each species affects this conclusion.

Parenthetically, it should be added that most studies using amino acid data to estimate evolutionary rates assume that the mammals have a common ancestor 75 million years ago. But in the Paleocene, there are already some 20 distinct genera of Primates (Szalay 1968), so the starting point of their time scale would seem to be highly doubtful. This assumption would also seem to be non-Darwinian, since it assumes most of the mammalian characteristics are due to common ancestry and not natural selection. The mammals and even the eutherian mammals may be polyphyletic (Reed 1960), which would wreak further havoc with these evolutionary rates.

For the analysis of genetic variation within a species, any model obviously has to consider several different breeding populations, but the relationships between them can be assumed to be different. Wright's general equations of gene frequency distributions were based on an island model of several populations with either no gene flow or a constant amount of gene flow among all of them. Wright has also developed an isolation by distance model, but only the simpler island model can deal with all the forces of evolution. This seems to be one of the major problems of genetic theory, that is, to develop analytic models of several populations that can determine the effects of selection, migration, mutation, and genetic drift when they are considered simultaneously.

More recently, Roberts and Hiorns (1962) first developed a matrix model of migration, which has subsequently been investigated in detail by Hiorns et al. (1968), Bodmer and Cavalli-Sforza (1968), and Maruyama (1970c), among others. The analysis of population subdivisions by F statistics has also been recently advanced by Wright (1965), Allen (1965), and Nei (1965), and this type of analysis has been applied to the blood group variation in Japan by Nei and Imaizumi (1966) and to that of the Papago Indians by Workman and Niswander (1970). All of these models have resulted in a better understanding of the role of migration in maintaining genetic variation, and in some cases, population size and consequently genetic drift have also been considered. But most of the genetic variation is assumed to be due to random processes, so that no realistic scheme of selection has been incorporated into them. Thoma (1970) has applied Nei's methods to the blood group variation in Europe, but although he includes a discussion and estimation of selection, it is not very germane to his correlation analysis. On the other hand, Morton and his associates (Yasuda and Morton 1967, Morton, Miki, and Yee 1968, Imaizumi and Morton 1969, Imaizumi, Morton, and Harris 1970) have discussed selection as part of their application of Malécot's general equations to the genetic variation in several countries, including Switzerland, Sweden, Belgium, Japan, Brazil, and most recently, England (references in Imaizumi and Morton 1969 and Imaizumi, Morton, and Harris, 1970); however, they have not been able to estimate the selective effects of the gene substitutions.

Although most of these studies analyze the genetic variation among units that approximate the usual definition of a breeding population, it is possible to consider the gene frequencies of "populations" at many other levels. In fact, most of the gene frequency data that exist for the human species refer to units larger than breeding isolates, and these units are frequently political and not social. Yasuda and Morton (1967) have also commented on this discrepancy between genetic data and breeding isolates and state further that the data from Switzerland are the single large study that is amenable to their type of analysis. The gene frequencies of the actual human breeding isolates, or units most closely conforming to the ideal definition of this unit, in most parts of the world usually appear to have no consistent trends or differences, and the variation appears to be erratic and random. At this level, gene drift is frequently invoked as an explanation—as it should be—but the previously cited studies by Morton and his associates are the most comprehensive attempts to date to make order out of the seeming disorder of the gene frequencies of human isolates. In addition, these isolates are usually small and the samples taken from them even smaller; thus, sampling variation complicates the analysis at this level, and the partitioning of genetic variation into sampling and actual variation is one of the major problems.

On the other hand, it is possible to group human populations into larger units—tribes, nations, districts, races, and so forth—and at these higher levels, the genetic variation among the units is frequently more systematic and regular. When the major continental areas are compared, there are frequently consistent differences among them. If this variation is plotted along any linear transect, the resulting cline in gene frequencies will exhibit distinct trends. When irregularities occur, they frequently have some historical explanation; but it is also often the case that the variation has no readily apparent explanation. For example, if the variation in the R_0 chromosome is plotted between Central Africa and Europe, it seems highly erratic in the intermediate populations, although at the two end points, Africa and Europe, there are constant large differences in the frequency of this chromosome.

Nevertheless, as one increases the size and geographical range of the populations to which gene frequencies are assigned, the variation tends to get more regular. It seems that this larger scale regular variation is most appropriately studied by deterministic equations, while at the level of the actual isolates within a rather circumscribed area, the variation will be due, to a much greater extent, to random processes. To some extent, this point of view can alleviate the selection versus drift argument. Although the larger units are not breeding populations, they can be treated as such; and mutation, selection, population size, and migration can be discussed with reference to these larger units as a reasonable approximation. Hopefully, these approximations will work better than we expect.

At whatever level population is defined, all models make assumptions as to the nature and presence of equilibria for both gene frequencies and populations. The early models of population genetics that investigated gene frequency change assumed that the population size remained constant. For the most part, the Fisher-Wright-Haldane theory of genetic evolution was concerned with gene change within a single population; and, as has been discussed previously, the current non-Darwinian models of species evolution make the same assumption and deal with evolution only within this restricted framework. If we consider several populations and the genetic variability among them, then it is also simplest to assume that the populations are in equilibrium. The genetic variability among the populations will then be a function of the forces of gene frequency change, not of population differences. However, even with all these assumptions, the formal mathematics of the genetic variation among several populations is still intractable for most problems that consider all the forces of evolution simultaneously. Matrix models have been developed to handle migration and gene drift (Bodmer and Cavalli-Sforza 1968, Maruyama 1970a), but selection is still a problem. Thus, recourse to simulation with various numerical values for the parameters seems to be the most feasible approach to obtain some idea of the equilibria and their stability. Nevertheless, these models are only rough approximations for most human gene frequency variation, since most human populations have not been constant in size or territory in the last few thousand years. The pattern of genetic variation within the species has been determined, to a large extent, by this instability, and many of the gene clines are due to the increase and extension of territory of some populations at the expense of others. Haldane (1961) gave many reasons for suspecting that many gene frequencies are not near equilibrium. On the other hand, the entire species has been relatively constant until very recently. Coale (1964) has pointed out that the human population has only increased by twelvefold since the time of Julius Caesar, which implies a 2 to 3 percent increase per generation. The assumption of a constant population size does not seem too outrageous with this average increase.

MODELS OF POPULATION HISTORY

While the models of genetic change that have been previously discussed attempt to develop interpretations of the process by which the forces of evolution direct or determine the changes in gene frequencies, another whole group of models of evolution attempts to reconstruct historical events. The latter usually make the assumption that the process of evolution is constant, and in addition, they assume that the population is continually increasing, or at least that the number of populations is continually increasing. These models have been applied to a wide variety of biological problems under the name of numerical taxonomy and have been developed in detail for human history by Cavalli-Sforza and Edwards (1963); in precomputer times, Spuhler (1954) attempted the same thing, and many uses of Mahalanobis's D^2 have constructed the same type of tree diagram. These tree diagrams imply that evolution has primarily been a branching process. This implies further that the differences among the units are due to their budding off from each other and remaining relatively isolated, so that evolutionary forces can operate on their gene frequencies. The model must then go further and imply that gene frequency change is constant, or in the least that the changes for all loci cluster around some mean value. Such a model of the changes through time of the population structure of a species, or any other group, has been applied indiscriminately to all the genetic differences within the human species and to those among the higher primates. It may apply to some and not others, depending on the population growth in the time span encompassed by the model. The Hutterites would seem to be one of the best fits for this model of population expansion, but there seems to be enough gene flow among the colonies to make the model inappropriate even for the Hutterites (Steinberg et al. 1967). On the other hand, the Australian aborigines have been relatively stable in population and territory for the past ten thousand years, and their genetic differences make

47

little sense in terms of this kind of phylogenetic model (Kirk and Sanghvi [n.d.]). Similarly, the genetic differences among South American Indian tribes result in a set of phylogenetic trees that contribute little to our understanding of human history in South America (Fitch and Neel 1969).

Cavalli-Sforza and Edwards (1963) have analyzed both the differences in blood group genes and anthropometric traits among the major groups of the human species by this type of cluster taxonomy.Their two tree diagrams are very different, and the question arises as to why. Perhaps by combining the two or adding further traits or genes, one could get a closer approximation of the "true" phylogeny, but it is more likely that there is no "true" phylogeny and that the genetic differences in both blood groups and anthropometric traits are not caused by this kind of process. All of these techniques of numerical taxonomy result in reconstructions of the population history of the groups involved. They are attempts to use gene frequencies to determine population history but are causally backward. If the problem is to reconstruct population history, there are more relevant data and better ways to do it. The population structure of any species or group is one of the factors that can effect gene frequency change. It may affect the frequencies at various loci differently. But in any case, it would be highly unlikely that the genetic differences for any locus are solely due to, and therefore reflect accurately, the population history of the groups, or that the average gene frequency difference would reflect the history. A phylogenetic tree can be constructed from genetic data by many different methods, but there is no way to test their utility or judge among them. In most studies that reconstruct trees, the concordances with known history are emphasized, but the discrepancies, which are usually as numerous, are disregarded.

Despite assertions or beliefs to the contrary, the genes of any human population have little effect on their population's ability to increase, and the differences in growth rates among human populations are not due to genes. The forces that control population growth are ecological, not genetic. Thus, to reconstruct human history, cultural, ethnological, ecological, archaeological, linguistic, and many other kinds of data are more relevant to the size, territory, and interrelations of human populations. With some idea of the populations' history in a particular area, one can then include this reconstruction in any interpretation of the genetic variability among these populations. The simplest model can be seen when the populations are relatively stable and the genetic variation at equilibrium is due primarily to a balance of migration and differences in natural selection among the populations.

GENETIC ANALYSIS OF THE HEMOGLOBIN AND G6PD LOCI

To illustrate the principles that have been presented thus far, the remainder of this chapter will discuss some preliminary, inconclusive analyses of genetic variation at several different levels of human populations. Figure 7 shows the cline in the frequency of the hemoglobin S gene among the paramount chiefdoms in the interior of Liberia. Although the tribes vary significantly in their hemoglobin S frequencies, it can be seen that the cline is gradual, with the frequency more determined by geography than by tribe. Within the paramount chiefdoms, the village frequencies vary significantly, but by combining these frequencies, the variation is smoothed. This cline is presumably due to the wave of advance of the hemoglobin S gene, since malaria is equally endemic throughout Liberia. And its smoothness is due to the stability of the populations in the time since this gene began to diffuse among them.

Figure 8 shows the clines in the frequencies of thalassemia and the glucose-6-phosphate dehydrogenase (G6PD) deficiency in a linear series of populations in central Sardinia. Since malaria is endemic on the east and west coasts, but not in the central highlands, the frequencies of both genes are higher on the coasts and lower in the mountains. Since the populations of Sardinia have been relatively stable in the last two thousand years, it seems reasonable to assume that the gene frequencies for these two conditions are close to equilibrium, which is due to a balance of migration and selective pressures. However, the clines seem to be more erratic than the hemoglobin S cline in Liberia, so that random factors are more effective. This would seem to be expected, since many populations were combined to produce the Liberian cline. The cline for thalassemia has been replicated with reasonable numerical estimates for the fitness values of the genotypes and migration (Livingstone 1969b), but the G6PD locus raises new problems.

Siniscalco et al. (1966) have reviewed the Sardinian data, and their estimates for the fitnesses differ significantly from my previous ones (Livingstone 1964a). For all their models, they have set the fitness of the

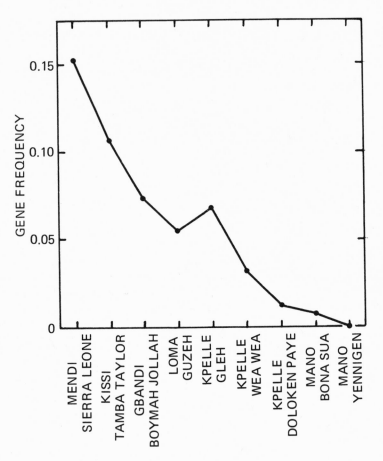

Note: The chiefdoms are aligned in an approximate linear sequence, and the decrease in the gene frequency is from northwest to southeast.

FIGURE 7. The cline in the frequency of the hemoglobin S gene in the paramount chiefdoms of the interior of Liberia.

G6PD deficient hemizygote and homozygote as greater than their normal counterparts, and in two of the three models, they estimate the fitness of the deficient heterozygote to be intermediate. With these sets of fitness values, there is no equilibrium frequency close to the average values found in human populations, and in the two cases with an intermediate fitness for the heterozygote, the G6PD deficient allele will completely replace the normal one. Siniscalco and his associates state that there is no reason to suppose that the frequencies of the world's populations would be near equilibrium; but since it takes about 200 generations, or 4,000–5,000 years,

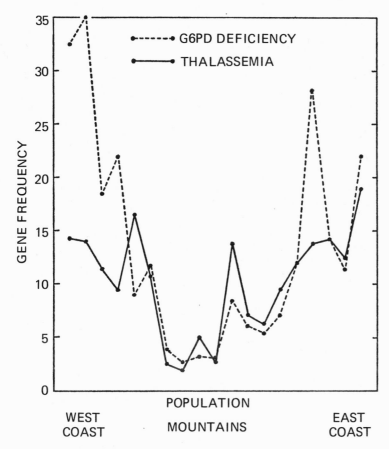

Note: The populations are arranged in a linear sequence from about Oristano on the west coast to Posada on the east coast.

FIGURE 8. The clines in the frequencies of the thalassemia and glucose-6-phosphate dehydrogenase deficiency genes in central Sardinia.

to attain equilibrium, it seems that a considerable number of populations should be more than halfway there. The Kurdistan Jews, perhaps some other Jewish populations, and some Arab populations of oases in eastern Saudi Arabia have frequencies of the G6PD deficiency greater than 0.5, but surely more high frequencies would be expected. The fact that most G6PD deficiency frequencies in human populations are less than 0.5 seems to strongly suggest that there is a stable equilibrium close to the average high frequency in malarious areas. If this is true, it implies that the deficient hemizygote and homozygote are less fit than normals and that the female heterozygote has the highest fitness. Of course, selection at this locus varies enormously, even among populations in malarious areas, since different deficient alleles seem to be selected in different areas, for example, A- in Africa and B- in the Mediterranean. However, in Sardinia, the deficiency frequencies cluster markedly around a mean value, so that as a first approximation, the fitness values can be equated in the populations of the coastal lowlands.

To test various sets of fitness values, a computer program for the G6PD cline was developed for a set of 50 populations with different fitness values and a given amount of migration between them. I have not attempted to find data on migration in Sardinia but have set the total amount at 0.25 for most runs. Of this total migration, 0.8 occurs between adjacent populations, 0.18 occurs between those adjacent to the adjacent ones, and 0.02 is randomly distributed among populations within five on either side. The boundary populations raise problems, but the migration has simply been eliminated if the appropriate populations did not exist. This amount and distribution of migration is considered to be the approximate average of peasant populations in Europe.

TABLE 7
VARIOUS ESTIMATES OF THE
G6PD GENOTYPE FITNESSES

| Estimate | Genotype (d = deficient allele) | | | | |
	D-	d-	DD	Dd	dd
Siniscalco et al., Model I	0.96	1.04	0.96	1.00	1.04
Siniscalco et al., Model II	0.95	1.01	0.95	1.00	1.01
Siniscalco et al., Model III	0.94	0.98	0.94	1.00	0.98
Balanced polymorphism, Model I	1.00	0.95	1.00	1.07	0.95
Balanced polymorphism, Model II	1.00	0.97	1.00	1.07	0.97

SOURCE: After Siniscalco et al. (1966).

The five sets of fitness values that were used are shown on Table 7. These fitness values were assigned to the coastal populations, and for all runs, the highland populations were assigned the following fitnesses: D- = DD = 1.00, d- = dd = 0.90, and Dd = 0.98. Malaria is not endemic in the highlands of Sardinia, but the fava bean seems to be cultivated and/or eaten there, so that the G6PD deficient genotypes should have a very low fitness there. For some runs, there were 10 highland populations in the middle of the cline, and for others, 20 were assumed. For all runs, the frequencies of the G6PD deficient allele in all 50 populations were started at either zero or very low frequencies that were below equilibrium in all cases. Hence, for the first few generations, the clines were similar for all models of fitness values but began to diverge as they approached equilibrium. Figure 9 shows the cline after 120 generations for

FIGURE 9. The cline in the frequency of the G6PD deficiency after 120 generations with a migration rate of 0.5 and the fitnesses of the Balanced Polymorphism I model in populations 1 to 20 and 41 to 50. *Source:* After Siniscalco et al. (1966).

Note: In this and all further G6PD simulated clines, the populations in the central area were assigned the fitnesses 0.9 for homozygous and hemizygous G6PD deficients and 0.98 for the G6PD heterozygotes.

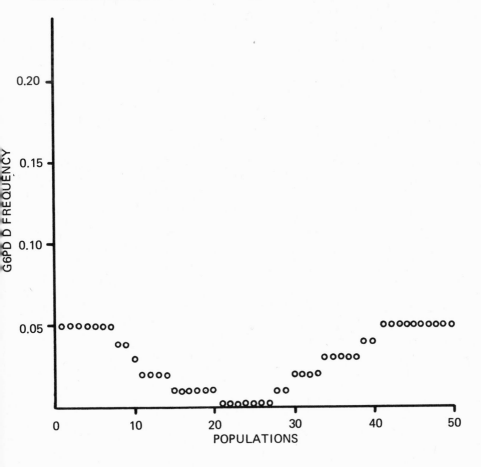

the Balanced Polymorphism I fitnesses when it is close to equilibrium. For this run, migration was set at 0.5, and it can be seen that this large amount of migration offsets the selective pressures to a greater degree than occurs in Sardinia. This results in a cline that is too gradual and has frequencies that are too low. Figure 10 shows the cline after 480 generations for the same set of fitnesses but with a total migration rate of 0.25. The cline approached this shape by the eightieth generation and remained there for 400 generations, so it appears to be equilibrium. In this case, differential selection more than offsets migration, although the fact that 20 populations were assigned the low fitnesses of the nonmalarious mountain region has also contributed to the sharpness of the cline. On the other hand, Figure 10 also shows the cline after 300 generations for the Balanced Polymorphism II fitnesses and 0.25 migration. Although far less erratic than the actual cline, these values seem to replicate it most closely. Several runs were also made with the fitness values of Siniscalco et al. (1966), but in all cases, frequencies of the G6PD deficiency greater than 0.50 occurred by 50 to 80 generations. Their Model I has slightly greater differences in fitness than Model II and so increases faster. Figure 11 shows the cline for their Model II after 80 generations with 0.25 migration. After 60 generations, there were frequencies greater than 0.50, and by generation 80, some are rapidly approaching 1.0. Since 80 generations is perhaps 2,000 years, this implies that malaria has become a selective force very recently in Sardinia. In addition, it would imply further that the cline is highly unstable. For these reasons, it seems that balanced polymorphism is a more reasonable alternative.

To a large extent, these isolated examples of consistent variations in gene frequencies for the hemoglobin S, thalassemia, and G6PD deficiency are characteristic of the distributions of these genes throughout the world. For other loci that are now being discovered and becoming known in as much detail, the geographical variation is not as continuous nor as consistent, and the question arises as to why. Although the various blood group genes are also characterized by having clinal distributions, most frequently their distributions are quite erratic and thus seem to be more like the distributions of most other biochemical traits and not like the malaria-related red cell defects. Two factors are involved: first, the differences in fitness among the genotypes for the red cell defects are greater than those for other loci that are polymorphic; second, the differences in fitness between homozygous normals and heterozygotes is due primarily

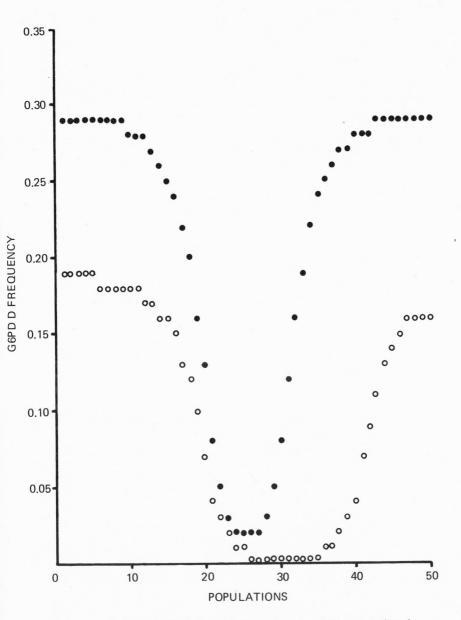

Note: (ooooo) represents the Balanced Polymorphism I model in populations 1 to 20 and 41 to 50, while (●●●●●) represents the Balanced Polymorphism II model in populations 1 to 20 and 31 to 50, the first being after 480 generations, and the latter, after 300 generations.

FIGURE 10. The clines in the G6PD deficiency with a migration rate of 0.25. Source: After Siniscalco et al. (1966).

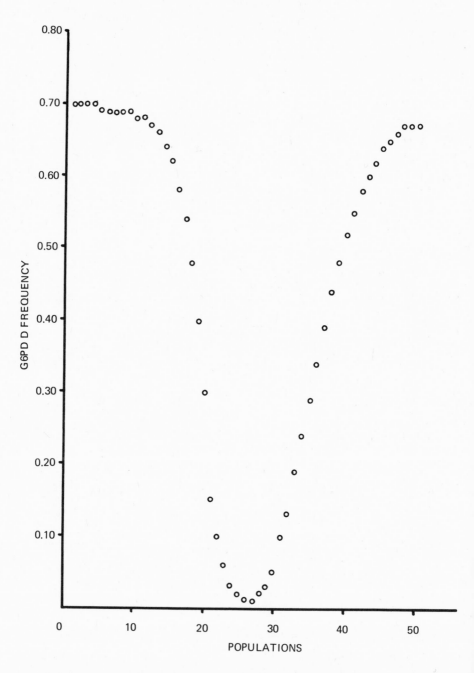

FIGURE 11. The G6PD cline for the fitnesses of Siniscalco et al.'s (1966) Model II after 80 generations with a migration rate of 0.25.

to one factor, malaria. With greater fitness differences, the gene frequency change due to systemic pressures is greater, and with one environmental factor determining equilibrium, these frequencies would approach the different possible equilibria faster and remain there. If, as seems more likely for the ABO blood groups, a great number of diseases and other physiological factors all affect the fitnesses of the genotypes, then it would be very unlikely that the effects of these many factors would vary concordantly among human populations. This would probably result in erratic variation, although major continental areas may exhibit consistent differences. For example, the R_0 gene is consistently high in Subsaharan African populations and low in European ones. But in the populations of North Africa and the Sahara, among whom the R_0 frequency decreases rapidly, the cline is quite erratic. Barnicot (1963) examined R_0 variation in East Africa, where it declines rapidly in Ethiopian populations, but the variation does not seem to reflect any readily apparent explanation.

GEOGRAPHIC DISTANCE AND GENETIC VARIATION

Another factor involved in these differing patterns of genetic variation is the size of the populations to which gene frequencies are assigned. Much of the variation in the red cell defects seems to be random when small individual isolates are examined. This may be due to the founder effect in recently formed isolates or to the fact that the total population has always been partitioned into small isolates. The high frequency of the hemoglobin S gene in the Brandywine isolate seems to be due to the founder effect (Livingstone 1969a), and the variability in the G6PD deficiency among Negro populations in Nova Scotia would seem to be another example. Their G6PD deficiency frequencies vary from 0.02 to 0.27 (Langley, Todd, and Bishop 1969). Obviously, there is no influence of malaria on these frequencies, so they seem to be far from equilibrium in contrast to the populations of Sardinia. All of the Nova Scotian Negro populations originated from migration from the United States after the War of 1812, and the population has increased from 2,000 then to 12,000 today, or approximately 35 percent per generation for eight generations. Barrai and I simulated this founder effect by beginning the populations as random samples of 100 from a parent population with a G6PD deficiency frequency of 0.2, which seems to be a reasonable approximation to the founding of the Nova Scotian isolates. If the fitness of the hemizygote and homozygote for the deficiency is estimated to be 0.9, then the simulated means were very similar to the actual mean, while the variances were somewhat larger. The mean and variance of the deficiency for the eight isolates reported by Langley, Todd, and Bishop (1969) are 0.163 and 0.0058, and for two runs of eight isolates each, we obtained means of 0.154 and 0.165 and variances of 0.0118 and 0.0158.

Figure 12 shows the hemoglobin S gene frequency distribution for the individual villages investigated by Burke, de Bock, and de Wulf (1958) in the Congo. Since these appear to be almost all the villages of five con-

FIGURE 12. The distribution of gene frequencies for the hemoglobin S allele among the villages of the lower Kwilu River area of the Congo.

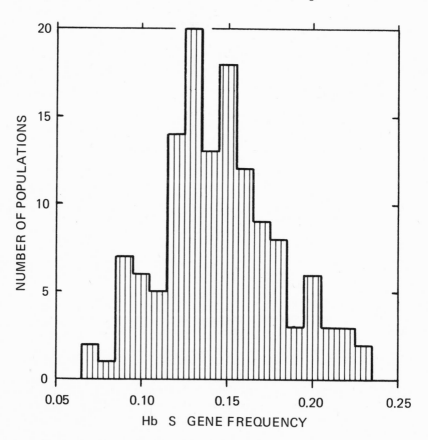

tiguous districts, this survey is the most comprehensive sampling of any population for this gene. The variation seems to be almost normally distributed about a mean of 0.145, which is the pattern of variation expected for Wright's island model with a balance between selection and drift. However, many of the samples are small, so there is a problem as to how much is sampling variation and how much is true variation among the populations. The fact that the investigators attempted to test the entire village in most cases also complicates the partitioning of the variance. Dr. W. A. Ericson of the Department of Statistics of the University of Michigan obtained the following unbiased estimate of the variance: given k populations with gene frequencies, $p_1 \ldots p_k$, and estimates of these, $p'_1 \ldots p'_k$, each of which is based on n_i individuals, and by taking the expected value of

$$s^2 = 1/k \sum_1^k (p'_i - \bar{p}')^2$$

where

$$\bar{p}' = 1/k \sum_1^k p'_i,$$

then with

$$\bar{p} = 1/k \sum_1^k p_i,$$

the estimate of

$$\sigma^2 = 1/k \sum_1^k (p_i - \bar{p})^2$$

is:

$$\sigma^2 = s^2 - [(k-1)/k^2] \sum_1^k p'_i(1 - p'_i)/(n_i - 1).$$

This is an estimate of the unweighted variance of the gene frequencies. Most genetic theory uses a weighted variance, but with comparable and relatively complete samples, this unbiased unweighted estimate seems to be closest to the true variance of the gene frequencies. However, Wright's formula for the relationship between the inbreeding coefficient and the genetic variance, $F = \sigma^2/\bar{p}(1 - \bar{p})$, may require a weighted variance.

For the Congo villages and the hemoglobin S gene, $F = 0.0039$; this is somewhat smaller than the values for the Papago (Workman and Niswander 1970) and intermediate for those calculated by Imaizumi and Morton (1969) on much larger clusters of isolates. The distribution of the frequencies around the mean value seems to indicate that random processes are tending to increase the variance, while the systemic pressures, migration and selection, are tending to decrease it. There is a slight north-south cline in the frequencies with the northernmost district having an average frequency of 0.157 and the southernmost of the five districts having an average of 0.132. Hence, selection probably varies within the area, which would tend to increase the variance. In addition, gene drift, the founder effect, and nonrandom migration are also involved in increasing the variance.

To determine how F varies with distance, Yasuda and Morton's (1967) formula for the coefficient of kinship was calculated for various distances. This formula is based on the covariance of the gene frequencies for populations grouped according to the distance between them. It is derived from Malécot's general theory of population structure, and Malécot himself (1969) has pointed out this application of his theory. Morton, Miki, and Yee (1968) have developed another method of calculating the coefficient of kinship (ϕ), which is based on Yasuda's theory of mating types. They have obtained comparable results for Switzerland by the two methods, but other data, such as that from Sweden (Beckman 1959), were stated to not be amenable to the first method (Yasuda and Morton 1967), while they have been used for the second (Imaizumi and Morton 1969).

Maps of the Lower Kwilu River area of the Congo on a scale of 1/250,000 were generously provided by the Army Map Service, but only 101 of the 132 villages could be located. The distance between villages was computed as a straight line in miles from their latitudes and longitudes. Table 8 shows the results for 10 groupings.

No discernible relationship between kinship and distance seems to be present in this analysis of the data. Different groupings were also tried, but the same absence of any trend always occurred. Motulsky, Vandepitte, and Fraser (1966) examined six villages of the Bayaka, a neighboring tribe of Central Bantu, for the hemoglobin S and G6PD deficiency genes, and there is also no correlation between distance and the absolute difference in gene frequency for this small sample. On the other hand,

Frank B. Livingstone

there is a significant correlation between hemoglobin S and G6PD deficiency gene frequencies, which is some evidence that local malaria selection may be the major factor contributing to the genetic differences.

This type of kinship and distance analysis depends on the mating structure of the populations and the relationship of the groupings to the average distance between marriage partners. From an anthropological viewpoint, it would seem unexpected that the great variety of marriage systems could be made to conform to a single equation. And there does seem to be some disagreement as to the application of Malécot's model.

TABLE 8
ESTIMATES OF THE COEFFICIENT OF KINSHIP (ϕ)
FOR 101 VILLAGES IN THE CENTRAL CONGO

Distance (miles)	Number of Pair Comparisons	Coefficient of Kinship (ϕ)
0–5	287	0.000656
5–10	632	−0.000142
10–15	667	−0.000588
15–20	597	0.000669
20–25	579	−0.000164
25–30	511	−0.000439
30–35	381	0.000428
35–40	311	0.000199
40–45	315	−0.000910
45–50	770	−0.000148

Yasuda and Morton (1967) state that the groupings should be within the "predictable" part of the curve, or, in other words, the width of the individual group should be much less than σ, the standard deviation of the marriage distance; however, Malécot (1969) insists his formula only holds for distances and hence groupings that are much greater than σ. Assuming isotropic migration and that the married couple will live in the ancestral village of one of the pair, the average marriage distance will be twice the parent-offspring distance.

The Central Bantu of the Congo is made up of several tribes, including the Bayanzi, Bambala, Bahungana, and Bangongo tested by Burke, de

Bock, and de Wulf (1958). All of these tribes have a marriage system based on some type of exchange or alliance (De Sousberghe 1955), which could be called prescriptive father's sister's daughter marriage. De Beaucorps (1933) found that the marriage rule among the Bayanzi is "the maternal grandfather of the bride is the maternal uncle of the groom," which can be viewed as a delayed exchange marriage among matrilineages. De Beaucorps's work also showed that the effective size of the clan and perhaps the breeding isolate is quite small and most likely under 200. Despite much suggestive evidence, I have not been able to find any data for the average marriage distance for these tribes. However, Douglas (1963) has tabulated the marriages for the Lele, who have a similar culture and marriage system and are about 200 miles away up the Kasai. From Douglas's map, the marriage distance could be estimated for 42 marriages, and the average distance is 5.7 miles. Because of the exchange marital relations between clans, marriage is also not simply a function of distance. A comparable study by Gajdusek and Reid (1961) on the marriages of a Fore village in New Guinea, which is also made up of primitive agriculturalists, has an average marriage distance of 3.0 miles. Both of these estimates are similar to the estimate of 4.0 miles for a rural village in Sweden in 1815 cited in Yasuda and Morton (1967) and that of 2.8 miles for rural Japanese farmers in the nineteenth century (Beardsley, Hall, and Ward 1959), which now has increased to 6.0 miles. Hammel's data from a district of Peru also has an average distance of 6.9 miles (Hammel 1964). On the other hand, there are small isolated tribes with very much smaller average marriage distances; for example, the Purum marriages recorded in Needham (1958) have an average marriage distance of 0.67 miles, but only some of these villages could be identified.

These distances for agriculturalists contrast sharply with those for hunters and gatherers. For the marriages on Groote Eylandt (Rose 1960) and the stated marriage alliances between clans for the Murngin recorded in Warner (1937) and mapped by White (1963), the average marriage distances are 22 and 26 miles, respectively. Cavalli-Sforza's (1968) recent data on the Babinga Pygmies also have an average marriage distance of 26 miles. With agriculture, the marriage distance thus seems to have decreased significantly but with industrialization is now increasing rapidly.

For this Congo population, an estimate of σ of 5.0 would not seem unreasonable. The systemic pressure for the hemoglobin S gene is due almost entirely to selection and can be calculated with some reasonable assumptions. SS homozygotes have a fitness of zero in most of tropical Africa. For the mean gene frequency of 0.145 in the Congo, the selection against the AA homozygote would be 0.169 if this mean frequency were equilibrium. The systemic pressure is thus $u = 0.169/(1.0 + 0.169) = 0.145$ (Yasuda and Morton 1967), which is perhaps the greatest selective pressure for any human locus. In the formula $u = (b\sigma)^2/2$, we can substitute $u = 0.145$, $b = 0.0168$. This is the coefficient of the exponential decrease of the kinship coefficient with distance. This value is not very different from the values for the ABO blood groups in Switzerland, and it is intermediate for the values of b for other populations (Imaizumi and Morton 1969). Since there seems to be no association of gene frequencies with distance, there is apparently no explanation for this discrepancy.

For the gene frequency distribution shown in Figure 12, the systemic pressure that is offsetting random drift can also be calculated for Wright's island model. If we assume that this pressure is migration, then the formula, $F = 1/(4Nm + 1)$, holds. With $m = 0.25$ and the previously calculated $F = 0.0039$, then $N = 255$, which seems close to reality. If the gene frequency distribution is assumed to be a steady state that is balanced by constant selection, Li (1955) gives the general formula derived by Wright; but to my knowledge, it cannot be integrated and thus the constant cannot be evaluated. However, the value of the gene frequency distribution at 0.1 is about one-third that at 0.15, so that if these two values are equated, the constant cancels. With the above values of the selection coefficients, $N = 56$, and this is smaller than that necessary for migration but still within the range of possible real values.

The preceding analyses of the hemoglobin S gene frequencies from a small part of the Congo indicate that many of the theoretical genetic parameters can be made to "fit" data. The fact that for these data several different models yield estimates of genetic parameters comparable to those found in other populations raises problems as to the interpretation of the estimates, the major one being the question of how much these estimates are simply artifacts of the arithmetic. For example, for the variation in gene frequencies of any set of populations, one would obtain a value of F by the Wright-Wahlund formula, which would look reasonable. I have calculated the value of F from the genetic variance for the studies shown on Table 9 and for many other populations; and, although these F values all seem to fall within acceptable limits, they do not seem to show any consistency among themselves. For the same set of isolates, the different loci, or even alleles within a locus, frequently have very disparate F values. On the other hand, the parameters of the equation relating kinship to distance used by Yasuda and Morton (1967) can attain unrealistic values and frequently do.

Despite this plethora of models, we are still unable to explain most gene frequency variation at the level of the individual isolate. In particular, there is often no correlation of gene frequency differences with geographic distance, linguistic differences, or other measures of cultural differences. Table 9 shows the correlations between the absolute value of the gene frequency differences and geographic distance. The use of the absolute value of each difference has been criticized (Giles 1966). Admittedly, this is the simplest or easiest model of analysis, but it is nevertheless a direct measure of gene frequency variation. It is possible to apply more sophisticated correlation techniques or other methods of analysis to this data, but there is some question as to how much they elucidate the causes of genetic variation. The construction of phylogenetic trees, the compilation of F statistics, and the study of kinship and distance are all techniques that use gene frequency differences to develop measures of population structure. In a sense, they are attempts to use gene frequencies for other problems and are not direct attacks on gene frequency variation, particularly with regard to the idiosyncracies of the individual locus. On the other hand, the simple correlation of gene frequency differences with distance seems to indicate how much of this variation is explained by geographic factors among a set of particular populations.

Some of the correlations shown on Table 9 border on statistical significance. However, the fact that they are almost uniformly nonsignificant seems to be considerable evidence for the random nature of genetic differences at the level of the individal isolate when it is compared with neighboring similar isolates. The evidence of Giles et al. (1966) points to the same conclusion, although Howells (1966a) found significant correlations between distance and various anthropometric traits in the same area of Melanesia. Friedlaender (1971) has more recently found a decrease of the coefficient of kinship (ϕ) with distance. It is not stated how many comparisons are in each of the nine groupings, but with only 18 populations, there would be very few in some of them. Yasuda and Morton's (1967) covariance formula for the coefficient of kinship (ϕ) was computed for the studies on Table 9, using five groupings. Even with this

TABLE 9

CORRELATION COEFFICIENTS OF THE ABSOLUTE VALUE OF GENE FREQUENCY DIFFERENCES FOR SEVERAL BLOOD GROUP ALLELES AND GEOGRAPHICAL DISTANCE

Number of Population		O	A	B	Ms	NS	Ns	R_1	R_2	R_0	r
23	Dalecarlia, Sweden*	−0.081	−0.096	−0.005	—	—	—	—	—	—	0.135
20	Markham River, New Guinea†	0.069	0.053	0.018	0.248	0.224	0.369	0.386	0.370	0.085	—
11	Sepik River, New Guinea‡	−0.116	−0.183	0.045	0.172	0.414	0.055	−0.114	−0.136	−0.042	—
16	Enga, New Guinea§	0.358	0.375	0.168	−0.096	0.177	0.121	0.147	0.132	0.106	—
16	Kagoshima||	0.060	−0.083	−0.004	—	—	—	—	—	—	—
14	Tokushima||	0.053	0.092	0.053	—	—	—	—	—	—	—

* Beckman and Martensson (1958).
† Giles et al. (1966).
‡ Simmons et al. (1965b).
§ Macintosh, Walsh, and Kooptzoff (1958).
|| Nei and Imaizumi (1966).

small number of groupings, there were only 10 paired comparisons in some groupings, and the maximum was about 100. The ϕ coefficients ranged from ± 0.01 to 0.0001, but there was no apparent association with distance. Thus, whether the important determinant of genetic variation is genetic drift or the systemic pressures of selection, migration, and perhaps mutation depends to a considerable extent on the populational level being examined. Among the small isolates of the human species, genetic drift may well be most important, but this does not imply that the major genetic differences within this species are also due to drift.

4

Genetics of Isolate Populations

Département d'Anthropologie
Université de Montréal

In one of the first systematic studies of an isolate population, Böök (1956) pointed out: "Concerning human populations [the] development [of population genetics] has been restricted almost exclusively to theoretical frameworks. . . . rather few attempts have been made to test the theories on actual populations." However, the results of research undertaken during the last 15 years are more positive; much of it has been done in the field, so that theory has had to collate with many real situations. This applies particularly to gene flow analysis and to the study of migration and of isolate populations. Since sociodemographic methods have become more varied and more accurate, the relationship between theoretical models and observation has become closer in this field. As a result of simulation methods, general theory itself has come closer to the observation.

The bridge between theory and observation is not yet perfect, and a gap remains, due to difficulties encountered in measuring all the relevant parameters, as well as to the structural diversity of populations. Current research on small isolated populations is attempting to resolve these difficulties by interrelating the knowledge of their sociodemographic structure, sociocultural observations, and standardized biological and biometric data.

In a discussion of the "genetics of isolate populations," it is first necessary to delineate the meaning of this expression. Many uncertainties are the result of loose definitions, and the term "isolate" has been variously defined. This is no doubt because this apparently simple notion covers a diverse and complex reality. Someone should do for "isolate" what Kroeber has done for "culture"—write a book containing all the definitions given by different authors. We would then notice that since Wahlund coined the term, "isolate" has been used a great deal to say many things, so much so that after having once been helpful, it now seems confusing, to the point where one is tempted to abandon it altogether. But this is one of the signs of progress in the practical and theoretical understanding of isolated populations—what appeared to be simple some time ago now seems more complex. Scientific progress often involves dividing one category into several more accurate ones. The shift from theory to observation is reflected in the diversification of the term "isolate" and the need for new definitions.

As Dahlberg used the term, an "isolate" referred to an abstract "breeding unit": it was panmictic, having no prescribed or forbidden marriages and took no account of the differential family size. Observation on real populations led to a redefinition of "isolate" as those human groups whose main characteristics were their isolation and small size, such as the Ivad (Nemeskéri and Thoma 1961) and other groups. In this case, one considers the whole of an isolated population that is itself several times the size of a breeding unit. Within this "isolate," one must then estimate, or count directly, the "effective breeding population."

Roberts (1963), on the other hand, suggested that the term "isolate" be restricted to "those breeding entities within a culturally homogeneous population which, by their existence, promote genetic heterogeneity among one another and homogeneity within themselves." He thus eliminated small homogenous isolated populations and subgroups of large populations, geographically and socially defined. But here again, we come up against a lack of precision due to too much precision—which social barriers result in intrapopulational genetic heterogeneity among such

68

"isolates," and which do not? We must think of an abstract "isolate," without social and geographical barriers, resulting from the limitation of effective size and of intrapopulation breeding units, as in certain large urban or peasant populations.

All definitions of isolates imply a discontinuity where none exists. The demographic structure of a population is the result of a series of independent variables: size, rate of immigration, differential fertility, sex ratio, marriage rules, and so forth. The value of each of these parameters may be located between two theoretical poles. Their interaction determines the theoretical probability of genetic drift, the proportion of homozygotes/heterozygotes, the rate and direction of selection, and the changes in the gene frequency of the population. Field research tries to measure certain of these variables, and the values of other variables can be inferred through theoretical considerations. All human populations deviate from the general panmictic model (a randomly mating population, of unlimited dimension, with no selection or mutations or gene flow). It is useless to try to define the specific limits of an isolate and more realistic to consider that there are certain specific populations that deviate from the general panmictic model, primarily because of their small size and isolation. Here, the determination of the degree of isolation is a more important problem than the defining of an isolate. Since the other aspects of population structures may also vary, we must deal with many situations, each one with its unique evolutionary consequences. The observation of reality adds much complexity to the more simple models, although these aid us in understanding this complexity. However, the great number of random events to be taken into account during observation often makes deterministic models hazardous. It is, then, in combining observation with the methods of simulation that the scientist can draw closer to reality and understand it better.

THE OBSERVATION OF
HUMAN POPULATIONS

Putting some order into all the works on isolated populations is a difficult task. Many problems are dealt with: consanguinity, pathology, genetic load, genetic drift, and selection. As for the population studies, their main features (size, rate of migration, genetic barriers, demography, historical evolution, and social structure) are very diverse.

We might shed some light on the subject by taking the social structure of these populations as our basis. By *structure*, we mean the following variables: demography, social and geographical barriers and their influence on marriage patterns, and the relation between social organization and the selection of spouses. Human groups can be isolated from each other by many different kinds of barriers. Some are purely geographic, as in islands or in mountains. However, even in primitive societies, barriers of this type are transgressed due to a more or less important mobility and to institutionalized exchanges. Social rules also play a very important role: racial antagonism, linguistic differences, and religious or political affinities serve as social boundaries to the gene flow between populations.

Besides these negative rules, some more positive grouping factors, based on the social structure and on the demographic characteristics of each group, occur among all societies—the balance of repulsion and choice appears as a regulatory mechanism at the interface between human groups. In some cases, this interface is well defined, because a group is isolated from the others by the different barriers working in conjunction. More frequently, the situation becomes highly complex, and the social reality goes far away from any simple model. We must also not forget that there can be isolation without reference to any real boundary. At the limit, if each individual in a large society can only marry people from a limited circle, social as well as geographic, the circles of the different members of the society are not superposed. Limitation of the choice of mates occurs without "isolate." Isolation by distance as described for animal species is a good example of that situation, but in human societies, there is a large diversity of "distances."

In the field, the situation is less complicated genetically. The description of the pattern of genetic variation in a population does not require the understanding of the social mechanisms that underlie it. However, direct census and genealogical information may not reveal the breakdown of the geographical or social barriers that results in the flow of genes from outside the population and their diffusion.

More difficult is the diagnosis and the measurement of the various kinds of social distances, of their influence on mating behavior and genetic exchanges. The consistency of work on isolated populations is due mostly to the fact that this structure is accessible through direct research.

Data that are difficult to obtain in complex populations can be more easily obtained in small groups. The dynamic processes peculiar to a given population, and the social and ecological factors on which they depend, can be studied in their true interrelation: genetic structure and social organization are observed as reality and not as probabilities derived from theoretical models.

We shall present a few studies dealing with isolated human populations, classifying them according to the data relative to their structure. However, this is an approximate classification that could be improved by further refinement.

Simple Cases

Some populations come very close to the simplest model—an endogamous group of some hundreds of individuals having lived in isolation over many generations. The best example is the Eskimo isolate of Thule (Sutter and Tabah 1956). But we still lack an inventory of those populations that can be studied from this point of view, and case studies of this type remain scarce. On the other hand, these cases themselves may vary by the length of time they have remained isolated, by the events that have marked their origin, and above all, by their rules of social organization. Thus, the rate of consanguinity is not as high among certain groups like the Eskimo or the Ramah Navajo (Spuhler and Kluckhohn 1953) than among others like the Dunker (Glass et al. 1952). The relation between the size of a given population and its rate of consanguinity is, therefore, quite variable, which implies, at least theoretically, important consequences of the dynamic processes in these groups. It should also be noted that these observations make us cautious about the value of Dahlberg's formula for the estimation of the size of "isolates" as a function of their consanguinity (Morton 1955).

Great differences also exist in the historical stability of these populations. For some, like the Pitcairn of Kisar, there was a small founder population. Extremely endogamous, these people have developed in almost complete isolation. The original group was racially mixed, so that their present biological characteristics derive from a racial admixture of known quantity and origin, followed by lengthy isolation.

Tristan da Cunha is another peculiar case. Its demographic fluctuations are better known than most, and Roberts (1968b) has been able to show their role in the process of genetic drift. On the other hand, Ivad (Nemeskéri and Thoma 1961) has known gradual development, the departure of certain lineages being associated with an increased opening up of the group. We cannot mention here all the studies concerning small endogamous groups, but each one is peculiar in some respect (see, for example, Bonné 1963, Smith 1960, Sutter 1967, Chapman and Jacquard 1971).

The importance of demographic phenomena, especially of differential fertility and the rate of population increase, is recognized for the evolution of genetic structure. But our information about these factors is very poor. Among all theoretically possible situations, only a few are illustrated by concrete observation, and quite often these studies are incomplete, centered as they often are on one particular problem. Nowadays, at a time when demographic variables are undergoing great change, small isolated populations offer a particularly favorable field in which to study the biological consequence of present-day socioeconomic transformation. But groups living in extreme isolation are very few and are marginal cases. More commonly, "isolated" populations are caught in a network of influences in which isolating barriers and gene flow both play a role.

Subdivided Isolated Populations

One of the most fruitful situations is one in which a human group, be it geographic, linguistic, or religious, is divided into subgroups having practically no genetic exchange with the outside, and who have, among themselves, only limited communication that the observer can determine with precision. Giles, Walsh, and Bradley (1966) have profitably studied this type of situation in New Guinea. The comparison of subgroups, characterized by an "undistinguishable environment and an original population unity," permits them to trace the differences between subgroups to the phenomenon of genetic drift. The same holds true for the Hutterites (Mange 1964), for the Bedik (Gomila 1971), and for the three parishes studied by Böök (1956).

Subdivided isolated populations are most commonly found in peasant societies, where social organization is intimately related to settlement patterns. This can be illustrated through the case of Saint-Barthélemy, a small island peopled by approximately 200 inhabitants, most of them being Whites of French origin. Since at least 125 years ago, the endogamy of the island is close to 100 percent. However, this isolated group is not a

single unit—the island is subdivided into two parishes, each one subdivided into several settlements (Benoist 1964, 1966). The examination
of the parochial records and the direct census of all the population show
us some important facts. The parishes are highly endogamous, with more
than 90 percent of all the marriages occurring between people born in the
same parish. Some districts are endogamous, some are not, but on the
eastern side of the island ("au Vent"), the parish as a whole constitutes
a Mendelian population. On the western side, this is not so. Some districts "sous le Vent" are more or less isolated (see Figure 13). Therefore,
although Saint-Barthélemy as a whole is an isolated island, its population
is subdivided into two "isolates," one of which is further subdivided into
several partially isolated subgroups.

The structure of Saint-Barthélemy is even more complicated due to
the settlement on a neighboring island (St. Thomas in the U.S. Virgin
Islands) of people originating from Saint-Barthélemy, where they created
a new isolated group. While Saint-Barthélemy is quite protected from

FIGURE 13. Genetic barriers in Saint-Barthélemy.

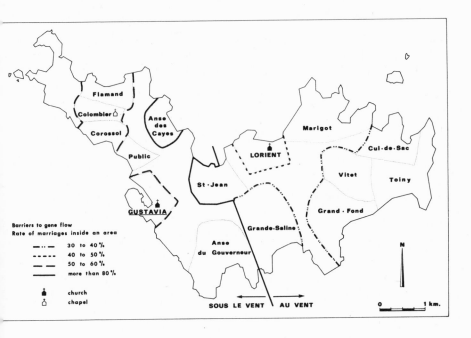

genetic admixture from outside, the group of St. Thomas is more open, especially through marriage with white people from other countries (Dyke 1970). This group also maintains a strong relationship with Saint-Barthélemy, where many people come to marry in their parish, and acts as an intermediate between Saint-Barthélemy and the outside world. For genetic purposes, this situation is highly favorable—well defined isolation, combined with a small amount of recognized gene flow occurring in a subdivided community, gives many opportunities for a careful examination of evolutionary dynamics and its social regulation.

In contrast, there are many "primitive" populations, apparently autonomous, among whom gene flow occurs at variable intervals. In ignorance of their recent history, we might have considered such populations as being isolated. Salzano, Neel, and Maybury-Lewis (1967), Neel and Salzano (1967), and Ward and Neel (1970b) have documented the results of this temporary segmentation of a "breeding unit" in a process of "fission/fusion." Random factors play a major role in the biological evolution of these groups without any of the subgroups being an isolate. In this population structure, the isolation of subpopulations, although only partial, is still an important evolutionary factor.

Semi-Isolated Populations

Local genetic differentiation may occur among partially isolated subpopulations. The calculated or direct estimation of the effective population size and of the rate of migration makes it possible to appraise the part played by random genetic drift in this differentiation. This is the case with the Peruvian communities investigated by Lasker and Kaplan (1964), with the Cashinahua studied by Johnston et al. (1969), as well as with the French Canadians living in Quebec and in the Acadia region, and now being studied. A number of studies have dealt with situations of this type, but have approached them from different theoretical perspectives: Laughlin (1950) on the Eskimos, Blumberg et al. (1964) on Quebec Indians, and Arends et al. (1967) on the Yanomama of the upper Orinoco region.

Interpretation based exclusively on the simplest models can lead to erroneous conclusions. The balance between differentiation and homogenization is perpetually open to question. This is one of the conclusions reached by Hiorns et al. (1969), who studied a series of neighboring parishes of the Otmoor district in Oxfordshire. They found that the rate of convergence of those populations who communicate among themselves induces a homogenization of all the villages at a rate that counterbalances their diversification. On the other hand, we must not forget that local differences in gene frequencies seem necessary between small communities, even if the problem of sampling has been solved. We must carefully examine their importance before coming to any conclusions concerning the respective roles of drift and selection in the differences found between partial subdivisions of a population. The recent works of Smith (1969) and Cavalli-Sforza (1969a) also tackle the theoretical side of this question.

These semi-isolated populations differ very little from complex societies, which, because of the social and ecological forces at work, are not perfectly homogeneous. Is this not the case with all human societies?

Isolated Populations and Complex Societies

Within vast populations living in a land with no major geographical barriers, developing subgroups can be traced in only two ways: by the statistical evaluation of consanguinity or by intensive study of geographical or social communities. The factors restricting individual mobility and the existence of marriage in-groups tend to maintain isolates in Dahlberg's sense. Field studies can analyze them by finding the lineages between which preferential marriages are still practiced for a number of reasons.

Works of a more general nature (Sutter and Tabah 1955a, Frota-Pessoa 1957) use demographical statistics and Dahlberg's formula to estimate the size of isolates. Results are often disappointing and contradictory, varying more according to what was assumed in the first place than according to the populations under study. Consequently, several books, mainly methodological, have been written, with the aim of tracking down groups of endogamous descent in peasant or urban societies. The transition, mentioned in the previous paragraph, is not clear-cut, and certain situations discussed are similar to those found in semi-isolated populations. Switzerland, for instance, has conditions that have been the object of research concerning hereditary pathology (Klein and Ammann 1964) or anthropology (Hulse 1957). The same holds true for Hungary (Walter and Nemeskéri 1967), Yugoslavia (Dolinar 1965), and Sweden

(Larson 1955). Cavalli-Sforza's work (1969a) on the Parma Valley is of the same nature.

All these studies concern populations with written records dating back several centuries. The reconstruction of genealogies and the exact description of demographic events are hence possible. The situation is less clear than it is in more simple cases, but the possibilities of accurate documentation offset the negative aspects. More and more works based on archives are being written for medical (Hammond and Jackson 1957, Woolf et al. 1955), demographic (Mugnier, Sutter, and Cox 1966, Charbonneau 1970), and anthropological purposes (Gomila and Guyon 1969).

The tendency here is toward a real dissection of complex societies, and data can be more or less directly used for genetic purposes. But these are difficult studies because of the quantity of information that has to be controlled, as well as the considerable variation that significant elements (like consanguinity and migration) have known over time; variations of the level of isolation become a part of a complex set of interacting variables.

METHODOLOGICAL PROGRESS AND THE EVOLUTION OF THEORETICAL THOUGHT

The improvement of methods, greater precision of observation, and the confrontation of theory with real situations have changed our knowledge and our perspectives; above all, recent works attest to a desire to go beyond the more simple concepts that had been useful in the beginning. For example, an attempt to measure consanguinity through the frequency of marriages between individuals having the same name (Crow and Mange 1965) has been applied to the Hutterites. Lasker (1969) has also proposed the calculation of an "expected isonymy," which is the random component of isonymy. This provides an estimate of the size of the "breeding population" or, at least, the size of several "breeding populations." A series of data (genealogies, archives, and inscriptions found on tombstones) helps us measure endogamy over a relatively long period of time. These results are valid only if the nonrandom component is very small compared with the random one and if surnames are regularly transmitted. In small populations with good archives, we could probably compare the consanguinity obtained from genealogy with the one obtained from isonymy. It would give us precious quantitative data on social structure, especially on residential rules. But in the overall picture, there is no doubt that the genealogical and social-demographical methods have known the greatest progress. The gathering of data and their analysis have become more systematic, and computers allow us to work on large groups.

The direct study of archives has been perfected by specialists in the field of historical demography (Fleury and Henry 1965). Mechanographic methods have been used for the demographic analysis of small-scale isolated populations (Sutter and Tabah 1956, Mugnier, Sutter, and Cox 1966). But it is particularly the reconstruction (with the help of a computer) of genealogies on the basis of archives that has yielded good results. It has thus been possible to retrace with great accuracy the demographic history of populations (birth rate, migrations, and differential fertility), as well as the evolution of their consanguinity. For example, this kind of research is now proceeding in seven French-Canadian communities (Gomila and Guyon 1969). Biological results can be associated with individuals and, therefore, can be analyzed by taking account of the subjects' relationships. This helps us utilize samples that include related persons.

The study of social contexts has become much more sophisticated since the last decade, yet the question remains—is this the case for strictly biological data? The discovery of an increasing number of genetic systems that are relatively easy to identify in a laboratory has overshadowed the works devoted to morphological characteristics. The problem peculiar to research on small-scale isolated populations leads scientists to seek support in undisputable genetic facts. On the other hand, our poor knowledge of the transmission of biometric characteristics discourages their use. But, inversely, we wonder if we could not study these factors in the tradition of Hulse (1957), Mange (1964), and Gomila (1971)—isolated populations may well help in our understanding of their genetic bases. The same is true for any populations from which the genealogies are well known.

Another field of methodology has also been developed, namely, the techniques used for computer simulation. Here, it is theory that keeps close to observation. Classical mathematical treatment, even of the most elaborate kind, comes up against the complexity and diversity of random factors. Without dwelling on this topic, which is treated in detail in Chapters 10 and 11, this approach permits the introduction of the chance factor on an individual level at the same rate that was statistically found in the survey of a large-scale population. Population simulation brings us closer to reality than most mathematical models. With further developments of these techniques, the evolution of the genetic structure of artificial populations will, consequently, give us an exact image of that of real ones.

It appears, then, that as a whole, recent research has allowed us to voluntarily leave behind simplified models for more complex analysis of facts, and this, in turn, has led to connecting interrelated phenomena that used to be studied separately. In order to imprint a certain unity to our brief description of this change, we can set it within the general framework of the evolution that small-scale populations have known.

Within these populations, a reduction of size does not, of course, directly alter the frequency of genes, nor does it affect the relation, established by the Hardy-Weinberg law, between the frequency of genes and that of genotypes. However, limited size does affect the evolution of genetic structure and genotypic structure. Chance variations tend to eliminate alleles and to fix only one of them at a speed inversely proportional to the size of the population. The rate of consanguinity increases in random marriages, which implies a reduced number of heterozygotes in the successive new generation. With time, the population tends to become increasingly more homozygous. Moreover, marriage rules often prescribe the choice of a spouse who is related, which increases the pressure in the same direction.

Thus, data obtained by different methods all lead to these fundamental problems: to determine the coefficient of kinship in a given population and to measure the probability and the results of genetic drift. Research contributes information on two important subjects: (1) the comparison, with the help of sociodemographical data, of real populations with the theoretical models of small-scale isolated populations, and (2) the detection of the biological effects of the factors that bring these populations closer to, or further away from, the evolutive scheme.

As no human population exactly conforms to the extreme models of an isolate or of a population of unlimited size, all studies are limited to a certain part of the continuum, the two poles of which are these models. But it is becoming increasingly evident that it is this continuum that is interesting, rather than its pole. The observation of small-scale populations thus becomes part of a wider study concerning the structure of populations and the meaning of their evolution (Jacquard 1970b). All research dealing with human genetics should be concerned with populations whose structure is well known—no valid sampling can be made without this, whether it is for the study of genetic polymorphism or for that of biometric variations. It is the time for the study of the effects of consanguinity on the genetic heritage, the selective value of polymorphism, or the rate of mutation of recessive lethal genes.

The study of isolates has played a pioneering role by its direct research of data that can be applied both to a population as a whole and to the individuals it comprises (Sutter 1967). This is especially true in those cases where good written records covering many generations are available. Furthermore, it is not only by renewing the general outlook of research that the studies of small-scale populations have contributed to our knowledge of the biology of populations. More specifically, these studies have also contributed to our understanding of the evolutionary process of small-scale populations. We shall now appraise both the success and the limits of their contribution.

The conditions peculiar to small-scale populations first led research workers to examine, with good results, the role played by genetic drift in the "microevolution" of human populations. These investigators have been able to show significant differences in the frequency of genes between isolated groups and their population of origin or between subpopulations (Glass et al. 1952, Lasker 1969, Lasker and Kaplan 1964, Benoist 1964, 1966, Cavalli-Sforza, Barrai, and Edwards 1964, Giles, Walsh, and Bradley 1966, Cavalli-Sforza 1969a, Morton et al. 1972). These differences have been traced to genetic drift for two main reasons: (1) the theoretical probability of drift within the groups being observed in relation to its demographic characteristics, and (2) the elimination of disturbing factors, such as migration and selection, by the choice of the group to be studied.

But, if it has been proved that drift plays a role in the genetic transformation of human populations (to quote Cavalli-Sforza 1969), "the relative importance of drift and natural selection in determining the course of evolution remains to be assessed." And this is one of the more important shortcomings of studies concerning small-scale populations. For during the 1960s, the influence of selection on a great number of genetic markers and on the maintenance of polymorphism has clearly been shown (Brues 1963, Livingstone 1960, Chung and Morton 1961,

79

Morton, Krieger, and Mi 1966, Vogel and Chakravartiim 1966, Allison 1964).

The relationship between selection and phenomena peculiar to small populations, however, is very complex. Local variations in the coefficients of selection may exist. There is also a relationship between the proportion of homozygotes/heterozygotes and selection, and this proportion is affected both by consanguinity and drift. Some authors have attempted to determine the respective roles of chance fluctuation and of drift in interregional variations of gene frequency by using the method of probabilities (Nei 1965, Nei and Imaizumi 1966, Thoma 1969). Considering the results of these works, we must admit that *small isolated populations can lead to erroneous interpretations concerning the influence of selection* on their transformation. Here again, the methods of simulation may prove to be very fruitful.

The mechanisms leading to genetic drift are many (Roberts 1968b). History, unforeseeable events, and social organization also have an importance. The study of isolates provides many examples of the permanent interaction between social and biological factors. The biological observations cannot be explained without reference to the social organization and historical events (Benoist 1966). To quote Neel and Salzano (1967): "aspects of the social organization of the group . . . may be an important factor in determining the composition of the new group." We often ignore correlations between the place of individuals within their social organization and their hereditary characteristics, particularly in the field of behavior. The few known comparisons between migrant individuals and their initial group show that this is a selective factor that must not be neglected. To a certain extent, drift by the founder effect may have a selective origin.

But if studies concerning genetic drift have yielded quite satisfying results, there is another field where research has turned out to be disappointing and contradictory—genetic polymorphism and biometric variability rarely give evidence of expected homozygosis. Neel and Salzano (1967) have recently commented on this apparently paradoxical result and have taken up part of the research concerning this question. We have here a most complex problem both in theory and in practice. This question could also be studied from another angle—by the observation of heterosis resulting from the breaking up of isolates (Hulse 1957, Gomila 1971). In spite of some seemingly positive findings, we are still not sure what mechanisms intervene: it is difficult to appreciate the exact relative importance of heterosis and of selection or migration.

The fact that we very rarely observe the loss of genes without any selective value within small populations can be due to only two reasons: first, either the structure of these populations is more remote from the model of an isolate than we believe, or second, selection is much more important than we think. Of course, this brings up the question of what role is played by selection in the maintenance of human polymorphism.

But we could also ask ourselves if we have not neglected another area of observation that would consist, with the help of the many genetic markers that we now know, in the direct inventory of genotypic structure in small-scale populations. Scientists have always paid more attention to the frequency of genes than to that of genotypes. This can, however, be directly observed to a certain extent. It would be interesting to compare observation and probability in small groups, particularly in the racially-mixed ones. No doubt we would come up against some difficulty in establishing tests of statistical comparison in small populations.

As we end this survey, some general features seem to emerge. The most interesting one, no doubt, is the dialectic movement between theory and observation. First, theory gives us very simplified models. We observe reality in order to find cases that approximate these models. And then, reality makes us construct more elaborate theoretical frameworks, which in turn are modified by reality. This has been the case of the studies dealing with small isolated populations where, besides the direct contribution due to work on the more simple cases, we can see a shift in the center of interest. Semi-isolated and complex societies come into the foreground, as theory and method become more sophisticated. This can be seen in the fieldwork being done, as well as in theoretical preoccupations (Morton 1968). And, one may think that future progress in the knowledge of the factors that govern the evolution of human populations will come more and more from the study of subdivided populations, of these isolated regional groups within which different forces act simultaneously according to a wide range of possible variations.

5
Inbreeding in Human Populations[1]

R U S S E L L   M.   R E I D

Department of Anthropology
University of Texas at Austin

"Theoretical population genetics is concerned with model building. Any model of nature is an oversimplification, as is any verbal description of a natural process. A model is an attempt to abstract from nature some significant aspect of the true situation" (Crow and Kimura 1970:3). The more basic models of population genetics assume that members of the population mate at random and have equal reproductive potential. In other words, each act of fertilization represents the union of two gametes, each of which was randomly chosen from the vast array of gametes that could potentially be produced by the adult members of the population. While nonrandom mating of various forms is often found in nature, it is of special interest to the anthropological geneticist because of the anthropologist's broader interest in human marriage. Since human mating is often associated with the social institution of marriage, nonrandom mating emerges as one of the many manifestations of cultural behavior.

It is a universal feature of human society that marriage between certain relatives is prohibited. In some human societies, this prohibition is complemented by a preference for marriage between certain other relatives.

Such preferences generally take one of two possible forms. In the more common form, marriage between children of siblings of the same sex (parallel cousins) is prohibited. These parallel cousins are often addressed by the same kinship terms as siblings. Complementing this prohibition .s a preference for marriage between offspring of siblings of opposite sex (cross cousins). In some such societies, these cross cousins may be addressed by the same kinship terms as sibs-in-law or spouses. The execution of such preferences results in a series of marriages between pairs of kin-based groups. This persistent relationship between such groups is referred to as "marriage alliance" (Dumont 1968). In contrast to the relatively widespread systems of marriage alliance is the preference for patrilateral parallel cousin marriage (marriage of a man to his father's brother's daughter) found in some Islamic societies of the Middle East (Murphy and Kasdan 1959). This preference, in sharp contrast to the nature of alliance systems, reflects a tendency toward patrilineal descent group endogamy.

This chapter deals with consanguineous marriage and inbreeding in human populations and the relevant mathematical models of population genetics. Included first is a discussion of the concept of inbreeding and the means by which it is quantified, that is, the "inbreeding coefficient." The two widely used formulations of this coefficient are compared by reference to three hypothetical cases. Second is a discussion of the methods by which this coefficient is estimated for an individual and for a total population. This includes a discussion of pedigree studies, isonomy, and bioassay. The third section deals with the occurrence of consanguineous marriage and inbreeding in human populations. Fourth is an examination of the theoretical and empirical effects of inbreeding. The chapter concludes with a discussion of human inbreeding as "cultural behavior."

THE CONCEPT OF INBREEDING

Definitions

For the geneticist, *consanguinity* refers to a relationship between two individuals sharing one or more common ancestors. Consanguineous mating and consanguineous marriage refer, respectively, to mating and marriage between individuals so related. The human geneticist should be cautioned that this definition of consanguinity is not shared by social anthropologists. Morgan (1871) felt that kinship was based on folk knowledge of biological consanguinity. Van Gennep (1906), by contrast, saw the need to distinguish between *parenté sociale* and *parenté physique*, because the consanguineous ties of relevance to kinship relationships in any particular society need not be the same as either real biological consanguinity or the society's folk concepts of biological consanguinity. This approach was followed by Malinowski (1913:182): "consanguinity (as a sociological concept) is, therefore, not the physiological bond of common blood, it is the social acknowledgment and interpretation of it."

Inbreeding is a genetic consequence of biologically consanguineous matings, and the offspring of biologically consanguineous matings are said to be inbred. In a series of papers published in the *American Naturalist* between 1913 and 1917, Pearl expressed a need for a coefficient by which the geneticist could quantify the degree of inbreeding. Two major formulations of an inbreeding coefficient have subsequently been proposed. For some purposes, these two approaches may be used interchangeably.

The first of these formulations is that of Wright (1921, 1922), which states that the inbreeding coefficient (f) is the correlation between uniting gametes. "If there is *assortative mating from any cause* [italics added], there will be some correlation between the gametes which unite. Represent this correlation by f" (Wright 1921:118). The words "assortative mating from any cause" have been emphasized to show that from the onset, Wright saw applications of this coefficient beyond the problem of parental consanguinity. Indeed, Part III of the same paper by Wright deals with the contribution to f of assortative mating for phenotypic similarity. Likewise, Wright (1921) suggested the importance of "mating within local races" as a form of assortative mating contributing to this f coefficient. This suggestion anticipated later work on the genetics of subdivided populations (Wahlund 1928, Wright 1931, Yasuda 1968b) and on isolation by distance (Wright 1943).

The second major approach to the inbreeding coefficient, based on probabilities rather than on correlations, was developed by Haldane and Moshinsky (1939), Cotterman (1940), and Malécot (1948). By their approach, the inbreeding coefficient is the probability that the homologous genes of uniting gametes are identical by descent from one or more

85

common ancestors. This approach, unlike Wright's, limits the coefficient to the problem of parental consanguinity.

When we are concerned with the contributions to inbreeding of a particular form of consanguineous mating, these two approaches yield the same coefficient. Likewise, if we are concerned with an infinite population in which the only departure from random mating is parental consanguinity, then these approaches are interchangeable. Beyond those conditions, there are important differences between these two formulations of the inbreeding coefficient. We will deal with both formulations in more detail by looking at a series of hypothetical situations.

Case I: An Infinitely Large Inbred Population

Assume we have a population of infinite size in which some consanguineous mating occurs. An individual whose two homologous genes at a particular locus are identical by descent from the common ancestors of his parents is said by Cotterman (1940) to be autozygous. When the homologous genes of an individual are of independent ancestry (even though the individual may be homozygous), he is said to be allozygous. By Malécot's definition, the inbreeding coefficient, f, is the probability that the homologous genes of an individual are identical by common descent. In other words, f is the probability of autozygosity. Under the Hardy-Weinberg conditions of infinite population size and random mating, all individuals would be allozygous. Thus, f would be zero. However, when f is nonzero, we must adjust the Hardy-Weinberg expectations. For alleles A and B, with frequencies p and q, respectively, the expected genotype distributions are shown in Table 10. These frequencies illustrate the

TABLE 10

EXPECTED GENOTYPE FREQUENCIES IN AN INFINITELY LARGE POPULATION WITH PARENTAL CONSANGUINITY

Genotype	Frequencies				
	Allozygous		Autozygous		Total
AA	$p^2(1-f)$	$+$	pf	$=$	$p^2 + pqf$
AB	$2pq(1-f)$			$=$	$2pq(1-f)$
BB	$q^2(1-f)$	$+$	qf	$=$	$q^2 + pqf$

consequences of parental consanguinity for genotype frequencies in an infinitely large population.

Now, if we assign metric values of a and b to the alleles A and B, respectively, we can calculate the correlation between uniting gametes in this infinitely large but inbred population (Table 11).

TABLE 11

VALUES USED IN CALCULATING THE CORRELATION BETWEEN UNITING GAMETES IN AN INFINITELY LARGE POPULATION WITH PARENTAL CONSANGUINITY

Sperm	Egg	Frequency	Value of Sperm = S	Value of Egg = E	S^2	E^2	SE
A	A	$p^2 + fpq$	a	a	a^2	a^2	a^2
A	B	$pq(1-f)$	a	b	a^2	b^2	ab
B	A	$pq(1-f)$	b	a	b^2	a^2	ab
B	B	$q^2 + fpq$	b	b	b^2	b^2	b^2

$$\overline{S} = \overline{E} = a(p^2 + fpq + pq - fpq) + b(q^2 + fpq + pq - fpq)$$
$$= ap + bq$$

$$\overline{S^2} = \overline{E^2} = a^2(p^2 + fpq + pq - fpq) + b^2(q^2 + fpq + pq - fpq)$$
$$= a^2p + b^2q$$

$$\overline{SE} = a^2(p^2 + fpq) + ab[2pq(1-f)] + b^2(q^2 + fpq)$$
$$= a^2p^2 + a^2fpq + ab2pq(1-f) + b^2q^2 + b^2fpq$$

$$r_{SE} = \frac{\overline{SE} - \overline{S}\,\overline{E}}{(\overline{S^2} - \overline{S}^2)(\overline{E^2} - \overline{E}^2)}$$
$$= \frac{fpq(a-b)^2}{pq(a-b)^2}$$
$$= f$$

Thus, the correlations between uniting gametes (Wright's f) is exactly equal to the probability of autozygosity (Malécot's f) under the stated conditions.

again, see Yasuda & Morton 1967: 251

87

Case II: Finite Randomly Mating Populations

Now let us assume that we have a finite population of N initially unrelated individuals who mate entirely at random (including self-fertilization). Under these conditions, the genotype of each member of the offspring generation is formed by randomly combining two genes sampled from the genes of the parental generation. The correlation between uniting gametes (Wright's f) would thus be zero. The probability of autozygosity (Malécot's f) would, however, only be zero in the initial generation. Among the first generation of offspring, this probability would be 1/2N. In other words, the probability of randomly choosing the same parental gene twice for any given offspring is 1/2N. As more and more members of the population are related by descent from common ancestors, the probability of autzygosity increases to

$$f_t = 1 - (1 - 1/2N)^t$$

in t generations. Note that the probability of randomly occurring autozygosity is slightly different when self-fertilization is not possible. It takes one additional generation before this probability is 1/2N, and thereafter it is

$$f_t = f_{t-1} + (1 - 2f_{t-1} + f_{t-2})/2N$$

(Crow and Kimura 1970:101–2).

In a randomly mating finite population, Wright and Malécot's formulations of the inbreeding coefficient seem to be in conflict, but in fact they are not, since, in this case, they refer to different kinds of relationships between gene frequencies and genotype frequencies. The correlation approach relates these frequencies within a single generation, while the probability-of-autozygosity approach relates the genotype frequencies of one generation to the gene frequencies of the initial generation. Thus, the probabilty already referred to, $1 - (1 - 1/2N)^t$, is the expected loss of heterozygosity after t generations due to random drift toward fixation. It does not imply a nonrandom pattern of genotype combinations within any given generation. If the gene frequencies are not randomly drifting— if, for example, the population is in a stable equilibrium—then we may ignore randomly occurring consanguineous matings, the resultant autozygosity, and the predicted loss of heterozygosity. From this, Crow and

Russell M. Reid

Kimura (1970:61) conclude that "inbreeding occurs when mates are more closely related than they would be if they had been chosen at random from the population."

Case III: Subdivided Populations

Imagine a society composed of two endogamous randomly mating subdivisions equal in size but displaying very different gene frequencies, as in Table 12. If a geneticist were to treat these two endogamous divisions as

TABLE 12
GENOTYPE FREQUENCIES IN A POPULATION
WITH TWO RANDOMLY MATING ENDOGAMOUS
SUBPOPULATIONS OF EQUAL SIZE

| | Observed Frequencies | | |
	Subpopulation I	Subpopulation II	Total
Allele A	0.9	0.1	0.5
Allele B	0.1	0.9	0.5
Genotype AA	0.81	0.01	0.41
Genotype AB	0.18	0.18	0.18
Genotype BB	0.01	0.81	0.41

a single population, then he would observe the frequencies in the total column. Since the observed total gene frequencies would yield an expected genotype distribution of 0.25, 0.50, and 0.25, respectively, for AA, AB, and BB, the geneticist might conclude that there is a very high level of inbreeding in the population. Indeed, if we view inbreeding as the correlation between uniting gametes, then this conclusion is correct. However, this need not imply inbreeding in the Malécot sense. Here again, the two formulations of the inbreeding coefficient yield very different answers.

why not equilibrium?

This problem has been treated in more general form by Wahlund (1928). He has shown that if a large population is divided into closed but randomly mating subpopulations, where $\bar{p}$ and $\bar{q}$ are the mean values of p and q in the various subpopulations and σ^2 is their variance, then the genotype frequencies for the total population are as indicated in Table 13.

From what we have seen in Cases I and II, it follows that for the total population, the correlation between uniting gametes (Wright's f coefficient) is $\sigma^2/\bar{p}\bar{q}$ (Wright 1951), while for the individual subpopulation, it is zero. Note that the correlation dealt with here, unlike Malécot's probability of autozygosity, depends on the particular pattern of gene frequency differences among the various subpopulations. This correlation might, therefore, vary from locus to locus.

TABLE 13

GENOTYPE FREQUENCIES IN A POPULATION PARTITIONED INTO ENDOGAMOUS RANDOMLY MATING SUBPOPULATIONS

Genotypes	Frequencies in Total Population
AA	$\bar{p}^2 + \sigma^2$
Aa	$2\bar{pq}(1 - \sigma^2/\bar{pq})$
aa	$\bar{q}^2 + \sigma^2$

If the various subpopulations all begin with the same gene frequencies, p_0 and q_0, which are equal to $\bar{p}$ and $\bar{q}$, and if the subsequent genetic differences resulted only from random genetic drift, then the variance used above is

$$\sigma^2 = \frac{p_0 q_0}{2N}$$

after one generation and

$$\sigma^2 = p_0 q_0 [1 - (1 - 1/2N)^t]$$

after t generations (Crow 1954). If we substitute these variances due to random changes in gene frequencies into Wahlund's formulas above, we get correlations between united gametes of

$$1/2N$$

after one generation and

$$1 - (1 - 1/2N)^t$$

after t generations. These are, as we saw in Case II, the probabilities of autozygosity in a randomly mating isolate of size N. Thus, if the differences between the subpopulations of Wahlund's model result entirely from drift, then the probability of autozygosity equals the correlation between uniting gametes for the total subdivided population. In this restricted case, the Wright approach and the Malécot approach are equivalent.

In real populations, we seldom find discretely bonded subpopulations. Rather, we see isolation by geographic and social distance in mate selection and movement between semi-isolated subpopulations. Wright (1943) and others have extended the mathematics reviewed here to cover these more complex situations.

It should be clear by now that the inbreeding coefficients of Wright and of Malécot are equivalent only under very special conditions. This is a point that is too easily overlooked by human geneticists dealing with inbreeding. Though both formulations yield parameters valuable to the study of human populations, we must be cautious in our choice of approaches. This choice, as we have seen, must depend on the nature of the study population and of the research problem.

METHODS OF ASCERTAINMENT OF INBREEDING

Pedigree Studies

Since it may be shown that the contribution to the inbreeding coefficient of any particular form of consanguineous mating is the same under either the Wright or the Malécot formulation, only the Malécot approach will be presented here, because it seems to me to be the easier to understand. The probability formulation may be understood as an extension of two basic situations. First, let us look at a single gametic generation (Figure 14). For any autosomal locus, A, the probability that the gene in a particular gamete produced by an individual, A_j, is an immediate replicate of the gene coming to that individual from a particular parental gamete, A_i, is exactly one-half. This can be coded as follows:

$$P\{A_i \equiv A_j\} = 1/2.$$

Second, let us look at two gametes, A_i and A_j, produced by the same individual (Figure 15). The probability that A_i and A_j are identical by common descent is

$$P\{A_i \equiv A_j\} = 1/2 + \frac{F}{2} = (1 + F)/2,$$

where F is the inbreeding coefficient of the individual (that is, the prob-

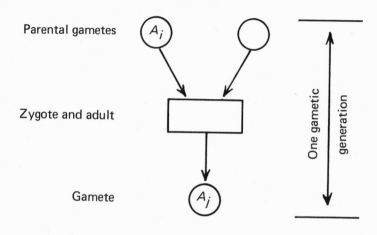

FIGURE 14. Genetic identity in a single gametic generation.

ability that A_m and A_p are identical by descent). Now, let us consider the genealogy illustrated in Figure 16. When the information given in Figures 15 and 16 is combined, we see that the probability that the genes of the uniting parental gametes are identical by descent from the common ancestor is

$$F = 1/2 \cdot 1/2 \cdot 1/2 \cdot \{(1 + F_A)/2\}1/2 \cdot 1/2$$
$$= (1/2)^6(1 - F_A),$$

where the power 6 is exactly the number of persons along the path through the common ancestor connecting the two parental gametes. Had there been more such paths through this or other common ancestors of the parents, then we would have summed over all such paths. Therefore, the general formula is

$$F = \sum(1/2)^n(1 + F_A),$$

where F_A is the inbreeding coefficient of a particular common ancestor and n is the number of persons along the genealogical paths between the parental gametes through that ancestor.

The genealogy illustrated in Figure 17 shows a birth to a couple related as first cousins.

92

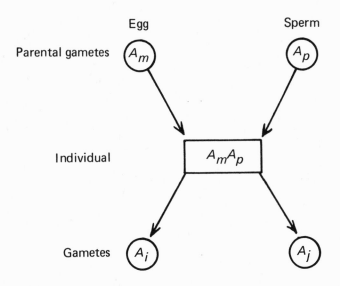

Egg | Sperm

Parental gametes $\quad (A_m) \qquad\qquad\qquad (A_p)$

Individual $\qquad\qquad \boxed{A_m A_p}$

Gametes $\qquad (A_i) \qquad\qquad\qquad (A_j)$

FIGURE 15. Genetic identity in two gametes produced by a single individual.

$$F_0 = (1/2)^5(1 + F_1) + (1/2)^5(1 + F_2)$$
$$= (1/2)^4 + (1/2)^5(F_1 + F_2)$$
$$= (1/2)^4\{1 + (F_1 + F_2)/2\}$$

If the ancestors were not inbred, then the inbreeding coefficient of the offspring becomes

$$F_0 = (1/2)^4 = 1/16.$$

The procedure differs only slightly in the case of X-linkage. First, only females normally have two X chromosomes, so it is only for female offspring that we can have X-chromosome inbreeding. Second, consider one gametic generation of a male (Figure 18).

We see that

$$P\{X_i \equiv X_j\} = 1,$$

where X_j is an X-linked gene that a man received from his mother and X_i is the X-linked gene that he passes to his daughter. In contrast, the

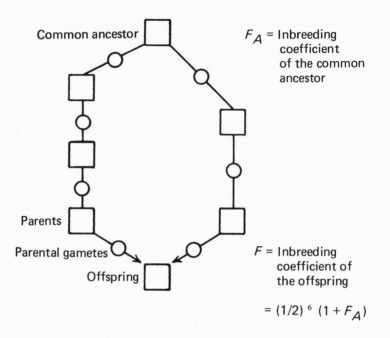

F_A = Inbreeding coefficient of the common ancestor

F = Inbreeding coefficient of the offspring

$$= (1/2)^6 (1 + F_A)$$

FIGURE 16. Probability of autozygosity.

FIGURE 17. Paths to common ancestors in a mating between first cousins.

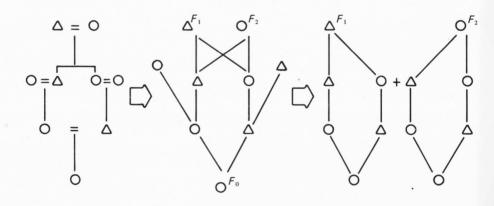

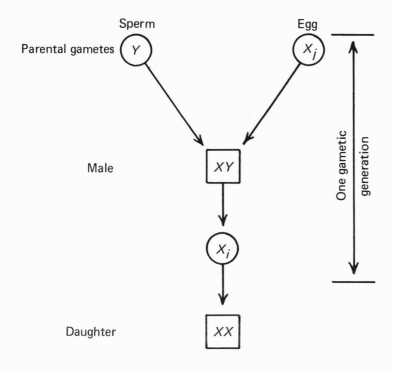

FIGURE 18. Sex chromosomes in a single male gametic generation.

probability that X_i is a replicate of the gene he received from his father is zero. Likewise, the probability that he will pass on a replicate of X_j to his son is zero. From this, it follows that in calculating X-linked inbreeding coefficients, F_x, we can (1) define F_x only for females, (2) ignore all genealogical paths with two males in succession, and (3) for the remaining paths, use the same formula as for autosomal loci, except that n is now the number of females along the path.

In the example of the girl born to a man and his mother's brother's daughter shown in Figure 17, we need consider only the path through the grandmother of the couple. There are only three females along that path. Thus, the X-linked inbreeding coefficient of the daughter is

$$F_x = (1/2)^3(1 + F_{xA}),$$

where F_{xA} is the X-linked inbreeding coefficient of the female ancestor.

F for linkage? Y-linkage too [handwritten marginal note]

95

Though the procedure just described is, in fact, quite simple, we must adopt some systematic approach to the recording and analysis of those data when we are dealing with a large number of complex genealogies. Kudo (1962) and Kudo and Sakaguchi (1963) have proposed a very useful procedure for this purpose. By their method, six generations of the ancestry of an individual may be represented by a 32×32 matrix, allowing very simple calculation of the individual's inbreeding coefficient. This procedure readily yields itself to computer analysis. MacCluer et al. (1967) developed a program based on Kudo's method. Other computer programs designed to calculate inbreeding coefficients from pedigree data have been reported by Mange (1969) and MacLean (1969). When choosing between estimating inbreeding coefficients by hand or by computer, it is necessary to determine if the time needed to organize the genealogies into the form required by the program is less than that required for a hand calculation. Ideally, such decisions should be made before the collection of data, so that the original recording procedure requires minimal reorganization of the data into the form required for analysis.

Using the pedigree method, we may calculate the individual inbreeding coefficient, F, for each member of the population. Having done this, the population inbreeding coefficient, f, is the arithmetic mean of the individual inbreeding coefficients:

$$f = \bar{F} = \frac{\Sigma F}{N}.$$

The value calculated is the Malécot coefficient of inbreeding, even if the correlation approach had been used in calculating the individual F values. This is true because the pedigree approach is concerned only with common ancestry. One consequence is the assumption that F is zero for persons whose parents are unrelated. However, under the Wright approach, the correlation between the uniting gametes of these nonconsanguineous births could be (1) positive, as in a subdivided population, or (2) zero, as in an infinite population combining consanguineous and random mating, or (3) negative, as in a finite randomly mating population. This can be seen from a review of the three cases in the preceding section of this chapter. Unfortunately, the pedigree approach gives us no

Russell M. Reid

method for calculating the contribution of the nonconsanguineous births to Wright's inbreeding coefficient.

Crow, in a personal communication to Allen (Allen 1965), has offered a solution to the problem of randomly occurring consanguineous matings in finite populations. He suggests that the contribution of parental consanguinity to the correlation between uniting gametes is the nonrandom component, f_n, of the probability of autozygosity:

$$f_n = \frac{f - f_r}{1 - f_r},$$

where f is the actual probability of autozygosity calculated as the mean of the individual F values, and f_r is the probability of autozygosity expected under random mating. This adjustment for "background" inbreeding is important to investigations of consanguineous mating in very small isolates, as, for example, the Samaritans (Bonné 1962). Indeed, this random component of inbreeding would be difficult to estimate for any population other than a small and easily definable isolate. Crow's formula shown above is modeled after Wright's (1965) formula for the mean coefficient of kinship within the subpopulations of a hierarchically subdivided population.

Isonomy

Crow and Mange (1965) provide us with an approach to estimating population inbreeding coefficients by using the frequency of marriages between persons with identical surnames—*isonomy*. The approach assumes that spouses are chosen without regard to surnames. Any increase over the randomly expected frequency of isonomous matings is thus viewed to result from consanguineous mating.

In human societies, it is often the case that surnames are an important consideration in the choice of spouses. In South India, for example (Reid 1971), we see strong preferences for consanguineous marriage linked with a total prohibition of isonomous marriage. Thus, the isonomy approach would have yielded an estimated inbreeding coefficient of zero. Though this is clearly an extreme case, less extreme deficiencies in the approach have been seen in other populations (Cavalli-Sforza and Bodmer 1971).

97

Bioassay

Another approach to estimating the population inbreeding coefficient (in Wright's sense) uses the observed deviation of phenotype proportions or mating type proportions from those expected under the Hardy-Weinberg theorem. Such a method, *bioassay,* has been proposed by Morton and Yasuda (1962) and developed further by Yasuda (1968a, 1969a). This approach uses "the method of maximum likelihood" to find the inbreeding coefficient and allele frequencies with the highest probability of producing the observed data. This mode of estimation involves the use of derivatives of log functions and thus an understanding of the procedure requires a knowledge of differential calculus. Interested readers are encouraged to refer to the References for information on this powerful and important approach to the estimation of inbreeding coefficients and gene frequencies.

OCCURRENCE OF INBREEDING IN HUMAN POPULATIONS

Table 14 groups various human populations according to their reported levels of inbreeding. There is no record of a human population in

TABLE 14
INBREEDING COEFFICIENTS OF
VARIOUS HUMAN POPULATIONS

Populations with $f < 0.00001$	
The Netherlands	Polman (1951)
Panama	Freire-Maia (1968)
Populations with f Between 0.00001 and 0.0001	
Czechoslovakia (Brno) after 1950	Zahálková and Preis (1970)
United States (Roman Catholic)	Freire-Maia (1968)
Populations with f Between 0.0001 and 0.001	
Belgium	Twisselmann (1961)
Czechoslovakia (Brno) before 1950	Zahálková and Preis (1970)
Italy (Northern)	Moroni (1966)
Switzerland	Morton and Hussels (1970)

Russell M. Reid

TABLE 14, cont'd.

Canada (French)	Freire-Maia (1968)
Canada (Roman Catholic)	Freire-Maia (1968)
Chile (Roman Catholic)	Freire-Maia (1968)
Uruguay (Roman Catholic)	Freire-Maia (1968)
Argentina (Roman Catholic)	Freire-Maia (1968)
Cuba (Roman Catholic)	Freire-Maia (1968)
Mexico (Roman Catholic)	Freire-Maia (1968)
Bolivia (Roman Catholic)	Freire-Maia (1968)
Brazil (Roman Catholic)	Saldanha (1960)

Populations with f Between 0.001 and 0.01

Japan (various)	Schull and Neel (1965)
France (Loir-et-Cher and Finistère)	Sutter and Tabah (1955b)
Hungary (Ivad)	Nemeskéri and Thoma (1961)
Italy (Sardinia and Aeolian Islands)	Moroni (1966)
Spain	Cisternas and Moroni (1967)
United States (Watauga Co., North Carolina)	Herndon and Kerley (1952)
United States (Mormon)	Woolf et al. (1956)
United States (Ramah Navajo)	Spuhler and Kluckhohn (1953)
India (Bombay)	Sanghvi, Varde, and Master (1956)
Brazil (Northeastern) from pedigrees	Yasuda (1969a)

Populations with f Between 0.01 and 0.05

Japan (Hosojima)	Iskikuni et al. (1960)
India (Coastal Andhra Pradesh)	Dronamraju (1964)
India (Rural Andhra Pradesh)	Sanghvi (1966)
India (Kavanur Village, Madras)	Centerwall et al. (1969)
India (Telaga Caste, Andhra Pradesh)	Reid (1971)
Jordan and Israel (Samaritans)	Bonné (1962)
Egypt (Nubia)	Strouhal (1971), Hussien (1971)
Guinea (Fouta-Djallon)	Cantrelle and Dupire (1964)
United States (Dunkers, Pennsylvania)	Glass et al. (1952)
United States (Hutterites, South Dakota and Minnesota)	Mange (1964)
Tristan da Cunha	Roberts (1967)
Brazil (Xavante)	Neel et al. (1964)
Brazil (Northeastern) from bioassay	Yasuda (1969a)

Other Populations with Close Consanguineous Marriage for Which No Inbreeding Coefficients Are Available

Australia (Aborigines)	Radcliffe-Brown (1913)
Ceylon	Tambiah (1958)
Burma (various tribes)	Leach (1961)
Bedouins	Murphy and Kasdan (1959)

which the inbreeding coefficient is greater than 0.05, and most human populations have inbreeding coefficients below 0.005. From Table 14 and the available ethnographic data, we find that there is a chain of populations in the circum-Indian Ocean area—from the aboriginal population of Australia through the tribal groups of Southeast Asia, the populations of Ceylon and southern India, the Middle East, and into Africa—in which traditional social custom encourages close consanguineous marriage. These populations, and a few scattered elsewhere, have the world's highest human inbreeding coefficients.

The high inbreeding coefficients reported for extremely small isolates may be misleading. The 270 inhabitants of the island of Tristan da Cunha are the descendants of 15 persons arriving on the island between 1816 and 1908. Roberts (1967) reports that the probability of autozygosity among the present population is 0.0403, while a probability of 0.0330 would be expected in a randomly mating population derived from 15 founder ancestors. Using Crow's adjustment for this random background inbreeding, we derive a nonrandom component of the probability of autozygosity as follows:

$$f_n = \frac{f - f_r}{1 - f_r}$$
$$= \frac{0.0403 - 0.0330}{1 - 0.0330}$$
$$= 0.0075.$$

As we have seen, it is this nonrandom autozygosity that results in departures from the Hardy-Weinberg law within any given generation. This nonrandom component becomes especially large in the presence of social preferences for close consanguineous marriage. Bonné (1963) has shown that close consanguineous marriage is far more common in the extremely small Samaritan population than would be expected under random mating. This high frequency of consanguineous marriage and high inbreeding coefficient were partially ascribed to the social preference for close consanguineous marriage. This is, likewise, true for the much larger population of southern India (Reid 1971).

Less is known of the native populations of the New World. Although their traditional systems of classification of relatives are often consistent with close consanguineous marriages, their traditional marriage patterns had often undergone vast changes by the time they were carefully studied.

Russell M. Reid

The high inbreeding coefficients reported for the Navajo (Spuhler and Kluckhohn 1953) and the Xavante (Neel et al. 1964), as well as the ethnographic work of Strong (1929) with the Naskapi and Hallowell (1937) in the Lake Winnipeg area, to cite only a few, suggest that consanguineous marriage was common in many of the precolonial populations of the New World.

With one exception, the figures in Table 14 are based on pedigree studies. That exception is the high figure from northeastern Brazil, which is based on bioassay (Yasuda 1969b). The value computed from pedigrees in the same population was less than half that calculated from bioassay. A portion of the remaining coefficient could be accounted for by racial endogamy (the population contains Brazilian Indians in addition to persons of European and African ancestry); but, 34 percent of the total inbreeding coefficient from mating type bioassay could not be accounted for. Yasuda refers to this as unascertained consanguinity. We must, however, remember that while bioassay measures Wright's correlation between uniting gametes, the pedigree study of consanguineous couples measures Malécot's probability of autozygosity. We have seen in Case III that for Wright and Malécot's inbreeding coefficients to be identical in a subdivided population, it is necessary for the genetic differences between the subpopulations to be the result of drift from initially equal frequencies. This is clearly not the case in a national population composed of Negroes, Indians, and Caucasians. Under these real conditions, we can even question the validity of a single bioassay drawn from data on a number of different loci. In a collection of subpopulations of independent origins, the correlation between uniting gametes would be expected to vary from locus to locus. It is not surprising that a composite estimate based on several loci in such a complex population should contain large components that cannot be accounted for. Such situations should not be viewed as evidence for shortcomings in a well-executed pedigree study. In contrast, the situation reported by Yasuda points to the inherent differences between the two formulations of the inbreeding coefficient.

Social anthropologists and the geneticists dealing with close consanguineous marriage agree that *only a minority of the marriages are of the socially preferred type*. Indeed, it is clear from computer simulation studies (Kunstadter et al. 1963) that this must be the case. The upper limit on the frequency of marriages meeting a society's preference is based on the demographic availability of persons of the appropriate age, sex, and genealogical or kinship relationship. Several authors (Barrai, Cavalli-Sforza, and Moroni 1962, Hajnal 1963, Cavalli-Sforza, Kimura, and Barrai 1966, Schull and MacCluer 1968, Reid 1971) present mathematical models predicting the availability of various kinds of genealogical relatives. Among the very large but inbred populations of southern India, a majority of the marriages are between persons with no known common ancestry (Reid 1971). While the inbreeding coefficient for the total population may remain low, the variance of individual values may be quite high. As a consequence, human inbreeding cannot be treated as a system of mating in which all matings are genealogically identical. It may be that the extremely wide range of individual inbreeding coefficients is far more important than the relatively low population averages attained even in populations preferring close consanguineous marriage. In other words, the difference between highly inbred and noninbred persons of the same population may be of greater biological importance than the difference between a population with an inbreeding coefficient of 0.02 and another with a coefficient of 0.0002.

concentrate on individuals with a high 'F'

THEORETICAL AND EMPIRICAL EFFECTS OF INBREEDING

Effects of Inbreeding on Genotype Frequencies

The primary level at which inbreeding affects the mathematics of population genetics is in the relationship between allele frequencies and genotype frequencies. To view this, we may assume a genetic locus where A represents any particular allele with a frequency of q, and A' represents the set of all other alleles at that locus. In an inbred population lacking differential fertility for the genotypes in question, we can expect the genotypic frequencies illustrated in Table 15. The inbreeding coefficient, f, is

TABLE 15
EXPECTED GENOTYPE FREQUENCIES
UNDER INBREEDING

Genotypes	Frequencies
Homozygote AA	$q^2 + fq(1 - q)$
Heterozygote AA'	$2q(1 - q)$

thus the fraction by which the frequency of heterozygotes is reduced as a result of consanguineous mating. The departure from the Hardy-Weinberg prediction for the frequency of homozygotes is

$$\text{Departure} = fq(1 - q) = f(q - q^2).$$

This departure, a simple quadratic function of the allele frequency q, reaches its maximum value when $q = 1/2$. For that value of q, the frequency of the AA genotype deviates from the Hardy-Weinberg predictions by a value of $0.25f$. If f has a value of 0.025 (a level of inbreeding similar to those seen in southern India), then the maximum inbreeding departure from the predicted frequency of individuals homozygous for a given allele would be $+0.00625$. The maximum departure from the predicted frequency of a particular heterozygous genotype would be -0.0125. Table 16 illustrates this maximum effect of an inbreeding coefficient of 0.025.

TABLE 16
MAXIMUM EFFECTS OF f VALUE OF 0.025 ON
GENOTYPE FREQUENCIES AT A SINGLE LOCUS*

Genotypes	Frequencies	
	$f = 0$	$f = 0.025$
AA	0.25	0.25625
AA'	0.50	0.4875

* The frequency of the A allele is 0.50.

Though the inbreeding departure is greatest for mid-range gene frequencies, these departures are small when compared with the Hardy-Weinberg expectations in that region. However, as the gene frequencies approach zero, the inbreeding departures become quite large in relation to the Hardy-Weinberg predicted values. For small values of q, the frequency of the heterozygote AA approaches

$$\text{Frequency of AA} \approx q^2 + fq = q(q + f),$$

and with even greater reduction of the value of q,

$$\text{Frequency of AA} \approx fq.$$

Thus, for alleles sufficiently rare, even the modest inbreeding coefficients found in some human populations can become a primary factor in predicting genotype frequencies.

Effects of Inbreeding on Genetic Equilibrium

By elevating the frequency of occurrence of homozygous individuals, inbreeding alters the efficiency of selection. For example, selection against homozygous recessives will alter the gene frequency, q, in one generation, as the following equation shows:

$$\Delta q = q_{n+1} - q_n = \frac{H/2 + R(1-s)}{1 - sR} - q_n,$$

where

$$q_n = \text{the frequency of the A allele in the } n \text{ generation,}$$
$$q_{n+1} = \text{the frequency of the A allele in the next generation,}$$
$$s = \text{the intensity of selection against the AA genotype,}$$
$$H = \text{the frequency of heterozygous AA' before selection, and}$$
$$R = \text{the frequency of homozygous AA before selection.}$$

The fraction q_{n+1} is composed of half the frequency of the heterozygous genotype plus the frequency of the homozygous AA' genotype after selection. The numerator of the fraction can be rewritten $(H/2 + R) - sR$, where $(H/2 + R)$ is q_n, the frequency of A before selection. Thus:

$$\Delta q = \frac{q_n - sR}{1 - sR} - q_n,$$

or,

$$\Delta q = \frac{-s(1 - q_n)R}{1 - sR}.$$

If this loss due to selection is balanced by a gain due to a mutation at a rate of μ, then the change per generation is

$$\Delta q = \text{change due to mutation} + \text{change due to selection,}$$

$$\Delta q = \mu(1 - q_n) - \frac{s(1 - q_n)R}{1 - sR}$$

$$= \frac{(1 - q_n)[\mu - R(\mu s + s)]}{1 - sR}.$$

Russell M. Reid

At equilibrium, Δq becomes zero. This will occur either if q_n has a value of one, or if

$$\hat{R} = \frac{\mu}{s(\mu + 1)} \approx \frac{\mu}{s}.$$

The frequency of occurrence of the homozygous AA genotype at such an equilibrium, $\hat{R}$, is thus unaffected by inbreeding. However, the gene frequency, $\hat{q}$, necessary to obtain that equilibrium genotype frequency, will depend on inbreeding. By solving the quadratic equation

$$\hat{q}^2 + f\hat{q}(1 - \hat{q}) = \frac{\mu}{s}$$

$$\therefore (1 - f)\hat{q}^2 + f\hat{q} - \frac{\mu}{s} = 0,$$

we obtain (according to Haldane 1940):

$$\hat{q} = \frac{-f + \sqrt{f^2 + 4(1 - f)\mu/s}}{2(1 - f)}.$$

In the absence of inbreeding (for $f = 0$), this formula reduces to

$$\hat{q} = \sqrt{\mu/s}.$$

Figure 19 illustrates the effects of inbreeding ($f = 0.025$) on this equilibrium for a mutation rate of $\mu = 0.00002$. This gives us some idea of the importance of inbreeding for genetic equilibrium in a population large enough so that a recurrent mutation can have predictable effects on evolutionary processes.

Effects of Inbreeding on Mean Phenotypic Values

If we take a simple quantitative trait under the genetic control of a single locus with two alleles, we see the pattern in Table 17. Here, the phenotypic values, P_1 and P_2, have been rewritten as P_0 plus some multiple of α, where α is half the difference between P_2 and P_0. This yields the code values for the phenotypes of 0, k, and 2. This coding is useful because

$$\text{Mean Phenotype} = P_0 + (\text{Mean Code})\alpha.$$

This simplifies our problem.

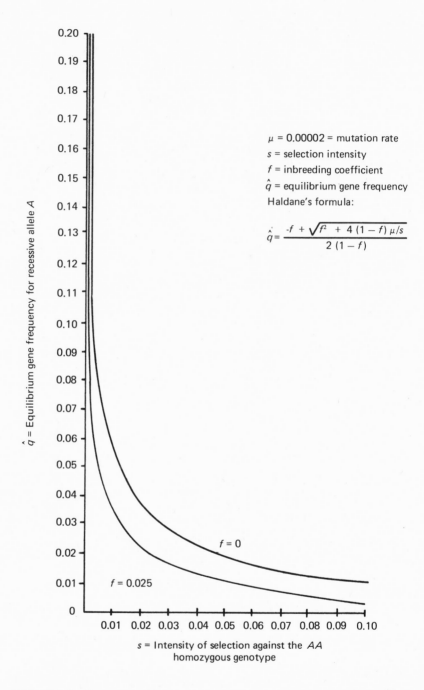

FIGURE 19. Genetic equilibrium under a balance between mutation and selection against homozygous recessives with inbreeding based on Haldane's (1940) formula.

$$\text{Mean Code} = 2(q^2 + fpq) + k2pq(1 - f)$$
$$= 2q^2 + 2fpq + 2kpq - 2kfpq$$
$$= 2(q^2 + kpq) + 2fpq(1 - k).$$

If the trait under study is perfectly additive, then P_1 falls midway between P_0 and P_2; that is, $P_1 = P_0 + \alpha$. In that case,

$$k = 1,$$
$$\text{Mean Code} = 2(q^2 + pq)$$
$$= 2q.$$

Therefore, the mean phenotype,

$$\text{Mean Phenotype} = P_0 + 2q\alpha$$

is independent of the value of f. *The mean phenotype of a perfectly additive trait will in no way be affected by inbreeding in the population.*

TABLE 17
PHENOTYPIC CODES FOR CALCULATING THE MEAN PHENOTYPE UNDER INBREEDING

Genotypes	Frequencies	Phenotypes	Code
AA	$q^2 + fpq$	$P_2 = P_0 + 2a$	2
Aa	$2pq(1 - f)$	$P_1 = P_0 + ka$	k
aa	$p^2 + fpq$	$P_0 = P_0 + 0a$	0

For all values of $k > 1$ (that is, when A is dominant to a), the portion of the mean code containing the inbreeding coefficient, $2fpq(1 - k)$, is negative. This tells us that inbreeding will depress the mean phenotype by a value of $2fpq(1 - k)\alpha$. When A is recessive (that is, when $k < 1$), then the expression $2fpq(1 - k)$ is positive, and the mean phenotypic value in the population will be elevated by inbreeding.

This process has, in general, been referred to as "inbreeding depression," a name that is perhaps inappropriate in view of the elevation of mean values in the recessive case. However, for inbreeding to result in inbreeding depression of mean phenotypic values, there must exist a nonadditive component to the phenotypic variance of that trait.

For any given set of gene frequencies and a dominance coefficient, the relation between the mean phenotype and the inbreeding coefficient is a simple linear function:

$$\text{Mean Phenotype} = C_1 + C_2 f,$$

where

$$C_1 = P_0 + 2(q^2 + kpq), \text{ and}$$
$$C_2 = 2pq(1 - k).$$

The value C_1 would be the mean of the same population under random mating, and C_2 would be the slope of the graph of the mean phenotype as a function of f.

If we shift to multilocus problems, then this simple linear relation persists only as long as interactions between the various loci are additive. With epistatic interactions between the loci contributing to the phenotype, the graph of the mean as a function of inbreeding becomes curvilinear (Crow and Kimura 1970).

We have seen that the genetic contribution to the phenotypic mean is dependent on the gene frequencies, the inbreeding coefficient, the degree of dominance, and, for a multilocus problem, epistasis. It is not possible to document inbreeding effects by comparing an inbred population to a random-bred population, because we have no assurance that the two populations have the same gene frequencies. As an alternative, we may make use of the considerable degree of variability found in the individual inbreeding coefficients of the members of a single population. We may, for example, examine the highly inbred members of the population and compare them with the remainder of the population or with the population as a whole. As long as these highly inbred individuals are scattered randomly throughout the population and not concentrated in particular genealogical lines or subpopulations, differences in gene frequencies or environmental factors are not expected to obscure the effects of inbreeding.

A variety of studies using this approach (Morton 1958, Schull and Neel 1963, 1965, Barrai, Cavalli-Sforza, and Mainardi 1964, Schork 1964, Schreider 1967, Krieger 1969, Strouhal 1971) have documented small and sometimes statistically insignificant depressions of mean values for various aspects of body size among inbred individuals. More striking inbreeding effects have been recorded for diastolic blood pressure (Krieger 1969) and neuromuscular development and skills as measured in age when walking and talking, as well as psychometric test scores and school performance

(Schull and Neel 1965). From the earlier discussion of inbreeding depression, this would imply that the variance for these latter traits contains a significant nonadditive genetic component. These inbreeding effects are especially important for contrasts between highly inbred and noninbred members of the same population. Direct comparisons of various traits to find which show the greatest inbreeding depression may be extremely misleading. The compared traits may be influenced to different degrees by socioeconomic correlates with inbreeding (Schull and Neel 1965). Further, scale differences between these traits make direct comparisons of percentage depression of mean values meaningless. Even if all metric traits under study could be converted to true linear scales, it would still be preferable to measure inbreeding depression as a percentage of the standard deviation of the trait rather than of the mean of the trait. Without such an analysis of the data, any conclusions about the relative importance of inbreeding for various metric traits should be considered tentative.

Effects of Inbreeding on Phenotypic Variance

We may rewrite the predicted genotype frequencies from Table 17 as follows:

Frequency of $Aa = 2(pq - fpq) = H,$
Frequency of $AA = q^2 + pq - pq + fpq = q - H/2,$ and
Frequency of $aa = p^2 + pq - pq + fpq = p - H/2.$

Again, the phenotypes may be expressed by the equation

$$P_i = P_o + X_i\alpha,$$

where P_o and α are constant and X_i is the appropriate code value. Thus, the phenotypic variance is

$$\sigma_p^2 = \alpha^2\sigma_x^2,$$

where σ_x^2 is the variance of the codes.

From Table 18, we can see that

$$\sigma_x^2 = \overline{X^2} - \overline{X}^2$$
$$= 4(q - H/2) + k^2H - [2(q - H/2) + kH]^2.$$

With minimal difficulty, it can be shown that this becomes

$$\sigma_x^2 = 4q(1 - q) - H + H(k - 1)[k + 1 - 4q - H(k - 1)].$$

Remembering that the phenotypic variance is

$$\sigma_p^2 = \alpha^2 \sigma_x^2,$$

that the frequency of heterozygotes is

$$H = 2q(1 - q)(1 - f),$$

and that k tells us the degree to which A is the dominant allele, we can now see the effects of inbreeding on phenotypic variance for a given degree of dominance. For example, if k has a value of 1—that is, if we are dealing with a perfectly additive trait—then

$$\sigma_x^2 = 4q(1 - q) - H$$
$$= 4q(1 - q) - 2q(1 - q)(1 - f)$$
$$= 2q(1 - q)(1 + f).$$

Therefore,

$$\sigma_p^2 = \alpha^2 2q(1 - q)(1 + f).$$

For an additive trait, inbreeding will increase the phenotypic variance for all gene frequencies. This may be seen in Figure 20.

TABLE 18
PHENOTYPIC CODES FOR CALCULATING
VARIANCE UNDER INBREEDING

Genotypes	Frequencies	X = Phenotypic Codes
AA	$q - H/2$	2
Aa	H	k
aa	$p - H/2$	0

Suppose, however, that we are dealing with a perfectly dominant trait. Then k would have a value of 2. Now, we see that

$$\sigma_x^2 = 4q(1 - q) - H + H(3 - 4q - H)$$
$$= 4q(1 - q) + H(2 - 4q - H)$$

and

$$\sigma_p^2 = \alpha^2[4q(1 - q) + H(2 - 4q - H)].$$

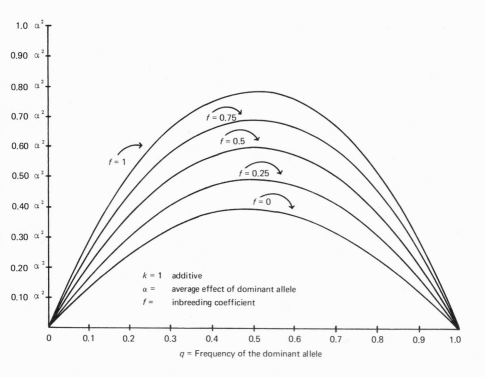

FIGURE 20. Total variance arising from a single locus with two alleles as a function of gene frequencies and degree of inbreeding (additive).

If we were to substitute for H as before, we would see that when q is small (say, below 0.3), the variance decreases as inbreeding increases. However, if q is large (say, over 0.5), then variance increases as the inbreeding coefficient increases. In other words, inbreeding will increase the phenotypic variance arising from a common dominant allele but decrease the variance arising from a rare dominant allele. It is, therefore, impossible to predict the effects of inbreeding on the variance of a complex metric trait without a considerable amount of preliminary information on the genetic sources of the variance. The dominance case may be seen graphically in Figure 21. In this graph and others using other degrees of dominance, it is possible to see that while dominance tends to skew the variance curves so that the maximum variance is achieved when the dominant allele is the less frequent, inbreeding tends to recentralize these curves. Inbreeding effects

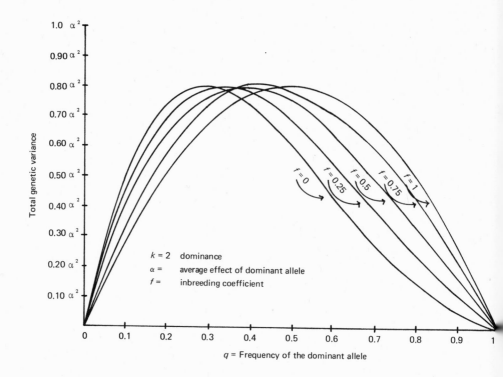

FIGURE 21. Total variance arising from a single locus with two alleles as a function of gene frequencies and degree of inbreeding (dominance).

on the variance of a metric trait have been shown for tooth diameter by Niswander and Chung (1965).

A potential use of inbreeding data is as a supplement to heritability studies. A heritability study attempts to partially account for the sources of variance for a particular phenotype trait in a particular population. Specifically, such studies attempt to evaluate the contribution of additive genetic effects to the total variability of the trait. We have seen that non-additive genetic sources of variance, that is, dominance and epistasis, introduce predictable relationships between inbreeding and phenotypic means and variances. Thus, the effects of inbreeding on means and variances have potential value in testing for nonadditive genetic factors. Such information could augment the usually narrow view offered by heritability studies. Barrai, Cavalli-Sforza, and Mainardi (1964) offer an example of such a use for inbreeding data.

Russell M. Reid

Inbreeding Effects on Morbidity and Mortality

Significant increases in morbidity and rates of congenital anomalies among offspring of close consanguineous matings have been reported for Japan (Schull 1958, Neel and Schull 1962, Schull and Neel 1965), for India (Centerwall and Centerwall 1966), for the United States (Adams and Neel 1967), and for Czechoslovakia (Seemánová 1971). In populations such as those in southern India, in which close consanguineous marriage is preferred and common, inbreeding becomes a very important factor in the occurrence of such anomalies. In their study of 1,037 new-born infants at the Christian Medical College Hospital, Vellore, South India, Centerwall and Centerwall found that two-thirds of the 23 major congenital anomalies occurred in the 37.4 percent of the births that were to consanguineous couples. In a larger sample of pediatric outpatients, they found similar patterns of occurrence for such anomalies, as well as for mental retardation.

When selection favors homozygous individuals, an unstable equi-librium results. The ultimate fate is the fixation of one allele at the locus and the elimination of all others. By contrast, selection favoring hetero-zygous individuals leads to a stable equilibrium and the maintenance of the polymorphism. If an old population is found to be polymorphic at a particular locus, then it is unlikely that selection on that locus favors homozygosity. In such an old population, we would not expect inbreeding to lower mortality rates. Inbreeding might, however, be expected to ele-vate mortality rates as a result of selection on polymorphic loci favoring heterozygosity. In Japan (Schull and Neel 1962, 1965, 1966, Schull et al. 1970a, Neel and Schull 1962, Yamaguchi et al. 1970), in India (Reid 1971), in Brazil (Marcallo et al. 1964), in Egyptian Nubia (Hussien 1971), and in Czechoslovakia (Seemánová 1971), inbred children were found to be subjected to higher mortality rates than noninbred children from the same population. Again we see the importance of variability in individual inbreeding coefficients within single populations. It is curious that in at least three of these populations, the consanguineous couples seem to produce more livebirths per couple than the nonconsanguineous couples (Schull et al. 1970b, Reid 1971, Hussien 1971). In these three cases, the birth rates of consanguineous couples were elevated at least enough to compensate for the higher mortality rates among their live-born offspring. This is not intended to imply that couples elevate their

113

birth rate in response to deaths among their offspring. Indeed, other studies (Newcombe and Rhynas 1962, Reed 1971) raise serious doubts about the couples' ability to compensate for offspring deaths by elevating their birth rates. It is very likely that the interpersonal relations in a consanguineous marriage (especially in Indian societies) are so different from those in a nonconsanguineous marriage that we should expect their fertility performances to differ (Reid 1971).

INBREEDING AS CULTURAL BEHAVIOR

The point was made earlier that the highest levels of inbreeding known for human populations are associated with rather strong social preference for close consanguineous marriage. This points to human inbreeding as a product of cultural behavior. Figure 22 illustrates one way of thinking about cultural behavior.

Tyler (1969), in his introduction to *Cognitive Anthropology*, has contrasted cultural anthropology as a natural science interested in the description of discrete material phenomena with cultural anthropology as a formal science interested in the discovery of the sets of logical principles that order material phenomena. We may follow his lead by contrasting

FIGURE 22. Components of culture.

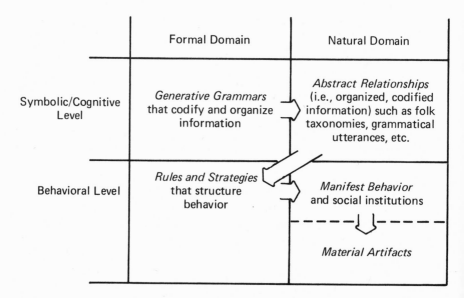

the natural as opposed to the formal aspects of culture. The former would include the various sorts of material phenomena referred to in many traditional definitions of culture. The latter would refer to certain underlying principles that give pattern to these material phenomena. Figure 22 recognizes two levels of culture—a symbolic or cognitive level and a behavioral level. At the symbolic or cognitive level, we are concerned with the way in which a society codifies and organizes information into abstract relationships. At the behavioral level, we are concerned with a body of rules and strategies governing behavior in a society and the patterns of behavior and artifacts resulting from these rules. The horizontal arrows on Figure 22 are, perhaps, self-explanatory, in that they reflect the relationships between the logical principles, rules, and strategies in the Formal Domain and the resultant observed patterns in the Natural Domain. The diagonal arrow leading from Abstract Relationships to the behavioral Rules and Strategies indicates that these rules and strategies are stated in terms of the categories and relationships generated at the symbolic or cognitive level. No claim is made that manifest behavior can be fully accounted for by the component of this model. Extracultural factors must also be considered. For example, the selection of a particular agricultural strategy to follow in a given year might depend on the rainfall pattern that year. Other aspects of manifest behavior might be partially or totally accounted for by the biological nature of the human species or by genetic variability within the species. Nor is it claimed that all study of cultural behavior must trace the behavior patterns to an underlying cognitive process. The point of this particular view of culture is that it focuses on those aspects of behavior that are ultimately patterned, at least partially, by cognitive processes.

Certain aspects of human mating behavior meet these criteria for cultural behavior, while others do not. The absence of self-fertilization is an obvious consequence of the biological nature of the species. The avoidance of incest, by contrast, is an example of cultural behavior resulting from an interplay between the cognitive systems by which the relevant information is codified and organized to define such categories as "sister" and a corpus of behavioral rules including the rule that "a man may not marry or have sexual relations with his sister." The endogamy of a Hindu caste, the exogamy of a clan or village, the preference for or prohibition of marriage between certain kinds of close consanguines, and assortative marriage with respect to age or phenotypic similarity are all areas of cultural behavior giving rise to nonrandom patterns of mating. Indeed, most are problems of traditional concern to the cultural anthropologist.

The relationship between rules or strategies of behavior and cognitive patterns in the context of marriage has been recognized since the beginning of the scientific study of kinship systems. In *Systems of Consanguinity and Affinity of the Human Family*, Morgan (1871) expressed the belief that kinship terminologies reflect behavior and that if a terminology cannot be understood from present behavior, it must reflect past behavior. Rivers (1907, 1914) noted the relationship between preferential cross-cousin marriage and the patterns of kinship classification of cousins. As with Morgan, he felt that terminology reflected behavior, but, in his view, the marriage rules caused the patterning of the terminology systems. Though more recent writers have been reluctant to speak of such cause and effect relationships or to explain terminologies by reference to past rules of behavior, the relationship between marriage behavior and kinship terminologies is still recognized.

In some cases, it has been possible to cite political or economic motivations for particular forms of close consanguineous marriage. For example, in a society where membership in descent groups is matrilineal but where succession to authority or inheritance of property follows a male line, it is possible for two lineages to monopolize that authority or property by marrying the heir to his father's sister's daughter. Dumont (1957) gives the example of two matrilineages of the Nangudi Vellalar of southern India who have monopolized the chiefdomship for eight generations by this strategy. Such examples of clear-cut economic or political motivations are far too rare to be pointed out as general "causes" of preferences for close consanguineous marriages. These problems of the social regulation of marriage among the Telaga Kapus of southern India have been dealt with elsewhere in some detail (Reid 1971).

Since cultural behavior is the central unifying concern of anthropology, then human mating behavior might be viewed as one of the logical focal points of anthropological genetics. It is especially in the study of mating behavior that we see the impact of culture on genetic processes.

NOTE

1. This paper was prepared with the support of NSF-USDP Grant GU1598 to the University of Texas at Austin, Austin, Texas.

6

Genetic Analyses of Hybrid Populations

P. L. WORKMAN

Department of Pediatrics
Mount Sinai School of Medicine

Department of Anthropology
University of Massachusetts

The pattern of genetic variation within and between populations results primarily from the interaction of four factors: mutation, selection, migration, and genetic drift (Wright 1955). Such rare chance events as catastrophes reducing population size and isolated instances of migration (Gajdusek 1964) may also have marked local effects. Gene migration (gene flow) resulting from intermixture among individuals from different populations leads to (1) an increase in genetic variability within populations and (2) a decrease in genetic differences between populations. In other words, migration causes populations to become more alike, as opposed to the diversifying effect of genetic drift in partially isolated populations of finite size. Migration also makes it possible for mutants arising in one population to be exposed to new genetic backgrounds in many different environments. In this role, migration among populations acts to increase the adaptive potential of the species, just as segregation and

117

recombination provide new opportunities for adaptive combinations of genes within a population.

Empirical studies of the effect of gene flow on genetic variability in human populations have been extremely limited. There has been some attempt to collect data on migration rates and population size (Lasker and Kaplan 1964, Lasker 1960a, Spuhler and Clark 1961) that can be incorporated into the mathematical models of drift and migration (Wright 1969). Only a few studies, however, have considered data that could be used to describe the effects of migration on within- and between-population variability (Lasker 1960b, 1962). In addition, it is usually assumed that migrants comprise a random sample from their population. Although there are theoretical analyses of the consequences of differential migration of genotypes (Haldane 1930, Parsons 1963), there are no relevant data.

There have been, however, many studies in which a historical process of gene flow has been considered by an analysis of the distribution of gene frequencies among populations. In some cases, a pattern of genetic variation over an extensive geographic region can be informative. The distribution of the frequency of the B allele (ABO locus) in Europe has been shown to reflect intermixture resulting from the Mongolian incursions between the fifth and fifteenth centuries (Candela 1942). The distribution of gene frequencies over an extended geographical region can be depicted by a so-called isogenic map, analogous to a geographical contour map. For example, suppose that a mutation arose that had a selective advantage in the region in and around its population of origin and that it diffused out into the surrounding populations, by intermixture, at approximately equal rates. On a map of the region, lines drawn that connected populations with equivalent frequencies of the mutant allele would form a series of concentric circles, with their center—the region of highest frequency—in the population in which the mutation originated. Isogenic and isophenic maps (with contours connecting areas of equal phenotypic proportions) were used by Birdsell (1950) in his discussion of the origin of the Australian aborigines and their patterns of historical intermixture.

This chapter will focus on the process of gene flow as it relates to the formation of distinct hybrid populations or to groups of intermixing populations. Several genetic models that can be used for the analysis of gene flow in such populations will be discussed. In particular, data on gene frequencies in a hybrid population and in the populations from which the hybrid population is known to be derived can be used to estimate the proportions of the hybrid gene pool contributed by each parental population. In addition, it is sometimes possible to estimate the rates of intermixture per generation and the distribution of gene frequencies in past and future generations (if current intermixture rates are known). Quantitative observations may provide support for genetic analyses or may be used to determine whether the hybrid population is in genetic equilibrium. Analyses of gene flow have also been used to detect genes that may have been subjected to differential selective pressures in the hybrid and parental environments. Finally, estimates of individual differences in ancestry can be used to determine the extent of differences in parental contributions to variation in quantitative traits in a hybrid population.

ESTIMATES OF THE ANCESTRY OF HYBRID POPULATIONS

All models used to describe the genetic structure of populations are, necessarily, idealized abstractions from reality. For example, the distribution of phenotypes in a sample, $(AA, Aa, aa) = (P,H,Q)$, is usually compared with frequencies predicted by the Hardy-Weinberg law (p^2, $2pq$, q^2). The sample may actually be drawn from a political unit of population (country, city, and so forth), itself a finite, stratified, partially exogamous "population" within which mating is nonrandom and selection and drift are present. Nevertheless, the Hardy-Weinberg model appears to fit the data almost all of the time, suggesting its relative insensitivity to a wide range of deviations from the idealized conditions. On the other hand, diverse factors acting on gene frequencies may, under many circumstances, effectively nullify the effect of any one factor, unless it is sufficiently strong (Workman 1969). Paradoxically, then, simple models seem to work for very simple or very complex situations. Similarly, elementary models of gene flow, also highly idealized abstractions, generally provide an adequate deterministic description of genetic exchange among populations, even when the idealized assumptions are violated.

The simplest model of gene flow is one in which migrants from two distinct parental populations, say P_1 and P_2, in proportions m and $1 - m$, establish a distinct hybrid population, H, as represented in Figure 23a. Consider a gene A, whose frequencies in P_1 and P_2 are q_1 and q_2. Then, the frequency of A in H, say q_H, is just the average gene frequency of all migrants, or,

$$q_H = mq_1 + (1 - m)q_2. \tag{1}$$

If we know the frequencies of A in both the parental and the hybrid populations, then an estimate of m is given by

$$m = \frac{q_H - q_2}{q_1 - q_2}, \tag{2}$$

as shown by Bernstein (1931). This model requires no assumptions about the historical pattern of intermixture—that is, m describes the proportion of the total gene pool of H derived from P_1, whether the hybrid was the result of a single instance of migration or the consequence of many generations of gene flow in varying proportions from both P_1 and P_2, as represented in Figure 23b.

FIGURE 23. Simple models of gene flow.

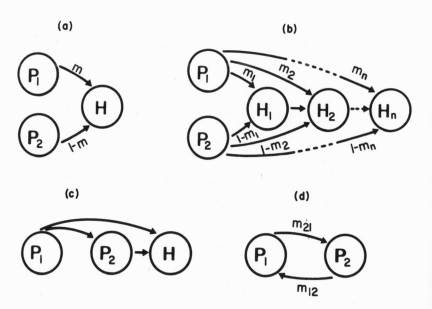

Equations 1 and 2 may also be used to describe systems of "one-way" gene flow from a donor population, P_1, into a recipient population P_2 (Figure 23c). In other words, P_2 and H describe the recipient population before and after gene flow. For example, Negroes in the United States may be viewed either as a distinct hybrid population formed by intermixture among Europeans and West Africans or as an example of one-way gene flow from Europeans into an African population. The gene flow is described as one-way because a person with any proportion of African ancestry is generally regarded as Negro (a social, not a biological, definition), and there is no evidence of a significant amount of African genes in American Caucasians (Workman, Blumberg, and Cooper 1963, Reed 1969c).

Estimates of gene flow can sometimes be compared with genealogical observations. For example, the progeny of matings between individuals from P_1 and P_2 would have half of their genes from each parental population; therefore, in a sample of such progeny, the expected value of m would be 0.5. Pollitzer et al. (1962) studied the ABO blood group of 442 Cherokee Indians of mixed White and Indian ancestry. Genealogical information from the tribal records, giving the degree of ancestry of each Indian, provided a mean estimate of 47 percent White ancestry. In good agreement was a mean estimate of 50.2 percent White ancestry computed from the A, B, and O alleles, using Equation 2.

In most studies, independent estimates of ancestry are not available, and only genetic data can be used to obtain estimates of ancestral contributions to a hybrid population. Each allele at a locus, as well as genes at different loci, can be used to obtain an estimate of m by Equation 2. Given accurate estimates of the gene frequencies in the parental and hybrid populations, then all estimates of m should be identical. In practice, however, there can be considerable variation among the estimates. Several causes of such variation will be seen in the following example.

Contemporary Chileans are a dihybrid population for which different genetic estimates of the ancestral composition have been derived. Historical evidence suggests that Chileans derive almost all of their genes from two ancestral populations: American Indians (primarily Auracanian), and Europeans, primarily Spanish Castilians and Basques. Both historical and genetic studies suggest that at most, only an insignificant contribution could have come from Africans (Nagel and Soto 1964). In order to estimate the proportion of Indian ancestry, we need estimates of the gene frequencies in a sample of Chileans and in the ancestral populations.

Now, each Chilean may be assumed to have some true proportion of genes, say θ_i, derived from Indian ancestors. However, as will be discussed later, unless the population is in equilibrium, different individuals will have different values of θ_i $(0 \leqq \theta_i \leqq 1)$. Thus, different samples of Chileans may have unequal distributions of θ_i and hence different total proportions of Indian genes in their gene pools. This potential source of variation among estimates of m can be eliminated simply by ensuring that the frequencies of different genes in the Chileans are estimated from the same sample. However, if there is considerable variation in θ_i within a sample, then estimates of gene frequencies at loci where there is dominance, based on the square root of the proportion of recessives, can be very inaccurate (Kalmus 1969), and estimates of m based on the frequencies at such loci may be unreliable.

The determination of the correct ancestral gene frequencies involves problems that cannot be solved by careful sampling techniques. Europeans other than Spanish or Basque were known to be among the ancestors, but their origins and relative frequencies are not known. We also do not know if the Spanish and Basque ancestors were a random sample from that part of Europe or if they were more representative of particular geographic or social subdivisions of their populations. Reported gene frequencies in Spanish and Basque populations may not be representative of the frequencies in contemporary populations and, often, different samples must be used to obtain estimates of different parental gene frequencies. Finally, even if we knew the exact ancestral origins and had accurate estimates of current gene frequencies from a single large sample, there still remains the possibility that selection, drift, or migration has changed gene frequencies in the descendants of the original ancestral populations or in the hybrid population. Similar problems are posed when we attempt to describe the gene frequencies in the parental Indian population. Moreover, different Chilean subpopulations may have originated from different ancestral populations. Thus, any choice of ancestral frequencies introduces numerous sources of error, and some variation among estimates of m must be expected. In order to minimize these sources of error, we should choose only genes whose frequencies appear to be relatively uniform over the parental alternatives from which we can select. In addition, one can use various parental estimates in order to determine the effect of such errors on the magnitude of m (Roberts 1955). Finally, as a further pessimistic note, there is always the possibility of typing errors in the determination of the phenotypes of certain polymorphic traits.

Despite these problems, and even though different sources were used to obtain estimates of genes in both the parental and hybrid population, the variation among estimates of m in the Chileans is not very large. As shown in Table 19, the values are distributed closely about the median

TABLE 19
ESTIMATES OF THE INDIAN CONTRIBUTION TO THE
GENE POOL OF CONTEMPORARY CHILEANS

Allele	Data Source	Chilean (q_H)	Indian (q_I)	Spanish (q_2)	$\lvert q^1 - q^2 \rvert$	$m = \dfrac{q_H - q_2}{q_1 - q_2}$
Hp^1	*	0.530	0.790	0.380	0.410	0.36
$r(Rh)$	*	0.251	0.000	0.364	0.364	0.31
$r(Rh)$	†S	0.294	0.119	0.384	0.265	0.34
$R^1(Rh)$	*	0.469	0.693	0.411	0.282	0.31
$A(ABO)$	*	0.173	0.017	0.292	0.275	0.43
$A(ABO)$	†S, C	0.187	0.071	0.286	0.215	0.46
$O(ABO)$	†S	0.752	0.893	0.652	0.241	0.39
$t(PTC)$	†C	0.366	0.111	0.498	0.387	0.34
$M(MN)$	*	0.561	0.630	0.511	0.119	0.41

* Nagel and Soto (1964), Chileans from Santiago.
† Saldanha (1968), Chileans from Santiago (S) and Concepción (C).

and suggest that contemporary Chileans derive approximately 36 percent of their genes from Indians and 64 percent from Europeans. Although the data are not yet available, it would be extremely interesting to examine the distribution of ancestry in populations of different social classes and in different urban versus rural or coastal versus mountain areas. The Chilean data of Table 19 appear to be based on urban populations that, presumably, would have the highest degree of European ancestry.

Differences among ancestral contributions to subpopulations have been observed in other hybrid groups. For example, there appears to be considerable variation in the amount of European ancestry in different United States Negro populations, with the highest values occurring in northern urban areas. Estimates of m for the Fy^a allele and for the R^0 (cDe) and $R^1(CDe)$ alleles are shown in Table 20. The estimates of

TABLE 20
ESTIMATES OF EUROPEAN ANCESTRY IN DIFFERENT U.S. NEGRO POPULATIONS

Location	Reference	Gene Frequencies			Estimates of Intermixture		
		R^0(cDe)	R^1(CDe)	Fy^a	R^0	R^1	Fy^a
"Ancestral" Populations							
West Africa	Workman, Blumberg, and Cooper (1963)	0.599	0.069	0.000			
English White	Race and Sanger (1962)	0.026	0.420	0.414			
United States Negroes							
Charleston, S.C.	Pollitzer (1958)	0.558	0.087	0.016	0.072	0.051	0.037
James Is., S.C.	Pollitzer et al. (1964)	0.536	0.129	0.038	0.110	0.171	0.092
Sapelo Is., Ga.	Robinson et al. (1967)	—	—	0.039	—	—	0.094
Claxton, Ga.	Workman, Blumberg, and Cooper (1963)	0.535	0.103	0.046	0.112	0.097	0.106
Birmingham, Ala.	Casey et al. (1968)	0.511	0.081	—	0.154	0.034	—
Oakland, Calif.	Reed (1968)	0.486	0.161	0.094	0.197	0.262	0.227
Baltimore, Md.	Glass and Li (1953)	0.446	0.145	—	0.267	0.217	—
West Virginia	Juberg (1970)	0.476	0.147	0.100	0.215	0.229	0.252
New York, N.Y.	After Reed (1969a)	0.359	0.171	—	0.419	0.291	—
Detroit, Mich.	After Reed (1969a)	—	—	0.111	—	—	0.268

the parental frequencies of Fy^a assume the absence of that allele in Africans and hence are maximum estimates.

The general absence of Fy^a in African populations permits the assumption that no sampling error is involved in the assignment of the parental gene frequency. For such a locus, the variance of the estimate of m is considerably reduced (Reed 1969a). However, the Duffy locus is triallelic (Fy^a, Fy^b, Fy) and, often, individuals are typed with only a single antiserum as $Fy(a+)$ or $Fy(a-)$. If there is considerable heterogeneity in ancestry in a population, as already noted, the estimate of m may be biased due to the problem of dominance. For other genes that require estimation of the frequencies in all populations, the variance of an estimate of m is usually least when the differences between the parental populations, $|q_1 - q_2|$, are greatest (formulas for computing σ_m^2 are given by Reed 1969a). Thus, for the Chilean data of Table 19, the most reliable estimates would be provided by the Hp^1 and t alleles. For the U.S. Negroes (for example, Table 20), Reed has suggested that the Fy^a allele provides estimates with the smallest variance. Accurate African parental gene frequencies are very difficult (if not impossible) to obtain (Reed 1969a), but the Rh and Fy estimates are in fairly good agreement, and, in any case, the heterogeneity can be seen directly in the differences in Negro gene frequencies. The variation probably reflects both differences in the historical pattern of intermixture in these populations, as well as differential migration of individuals of mixed ancestry. In addition, heterogeneity in the African origins of Negroes in different parts of America may also be involved.

The estimates from different genes may also be combined to provide a single joint estimate of the ancestral contributions to the hybrid gene pool. Several alternative methods for obtaining such estimates are discussed by Elston (1971). A numerically simple method of obtaining a joint estimate would be to take a weighted mean of the estimates using the inverse of the variance of the estimates ($1/V_m$) (that is, the information per gene) as the weights.

The estimation of the relative ancestral contributions to a hybrid gene pool becomes rather complex when there are more than two parental populations. For example, for k, parental populations, $k - 1$ parameters must be estimated, and this requires data on $k - 1$ independent alleles. Thus, the analysis of a trihybrid population requires data on at least a triallelic locus, such as the ABO blood group, or on genes at two independent loci. In addition, since the analysis requires accurate estimates of k sets of parental gene frequencies, the sources of error discussed earlier are confounded.

For an analysis of a trihybrid population, an algebraic formula could be derived for data based on two independent alleles. In most cases, however, the variance of such an estimate would probably be very large. Moreover, given the large number of polymorphic traits that can be used to characterize populations, joint estimates can be based on the frequencies of many genes, and these would provide the best description of the origins of the hybrid population. A variety of methods have been devised for obtaining joint estimates, most requiring computing machines (Roberts and Hiorns 1962, 1965, Krieger et al. 1965, Elston 1971). Alternative methods have been shown to give generally similar results, but occasionally marked differences can occur (Elston 1971). One test of the relative accuracy of different methods has been suggested by Pollitzer (1964). If q_i ($i = 1, 2, \ldots k$) denotes the frequencies of a gene A in the parental populations, and m_i denotes the estimated contribution from population P_i, then the observed frequency in the hybrid, q_H, can be compared with the frequency predicted by the joint estimates, namely $\sum q_i m_i$. This provides values of chi-square for each gene that can be summed to give an overall chi-square. Different methods can be compared in terms of their total chi-squares, and the values for each gene can be used to determine whether any particular locus is causing a major proportion of the total deviation.

The development of methods for handling polyhybrid populations was stimulated by the recognition that there are large numbers of trihybrid populations of considerable anthropological interest. In the eastern United States, there are at least 35 trihybrid populations of Indian, African, and European origin. These groups vary widely in size (from 100 to 30,000, according to the 1950 census); in degree of subdivision, they inhabit more than 100 counties in 17 eastern states (Gilbert 1946, Price 1953, Beale 1957). These populations are generally isolated and highly inbred as a result of various social pressures (Berry 1963) and, consequently, are also of interest to geneticists because they often have high frequencies of rare recessive traits (Witkop et al. 1960, 1966).

Genetic analyses have also been used to determine the historical origins of a few of these trihybrid groups (Pollitzer 1964, Pollitzer, Menegaz-Bock, and Herrion 1966, Pollitzer et al. 1969). For example, Pollitzer

(1964) studied a relatively isolated North Carolina population of individuals who described themselves as Indian. Extreme morphological variation was observed; skin coloring ranged from light to dark, and hair form varied from very curly to straight. Different methods were used to estimate the ancestral origins from gene frequencies in the hybrid, with the assumption that the parental populations had frequencies similar to those in English Whites, Charleston Negroes, and Cherokee Indians. Three methods gave roughly similar estimates of the White, Negro, and Indian contributions: 43:41:16, 53:37:10, and 34:53:13. Thus, the population appears to have similar White and Negro components but considerably less Indian ancestry. Accurate estimates would probably be impossible to obtain, even if good estimates of the frequencies in the parental populations were available. The effect of a small founder population and subsequent genetic changes due to genetic drift and differential fertility causes gene frequencies to vary in unpredictable ways. In the Brandywine isolate in Maryland, Witkop et al. (1966) found that 10 of 26 alleles studied had frequencies outside the range of possible Negro, Indian, and White ancestral populations. In such cases, estimates of ancestry have to be based on those genes with frequencies within the range of parental frequencies, although these are also likely to have been changed over time.

Trihybrid models may also have a much wider use in the study of United States Negro populations. In the eastern United States, Negro populations appear to have little or no Indian ancestry (Glass 1955, Roberts 1955, Roberts and Hiorns 1962). However, genealogical studies indicate that Negroes in the lower Mississippi Valley may have a significant proportion of Indian ancestry and a lesser amount of European ancestry than Negroes to the east (Herskovitz 1930, Meier 1949). Unfortunately, there is not as yet genetic data that could be used to ascertain whether such heterogeneity in Indian ancestry really exists.

The Brazilian population—primarily descendants of three groups: native American Indians, Europeans, and Africans—also contains numerous hybrid subgroups differing in their ancestral origins. At the onset of western colonization in Brazil, in the early sixteenth century, there were, according to some estimates, at least 800,000 Indians, primarily of the Tupi-Guarini and Ge linguistic stocks living in the area. The Ge-speaking tribes, described as possessing a marginal culture, occupied the large central area of Brazil. The Tupi, with a Tropical Forest culture, lived

127

along the entire coast of Brazil and were the source of most of the Indian-White and Indian-Negro contact. Within a century and a half after colonization, most of the Tupi had either been absorbed into the new colony by the European settlers, had died from disease, or had fled into the central areas of the country (Smith and Marchant 1951). The Europeans who emigrated to Brazil were mostly of Portuguese, Italian, or Spanish origin. The majority of the Africans were derived from two cultural groups, the Sudanese and the Bantu.

The slave trade to Brazil started in the middle of the sixteenth century. By 1798, Brazil had 400,000 free Negroes and 1,582,000 Negro slaves out of a total of 3,250,000 inhabitants. Estimates of the total number of Negroes brought to Brazil vary between six million and eighteen million, but, unfortunately, all documents related to slavery were destroyed by decree in 1890, so that a precise history of the Negro in Brazil is impossible to obtain.

Intermixture among these groups has been at a high rate since the first days of colonization. Most of the crosses, originally, were Negro-White or Indian-White. Indian-Negro matings were infrequent because the Negroes settled in areas generally not inhabited by Indians, and gene flow among these groups must have been by way of intervening matings with Whites. One factor in promoting high rates of intermixture was the great excess of men over women in the first few centuries of colonization. Another factor that significantly increased the opportunity for intermixture was a large antislavery movement that grew throughout the nineteenth century. In 1850, restrictive laws were passed on slave importation, and in 1888, slavery was legally abolished throughout Brazil. The effect of the antislavery movement can be seen in the statistics of the city of São Paulo: 4,075 Negroes out of 15,471 were slaves in 1855; in 1887, the number had dropped to 493 slaves out of 44,030 Negroes (Morse 1953). According to the Brazilian census of 1950, there were 61.6 percent "White," 10.9 percent "Negro," 22.5 percent "Mulatto," and 5 percent "Indian" in a total population of almost 52 million. A comprehensive review of biological studies on the Brazilian populations is provided by Salzano and Freire-Maia (1970).

In particular, Salzano and his associates have carried out an extensive study of the population of Pôrto Alegre, in which they were able to analyze the proportion of White ancestry in the Negro population. Pôrto Alegre, the capital of Brazil's southernmost state, Rio Grande do Sul, was founded in 1752 by 60 White couples from the Azores. By the end of the eighteenth century, over half the inhabitants were Negro slaves. Because of a great influx of White immigrants in the nineteenth and twentieth centuries, the proportion of Negroes and Mulattoes had decreased to 29.2 percent by the end of the nineteenth century and to 14 percent by 1950. Indians have never been frequent in the area, and any Indian contribution to the Negro gene pool should be insignificant.

Table 21 shows the gene frequencies of several alleles in West Africans, Portuguese, and different groups from Pôrto Alegre. The classification into "Negro," "Dark Mulatto," "Light Mulatto," and "White" was based on skin color and several other Negroid features. The data show that individuals with greater manifestations of African morphological traits also have gene frequencies more characteristic of African populations. Since genes derived from Africa are not segregating independently, the Negro population is not in genetic equilibrium, and there are individual differences in ancestry. Similar heterogeneity in ancestry was observed in a Negro sample from Bahia (Saldanha 1957). The gene flow in this population is not entirely one-way. Salzano, Da Rocha, and Tondo (1968) examined the hemoglobins of 439 individuals classified, on morphological grounds, as White and found one AS and three AC individuals. However, the small proportion of African genes in the Whites (less than 0.5 percent) permits fairly accurate estimation of m using a model of one-way gene flow.

Using the Portuguese frequencies, the estimates of the proportion of White ancestry in the total Negroid population in Pôrto Alegre are 0.43 and 0.39 for the R^0 and R^1 alleles of the Rh locus. The estimates for the Hp^1 and Hb^s alleles are somewhat higher, 0.505 and 0.649, respectively. For reasons that will be considered later, the Rh alleles probably provide the best estimates of the accumulated gene flow from the White to the Negro.

In another study, Saldanha (1957) estimated that there was about 55 percent White ancestry in Negroes living in the States of Rio de Janeiro and São Paulo. Also, Ottensooser, Leon, and Cunha (1961), using the Gm^a (gamma globulin) allele, estimated 50 percent White ancestry in a different Negro sample from São Paulo. The slightly lower estimate from Pôrto Alegre might reflect some sort of sampling error; however, since a Negro sample from Bahia showed only 35 percent White ancestry (Saldanha 1957), the amount of White ancestry probably does vary some-

TABLE 21

GENE FREQUENCIES IN WEST AFRICANS, PORTUGUESE, AND WHITES AND NEGRO GROUPS FROM PÔRTO ALEGRE, BRAZIL

	Population	Hp^1	Gc^1	Hb^S	A	B	R^0	R^1	R^2	r
	West African Negroes	0.717	0.922	0.084	0.157	0.150	0.599	0.069	0.086	0.211
PÔRTO ALEGRE	Negroes	0.642	0.846	0.045	0.162	0.126	0.423	0.136	0.125	0.230
PÔRTO ALEGRE	Dark Mulattoes	0.555	0.846	0.030	0.199	0.081	0.376	0.236	0.123	0.212
PÔRTO ALEGRE	Light Mulattoes	0.457	0.840	0.014	0.181	0.116	0.288	0.225	0.204	0.270
PÔRTO ALEGRE	All Negroids	0.552	0.844	0.030	0.182	0.104	0.365	0.203	0.149	0.232
PÔRTO ALEGRE	Whites	0.385	0.710	0.001	0.254	0.056	0.065	0.418	0.153	0.342
	Portugal	0.390	—	0.000	0.304	0.066	0.052	0.416	0.107	0.403

SOURCES: *West African frequencies*—Salzano (1963), Workman, Blumberg, and Cooper (1963).
Brazilian frequencies—(*ABO, Rh*) Salzano (1963), Salzano, Sune, and Ferlauto (1967); (*HP*^{1}) Tondo, Mundt, and Salzano (1963), Schwartes et al. (1967); (*Hb*^{S}) Tondo and Salzano (1962); (*Gc*^{1}) Salzano and Hirschfeld (1965).
Portuguese frequencies—(*Hp*^{1}) Torrinha (1967); (*ABO*) Saldanha (1962); (*Rh*) Saldanha (1962), Sa (1962).

what among different Brazilian Negro populations, although the hetero-geneity is certainly much less than that observed among different United States Negro populations.

In the northeastern part of Brazil, there is a large trihybrid population of individuals called "Nordestinos," derived from intermixture among native Indians, both Tupi-Guarani and Ge-speaking groups, Whites (primarily Portuguese), and West African Negroes (Bantu and Sudanese). Saldanha (1962) analyzed a group of Nordestinos believed to have originated in the more northern areas. Indians now living in the states of Matto Grosso and Amazonas were taken as representative of the Indian base population. An analysis of gene frequencies at the Rh, ABO, and MN, Di, and PTC loci provided estimates that the proportions of Negro, Indian, and White ancestry in this population were 26 percent, 9 percent, and 65 percent, respectively (Roberts and Hiorns 1962). Elston (1971) obtained similar estimates from the same data by each of five different methods.

A second study of a population in this area was reported by Krieger et al. (1965). The number of individuals studied was large, but they originated from all over the northeast of Brazil and thus make up a rather heterogenous sample. Data for gene frequencies at 17 loci were analyzed jointly by a maximum likelihood method that gave estimates of 30 percent, 11 percent, and 59 percent for the parental contributions of Negroes, Indians, and Whites, respectively, in good agreement with the analyses of Saldanha's data. Each of the individuals in this study was classified into one of eight racial classes on the basis of various morphological characters, discriminating Caucasoid from Negroid phenotypes.

In each class, estimates of the White, Indian, and Negro contributions to the gene pool were obtained. In the "most Caucasoid" and "most Negroid" classes, the proportions of White ancestry were 70.8 percent and 27.9 percent, respectively, indicating that there is also considerable variation in ancestry among the Nordestinos.

In addition to the use of genealogical records or gene frequencies, analyses of morphological variation may also provide insight into the ancestral origins of a hybrid population. Pollitzer (1958) compared Negroes from Charleston, South Carolina, with West Africans and Charleston Whites; by using gene frequency data, he obtained chi-square estimates of genetic distance (Sanghvi 1953) and data on nine morphological traits, which provided an estimate of anthropometric distance by the D^2 method

131

of Mahalanobis. The results gave quite similar estimates of biological distances among these populations. Similarly, according to Pollitzer et al. (1964), anthropometric comparisons supported results from a gene frequency analysis that indicated that Negroes from James Island, South Carolina, had a higher proportion of White ancestry than did the Charleston Negroes.

Since some morphological characters, especially those with low heritabilities, may be especially susceptible to environmental variation (climatic, nutritional, altitudinal, and so forth), anthropometric distances based on an inappropriate set of traits may be quite different from genetic distances (Hiernaux 1966). Other traits, such as skin color, should be corrected for age and sex differences (Pollitzer et al. 1970). In a comparison of morphological variation in several hybrid groups with that observed in their parental populations, Trevor (1953) noted considerable differences among various metric characters in their ability to differentiate among parental and hybrid populations. One solution to this problem might be to derive anthropometric distances for traits of equivalent heritability and then combine these measures weighted by their heritabilities. Alternatively, one could derive the distances only for a set of traits from which those with the lowest heritabilities, or those with extremely large variances due to measurement errors, were eliminated.

Biological distances, whether genetic or anthropometric, will not provide accurate estimates of the ancestral contributions to the hybrid gene pool (Pollitzer 1964, Roberts and Hiorns 1962), unless the distances are approximately linear with the gene frequencies. In other words, suppose that d_{ij} is the biological distance between populations i and j and, for a dihybrid model, $d_{1H} + d_{2H} = d_{12}$. Then, an approximate estimate of the ancestral contribution from population 1 to population H is given by $d_{2H}/(d_{1H} + d_{2H})$, which corresponds to Equation 2. Cavalli-Sforza et al. (1969) suggest that their measure of genetic distance, based on an angular transformation of gene frequencies, can be used to obtain estimates of ancestry. This measure, however, gives very inaccurate estimates for gene frequencies less than 0.05 or greater than 0.95. Unfortunately, such extreme gene frequency values, especially 0.0 (or 1.0), are usually those with minimum variance and therefore provide the most information about ancestry. Thus, given the gene frequencies in the hybrid and parental populations, estimates of ancestry should be obtained by the methods previously described.

P. L. Workman

DYNAMIC MODELS OF INTERMIXTURE

The analysis of simple models constitutes the "statics" of intermixture studies, in that they provide only estimates of the total accumulated proportion of the hybrid gene pool derived from specified donor populations. In order to consider the historical process of intermixture, it is necessary to develop dynamic models incorporating both rates of intermixture, possible varying over time, and a specification of the total time during which intermixture has occurred. In addition, the simple models were limited to systems of one-way gene flow, in which the genetic structure of donor populations was assumed to remain unchanged. Given the geographical isolation of the hybrid from the ancestral populations, and given the size and complexity of the parental populations that reduced the likelihood for changes in their mean gene frequencies, such a simplification was warranted. However, such a model would not be appropriate for descriptions of genetic exchange among populations of moderate size inhabiting adjacent territory. Only totally endogamous populations would have their gene pools unaffected by immigration, and such isolates would not be of much importance during the course of human evolution. More generally applicable models would have to allow for reciprocal exchange among two or more populations (Figure 23d).

The most elementary dynamic model, involving one-way gene flow and constant rates of gene flow per generation, was developed by Glass and Li (1953) to describe the incorporation of Caucasian genes into the United States Negro gene pool. Suppose that q_1 denotes the frequency of an allele (A_1) in a hybrid population $(H^{(1)})$, which is derived from one generation of gene flow in proportion (m) from a population in which the frequency of A_1 is Q, into a population $(H^{(0)})$ in which the initial gene frequency is q_0. Then, as before,

$$q_1 = (1 - m)q_0 + mQ.$$

Since, in this model, the amount of gene flow (m) is constant, after a second generation of intermixture, the frequency in $H^{(2)}$, q_2, will be

$$\begin{aligned}
q_2 &= (1 - m)q_1 + mQ \\
&= (1 - m)[(1 - m)q_0 + mQ] + mQ \\
&= (1 - m)^2 q_0 + m(1 - m)Q + mQ.
\end{aligned}$$

The general expression after n generations, giving the frequency in $H^{(n)}$ (Glass and Li 1953), is

$$q_n = (1 - m)^n q_0 + [1 - (1 - m)^n] Q.$$

If the frequencies in the base population and the hybrid population are known, then the relation between the rate of gene flow and the number of generations of intermixture can be rewritten as

$$(1 - m)^n = \frac{q^n - Q}{q_0 - Q}. \tag{3}$$

Equation 3 applies when the generations are discrete. If the generations are considered overlapping, and consequently the gene flow is continuous, the relation between n and m is given by $e^{-nm} = (q_n - Q)/(q_0 - Q)$, which is a good approximation to Equation 3 when m is small and n is large.

Such a system described by Equation 3 always goes to an equilibrium in which the gene frequency of the hybrid is equal to that in the donor population. Since m is always less than 1.0, then $(1 - m) < 1.0$; therefore, as n increases, $(1 - m)^n$ decreases. In the limit as $n \rightarrow \infty$, $(1 - m)^n \rightarrow 0$, and consequently $q_n = Q$. In other words, if there were continuous gene flow from the White to the Negro population, in any amount $m > 0$, then, ultimately, the gene frequencies in the White and Negro populations would be identical. The rate of approach to this equilibrium state depends on both n and m.

Ten to 12 generations appears to be a reasonable estimate of the length of time during which there has been intermixture between Negroes and Whites in the United States. Workman, Blumberg, and Cooper (1963) obtained an estimate of 0.535 for the frequency of the R^0 allele (Rh locus) in a Negro population in Georgia. Assuming that the gene frequencies in the parental populations could be approximated by those in contemporary Georgia Whites and West African Negroes, the frequencies in the parental populations were taken to be 0.037 and 0.599 for Q and q_0, respectively. Total admixture, estimated by Equation 2, was found to be 11.4 percent. Using Equation 3 and an estimate of $n = 10$, this is equivalent to an average rate of 1.1 percent per generation.

In a Negro sample from Baltimore, also from data on the R^0 allele, the rate per generation was estimated to be about 2.5 percent (Glass 1955). Differences in rate estimates only reflect variation in accumulated White ancestry and should not be taken as descriptive of the historical process of intermixture. However, suppose these rates can be compared with independent observations of current frequencies of intermarriage. Then, an increase or decrease in historical rates can be postulated depending on whether current rates are lower or higher than those estimated by Equation 3. At a rate of 2.5 percent, 97.9 generations (at 27.5 years per generation) would be required to reduce the current Negro R^0 frequency of 0.446 to 0.063 (Glass and Li 1953). The real approach to equilibrium is probably much slower, since present intermixture rates appear to be considerably lower than those that must have occurred in the past (Heer 1967).

More complex models of interchange between two populations can be handled mathematically or by using computers. Roberts and Hiorns (1962) derived explicit formulas for two intermixing populations for a model with variable gene flow rates per generation and for models incorporating either discrete or continuous generations. Hainline (1963) used a computer to simulate a simple model of mutual exchange between two populations. She examined a number of different factors that could affect the rate of gene flow: differences in relative rates of exchange, differences in population size, increasing or decreasing population size, and variable rates of exchange per generation. The results suggested that both decreasing population size and variable rates of exchange could limit the utility of such models. Her results were applied to an examination of the present-day ABO blood group gene frequencies in Siksika, Sarsi, and Stoney American Indian tribes, among which, according to historical evidence, there has been mutual exchange. Since the B allele was absent in these tribes, the ABO locus could be treated as a diallelic locus. The frequencies of A in contemporary Siksika and Sarsi groups are 0.58 and 0.28, respectively, a difference of 30 percent. From historical records, it was concluded that 12 generations would be a good estimate of the number of generations of intermixture. If there had been an average rate of exchange of 5 percent, the initial differences would have had to exceed 100 percent, which is clearly impossible. At a rate of 4 percent, the initial differences would have to have been only 78 percent, so an average maximum rate of 4 percent can be postulated. However, there is also good evidence that the Sarsi have always been much less numerous than the Siksika. The computer results suggested that assumptions based on equal population size would overestimate the real exchange rates if the populations were, in fact, of significantly different sizes. Consequently, an average rate of about 3 percent was suggested as being more reasonable. This rate leads to a prediction of initial frequencies that are acceptable, given the expected range of ABO frequencies for Indian tribes in that area. A similar analysis was applied to Siksika-Stoney intermixture, and an estimate of $n = 12$, and $m = 1$ or 2 percent was obtained. These mathematical results were in good agreement with independent historical and anthropological evidence suggesting that the Stoney Indians had a lower rate of intermixture with the Siksika than did the Sarsi.

Roberts and Hiorns (1962) also provide a general method applicable to the study of an arbitrary number of mutually intermixing populations. Suppose that there are r intermixing populations, p_i $(i = 1, 2, \ldots r)$. Let m_{ij} denote the proportion of the ith population's gene pool that is contributed by the jth population (for example, Figure 23d). Equivalently, m_{ij} is the proportion of marriage partners who marry and live in i and who originated in population j. In other words, suppose that of every 100 matings in population i, 10 involve matings between individuals from populations i and j, so that 10 of 200 mates, or 5 percent, come from j. The proportion of the gene pool of i coming from j in that generation is therefore 5 percent. Thus, estimates of the rate of genetic exchange among populations, per generation, can be taken directly from data describing the origins of mates. For this model, we shall assume that m_{ij} is constant for all generations. If $q_i^{(n)}$ and $q_i^{(n+1)}$ are the frequencies of an allele in the ith population in generations n and $(n + 1)$, then $q_i^{(n)}$ and $q_i^{(n+1)}$ are related by the following recurrence equations:

$$q_1^{(n+1)} = m_{11}q_1^{(n)} + m_{12}q_2^{(n)} + \ldots + m_{1r}q_r^{(n)}$$
$$q_2^{(n+1)} = m_{21}q_1^{(n)} + m_{22}q_2^{(n)} + \ldots + m_{2r}q_r^{(n)}$$
$$\cdot \tag{4}$$
$$\cdot$$
$$q_r^{(n+1)} = m_{r1}q_1^{(n)} + m_{r2}q_2^{(n)} + \ldots + m_{rr}q_r^{(n)}.$$

Equation 4 can be written as a matrix equation:

$$Q^{(n+1)} = MQ^{(n)}. \tag{5}$$

Now, from Equation 5, $Q^{(1)} = MQ^{(0)}$, and $Q^{(2)} = MQ^{(1)} = M^2Q^{(0)}$. And, in general, we can formulate

$$Q^{(n)} = M^n Q^{(0)}. \tag{6}$$

The elements of M in Equation 5 are the rates of intermixture per generation. The elements of M^n, that is, the $m_{ij}^{(n)}$, have two interpretations: (1) $m_{ij}^{(n)}$ is the probability that an allele initially in the jth population will be in the ith population in generation n, or (2) $m_{ij}^{(n)}$ is the proportion of the individuals (or the gene pool) in the ith population descended from population j. The second interpretation simply means that the elements of M^n describe the origins of the total accumulated intermixture in generation n.

As described by Equation 4, $Q^{(n)}$ is a column vector ($r \times 1$) of the frequencies of a gene in each of r populations at generation n. For k independent alleles, k such vectors can be combined so that $Q^{(n)}$ becomes an $r \times k$ matrix. In the limit, as $n \to \infty$, all the values in a column of $Q^{(n)}$ will be identical so that all rows of $Q^{(n)}$ will be identical. In other words, the system of exchange proceeds to an equilibrium state at which the frequencies of any allele, $q_i^{(n)}$, are the same in all intermixing populations. This is analogous to the equilibrium state already described by Equation 3.

This model can be used to estimate the ancestral contributions to the gene pool of a polyhybrid population. Suppose that we wish to estimate the contributions from Indian, White, and African populations to a distinct trihybrid population, H. We let $Q^{(0)}$ denote the frequencies of any number of genes in the ancestral populations. Then, we consider a model of three intermixing populations for which sufficient intermixture has occurred so that the equilibrium state has been reached. The frequencies in $Q^{(n)}$, that is, at equilibrium, are assumed to be those in the trihybrid population, so that each column of $Q^{(n)}$ is the same and both $Q^{(n)}$ and M^n become (1×3) row vectors. Then, by standard statistical procedures, we can determine the elements of M^n, giving the accumulated contributions to H from each population. For the trihybrid population in the United States, we assumed no exchange between White and Indian and no gene flow from the Negro to either Whites or Indians. In this special case, because of certain properties of M, it is only possible to calculate the total amount of intermixture and not the rates per generation (Roberts and Hiorns 1962, 1965).

This model also enables us to consider various questions about the process of intermixture among populations. Some of these will be illustrated by a consideration of intermixture among three Nilotic populations of the southern Sudan—the Nuer, Dinka, and Shilluk, as described by

Roberts (1956) and Roberts and Hiorns (1962). Each of these groups includes many small villages and homesteads that form the basic units of the society. Neighboring villages are grouped into subtribal units, several of which form a tribe, occupying a continuous territory. In the Dinka, the breeding unit does not appear to be the village, the subtribe, or even the tribe itself, since the proportion of exogamous marriages in each of these units was 94 percent, 74 percent, and 20 percent, respectively. The Dinka, as a whole, in the tribes investigated, number about 30,000, and this, then, appears to be the total size of the effective unit. Each of the three populations may be considered to be an essentially random mating unit, although geographical distances between potential mates are likely to have some effect. There are barriers to interbreeding among these populations that result, in part, from linguistic differences. A sample of the marriages in each of the populations provided estimates of intermixture. Among 288 marriages in the Dinka villages, eight mates were Nuer and five were Shilluk; in Shilluk villages, out of 255 marriages, five mates were Dinka and none were Nuer; in 200 Nuer marriages, one mate was Shilluk and five were Dinka. These values, converted to percentages, are set into a table corresponding to the M matrix (Table 22).

TABLE 22

GENE FLOW (BASED ON INTERMIXTURE RATES) AMONG THREE NILOTIC POPULATIONS FROM THE SUDAN

Recipient Population	Donating Population		
	Nuer	Dinka	Shilluk
Nuer	0.9850	0.0125	0.0025
Dinka	0.0138	0.9775	0.0087
Shilluk	0.0000	0.0098	0.9902

SOURCE: After Roberts and Hiorns (1962).

The intermixture rates m_{ij} are assumed to be constant, so that given the present gene frequencies in these populations, it is possible to determine the gene frequencies that will occur at some future generation. For example, the present frequencies of the blood group gene, M, are 0.5750, 0.5670, and 0.5047 for the Nuer, Dinka, and Shilluk, respectively. It can be shown that at equilibrium, in each of these populations, the frequency of M will be 0.5464 but, as is evident from Figure 24, this value will be approached very slowly. Similarly, the frequencies at some past generation can also be found using Equation 5. In other words, the methods used above are simply applied to the inverse of the matrix of intermixture values.

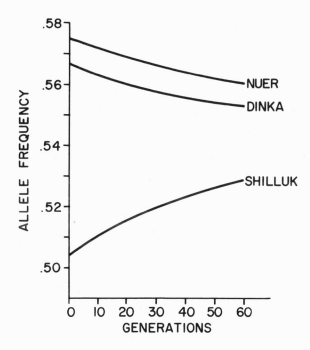

FIGURE 24. Approach to equilibrium resulting from gene flow among three Nilotic tribes. *Source:* After Roberts and Hiorns (1962).

The rates of gene flow in Table 22 might appear to be very small, and one might expect that such rates would have little effect. Suppose, however, that they continue for another 20 generations. Table 23 shows the matrix M^{20}, which gives the proportions of the gene pool of each population 20 generations later that will be derived from each ancestral population. The gene pool of the Dinka, for example, will derive one-third of its genes from the other base populations. As Roberts (1965) points out, " 'Ancestral' is a word that clearly needs applying with care to human populations."

The method of Roberts and Hiorns provides the most elementary deterministic model of intermixture among a set of r populations. Hiorns et al. (1969) extended the model by including a set of parameters, r_{ij}, denoting the proportion of common ancestry initially shared by each pair of populations. In order to account for matings with individuals not from one of the r populations, that is, exogamous matings, they also added an artificial $r + 1$ st population to represent the outside world. Their model was used to analyze the patterns of mating among eight Oxfordshire parishes as described in parish records spanning 250 years. This deterministic approach describes the reduction in variation among populations due to gene flow. However, it does not account for the dispersive effect of genetic drift which would be especially important in a small population among which gene flow was limited.

TABLE 23

ACCUMULATED GENE FLOW AFTER 20 GENERATIONS
OF INTERMIXTURE AMONG THREE NILOTIC TRIBES

Recipient Population	Donating Population		
	Nuer	Dinka	Shilluk
Nuer	0.7637	0.1810	0.0553
Dinka	0.1961	0.6693	0.1346
Shilluk	0.0195	0.1465	0.8340

SOURCE: After Roberts (1965).

The incorporation of drift into a model designed to deal with migration among a finite set of populations was presented by Bodmer and Cavalli-Sforza (1968). Similar treatments of this model, first discussed by Malécot, are given by Smith (1969) and Imaizumi, Morton, and Harris (1970). This "migration matrix" method yields predictions of kinship in successive generations, and if migration from the outside is of the order of 10 percent then the asymptotic approach to equilibrium may be very rapid. Since this method utilizes demographic data on the birthplaces of parents and offspring, it should prove to be a relatively inexpensive method for describing the population structure of contemporary subdivided populations.

P. L. *Workman*

INTERMIXTURE AND THE
DETECTION OF SELECTION

In the analyses considered thus far, it has been assumed that selective forces have not changed the gene frequencies in any of the populations, and, consequently, that all genes should provide similar estimates of gene flow. However, if a hybrid population derives a proportion of its genes from populations occupying distinctly different environments, then the selective pressures acting on genes in these populations might be quite different. For example, the high frequencies of the sickle-cell hemoglobin allele, Hb^S, in areas of West Africa, appear to be due to the selective advantage of sickle-cell heterozygotes, $Hb^A Hb^S$, in regions where malaria is endemic (Allison 1964). In the United States Negroes, in nonmalarial environments, the frequency of the sickle-cell allele should be reduced, not only by directional selection against the Hb^S allele, but also by the effects of intermixture with European populations in which Hb^S is absent. Thus, excepting rare circumstances in which the net effect of selective forces in different environments leaves intermixture estimates unchanged, any changes in gene frequency due to selection should result in anomalous estimates of gene flow.

The detection of changes due to a single generation of directional selection would generally require either unusually strong selective forces or unrealistically large sample sizes (Workman 1968, 1969). Studies of hybrid populations, however, may involve a comparison of gene frequencies in populations separated by many generations of gene flow; furthermore, the cumulative effect of directional selection over a long period of time might produce changes of sufficient magnitude to be detectable by comparisons among estimates derived from several independent genes. In other words, we may assume that all genes not affected by selection should produce similar estimates, but those that have been subjected to sufficiently intense directional selection for several generations should provide recognizably aberrant estimates. Thus, as first suggested by Glass and Li (1953), the analyses of hybrid populations may provide an opportunity to detect differences in the adaptive requirements of the environments of the hybrid and parental populations.

The above arguments are, of course, entirely theoretical. In reality, it would be impossible to provide conclusive evidence for selection by analyzing the variation among estimates of *m*. Sampling errors or variation due to genetic drift in a subpopulation could be distinguished by replication of the analyses in different hybrid subpopulations or by obtaining better estimates of the frequencies in the designated parental populations. Although more accurate historical descriptions of the origins of a hybrid might assist in getting better estimates of ancestral frequencies, there is really no way to account for errors in such frequencies related to founder effect or ignorance. Therefore, although selection can be one cause for aberrant estimates of intermixture, it is not the only cause. On the other hand, the number of polymorphisms that we can study is very large, and in a search for evidence for natural selection, any method that can pick out a small group of genes on which selection is more likely to have been operative should be especially useful.

The variation among estimates of Caucasian ancestry in an American Negro population was examined by Workman, Blumberg, and Cooper (1963). In so far as was possible, sources of variation in the estimates were controlled. In an essentially random sample of Whites and Negroes from Evans and Bullock counties in Georgia, estimates of the gene frequencies of a large number of polymorphic traits were determined (Cooper et al. 1963). Since the frequencies in Whites were very similar to those in English Whites, it was concluded that a model of one-way gene flow from the White into the Negro population provided an appropriate description of intermixture in this area. The gene frequencies reported for contemporary West Africans were assumed to correspond to those in the ancestral African populations. These frequencies, based on inadequate sampling in territories only generally described as having been the origin of American Negroes, provide the major source of error in any attempt to determine the relative parental contributions to the Negro gene pool (Reed 1969a). However, for studies designed to locate loci that have a greater-than-random chance of having been affected by selection, such errors are of less consequence.

The estimates of Caucasian ancestry, m, for a number of genes in this population are shown in Table 24. Only loci for which the ancestral frequencies differed by at least 0.09 were considered, in order to eliminate estimates that would have extensive sampling errors. There is obviously a very large range of values among the estimates. However, all but the last four (G6PD, Hp^1, T, and Hb^s) range between 0.0 and 0.218. Moreover, it can be shown that a joint estimate for the ABO locus is approximately 0.16, so that excluding the Inv^a allele, for which only limited African data

142

are available, most estimates lie between 0.07 and 0.167. As discussed earlier, the estimate with the lowest variance is provided by Fy^a, and if the absence of Fy^a in Africans were due to selection, or if Fy^a did occur at low frequencies in West Africa, then this estimate would be too large. In addition, the R^0 and R^1 alleles, which also have low variances because of the large differences in their parental frequencies, provide estimates very similar to that for Fy^a. Thus, it can be assumed that about 10 to 12 percent of the Negro gene pool in the population is derived from Caucasian genes. Variation among these lower estimates could be due to any number of sources, but they are in good general agreement. An estimate much lower than the best "neutral" estimates could also indicate selection, but in this population, that type of deviation could be at most 0.12 and would not be detected by this approach (Workman 1968).

Estimates from the G6PD, Hp^1, T, and Hb^s alleles appear to be quite

TABLE 24
ESTIMATES OF ACCUMULATED GENE FLOW FROM THE WHITE INTO THE NEGRO POPULATION IN EVANS AND BULLOCK COUNTIES, GEORGIA

Allele or Segment	*Difference in White and West African Frequencies*	*Estimate of* m
Inv^a	0.298	0.000
Gm^a	0.240	0.070
Gc^1	0.229	0.074
P	0.266	0.094
$R^1(CDe)$	0.357	0.095
A	0.098	0.107
Fy^a	0.422	0.109
$R^0(cDe)$	0.562	0.113
r(cde)	0.147	0.129
S	0.147	0.143
Jk^a	0.247	0.167
B	0.101	0.218
G6PD	0.18–0.21	0.34–0.44[*]
Hp^1	0.19–0.37	0.42–0.70[*]
T(PTC)	0.268	0.466
Hb^s	0.08–0.14	0.46–0.69[*]

Source: After Workman, Blumberg, and Cooper (1963) and Blumberg, Workman, and Hirschfeld (1964).

[*] These estimates are based on a range of West African frequencies: G6PD: 0.18–0.21; Hp^1: 0.60–0.78; Hb^s: 0.08–0.14.

discrepant, even if the lower values are considered. The G6PD estimates are probably underestimates. Much of the intermixture, at least in the early days of slavery, was probably between Caucasian males and Negro females. For an X-linked locus, White males would have contributed only one-third of the genes, in contrast to the one-half for autosomal genes. Thus, estimates based on an X-linked gene could be as low as two-thirds of those from autosomal genes. On the basis of this study alone, one would obtain a group of four genes that may have been affected by selective pressures that differ in African and American environments. The results could, of course, be due to sampling errors in determining the Negro frequencies in Georgia or to an incorrect choice of African frequencies. The former possibility can be tested by examining these genes in other United States Negro populations. Table 25 shows estimates based on the frequencies of G6PD and Hp^1 in different American Negro populations. All of the estimates are also markedly greater than those obtained for the Fy^a and R^0 alleles in other Negro populations (Table 20). Thus, sampling errors in American Negroes can be discounted as a cause of anomalous estimates for these alleles, leaving selection in Africa or America or erroneous ancestral frequencies as the most likely causes. The evidence for selection on the Hb^s allele in Africa has been reviewed by Allison (1964) and, similarly, both G6PD and Hp^1 appear to be associated with malarial environments (Motulsky 1965). Furthermore, among the estimates of m from Pôrto Alegre (Table 21), the figure based on Hb^s was considerably larger than those based on the Rh allele. For the T allele (PTC locus), both the American and African data are generally lacking, and only future study can determine the meaning of the high estimate for this allele. The extent to which deviant estimates of m actually derive from selective differences in the environments should be determined by independent studies of the kind outlined by Morton, Krieger, and Mi (1966).

Comparisons of estimates in a series of subpopulations can also be used to infer the possibility that selection has affected the estimates of m (Hertzog and Johnston 1968, Workman 1968). For example, Figure 25 shows the frequencies of the A_1, A_2, and B alleles in several West African, U.S. Negro, and U.S. White populations. The distribution of the A_1 allele in these populations suggests a lack of intermixture between Whites and Negroes, whereas the A_2 frequencies suggest considerable intermixture. The B allele gives estimates comparable to those provided by the Fy^a and

144

TABLE 25

ESTIMATES OF GENE FLOW FROM U.S. WHITES TO
U.S. NEGROES, BASED ON THE FREQUENCIES OF THE
Hp^1 AND G6PD ALLELES IN DIFFERENT
U.S. NEGRO POPULATIONS

G6PD (in males)				
City	Source	Sample Size	Trait Freq. (%)	m
Seattle	Motulsky (1965)	658	10.2	0.490
Chicago	Motulsky (1965)	130	11.1	0.445
Baltimore	Motulsky (1965)	144	14.6	0.270
Baltimore	Porter, Schulze, and McKusick (1962)	238	6.3	0.685
Memphis	Motulsky (1965)	97	16.5	0.175
New York	Motulsky (1965)	152	7.2	0.640
Claxton (Ga.)	Porter, Schulze, and McKusick (1962)	76	11.8	0.410
Oklahoma City	Kirkman and Henderson (1963)	79	10.1	0.495

G6PD in U.S. Whites = 0.0%
G6PD in West Africans (Motulsky 1965) = 20%

Hp^1				
City	Source	Sample Size	Gene Frequency	m
Seattle	Giblett (1959)	406	0.526	0.561
Seattle	Giblett and Brooks (1963)	1657	0.552	0.478
Cleveland	Giblett and Steinberg (1960)	178	0.539	0.519
Ann Arbor	Sutton et al. (1959)	43	0.590	0.355
Austin	Sutton and Karp (1964)	237	0.550	0.484
New York	Parker and Bearn (1961)	100	0.594	0.342
Claxton (Ga.)	Workman, Blumberg, and Cooper (1963)	164	0.520	0.581

Hp^1 in U.S. Whites = 0.39
Hp^1 in West Africans (Sutton et al. 1959, Parker and Bearn 1961) = 0.70

ALLELE POPULATION

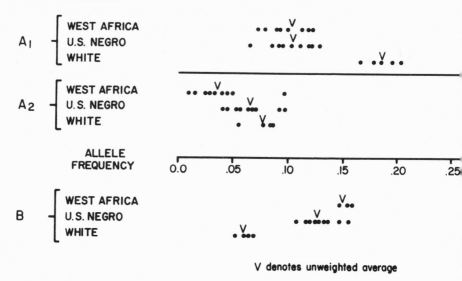

V denotes unweighted average

Note: The values for *B* in West Africans and in Whites are based on averages of a large number of studies.

FIGURE 25. The distribution of the frequencies of the ABO blood group alleles, A_1, A_2, and B, in different West African, U.S. Negro, and U.S. and English White populations. *Sources:* West Africa—Mourant, Kopec, and Domaniewska-Sobczak (1958); U.S. Negro—Mourant, Kopec, and Domaniewska-Sobczak (1958); U.S. Whites—Mourant, Kopec, and Domaniewska-Sobczak (1958), Cooper et al. (1963), Race and Sanger (1962), Gershowitz and Neel (1965).

Rh alleles. Together, these results support a hypothesis that selective forces have reduced the frequency of A_1 and raised the frequency of A_2 in American Negroes. The possibility of typing errors in the determination of A subtypes and problems with African frequencies cannot be discounted. Nevertheless, the data in Table 20 do suggest a need for further studies on the distribution of A_1 and A_2 frequencies and its possible relation to selection.

INDIVIDUAL VARIATION IN ANCESTRY

Each of the preceding analyses of gene flow required estimates of the gene frequencies at various polymorphic loci in two or more populations. Such data are usually obtained from determinations of the phenotypes of several polymorphisms in each individual in a more or less random sample of a population. The gene frequencies are estimated from the pooled proportions of the phenotypes in the total sample. If the population is in genetic equilibrium, the phenotypes are distributed at random in each individual, and all of the information about the genetic structure of the population is contained in the pooled phenotype and gene frequencies. In other words, the probability that an individual will have a specific set of phenotypes, say G_i, at each of k loci, is just the joint product, $\prod_{i=1}^{k} f(G_i)$, of the proportions of each of the phenotypes. However, if the population is not at equilibrium, then the joint distribution of phenotypes within an individual cannot be predicted for the pooled proportions, and, considerable information about the population structure may be contained in the individual joint distributions.

In several of the distinct hybrid populations already discussed, it was shown that both the morphological and genetic characteristics of African populations remained in association with individuals, and, therefore, that these populations were not in equilibrium. MacLean and Workman (1973a, 1973b) have developed methods for utilizing the information contained in the phenotypic distributions of individuals within a dihybrid population. Their results provide estimates of the ancestral origins of each individual in a hybrid population and an estimate of the contribution from each parental population to the variation among individuals in any quantitative trait. In addition, they provide a method for estimating the frequency distribution of ancestry among individuals, which can provide insight into the history of intermixture in the population. The essential features of their analysis, and some possible applications, will be summarized below.

The analysis requires estimates of the gene frequencies in two parental populations, P_0 and P_1, and a characterization of individuals in a distinct hybrid population formed by intermixture among migrants from P_0 and P_1 (for example, Figure 23b). Each individual in H has some proportion,

147

θ_i, of his genes derived from P_1 and the remainder, $1 - \theta_i$, from P_0. If a complete genealogy were available, then θ_i could be determined precisely. Lacking such information, the genetic observations of the individual, say G, are used to determine a conditional density function $q_i(\theta|G)$, which gives the probability that the individual has a proportion θ of his genes from P_1, assuming that he has the phenotypic array, G. In other words, $q_i(\theta|G)$ describes the ancestry of individual i in terms of a probability distribution. If there were no information about the individual, then all values of θ, $0 \leq \theta \leq 1$, would have to be assumed equally probable. The more information available, the more the values of θ near θ_i should have a higher probability, and those further from θ_i should have a lower probability. Geometrically, as the information increases, $q_i(\theta|G)$ goes from a uniform distribution (a straight line) to a curve, approximately symmetric about θ_i with a continuously decreasing variance. For this analysis, then, it is desirable to use as many genes as possible that have significant amounts of information, such as Fy^a and R^0 in the American Negroes. In addition, anthropometric measures in the parental and hybrid populations can be used to define an individual's anthropometric distance from P_0 and P_1, and this information can be incorporated into the estimate of $q_i(\theta|G)$.

The derivation of $q_i(\theta|G)$ is based on a Bayesian approach, and although no analytic solution can be obtained, numerical procedures for the computation of this function, requiring computing machines, are provided by MacLean and Workman (1973a). For each individual, a single point estimate of ancestry, say x_i, can also be obtained. For example, one might use the average likelihood so that $x_i = \int \theta q(\theta|G)\, d\theta$.

The distribution of ancestry among individuals in H could be obtained by combining the $q_i(\theta|G)$ or by making a frequency function from the x_i. A method for obtaining a more precise estimate of this distribution, say $g(\theta)$, is provided by MacLean and Workman (1973b). The form of $g(\theta)$ is determined by the historical pattern of intermixture in the hybrid, and, in some cases, knowledge of $g(\theta)$ may help in reconstructing that history.

For heritable quantitative traits, especially those whose environmental variation is, in part, the result of cultural factors, there appears to be no direct method for interpopulation comparisons. The genes controlling variation in such traits cannot be identified, and the effects of differing physical environments, the complications of social heredity, and genotype-environment interactions all make the prospect for such comparisons very remote. Thus, there appears to be no direct answer to such a question as: Are there genetic differences between populations, either in genes or in gene frequencies, with respect to such a quantitative trait (Thoday 1969, Bodmer and Cavalli-Sforza 1970)?

Suppose, however, that for some quantitative trait (anthropometric, physiological, or behavioral), we had scores for individuals in the hybrid population for whom estimates of $q_i(\theta|G)$, or x_i, were also available. The scores, s_i, can be regressed on the estimates of ancestry, x_i; formulas for the regression coefficients and their error estimates are provided by MacLean and Workman (1973a). The slope of the regression line should indicate the extent to which the parental populations differ in their mean additive gene effect on the quantitative scores. This approach provides an answer to a more limited question about interpopulation differences: Is the intrapopulation variation in a quantitative trait in a hybrid population related to individual differences in additive gene effects reflecting differences in ancestral origins?

In this procedure, especially for behavioral traits, care should be taken to ensure that there are no correlations between anthropometric traits and the scores for which adjustments have not been made. For example, this method might be used to relate ancestry to behavioral test scores in an American Negro population. Socioeconomic analysis should be used to guarantee that the cultural environment of the individuals in the hybrid sample is at least randomized with respect to ancestry. Moreover, if morphological appearances affect performance on behavioral tests for non-biological (that is, social) reasons, as seems likely, then scores on the behavioral tests can be regressed on ancestry only after elimination of the variation induced by such interactions. Given the variance and errors associated with the determination of African gene frequencies, then the use of genetic data alone in the estimation of $q_i(\theta|G)$, together with the necessity to correct for morphological-behavioral interactions, might not provide a regression with a variance sufficiently small to be meaningful. On the other hand, diseases such as hypertension are especially common in American Negroes (Howard and Holman 1970). A regression of a measure of hypertension, such as blood pressure, on estimates of ancestry based on both genetic and anthropometric observations might have an acceptably low variance. The slope should indicate the extent to which the observed high blood pressure derives from African ancestry or from the physical and cultural environments in which the American Negroes live.

This approach should be generally useful for assessing the impact of the environment on a hybrid population. Another application, for example, might be in a study of the mechanisms of high altitude adaptation in South American hybrid populations derived from Europeans and native Indians. With the ever increasing number of polymorphisms that can be used to characterize populations, and with more studies to provide better estimates of the gene frequencies in different populations, this method should become an increasingly reliable tool.

7

Human Genetic Distances and Human Mating Distances[1]

G A B R I E L   W.   L A S K E R

Department of Anatomy
Wayne State University School of Medicine

GENETIC DISTANCES

The genetic distance between two individuals (or between two populations) can be thought of as simply the amount of genetic information that the two individuals or groups are able to transmit to their offspring (that is, their total genetic constitution), divided into the amount of such information they do not hold in common. If the fraction held in common is so held by reason of common descent, the measure of genetic distance is also the measure of genetic or evolutionary divergence. The measurement of distance—the proportion of genetic information that differs—has been estimated both by direct measurements and by some ingenious indirect approaches.

To the extent that nucleic acids provide the chief genetic mode, through coded base sequences, the most direct measure of genetic distance is the comparison of specific DNA. Unfortunately, that advantage is offset, in part, by the problem of different informational value of different kinds of DNA and by the continuing technical difficulty of getting good measurements of DNA from large numbers of species. Hoyer, Mc-Carthy, and Bolton (1964), Martin and Hoyer (1967), and Kohne (1970) have tested the amount of complementary pairing in DNA of pairs of species. Such tests for DNA measure the extent to which specimens from two sources remain bound or dissociate under certain conditions. Some results are given in Table 26. Kohne believes that results from

TABLE 26
DISTANCE MEASUREMENTS AS A PERCENTAGE OF THE DISTANCE BETWEEN MAN AND RHESUS OR OTHER CERCOPITHECOID MONKEYS RECALCULATED FROM DATA ON VARIOUS TESTS

Test	Man and Gibbon	Man and Chimpanzee
Unfractionated DNA	71	26
A-T-rich DNA*	66	32
G-C-rich DNA*	58	19
Nonrepeated sequence of DNA†	61	25
Serum proteins‡	61	17
Serum albumin§	33	17

* From data of Martin and Hoyer (1967).
† From data of Kohne (1970, Table 6).
‡ From data of Goodman et al. (1970, Table 23, right-hand column).
§ From data of Sarich and Wilson (1967).

DNA with nonrepeating sequences are more meaningful in taxonomic studies than those from repeated sequences that have relatively less taxonomic significance. Thus, molecular systematics involves the relative weighting of traits, just as systematics based on morphology does.

The next step in surveys of genetic distance is the comparison of karyotypes. The degree of common origin is inferred from the communalities in the number, arm lengths, and other traits of the chromosomes. New methods of fluorescent staining hold forth promise that it will be possible to compare chromosomes between individuals and between species with respect to more characteristics than has heretofore been possible. Weighting various traits is also a problem with chromosomes. Thus, with respect to number, dealing with polyploidy may be a difficult question, since in a short time span—a single generation—there can be a large change in number of chromosomes with less genetic effect than, for example, some small alteration of a single chromosome. The problems posed in karyotypes by polyploidy and other types of duplication of chromosomes or their parts, like those posed in DNA by repeated sequences, exemplify the necessity of weighting the measurements according to their informational values.

The next level of study is the comparison of proteins and other molecules. Proteins can best be measured by counting differences in peptide sequences. What are the minimum number of changes in amino acid residues (or in the code that determines them) that can account for the differences in sequence between two forms of a protein? The unstated assumption of common origin and transformation over a near-minimum number of steps (a distance measurement equivalent to "as the crow flies") is usually taken for granted. These minimum mutational distances for comparison of cytochrome C, hemoglobins, and other genetically-determined organic products are among the most useful distance measurements available (Fitch and Margoliash 1967). The application of such distances to differences of two hemoglobins within the same individual (such as beta and delta hemoglobin polypeptide chains) and of two related molecules (such as myoglobin and hemoglobin) calls for an extension of the definition of genetic distance from the population and individual levels to the molecular level. Goodman et al. (1971) have derived several different phylogenetic trees. They are all similar in placing man and the anthropoid apes very close together and among the catarrhines, but the relative distances vary depending on which molecules are studied.

Differences in function between different cells of the same organism imply at least one more useful level at which the distance concept can be applied. In embryology, differentiation produces distances in the cells of different tissues that have much in common with the genetic distances of evolution. The analogy suggests that a general theory might well cover both kinds of differentiation, but the elaboration of such a theory is still largely unexplored.

To return to the proteins, indirect methods of analysis, such as immunological similarities, provide a less precise but relatively easy and hence widely applicable method of screening protein distances (Table 26). Goodman et al. (1970) have shown that these distances readily lend themselves to the construction of phylogenetic trees. Such trees can be based on quantitative analysis of a single protein (Sarich and Wilson 1967) or on the overall extent of immunological cross-reaction between blood serum that involves several proteins and hence gives average distances (Goodman et al. 1970). The data given in Table 26 are only examples. Depending on what methods are used, the tests yield different results. The quantitative methods measure only one protein, and evolution of that protein may not be the most characteristic. On the other hand, immunodiffusion tests several proteins, but the exact extent of the differences is not precisely known. Nevertheless, phylogenetic trees based on such studies, like those based on DNA, closely resemble the trees derived from the morphology of fossils in the palaeontological record. In fact, they can be combined (Lasker 1973). Use of the palaeontological record as a measure of genetic distance between species is, of course, equivalent to use of the known pedigree for the same purpose between individuals. The fossil record and the pedigree are the historical standards against which measurements by other methods are sometimes converted into units of time, such as years or generations.

MATING DISTANCES

Now we come to the other way of approaching genetic distances—especially in the case of man, where documentary evidence on mating patterns and breeding behavior can be, and has been, collected. The emphasis can be on the breeding pattern rather than on the genetic results. Thus, parthenogenesis of an animal or self-pollination of a plant without intervening mutation can be taken to give a distance of zero, meaning that there is no difference in genetic information. Random mating at the species level yields the maximum breeding distances normally encountered (although assortative mating for heterogamy could exceed this standard). Perhaps the generalized scale for distance should be conceived as zero for selfing and 1.00 for random mating. That leaves the range above unity for selective heterogamy and interspecific crosses. Such a scale can be seen as measuring the inverse of the inbreeding coefficient. The inbreeding coefficient, in turn, is a special kind of coefficient of kinship, a measurement of propinquity rather than of distance. The genetic challenge to demography is to determine the different kinds of social data that can be used for the measurement of distance or propinquity and to monitor the quality of

Gabriel W. Lasker

the information. What kind of answers can one get to the question "Who mates with whom?" Since most children are born in wedlock, the more usual form of the question is "Who marries whom?" Or, in studies of effective breeding, "Who are [or were] your mother and father?"

The idea of distance also immediately suggests that this be measured in kilometers. "Where was your mother born? Where was your father born? How far is it between those two sites?" If mankind were thought to be spread homogeneously over the globe but to vary genetically along steady clines, the statistics of answers to the last question would give a measure of distance directly transformable into genetic terms. In fact, the existence of large uninhabited areas and variations in population density have suggested a model other than isolation by distance. It is called the "island model" and supposes points of essentially zero area with whole populations at each. In such a model, the genetic distances are, of course, measured between populations. As so often happens, real situations are usually somewhat intermediate between these limiting models.

Equal mating distances do not necessarily imply the same degree of inbreeding because there is another dimension in human breeding distance: *social distance*. Caste, class, and culture (linguistic and religious affiliations) influence mate selection. The highest inbreeding cofficients for human populations occur both on tiny islands far from other inhabited places (such as Tristan da Cunha [Roberts 1969], the Wellesley Islands [Simmons, Tindale, and Birdsell 1962, Simmons, Graydon, and Tindale 1964], Pitcairn [Shapiro 1929], Saint-Barthélemy [Benoist 1964]) and in religious isolates, often in the midst of large populations (such as the Samaritans [Bonné 1963], Hutterites [Mange 1964], Old Order Amish [Cross and McKusick 1970, Juberg et al. 1971], and Dunkards [Glass et al. 1952]). Mountain valleys are sometimes highly endogamous, for example: Saas (Hussels 1969) and Canton Ticino (Hulse 1957) in Switzerland, Paracho (Lasker 1954) and Tlascala and San Pablo del Monte, Mexico (Halberstein and Crawford 1971), the Parma Valley in Italy (Cavalli-Sforza 1963), and the New Guinea Highlands (Giles, Walsh, and Bradley 1966, Giles, Wyber, and Walsh 1970).

In some instances, breeding isolation has been compared with biological differences from surrounding populations—especially in gene frequencies for red cell antigens (blood groups). Among the above, such studies show local differentiation among Tristanites, two groups of Wellesley Islanders, Saint-Barthélemy, Samaritans, Hutterites, Dunkards,

155

Tlascalans, several New Guinea populations, and the villages of the Parma Valley. Sharp differences between local isolates and surrounding populations with respect to gene frequencies appear as escarpments rather than gradual clines on maps of gene frequency distributions.

Even urban communities show some short breeding distances. Dunn and Dunn(1957) found both endogamy and distinctive gene frequencies in the Jewish quarter of Rome. Indeed, the greatest difficulty may be the measurement of *social distance* in the city. Coon (1966) once asked how one can draw clines for skin color in New York. The distances in cities are hardly at all geographic; they are largely in terms of ethnicity and economic status.

In just such situations, very indirect methods may be helpful. Crow and Mange (1965), Yasuda and Morton (1967), Hussels (1969), Morton and Hussels (1970), and Swedlund (1971), among others, have tried to apply data on surnames in distance studies. *Isonymy*, the likelihood of a surname to recur independently in two (affinal) lines in a pedigree, can be used to calculate a distance measurement that, on certain assumptions, can be translated into an "inbreeding coefficient." According to my studies, expected and observed isonymy are in fair agreement, which tends, in part, to justify such assumptions (Lasker 1969).

In a study of blood groups and leukemia in Boston, MacMahon and Folusiak (1958) showed that control for surnames served to discount the ethnic factor, that is, the frequencies of ABO blood groups were not significantly different from a control group matched individual by individual for the same surnames. Perhaps, in urban studies, data on surname frequencies and isonymy offer an approach to breeding distance, even though this is not amenable to direct methods (Lasker 1970). The ethnic factor in social distance may be partially controlled in this way, but one must also take such factors as patrilocal marriage into account in interpreting isonymy.

The time seems ripe for a study of the breeding structure of the whole human species. With improved prospects of communication with mainland China (a major segment of the human population), one might hope to characterize human breeding distances of each type of people of the world in socioeconomic terms: Western industrial workers, Asian peasants, Arctic hunters, and so forth; then, one could extrapolate from sample distance calculations by weighting according to the number of each such kind of individuals. A composite table of distribution of distances could be used, among other things, to calculate the time it would take for specific genes to diffuse under various assumptions concerning their fitness.

Genetic variability between mates can give impetus to evolution; it can also lead to the diseases of maternal-fetal incompatibility. Genetic similarity between mates can conserve interpopulation differences; it can also lead to homozygous recessive genotypes. The availability of genetic variability is a necessary resource for our descendants. The extent of such variability, how it is distributed within the species (and distances from other species), and the breeding structure of the species (which will determine the redistribution of the variability) are therefore dimensions whose extent concerns the biological future of man.

NOTE

1. Research supported in part by grant HD 04815, U.S. Public Health Service.

8
Measures of Population Distances[1]

W. W. HOWELLS

Peabody Museum
Harvard University

Numerical measures of distances among populations are the mirror of various ideas now circulating in anthropology and population genetics. They are used for different implied purposes, are based on different hypothetical premises, employ different kinds of material, and are applied to different population situations; questions of appropriateness of fit among these several categories can arise. With relation especially to these matters—purpose, premise, materials, populations—further comment on distinctions and definitions might be useful, especially for anthropologists.

BIOLOGICAL VERSUS GENETIC DISTANCES

The distinction between biological and genetic distances is an arbitrary one: they do not necessarily differ in form, but only in application and meaning. *Biological distances* refers to the classic D^2 of Mahalanobis:

multivariate measures of likeness or difference over a set of traits (usually metric) for purposes of organization and comparison among populations. They have often been used to infer relationships of a phylogenetic kind among the populations, but the questions they answer may, in fact, not have been asked; for purposes of this discussion, they have no necessary prior theoretical commitments.

Genetic distances, however, are model-bound, as distinguished from the model-free status of biological distances, and are directly related to measures of inbreeding, and so forth (see Chapter 7). Genetic distances (and Wright's *F* statistics) in ideal form assume a finite, pristine population, divided into more or less mutually isolated subpopulations that, for any given locus, are heterogeneous due to random effects. Allowance may be made for systematic pressures toward homogeneity, from mutual gene flow, from outside gene pressure from a foreign population, or from a common selective force. But the model is essentially one of an original parent population segmented by geography and undergoing random genetic drift. The genetic heterogeneity of the segments can be measured by estimators of inbreeding (such as loss of heterozygosity within the subpopulations compared with that which would be obtained in the whole population under panmixia) or by measures of distance, some of which are algebraically related to the above, as I have indicated.

SINGLE LOCUS VERSUS MULTILOCUS TRAITS

Both single locus and multilocus traits have been clearly recognized, but terms to distinguish the two have not been very satisfactory. The first class consists of those primary, gene-specific or "genetic" traits (for example, blood or serum characters). In such a polymorphism, an individual has an absolute phenotype, one of a set of clear alternatives, unmodified in ontogeny, and for a population of different alleles at a locus, it may be estimated very closely or even counted exactly. Essentially, each such trait is independent of others, and all are thus uncorrelated phenotypically. The second class is made up of secondary traits (physical measurements, but such things as skin color must be included). If we want a term to oppose "genetic," we might call them "somatic." (Other terms in use, "phenetic" and "habitus," have different connotations.) In them, the phenotype varies continuously, or seems to; the genotype cannot be read, and, in fact, the same phenotype may rest on different genotypes. The genetic component of variation is polygenic, which is the source of the continuous variation, and these traits have other special characters. Especially if such a trait has the form of a scaled measurement, it is *devised* by an investigator, rather than being discovered, like a blood system. In other words, the scale is an indirect measure of something— relating to shape, for example—that has no natural way of putting itself on record, like an antigenic reaction, or a straightforward observational category such as crumbly earwax.[2] Various measures may all relate to the basic, unmeasurable character and thus to each other: they are correlated, not independent, and the "character" is thought of as being like a factor in factor analysis.

FORMS OF DISTANCE MEASURE

In the multivariate case, the usual form is to obtain, from the original variables, standardized and uncorrelated variates—the differences in which may be summed into a single distance or, better, since they are orthogonal, used to find distances in a Euclidian space, as the square root of the sum of the squared differences. This was first done, using metric traits, in Pearson's Coefficient of Racial Likeness (Pearson 1926, Tildesley 1921). Mahalanobis, Pearson's student, pointed out its faults (especially the lack of orthogonality) to Pearson and eventually produced a solution in D^2 (Mahalanobis, Majumdar, and Rao 1949). Other transformations of the measurements may be used, such as multiple discriminant function scores, as long as they are uncorrelated. Most simply, a large number of measurements may be subjected to a *principal components analysis* and scored on these uncorrelated variates; this has the advantage that individuals as well as populations may be "distanced," and also, since the components remove the greatest proportion of total variance at each step, some of the last in the total set may be dropped with loss of a proportionately small amount of information.

Doing the same thing with noncontinuous traits took longer to solve. One straightforward solution was Sanghvi's (1953) summing of chi-squares over different loci (used recently, for example, by Workman and Niswander [1970] on the Papago). The problem, obviously, was not correlation among the traits, but quite the reverse: lack of correlation made standardizing and scaling difficult. A much used form is the angular transformation of Cavalli-Sforza and Edwards (1967). For any one locus, the frequencies of the several alleles are used to form a vector of unit length, so that for two populations, the sum of the square roots of the cross products of corresponding alleles gives the correlation between the two, in the form of the cosine of the angle between the vectors. This varies, of course, from 0 to 1.0, so the distance becomes 1 minus the cosine. (It is further transformed by converting the angle to radians and using the chord of the arc between the ends of the vectors as the distance in order to standardize the measure so that 1.0 equals one complete gene substitution.) This value can be used as before, additively with other loci, or to produce the Pythagorean distance from the root of the sum of the squares. The angular transformation attempts to correct for distortion arising when allele frequencies are very small, since the cosine changes somewhat more rapidly near 0° or 90°; this is not entirely successful.[3]

These particular single gene distances may stand either as biological distances or with the implications involved in genetic distances, already described. They are, in fact, directly related to Wahlund estimates of kinship among populations on the model of a subdivided population in which isolation and drift lead to reduction of the heterozygosity within the subpopulations. In fact, Cavalli-Sforza used the form of distance just described in several distance studies, but moved to a modification more specifically related to F statistics, that is, to an estimate of F_{ST} (see Note 3), in a study of African pygmies (Cavalli-Sforza et al. 1969).

Problems arise with the use of these distances, or F statistics, in populations at different levels; since small subpopulations will have a greater variance in gene frequencies among themselves, compared with comparisons of larger populations, this tends to make kinship coefficients or correlations appear lower (distances greater), whether these are in the form of genetic distances or F figures. Whether they are also subject to wider fluctuations in general results according to the number and nature of loci introduced, as compared with metric biological distances, is not known, but it seems likely. In both cases, of course, only a minute section of the genetic and other information is involved, but with metric traits especially, it is clear that different sets tend strongly to give the same results (Oxnard 1967), and that after combining a modest number of measurements in a generalized distance, redundancy sets in.

CLUSTERING

A necessary adjunct of distance measures is "clustering" procedures, since with more than a few populations, the table of mutual distances may have a number of dimensions and becomes incomprehensible anyway. Here again, procedures are tied to premises. For biological distances, clustering may be used simply to create an informative grouping of populations, while maintaining reserve as to taxonomic implications. For genetic distances especially, the very form of the distance implies departure from a common source, and the result of clustering or grouping is taken specifically as a phylogenetic tree; the model of connections (topology) has a good deal to do with the choice of method. The statistical aspects have been particularly well dealt with in a recent article by Kidd and Sgaramella-Zonta (1971). In the "minimum deviation" method of Fitch and Margoliash (1967), the desideratum is to make the total connecting line between two populations conform to their original mutual distance figure, expressing the amount of evolution by which the two have diverged. In the "minimum evolution" form of Cavalli-Sforza and Edwards (1967), the aim is to minimize the total length of "string" or connecting branches throughout the figure, based on the "random walk" model of population divergence. While migration and selection may be allowed as elements in this model, its heart is random genetic drift leading to gene substitution.

APPLICATIONS TO GENETIC TRAITS

In looking at recent test results, the interest is partly in seeing how they conform to authors' expectations and partly in what those expectations are: whether distance measures turn up findings not in conformity with what might be assumed on naïve premises. For example, do biological or genetic distances increase smoothly with increasing population remoteness or cultural isolation? Or, more important, do they imply the same thing when different levels of population division are under consideration?

At the basic level, we have cases of groups or villages converging on the model of genetic distance studies already considered; these groups are so closely connected that the history of their relationships is approximately known, and migration matrices of intermarriage can be made up. Such a study (by Ward and Neel [1970b]) on seven villages of the Makiritare

163

Indians of southern Venezuela used a Cavalli-Sforza-Edwards phylo-genetic tree based on 11 blood systems, with a result that agreed closely with the known pattern of village history (since 1910) and of village inter-marriage. Giles, in Chapter 17 of this book, refers to the study by Sinnett et al. (1970) on related clans around Wabag and Mt. Hagen, New Guinea, in which, again, a minimum-evolution tree from five systems fitted traditional history very well. Wyber (1970) reports that genetic distances (number of alleles not given) among seven Anwin villages of the North Fly area in New Guinea nicely correlated with geographic distances.

Ward and Neel (1970b) find that their picture of evolution fits best when all 11 of their systems are used in genetic distance; a subset of six (Rh, MNSs, Duffy, Kidd, Diego, Hp) is only fair, and another of five (P, Lewis, secretor, Gc, acid phosphatase and PGM_1) is rather poor; they promise a future locus-by-locus analysis. In addition, the intervillage distance for individual loci fluctuates considerably around what is pre-dicted for each from a broader study. (See Workman 1968 for a view of the selective significance of such fluctuations.)

So far so good: genetic distances in some cases reflect local phylogeny well and are even more suggestive in such a study as that of Friedlaender et al. (1971). But the genetic differentiation can be—and should be ex-pected to be (see Note 3)—to a significant degree independent of geog-raphy and the simple phylogenetic model. For hard evidence, Workman and Niswander (1970) found highly significant and "essentially random" blood gene differences among Papago Indian regional groups. And Giles demonstrates the surprising disparities among his Waffa villages, espe-cially in the ABO system, despite what must be a relatively recent isola-tion (in terms of generations) among the three groups, and despite the lack of any clear systematic effects.

Wyber (1970) and Fitch and Neel (1969) speak of "dispersive forces" leading to such local random genetic differentiation, which Fitch and Neel refer to as "noise" in the context of larger groupings. Wyber, while finding significant correlation of genetic distance with linear geographic distance, noted the importance of the noncorrelated component; for this component, he suggested a number of causes of random drift: selective action possibly leading to a selective homeostasis, and cultural effects, such as high isolation by endogamy, differential fertility related to po-lygamy, and the founder effect operating along family lines, not by random collections of individuals. Thus, genetic distance at this population level may have a considerable nonphylogenetic component, at least in magnitude, while it also may cover up population distinctions of importance at individual loci.

Fitch and Neel cover a broader level of population distribution, taking in 12 circum-isthmian American Indian tribes, for which, of course, the historical background of phylogenetic relations is not known, except for possible inferences from language. For these, six blood systems (material taken from the literature) were used in several clusterings (minimum string, minimum deviation, sequential splitting), with consistent and satisfying results (though not such as immediately to suggest a historical framework for the original peopling of the area). Apparently in contrast to these results, the authors drew attention to the strength of the "dispersive forces" determining the gene frequencies of individual villages within a tribe.

The final category is application to specifically unrelated populations on different continents. The prime case, which comes from Cavalli-Sforza and Edwards (1963) and Cavalli-Sforza, Barrai, and Edwards (1964), is entitled "analysis of human evolution" and is based on gene substitution by random genetic drift as the parameter of distance. In these articles and accompanying discussion, the difficulties of migration and hybridization and of parallel selection—as reducing expressed distance—are recognized, as is the problem of possible differential weighting on different systems subsumed. (Cavalli-Sforza and Edwards apparently felt that this problem of possible differential weighting, as in other cases, would be compensated for by generalizing the distance over a number of systems; they also applied a principal components analysis and the minimum string clustering.) In the main result, there is a general east-west division of human populations, with American Indians, Maoris, and Australians opposed to a western pair of branches, European and African, respectively. This leads to a map of hypothetical diffusion of modern man, with no stated root or origin (though it appears suspiciously close to the Garden of Eden).

Now, regardless of results, it is to be questioned whether distance measures based on these traits should be applied on such a scale, except as an exercise. I agree with Livingstone that there is no "true" phylogeny likely to be involved in the tree; furthermore, it is hard to believe that the actual process is one of simple genetic displacement by random drift. (Cavalli-Sforza himself has elsewhere [1967] reviewed the probable force of other factors, especially selection, in early human history.) By a different route, this has brought us back to the blood group "races" of Boyd and others and to the legitimacy of judging phylogenetic relationships by single-gene traits going far back into the past. Nonadaptiveness is a basic assumption but a questionable one. Selective effects on blood systems are surely too heavily discounted when such spans of space and time are in view.[4] Though the evidence is indirect, it has been pointed out that various blood or serum alleles must have been subjected episodically to severe selective pressure by endemic disease (most probably), and examples have been suggested, such as smallpox and the MN system (Hunt and Smedley 1965). The result would be to make populations, of any racial or tribal complexion, converge in their gene frequencies over a major area. Harpending (1971b) considers the case of the South African Bushmen and their Bantu neighbors. Opinions on their morphological likeness vary considerably, but it is agreed to be less than their serological likeness. Harpending concludes that the latter is suspect and that serological traits are not very reliable evidence for population history. This conclusion is also toxic to general models of human evolution based on gene substitution under drift.

There is another effect of probable importance, different from random genetic drift, but applicable to major geographical populations where it is possible that these have had episodes of very small population size. This is the bottle-necking effect of the founder principle when combined with unequal population expansions. Some of the blood systems weightiest in distance figures may have been so affected: we note the surprising differences in the frequency of the B gene in Giles's Waffa villages—departures that presumably fall in the category of drift and the founder effect among local populations (see also Neel's [1967] remarks, below, on the importance of relatedness among human founders). On a grand scale, it is difficult to believe that the tendency of the B antigen to be absent from certain major but marginal populations of the world (in Australia, Polynesia, America) is not systematic in this special sense. Brues (1964, for example) has emphasized this general tendency to lose the least frequent gene, even both A and B, for its importance to the early populations of the Americas. All these widespread populations were almost certainly subject to bottle-necking effects during migration, followed by population expansions. Australia, with an earliest occupation beyond 30,000 years, and America with the same at 20,000 years and probably more, might have been entered by isolated bands from Asian populations devoid of B before its general presence in the human population, though this seems like an antique idea. But the Polynesians must have arisen from some East Asiatic population, plentifully supplied with B, not over 5,000 years ago, developing specifically Polynesian culture; there were then successive Fijian and Tongan sojourns about 3,000 years ago under conditions of increasing isolation of the seed colony, followed by a further founding of central and eastern Polynesia after B had been lost entirely, since these are the areas of its absence.[5]

All this suggests strongly that the ABO locus, at least, is of dubious reliability for interpreting relationships over the long term and for populations not forming a structure. (And what term is actually "long" or "short" is probably indeterminate.[6]) Barnicot (1964) has cautioned against making historical inferences from gene distribution maps limited to single systems; indeed, information from such maps is likely to flow inward, toward the selective, clinal, or other arrangements of the system itself, rather than outward toward the history of major populations. At lower levels (intertribal and intratribal), gene distributions and genetic distances doubtless convey significant information, if of different kinds. Ward and Neel (1970b) found that, roughly, the average South American intertribal distance was half the average Cavalli-Sforza-Edwards worldwide distance, but that the intratribal (intervillage) mean distance was almost the same as the intertribal. This does not accord with the conceivable but naïve assumption, suggested above, that distances would increase linearly with inclusiveness of the level of population being compared. It does reflect the different bases of distances taken at those levels: (1) the considerable differentiation among subunits of a general tribal population that is smoothed over and not involved in the variance of distances among whole tribes, and (2) the special, nonrandom causes of genetic differentiation between major ethnic divisions. In addition, according to Harpending, there is no real model to dictate choice of the best form of genetic distance or relationship among several kinds (see discussion in Ward and Neel), nor are the sampling properties known for the kinds of distance in use, so that methodological and biological differences may be confused. Harpending (1971b) suggests that the meaningfulness of distances might be improved by trying to find worldwide base lines (that is, the average distance between two individuals chosen at random from any parts of the world) by way of standardizing things, but that it would be more direct, in effect, to move into F statistics: to express distances as equivalent inbreeding coefficients. Evidence that "polymorphic blood group alleles are not good indicators of population relationship is the kind of information which calculations of genetic distance would not reveal but which is immediately obvious when equivalent inbreeding coefficients are studied" (Harpending 1971b:78).

One usefulness of distances for generalizing genetic differences has been pointed out. If drift (Harpending 1971b) or hybridizing (Workman 1968) should produce the same distance estimates from all loci, then loci that depart markedly from the expected figures may be investigated for the effects of selection.

SOMATIC TRAITS: HERITABILITY

Somatic characters have an ontogenetic development and so express an environmental component of variation; in them, heritability is less than 100 percent and varies from character to character. This has been investigated a number of times but has been epitomized by Hiernaux (1963) in combining his results with those of Osborne and De George (1959). Osborne and De George's study consisted of measurements made on MZ and DZ adult twin pairs, with relative heritability being expressed by a high F ratio in an analysis of variance (that is, smaller relative MZ twin variance), signifying a stronger genetic component (see Table 27, taken from Hiernaux). Hiernaux's own data used Hutu males of Kivu province, Congo, in two samples, one of these populations being favored environmentally by better nutrition and less malaria in an upland environment. In Hiernaux's hypothesis, measured traits of least relative heritability would show the greatest standardized differences between the two samples; and, in fact, these differences did correspond inversely with Osborne and De George's ranking by greatest heritability (Tables 27 and 28). A stronger genetic component was indicated in stature, limb lengths, and face heights, and a weaker genetic component in trunk diameters, girths, and head measures.

In a study of Hutterite siblings (Howells 1966b), interfamily heterogeneity, both ethnically and environmentally, was reduced by the nature of the population as far as may ever be expected in human material. Intraclass sibling coefficients, as a measure of heritability on a simple polygenic basis, placed (as above) stature, nose height (face height could not be

168

used), and foot length close to the theoretical 0.50 for such measurements, with other limb lengths (and head length and breadth) a step
lower, near 0.40; trunk measures, facial breadths, body girths, and skin-
fold thicknesses placed on a descending scale down to 0.20.

All this applies to univariate measurements. Only the study by Hier-

TABLE 27
F RATIOS OF THE DZ AND MZ WITHIN PAIR
VARIANCES IN OSBORNE AND DE GEORGE'S MALE
SERIES AND DISTANCES BETWEEN THE
TWO HUTU SUBGROUPS*

Character	F Ratio of DZ and MZ Variances	Distance Between the Two Hutu Subgroups
Cephalic index	9.90	0.064
Total arm length	4.97	0.316
Stature	4.73	0.198
Total leg length	4.41	0.240
Nose height	4.03	0.273
Upper face height	3.49	0.145
Bigonial breadth	3.17	0.435
Forearm length	2.89	0.356
Upper arm length	2.68	0.219
Biocular width	2.39	0.387
Biacromial breadth	2.29	0.538
Chest breadth	2.17	0.623
Mouth width	1.86	0.451
Chest depth	1.83	1.419
Total face height	1.81	0.204
Interocular width	1.76	0.292
Max. calf girth	1.58	0.814
Bi-iliac breadth	1.50	0.509
Nose breadth	1.39	0.365
Upper arm girth	1.36	0.915
Weight	1.05	0.968
Bizygomatic breadth	0.99	0.356
Thigh girth	0.91	0.930
Head height	0.73	0.241
Head length	0.44	0.458

SOURCE: After Hiernaux (1963).
  * Characters are listed by decreasing F ratios.

TABLE 28
SIGIFICANCE OF THE *F* RATIOS OF THE DZ AND
MZ WITHIN PAIR VARIANCES IN OSBORNE AND
DE GEORGE'S MALE SERIES AND SIGNIFICANCE OF
THE DIFFERENCE BETWEEN THE TWO
HUTU SUBGROUPS*

Character	Significance of the F Ratio of DZ and MZ Variances	Significance of the Difference Between Hutu Subsamples
Cephalic index	**	
Total arm length	**	*
Stature	**	
Total leg length	**	
Nose height	**	*
Upper face height	**	
Bigonial breadth	**	*
Forearm length	*	**
Upper arm length	*	
Biocular width		**
Biacromial breadth	*	**
Chest breadth		**
Mouth width		**
Chest depth		**
Total face height		*
Interocular width		*
Max. calf girth		**
Bi-iliac breadth		**
Nose breadth		**
Upper arm girth		**
Weight		**
Bizygomatic breadth		*
Thigh girth		**
Head height		
Head length		**

SOURCE: After Hiernaux (1963).

*Two stars indicate *P* values below 0.01, one star *P* values below 0.05, no star *P* values above 0.05. Characters are listed by decreasing *F* ratios.

naux and one by Howells (1953) have attempted to find such distinctions in factor scores as opposed to raw measurements. In the latter case, oblique factors for long bone length and facial height gave sharply higher fraternal correlations (intraclass) than did factors for trunk breadths, facial breadths, and other head measures. The findings were not entirely satisfactory, since in this cosmopolitan American sample, interfamily heterogeneity of the data may have augmented the fraternal correlations. The main point, however, is that such continuous measures of size or shape, in raw or factor form, do show considerable differences in degree of heritability, which, in turn, bears on considerations of generalized distances based on somatic traits.

STUDIES COMBINING GENETIC AND SOMATIC TRAITS

Somatic traits, on one hand, and genetic and biological distances on the other have been used in parallel a number of times, usually producing congruous results (for an early example, see Sanghvi 1953). Only a few recent cases will be cited here, beginning with one that does not primarily provide distances but does illuminate some basic points—a study by Mc-Henry and Giles (1971). This study uses Giles's anthropometric data on his three Waffa villages for comparison with the serological results he has already reported. These are the notable facts:

(1) As Giles found with blood genes, there was a pronounced degree of morphological differentiation among the villages, with their presumably common ancestry and with no discernible causes of differentiation other than drift. The measurements giving significant intervillage F ratios indicated that the differentiation was a matter of shape, not of size (stature or weight). This agrees with Shapiro's (1939) finding for Japanese migrants to Hawaii; it does not, however, agree with the belief of Workman and Niswander (1970) that, following the failure of Schull, Yanase, and Nemoto (1962) to find local differentiation in size on the island of Kuroshima, Japan, anthropometric data would probably not have given signs of drift among the Papago.

(2) The single measurements with high F ratios tended definitely to be those high in heritability. (McHenry and Giles did an analysis of sibling correlations to judge heritability, and the strongly differentiated [intervillage] measurements corresponded only moderately well with high

heritability in these results. Inspecting their figures, I find a definitely better correspondence with those measurements giving a high genetic component in the study of Osborne and De George [1959] and possibly better still with my own Hutterite figures [1966b], material I believe less difficult to analyze in this way than the authors' own.) It will be remembered (above) that Hiernaux found the *least* "heritable" measures to show the greatest difference between two Hutu populations of common descent that live in strongly different environments. For the Waffa, without environmental differences, may we read an argument for drift, in the form of the founder effect, operating on measures with a strong genetic component?

(3) McHenry and Giles also did several discriminant analyses of the villages. In the most general, it was again measurements of high heritability that were pointed to by the discriminant vectors as being important in differentiation—leg lengths and proportions, foot breadth, head breadth, and upper face height. (Here again, I am judging heritability more on the basis of Osborne and De George and myself than on the authors' data.) When the authors used their own estimates of heritability to divide measurements into two sets—high and low in heritability—those with supposedly a stronger genetic component were only slightly more efficient in intervillage discrimination of individuals. When they used Osborne and De George to make the same kind of division, their figures indicate a more marked advantage for the more heritable measurements.

We may conclude that drift may operate significantly on the genetic component of such continuously varying traits, as it does on single gene characters. This reinforces the likelihood that the founder effect is the essential agent in differentiation, especially when group fission occurs by lineages rather than by really random individuals. Neel (1967) has stressed the importance of human social organization in this respect, giving a specific example of a Xavante splinter group, dominated by one large sibship and having other internal interrelationships. It actually joined an existing village, but had it founded a new village or tribe, it would have constituted a highly nonrandom sampling of its source. Because of this extra kind of distortion, in addition to the luck of the draw in a small sample (the meaning of the founder effect in animal species), Neel suggests that, for human studies, a "lineal effect" should be recognized in addition to the founder effect.

Friedlaender et al. (1971) have analyzed 18 villages of south central

Bougainville in the Solomon Islands. These villages are distributed, broadly speaking, along a sort of alley on the eastern side of the island, with a linguistically transitional tribe, the Simeku, occupying a bottleneck area near the middle, between north and south. These villages are particularly diverse linguistically (Austronesian and two non-Austronesian stocks represented), and although environmental differences are minor, social fragmentation is marked, with little marriage across major linguistic group lines. All those blood systems that are polymorphic in the area were significantly heterogeneous at the 0.001 level. Physically, the people give an impression of homogeneity, but anthropometry and discriminant analysis show them to be relatively diverse. Friedlaender et al. found some blood alleles to vary clinally, with a well-marked step at the Simeku region, some to have aberrant frequencies at the middle of the distribution, and some to fluctuate in no intelligible fashion.

Distances and clusterings (used in several different ways) gave highly congruous results between blood and anthropometry, as well as between both of these and linguistics. Language differences were better related to biology than was simple geographic distance, and at least as well with anthropometry as with blood. As Friedlaender et al. point out, this is a set of local populations with a generally known history and a linguistic situation that makes the model of simple branching evolution unacceptable on the face of it.

This model has, however, been applied on a worldwide scale by Cavalli-Sforza and Edwards (1963), as we have seen. In addition to the genetic tree, they used anthropometry, selecting 15 populations from the literature to match those composing the blood tree as closely as practical. The result gave enough resemblance between the two trees to encourage the authors in the feeling that better data and more complete agreement might support their broad view of evolution. Without commenting on this, I would like to mention material of my own (Howells 1973)—cranial populations also selected on a worldwide basis, measured with uniform technique and a large set of measurements and angles. These 17 populations were formed into trees, both by a successive merging method and, by the kindness of K. K. Kidd,[7] by the successive splitting as well. The results are very similar, a fact that Kidd finds interesting, since the two methods are probably more accurate at the first mergings and the first splits respectively. In either case, the tree is more satisfying than either of those in Cavalli-Sforza and Edwards, because it corresponds more closely to

173

geography. Crania are not amenable to fine-grain population studies, of course, but may in many ways be useful for distance studies. (One problem in comparing work on the living is that of attacking heritability; another, common to both, is how the polygenic and pleiotropic aspects of the genetic component in somatic traits may behave under drift, selection, or migration.)

The arrangement of populations using male skulls is shown in Figure 26 (that given by females is essentially the same). The distances here are based on discriminant functions. These, in turn, indicate where the bases of cranial differences lie. Africans, Europeans, Asiatics, and Australo-Melanesians, each appearing from the branchings to be major populations, have specific, distinct, and apparently rather deep-seated cranial traits. The tropical peoples are short-faced and narrow-skulled—this is the nature of major discrimination. But Australo-Melanesians have heavy supraorbitals and recessed nasalia that, however, are not flat; they are also prognathic. Africans have traits generally opposite to these. Such broad distinctions can be broken down further by factor analysis; for example, facial height and skull base breadth, though both characters of Asiatics especially, vary in individuals independently of one another; so do projection of the nose and of the midface generally. These appear to be the anatomically local patterns of individual genetic variation on which population differences are also constructed. (The possibility that they are environmentally induced seems remote, both from the pattern in factor analysis and from the different environments in which such cranially similar peoples as Tasmanians and Tolais of New Britain must have existed for some millenia.)

This is indeed a different picture of population differentiation from that seen in most of the studies described. Use of distances and clustering is important in bringing it out. But the case is special. It is unlikely that crania will ever be available for the study of the "dispersive forces" of differentiation among subpopulations like the Waffa (although Laughlin and Jørgensen [1956] managed this to a degree). Yet cranial skeletal traits should respond like other somatic traits. The problem posed in this case is another: the apparent persistence of major population differences in cranial form, over large regions, but more important, over long periods. It may seem like an old-fashioned view to think of "races" as unchanging except for mixture. But the evidence at present—whether from Europe, Australia (and also Southeast Asia), America, or South Africa—is in favor, rather

174

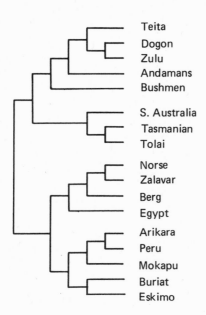

FIGURE 26.   Clustering of cranial populations by successive mergers.

than against, the existence of cranial differences much like those of today, going well back into the Pleistocene. This can be supported directly from the same multiple discriminant analysis. Such persistence of morphology over time, in what should be moderately labile polygenic characters, is not something for which the study of living populations has provided good answers.

NOTES

1. The final draft of this paper was done well after the School of American Research seminar and had the benefit of other papers prepared or published later (Kidd and Sgaramella-Zonta 1971, Friedlaender et al. 1971, McHenry and Giles 1971). In particular, I must acknowledge suggestions and criticisms from Henry Harpending, as well as discussions with him relating to his own dissertation (1971b).

2. The distinction is not complete: a numerical trait like abdominal bristles in *Drosophila* is a "natural" count. On the borderline fall occasional human traits like those of the dentition.

3. Details and algebra are taken from Cavalli-Sforza and Edwards (1967), Morton, Miki, and Yee (1968), Workman and Niswander (1970), Harpending (1971b), and personal comments. For a locus with two alleles, the population locus may be written as $(\sqrt{[p]}, \sqrt{[q]})$, so that the sum of squares $(p + q) = 1.00$.

The relation between two such unit population vectors, 1 and 2, is the sum of roots of the cross products.

$r = (\sqrt{[p_1 p_2]} + \sqrt{[q_1 q_2]}) =$ cosine of angle between vectors 1 and 2. The one-locus distance is taken first as $(1 - \cos\theta)$, i.e., increasing as vectors diverge toward 90°, in which case $r = 0$. Such a distance would, in the two-allele case, correspond to a complete gene substitution $(p_1 = 1.00, p_2 = 0.00)$. In the form used by Cavalli-Sforza and Edwards, the distance is taken as the *chord* of the arc between the ends of the vectors, made equal to 1.00 in the above case by converting the angle to radians (1 radian = $180°/\pi$), namely,

$$d = (2\sqrt{2}/\pi)\,(\sqrt{1 - \cos\theta}).$$

Now, as a Wahlund estimate of kinship in the framework of related subpopulations, the coefficient of kinship based on deviations of frequencies from the estimated mean allelic frequencies (for one allele) may be written

$$r_{1,2} = (p_1 - \bar{p})\,(p_2 - \bar{p})\,/\,\overline{pq},$$

which may be applied to the case of a single population as

$$r_{1,1} = (p_1 - \bar{p})^2\,/\,\overline{pq} = f,$$

which is the inbreeding coefficient. This may be compared with the generalized form

$$F_{ST} = \sigma^2{}_p\,/\,\overline{pq},$$

an F statistic estimating the effect of nonrandom mating due to subdivision of the population or reduction of local heterozygosis compared with Hardy-Weinberg expectation if the total population were panmictic.

It is worth noting (see especially Workman and Niswander) that the effects of nonrandom mating, leading to genetic differentiation as measured above, are present whether or not there are also systematic effects of drift or other causes leading to "kinship," which is what genetic distances aim to measure.

4. Even the central assumption of independence of different loci is in question, with multilocuous interactions (ABO, haptoglobin, Gc, Kidd, and Lewis) having been indicated (Sing and Shreffler 1970).

5. These events are strongly indicated from recent linguistic and archaeological analysis. Some other related Pacific populations fluctuate radically in the ABO system: Rennell and Bellona, outliers evidently colonized from western Polynesia where B probably survived, have a higher frequency of B than of A. Tench Island, north of New Ireland, has evidently been losing B and A from its small population; on the other hand, the Australian aboriginal inhabitants of Bentinck Island in the Gulf of Carpentaria have B and O only, with A absent.

6. Boyd's (1963) interesting paper, "Four Achievements of the Genetical Method in Physical Anthropology" (see also Crawford's Chapter 2) dealt with the Gypsies, the U.S. Negro population, the Lapps, and the Pygmy-Negrito populations of the tropics. The force of his demonstration as to genetic origins, clear in the first two classes that have migration histories of a few centuries only, is vitiated in the case of the Lapps by the tendency toward loss of B in isolated small groups, already discussed, and in that of the last case, because any possible continuity of Pygmies and Negritos would have been broken in an antiquity presumably comparable to that of the peopling of America. As to Negritos, I herewith swallow the words quoted by Crawford, having changed my views.

7. Kenneth K. Kidd: personal communication.

9
Genetic Distance
Among Southern African Populations

HENRY HARPENDING

Department of Anthropology
Yale University[1]

TREFOR JENKINS

South African Institute
for Medical Research
Johannesburg

Analysis of variation in gene frequencies within an area may have several purposes, and much of the ongoing disagreement about methodology in human population genetics may reflect as much a lack of clear perception of the purposes of the methodology as it does real conflict over substantive theoretical issues. A method of analysis should be directed toward answering questions, and these questions should be explicit.

There are two broad and overlapping areas of inquiry for which studies of regional gene frequency variation are pertinent. One is population structure—the study of the effects of internal migration, group composition, mating practices, and other factors on the amount and pattern of genetic drift within an area. The second is really population history. Here, the questions concern the degree of similarity among populations, where similarity may reflect either common ancestry or mate exchange. These two aspects of genetic similarity are ordinarily inseparable.

Studies of population structure typically focus on small and/or homogeneous areas. Under the assumption that the study population is near "equilibrium," that is, that a stationary distribution of gene frequencies has been reached, variation in gene frequencies or genotype frequencies is compared with predictions made by considering various demographic parameters of the population. Each marker locus yields a measure of the amount of drift. This measure is either Wahlund's coefficient of inbreeding (F_{ST} in Workman and Niswander [1970], F_W in Cavalli-Sforza [1969b], F in Harpending and Jenkins [1972b]), or the genotypic disequilibrium inbreeding coefficient of Li and Horvitz (1953) (F_{IT} in Workman and Niswander [1970], α in Yasuda [1968b] and Morton et al. [1971c]). In addition, the form of the regression or normalized genetic covariance—r in Harpending and Jenkins (1972b), $y(d)$ in Morton et al. (1971c)—is of interest, although it now seems that this regression is primarily a function of sample size, distribution, and the local inbreeding coefficient, rather than a function of the underlying population structure. This biological measure of drift is compared with predictions from any or all of the following demographic items: pedigrees, isonymy, the root mean square distance between birthplaces of parents or between parents and offspring (Malécot 1948, Azevêdo et al. 1969), a matrix of frequencies of gene exchange among areas or villages (Bodmer and Cavalli-Sforza 1968, Smith 1969, Morton 1969, Friedlaender 1971a, Harpending and Jenkins 1972b), and local effective population size.

Evaluation of the amount of concordance between predictions from demography and observed marker gene frequency variation has been equivocal, because of uncertainty about what constitutes reasonable agreement, and because of uncertainty in the interpretation of the predictive models. For example, Friedlaender (1971a) and Morton et al. (1971c) assume that inbreeding statistics given by the migration matrix model should correspond to Wahlund F statistics, while Harpending and Jenkins (1972b) modify their results to account for finite sample size. The difference between the corrected and uncorrected predictions is very large. As this approach is refined and applied to diverse groups it may lead to inferences about selection at loci which deviate significantly from predictions.

178

The second, or historical, approach to studying gene frequency variation has been applied to populations of all sizes from single tribes (Ward and Neel 1970a) to the whole world (Cavalli-Sforza and Edwards 1967). In these studies, group gene frequencies are converted into genetic "distances" among groups, and these distances are used to make a "genetic map" (Sanghvi, Kirk, and Balakrishnan 1971) or a cladogram, both of which provide a visible if anecdotal summary of the intergroup differences. This summary diagram is then compared intuitively with knowledge of mating patterns, ancestry, linguistic relationships, or other heuristic indicators of similarities among the groups.

There are many measures of genetic distance, all of which are reasonable. They are all related to one another, and none is likely to seriously mislead an investigator. Consideration of the notion of genetic similarity should, however, lead to some measure that has specifiable advantages. These may be that it lend itself equally well to the construction of cladograms and to the construction of genetic maps and that it be clearly related to genetic theory—that is, that it have more than anecdotal interpretation.

The genetic distance between two groups should be small if their gene frequencies are similar. There are a number of reasons why two groups should have similar gene frequencies, the more conspicuous of which are: (1) they shared a recent common ancestor; (2) they exchange genes; (3) they are large, so that little drift has occurred since their separation; and (4) their loci are or have been subject to similar selection pressure. Of these, the third reason is often overlooked. Since drift of mean gene frequencies of a subdivided group is nearly independent of mating patterns within the group (Ewens 1969), consideration of size makes reasonable the finding, for example, that genetic distances between villages within American Indian linguistic groups are as large as distances between linguistic groups.

The fourth cause of similar gene frequencies (similar selection histories of populations) is, in practice, not often cited to explain the results of studies. Many studies of genetic distance are of restricted homogeneous areas where there is no reason to suspect heterogeneity in selection pressures. Other selection environments, such as homogeneous selection over an area or random changes in the magnitude and intensity of directional selection, will not, in effect, be very different from drift. For these reasons and for others discussed in Cavalli-Sforza (1969), selection is usually not explicitly considered in studies of genetic distance, in which genetic drift is the presumed agent responsible for observed gene frequency differentiation. Within small areas, many kinds of selection would have little effect on the differentiation caused by drift, and even regional heterogeneity would be swamped by drift and migration unless it was very strong.

Genetic drift is described by kinship statistics, and these should be the basis of measures of genetic distance. The coefficient of kinship between two groups that are labeled i and j is written f_{ij} (or φ_{ij} in Morton et al. [1971c] and Harpending and Jenkins [1972b]). This coefficient has two interpretations that are often used interchangeably: (1) the probability that a random allele at a specified locus in population i is identical by descent to a random allele from the same locus in population j is f_{ij}; (2) the populations are undergoing genetic drift. There is some gene frequency P that is either the initial gene frequency before drift or else the gene frequency toward which systematic pressure is directing the frequencies in groups i and j. Then, f_{ij} is the normalized covariance between gene frequencies of any allele described by the model, that is,

$$f_{ij} = E\left[\frac{(p_i - P)(p_j - P)}{P(1 - P)}\right],$$

where p_i and p_j are the gene frequencies in groups i and j, and $E(\cdot)$ means expectation or average value of the term on which it operates.

The first definition of f_{ij} is applicable to individuals as well as to groups, and i may be the same or different from j. When i is the same as j, the second definition is a form of Wahlund's principle (Li 1955), and it also is applicable, with slight modification, to individuals as well as to groups (Harpending and Jenkins 1972b).

The second definition of the coefficient of kinship immediately suggests that a reasonable measure of genetic distance is

$$\Delta_{ij} = f_{ii} + f_{jj} - 2f_{ij}.$$

This is simply the squared Euclidean distance between populations i and j in a hyperspace whose axes are allelic frequencies scaled by dividing by the normalizing factor $\sqrt{[P(1 - P)]}$ as is appropriate for genetic drift.

COMPUTATION

The observed or sample coefficient of kinship between groups i and j is given as

$$r_{ij} = \frac{(P_i - \bar{P})(P_j - \bar{P})}{\bar{P}(1 - \bar{P})}$$

for any allele. (Morton et al. [1971c] use y instead of r for a similar coefficient.) In this expression, $\bar{P}$ is the weighted mean gene frequency of the allele in the study array; it provides an estimate of the "underlying" mean gene frequency P. The matrix of sample kinship coefficients is calculated for each allele, and these matrices are averaged to yield one overall matrix of sample coefficients. If all the alleles studied are subject to genetic drift with the same systematic pressure (imagined to be immigration from the outside world), then all alleles should give estimates of the same "true" r coefficients, subject only to chance deviations. Hence, Harpending and Jenkins (1972b) simply averaged the r matrices from all alleles they studied. It is probably better to give unequal weight to alleles by weighting estimates from different loci by the degrees of freedom at the locus, as when genetic distance is calculated as a chi-squared statistic. Morton et al. (1971c) propose a weighting method that depends on their own special programs but that may be a better way to reconcile the following kinds of consideration: (1) loci without dominant alleles are much more informative and should be given greater weight than loci like ABO, where much of the gene frequency variation may reflect estimation error; and (2) common alleles are more informative than rare alleles whose frequencies are much more subject to sampling error. For samples of the size common in anthropological studies, the difference between the gene frequencies of 0.3 and 0.4 is meaningful, while the difference between 0.03 and 0.04 is not. Whatever the method used to combine information from the various loci, the resulting matrix of sample relationship coefficient r_{ij} is then amenable to analysis in several ways; one may make a "tree" or one may examine its principle axes and make a "map."

TREES

Harpending and Jenkins (1972b) suggest that the expected or average value of a sample relationship coefficient is

$$E(r_{ij}) \cong \frac{f_{ij} + \bar{\bar{f}} - \bar{f}_i - \bar{f}_j}{1 - \bar{\bar{f}}}.$$

Here, $\bar{f}$ is random kinship within the sample. Writing w_i as the proportion of the total sample that is the ith population ($w_i = N_i / \sum_k N_k$, where N refers to census and not sample sizes), random kinship is

$$\bar{f} = \sum_{i,j} w_i w_j f_{ij}.$$

This is interpretable as the probability of identity by descent of two random alleles from the same locus or as a measure of the drift of sample mean gene frequencies $\bar{p}$ away from the prior mean P, that is,

$$\bar{f} = E\left[\frac{(\bar{p} - P)^2}{P(1 - P)}\right].$$

Similarly $\bar{f_i}$ is the random kinship of population i, that is,

$$\bar{f_i} = \sum_j w_j f_{ij}.$$

This is interpretable as the probability of identity by descent of a random allele from population i with a random allele from anywhere in the sample or, alternatively, as a measure of the similarity of the gene frequencies of population i to the sample mean gene frequencies. If no population is much more isolated than the others, it measures the relative size of population i.

The sample relationship coefficients then give a measure of distance between populations i and j as

$$d_{ij} = r_{ii} + r_{jj} - 2r_{ij}.$$

This measure has expected value

$$E(d_{ij}) \cong \frac{f_{ii} + f_{jj} - 2f_{ij}}{1 - \bar{f}} = \frac{\Delta_{ij}}{1 - \bar{f}},$$

which is the measure of distance suggested above, apart from the constant $(1 - \bar{f})$ in the denominator. Note that the circulation of this distance measure is like the calculation of a chi-squared statistic. With the summation referring to summation over all alleles,

$$d_{ij} \cong \sum\left(\frac{1}{\bar{p}(1 - \bar{p})}\right)[(p_i - \bar{p})^2 + (p_j - \bar{p})^2 - 2(p_i - \bar{p})(p_j - \bar{p})]$$

$$\approx \sum \frac{(p_i - p_j)^2}{\bar{p}},$$

since $\sum \bar{p}$ is an integer equal to the number of loci. However, it is preferable to compute first the matrix of kinship coefficients, because this matrix gives Wahlund F as the average diagonal element and because the eigenvectors of this matrix give a "genetic map" of the sample.

There are many routines that convert a table of distances into dendrograms or trees. Attempts to justify any particular routine as superior to others because of its "reconstruction" of evolution seem unsatisfactory and inapplicable to interbreeding human populations. We prefer a simple "maximum-linkage" technique, which is economical of computer time (Jenkins et al. 1971). The trees given by various techniques are usually similar in broad outline but differ in detail. It is difficult to evaluate or to say anything meaningful about differences among trees. Figure 27 shows trees produced from our material (see below) by the maximum and minimum linkage techniques (Jenkins et al. 1971).

MAPS

Much more satisfactory visual aids for the interpretation of genetic distances are provided by genetic maps (Morton et al. 1971c). A genetic map is simply the result of a principal components analysis of the kinship matrix. To do this, we transform gene frequencies into new, imaginary gene frequencies (more precisely, imaginary scaled deviations from the sample mean) that have the following properties: (1) a population's frequency of any of the imaginary genes has no relationship to its frequency on any of the others, that is, the gene frequencies are uncorrelated; and (2) the variability of the imaginary gene frequencies among the populations may be ranked in descending order, so that a plot of the populations on axes representing the two or three most variable genes gives a good picture of the biological relationships or distances among the populations.

For convenience, we work with three alleles, which may or may not be at the same locus, in three populations, but the procedure is perfectly general. We write, p, q, and r for the gene frequencies and label the populations with subscripts i, j, and k. Then, the kinship matrix is, apart from a scalar divisor (that is, three, because there are three alleles pooled):

$$R = \begin{matrix} r_{11} & r_{12} & r_{13} \\ r_{21} & r_{22} & r_{23} \\ r_{31} & r_{32} & r_{33}, \end{matrix}$$

where, for example,

$$r_{11} = \frac{(p_i - \bar{p})^2}{\bar{p}(1 - \bar{p})} + \frac{(q_i - \bar{q})^2}{\bar{q}(1 - \bar{q})} + \frac{(r_i - \bar{r})^2}{\bar{r}(1 - \bar{r})}$$

$$r_{12} = \frac{(p_i - \bar{p})(p_j - \bar{p})}{\bar{p}(1 - \bar{p})} + \frac{(q_i - \bar{q})(q_j - \bar{q})}{\bar{q}(1 - \bar{q})} + \frac{(r_i - \bar{r})(r_j - \bar{r})}{\bar{r}(1 - \bar{r})}$$

$$r_{22} = \frac{(p_j - \bar{p})^2}{\bar{p}(1 - \bar{p})} + \frac{(q_j - \bar{q})^2}{\bar{q}(1 - \bar{q})} + \frac{(r_j - \bar{r})^2}{\bar{r}(1 - \bar{r})}.$$

This may be written as the product of a matrix and its transpose:

$$R = \begin{pmatrix} \dfrac{(p_i - \bar{p})}{\sqrt{\bar{p}(1 - \bar{p})}} & \dfrac{(q_i - \bar{q})}{\sqrt{\bar{q}(1 - \bar{q})}} & \dfrac{(r_i - \bar{r})}{\sqrt{\bar{r}(1 - \bar{r})}} \\[2ex] \dfrac{(p_j - \bar{p})}{\sqrt{\bar{p}(1 - \bar{p})}} & \dfrac{(q_j - \bar{q})}{\sqrt{\bar{q}(1 - \bar{q})}} & \dfrac{(r_j - \bar{r})}{\sqrt{\bar{r}(1 - \bar{r})}} \\[2ex] \dfrac{(p_k - \bar{p})}{\sqrt{\bar{p}(1 - \bar{p})}} & \dfrac{(q_k - \bar{q})}{\sqrt{\bar{q}(1 - \bar{q})}} & \dfrac{(r_k - \bar{r})}{\sqrt{\bar{r}(1 - \bar{r})}} \end{pmatrix}$$

$$\begin{pmatrix} \dfrac{(p_i - \bar{p})}{\sqrt{\bar{p}(1 - \bar{p})}} & \dfrac{(p_j - \bar{p})}{\sqrt{\bar{p}(1 - \bar{p})}} & \dfrac{(p_k - \bar{p})}{\sqrt{\bar{p}(1 - \bar{p})}} \\[2ex] \dfrac{(q_i - \bar{q})}{\sqrt{\bar{q}(1 - \bar{q})}} & \dfrac{(q_j - \bar{q})}{\sqrt{\bar{q}(1 - \bar{q})}} & \dfrac{(q_k - \bar{q})}{\sqrt{\bar{q}(1 - \bar{q})}} \\[2ex] \dfrac{(r_i - \bar{r})}{\sqrt{\bar{r}(1 - \bar{r})}} & \dfrac{(r_j - \bar{r})}{\sqrt{\bar{r}(1 - \bar{r})}} & \dfrac{(r_k - \bar{r})}{\sqrt{\bar{r}(1 - \bar{r})}} \end{pmatrix}$$

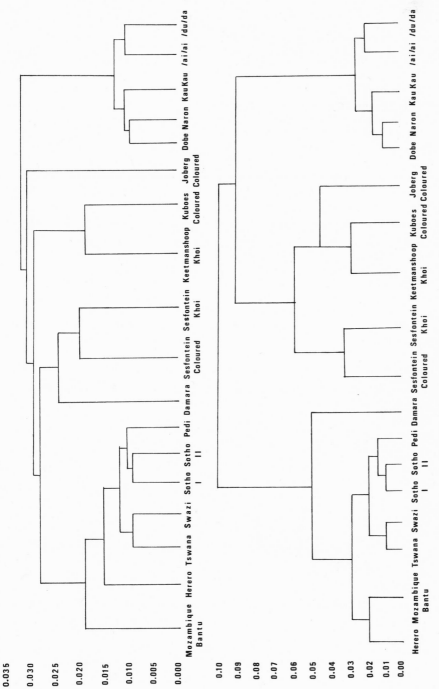

FIGURE 27. Maximum (top) and minimum (bottom) linkage χ^2 distances.

For future reference, we call the matrices on the right of this equation Z and Z^T, so $R = ZZ^T$.

We write our new, imaginary gene frequencies for population i as

$$e_{1i}\sqrt{\lambda_1}, e_{2i}\sqrt{\lambda_2}, e_{3i}\sqrt{\lambda_3}.$$

The reasons for this notation will be apparent. We wish our new frequencies to reconstruct the original kinship matrix R, that is,

$$R = \begin{pmatrix} e_{1i}\sqrt{\lambda_1} & e_{2i}\sqrt{\lambda_2} & e_{3i}\sqrt{\lambda_3} \\ e_{1j}\sqrt{\lambda_1} & e_{2j}\sqrt{\lambda_2} & e_{3j}\sqrt{\lambda_3} \\ e_{1k}\sqrt{\lambda_1} & e_{2k}\sqrt{\lambda_2} & e_{3k}\sqrt{\lambda_3} \end{pmatrix} \begin{pmatrix} e_{1i}\sqrt{\lambda_1} & e_{1j}\sqrt{\lambda_1} & e_{1k}\sqrt{\lambda_1} \\ e_{2i}\sqrt{\lambda_2} & e_{2j}\sqrt{\lambda_2} & e_{2k}\sqrt{\lambda_2} \\ e_{3i}\sqrt{\lambda_3} & e_{3j}\sqrt{\lambda_3} & e_{3k}\sqrt{\lambda_3} \end{pmatrix}$$

Write E as a matrix consisting of the column vectors e_{1-}, e_{2-}, e_{3-}, and scale these vectors so that the sum of squares of their elements is one and the magnitudes of the λ's express the variability of the new gene frequencies; then the previous matrix equality may be written

$$R = \begin{pmatrix} e_{1i} & e_{2i} & e_{3i} \\ e_{1j} & e_{2j} & e_{3j} \\ e_{1k} & e_{2k} & e_{3k} \end{pmatrix} \begin{pmatrix} \lambda_1 & 0 & 0 \\ 0 & \lambda_2 & 0 \\ 0 & 0 & \lambda_3 \end{pmatrix} \begin{pmatrix} e_{1i} & e_{1j} & e_{1k} \\ e_{2i} & e_{2j} & e_{2k} \\ e_{3i} & e_{3j} & e_{3k} \end{pmatrix}$$

or

$$R = E\Lambda E^T,$$

where Λ is a diagonal matrix with elements λ_1, λ_2, λ_3.

Since the matrix R was written originally as the product of a matrix and its transpose, it is symmetric and positive semidefinite. The matrix E and numbers λ are the eigenvectors and eigenvalues of R. A discussion of the algebra of eigenvectors and eigenvalues as used here may be found in Tatsuoka (1971). Because R is symmetric, the matrix E is orthogonal, that is, $EE^T = I$, or, in our terms, the imaginary gene frequencies are uncorrelated. Further, since R is positive semidefinite, the eigenvalues are all greater than or equal to zero. At least one will be zero, because k populations occupy a space of $k - 1$ or fewer dimensions, and several more may be zero if fewer independent alleles than populations are studied.

If the eigenvalues and their associated vectors are arranged and labeled in descending order of magnitude, the imaginary gene frequencies $e_{1i}\sqrt{\lambda_1}$, $e_{1j}\sqrt{\lambda_1}$, $e_{1k}\sqrt{\lambda_1}$ will array the populations along an axis, a rotation of the original gene frequency axes, along which the dispersion is maximized. The second set of imaginary frequencies, $e_{2i}\sqrt{\lambda_2}$, $e_{2j}\sqrt{\lambda_2}$,

$e_{2k}\sqrt{\lambda_2}$, gives a second axis at right angles to the first, along which dispersion is again maximized, after the variation accounted for by the first axis has been removed. The first two or three axes found in this way then provide the "best" reduced dimension picture of the "distance" relations among the groups.

Several remarks concerning the relation of this procedure to ordinary principal components analysis are in order. In many studies, when the positions of objects on component axes are shown, the eigenvectors themselves are plotted, rather than the eigenvectors multiplied by the square root of the corresponding eigenvalue. Since the eigenvectors are scaled so that the sum of their squared elements is equal to one, the plots appear spherical; this may be misleading if the eigenvalues—the magnitudes of dispersion along the corresponding axes—are very different.

Principal components analysis is widely used to array objects in a new space when these objects have been measured on a number of metric traits. Often the reduced-space representation is very satisfactory, since much of the variation can be accounted for by a few components, usually identifiable as size, robusticity, linearity, and so forth. When this method of analysis is used in this population-genetic context, there is no reason to expect that a small number of new variables will account for the relations among the groups in a satisfactory manner, since under pure drift, no locus should be correlated in any way with any other locus. This method should be valuable, on the other hand, in identifying clusters of related groups, since relatedness should be the only factor introducing correlations among groups. In morphometric studies, items like total size seem to become confounded with relatedness.

In morphometric studies, a decision must be made whether to find components of the correlation matrix, which gives all variables equal weight, or of the covariance matrix, which weights variables by their magnitude. Here, gene frequency covariances are divided by the scaling factor $\bar{p}(1 - \bar{p})$ derived from genetic drift theory. This may not be the most appropriate procedure if the object is discrimination, but it has the advantage that it articulates distance analysis with genetic theory and that it provides a map optimally corresponding to the population structure that determines drift.

Finally, in ordinary components analysis, a covariance or correlation matrix among the variables is computed, the eigenvalues and eigenvectors determined, and the component scores (our imaginary gene frequencies) determined by multiplying the eigenvectors by the variable values for each object. The procedure described here is a shortcut and offers further advantage of yielding a distance matrix (if desired) and population structure statistics along the way. It is particularly useful, and economical of computing effort, when many more alleles than populations are studied.

PLOTTING ALLELES

It will usually be of considerable interest to go back and look at the relations among the alleles as well as among the populations. Coordinates for alleles along imaginary axes of greatest variation may be obtained from the eigenvectors of the matrix R by simple matrix multiplication; these coordinates will be eigenvectors of the scaled matrix of covariances among allele frequencies, which we write S.

The matrix Z defined on p. 186 of scaled data values will have k rows and p columns, where p is the number of alleles and k is the number of populations under study. Apart from scalar divisors, the k by k matrix R is equal to Z postmultiplied by its transpose, while the p by p matrix S is equal to Z premultiplied by its transpose. If k is much smaller than p, that is, if there are many more alleles than populations, there are, at most, k eigenvectors of R, imaginary gene frequencies along which the populations are arrayed. These will always be sufficient to reconstruct the kinship or distance matrices, since k populations occupy a hyperspace of, at most, $k - 1$ dimensions. For example, in the three-population example, no matter how many alleles are studied, three populations define a two dimensional space, and distances between them may be drawn exactly in two dimensions. In general, the dimension of the space occupied by k populations defined on p allele frequencies is the minimum of $k - 1$ and p, so that either the S or R matrix contains all the information available about kinship and genetic distance. If, as in this study, k is much smaller than p, it is much more convenient to work with the matrix R. If, on the other hand, p is much smaller than k, it is convenient to work with the scaled covariance matrix among alleles S.

The important algebraic result that allows the use of either matrix for this analysis is that S and R have exactly the same set of nonzero eigenvalues. This means that the dimensions of the space in which the populations are located are exactly the same, whether we imagine populations as points on axes corresponding to gene frequencies, or whether we imagine gene frequencies as points on axes corresponding to populations. Further, the eigenvectors of one are given by multiplying the corresponding eigenvectors of the other by the scaled data matrix Z (Dempster 1969). In matrix notation, let the number of nonzero eigenvalues of S and R be l. Then the l by p matrix of eigenvectors of S is given by the product of the l by k matrix of eigenvectors of R postmultiplied by the k by p matrix of scaled data Z. In general these will have to be rescaled. Then, the p-element eigenvectors of S corresponding to the first few largest eigenvalues give an optimum graphic portrayal of the correlations among the alleles and of their contributions to genetic distances along the corresponding axes.

NUMERICAL EXAMPLE

A numerical example of this procedure using three populations and three gene frequencies may clarify the meaning of the operations. Let populations I, J, and K have gene frequencies p, q, and r as follows:

	I	J	K		
p	0.4	0.8	0.6	$\bar{p} = 0.6$	$\bar{p}(1 - \bar{p}) = 0.24$
q	0.5	0.2	0.8	$\bar{q} = 0.5$	$\bar{q}(1 - \bar{q}) = 0.25$
r	0.5	0.5	0.8	$\bar{r} = 0.6$	$\bar{r}(1 - \bar{r}) = 0.24.$

First, the kinship matrices are formed for each allele, as

$$R_p = \begin{matrix} 0.17 & -0.17 & 0.00 \\ -0.17 & 0.17 & 0.00 \\ 0.00 & 0.00 & 0.00 \end{matrix} \qquad R_q = \begin{matrix} 0.00 & 0.00 & 0.00 \\ 0.00 & 0.36 & -0.36 \\ 0.00 & -0.36 & 0.36 \end{matrix}$$

$$R_r = \begin{matrix} 0.04 & 0.04 & -0.08 \\ 0.04 & 0.04 & -0.08 \\ -0.08 & -0.08 & 0.16, \end{matrix}$$

and averaged:

$$R = \begin{matrix} 0.07 & -0.04 & -0.03 \\ -0.04 & 0.19 & -0.15 \\ -0.03 & -0.15 & 0.18. \end{matrix}$$

Inspection of this matrix shows that the average diagonal element, Wahlund F, is 0.15, which is of the order of those found for comparisons among major racial groups. Second, the inbreeding coefficient of the first population (r_{11}) is small, implying that it is nearest the center of the swarm. Third, the sum of any row or column is zero. In general, it is true that sample random kinship $\bar{r} = \sum_{ij} w_i w_j r_{ij}$, or random kinship of subpopulation j, $\bar{r}_j = \sum_k w_k r_{jk}$, is zero. This corresponds to the intuitive notion that the correlation between two random populations is zero, since correlation is calculated from observed sample mean gene frequencies.

The eigenvectors and eigenvalues of this matrix are:

$$\lambda_1 = 0.34 \qquad e_{1I} = -0.03 \qquad e_{1j} = 0.72 \qquad e_{1k} = -0.69$$
$$\lambda_2 = 0.10 \qquad e_{2I} = 0.82 \qquad e_{2j} = -0.38 \qquad e_{2k} = -0.43$$
$$\lambda_3 = 0.00 \qquad\qquad\quad — \qquad\qquad\qquad — \qquad\qquad\qquad —$$

The sum of the eigenvalues, 0.44, is the sum of the diagonal elements of the original matrix. The eigenvalues measure the dispersion along the new axes; the total dispersion is preserved under the rotation and new representation and given by the sum of the eigenvalues. The third eigenvalue is zero, implying that the three populations occupy a space of only two dimensions, as is obvious. The two eigenvectors corresponding to the two positive eigenvalues are natural coordinate systems for showing the relations among the groups. The squares of the elements of each vector sum to one, so the dispersion along each axis will be the same if the vectors are plotted. More naturally, each vector should be multiplied by the square root of its eigenvalue to show "true" relations (Figure 28).

FIGURE 28. Distance relations among three hypothetical populations.

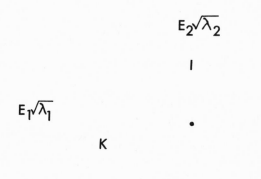

Now, to obtain graphic representation of the relations among the alleles, we obtain the eigenvectors of S from those of R.

$$Z = \begin{pmatrix} \dfrac{(0.4-0.6)}{\sqrt{0.24}} & 0 & \dfrac{(0.5-0.6)}{\sqrt{0.24}} \\[2ex] \dfrac{(0.8-0.6)}{\sqrt{0.24}} & \dfrac{(0.2-0.5)}{\sqrt{0.25}} & \dfrac{(0.5-0.6)}{\sqrt{0.24}} \\[2ex] 0 & \dfrac{(0.8-0.5)}{\sqrt{0.25}} & \dfrac{(0.8-0.6)}{\sqrt{0.24}} \end{pmatrix},$$

$$E^T = \begin{pmatrix} -0.03 & 0.72 & -0.69 \\ 0.82 & -0.38 & -0.43 \\ - & - & - \end{pmatrix},$$

and

$$\begin{matrix} & p & q & r \\ E^T Z = & \begin{pmatrix} 0.30 & -0.85 & -0.42 \\ -0.16 & 0 & -0.24 \\ - & - & - \end{pmatrix}, \end{matrix}$$

approximately. The rows of $E^T Z$ are eigenvectors corresponding to the two nonzero eigenvalues of the scaled covariance matrix among alleles given by $S = Z^T Z$, apart from some scalar row multipliers to make the sum of squares of each vector equal to unity. These relations are shown in Figure 29. The axes are the same in Figures 28 and 29 and reveal immediately, for example, that allele q contains no information for telling population I from J and K, or that allele q is very low in population j.

FIGURE 29. Relations among alleles.

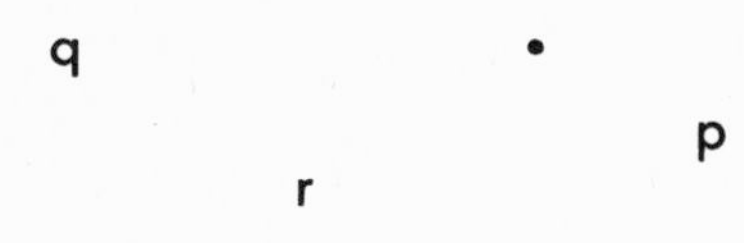

ANALYSIS OF SOUTHERN AFRICAN DATA

We have applied these techniques to data on 15 marker loci from 18 populations in South Africa (Jenkins, Zoutendyk, and Steinberg 1970, Jenkins et al. 1971, Jenkins and Steinberg, unpublished data). These publications will present the results of the various genetic analyses in detail.

The populations studied fall into four main subdivisions; San, Khoi, Bantu, and Colored. We use the new terminology of San for "Bushman" and Khoi for "Hottentot." The provenance of the samples from the Bantu-speaking peoples has been given in Jenkins, Zoutendyk, and Steinberg (1970), except for the Herero sample, which was collected by Harpending during fieldwork in northwest Botswana with !Kung San. The samples from !Kung, Naron, the three groups from Sesfontein, southwest Africa (Damara, Sesfontein Colored, and Khoi), and the Johannesburg Colored are described in Jenkins et al. (1971) and Harpending and Jenkins (1972b). The Khoi from Keetmanshoop, Southwest Africa, and the Colored from Kuboes are described in Jenkins and Corfield (1972). The 18 populations are shown in Figure 30.

Since we are interested in the distance relations among these populations, we have treated them as if they had equal weight in the calculation of the R matrix given in Table 29. If this were a study of population struc-

FIGURE 30. Location of populations in southern Africa.

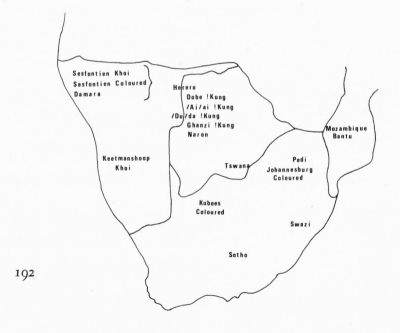

TABLE 29

RELATIONSHIP MATRIX AMONG 18 SOUTHERN AFRICAN POPULATIONS ($\times 10^3$)

	1	2	3	4	5	6	7	8	9	10	11	12	13	14	15	16	17	18
1.	056																	
2.	047	070																
3.	060	070	098															
4.	038	037	057	057														
5.	036	035	045	038	040													
6.	−010	−014	−006	−008	−009	041												
7.	001	−004	−008	009	001	009	060											
8.	−032	−043	−041	−036	−034	011	−018	088										
9.	−024	−013	−027	−024	−014	−003	−015	015	309									
10.	−012	−017	−023	−021	−013	−003	−007	011	011	021								
11.	−016	−013	−022	−018	−013	−001	−012	011	010	010	018							
12.	−024	−017	−026	−021	−014	000	−006	003	013	017	017	033						
13.	−018	−025	−035	−027	−016	−014	−016	024	019	019	014	012	037					
14.	−030	−030	−036	−028	−020	−004	−015	009	017	020	018	026	021	044				
15.	−025	−030	−026	−019	−022	027	−003	043	006	003	003	003	−000	002	051			
16.	−013	−019	−023	−002	−012	012	004	−027	−020	−010	008	−010	−010	000	−009	144		
17.	001	−007	−007	011	002	013	040	−023	028	−021	−017	−024	−023	−019	−010	043	102	
18.	−037	−028	−050	−043	−030	−018	−020	039	038	016	017	017	038	025	006	−020	−034	084

ture, attention would have to be given to the varying census sizes of these groups and to the biases in these relationship statistics from the variability in sample sizes. For our purposes here, those considerations are not important, since the genetic distances do not depend (very much) on how mean gene frequencies are defined, or on the niceties of biased versus unbiased estimates of R. Nevertheless, it is of some note that F_{ST}, or Wahlund F, for all these groups considered together is only 0.06, which is on the order of that found within single tribes or small areas among tropical gardeners (Friedlaender 1971a), and that F_{ST} calculated by weighting groups by census size would be even smaller.

The eigenvalues of this matrix are plotted in descending order in Figure 31. Since the average allele has a scaled variance of 0.06, we may, as a rule of thumb, consider a dimension corresponding to an eigenvalue greater than this to be significant. There are only five such eigenvalues, but the first two or three seem clearly larger than the others. Most of the variation will be described by the first two or three axes, but it will be worth-

FIGURE 31. Eigenvalues of R.

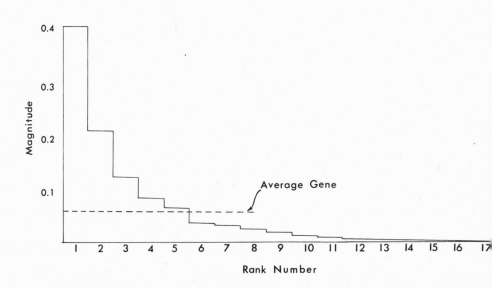

while to examine the others to see if any one group or cluster of groups is being differentiated by this axis.

The 18 groups are plotted on dimensions corresponding to the first two eigenvectors in Figure 32, and the alleles used are plotted on the first two eigenvectors of the S matrix in Figure 33. The first four eigenvectors of R are given in Table 30, along with the corresponding eigenvalues.

RELATIONS AMONG POPULATIONS

The first axis in Figure 32 is clearly differentiating Bantu-speaking and Khoisan-speaking peoples. It is worthy of note that the extreme Khoisan population, the /Du/da !Kung, is the !Kung population most isolated

FIGURE 32. Populations plotted on first two scaled eigenvectors.

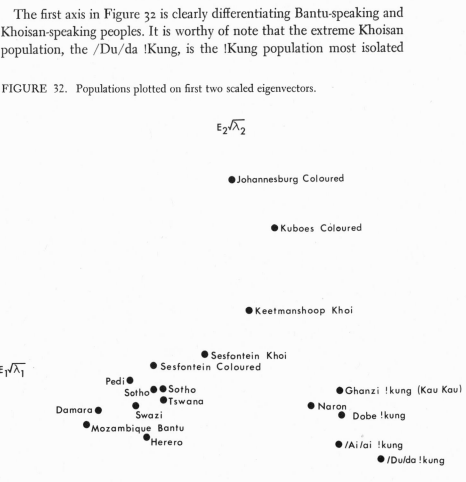

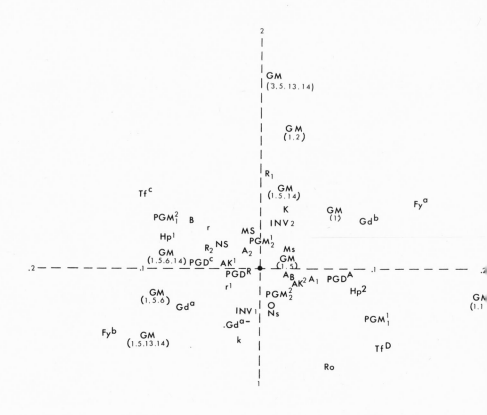

FIGURE 33. Plot of alleles on first two eigenvectors of S (eigenvectors not scaled).

from contact with Tswana and Herero Bantu-speakers. The Mozambique Bantu sample is at the other extreme of the first axis, confirming the low Khoisan admixture into this sample deduced by Jenkins, Zoutendyk, and Steinberg (1970). The ordering of the other Bantu groups on this axis also conforms to the admixture estimates in that publication.

The second axis in Figure 32 is just as clearly revealing non-African admixture. The Johannesburg Colored population is highest on this dimension, followed by that of Kuboes, also from South Africa, the Khoi from Keetmanshoop in southern Southwest Africa, and last by the populations at Sesfontein in the extreme northwest part of Southwest Africa,

TABLE 30
EIGENVECTORS OF KINSHIP MATRIX

	Eigenvectors			
Population	1	2	3	4
1. Dobe !Kung	0.31	−0.15	−0.03	0.06
2. /Ai/ai !Kung	0.32	−0.23	−0.13	0.00
3. /Du/da !Kung	0.42	−0.26	0.00	0.22
4. Ghanzi !Kung	0.32	−0.05	0.01	0.05
5. Naron	0.25	−0.12	−0.06	−0.05
6. Sesfontein Khoi	−0.03	0.08	0.41	0.06
7. Keetmanshoop Khoi	0.09	0.23	0.26	−0.47
8. Damara	−0.31	−0.10	0.37	0.42
9. Herero	−0.19	−0.15	−0.10	−0.10
10. Tswana	−0.14	−0.07	−0.09	−0.09
11. Sotho I	−0.14	−0.06	−0.09	−0.05
12. Sotho II	−0.16	−0.06	−0.12	−0.18
13. Swazi	−0.21	−0.09	−0.17	−0.07
14. Pedi	−0.22	−0.01	−0.20	−0.15
15. Sesfontein Colored	−0.17	0.03	0.39	0.36
16. Johannesburg Colored	0.04	0.65	−0.49	0.46
17. Kuboes Colored	0.15	0.52	0.25	−0.33
18. Mozambique Bantu	−0.33	−0.16	−0.20	−0.12
Eigenvalue	0.41	0.22	0.13	0.08
Cumulative percent of total kinship	38	58	70	78

furthest from areas of dense European settlement. The samples from Sesfontein and Keetmanshoop labeled Khoi were chosen as people who claimed four Khoi grandparents. In general, this analysis shows that such individuals are not significantly "purer" Khoi and that, indeed, the Khoi and Colored groups are not genetically distinguishable. This point is reinforced by the location in Figure 32 of the Naron, who are hunter-gatherers of the central Kalahari Desert around Ghanzi, Botswana, and who speak a language mutually intelligible with Nama; in other words, they are linguistically Khoi. The results of this analysis suggest that there are no significant differences between the San and Khoi (or "Bushman" and "Hottentot") peoples of South Africa and that some of the ascribed differences are the results of admixture, a different way of life with a different diet, and so forth. The populations in southwest Africa who call themselves Khoi seem fully genetically allied with the Colored populations around them. However, these findings are subject to different possi-

$E_3\sqrt{\lambda_3}$

Sesfontein Coloured
● ●Sesfontein Khoi
Damara ●

Keetmanshoop Khoi ●   ● Kuboes Coloured

Naron
Dobe !Kung   ●Ghanzi !Kung
$E_2\sqrt{\lambda_2}$ /Du/da !Kung●   ●   ●●(Tswana, Sotho I, Sotho II)

/Ai/ai !Kung ●   ●Herero
Mozambique Bantu ●   ●   ● Pedi
Swazi

Johannesburg Coloured●

FIGURE 34. Populations plotted on second and third scaled eigenvectors.

ble interpretations, especially when the third dimension is considered. Figure 34 shows these populations arrayed on axes 2 and 3. When looking at this, it should be kept in mind that the San and Khoi-Colored are separated on axis 1 from the Bantu and that the Damara are good Bantu on the first axis.

The San (including the Naron) and the Bantu groups are indifferent on the third axis; on it, the Johannesburg Colored population is alone at one extreme, while the rest of the Damara-Khoi-Colored complex occupies the other. This might be taken to indicate that the composition of the Johannesburg population is basically different from that of the other Colored groups in southern Africa, possibly reflecting Malay admixture. On this axis, the Damara are in the midst of the Khoi-Colored complex, while on the first two axes, they are clearly Bantu. This confirms their puzzling status among these populations and indicates that an extension of this analysis to include populations from the rest of the continent would be useful. See Jenkins et al. (1971) for a discussion of the Damara.

The contribution of the alleles studied to the variation along each of the axes is shown graphically in Figure 33. Such a presentation immediately identifies alleles highly associated with San to be $Gm^{1,13}$, Fy^a, Tf^D, Hp^2, and $PGM_1{}^1$, and alleles indicative of extra-African admixture to be $Gm^{3,5,13,14}$, $Gm^{1,2}$, R_1, Tf^G, and so forth. This kind of representation seems to us very useful for studies of genetic distance among heterogeneous groups, since allelic variation is comprehensible at a glance. A collection of plots such as this from various areas might provide the simplest way to scan for associations among alleles consistent over different areas.

NOTE

1. Present address: Department of Anthropology, University of New Mexico.

10
Computer Simulation
of Demographic Processes[1]

FRANCIS E. JOHNSTON
Department of Anthropology
Temple University, Philadelphia
MORRIS E. ALBERS
University of Texas at Austin

The methods used in the study of population genetics have been, since its onset, quantitative ones. Shortly after the turn of the century, Hardy and Weinberg's independent demonstrations of the relationships between the gene frequencies of the parental generation and the genotype frequencies of their offspring involved the expansion of the simple binomial in the simple form $(pA^1 + qA^2)^2$. From this beginning, the discipline advanced rapidly, and subsequent years have seen the development of an elegant body of mathematical theory expressing the relationships between various mechanisms of the evolutionary process and the dynamics of genes within and among Mendelian populations (see, for example, Fisher 1930, Wright 1969).

Despite the early recognition of the essentially mathematical nature of these dynamics and the emphasis on their theoretical delineation, the solutions of problems arising out of evolutionary studies have, in most cases, yet to be achieved. This is particularly evident whenever the interactions between mechanisms that involve stochastic aspects, and their effects on the gene pool, are being considered. The mathematical complexity involved in attempting to analyze and model an involved system composed of a number of independently varying components has necessitated assumptions that, more often than not, reduce the applicability of the theory to the real world of human populations in their ecological settings. Attempts to determine the effecive breeding size of a population (Wright 1969) illustrate the problems involved here.

The results of the attempts to cope with the above problems have been evident in the existence of a massive literature on theoretical aspects of evolutionary dynamics. This literature is based heavily on experiments with laboratory populations on organisms with simplified population structures and is accompanied by a general lack of knowledge about similar problems among human groups.

DEMOGRAPHY AND POPULATION GENETICS

In its most restrictive meaning, *demography* refers to numerical data on human populations; traditionally, this means the listing of age, sex, and other distributions, along with the construction of a life table, from which the statistical probability of living from one age to another may be calculated. However, with the increasing realization by population geneticists that such data are relevant in their research, a more dynamic view of demography has come into being. Population structure is seen not only as a static parameter to be described, but also as a rather sensitive indicator of ongoing processes that are directly relevant to evolutionary processes. Thus, Bodmer and Lederberg (1967) recognize a broadening of demographic concepts from the ". . . usual, narrower sense . . ." of correlates of mortality and fertility to the ". . . statistical study of populations."

The implications arising out of this broader view have led to the formulation of a distinct subfield of human population genetics that we may call "demographic genetics." Those who conduct research within this subfield recognize the fact that the usual demographic parameters—for example, age and sex distributions, life expectancies, fertility among various classes of the population, migration and intrapopulation mobility, and so forth—on the one hand are the results of past evolutionary processes and on the other are determinants of the future course of evolution. Viewed in this way, a significant amount of information about microevolutionary dynamics in a particular group may be gained even before the investigator knows any single allele frequency.

Thus, Crow (1958) has demonstrated that the effectiveness of natural selection in a population may be inferred from measures of differential fertility and prereproductive mortality. Using this concept, Spuhler (1963) has demonstrated the existence of correlations with the technological and economic levels of human populations; in general, the trend is for increased selection through differential fertility, and reduction in selection through death before attainment of puberty, with increased levels of technology.

Demographic genetics has assumed even new dimensions with increased concern by investigators of the roles of human behavior in determining mate choice, village stability, population mobility, and so forth. As in any species, the probability of mating between any two individuals reduces with an increase in the geographical distance between them or in the distance between their birthplaces. However, man's cultural values impose another set of determinants that interferes with simple distance functions and that involves the concept of "social distance." Marriage partners are selected within a context of cultural acceptability that may grossly distort the systematic spread of genes within the population. Out-migration and in-migration are also culturally determined, and variations in their intensity among populations are powerful determinants of gene frequency dynamics. Clearly, anthropological data must be carefully integrated into more conventional demographic data in analyzing a population, a fact recognized by numerous investigators in recent years (Roberts 1965, Neel and Salzano 1967, Neel and Ward 1970).

MODELS AND SIMULATION IN HUMAN POPULATION GENETICS

Scientific model may be defined as the "simplified representation of a real physical system" (Friedenberg 1968). In a very real sense, any reduction of raw data represents a model, though perhaps a simplified one. Thus, the calculation of mean stature in a sample, and the variance about the mean, is a model that represents the distribution of stature within the group studied.

Model-building serves two purposes. First, it provides a simplified representation of what may be a very complex mass of data, a representation that will allow one to view the data and the system they represent in a more comprehensible and comprehensive way. Second, model-building also demonstrates an understanding of the system being studied, providing that the model constructed is adequate to explain its operation. An accurate model indicates that the system it represents is understood by the investigator and that it can be reduced to a series of steps along a flow diagram.

Once the model is constructed, and once the investigator is satisfied that it does, in fact, represent the raw data, it is possible to operate the model by varying the values of its parameters. In this way, the system so represented is "simulated" and a quasi-experimental level is attained. Thus, the models that represent the changes in gene frequency due to natural selection depend on values for selection intensity, frequencies for the alleles segregating at that locus in the population, and an understanding of the mode of inheritance involved (Falconer 1961). If these can be determined for a population, certain predictions can be made about the process of evolution. Environmental changes may be simulated by altering the intensity of selection, leading to different conclusions under the new set of conditions. This, of course, is a very simple model and resultant simulation, but it nonetheless represents the procedures involved. Obviously, the ultimate changes in gene frequency are the result of the interaction of the entire range of evolutionary mechanisms, and the model becomes far more complex very rapidly.

The conceptual approach to model-building and subsequent simulation is heavily laced with the theory and language of systems analysis. While it is sufficient here to consider a system as an "arbitrary segment of the world about us" (Friedenberg 1968), it is important to note that systems theory is quite elaborate, if largely at the conceptual level, and has been applied to biological phenomena (Bertalanffy 1968, Maruyama 1968).

The emphasis on quantitative theory among population geneticists has resulted in the development of models representing the operation of evolutionary mechanisms at all levels of complexity. These involve, for example, individual mechanisms, such as natural selection, as well as some of the more simple interactions, as those between mutation and selection (Falconer 1961). Or we may also note various models predicting the probable effects of genetic drift under various population models.

Simplified models such as the above have been widely used by population geneticists and form the basis for the approach to genetic variation characteristic of the discipline. At the same time, it is recognized that they are, without exception, overly simplistic and only partially applicable to real situations. In other words, they are unable to account for a large enough proportion of observed variation to serve as adequate models of natural populations approaching the structural complexity seen among man.

The advent of high speed electronic computers provided a new medium for the investigation of problems in human population genetics. Brues (1963) remarks the increased sophistication in her study of the distribution of alleles at the ABO locus over an earlier analysis that she carried out on a desk calculator (Brues 1954). Computers are able to handle with ease a wide variety of genetic analyses, ranging from the analysis of linkage among natural populations to the construction of a taxonomic scheme based on genetic distances.

Using computers has reduced computation time to a matter of seconds, and this has made possible newer approaches to model-building. The complexity that immediately arises when interactions among components are to be studied is of no consequence when a computer is used. Models may be constructed that represent reality more accurately by including all necessary subsystems. For it is only when a sufficient number of subsystems are identified and included that significant interactions become revealed; at that time, the model comes as close to the real situation as it can be (Heinmets 1969).

Computers also permit the simulation of ever-larger systems. Simulated biological systems range from the kinetics of electron transport in mitochondrial membranes (Pring 1969) to an ecosystem occupied by grazing livestock (Goodall 1969). In the behavioral sciences, simulation has become an important tool in sociology, geography, and economics.

Basically, simulations may be used in two ways. First, they may predict the behavior of a system prospectively, leading to operational decisions, or retrospectively, leading to historical reconstructions. Second, they may be used in a synchronic sense to study the effects of interactions among components by means of "experimental" manipulation of the parameters. The problem being investigated, of course, determines the approach carried out.

The complexity of human genetic systems, especially at the population level, makes a computer simulation all the more valuable as a research tool. The value is increased through the realization that the transmission of genes between generations is often markedly affected by the occurrence of random events, genetically speaking, that operate at all levels and that have important interactions with more deterministic ones, such as selection.

The necessary inclusion of demographic and cultural components into any system designed to model a human population enlarges the scope of the problem to where it can be approached only through the use of the most sophisticated analytic techniques. Of particular relevance is the simulation of the genetic systems of those populations frequently referred to as being of "anthropological importance." Such groups are usually relatively small in number and tend to be rather isolated from their closest neighbors. Their gene pools are often markedly affected by various natural events that occur, such as disasters or epidemics, as well as by migrations, village splitting, and so forth. Systematic deviations from random mating may accompany the adherence to a rigidly defined social system; more often than not, they may require the expertise of a social anthropologist to assist in describing the structure of the system, as well as any deviations from it. The rapid acculturation of such groups, accelerating in recent years, instills some urgency into the need for their study.

Since the emergence of anthropology as a recognized discipline, anthropologists have usually been involved with small primitive groups. However, not all investigators have been oriented toward gathering the kinds of demographic data, to say nothing of observations on the genetic structure, necessary for an analysis of the group, with the eventual aim of model-building. The concern of social anthropologists with the ideals of human social systems has all too often masked the reality that preferential patterns are frquently not adhered to (Kunstadter et al. 1963).

In the past decade, anthropologists and human geneticists have begun to focus more intently on small primitive groups as providing the basis for model-building in human evolution. Supported by detailed and replicable data, they have turned to a more theoretical approach to such groups, which has led, in turn, to the development of models representing the existing biocultural interactions.

The simulation of human demographic systems has not in any way been limited to genetically significant variables. For example, in 1963, Kunstadter and his associates constructed an arbitrary population and simulated marriages for periods of up to 740 years; their purpose was to study the effects of variability in the demographic profile and in marriage preference on the frequency of cross-cousin marriages over time. Using several models, Heer and Smith (1968, 1969) examined, through simulation techniques, the relationship between the intrinsic rate of natural increase in population size and mortality. Perrin and Sheps (1964) and Sheps and Perrin (1966) have presented the results of simulations of reproduction in females under a number of conditions of mortality and fetal wastage, the result expressed as distributions of fertility.

The above studies serve to demonstrate the range of problems that may be investigated through the simulation of demographic parameters in populations. In some, demographic variation was a determinant of biological processes and, in others, of sociocultural ones. In simulations of demographic variables of genetic consequence, the concern is with the effects on gene frequency over successive generations.

APPROACHES TO GENETIC SIMULATIONS

Levin (1969) notes that simulations may be classified into three categories. First are *deterministic* ones, in which the outcome is the solution of an algebraic equation or other mathematical statement and is based on the values assigned to the elements of the statement. In other words, the results depend entirely on the values given to the parameters; only one solution exists for each combination of values. The equations of natural selection provide us with one example out of an almost countless number. The change in frequency due to selection depends on the values selected for fitness and for the initial gene frequency.

The second class of simulations are those called *stochastic*. They derive their name from the fact that the outcome of a specific run is but one of several possible results with identical input values. The results are determined by the probabilities of occurrence of a number of component events rather than by an algebraic equation. Stochastic simulations gain their power from this feature and from the fact that mathematical manipulations are, when present, of the simplest kind. They are typified by *Monte Carlo* techniques, a method that will be described in some detail below.

The third class of simulations are called *partial deterministic/stochastic*. As suggested by the name, they combine deterministic elements with stochastic ones, the choice being whatever is appropriate for the process being considered. Obviously, most large-scale simulations are of this type, since the simulation of some processes is best accomplished by mathematical manipulations and, of others, by probabilistic approaches.

Genetic simulations of entire populations have received their greatest stimulus from the development of Monte Carlo methods. Since many processes in the chain of events constituting human evolution are based on sampling phenomena, they are distribution-dependent, and the outcomes are heavily influenced by probability functions. Any approach that uses probability in reaching a solution is bound to carry an initially greater theoretical impact. Thus, while there have been but a handful of attempts to simulate the interaction of demographic, genetic, and other evolutionary mechanisms, each has relied heavily on Monte Carlo methods.

The basic feature of the Monte Carlo technique is its employment of a random number decision-making process—that is, a random number, from among a specified range, is selected or generated by the computer. It is then compared with a number that corresponds to the probability of occurrence of an event; this comparison forms the basis for a yes or no decision for that occurrence. Suppose, as an example, that the probability of dying at some time for an individual is 0.75, and our simulation must determine whether or not that individual lives. (Note that this probability might have been obtained from the inspection of a life table.) A random number is then generated from a range of, say, 1 through 999. If the number is 750 or less, the individual in question dies; if it is greater than 750, he lives. The probability of selecting at random from this range a number that is 750 or less is 750/999, or virtually 0.75. Thus, the probability of death will equal the observed probability through construction of the random number decision-making process. A different probability would simply result in the selection of a correspondingly different number as the cut-off point.

The essence of the Monte Carlo method lies in the fact that the outcome is not determined. In the example above, it is possible for the individual in question to live, and one will expect deviations to occur. If the simulation is considering a number of individuals with probabilities of dying of 0.75, the proportion actually doing so, in the simulation, would tend to approach 75 percent as the number examined increased.

Thus, in a Monte Carlo simulation, while the direction of a process may be estimated from the associated probabilities, variations can occur that will alter the outcome. The advantages in dealing with something

208

like genetic drift are obvious. Of course, as noted above, most simulations are best conducted through the use of a combination of deterministic and Monte Carlo functions. As the simulation proceeds along a series of steps in the flow diagram, each element, and the outcome resulting from its operation, determines the progress to the next step.

There are cautions to be observed in using Monte Carlo techniques, apart from the one applicable to all—that the model employed actually account for all relevant processes. It is essential to know the probabilities associated with a particular event; if the assigned values are unrealistic, bizarre outcomes may result that will simulate nothing and only vitiate the entire process. As with any model-building, it is necessary to carefully study all the data and then construct the model within a sound genetic, demographic, and cultural framework. Regardless of the sophistication of the simulation and the completeness of the model, erroneous input parameters will result in nothing more than an exercise in futility. The model must be built on a foundation of accurate data.

On a more technical level, it is important to understand that the random number generator of the computer does not produce a strictly random sequence. Schull (1969) has reported serial correlations among supposedly random numbers as high as 0.10. This may bias the results of a series of Monte Carlo decisions when one individual is taken through a number of consecutive steps. On the other hand, these problems may be dealt with quite effectively by making all decisions for a particular event at the same time and for everyone in the artificial population. From a programming standpoint, this latter procedure is logically less difficult and more efficient.

Simulations that rely on random number decisions should not be thought of as reconstructing history. Neither should they be used to predict future courses, except in probabilistic terms. The iteration of a simulation from the same initial point should, as the number increases, indicate the distribution of outcomes. Such a simulation, however, is best considered as an "experiment" in which the parameters may be altered and complex interactions viewed.

Genetic simulations of populations date only from 1957, with the development of a Monte Carlo model by Fraser (1957) and its application to a study of the effects of linkage on natural selection. Fraser's model was not of a population in an inclusive sense, and demographic variables were not considered. The first reported simulation of a total genetic system of a population, including demographic components, was that of

Cavalli-Sforza (Cavalli-Sforza and Zei 1967). For its time, the model was unique in that it simulated a real population living in the mountain valleys of northern Italy. Spouse selection depended on geographic location, age, sex, and "social conditions." The problems investigated revolved about genetic drift and inbreeding.

Computerized simulations using Monte Carlo models have likewise been conducted by MacCluer (1967), who has recently completed a sophisticated model, involving cultural variables, for the Yanomama Indians of Venezuela. She has also utilized simulation techniques to analyze the development of inbreeding and to examine estimates of effective population size in a model based on Japanese population data (MacCluer and Schull 1970a, 1970b).

THE GENETIC SIMULATION OF THE PERUVIAN CASHINAHUA

This section will present, as an example, a simulation developed in our laboratory (from 1969 to 1971) that grew out of studies on the interaction of sociocultural mechanisms, genetic drift, and natural selection in human populations. We chose to simulate a real population in the belief that a functioning biocultural unit would permit a more realistic simulation, would allow for a more realistic assemblage of input data, and would result in a better understanding of microevolutionary processes in a specific level of population and economic complexity.

The population chosen for modeling was the Peruvian Cashinahua (Johnston 1970b, Johnston and Kensinger 1971, Johnston et al. 1968, 1969a, 1969b); this choice was made for several reasons. First, our studies had collected sufficient biological and cultural data to suggest that a model could be developed that would be sufficiently accurate for genetic simulation. Second, small, almost isolated groups may be represented by a simpler model as a first step in studying evolutionary processes at the level of component interactions. Finally, the interaction of the components of the genetic systems of small primitive groups has not been systematically studied. In attempting to understand human genetic systems at different levels of ecological complexity and cultural variation, the small primitive group is a logical choice for a beginning. (As a practical matter, numerically small populations require less computer memory.)

The simulation to be described uses a model with parameters that account for the greatest portion of genetic variation in the Cashinahua gene pool. These may be grouped into three kinds. First, there are cultural factors that, by and large, affect spouse selection and cause deviation from a random mating model. These include aspects of social structure, rules governing spouse selection, and rules of residence. Of particular importance here is not only the parameterization of an ideal system, but also the necessity of allowing for observed violations of the "rules." Next are those stochastic factors that operate at the levels of the genotype and the individual gene. Included here are differential migration into the population, as well as the occurrence of death irrespective of genetic constitution. This is an important variable in a population with a very high death rate from causes unrelated to the genotypes present. The third set of factors constitutes natural selection operating through differential fertility and mortality.

With such a model, evolutionary processes can be simulated on the computer. The real population, as observed, forms the initial core of the simulation. The individuals so represented simulate reproduction within the constraints of the parameters constituting the model and eventually die. Gradually, this results in the replacement of the original "real" population by a group of artificial individuals.

The basic data set consists of the representation, on computer cards (tape is more efficient for larger populations or for long-term simulations, such as for 100 generations), of those Cashinahua existing in 1966. At that time, the population numbered 207. Space is provided for the storage of genetic information at 14 loci, one of which is used for the recording of sex and the transmission of the sex chromosomes. At the other 13 locations, the genes determined by our studies were entered; if the data were not available for certain loci or individuals, the loci or individuals were assigned in such a way as to maintain observed gene frequencies for the population. If individuals with missing data had relatives in the population with known genes at the loci in question, genotypes were assigned by random number decisions of possible gene combinations arising through segregation.

Each genotype as a single locus is assigned a fitness from among a range of 0 to 1.000. These fitnesses may be altered, and their manipulation permits the studying of natural selection in the population. Each individual is assigned an overall fitness for his or her "genome," calculated as the thirteenth root of the product of the individual values for each loci.

If the focus is on fewer loci, then the appropriate computation can be made accordingly.

TABLE 31

DEMOGRAPHIC VARIABLES USED IN COMPUTER
SIMULATION OF PERUVIAN CASHINAHUA

Age	Paternal grandfather's I.D.
Sex	Paternal grandmother's I.D.
Spouse 1 I.D.	Maternal grandfather's I.D.
Spouse 2 I.D.	Maternal grandmother's I.D.
Father's I.D.	Village
Mother's I.D.	Moiety

Table 31 lists the demographic profile of each individual, with characterization by residence and kinship variables, as well as by age and sex. This permits determination of kinship, in addition to its use in spouse selection. Those determinants used were found to be the ones significant in spouse selection from the 10 years of detailed data collected by Kenneth Kensinger.

The model developed (Figure 35) is seen as a series of components, independently varying but with the events in one component determining the progress to the next. This model represents one year, and, hence, it is cyclical and continuous, proceeding for each individual until death, at which time he or she is removed from the population. Each individual is examined at each step every year by the computer, and a series of decisions is made, based on mathematical functions or random number selections.

The simulation starts with mate selection, with all unmarried eligible individuals being assigned spouses, based on a number of criteria. First, of course, is age, with marriage occurring early. Marriage is valued among the Cashinahua and closely follows passage through puberty rites. Our data showed no unmarried female over age 14 or male over 19. Thus, eligibility commences at age 15 for the females and 17 for the males. As the Cashinahua practice polygyny, already-married males may marry once again. In accordance with our detailed records, marriage eligibility is immediate following the death of a spouse for either males or females. The other rules governing mate selection among the Cashinahua, which are included in the simulation, are moiety exogamy, generation, and village endogamy.

(1) *Moiety exogamy*. All Cashinahua, whether residing in Brazil or in Peru, are lifetime members of the moiety of their fathers (that is, descent is patrilineal), and there are two such kin groups. With respect to moiety, marriage is exogamous; in other words, it is strongly preferred that a spouse be a member of the opposite group. A marriage that violates this rule is viewed as being "incestuous" by the Cashinahua, although,

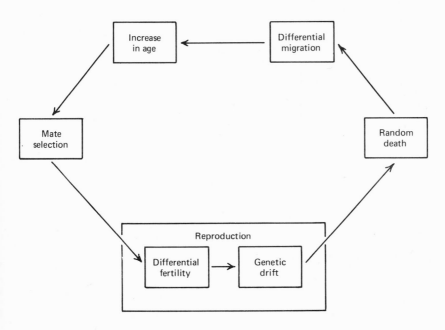

FIGURE 35. Model of genetic system for the Peruvian Cashinahua.

of course, the incest is social rather than biological. The most preferred marriage is to a cross cousin, who will be a member of the opposite moiety, although enough individuals are available to ensure a true cross cousin for only a small percentage of the marriages. In the simulation of the Peruvian Cashinahua, moiety membership is specified for each individual.

(2) *Generation*. Marriage is not allowed with anyone from the generation on either side of the individual in question, that is, with anyone

falling into the generation of his or her parents or offspring. Although generation is not a variable in the simulation, the age of each individual permits this rule to be observed. The individual being examined and eligible for marriage is not assigned a spouse whose age is 16 to 32 years older or younger than himself.

(3) *Village endogamy*. In 1966, the Cashinahua were grouped into three small villages, each ranging in population from 34 to 122. Marriage is preferred with someone from the same village; since the Cashinahua are matrilocal with respect to residence, village endogamy ensures that a man will remain in the village of his kinsmen, since descent is traced through the paternal line. The village in which each individual resides is a variable in the simulation.

Thus, the most desirable spouse for a man would be a female cross cousin from the same village, unmarried, and within 16 years of his own age. Clearly, this list of qualifications cannot be met in such a small population; the value placed on early marriage results in a situation that is resolved, when necessary, by marriage to someone who falls outside of this ideal class. Our data (Johnston et al. 1969a) reveal that, with respect to moiety and village, 17 percent of the marriages recorded were considered socially incestuous.

It is important that a simulation reflect, as much as possible, the observed realities. In the case of the simulation of the Peruvian Cashinahua, it is therefore necessary that the selection of a spouse conform to socially-sanctioned preferences, where possible, but allow deviations on the order observed. In addition, not all deviations are considered of equal significance, and some could be tolerated more readily than others. For example, biological incest, that is, marriage with one's parent or offspring, is strictly forbidden and strictly observed. To allow for deviations in the order in which they were permissible, yet to conform where possible to preferential patterns, the simulation is run in such a way that the computer evaluates each potential spouse in terms of marriage suitability with respect to the propositus. The evaluation is expressed as a priority score, derived from ethnographic records: *five points* indicates a cross cousin; *four points*, a member of the other moiety residing in the same village; *three points*, a member of the other moiety residing in another village; *two points*, a member of the same moiety residing in the same village; and *one point*, a member of the same moiety residing in another village. The person with the highest priority who is first encountered by the computer is assigned to the individual as his or her spouse. If there is no eligible spouse, the individual is not married during this simulated year.

After all unmarried individuals in the computerized population are assigned spouses, if possible, the simulation proceeds to the next step in the model, corresponding to reproductive performance and composed of three aspects, presented in Figure 35 as two components. First is differential fertility without respect to genotype, that is, not selective in nature. The average interval between successive birth approximated two years; hence, in a given year, a couple has one chance in two of producing an offspring in this aspect of differential fertility. A random number between 1 and 999 is generated; if it is 500 or greater, the marriage does not result in an offspring for that year. If the number is less than 500, reproductive performance then becomes a function of differential fertility due to parental genotypes; in other words, natural selection comes into play. The fitness of the mating is calculated as the square root of the product of the fitnesses of the parents. This fitness becomes the probability of producing an offspring, during that simulated year, because of factors associated with the genotypes of the parents. Reproductive "success" is determined through another random number decision, the cut-off point being, as usual, the probability.

The second aspect of reproductive performance, and its effect on the transmission of genes to offspring, is genetic drift. Here we mean genetic drift in the strict sense, that is, deviation in the frequencies of alleles transmitted from those expected because of effects due to gametic sampling. For each locus, one of the two alleles is selected at random from each parent as the one to be passed to that offspring. This includes the location in the computer memory at which sex is determined. In the simulation, all marriages are examined in this order and offspring assigned, with appropriate genotypes, to those parents who proceed successfully through the steps. Each offspring is assigned to the moiety of his father and the village of his parents; age is determined from the year of birth.

The next step in the simulation is the selection of individuals to die without respect to genotype. In populations exposed to persistent and strong pressures from disease, natural disaster, and so forth, without the benefits of modern medical care, many deaths occur that are unrelated to the genotypes of the individual. The genetic effects of this random removal are not predictable and may be grouped along with those stochastic processes that can affect the gene pools of small populations.

In the model and its simulation, each individual is examined, and a random number decides whether he will "live" or "die" during that year. The probability of living or dying is a function of age and is determined by the observed mortality rates for age cohorts. These rates were observed to be very high during infancy, dropping to lower values during the third and fourth decades and rising again thereafter (Johnston et al. 1969a).

Following the preceding step, the simulation then goes on to the final component in the cycle; the age of every individual in the population is advanced by one year. The entire series of steps previously described is repeated as many times as desired to simulate any number of years. The simulation may be stopped whenever desired and the population as it exists at that time examined. Gene frequencies may be determined, the demographic profile analyzed, and so forth.

In attempting to simulate the observed situation as closely as possible, another component of the model may be brought into operation whenever desired. The Cashinahua of Peru, though they may be thought of as an "isolate," are similar to most such human groups in that migrants are accepted into their number from time to time and individuals occasionally leave the population. The newcomers are always Cashinahua from Brazil, who come to Peru as an escape from the more intense acculturation experienced in Brazil. Those who move in the opposite direction are many fewer, but they represent individuals who desire the technological advantages associated with increased contact with Brazilians.

The migrations just described are genetically significant in small populations. The effects on gene frequency are magnified by the fact that the migrants come or go not as individuals but as families. Thus, they are not random samples of the genotypes of the populations being left or entered, but represent constellations of similar genomes. Likewise, the migrants settle among the Peruvian Cashinahua not randomly but as family groups in villages. The effects of differential migration can be quite marked and may be documented among the Peruvian Cashinahua (Johnston et al. 1969a, Johnston 1970a). The simulation provides for gene flow into the population through the introduction of a specified number of migrants whenever desired. The routine used generates a "family" of individuals with genotypes produced through simulated transmission of genes.

In summary, the model described above permits the simulation of evolutionary processes within a specific human population. It includes

216

demographic and cultural parameters and permits the analysis of the effects of their interactions with each other, with parameters representing selective pressures, and with simulated environmental effects.

CONCLUDING REMARKS

The simulation, by means of high-speed computers, of the demographic and genetic processes of a population permits investigators to analyze the interactions of components of the systems in ways not possible through other approaches. However, the development of such a simulation is not an end in itself, but rather a beginning. The analysis of specific groups in known ecological and cultural settings will permit the study of human population dynamics in ways that perhaps approach the controlled experiments of the laboratory.

Although simulations involving Monte Carlo techniques that view the population en toto represent valuable additions to available analytic methodology, certain cautions must be exercised. Comprehensive demographic observations are essential, and their collection requires a sensitivity that, while inherent in the anthropological approach, is not always evident in the data. Model-building requires a knowledge of the system as a whole, as well as those components that contribute significantly to it.

Finally, agreement among researchers using simulations is vital in order to permit comparability of conclusions. How are the seemingly endless pages of output data to be analyzed? What lengths of time are to be used in simulation runs? How many iterations of a particular simulation are desirable or necessary in a particular experiment?

The technology for complex simulations now exists, and the need for analysis based on these simulations is readily apparent. However, they must be brought to a level of use that is truly analytic and not presented merely as a tour de force. In other words, much thought will have to be given to the entire subject if the simulation of a population and its genetic structure is to become an important tool in human biology.

NOTE

1. The authors' research reported herein was supported by grants GU-1598 and GS-3038 from the National Science Foundation.

11

Computer Simulation
in Anthropology and Human Genetics[1]

JEAN W. MacCLUER

Department of Anthropology
The Pennsylvania State University

Those who study small human populations are all too familiar with the problems involved in attempting to draw conclusions from limited data. The investigator who wishes to analyze the demographic, genetic, or cultural characteristics of a small population is hampered by the fact that random fluctuations in the relevant parameters may swamp systematic trends that he is trying to measure. In an effort to increase sample size, he may pool data from several sources; first, however, he must ask whether the data from the various sources are equally reliable, and, in fact, whether, for purposes of the analysis, the populations are similar enough that they may legitimately be pooled. These are problems that arise simply by virtue of the small size of populations; if, in addition, a population is technologically primitive, then one must contend with a large number of practical difficulties in the collection of data before the stage of analysis is even reached. The likelihood is high that data collected under these less than ideal conditions will be incomplete and not internally consistent.

With increasing frequency, small populations are being analyzed with computer simulation models, which are being used to assess the reliability and consistency of data, to formulate and test theories about population structure, and to decide whether specific populations conform to the assumptions and predictions of existing theories. The purposes of this chapter are threefold: to describe the characteristics of various types of computer simulation models used by anthropologists, human geneticists, and demographers; to discuss the kinds of problems that may be approached by simulation; and to review the models and results of some computer simulation experiments with human populations.

TYPES OF SIMULATION MODELS

Computer simulation models of human populations have certain characteristics in common. They begin with a set of assumptions about population structure and a set of rules for making decisions about changes in that structure through time. The assumptions and rules are generally given in terms of statements in a computer program, together with input data that may be varied from one experiment to another.

These computer models may be categorized in numerous ways. Depending on the kinds of assumptions that are made about population structure, a model may be primarily demographic, genetic, anthropological, economic, ecological, or a combination of these. For example, a model in which a population is defined solely in terms of its age and sex distribution, together with a schedule of birth and death rates, is a demographic model. If, in addition, a distribution of genotypes and their fitnesses is defined for some locus in the population, then the model is a genetic-demographic one. The level of complexity may be further increased by introducing a set of mating rules and perhaps clan structure, so that the model becomes genetic-demographic-anthropological. There is no limit, at least in theory, to the degree of complexity of a model. In practice, however, the results of experiments may be extremely difficult to interpret if the model is very complex. Among investigators who have experience with computer simulation models, it is generally agreed that the assumptions should be limited to those believed to have a direct bearing on the problem to be investigated.

Computer simulation models may also be classified as either stochastic (Monte Carlo) or deterministic, according to the way in which decisions are made. As an example, suppose that a model defines a population size n at time t, and consider the following two rules for determining population size at time $t + 1$:

Rule 1: Increase population size by an amount Kn, where K is a constant rate of increase.

Rule 2: Increase population size by an amount Rn, where R is a random rate of increase, with a mean value of K and a variance of V_K. R may vary from one time t to the next.

Rule 1 is a deterministic rule, and Rule 2 is a stochastic one, with the outcome dependent on the value of a random number that is generated in the computer at the time the decision is to be made. Many computer models of human populations contain both deterministic and stochastic rules.

The distinction of macrosimulation or microsimulation model is often made to indicate the size of the unit that is used as the basis for decision making. A model that treats the entire population as a unit for purposes of decision making (as in Rules 1 and 2 above) is a macromodel. If decisions are made for each member of the population, so that changes in population structure are a function of the events that occur to each individual, then the model is a micromodel. To continue with the example used in the preceding paragraph, in a microsimulation model the size of the population at time $t + 1$ might be determined according to the following rule:

Rule 3: Generate a random number R for each person in the population and compare it with an age- and sex-specific probability of dying, D. If $R < D$, the individual dies; otherwise, he survives. Similarly, new individuals may be born into the population. The size of the population at time $t + 1$ is then equal to n minus the number of deaths plus the number of births.

Thus, a macromodel records the characteristics of the entire population without distinguishing its members, whereas a micromodel tabulates the characteristics of each individual in the population.

Simulation models of human populations may differ from each other in several other respects: In some micromodels, all decisions for all members of the population are made for a specified time interval (one year, one generation), and then the entire process is repeated for the next time

221

interval, until the specified length of time has been simulated. In other models, all or most decisions are made for an individual at the time of his birth. The relative merits of these two approaches will be discussed in a later section. Some simulation models are designed for specific problems and are not readily adapted for other purposes, whereas others are large, complex models with many assumptions about population structure and many stochastic rules for determining changes in that structure. Although, as mentioned earlier, it may be difficult to interpret the results of experiments with such complex models, there are many problems for which a simpler model would be inadequate. In these cases, simple models may sometimes be used in conjunction with the complex one as a means of identifying sources of variation in experiments with the larger model with a minimum expenditure of computer time. Finally, simulation models may differ according to whether they are designed for use with specific real populations or with generalized or hypothetical ones. Many models may be used for experiments with either real or hypothetical populations. If a model is intended to simulate the structure of some actual population, then it must be validated, that is, known characteristics of the actual population must be compared with those of artificial populations created by simulation to be sure that the model is an accurate representation of reality. The characteristics chosen for validation will vary with the problem being investigated. (For a more extensive discussion of the validation of computer models, see Naylor et al. 1966.)

TYPES OF PROBLEMS SUITED TO INVESTIGATION BY SIMULATION

Computer simulation is a potentially useful technique for solving almost any problem that cannot be treated analytically. The following enumeration indicates the wide range of applicability of computer simulation to problems involving human population structure.

(1) Determine whether the observed distribution of some characteristic in a population can be accounted for on the basis of chance alone. When there is no analytical method for predicting the expected variation in population parameters, simulation can be used to generate these expectations. Geneticists, for example, might be interested in detecting nonrandomness in the geographical distribution of genotypes or in the frequencies of consanguineous marriage; anthropologists, in deciding

whether observed differences in mating practices between clans might be accounted for simply on the basis of chance fluctuations in demographic structure; demographers, in determining whether the distribution of a small population by age and sex deviates significantly from some stable age-sex distribution, or whether there are nonrandom seasonal fluctuations in the secondary sex ratio.

(2) Examine which characteristics of a population are likely to vary widely through time and between populations, and which are more stable. Determine the distribution of population parameters such as generation length, completed family size, birth interval, age at marriage, number of spouses, and rate of growth of a population or its subdivisions (clans, surnames, genotypes, villages).

(3) Determine whether the data that have been collected for a population are internally consistent. For example, if births, deaths, marriages, and migrations occur at the estimated rates, will the resulting population growth rate be consistent with actual records of population growth? If females are assumed to reproduce at certain age-specific rates, will the resulting distribution of completed family sizes resemble. the observed distribution?

(4) Evaluate how closely a population can adhere to its stated rules for mating, migration, reproduction, and so forth. For example, it might be possible to show by simulation that although cross-cousin marriages are preferred in a population, only a small proportion of marriages will normally be of the preferred type, with population size decreasing rapidly if the rule is strictly adhered to.

(5) Estimate certain genetic and demographic parameters in small populations. For example, computer simulation may be used to estimate the rate of gene frequency drift, the pedigree inbreeding coefficient in a population with insufficient pedigree depth, the average deviation of genotype frequencies from Hardy-Weinberg proportions, the migration rate necessary to account for observed geographical distributions of populations, or the minimum size at which a population is able to maintain itself under specified vital rates.

(6) Determine the relationship between certain genetic and demographic parameters in model human populations of various types: the decrease in coefficient of kinship with distance, the relationship between migration rates and genetic distances, or the similarity of the inbreeding coefficient as measured by isonomy and from pedigrees.

(7) Establish the consequences for a population of various short- and long-term perturbations in its structure. For example, which of two alternate methods of decreasing the rate of population growth will be most effective? What will be the effect of a famine, plague, or other catastrophe on population structure? What changes will occur in the structure of a primitive population into which modern medical practices are introduced?

As implied in some of the preceding examples, computer simulation may be used to arrive at generalizations about the structure of human populations of various types. In addition, simulation experiments may be used to extend existing data on small populations, thus allowing a more detailed analysis than would be possible by studying the original data alone. Finally, computer simulation models may be of value in both prospective and retrospective investigations of human population dynamics, that is, they may be used either to predict the future course of a population or to reconstruct its past. The conclusions of prospective studies are perhaps less tenuous than those of retrospective ones, since in the former case, one must merely determine the distribution of possible consequences of a given strategy, whereas in the latter, one must decide, often by trial and error, what kinds of strategies are likely to have produced the present structure of the population. However, retrospective studies have the advantage that simulation results may be verified against currently available information on the structure of the real population. Anthropologists and human geneticists are generally more concerned with restrospective studies than with prospective ones for two reasons. First, predictions of future structure may require unobtainable information about the rules that will govern future population change, and second, the validity of prospective models often cannot be tested until some time in the distant future.

MODELS AND RESULTS

 The following review includes a description of those computer simulation models that have been used in anthropological and genetic studies of human populations. Both anthropologists and geneticists are becoming increasingly interested in the demographic structure of human populations; therefore, a number of simulation models are presented here whose focus is primarily demographic. No mention has been made of the many interesting models of multilocus genetic systems (Fraser 1957, Martin and Cockerham 1960, Sved 1968, Fraser and Burnell 1970, Franklin and Lewontin 1970). Because the process of developing and testing a complex simulation model can be expensive and time consuming, there are several models that have been described in the literature for which no experimental results are available. The emphasis in the following discussion is on models that have actually been applied to some problem of human population structure. Since much of the work on simulation of human populations is quite recent, a number of references have been made to investigations that are not yet published. The discussion has been organized according to the types of problems to which simulation models have been applied. This approach is admittedly somewhat artificial, since some models have been used for more than one type of problem.

Mating Structure

The first use of computer simulation in anthropology was by Kunstadter et al. (1963), who investigated preferential marriage patterns in populations with different age-specific marriage rates. They used a stochastic microsimulation model to estimate the expected proportion of mother's brother's daughter (MBD) marriages for populations in which this is the preferred marriage type. Beginning with populations of sizes 100, 200, and 300, equally divided between males and females, they simulated changes in population structure over periods as long as 740 years by subjecting individuals to age-specific probabilities of marrying, reproducing, and dying. Mortality rates were chosen to correspond to a mean expectation of life at birth of 25 years, and marital fertility rates were derived from data for populations not yet affected by modern medical practices. Two age-specific marriage schedules were used, corresponding to early and late median age at marriage. It was found that when marriages in the artificial populations were allowed to occur at random with respect to relationship of spouses, only 1 to 2 percent were of the ideal type. However, when there was a strong preference, 27 to 28 percent of the marriages in the artificial populations were of the ideal type, a figure much higher than that observed in real populations claiming to have a preferred marriage type. When a strong preference for MBD marriages was imposed in the simulations, a number of trends were observed. The proportion of marriages that were of the ideal type was found to be higher in large populations than in smaller ones. Age at marriage also affected the frequency of ideal marriages, more such marriages occurring when age at marriage was low.

A second attempt was made by Gilbert and Hammel (1966) to determine the relationship between population structure and the frequency of a particular type of cousin marriage, in this case, father's brother's daughter (FBD). Their program, also a stochastic microsimulation model, created a population list, beginning with populations of 120, 240, or 360 individuals under age 40, each person identified by residence, sex, father, and mother. The age of each person could also be determined from his position in the list. Simulations were done under a variety of initial conditions, each run continuing until 1,000 marriages had been contracted. Throughout each run, population size was held nearly constant. Mate choice was a function of residences, ages, and the age differences of prospective mates. Probabilities of group endogamy were varied from run to run. Marriages between parent and child, sibs, uncle and niece, and aunt and nephew were prohibited, but otherwise, marriages were random with respect to relationship of spouses. Using this model, Gilbert and Hammel tried to determine to what extent the supposed preference for FBD marriages in a Near Eastern population was simply a by-product of territorial endogamy. They found that although the frequency of FBD marriages in the actual population was 9 to 12 percent, the simulation predicted only about 4 to 5 percent. They compared these results with the predictions of a mathematical model that did not take into account the similarity in ages of spouses. They were also interested in more general problems, such as the extent to which the rate of FBD marriages may be influenced by the number of groups involved in exchange of women, by group sizes, by postmarital residence rules, and by degree of preference for territorial endogamy.

More recently, computer simulation has been used to study the demographic structure of a primitive population, the Yanomama Indians of Venezuela and Brazil. MacCluer et al. (1971) developed a stochastic simulation model of a polygynous society in which there were marriage-based alliances between sibships, a preference for village endogamy, and a requirement for lineage exogamy. Individuals in the population were identified by date of birth (and death); sex; marital status; village; lineage; identity of parents, grandparents, and great-grandparents; and (for females) number of livebirths. The initial population consisted of individuals identified in censuses of four interrelated villages ranging in size from 50 to 244. This simulation model differed from the previous two in that the composition of the initial population was not a hypothetical one but was identical to that of four actual Yanomama villages. Rough estimates of age-specific birth, death, and marriage rates, required as input for the simulation, were obtained from field observations, as were arrays of lineage and village preferences for mating. A series of runs was done, each run simulating 200 years of births, deaths, and marriages. Initial conditions were held constant from run to run, but each run was done with a different set of random numbers. On the basis of comparisons between certain demographic characteristics of the artificial and real populations (age at maternity, age at paternity, mean birth interval, completed family size, age difference between spouses), it was decided that the model was a reasonably accurate representation of reality and that data derived from the model could be used in a more detailed analysis of Yanomama mating structure. It was estimated by simulation that one-third of Yanomama marriages may be between first or second cousins and that in spite of a strong preference for village endogamy, perhaps one-sixth of the marriages are village exogamous. Wife trading is common in the real population, with the result that nearly all men are married at some time during their lives. From the simulations, it was concluded that if there were no wife trading, nearly 30 percent of the males would complete the reproductive period without marrying. In the process of validating the model, it was discovered that sibship size is an important factor in determining a man's ability to obtain wives. Therefore, a few men have many more wives, children, and grandchildren than the average, and, as a consequence, the father-son correlation in fertility for the real population is high (0.258). Finally, the frequency of cousin marriages was examined through time in the artificial populations. The proportion of first cousin marriages fluctuated rather widely, and it was concluded that caution should be used in interpreting figures computed for real populations at a single point in time.

The effects of incest prohibitions and clan proscriptions on the growth of small populations have been studied by Morgan.[2] Using a simulation model that incorporated age-specific fertility and mortality rates, he began with an initial population of size 200 and subjected it to a schedule of low fertility and mortality over periods of up to 600 years. He investigated the effects of no remarriage after the death of a spouse, exclusion of clan endogamy, and incest prohibitions that exclude matings of first cousins, grandparent-grandchild, and closer. Preliminary results indicate that (1) remarriage had only a small effect on population growth; (2) as expected, populations that were subjected to clan proscription rules died out sooner than those that were not; and (3) somewhat surprisingly, populations survived longer when incest was prohibited. It was tentatively suggested that incest prohibition might affect population growth by changing the distribution of age differences between mates.

The relationship between mating structure and population growth has also been investigated by Cannings and Skolnick (in press). In their model, unlike the models described above, the ages at marriage and death of each individual were generated at the time of his birth, and the entire reproductive history of a couple was determined at once. This method has the advantage of increased efficiency, since the number of decisions involved is minimal. In addition, certain kinds of variability in vital rates (for example, birth rates that are dependent on birth interval) may be dealt with more conveniently. On the other hand, it may be more difficult with a model of this type to vary vital rates through time, for example, as a function of the size or age composition of the population. Comparisons of the results of this model with those of other models have yet to be made, but they should prove interesting. Cannings and Skolnick also investigated five different mating systems in populations of various sizes: random mating, four-clan exogamous, two-clan exogamous, an Australian aboriginal mating system, and a four-clan cycling system. Their preliminary results suggest that population growth rate varies widely depending on initial population size and mating system.

Pollard (1969) developed a stochastic macrosimulation model of demographic structure that incorporated marriage and compared its predictions with those of theoretical models. The population consisted of single males, single females, and married couples grouped according to age. Changes in the structure of the initial population were determined at regular intervals by subjecting the population to constant age-specific probabilities of change. The number of marriages between a male age x and a female age y was assumed to be equal to the minimum of the number of men age x desiring to marry women age y and the number of women age y desiring to marry men age x. The model has been applied to only a limited extent (to the projection of the 1960 population of Australia over three two-year time periods), primarily because of the large amount of computer time required to calculate the desired covariances between the sizes of each subgroup of the population. Pollard concluded that fluctuations in demographic parameters are caused by (1) statistical fluctuations due to finite population size and (2) random fluctuations in the rates of vital events.

Consanguinity

Several attempts have been made to investigate inbreeding in human populations by computer simulation. Cavalli-Sforza and Zei (1967) simulated the structure of 22 villages in the Parma Valley in Northern Italy (see also Cavalli-Sforza 1969a). Decisions were made every 10 years for each member of the population. In their model, the choice of a mate was a function of age, residence, and social status of the prospective spouses. Incest was prohibited, but other consanguineous marriages were allowed to occur on a random basis. The relatedness of married couples was computed in both the real and artificial populations, ignoring consanguinity more distant than third cousins. It was suggested that if the frequencies of various types of consanguineous marriages were similar in the real and artificial populations, then it would be sufficient to assume that in the Parma Valley, marriage preferences are determined only by age, residence, and social status and do not depend directly on the relationship of potential spouses. However, rather large discrepancies were found between the artificial and real populations in frequencies of matings in which the number of steps back to the common ancestor was different for the two spouses (that is, uncle-niece, first cousins once removed, second cousins once removed). It was suggested that this difference might be attributed to the excessively large variance in male generation time in the artificial population. In addition, the frequencies of first and second cousin marriages were slightly lower in the real population than in the artificial one.

A similar analysis was done by MacCluer and Schull (1970b), using a model described by MacCluer (1967, 1968) to investigate consanguinity in the population of Hirado, a small Japanese island. In this model, the initial population consisted of a random sample of size 200 or 400, stratified by age and sex, drawn from the actual population. Several different random samples were used to test the effect of differences in the initial populations. Decisions were made for each individual on a yearly basis over a period of 400 years. The relatedness of spouses was calculated for both the real and the artificial populations, disregarding relationships beyond second cousins. First cousin marriages were classified according to type (MBD, MZD, FBD, FZD) and marriages between first cousins once removed according to whether the male or female spouse was further removed from the common ancestor. Comparisons of frequencies of consanguineous marriage were made not only between the real and artificial populations, but also with the predictions of a theoretical model developed by Hajnal (1963). It was found that the relative frequencies of the four types of first cousin marriages and the two types of marriages between first cousins once removed were similar for the real population, the artificial populations, and the Hajnal predictions. However, neither the simulations nor the Hajnal model predicted the observed proportion of $1:1\frac{1}{2}:2$ cousin marriages, the real population having an excess of first cousin marriages (or a deficiency of second). It was concluded that this result was not likely to have been caused by underreporting and that cultural factors might be responsible. The simulation results were also used to test the ability of the Hajnal model (and an earlier model developed by Dahlberg [1929]) to predict isolate size from the frequencies of consanguineous marriage. In addition, the mean pedigree coefficient of inbreeding was calculated for one artificial pedigree to a depth of seven ancestral generations, and the contribution of remote consanguinity was evaluated. It was found that at the end of 300 years, the mean F was 0.066 and still increasing rapidly, with about 15 percent of the total contributed by the seventh generation. This result was assumed to have only limited applicability to real populations, since the artificial population was closed to immigration, and its size was never greater than 200.

In a further application of the model described in the previous section, MacCluer and Neel (in preparation) have attempted to estimate the probable level of inbreeding in the Yanomama Indians and the amount of stochastic variation to be expected in mean F under constant input conditions and constant vital rates. They computed mean F in five artificial pedigrees, all of which began with the same population of 451 individuals and which varied in size from 303 to 552 at the end of 400 years of simulation. The population consisted of four villages, with some migration between villages but no exchange with the outside world. In these five runs, the seven-generation inbreeding coefficient at the end of 400 years ranged from about 0.025 to 0.045. There were wide fluctuations through time and between runs in mean F, thus indicating that an extremely large number of runs would be necessary to get a very precise estimate of mean F for the Yanomama. An additional set of runs was done with migration from the outside in an attempt to provide a lower limit to the estimate of mean F. In an investigation of remote consanguinity, it was found that 15 to 20 percent of the total inbreeding (calculated on the basis of seven ancestral generations) was contributed by the most remote generation, a finding consistent with that in the Japanese study discussed earlier. In addition, it was discovered that as a consequence of marriage preferences of the Yanomama, there were complex multiple relationships between individuals, the average person having 33.4 common ancestors in the seventh generation, in addition to those in more recent generations.

Fertility and Population Growth

Although fertility simulation models have been used by demographers for several years, anthropologists and geneticists have just begun to apply simulation techniques to the investigation of fertility and population growth. Skolnick and Cannings (in press) have used the model described earlier to study the effectiveness of child spacing as a means of regulating the size of primitive human populations. Their program includes as random variables (1) age-specific fertility and (2) a period of postpartum sterility, with birth interval a function of pregnancy outcome (fetal death or livebirth) and survival of the child through infancy. Skolnick and Cannings did four simulations of each of the mating systems listed earlier; two of the runs for each system assumed no correlation between length of sterile period and population size (as measured by number of marriages), and two runs assumed that the sterile period was reduced as population size increased. In every case, regulation of the sterile period was effective as a means of population control, with the required adjustment ranging between sterile periods of 2.1 and 2.9 years. Skolnick and Cannings suggest a possible mechanism by which actual primitive populations might adjust their child spacing as a function of population size. It is known that some societies have a taboo against coitus during lactation, and there is some indication that lactation reduces the probability of conception. If food supply per person is limited, then mothers might continue to nurse their children for a longer period of time than when food is abundant, and the interval between births might be increased. If total food supply remains relatively constant, this suggests a feedback mechanism, whereby as population size increases, there is a lengthening of birth intervals, which leads to a decline in population numbers.

Zubrow (1971a, 1971b, 1971c) has simulated population growth and dispersal over a geographical area in which there are regional differences in carrying capacity. In the model, settlements were located on a 25 x 25 grid representing the Hay Hollow Valley in eastern Arizona, a region that, according to archaeological evidence, was inhabited from A.D. 200 to 1400. Each of the 625 squares in the grid was assigned a microhabitat. Input data included birth, death, and migration rates, maximum settlement size, rate of growth of resources, proportion of total resources consumed, and nonresource variables that controlled population longevity. Simulations were begun in A.D. 200 with a single population of size 50. During each run, settlement sizes increased until the carrying capacity was reached, and new populations budded off. Each new population was located in the best available microhabitat. Simulations were done under a variety of initial conditions for the 1200-year period from A.D. 200 to 1400. Several variables were plotted through time (population size for each microhabitat, total population size, number of sites), and comparisons were made with the archaeological record.

Cannings and Skolnick[3] and Morgan (1969) have investigated other aspects of the growth of small human populations. In their simulations, Cannings and Skolnick have found that populations may maintain a reasonably constant size over long periods of time and then experience a sudden rapid increase, or else decrease to extinction. They are studying the relationships between this phenomenon and the mating system and age structure of populations. Morgan has studied the survival of small populations that are closed to migration and that have an intrinsic rate of increase of 0.5 percent per year. Using a stochastic microsimulation model, he has simulated the growth of populations at different fertility and mortality levels, beginning with populations of either 100 or 200 individuals. He has found that the growth rates experienced by the artificial populations were, in general, lower than the rate predicted from the life table data. His results further suggested that populations subjected to low fertility and mortality schedules are more stable with respect to long-term survival than are those experiencing high fertility and mortality.

A number of demographic simulation models have been developed whose primary emphasis is on the events of the human reproductive period. These models, which have many features in common, are used to

232

simulate the complete reproductive histories of a specified number of women or couples. The events that occur to a woman are determined solely from input parameters and are independent of the events that occur to any other individual so that, for example, the probability of marriage does not depend on the availability of an appropriate mate. The usual procedure is to simulate the entire reproductive history of a given woman before considering the next woman on the list. Unlike most anthropological and genetic simulation models, the events of the reproductive period are generally dealt with in considerable detail, and only short time periods (for example, 35 years) are simulated. At a given point in her reproductive period, a woman may be assigned with specified probabilities to any one of a number of states: (1) nonpregnant, fecundable, (2) pregnant, (3) postpartum sterile period associated with livebirth, stillbirth, or abortion (in one model, abortions are classified as spontaneous, induced legal, or induced criminal), or (4) secondary sterility near the end of the reproductive period. Monthly probabilities of passing from one to another of these states may be a function of the age and parity of the woman (and her husband) or the duration of marriage. The length of the reproductive period may be determined by specifying probabilities of marriage, divorce, widowhood, remarriage, menopause, and death, all of which may depend on age or duration of marriage. Such models have been used in attempts to match data from actual populations, to investigate changes in various measures of fertility as a function of underlying probabilities, and to predict the success of alternative methods of family limitation. One of the major difficulties in the application of these models is the lack of appropriate input data for any single population.

One of the first fertility simulation models was developed by Perrin and Sheps (1963, 1964) and later extended by Ridley and Sheps (1965, 1966), Sheps and Ridley (1965), and Ridley et al. (1967a). This model has been used to investigate (1) the interval between births as a function of parity of mother and number of years observed within the reproductive period, (2) the effects of changes in age at marriage on natality, (3) the effects on natality of decreases in the incidence of marital dissolution as life expectancy increases, and (4) the effects on natality of alternative methods of family planning. It has also been used in an effort to simulate natality levels characteristic of India.

A similar model, developed originally by Hyrenius and Adolfsson (1964), has undergone extensive testing with periodic modification of the basic program (Hyrenius, Adolfsson, and Holmberg 1966, Holmberg 1970). Some versions of the model have introduced time changes in vital rates, so that various aspects of population dynamics may be examined (Hyrenius, Holmberg, and Carlsson 1967, Holmberg 1968). Holmberg (1970) has investigated the variability in certain fertility measures between simulation runs under both constant and variable input conditions and has examined fertility patterns under two different methods of contraception. In attempting to simulate demographic changes in Sweden for a period of more than 200 years, Holmberg (1968) found that the demographic transition can be simulated satisfactorily only if input probabilities are allowed to change continuously, rather than in discrete steps.

A third fertility simulation model, developed by Jacquard (1967), has been used to study the probable success of contraception of varying degrees of effectiveness, where success is measured for individual families and for the total population. He found that at the lowest level of contraceptive effectiveness (50 percent before the birth of the last wanted child, 70 percent thereafter), the net reproduction rate was almost independent of the desired family size. When the effectiveness of contraception was increased to 90 percent before the birth of the last wanted child and 95 percent thereafter, population growth could be maintained at an economically sound level, but the rate of individual family planning success was low. This model has been used by Bodmer and Jacquard (1968) to identify factors that contribute to the variance in family size and to determine the amount of variability contributed by each factor. They also have applied it to the Hutterites. Jacquard (1970a) discussed the Poisson distribution of family sizes that is commonly used by geneticists, as well as possible sources of deviation from this distribution. Such sources include postpartum sterility, variable age at menopause, family planning, and variable age at marriage. To illustrate the effects of such factors on the distribution of family sizes (as measured by the ratio of variance to mean), he did a series of simulation runs using the model mentioned above and assuming various levels of contraceptive effectiveness ranging from zero (no contraception) to 99 percent. He showed that as contraceptive effectiveness increased, the ratio of variance in family size to mean family size decreased. In the light of these results, he discussed the time changes in distribution of family size that have occurred in both the United States and France and the large ratios of variance to mean family size that were observed in the data.

Jean W. MacCluer

A fertility simulation model developed by Barrett (1967, 1969) has been used to investigate possible sources of bias in the measurement of certain fertility parameters. Barrett (1971) has generated data by simulation, made estimates of various demographic parameters on the basis of this data, and compared the estimates with those derived from theoretical models. He was able to show that the renewal theory of Perrin and Sheps (1964) overestimated the mean birth interval by 0.6 months for each birth interval after the sixth interval for women who marry at age 20, the discrepancy resulting from the assumption of an infinite reproductive period in the renewal formulas. In comparing methods of estimating proportions of women sterile at various ages, he found that a greater bias is introduced by using age at last conception than by using proportions sterile at marriage. Finally, he examined the relationship between increased numbers of fetal deaths and increased numbers of pregnancies.

Potter and Sakoda (1966) have used a macrosimulation model to study fertility in a homogeneous cohort of ten million married couples. The model was deterministic, except that the duration of postpartum sterility following a livebirth was a random variable with a probability distribution. There was no death or divorce, and fecundability did not vary directly with age but only with duration of marriage and parity. Reproductive periods were simulated as a series of one-month intervals. The population was subdivided into various states, and the proportions in each state changed through time according to a matrix of transition probabilities. The model was applied to couples in the present United States population who practice contraception, who are average in fecundity and in the length of their reproductive periods, and who do not breast-feed their children.

Heer and Smith (1968, 1969) have used several computer models to examine the relationships between mortality level, population increase, and desired family size, assuming that couples have a perfect method of birth control and that they want to be very certain that at least one son (or two children) survives to the father's sixty-fifth birthday. Their models assumed a constant age at marriage of 20 for males and 17 for females and a sex ratio of 0.513 (male births divided by total births). The models varied according to the degree of certainty desired by the parents, whether death of a child was assumed to be independent of deaths of his sibs, whether death of parents was taken into account, and whether women differed in fecundity. Simulation runs were done at each of 24 levels of mortality taken from United Nations model life tables (1955). The rate of population growth was found to be greatest at intermediate mortality levels, which are similar to those of most of the underdeveloped countries. Their results indicate that a further reduction in mortality in these countries might actually reduce their rate of growth, because as mortality declines, fewer births are required to assure the survival of offspring who can support their parents in old age.

A computer model that is more comprehensive than the fertility simulation models previously discussed has been used by Horvitz et al. (1971) to study problems involving human reproduction. The initial population for their simulations is created by a program that requires as input the relative frequencies of age-sex-marital status groups, population size, and probabilities associated with marriage and reproduction. One version of the model records the composition of family groups and requires that all marriages take place between members of the computer population (closed model). In a second version (open model), the initial population may be thought of as a random sample of individuals from some larger population, and family relationships are disregarded. Thus, it is possible to simulate certain characteristics of very large populations while maintaining the advantages of a microsimulation model. Probabilities of birth, death, marriage, and divorce are specified on a monthly basis, and summary tables of selected population characteristics are printed out at regular intervals during the simulation. The model has been applied to (1) evaluating the influence of several types of sterilization programs on the birth rate in a population whose demographic characteristics were similar to that of the United States in 1950, and (2) investigating the relationship between the distribution of ages at first marriage and female fertility in a population similar to the United States population of 1950–60.

Estimation of Vital Rates

Dyke and MacCluer (in manuscript) have used computer simulation to estimate age-specific fertility and mortality rates in the population of Northside, a French-derived isolate on St. Thomas in the U.S. Virgin Islands. Their estimates were based on birth, death, and marriage records for the years 1916 to 1966. Because the population was so small (increasing from 202 in 1916 to 657 in 1966), the numbers of births and deaths recorded for Northside in this 50-year period were insufficient to estimate age-specific birth and death rates directly. In addition, although there was accurate recording of births, death registration was incomplete. The estimation of birth and death rates by simulation proceeded in two steps. First, a small simulation program was used to estimate a mortality schedule. The initial population in this model was given the age and sex composition of the 1916 Northside population. During the simulation, this population was incremented yearly by a number of newborn males and females corresponding to the actual numbers of births recorded in Northside for the years 1917 to 1966. In each year of the simulation, individuals were exposed to age- and sex-specific probabilities of death that were derived from model life tables compiled by Coale and Demeny (1966). A graded series of mortality levels was used, and the level that most accurately reproduced the observed growth of the population over the 50-year period was used as the estimate of age-specific mortality for Northside. Because of the large variance in growth rate between simulations, even under the same initial conditions, it was necessary to do 25 replicates at a single mortality level in order to get a reliable estimate of mean growth rate. In the second step of the estimation procedure, a more complex simulation program was used, similar to the ones described by MacCluer (1967) and MacCluer, Neel, and Chagnon (1971). Again, the initial population was that of Northside in 1916. The death rates used as input were those estimated in the first step, and preliminary estimates of birth rates were derived from the data. Births, deaths, and marriages were simulated over a 50-year period. Birth probabilities were adjusted empirically from one set of simulation runs to the next, until population growth rates, as well as other demographic characteristics, were similar in the real and simulated populations. The birth rates that produced the best fit to the real population data were taken as the estimate of age-specific probabilities of reproducing.

Selection

A number of simulation models have been used to detect selection in human populations, to determine selection intensities necessary to account for observed geographical distributions of genes, or to examine the effect of selection through time in the presence of other evolutionary forces. Brues (1963) was the first person to use computer simulation to study the genetic structure of human populations. Extending an earlier study that was done on a desk calculator (Brues 1954), she estimated the selection pressures required to produce the present world-wide distribution of the ABO blood group genes, taking into account maternal-fetal incompatibility with respect to this locus. The model specified random union of gametes and nonoverlapping generations. Each experiment consisted of 60 simulation runs, 20 runs at each of three population sizes: 40-50, 80-100, or 160-200 breeding adults. All simulations were started with gene frequencies of 0.25A and 0.15B and were allowed to run for 20 generations in order to observe the effects of drift. A number of interesting results emerged. First, with maternal-fetal incompatibility, but in the absence of other selection, populations rapidly approach fixation. Therefore, it is unlikely that the ABO polymorphism is unstable and is merely in a stage of transition. Second, when the genotype AB is given a selective advantage in the presence of incompatibility and all other genotypes are assumed to have equal but lower fitnesses, populations diverge from their initial frequency, tending toward loss or fixation of the O gene. Third, in order to simulate the observed distribution of ABO frequencies in the world, the required selection coefficients were $OO = 0.79$, $AA = 0.74$, $BB = 0.66$, $OA = 0.89$, $OB = 0.86$, and $AB = 1.00$, with the heterozygote in every case being more fit than either of the corresponding homozygotes. Brues concluded that since the ABO polymorphism appears to be maintained by a selective difference between heterozygotes and homozygotes, it is not very useful to collect population data in which only phenotypes may be distinguished; instead, attention should be centered on the collection of family data.

The maintenance of the Rh blood group polymorphism was investigated by Levin (1967). He used both deterministic and stochastic simulation models to study the effects of various levels of reproductive compensation on gene frequency change in the presence of selection against the Rh-negative allele. Simulations of 100 generations each were done at two levels of selection and three levels of reproductive compensation, with initial gene frequencies ranging from 0.2 to 0.8. Levin concluded that variation in the rate of reproductive compensation between populations could account for the large variation in Rh frequencies and for long-term maintenance of the Rh polymorphism.

Livingstone (1969c) has used a deterministic macrosimulation model incorporating selection, mutation, and gene flow in an investigation of the evolution of skin color differences. In the model, skin color was assumed to be determined by four loci, two of which subtracted from the total amount of melanin and two of which added to the total. Two levels of dominance (0 to 80 percent) were used. He found that with optimizing selection and with, at most, a 6 percent difference between the maximum and minimum fitnesses assigned to the various phenotypes, the evolution of the present range of human skin color differences would require about 800 generations with no dominance and about 1,500 generations with 80 percent dominance. If isolates were assumed to be arranged in linear order, then significant differences in skin color could persist even in the presence of 5 percent migration per generation.

Another simulation model has been used by Livingstone (1969a) to determine the fate of a deleterious gene in a small founder population that subsequently experiences rapid growth. Beginning with initial populations of sizes 20, 40, and 80, he allowed doubling of population size for each of the first few generations, with a slower but still sizable rate of increase thereafter. Each initial population contained one or two copies of a recessive lethal (or nearly lethal) gene. After 10 generations, the lethal gene had increased in frequency in a number of the populations. The model was applied to the Brandywine isolate in southeast Maryland, in which the sickle-cell gene has a frequency of 0.1. Since falciparum malaria is not endemic in this region, one would not expect the sickle-cell gene to be maintained in this population at such a high frequency. It was shown by simulation, however, that there is no need to postulate a selective advantage for the sickle-cell heterozygote in order to account for the high frequency of the sickle-cell gene. If the gene were present in the small founding population about 10 generations ago, it could have reached its present frequency by chance alone as the population experienced rapid growth.

In an attempt to account for the geographical distribution of β hemoglobin variants, Livingstone (1969b) has constructed a computer model that simulates gene flow among populations arranged in a linear sequence. Fitnesses of genotypes were chosen to duplicate those associated with β thalassemia and hemoglobins S, C, and E, with fitness being allowed to vary from one end of the linear array to the other according to known geographical variations in selection pressures. It was concluded that major population movements must be postulated in order to account for the spread of hemoglobin S through Africa and of hemoglobin E through Southeast Asia, whereas large amounts of local migration seem to be responsible for maintaining the cline for thalassemia in Sardinia.

Williams (1965), using a stochastic simulation model developed by Levin in 1965, has studied the maintenance of genetic polymorphisms in hunting-gathering societies and has attempted to define the conditions under which clines might be detected. In the model, hunting-gathering bands were assumed to be arranged in a matrix of hexagonal cells in such a way that each band could have as many as six adjacent neighboring bands. The number of bands, their sizes, and their arrangement in the matrix were specified at the beginning of each simulation, as were the mating pattern between bands and the numbers and fitnesses of individuals of each sex and genotype. The lengths of the simulations varied from 20 to 400 generations; population size was held constant throughout each run. Among the more interesting findings were: (1) polymorphism can be maintained in populations of this type by regional differences in selection pressures; (2) if the region is very small, it might not be possible to detect local differences in gene frequencies, although a polymorphism could still be maintained; (3) even though the existence of clines might be established, it would be difficult to determine their shapes; and (4) the variance effective size of these populations is relatively large.

Johnston and Albers (Chapter 10) have described a stochastic simulation model of the Peruvian Cashinahua that incorporates cultural, demographic, and genetic parameters. Each individual is assigned a genotype at each of 13 actual loci for which data are available in the real population. Although it has not yet been applied to genetic problems, the model may include selection in the form of differential fertility or mortality, as well as genetic drift, at any of the 13 loci.

The first genetic simulation model to include age structure was described by Schull and Levin (1964). In this model, members of the population were identified by genotype (a single locus with two alleles), sex, and age set (there were three age sets of 10 years each). Probabilities of reproducing and dying could depend on sex, genotype, and age set. Emigration occurred by random removal of individuals from the population, and immigrants were drawn from a population of infinite size (that is, a population having a structure invariant through time). The mating structure permitted a certain amount of generation overlap. Preliminary experiments were done with populations of effective size 50 to 200, constant through time. To illustrate the use of the model, Schull and Levin investigated (1) the effect of discrete overlapping of generations on genetic drift, (2) gene frequency change at a locus with incomplete selection against one homozygote, and reproductive compensation (for example, albinism among the Hopi and San Blas Indians), (3) gene frequency change at a locus with complete selection against one homozygote and 20 percent selection against the other (for example, sickle-cell anemia), and (4) gene frequency change at a locus for which fertility is a function of mating type rather than genotype. For each experiment, the mean and range in gene frequencies were plotted for 200 generations, and, where possible, comparisons were made with the predictions of deterministic models.

In an effort to determine whether recessive lethal genes may be detected by an examination of intervals between livebirths, Rossman and Schull[4] are simulating the reproductive histories of 50,000 marriages. A genotype is assigned to each child at birth; if the genotype is homozygous recessive, the child is stillborn. The interval to each birth is randomly generated from a specified distribution of birth intervals and is a function only of the outcome of the previous pregnancy. Experiments will be done with a variety of gene frequencies and birth interval distributions in an attempt to demonstrate the conditions under which a recessive lethal gene produces a measurable lengthening of livebirth intervals.

Anderson and King (1970) have constructed a deterministic macrosimulation model of age-specified selection on the genotypes in a population. Although it was not applied specifically to man, the model is flexible and general enough that it could provide useful information on the action of selection in human populations. For each genotype, a life table was defined that specified viability and fecundity by age class. The population was represented by a matrix in which the numbers of individuals of each genotype and age class were given. Fecundities and viabilities appeared as a matrix of transition probabilities, and the process of population growth through time was simulated by a series of matrix multiplications. To illustrate the use of the model, Anderson and King have simulated age-specific selection under both exponential and logistic population growth. With exponential growth, they assumed (1) equal viabilities across all genotypes, (2) a selective advantage in fecundity for the heterozygote, and (3) an advantage in initial population size for one of the homozygotes. For 25 breeding intervals, they showed the oscillations in progeny size and age distribution by genotype and the change in gene frequency through time. In the simulation of logistic growth, they assumed (1) identical viabilities for each genotype, (2) a selective advantage in fecundity for one

241

homozygote (AA), (3) carrying capacities of 500, 750, and 1,000 for AA, AB, and BB, respectively, and (4) initial numbers of $AA = 9$, $AB = 3$, and $BB = 1$. Under these conditions, the population growth curve deviated from its expected sigmoid shape, showing a plateau at the point where it might have been expected to grow most rapidly. In a subsequent paper (King and Anderson 1971), the investigation was extended to include more complex interactions between density-independent and density-regulated components of age-specific selection during logistic population growth, and the consequences of selection in a variable environment were considered.

Gene Flow and Genetic Drift

The simulation models discussed in this section all assume that there are no genetically determined differences in viability or fertility among individuals. They have been designed to investigate the effects of gene flow or genetic drift, either separately or in combination, on the genetic structure of actual or hypothetical human populations.

Cavalli-Sforza and Zei (1967) have used computer simulation in an attempt to explain the observed distribution of ABO, Rh, and MN blood groups in the populations of the Parma Valley in Italy (see also Cavalli-Sforza 1969a, Cavalli-Sforza and Bodmer 1971). In the model, which was described in an earlier section, the sizes and migration patterns of 22 villages were taken from actual data. Migration was assumed to occur only at marriage. Members of the initial population were assigned genotypes for the ABO, Rh, and MN loci, with frequencies corresponding to those in the real population. All villages were assumed to have the same gene frequencies initially. After 15 generations of simulation, the variation in gene frequencies between villages was approximately the same as that observed in reality. Therefore, it was concluded that in the presence of migration, genetic drift alone was sufficient to explain the observed variability between villages and that there was no need to invoke selection as an explanation.

Neel and Ward (1972), in an analysis of genotype distributions in Yanomama villages, observed that for many loci, the average frequency of heterozygotes within villages was greater than the proportion predicted by the Hardy-Weinberg law (that is, F_{IS} was often negative). In an attempt to explain these negative values of F_{IS}, MacCluer and Neel (in preparation) computed F statistics for artificial pedigrees based on four Yanomama villages. The simulation model and the initial population were described above. Despite the lack of genetically determined differences in fertility or mortality, F_{IS} values in the artificial populations were also consistently negative. Therefore, it was not necessary to invoke systematic selection pressures to account for the negative F_{IS} values found in the Yanomama. Moreover, the excess of heterozygotes could not be accounted for by avoidance of close consanguinity, since the mean coefficient of kinship for married couples in the simulation was higher than that for random couples. Investigation of this problem continues both in the Yanomama population and in simulations of model populations (described below).

MacCluer (in press) has investigated the action of gene flow and genetic drift in hypothetical populations subjected to high fertility and mortality with five different yearly rates of migration between subdivisions. The simulation program was a modification of programs described previously (MacCluer 1967, MacCluer, Neel, and Chagnon 1971). The initial population of 400 people was divided into four villages of 50 males and 50 females each, all with identical age-sex structures and family compositions. Gene frequency change was simulated for 60 loci in each artificial pedigree over a 200-year period, and genetic distances and F statistics were computed. Five results of the simulation were noted. First, as expected, genetic differentiation was greatest when villages were isolated from each other; however, even when villages were exchanging migrants at a rate as high as 0.125 percent per year for 200 years, genetic differentiation between villages was not noticeably diminished. Second, when pairwise genetic distances and F_{ST}'s were calculated for a pedigree from several sets of 10 or 20 loci each, the results were quite variable, even though all loci began at a frequency of 0.5 and all were selectively neutral. Third, F_{ST}'s calculated from $\sigma^2/\bar{p}\bar{q}$ and $(F_{IT} - F_{IS})/(1 - F_{IS})$ were nearly identical, as would be expected for randomly differentiating subpopulations. Fourth, mean F_{IS} was consistently negative, as was the case in the Yanomama studies described above. Finally, F_{IS} and F_{IT} varied widely between loci and through time. Therefore, data from real populations that are based on only a few loci at a single point in time must be interpreted with caution.

In order to estimate the expected rate of gene frequency drift in a small population, MacCluer and Schull (1970a) used the computer model and the initial population described above and in MacCluer and

243

Schull (1970b). They generated sets of five artificial pedigrees, each 400 years in length and each beginning with the same initial population. Since each individual had a genotype, it was possible to compute gene frequency through time for each of these pedigrees, and then to calculate the variance in gene frequency through time between runs. By substituting this variance into the equation

$$\sigma q^2 = p_0 q_0 [1 - (1 - \tfrac{1}{2}N_e)^t],$$

where $p_0 = q_0 = 0.5$ and $t =$ generation time, N_e could be computed through time. These estimates were found to compare favorably with estimates made from demographic data. The effect of avoidance of incest on drift was determined by comparing the above estimates with those from another set of simulations in which matings between sibs and half sibs were allowed. Recently, more sophisticated analyses have been done, with N_e calculated on the basis of 60 to 100 loci for each of a series of artificial pedigrees.

Dyke (in manuscript) has used simulation to estimate N_e for the Northside French population of St.Thomas, U.S. Virgin Islands. Gene segregation has been simulated for 1,000 loci, using the actual pedigree of the St. Thomas population over a period of about 100 years. It was found that at least for this pedigree, 200 loci were required to yield a reasonably stable estimate of N_e.

Giesel (1971) developed equations that predict the rate of gene frequency drift in a stationary population with overlapping generations but discrete age classes. He compared predictions of this model with the results of computer simulations run for 45 mating seasons. With cross-generational mating, he found that until there is a decay in differences in the amount of inbreeding between age classes, the rate of drift is slowed by the presence in the population of older, less inbred individuals.

Several deterministic simulation models have been used to study gene flow. Hainline (1963) developed a simple macrosimulation model of genetic exchange between two populations and examined the rate of approach to genetic homogeneity when (1) populations were of unequal sizes; (2) population sizes changed through time; or (3) the rate of gene flow changed through time. She used the model to explain the present frequencies of the ABO and MN blood group genes in the Siksika (Blackfoot), Sarsi, and Stoney American Indian tribes and concluded that the data were consistent with a rate of exchange of about 3 percent per generation, beginning in about 1700.

Imaizumi, Morton, and Harris (1970) have investigated isolation by distance in populations arranged in various geometric configurations. They have used a deterministic computer model to derive the coefficient of kinship and other quantities from recurrence equations given a migration matrix, a systematic pressure, and a vector of effective population sizes; they have also established the relationship between coefficient of kinship and linear distance under the stepping-stone model of population structure. According to their study, when distances were short enough that kinship was not negligible, estimates based on asymptotic decline of kinship with distance were inaccurate.

The isolation by distance model has also been analyzed by Rohlf and Schnell (1971). Using a stochastic simulation model, they began with individuals uniformly distributed over a two-dimensional grid. Genotypes for members of the initial population were selected at random from a Hardy-Weinberg distribution, and a neighborhood size was specified at the beginning of each simulation. Changes in gene and genotype frequencies were simulated over a number of generations for several sets of initial conditions (shape of grid, mating pattern, and neighborhood size were varied). Both temporal and geographical distributions of gene frequencies were examined, and results were compared with the predictions of Wright's (1943) model. It was found first, that the observed rate of decrease in heterozygosity did not correspond to that predicted by Wright, and second, that the geographic distribution of gene frequencies became established early and persisted for many generations.

Social Interaction

Computer simulation models of social interaction have been used since the early 1950s. Although many of these models are designed for the study of small group behavior, a few may be applied to small human populations. In 1953, Hägerstrand did a computer simulation of the spatial and social diffusion of an innovation in Sweden. A summary of other diffusion simulation studies is presented in Hanneman et al. (1969) and Rogers (1969). These investigators have built a microsimulation model of innovation diffusion in a peasant village and have compared simulation results with the diffusion of awareness of 2, 4-D weed spray in the small, isolated

Colombian village of Pueblo Viejo. In the model, village members were divided into cliques. Seven individuals in the initial population were "knowers," and of these, four were "tellers." Information could enter the village through two external channels, and an individual could become a knower either by contact with a teller or from an external channel. The probability of becoming a knower varied from one clique to another, and the number of contacts per year between tellers and knowers was varied until the simulation output matched the actual data as nearly as possible. It was found, however, that when the cumulative number of knowers was plotted over a 10-year period, the curve derived from actual data was sigmoid in shape, whereas the simulations produced curves that increased rather sharply at first and then approached an asymptote. Possible reasons for this discrepancy were that in the model, there was no time lag between awareness and adoption of the innovation; no variability was allowed between tellers in the number of contacts per year; nonknowers were not allowed to seek out tellers; and, by chance, tellers often contacted individuals who were already knowers.

Rainio (1966) has developed a simplified model of social interaction and has applied it to an analysis of sociometric changes in small groups. The model would be equally appropriate for analyzing social structure in small populations. Rainio used a computer program to simulate social contact between pairs of individuals in a group. At the time of contact, individuals were assigned a behavior A or $\bar{A}$ with probabilities p_A and $p_{\bar{A}}$, where these two behavior patterns were assumed to be incompatible. If the individuals in contact had the same behavior, both were rewarded, and the probability of a subsequent contact between the two was increased; if the behavior of the two individuals differed, both were punished, and subsequent contact was less likely. The probilities p_A and $p_{\bar{A}}$ for an individual were altered according to the outcomes of previous contacts. The model was used with some success in an attempt to reproduce changing friendship patterns (expressed as sociograms) in groups of school children. It was suggested that the model could also be applied to studies of social influence and leadership, socialization, or the origin of conflicts.

Gullahorn and Gullahorn (1964, 1965) have developed a simulation model of social behavior based on the theory of Homans (1961). Their model is considerably more complex than that of Rainio, since it allows individuals to participate in a wide range of activities, to belong to a number of groups, and to have a variety of opinions. Furthermore, the behavior of an individual may vary according to his age, sex, education, ability, and so forth. However, this model has apparently been applied only to groups of two or three people, and until it has been expanded, it will probably have little utility in human population studies.

Other Uses of Simulation

Finally, this chapter will mention some simulation studies in other disciplines, as well as review articles and discussions of techniques and rationale, all of which may provide valuable information on the construction and use of human population models. Orcutt et al. (1961) have experimented with a stochastic microsimulation model of the U.S. economy, and Naylor et al. (1966) have described some of the uses of simulation in economics. The problems involved in simulation of social systems have been discussed by Orcutt (1963, 1965) and Beshers (1965, 1967), while Raser (1969) has reviewed simulation and gaming in the social sciences. In one of a series of monographs, Hyrenius (1965) has listed some general characteristics of demographic simulation models. Several applications of simulation to the solution of demographic problems have been given by Keyfitz (1968); and van de Walle and Knodel (1970) have published a simulation program to be used in teaching population dynamics. Hays (1965) has given an overview of simulation and modeling for anthropologists, while in the field of human genetics, Jacquard (1970b), Cavalli-Sforza and Bodmer (1971), Levin (1969), and Schull (1969) have discussed certain applications of simulation models. Further contributions have been made by Watt (1968) in describing the use of simulation in problems of resource management, and by Heinmets (1969) in editing a collection of articles on the uses of simulation in biology.

A number of books and articles have been written on simulation methodology, random number generation, and statistical techniques. Of particular interest are books by Naylor et al. (1966), Naylor (1969), Martin (1968), and Emshoff and Sisson (1970), and articles by Zellner (1965) and Hurtubise (1969).

SUMMARY

Computer simulation models have been widely used in anthropology and human genetics. In this chapter, the characteristics of various types of computer models have been described; consideration has been given to the types of problems for which simulation may be used; and some models and results have been presented.

NOTES

1. This work has been supported by grant GS–27382 A#1 of the National Science Foundation. I wish to express my gratitude to Dr. Bennett Dyke for his careful criticism of the manuscript and to the many people who allowed me to mention their unpublished work.

2. Kenneth Morgan 1972: personal communication.

3. Chris Cannings and Mark H. Skolnick 1972: personal communication.

4. David Rossman and William J. Schull 1972: personal communication.

The Feasibility of Demographic Studies in "Anthropological" Populations[1]

NANCY HOWELL

Office of Population Research
Princeton University

Making demographic studies of the kind of people that anthropologists classically study (that is, small groups of people who are not literate or timekeepers) can never be easy. It is one of the injustices of life that anthropologists, whose training tends not to prepare them to carry out demographic studies, are faced with precisely the most difficult circumstances in which to study a population, because the numbers are small, the information is scarce, and one doesn't know what to expect to find. Under these trying circumstances, the most sophisticated methodology and the most refined hypotheses are needed in order to learn anything at all.

As a demographer who has been coping with the frustrations of studying such a population, my own research over the past few years can serve as a model of the kind of approach that seems to be needed. I have made a field collection of data among the people who live in a particular geographical area of the Kalahari Desert (Howell 1973). During most of the time that they were under observation, there were between 350 and 500 individuals who are culturally and linguistically !Kung Bushmen, or *zun/wasi*, as they call themselves. These desert-living hunting and gathering people have experienced a minimum, though not an absence, of disruption of their age-old way of life.

Archaeological studies conducted by Yellen (1971) indicate that there has been continuous occupation of the area by people with a way of life similar to that of the !Kung for thousands of years. My studies of these people are focused on questions concerning the maintenance of the population over long periods of time.

Two basic questions motivate this research: What levels and patterns of mortality and what levels and patterns of fertility have formed this population and maintained it in the long run? How is this population pattern both a cause and an effect of the overall organization of !Kung life? The minor questions of the research, which are, as usual, the ones that actually take up most of the time and energy of the investigation, consist of how to measure or estimate the parameters from existing information, how to assess the plausibility or accuracy of findings, and how to correct for under-reporting, misestimation, or random fluctuations in the small numbers we have to work with in order to turn out useful results.

This time-consuming and in many ways tedious empirical study of the *zun/wasi* seems justified, first of all, because this small population happens to be one of the surviving, relatively undisturbed hunting and gathering societies; as such, it may give us insights about the kinds of population patterns that existed when hunting and gathering was the only economic arrangement that the human species had. A second reason for this research is to assess how much simplification of demographic methodology is possible in this kind of situation, while at the same time retaining a level of accuracy high enough that the studies are worth doing. Such an assessment will not be possible until after the conclusion of the empirical study.

Instead, this chapter presents a set of null hypotheses in the form of a summary of the knowledge of human populations in general that has been developed by demographers over the past 50 years. To the extent to which this general knowledge of all human populations can be said to apply to primitive populations, it can serve as a framework within which many substantial shortcuts of empirical and theoretical work can be made. Indeed, to the extent that the population processes of primitive people are just the same as those of all other human beings, empirical studies are not even necessary for an intelligent discussion of the demographic side of the demographic-ecological equation. That would be an extremely felicitous conclusion to reach, not only because empirical studies are so difficult to do in remote areas with small populations, but because much of the target phenomena—that of prehistory—is completely beyond our range of data collection.

Unfortunately, the only kinds of populations that are ever reported to fall outside of the known human range that will be described here are precisely those that anthropologists study, and anthropologists are usually the source of the report. Thus, Rose (1968) seems to believe that the Total Fertility Rate of the population of Groote Eyland was approximately 18, and Birdsell (1968) thinks that fertility in Australia was so high in the precontact period, and mortality so low, that infanticide had to be practiced on 15 to 50 percent of the births. These statements, if they are meant to characterize the populations over the long run and are not simply unusual temporary conditions, are very suspicious to a demographer because they are well outside the known range within which reliably studied populations vary. There is a long tradition in empirical demography of finding that in country after country, the amount of variation from central tendencies decreased along with improvements in the quality of data and analysis. In other words, deviations have often come from bad reporting rather than from the population itself, and this is the question we have to ask about primitive populations.

A good starting point now would be, first, to spell out very explicitly some of the observed central trends and constraints on population processes and composition that are known to set limits on the amount of variation that exists in all the reliably studied populations in the long run, and, second, to spell out situations that would be surprising if they were seen to occur. To start with one of the most simple ones, let us consider the sex ratio at birth. In known populations where the information about livebirths is reliable, the sex ratio at birth varies between 102 and 107 males per 100 females. Differences in sex ratio at birth have been shown to be persistent for particular countries over a long period of time and have been subjected to causal analysis (Teitelbaum 1970). The number of births needed to analyze variant patterns in sex ratio at birth start in the tens of thousands, because the size of the expected differences, although persistent, is small. The chance that an anthropologist could establish a variant pattern in sex ratio at birth in a small population fades when one clearly faces the fact that births will be produced in the population in question at a rate between about 20 to 50 per 1,000 persons per year. In a population of 1,000 persons, therefore, one would have to collect completely accurate information on all the births that occur for a minimum of 20 years before having as many as 1,000 births to test a hypothesis of a particular sex ratio at birth. If one observes 60 males born in 100 livebirths, the sensible response is to go to a table of the normal distribution to see how often that outcome is likely to occur by chance in a population of a particular size, given that the true probability of a male birth is 0.525 (a central estimate of probability), rather than using 0.60 as the "best estimate" of the sex ratio for that population over the long run.

Another area in which one is unlikely to turn up a significant finding in a small population is in the question of seasonality of births. Certainly seasonality of births is commonly observed in large populations where the information is good, but the ratio of births per month in one portion of the year to that in another tends to be near unity and could not be detected in populations of a few thousands where births are observed for only a few years. Only if the differences in births by season were extremely large would the pattern be detectable in a small population. Such a large difference between seasons should be surprising and should be labeled as one of these rare phenomena that should be very carefully investigated if discovered.

Next, let us consider the age distribution of fertility. Among men, there is little to say on this topic. Fertility starts after puberty and declines very slowly, persisting into old age. There are enormous differences in societal and cultural management of fatherhood, and this is one of the areas in which almost any arrangement is possible, because societies have great freedom from biological necessity in making satisfactory arrangements.

Among women, there is considerable regularity in age-specific fertility among all the human groups that have been studied. Fertility is very rare before the age of 15, but from ages 15 to 19, it increases sharply, reaching a high point in the early 20s; then it declines slowly to the early 30s, when the decline becomes sharper. Only a small proportion of births occur to women over 40, and by the age of 50, the amount of fertility remaining is insignificant (Henry 1961).

There is only one way for a population to achieve very high fertility.

252

The women must all enter sexual unions early (that is, before the age of 20), and stay in a sexual union until the fertile period is over, and have minimally short intervals between births. Individual intervals cannot become much shorter than one year, because time is required for conception to occur, for the pregnancy to develop to term, and for ovulation to be resumed after a birth. Realistically, the intervals cannot average less than about 18 months among highly fecund women who do not breast-feed their children and are more likely to be 24 to 36 months, on the average, for women who are involved in prolonged lactation. And, again, realistically, the probability of conception per month declines for older women as their fecundity is reduced by forces beyond their control (Sheps 1964). The total length of the fertile period for the average women is not 30 years (the difference between age 15 and age 45, which is the age range in which essentially all fertility occurs), but a much shorter period, on the order of 20 or 25 years. This is true because the loss of fertility is not experienced promptly at menopause but accumulates up to that point. Some women never achieve fecundity at all, some start to lose their fecundity at age 20, and this proportion *cumulates* throughout the childbearing years.

The highest Total Fertility observed in the world today occurs among the Hutterites of the United States and Canada. This population has the astonishing high rate of 10.4 livebirths born to a woman who survives to the end of the childbearing years (Sheps 1965). The Hutterite population, however, is one that has excellent health conditions and very low mortality. The incidence of infant mortality is very low, and this tends to increase the length of birth intervals on the average. Babies who die at birth or soon after are typically followed by a shorter interval to the next birth than surviving babies, who contribute to postpartum infertility. In primitive populations, where the mortality will almost surely be much higher than the Hutterite levels, Total Fertility could be expected to exceed the Hutterite levels to some extent, if all other factors were the same (Ridley 1967b). The Hutterite Total Fertility Rate has been approached by a number of other well-studied populations, such as the French Canadian population, but cannot be exceeded by much, if any, given the biological capacity of the human species (Henry 1961).

While there is only one way to maximize fertility (by taking the extreme position on all of the fertility relevant variables simultaneously), there are a number of different routes to less-than-maximum fertility. Davis and

Blake (1956) classified fertility-reducing behaviors in a form that should be useful to anthropologists, and Ridley (in preparation) reclassified the Davis and Blake list into those that operate by affecting the number of years that women are exposed to the risk of pregnancy and those that affect the probability of conception (or livebirth) per month within the fertile period. The first group of variables are primarily concerned with the practice of celibacy or sexual union throughout a woman's life. Age at marriage, stability of marriage, incidence of divorce and widowhood, and practices relative to remarriage for divorcees and widows are the usual forms in which we study the question of the length of the fertile period. The second group of variables are those that influence the frequency of pregnancy or livebirth during the fertile part of the life span, such as frequency of coitus, periods of abstinence, use of contraception and deliberate abortion, and so on.

One societal way of arranging things that leads to less-than-maximum fertility, then, is a pattern of late marriage for women or no marriage for some proportion of the potentially fertile population. This pattern has been the major way in which European populations reduced fertility in the early stages of the long-range fertility decline. This arrangement can be combined with high marital fertility for those who do marry (as in Ireland), or some moderate pattern. With all the various fertility controlling mechanisms that societies resort to, it is striking that the mean age of the childbearing schedule for women varies only between about 26 and 33 years, with the age of 30 making a useful estimate for any population where the true figure is unknown (Coale 1972).

The complex interrelationships that exist between these different variables have been investigated in real populations and have been simulated using computer models of reproduction. There are many interesting possibilities for anthropological research using knowledge of a society's practices concerning the fertility variables and fitting these into simulation models, even where the numbers are too small or for some reason are not available for empirical study of the same questions (Ridley and Sheps 1966, MacCluer 1967).

Now let us turn to a similar consideration of human mortality. One misperception of the process of mortality that can be set to rest is the belief that a high level of mortality leads to a particularly strong and vigorous population, because the weak people simply die. It can easily be shown, however, that mortality is the extreme of a process that also includes morbidity as a stage. The more mortality there is in a population, the more morbidity there will be. The individual who survives an illness that carries off others is likely to be a weakened and scarred person, vigorous only relative to his dead comrades, and much worse off than people in other populations who avoided both the mortality and morbidity.

The level of mortality that affects people at one age is very highly correlated with the level of mortality at all other ages. The factors that cause mortality to be high in infancy also cause high mortality in childhood, in adulthood, and in old age. When mortality conditions change, as they have all over the world in recent times, they affect mortality at all ages. These changes are not *linear*, that is, they do not change mortality the same amount at all ages. They are, however, predictable in more complex ways.

The overwhelming finding that has emerged from cross-national and cross-time comparisons of populations is that human mortality is an extraordinarily predictable and regular process. It is not quite true that all human populations experience mortality in the same way. During extremely disrupted periods, like those of war, famine, or epidemic disease, death can come in atypical ways. We can imagine a situation in which all of the able-bodied adult men are killed in a war or industrial accident, or one in which the Pharaoh orders all the male children born in a certain year to be killed, or one in which all the adolescent maidens are sacrificed. But while anything *can* happen, mostly it doesn't happen. Where the causes of death are many, the shape of mortality curves is highly predictable.

The basic tool we have for the analysis of mortality is the life table (which is a euphemism for its proper name, a death table). To make a life table, we ignore the renewal processes completely and simply analyze what happens to a group of people, conventionally 100,000 people, who are born together and subjected to a certain schedule of mortality. To see the implications of mortality in a real population, we estimate the probability of dying in each age interval (which can be one year or five years long) by counting the number of people who start the interval and those who die during the interval. This gives us a measure of the probability of death in the interval. Multiplying the number who start the first interval, that of age zero, by the probability of dying during the interval gives the number out of 100,000 who will die in infancy. Subtracting that number from 100,000 gives us the number who will start the next interval, that of year one, and who will be subject to the probability of dying during that interval. Calculating the next number of deaths and subtracting the deaths from the number who started the interval gives the number who start the next interval, and so on. This process is continued until there are no more people alive at the beginning of an interval. From these numbers, it is possible to calculate the number of years left to live at each age by members of the original 100,000, and one can (and does) calculate a measure of the average number of years left to live by people who start each interval. This measure is called the expectation of life at age x and is calculated for each age. The first of these, the expectation of life at birth, is the best single number measure of mortality there is, as it is free from distortions due to the age compositions of the population; furthermore, it has a clear-cut and intuitively interesting interpretation, that is, the number of years that the average person born into the society will live.

Hundreds of accurate life tables have been calculated to examine the implications for cohorts of the mortality experience of national populations at a certain point in time. From these hundreds of accurate life tables, an analytic tool called Model Life Tables has been constructed to spell out the central tendencies of the mortality experience in all known human populations (Coale and Demeny 1966). The life tables are printed out in a large book, one table for every 2.5-year change in the expectation of life at birth for females, starting with 20 years and ending with 77.5.

Certain general observations about mortality emerge from the Model Life Tables. Maximum life span, which is investigated by looking at the age of the oldest living person in the population, does not vary widely between populations, even though they may have drastically different mortality patterns. The probability of dying in the next year of life increases every year after the age of 10, sharply so in old age, so that finally around the age of 110, the probability of dying in the next year reaches totality. In very advanced populations and in backward populations, therefore, the oldest living person may be as old as 110, simply because there is a nonzero probability of reaching that age. The proportion of people who reach very old age will, of course, differ sharply. And anthropologists should keep in mind that small numbers make observations difficult to interpret. As an example, if there were one chance in a million of reaching the age of 110, one would expect to find several 110-year-old people at a time in a large nation, while in a population that numbered only a thousand, one might have to wait around century after century before observing a similar number of people. This would be true even if the mortality levels of the two populations were the same.

The age pattern of experience with mortality is very predictable. Mortality is extremely high at birth and high throughout the first year of life, declining steadily. The probability of dying in each year declines regularly from one year to the next but is still a major factor throughout childhood, until it reaches the lifelong low point, around the age of 10 years. Between the ages of 10 and 50, mortality curves are typically flat, with a very slow increase. This is true for both males and females, and it is worth pointing out explicitly that while maternal mortality is a significant cause of death during the middle years of life, mortality in general is low at these ages in all populations, relative to childhood and to old age. After the age of 50 or so, the probability of dying in each age segment starts increasing more rapidly, and this increase accelerates until there are no more members of the population left to die.

While the shape of mortality curves is similar for men and women, there is a well established tendency for women to have a better chance of survival at all ages than men of the same population. The Model Life Tables report the central tendencies of mortality for males and females separately because of these fairly small but consistent differences in age-specific mortality for the two sexes. In general, women are the hardier sex. On the average, they experience almost four years more expectation of life at birth than the men who share the same conditions with them in very favorable mortality conditions (where the expectation of life at birth is over 60 years) and show less advantage but still a consistent one, averaging about two years of expectation of life at birth under severe mortality conditions. The only condition in which women generally have higher mortality than men is in the early childbearing years (15 to 30, approximately) for populations of high mortality. Since mortality is relatively low at this period of life in general, women overall still live longer than the men of the same population. This observation is a generalization based on the observation of large well-studied populations and is not intended to suggest that other patterns cannot exist, only that they should surprise us. Where female infanticide is practiced, for instance, infant mortality is obviously going to be higher for females than males. Populations that severely handicap females at any stage of the life process, by restriction of food or access to medical care, for example, may show higher mortality for females, as happens in parts of contemporary India. The re-

sexual division of Labor?

ports of New Guinea field workers that women die much earlier than men would have to be taken seriously in this context.

Having specified some of the central tendencies of fertility and mortality that are found for well-studied populations, we can now consider the ways in which these patterns combine to produce varying populations. We are fortunate as students of "primitive" populations to be able to make use of the results of Stable Population Theory.

In the same large book that contains the Model Life Tables previously discussed (Coale and Demeny 1966), there are four sets of Model Stable Populations. These Model Stable Populations consist of the complete age-sex pyramid and vital rates (such as birth rates, death rates, growth rates, and so forth) that would be produced by the unique combination of a particular Model Life Table with particular schedules of fertility, combined without change over a long period of time. Only the first set of these Model Stable Populations, that called "West," need concern us.

These descriptions of hypothetical populations are particularly useful for anthropologists and others interested in studying the population processes of primitive societies. Fortunately for us, without going to the trouble of programming a computer simulation especially made for the situation that we want to consider, we can learn a great deal about the long-run implications of the combination of patterns of mortality with patterns of fertility. One need only accept two assumptions about the target population in order to use the Stable Models. First, one must accept the fact that the population is characterized by fertility and mortality patterns conforming to the range described above. Second, one must assume that whatever the fertility and mortality processes are, they have not changed systematically during the previous century. This second assumption is a substantial stumbling block to use of Stable Models for populations in developing countries, where public health programs will almost surely have changed the mortality conditions substantially during the recent past and where birth-control programs may currently be changing fertility patterns. This is much less of a problem for populations like the Bushmen, who are extremely remote and may be among the last people in the world to be affected by the recent declines in mortality. In any case, one is often interested in the long-range implications of population processes, rather than recent shifts, so that the Stable Models may be useful even if the contemporary situation is changing.

To use Stable Population Models, we start by eliminating (or rather

Nancy Howell — realistic?

setting aside) migration as a population process. This is necessary because migration does not have nice mathematical properties that make it very predictable in its effects, as the biological processes of birth and death do. In the absence of migration (or "for a closed population," as we tend to put it), the age distribution (which includes all the static aspects of population composition) is completely determined by a certain level of fertility plus a certain level of mortality, provided that they remain constant for a period of something less than 200 years. To put this another way, if you started with two populations with very different age distributions (and they can be of any improbable shape, provided that at least some people are in the reproductive years) and applied the same fertility and mortality to them, they will be identical in all respects except total size within 200 years. In fact, they will converge very quickly at first, and more slowly in the later stages, so that they will be very similar as soon as the whole population has been replaced (perhaps 80 years later). To restate the Stable Population Theory in the form that makes it most useful for the study of small and remote populations, one can say that in the absence of migration, the long-term persistence of a certain pattern of fertility and mortality forms a population with one and only one kind of shape. The fertility and mortality levels need not be entirely unchanging: they can fluctuate within a certain range on a random basis from one year to another, provided that they are not systematically changing in a certain direction. The fertility and mortality certainly do *not* have to be equal to one another, that is, the population can be growing or even declining, as long as it is doing so as the result of the difference between long-standing fertility and mortality levels. The special case in which the population is not growing because birth and death processes are equal is called a stationary population and is simply one stable population in a field of many.

Under stable population conditions, the static view of a population, which is what results from a census, and the dynamic view, which is formed from the study of birth and death processes, are two aspects of the same reality. Each has to be consistent with the other, and any two out of age composition, fertility, and mortality tells what the other one has to be.

These interrelations between variables provide the basis on which Stable Model Populations are useful, that is, they allow us to check the internal consistency of a number of statements about population or to determine the consequences of statements about population. For example,

259

Silberbauer (1965), in the *Bushman Survey Report*, describes a population of Naron Bushmen who live to the south of the group that I
studied. After discussing the difficulties of gaining accurate information
about the population, Silberbauer gives an age distribution and some indications of the fertility and mortality. A comparison of the age distribution given with the Stable Model Population produced by fertility and
mortality patterns such as he describes shows that those processes would
not produce an age distribution of that sort in the long run. The comparison with the Stable Model does not tell what part of his description is
wrong but only that there is a long-run incompatibility between that age
distribution, that level of fertility, and that mortality.

Similarly, Neel and Chagnon (1968) report very low fertility for the
Xavante and Yanomama peoples and a high level of infant and childhood
mortality. Over the long run, these populations must therefore be growing very slowly or even declining in size. Such populations have an age
distribution with a relatively large proportion of the population at older
ages, and the age pyramid diagram is steepsided. The age distribution
given, however, is that of a young population, with large proportions of
children and young people. The Stable Models, by acting as a template
against which to compare the empirical population, shows that we cannot
accept the hypothesis that the population has been produced by the long-
range continuation of the fertility and mortality described.

Neel and Chagnon have not clarified the source of the inconsistency in
a direct way. Probably due to the same dissatisfaction that any investigator
would feel when faced with the empirical investigation of such small-scale
remote societies, they have joined with MacCluer to pursue the study
of the Xavante and Yanomama peoples through computer simulation
models (MacCluer, Neel, and Chagnon 1971). Rather than try to establish the population composition and processes entirely from what one
sees in the field, the computer simulation approach requires using the field
situation primarily to estimate parameters. The computer models are then
used to test the internal consistency of various statements about the population, to study long-range implications, and to assess the effects of
variability in patterns over the long run. Some such strategy of combining
empirically-based estimates of parameters with computer or other models
of how the parameters fit together seems to be an essential part of the
solution of demographic problems for primitive populations. Indeed, one
could argue that the need for such a strategy brings a useful corrective to

why not?

the tendency that prevails in demography as a whole—that is, to treat all ? intellectual problems as empirical ones, which has led to a kind of atheoretical bias in demography.

In this context, then, I would like to spell out some of the hypotheses that have been developed for and out of the Bushman study. As a strategy, I recommend formulating whole sets of hypotheses before even going to the field; in fact, the study developed with only primitive hypotheses before the field trip, with all of the more general ones being developed during the analysis phase of the project.

The hypotheses formulated before going to the field for data collection could be expressed simply: we suspected that the belief that life under hunting and gathering conditions was "nasty, brutish, and short" was simply not so. Mortality was guessed to be moderate, and fertility was therefore also supposed to be moderate rather than high, since the Bushman population had neither filled the world since the Pleistocene nor gone to extinction. The moderate fertility seemed to be accomplished by means that affected the spacing of births rather than the length of the fertile period of life in women. These vague hypotheses have been amply supported in the years of research that followed.

The following list of hypotheses, developed during the Bushman study, are meant to apply to the whole range of hunting and gathering populations, contemporary and prehistoric. They are offered here, not to test them or to discuss them in any detail, but to urge, by example, the practice of formulating both general and specific hypotheses about primitive populations as a framework within which empirical data can be collected, collated, and permitted to surprise us. The hypotheses are:

(1) That hunting and gathering peoples will be characterized by the same basic biological equipment as other people currently living: that the rate of maturation, age-specific susceptibility to death from given environmental conditions, and age-specific probability of conception and live-birth will be within the already known range of these variables, all other things being equal;

(2) That mortality is the exogenous variable in hunting and gathering ? populations, the controlling variable to which other variables like fertility and migration have to adjust;

(3) That mortality will vary in primitive populations between the highest level for which our limited human fertility can compensate, that

is, an expectation of life at birth of about 18 to 20 years to about 35 or 40 years for very favorable environments like the Kalahari Desert;

primitive and prehistoric

(4) That people have very little ability to deliberately affect mortality;

(5) That fertility will range from high to moderate, that is, total fertilities of about 10 down to about five;

(6) That people have considerable ability to influence fertility consciously and unconsciously;

(7) That population growth will be more frequent and more substantial in populations where mortality is moderate than those where it is high;

(8) That migration will be used as an adjustment mechanism for whole populations when mortality conditions worsen and for segments of societies that are growing;

(9) That populations at moderate mortality levels (like the Bushmen) will reproduce at less than the biological maximum and will arrange their societies to permit fertility-reducing customs such as optional marriage, periods of celibacy in marriage, and lack of widow remarriage, while populations that consistently have high mortality rates will require customs that lead to maximum fertility (one should be able to locate societies that have adjusted to consistently high mortality by their fertility-maximizing institutions);

(10) Finally, that adjustment to demographic realities will constrain hunting and gathering societies in basic ways and that similarities in demographic conditions will produce identifiable "types" of hunting and gathering societies that will have more in common than simply their vital rates. Institutions like religion and kinship will show the effects of demographic processes, and these similarities will be detectable between societies within similar demographic processes, even if there is considerable cultural distance.

Realistic to assume range of large populations set the bounds for small population? what local adaptations and local rates?

13
Historical Demography of a Navajo Community[1]

KENNETH MORGAN

Department of Anthropology
University of New Mexico

Generally cultural evolution is characterized by the development of more effective means of energy transformation, higher levels of sociocultural integration, and greater adaptional potential. The other aspect of cultural evolution, the specific, refers to the adaptive modification of particular cultures. According to Sahlins (1960:24), "Logically as well as empirically, it follows that as the problems of survival vary, cultures accordingly change, that culture undergoes phylogenetic adaptive development." Faced with environmental changes due to nature and the presence of other cultures, particular cultures frequently develop special features solely for the preservation of their basic structures and orientations (Harding 1960).

From the time of the emergence of culture until the beginning of the Neolithic Revolution, human populations were small and widely dispersed. During this period, an estimated 12 to 32 billion births occurred. By around 6000 B.C., it is estimated that the human population totaled about five million (Desmond 1965). The characteristic level of sociocultural integration for the Paleolithic era was the band. Throughout this longest period of human evolution, there were no forms of economy more advanced than hunting-gathering (Service 1962). Given the limited technological capacity of band culture, we might suppose that the demographic history of any given group was strongly influenced by the natural environment. The history of band populations had probably been one of extensive reshuffling of membership over long periods of time and fluctuations in size over shorter periods. Today, few representatives of these populations remain. With the rise of tribal and, later, more advanced stages of cultural evolution, the only hunting-gathering bands to survive cultural transformation or extinction were those pushed into marginal areas of little economic significance. However, as these areas and their primitive societies become the concern of the more dominant cultures, the primitive populations must develop new effective modes of adaptation, or they will disappear.

The focus of this chapter is the transitional character of a small, growing American Indian population. The Ramah Navajo band constituted the founding of this population in the American Southwest between 1869 and 1890. The territory of the Ramah Navajo has never been included within the boundaries of the Navajo Reservation proper, and it is separated from other Navajo groups contiguous to the reservation by intervening populations of non-Navajos. In many respects, the community still follows traditional Navajo ways of life. With regard to the influences of American culture, acculturation of the Ramah Navajo proceeded very slowly during the earlier decades of their history and has accelerated only in very recent decades.

Since 1870, when the total population is estimated to have numbered approximately 10,000, the Navajo Tribe has experienced very rapid and sustained growth. Today, the Reservation Navajo area population is in excess of 130,000 individuals. Furthermore, growth of the Ramah Navajo population has proved to be even more dramatic than that of the Reservation Navajo. This community, which has experienced periods of high mortality and some deterioration of its environment, has grown from approximately 100 individuals in 1890 to around 1,400 in 1971.

It is to be expected that a particular culture's responses to major environmental changes will include modification of its demographic structure. In turn, changes in demographic structure will modify the operation of evolutionary forces in a small population. The demographic history of the Ramah Navajo population is characterized by changing patterns of fertility, mortality, and migration. Furthermore, the information on this population is endowed with historical perspective, considerable accuracy, and detail with regard to both its demography and ethnography. The Ramah Navajo community is considered *transitional* in the sense that it originated as a small natural community of a widely dispersed primitive society and has developed into a larger, still-growing population with decreased isolation from, and increased dependency on, a dominant, more powerful society. Although confronted by continuing acculturative pressures, a growing population, and limited local resources, this community is attempting to preserve traditional ways of life. It is hoped that this study will provide some insights into the kinds of responses and their implications for genetic demographic models of small human populations in cultural transition.[2]

HISTORY, ECOLOGY, AND TECHNOLOGY

As of 1 January 1971, the Navajo population of the Navajo area was estimated to be 129,422 individuals—64,070 males and 65,352 females (Navajo Area Population Register 1970). Representing about one-fifth of the Indian population of the United States in the early 1960s, most of the Navajo reside in a reservation area of approximately 24,000 square miles, which extends over northeastern Arizona, northwestern New Mexico, and parts of southern Utah. In addition, many Navajos live on lands adjacent to the reservation boundaries, particularly to the east and south. Estimates of the population by administrative districts and major communities in the Navajo area on 1 April 1971 are given in Figure 36. However, substantial numbers of Navajos are in permanent residence beyond the boundaries of the reservation, primarily in a few major cities of the United States, and in temporary residence throughout the western States during the late spring and summer months while engaged in migratory agricultural work. The estimated proportion of total Navajos enrolled in the tribe who constituted the reservation-proper population was four-fifths in 1950 and two-thirds in 1960 (Johnston 1966).

The Ramah Navajo community, which is the focus of this study, is located on nonreservation lands about 75 miles east and south of "Big Navajo" (the Navajo reservation). Presently, the Ramah Navajo community numbers almost 1,500 individuals.

With respect to most indices of acculturation, the Navajo have re-

265

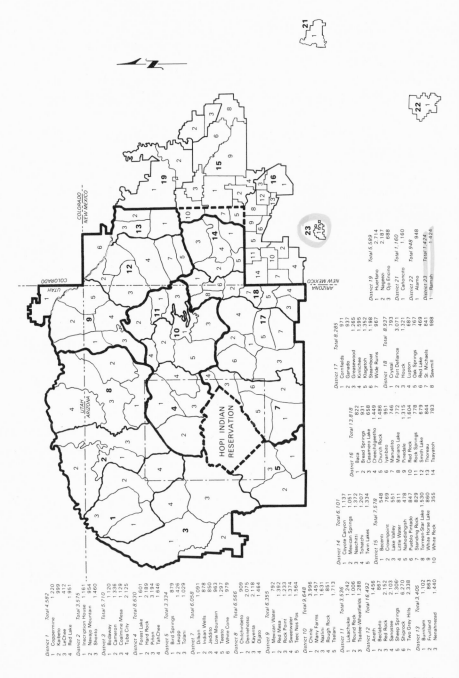

FIGURE 36. Estimates of population in the Navajo area by administrative districts and major communities on 1 April 1971. Source: Office of Information & Statistics, Bureau of Indian Affairs.

mained one of the least acculturated groups in the United States. Johnston regards the Navajo as typical of populations of the underdeveloped regions of the world, for they still maintain many values that are common to preliterate, preindustrial peoples. Typical of the manifestations of traditional values is a high rate of fertility. Combined with reduced mortality, this high fertility has led to a large population increase over the past one hundred years. The average annual rate of growth between 1870 and 1957 has been estimated at 2.33 percent (Johnston 1966). The estimate for the period 1950 through 1961–62 is even higher—2.56 percent per annum. Since January 1965, the Bureau of Indian Affairs, Navajo Agency, has been projecting the Navajo area population—with yearly adjustments for the ages under five years—at an annual rate of growth of 2.5 percent (Wise 1972). As will be seen, the Ramah Navajo population has experienced even more remarkable rates of growth.

A Brief Summary of Navajo History

Kluckhohn and Leighton (1962) provide a good discussion of the history of the Navajo people. The following summary of their material is presented as background information on the origins of the Ramah Navajo band. Other excellent sources of information on the history of the Navajo Tribe are to be found in the works of Johnston (1966) and Young (1961, 1968).

The Navajo and Apache are Athapaskan-speaking peoples whose ancestors arrived in the Southwest after A.D. 1000. The ancestors of the Navajo and Apache were originally hunting-gathering bands that ranged over extensive, forested regions of Alaska and western Canada. In their migration to the mountain, steppe, and desert zones of the Southwest, the ancestral populations acquired traits of the Intermontane and Plains cultures.

Navajo culture is syncretic. Agricultural techniques, weaving, and a matrilineal clan system developed from the early contacts with Pueblo peoples. Even the complex ceremonialism of the Navajo is, to some extent, a development of the early eras of Pueblo contact. Consolidation of the many different traits acquired from the Pueblos and other neighboring tribes into an independent, sociocultural organization of Navajos began before the eighteenth century, although a Navajo "tribe," in the true political sense, did not exist at that time (Hill 1940).

267

Significant developments in various aspects of Navajo culture again took place during the Spanish-Mexican period (1626–1846). The introduction of domesticated animals, particularly sheep and goats along with some horses and cattle, and the associated complex of pastoral traits was the result of contact with European culture primarily by way of Pueblo influences. Intensive contact with Pueblo peoples brought the Navajo new techniques in agriculture, weaving, and pottery making. In addition, Navajo social organization underwent modification, and new elements appeared in Navajo myth and ritual. An increase in the Navajo population was supported by the changes in ecological exploitation. Agricultural surpluses, livestock, and their derived products provided a source of wealth that extended the range of economic activities. This wealth fostered increased trading with other peoples and permitted the acquisition of metal tools and other manufactured goods. Gradually, the technological and economic transition of Navajo culture brought about a dependency on materials and manufactured articles of the European and American markets.

By the time the United States officials and settlers arrived to take possession of the southwestern territories from Mexico in 1846, the Navajo were adept at mounting raiding expeditions for the capture of livestock and occasional slaves. With the arrival of larger numbers of American settlers in the Southwest, punitive expeditions against the Navajo became the rule in response to perceived "treaty" violations (McNitt 1972).

The true character of Navajo social organization, it must be emphasized, was not appreciated by the Spanish, Mexican, and American governments. There was no political unit larger than the numerous, small communities of Navajos. The governments erred in assuming that they were dealing with a Navajo "nation." No collection of Navajo communities or individuals ever had the interest, much less the power, to represent all Navajos (Hill 1940, McNitt 1972).

In June 1863, Colonel Kit Carson entered Navajo country with specific instructions to destroy all crops, fruit trees, and livestock that could be found. The results of these forays were disastrous for the Navajo; by the following spring, the Navajos who had not been captured were faced with impending starvation. The first Navajo prisoners were sent back to their people with a message from Carson: Surrender at Fort Defiance, Arizona, or face eventual death.

268

Kenneth Morgan

In early 1864, Navajos began to surrender in substantial numbers at Fort Defiance. During the next two years, more than 8,000 Navajos were forced to make the "Long Walk" of 300 miles from Fort Defiance to Fort Sumner, New Mexico. A number of Navajo bands managed to escape captivity by scattering into inaccessible regions of their territory, but the overwhelming majority of Navajos, along with a much smaller number of Apaches who were brought to Fort Sumner in 1863, were to experience the miseries and degradation of mass captivity during the four-year period from 1864 to 1868.

June 1968 marked the centennial of the signing of the treaty of peace and the release of the Navajos from captivity. The reservation area designated to them in 1868 contained less than one-quarter of the area they had occupied before captivity.[3] Those who returned to homes that were within the boundaries of the new reservation found the dwellings destroyed and the livestock removed. Many of the Navajos were forced to migrate from place to place in search of land to plant some crops or graze what few stock they had managed to retain. Delays in government issue of seed, tools, and livestock, and the crop destruction caused by the late snow and drought of 1868, forced the army to continue regular distribution of rations at Fort Wingate and Fort Defiance to large numbers of destitute Navajos.

Finally, in the fall of 1869, the first general distribution of sheep took place at Fort Defiance. The Navajos, however, still had to face several years of severe drought, forcing many of them to migrate again. In the 1868-1888 20-year period that followed the release of the Navajo from captivity, the founding of the Ramah Navajo community can be documented.

The Ramah Area and the Navajo Community

Located in the southern part of the northwestern quarter of New Mexico, the territory presently occupied by the Ramah Navajo is scattered over a region bounded on the west by the Zuni Indian Reservation line and extending southward and eastward from the Mormon village of Ramah. The Ramah Navajo Chapter is represented on the Navajo Tribal Council by a single delegate elected by the members of the community. The territory, on the other hand, has never been included within the boundaries of the Navajo Reservation (see Figure 36). In addition, the Ramah Navajo are separated from other Navajo groups contiguous to

269

"Big Navajo" by intervening populations of Pueblo Indians, Spanish Americans, and Anglo Americans. The Mormon farming community of Ramah numbered about 300 individuals during the mid-1960s. Detailed information on the history of the community and its jurisdiction has been provided elsewhere (Morgan 1968, Kluckhohn 1966).

The Ramah area, as defined by Landgraf (1954), includes Indian and non-Indian populations and approximates a rectangle of about 18 miles from east to west by about 30 miles from north to south. Within this area of approximately 504 square miles, only a little more than half of all the land is available to members of the Navajo community. The better sections of the area are located almost exclusively in the most northern and eastern localities—for instance, the Mormon farming community and village are located in the two northwestern localities. The better lands are controlled by non-Indians, although they originally were the territory of the Ramah Navajo band before and into the Navajo founding period.

The geographical environment of the Ramah area has been described in detail by Landgraf. The area ranges from 7,000 feet above sea level in the southwest to 8,000 feet in the northwest and is characterized by mesas, extensive lava plains and flat drainages, and small canyons cut into semi-arid land. The wild vegetation of the area is composed of piñon and juniper trees, as well as numerous species of annual and perennial wild plants.

The environment of the Ramah area is effectively semiarid. Precipitation is very irregular with regard to both temporal and spatial patterns. The evaporation rate and alkali contents of the soils are high. Water supplies from sources other than precipitation are comparatively meager. Furthermore, the geological structure of the area results in the rapid movement of ground water to depths effectively beyond surface use. Thus, rainfall becomes "the primary, hazardous variable" affecting the economy of this region (Landgraf).

Landgraf's study indicated that by 1941, the Ramah area was unsuitable for agricultural pursuits. The ecology of the Ramah region would not long support any population dependent on plant cultivation. Although the region appeared more suitable for relatively open grazing, it was obvious that all parts of the area had suffered decreases in the quality and carrying-capacity of the land. The most pervasive factor in the deterioration of the land seems to have resulted from the overgrazing of grass and other forage plants. Secondary in importance were the effects of plowing, followed by the abandoning of fields in Mormon farming practices. Furthermore, destructive hunting of wild animal life has been practiced by inhabitants of the area since the 1870s. By 1941, hunting of larger game animals could no longer provide any regular proportion of local food income.

The technological history of the Ramah Navajo is one of an early and progressive movement away from a hunting-gathering culture. The Navajo economic patterns of 1941 included wagework, various types of subsistence farming, and livestock husbandry. Recent economic patterns may be appreciated from the summary of the labor force survey conducted in September 1963 as a part of the Ramah Chapter Community Census. Of the total 413 adults (both sexes included) surveyed, 220 individuals— or almost half of the adults—were engaged in seasonal employment as their main source of income. Only 65 adults held steady employment, while 90 individuals received their main support from welfare and other assistance benefits. The remaining individuals included 34 students engaged in part-time employment at school facilities and four individuals in the armed services. (For additional details on the economy of the Ramah Navajo community, see Morgan 1968.)

Growth of the land-based subsistence economy has not been able to keep up with the growth of the population. Not only has the size of the Ramah Navajo land base been effectively limited, but the Ramah area has suffered ecological deterioration. In addition, there is a declining American market for poorer quality lambs and wool, which are the products of outmoded practices employed by many Ramah Navajos. Good farming land is scarce, and most horticultural practices remain unsophisticated and often are self-defeating in the long run. In recent years, wagework and welfare have increased in importance as sources of income. But for most families, wagework still follows a sporadic pattern, and there are very few opportunities open to the Navajos for regular, substantial employment in the Ramah area. Very recently, however, increased employment opportunities have resulted from the establishment of the Ramah Navajo Bureau of Indian Affairs offices and the Ramah Navajo High School in July 1970. This has also resulted in a small influx of Ramah Navajos back into the community.

There are three ecologically distinct regions of physiographic unity in the Ramah area that dictate variously successful economic pursuits. Reynolds, Lamphere, and Cook (1967) point out that categories of wealth in the Ramah Navajo community generally correspond to ecological dis-

271

tribution of land holdings among families. The wealthier Navajos engage in little farming but control the larger flocks of sheep numbering over 300 head. These families control portions of land that are located in the lava bed zones. In addition, some members of these families participate in steady wagework. Solely on the basis of sheep holdings, the wealthier class is also the smallest, containing, perhaps, 5 to 10 percent of all families (Kluckhohn 1966).

The average-income families cultivate larger fields on the drainage bottoms of the "hill and valley" locality and graze flocks of 100 to 300 head of sheep on the hills. Some of these people engage in occasional wagework and also receive some welfare. In recent decades, they have represented about 15 to 20 percent of all families.

Finally, the poorer families have land that is generally located in the poorest ecological zone, for example, in the southwestern corner of the Ramah area. They have few sheep, if any, do some farming, engage in occasional wagework, and are the recipients of sizable amounts of welfare. In 1949 and 1951, 44 percent of Ramah Navajo families owned no sheep. An additional 29 to 37 percent had flocks numbering 100 head or less. Thus, if the conditions of the 1950s represent approximately those of the 1960s in the Ramah Navajo community, as many as three-fourths of all families would be placed in the "poor" category.

It must be pointed out, however, that "families" do not exactly correspond to the main units of Navajo social organization in the Ramah community (Reynolds, Lamphere, and Cook). The natural unit on which to base a rigorous discussion of the distribution of wealth in the community would seem to be the residence group. Unfortunately, this type of analysis is not presently available. Finally, with the fragmentation of the larger cooperative units (or "outfits")[4] since about the 1940s, the very large flocks of sheep, those numbering in the thousands, are no longer present. The trend toward more numerous and smaller herds in recent decades reflects primarily the fragmentation of outfits.

DEMOGRAPHIC HISTORY OF THE RAMAH NAVAJO

From documentary evidence, it can be concluded that in the beginning of the eighteenth century, the territory of the Navajo included or extended

272

very close to the northern region of the Ramah area. Older Navajo informants attested to hunting and farming in the Ramah region from about 1840 onward. Before the period of captivity at Fort Sumner, fields were planted by several Navajo families just above the head of the present-day Ramah reservoir, as well as in the vicinity of Nutria and Pescado (which are present-day Zuni farming villages).[5]

Following their release from captivity, seven families of the original residents returned to the Ramah region (Landgraf 1954). During the founding period of the population (about 1869 to 1890), this core group was joined by male relatives, their wives, and children. Many of the founder males were biological or clan relatives. By the end of the founding period, there were approximately 70 living individuals residing in the population who constituted about 11 families.[6] Early in this first period, families lived in small residence units scattered in the northern part of the Ramah area.

The founding period was characterized by fluctuating residence for many individuals and some families—a reflection of the generally disruptive conditions that began about two decades before Navajo captivity at Fort Sumner and continued throughout most of the founding period. Furthermore, the period of 1876 through 1882 saw the arrival of Mormon missionaries to the Ramah region and the establishment of Ramah village by the Mormons. Additional Anglo American and Spanish American communities bordering the Ramah area became well established after 1890.

During the period from 1890 through the early 1920s, large numbers (relative to the Ramah Navajo population at that time) of non-Indian settlers moved into and adjacent to the territory that was the domain of the Ramah Navajo band. The Navajo community could not effectively counter the increasing infringement of its territorial rights and, typically, responded by scattering into localities toward the south. The territory of the Ramah Navajo community became restricted, generally, to regions unsuitable for farming or cattle grazing.

During the stabilization period, about 1890–1920, the Navajo population received no new biological families. The volume of migration was small and composed mostly of in-migrating males, along with a few children who accompanied an in-migrating parent or who came to live with relatives upon the death of a mother. Since 1890 (except for a few recent adult migrants), adults have generally entered the population through

273

marriage. The former adults, however, are relatives of previous migrants to the community.

Only one allotment of land from public domain was made to a Navajo individual before 1920. Almost all of the granting of allotments by the government to the Ramah Navajos took place from 1920 through the 1930s. The allotment period, about 1920–40, is characterized by the beginning of a rise in the volume of migration with respect to the Ramah Navajo population. After this period, the pattern of migration shows movement of entire families as well as young adult individuals to and from the Ramah Navajo community.

The last 24 years, about 1940–64, make up the fourth period of Ramah Navajo history. During this period, fragmentation of the original Ramah Navajo outfits occurred (Reynolds, Lamphere, and Cook 1967). This fragmentation is, in part, a result of the death of the heads of outfits, who were members of the first two generations, and the dispersion of sibling groups of the recent generations of Ramah Navajos. This dispersion has come about through marriage and increased opportunities for wagework, education, and travel. In addition to these factors that have contributed to the reduction of the area maintained by an outfit and to the dispersion of its members over the entire Ramah territory, population growth may be implicated. Thus, an increasing population has become a burden for the limited resources of land, sheep, and water controlled by the community. However, these developments do *not* imply a "disintegration" of the Ramah Navajo population. Rather, diachronic analysis of the residence-group cycle demonstrates "that social units among the Navajo are coherently organized to form a system in which synchronic variation is an important characteristic. . . . As growth and fission continue over another generation, a dispersed sibling group becomes an outfit. These outfits eventually break up, and new ones are formed to include those who are related to common grandparents of a later generation" (Reynolds, Lamphere, and Cook 1967: 198).

Growth of the Ramah Navajo Population

The history of the Ramah Navajo, we have noted, may be conveniently divided into four periods that span the years 1869 through 1964. We now want to consider some general patterns of growth of the Ramah Navajo population. The basic data for various demographic estimates are given

TABLE 32

DISTRIBUTIONS OF EVENTS OCCURRING WITH REFERENCE TO THE RAMAH NAVAJO POPULATION FROM THE FOUNDING PERIOD (1869–89) TO THE CLOSING DATE OF THE CENSUS DATA (31 DECEMBER 1964)

Distribution of Individuals According to Type of Event

Periods: Intervals of Years	Livebirths			In-migrants		Deaths			Out-migrants	
	Males	Females	Sex Not Known	Males	Females	Males	Females	Sex Not Known	Males	Females
1869–89	12	18	—	25	24	4	4	—	—	—
1890–94	15	17	—	3	2	2	4	—	—	—
1895–99	20	20	1	2	—	2	3	—	—	—
1900–04	27	19	3	1	1	3	3	1	1	—
1905–09	27	21	—	1	—	7	6	3	—	—
1910–14	21	22	1	1	1	12	5	1	1	—
1915–19	37	40	2	5	1	18	16	2	1	—
1920–24	36	38	3	—	—	18	20	3	—	—
1925–29	33	37	—	2	—	21	23	—	1	—
1930–34	42	43	1	4	5	23	16	1	2	3
1935–39	55	59	—	9	5	24	20	1	3	5
1940–44	59	74	1	6	8	30	30	—	9	8
1945–49	67	68	—	7	8	21	25	—	10	—
1950–54	72	74	—	12	19	23	19	1	12	15
1955–59	83	85	1	8	9	18	7	—	6	6
1960–64	102	98	—	8	10	18	14	—	6	6
1869–1964	708	733	13	94	93	244	215	13	52	43

in Table 32. Events are grouped into five-year periods, except for the first period, the founding period, which spans 21 years for the purpose of this study. The method used in composing the migration distributions is presented in detail in a later section.

The demographic history of the Ramah Navajo is not that of a closed population. During the founding period, the growth of the population was primarily the result of in-migration. Most of the in-migrating individuals were adults who had already contracted fertile matings before their entrance into the population. In addition, during these earlier years, there must have been strong social pressures to stabilize interfamily relationships by marriage. Characteristically, the founding of small, human populations is selective. Although there is some bias toward the preferential inclusion of fertile young adults in the data for the founding period, undoubtedly the actual conditions of this period supported early marriages, large families, and polygamy. With the emphasis on the development of larger cooperative units, or outfits, an individual did not remain unmated for long—socioeconomic considerations dictated the arrangement of marriages by parents, and, especially, maternal uncles. In addition, large families were desirable and not a burden to a society that was organized into cooperative units (including many nuclear families) and was directed toward the exploitation of a new and extensive territory.

Thus, the conditions of the founding period and the early years of the stabilization period favored a "cohort" of potentially highly fertile individuals. That this situation was actually realized may be seen in the various estimates of population growth given in Table 33. Note, further, that the annual rates of growth for the stabilization period, 1890–1919, decline steadily except for the decade of 1910–19. The large decline for 1910–14 reflects two factors: (1) a decrease in male livebirths relative to the preceding five-year values, and (2) an increase in the number of male deaths. The average annual rates of growth during the allotment period, 1920–39, fluctuate considerably. As will be shown shortly, the periods falling within the years 1915–44 are characterized by higher levels of mortality than those of the preceding or following periods. Finally, we note the trend of increasing average annual rates of growth that characterize the fourth period of Ramah Navajo history. The years of 1945–64 are characterized by a strong trend of declining mortality and a weak trend of apparently declining fertility. Assuming a total population of 1,444 individuals as of 15 October 1971, and a census figure of 1,047 for September–

TABLE 33
ANNUAL RATES OF GROWTH FOR FIVE-YEAR PERIODS
OF THE SEX-KNOWN AND TOTAL POPULATIONS
OF THE RAMAH NAVAJO, 1890–1964

Intervals of Years	Annual Rates of Growth (Percent)*		
	Males	Females	Total†
1890–94	7.91	6.66	7.25
1895–99	6.84	5.57	6.34
1900–04	5.97	4.35	5.36
1905–09	4.08	3.17	3.31
1910–14	1.52	3.24	2.36
1915–19	3.43	3.78	3.61
1920–24	2.32	2.34	2.34
1925–29	1.52	1.65	1.60
1930–34	2.25	3.33	2.85
1935–39	3.43	3.58	3.46
1940–44	2.11	3.45	2.81
1945–49	3.05	2.71	2.87
1950–54	2.99	3.21	3.11
1955–59	3.48	3.70	3.60
1960–64	3.73	3.36	3.53

* The rate is $r_i = \dfrac{\log_e (P_i/P_{i-1})}{n} \times 100$, where P_i is the living population at the end of the ith period, P_{i-1} is the living population at the end of the preceding period, and $n = 5$, or the number of years in a period. Thus, the formula:

$$\frac{P_i}{P_{i-1}} = e^{rn}.$$

† Includes sex-unknown births and deaths.

October 1963—both figures may be overestimates—we arrive at an average annual rate of growth of 4.0 percent.

The growth rates of Table 33 are generally very high. Thus, the first doubling of the population took place within 10 to 15 years after the end of the founding period, as shown in Table 34. After this initial period of very high fertility, growth slowed somewhat, and the second doubling of the population occurred about 15 to 20 years later. By this time, the population had already entered the periods of relatively high mortality, and a third doubling of the population did not take place until an additional 25 to 30 years had passed. By the end of the final period, 1960–64, the population had almost again doubled in size for the fourth time since the end of the founding period.

Census estimates for the Ramah Navajo obtained after the close of my field research in 1966 are not consistent. Thus, Figure 36 shows an estimated 1,424 individuals as of 1 April 1971. However, a report from the Ramah Navajo Bureau of Indian Affairs (BIA) offices prepared in 1971 implies that the Ramah population numbered only 1,399 individuals for April 1971. The figure of 1,444 as of 15 October 1971 was supplied by an office worker at the Ramah Navajo BIA and is thus more consistent with the Navajo Area BIA estimate shown in Figure 36. Nevertheless, the Ramah BIA report prepared in the fall of 1971 projects the population at a rate of very nearly 4.0 percent per annum.

TABLE 34
SIZE OF THE TOTAL RAMAH NAVAJO POPULATION
AT THE END OF THE FOUNDING PERIOD AND EACH
SUBSEQUENT FIVE-YEAR PERIOD, FOR THE
YEARS 1889–1964

Year	Total Population at End of Year	Year	Total Population at End of Year
1889	71	1929	354
1894	102	1934	408
1899	140	1939	485
1904	183	1944	558
1909	216	1949	644
1914	243	1954	752
1919	291	1959	900
1924	327	1964	1,074

Migration and Stability of Residence[7]

The rate of population growth, as defined in Table 33, is a combination of natural increase and net migration. The Ramah Navajo population is obviously not a "closed" population; thus, the contribution of net migration to population growth must be assessed.

With regard to numbers of individuals, migration contributes little to immediate population growth after the founding period. Thus, from the data given in Table 32, in-migration after 1889 contributed a total of 138 individuals, while out-migration resulted in a loss of 95 individuals—a net gain of 43 individuals due to migration between the end of 1889 and the end of 1964. During this same period, there were 1,424 livebirths and 464 deaths, resulting in a net gain of 960 individuals. But, more important, the history of migration displays some interesting patterns with regard to sociohistorical changes in the population.

Characteristically, the founding period has the highest rates of in-migration and—partly because of the method used in composing the population data—exhibits no out-migration. Furthermore, only a single individual from the founding period population, a founder male, emigrated permanently. The first instance of permanent out-migration did not occur until the period 1900–04. This individual was a male; female out-migration, as defined in this study, did not begin until the end of the allotment period, during 1935–39.

Traditionally, in a matrilineal society, matrilocality would be preferred, following, in some instances, a short period of bilocality during the early years of marriage. Thus, higher rates of in-migration and out-migration would be expected for males, in comparison with females, under social conditions that supported the building up of large matrilineal units. The migration rates before the fourth period of Ramah Navajo history, shown in Table 35, are consistent with these expectations. However, since marital residence choice is dependent on the opportunities for male resource control in a Navajo communtiy, changes in the residence pattern will result from modifications of social organization that affect resource control and authority.

The shift toward higher volumes of female migration during approximately the first half of the fourth historical period (see Table 35) reflects the fissioning of the large cooperative units, accompanied by a diminished significance of matrilocality. In general, the residence cycle, the character of resource control, and the delegation of authority within an extended family result, over the long run, in a distinction between Navajo social organization and other matrilineal systems (Reynolds, Lamphere, and Cook 1967). Dispersed extended families do not permit the building up of large corporate matrilineages. Since Navajo livestock economy is based on small animals, and since ownership is maintained by both male and female individuals, especially during the recent history of the Ramah com-

TABLE 35
AVERAGE ESTIMATES OF CRUDE RATES OF
IN-MIGRATION, OUT-MIGRATION, AND NET
MIGRATION FOR EACH FIVE-YEAR PERIOD OF
THE RAMAH NAVAJO POPULATION, 1890–1964*

Historical Period and Intervals of Years	Average Annual Crude Migration Rates (per 1,000 mid-interval population)†						
	In-migration			Out-migration			Net
	Males	Fe-males	Both Sexes	Males	Fe-males	Both Sexes	Both Sexes
Stabilization period							
1890–94	7.1	4.7	11.8	—	—	—	+11.8
1895–99	3.4	—	3.4	—	—	—	+ 3.4
1900–04	1.3	1.3	2.6	1.3	—	1.3	+ 1.3
1905–09	1.0	—	1.0	—	—	—	+ 1.0
1910–14	0.9	0.9	1.8	0.9	—	0.9	+ 0.9
1915–19	3.8	0.8	4.6	0.8	—	0.8	+ 3.8
Allotment period							
1920–24	—	—	—	—	—	—	—
1925–29	1.2	—	1.2	0.6	—	0.6	+ 0.6
1930–34	2.1	2.6	4.7	1.0	—	1.0	+ 3.7
1935–39	4.0	2.3	6.3	1.4	1.4	2.8	+ 3.5
Fragmentation of outfits							
1940–44	2.3	3.1	5.4	3.5	1.9	5.4	+ 0.0
1945–49	2.3	2.7	5.0	3.3	2.7	6.0	− 1.0
1950–54	3.4	5.5	8.9	3.4	4.3	7.7	+ 1.2
1955–59	1.9	2.2	4.1	1.5	1.5	3.0	+ 1.1
1960–64	1.6	2.0	3.6	1.2	1.2	2.4	+ 1.2

* The mid-interval (or mid-period, demographic) population is calculated for the ith interval as follows:

$$P_i = P_{i-1}(e^{2.5r_i}),$$

where P_{i-1} and r_i are as defined at the foot of Table 33.

† As an example calculation of an average annual crude rate, let us take the male in-migration rate for the ith interval; thus:

[1000 × ⅕(number of male immigrants, ith interval)]/$\overline{P}_i$.

All of the rates for the ith interval (or demographic period of 5 years) have the same base, that is, the estimated mid-interval population, $\overline{P}_i$.

munity, the result is an emphasis on individual rather than corporate livestock ownership and on the use-rights to land. The livestock belonging to the individuals of a residence group are controlled by the oldest male. In passing control of resources to another member of his camp, this male will always favor his wife, son, or son-in-law over his matrilineal relatives. Continued over several generations, resource control can be seen to pass to males who are members of different matrilineages. The building up of large matrilineal units is thereby prevented. At the same time, the residence group receives support as the main unit of Navajo social organization (Reynolds, Lamphere, and Cook).

However, we again want to emphasize that the system of Navajo social units is characterized by coherent organization and synchronic variation. Thus, the "fission-fusion" nature of outfit development during the history of a Navajo community is to be considered an orderly and recurrent phenomenon of Navajo social organization. Most probably, the apparent reduction and stabilization of migration rates during the last part of the fourth historical period (1955–64), as shown in Table 35, reflect the beginning of fusion of extended family residence groups into new outfits— according to Reynolds and his associates, "the present fourth- and fifth-generation sibling groups are beginning to form new outfits, with third-generation males as heads."

The majority of in-migration during the period 1890–1950 followed upon an earlier arranged marriage (Kluckhohn 1956). Much of the remaining in-migration during these years "was simply an extension of patterns of relationship established in the 'founding' period."[8] Since the 1940s, a large proportion of the immigrants have been young children. Likewise, out-migration since the 1940s also reflects the movement of young families, in addition to the predominant pattern of migration upon marriage. Ramah males who have married out of the population often return with their wives and few young children to reside in the population, with varying permanency depending on the occupation of the husband and his opportunity to gain control of resources within the extended family. A number of individuals still retain ownership in small livestock and homes in the community but reside out of the population for the greater amount of the time.

In general, once the family becomes stabilized in the socioeconomic network of a community, subsequent residence changes are rare, except for visiting in the community of the other spouse for as much as several months out of a year (Kluckhohn 1956). Of course, the opportunities to visit in the Ramah community vary with the distance of the family's non-Ramah residence from the community. And the increasing opportunities for education, travel, and employment outside of the Ramah area in recent decades make it unlikely that the recent out-migration upon marriage will result eventually in the return of many of these individuals—with or without their families—to the community. Recently, however, there has been an influx of Ramah Navajos back into the community as a result of increased employment opportunities in July 1970.

One aspect of migration that deserves some additional consideration is the age distribution of migrating individuals. Discrepancies that arise between investigators in the estimation of in-migration and out-migration rates can often be attributed to different criteria used for the inclusion or exclusion of an individual from "membership" in the population. These criteria are based, to some extent, on the age of the individual at the time of change in status and his length of stay in the population. Both of these attributes of migration, in addition, have significance for population growth and the operation of evolutionary forces.

Thus, in-migration before the reproductive age (before age 14) does not immediately contribute to the effective breeding size of the population. My previous calculations (Morgan 1968) show that 41.2 percent of all in-migration between 1869 and 1964 is distributed among the ages under 15 years. In addition, the younger the child at the time of his entrance into the population, the more probable it is that his mortality experience, opportunities for mating, and so forth will be similar to those of an individual born in the population. Especially for females, in-migration after age 40 effectively denies them the opportunity to contribute to the population, except, of course, by way of immigrant offspring. Thus, 4.8 percent of all immigrants were age 40 or older at their time of entrance into the population. The remaining proportion of in-migration, 54 percent, is distributed among the ages at risk for reproduction. Some of these individuals enter the community with a growing family and will continue their reproduction as members of the community. Those individuals who enter the population during the reproductive years upon marriage, while engaged in a stable productive marriage or at high risk for mating within the population, extend the effective mating pool beyond the areal boundaries of the community. Of course, after the founding period and the first five years of the stabilization period, this additional "immediate" source of mates was relatively small in proportion to the total population. On the other hand, these individuals are genetically important because they are the survivors of early mortality pressures, and almost all of them contributed offspring who remained in the population for varying lengths of time.

Similar considerations apply with regard to age at time of permanent out-migration. Thus, out-migration before the reproductive age (under 14 years) will affect the composition of the mating pool at some later date. This group of emigrants composes 33.7 percent of all out-migration. Individuals who leave the population at age 40 or older—8.4 percent of all out-migration—are of minor significance. In general, if an individual and his immediate family are well integrated in the socioeconomic networks of the community, it is rather unlikely that they will emigrate. The remaining out-migration, about 58 percent, is distributed among the reproductive ages, and most of this among the ages 15 through 29 years. The bulk of this out-migration—as well as that of the temporary migration that is not estimated by these procedures—follows upon a first marriage to a non-Ramah individual. In the early half of the fourth historical period, out-migration during the productive years of life, along with movement of children, also reflects economic considerations.

The probability that an immigrant individual will contribute offspring to the population, and the degree of his contribution, will depend on his age at time of in-migration and his length of stay in the population. As previously mentioned, only one male of the total founding period population (with the exception of prefounders, who are not included in the population figures) emigrated permanently from the community. Of the total of 95 emigrants, 60, or about 63 percent, were born in the population. Thus, nonresident-born individuals (immigrants) who do not remain in the population until death constituted approximately 37 percent of the out-migration total. Furthermore, if we exclude the single founder individual, then these remaining 34 emigrants (18 males and 16 females) were drawn from a total of 138 immigrants who entered the population at various times after the founding period and at various ages. Therefore, almost one-fourth (24.6 percent) of the individuals who were judged to have entered the population as immigrants for 1890 to 1964 subsequently left the population before death, whereas only about 4 percent of the resident-born individuals, during this same period of 1890–1964, were judged to have emigrated.

PATTERNS OF MORTALITY
AND FERTILITY

Mortality during the prereproductive ages and during the reproductive period is obviously of some interest to students of genetic demography. In the following discussion, some detailed consideration will be given to mortality before the age of 15.

The mortality experience of many Navajo communities probably has not differed greatly from that of the Ramah Navajo. However, in order to obtain more adequate estimates of death rates, it has been necessary to use only Ramah-born individuals—which includes both home and hospital births—as the population at risk. In composing the mortality data, emigrant individuals were excluded if age at death could not be computed or if there was considerable uncertainty as to whether or not the individual was alive at the end of 1964. Finally, the population at risk has been further restricted to male and female livebirths that occurred after 1889 (Table 36).

The distribution of these individuals by cohort of birth and age at death (if deceased) is provided for males and females separately in my previous work (Morgan 1968). The informative births total 1,387 out of 1,411 Ramah sex-known livebirths for the period 1890 to 1964. The proportion of all informative livebirths that have resulted in death by the end of 1964 comes to about 27 percent for 75 years of population data.

One pattern that emerges from a comparison of the sex-specific totals of Table 36 and from a comparison of the total sex-specific age-at-death distributions is the generally greater mortality experience of Ramah Navajo males. In addition, we note that the overall sex ratio of livebirths is biased in favor of more females (Table 32). Fluctuations in vital rates are to be expected in small populations, especially over short intervals of time. We note the major deficiency of male livebirths for the five-year period of 1940–44, but we will postpone a discussion of sex-ratio biases and fluctuations to a later section.[9] By way of summarizing the fact that mortality among Ramah Navajo males born from 1890 through 1964 is higher than it is for females, we note that the percentage of all male, informative livebirths that resulted in death by the end of 1964 comes to almost 30 percent, while the corresponding value for females is about 24 percent.

In the absence of short-term, major fluctuations in mortality—occa-

TABLE 36
SUMMARY DATA ON THE COMPOSITION OF
MORTALITY DISTRIBUTIONS AND DISTRIBUTION
OF INFORMATIVE SEX-KNOWN LIVEBIRTHS FOR
THE RAMAH NAVAJO POPULATION, 1890–1964

Birth Cohort (interval of birth years)	Interval of Maximum Age (as of 31 December 1964) in Years	Number of Informative Events (end of 1964)					
		Births		Deaths		Alive	
		Males	Females	Males	Females	Males	Females
1890–94	70–74	14	17	10	12	4	5
1895–99	65–69	20	20	13	11	7	9
1900–04	60–64	25	19	20	7	5	12
1905–09	55–59	27	21	19	14	8	7
1910–14	50–54	21	21	14	9	7	12
1915–19	45–49	37	39	16	18	21	21
1920–24	40–44	36	37	21	11	15	26
1925–29	35–39	32	37	13	14	19	23
1930–34	30–34	41	42	13	12	28	30
1935–39	25–29	54	55	17	11	37	44
1940–44	20–24	59	73	15	23	44	50
1945–49	15–19	64	66	14	14	50	52
1950–54	10–14	71	72	8	5	63	67
1955–59	5– 9	82	85	5	1	77	84
1960–64	0– 4	102	98	7	8	95	90
Totals	—	685	702	205	170	480	532
Both sexes	—	1,387		375		1,012	

sioned, for example, by epidemics—we might envision a probable age
pattern of mortality in a population living under primitive technological
conditions. We would expect infant and early-childhood mortality to be
higher than it is among the industrialized nations of the modern era. But,
in the absence of new communicable diseases introduced by Europeans,
we do not know how high these rates would have been nor the degree of
salutary effects accrued from the low-density residence pattern of Navajo
communities before, during, and after the introduction of new diseases.
Neel and Chagnon (1968:687) have suggested that:

> Characteristic of contemporary primitive man (and perhaps of prim-
> itive man for an extended period of human prehistory) is a period of

"intermediate" *effective* fertility and early mortality. With the advent of agriculture, and the ascendancy of religions emphasizing fruitfulness, a period of higher fertility with a corresponding increase in prereproductive mortality was introduced.

In addition to prereproductive mortality, we must also consider mortality associated with reproduction and other activities of the productive years of life. In the earlier periods of Ramah Navajo history, there seems to have been appreciable maternal mortality because of childbirth during the younger ages of the reproductive period. In recent years, very few women have died in childbirth or from its complications. For males, during their most productive years of life, mortality must have been occasioned by the risks of accidental death to which they were exposed as hunters, warriors, and traders and the diseases to which they were exposed by way of contacts with other groups. This is not to say that disease selection was not significant in the "primitive" environments. Rather, we would suggest that during the historical eras, increasing contacts with other cultures exposed primitive populations to new or more virulent diseases that, supported by higher densities of growing populations in some of these cases, brought about increased levels of mortality. In the case of the Ramah Navajo, this intermediate period of high mortality has ended. As we will show, data on recent years suggest that this population has begun to experience relatively lower mortality.

Our next consideration, then, is the historical pattern of prereproductive mortality—defined, here, by deaths before age 14—of the Ramah Navajo population. Primarily because of the small number of relevant observations for any given five-year birth cohort during most of the history of this population, we have grouped the cohorts in certain ways to provide a clearer picture of patterns of prereproductive mortality. Table 37 provides estimates of infant death rates and early-childhood death ratios—an expression of the probability of death before age five for those individuals who survived infancy—for various groups of livebirths. The infant death rate is a very sensitive indicator of changes in mortality, but accurate data are difficult to obtain in preliterate societies. Some loss of information may be expected for the earliest cohorts, although this would not be very great in the Ramah data. However, some deaths that were reported to have occurred at age one or two years may have been infant deaths, and conversely. With regard to sex-unknown livebirths, which were excluded from the analyses, we note that they were few in total (Table 32), resulted

Kenneth Morgan

TABLE 37
ESTIMATES OF INFANT DEATH RATES AND
PROBABILITY OF EARLY-CHILDHOOD MORTALITY FOR
VARIOUS GROUPS OF BIRTH COHORTS OF THE
RAMAH NAVAJO POPULATION, 1890–1964

Birth-cohort Group (interval of birth years)	Infant Death Rates* (per 1,000 births)			Early-childhood Death Ratios† (per 1,000 suvivors)		
	Males	Females	Total‡	Males	Females	Total‡
1890–1909	93	26	60	51	67	59
1910–24	74	103	89	172	80	126
1925–39	118	164	141	98	71	85
1940–49	114	151	133	110	102	106
1945–54	67	87	77	87	48	68
1950–59	39	25	32	48	13	31
1955–63	31	55	43	—	—	—

* Computed as follows: $\dfrac{(\text{deaths prior to 1 year of age})}{(\text{number of births})} \times 1000$.

† Computed as follows: $\dfrac{(\text{deaths, ages 1–4 years}) \times 1000}{(\text{number of births}) - (\text{deaths prior to 1 year})}$.

‡ Sexes combined.

in deaths in general before age five, and have been included in the calculations of crude vital rates in a later section.

Although the infant death rates can serve, in a general way, both for
period and cohort comparisons, this is not the case with the early-
childhood death probabilities, because some deaths at older ages extend
into the more recent period of time adjacent to the interval of birth years
from which these individuals were drawn. Thus—and especially during
periods of rapid population growth and rapid changes in mortality—
changes in the probabilities of death at older ages for a given cohort of
births would *appear* to precede those at earlier ages. Taking these facts
into consideration, comparisons of the *total* values of the two different
measures of mortality given in Table 37 suggest that the probabilities of
infant mortality and early-childhood mortality are similar to one another
—of the same order of magnitude—for the *same* actual periods of time in
the history of this population. The infant death rates, however, display a
clearer picture of secular patterns of mortality during the history of the

Ramah Navajo population after 1889. Thus, infant death rates rise from "intermediate" values, enter a period of relatively higher values, begin to decline in the late 1940s, and, finally, drop to their lowest values after 1949. When grouped into smaller intervals of five years, infant death rates exhibit a fair amount of fluctuation. This is true even for the years of birth 1950–63; random fluctuations in vital rates are to be expected. More important, the historical pattern of mortality suggested by the changes in the infant death rates is corroborated by additional analyses.

In general, infant mortality is, by far, responsible for the largest number of deaths occurring during the prereproductive period. In fact, the totals of the age-at-death distributions show that almost one-third of all informative deaths for the years 1890 to 1964 were contributed by infant mortality. This proportion is, of course, reflecting the comparative youthfulness of the population. Furthermore, it should not be taken to be an estimate derived from a stable population. The estimates provided in Table 37 show that during the years of high mortality, an average of almost 15 percent of the livebirths will be lost from the population, by death, before they complete their first year of life. Furthermore, with the exception of the values for 1890–1909 and 1950–59, male infants would seem to fare better than female infants during periods of higher infant mortality. This sex-differential pattern of infant mortality is strong enough in some periods to exert an effect on the estimates of the proportion of livebirths that resulted in death after birth and through the fourth year of life. Table 38 provides comparisons of the probabilities of dying during the first 5-year period and the remaining 10-year period of childhood for different groups of birth cohorts. All of these data on mortality during childhood, along with the infant death rates, show a clear advantage of females as compared with males in declining mortality.

The historical pattern of total mortality in the Ramah Navajo population, 1890–1964, is shown in Table 39. We may suppose that before the introduction of infectious diseases by other cultures, the small primitive populations of the dispersed Navajo groups experienced "intermediate" or relatively lower mortality before the reproductive period. The Ramah Navajo population before 1905 shows such intermediate death rates that probably find part of their explanation in the dispersed character of the band and in the relative isolation of the entire community. Crude death rates had clearly risen before the end of the stabilization period, resulting in the very high values throughout the period 1915–29. High mortality

288

TABLE 38
ESTIMATES OF MORTALITY RATES FOR THE AGE
INTERVALS OF 0–4 AND 5–14 FOR VARIOUS GROUPS
OF BIRTH COHORTS OF THE RAMAH NAVAJO
POPULATION, 1890–1964

Birth-cohort Group (interval of birth years)	Mortality Rates, Ages 0–4 (per 1,000 livebirths)			Mortality Rates, Ages 5–14* (per 1,000 survivors)		
	Males	Females	Total†	Males	Females	Total†
1890–1909	140	91	116	135	86	111
1910–24	234	175	205	97	113	105
1925–39	205	224	215	89	10	50
1940–49	211	237	224	31	19	25
1945–54	148	130	139	—	—	—
1950–59	85	38	62	—	—	—

* Survivors = (number of births) − (deaths prior to age 5 years).
† Sexes combined.

TABLE 39
AVERAGE ESTIMATES OF ANNUAL CRUDE RATES OF
DEATH FOR EACH FIVE-YEAR PERIOD OF THE
RAMAH NAVAJO POPULATION, 1890–1964*

Five-year Period: Interval of Years	Mid-period Population Estimate†	Average Annual Crude Death Rate‡	Five-year Period: Interval of Years	Mid-period Population Estimate†	Average Annual Crude Death Rate‡
1890–94	85.1	14.1	1930–34	380.1	20.5
1895–99	119.5	8.4	1935–39	445.0	20.2
1900–04	160.1	8.7	1940–44	520.2	23.4
1905–09	198.8	16.1	1945–49	599.6	15.3
1910–14	229.1	15.7	1950–54	696.2	12.0
1915–19	265.9	27.1	1955–59	822.8	6.3
1920–24	308.4	26.6	1960–64	982.8	6.5
1925–29	340.3	25.8			

* Calculated from the data given in Table 32, including sex-unknown births and deaths.

† See Table 35 for formula and definitions.

‡ Calculated as follows: $\frac{1}{5} \cdot \frac{(\text{Deaths during the } i\text{th period}) \times 1,000}{(\text{Mid-period population of the } i\text{th period})}$.

is sustained, but at a somewhat lower level, through the early 1940s. Undoubtedly, the high mortality periods of the years 1915–29 reflect the high tolls exacted from the older individuals by tuberculosis and the overall increased mortality—which was most severe for the very young—occasioned by the influenza pandemic of 1918 and the secondary outbreaks of this disease in 1919 and in the 1920s. In the past, respiratory and intestinal ailments have, in general, been the major causes of mortality, especially among the young. But, while maternal mortality, along with tuberculosis, has essentially disappeared from this population, accidental deaths among older individuals (for example, deaths involving alcohol and a motor vehicle and deaths from occupational hazards) do not seem to be decreasing. So-called childhood diseases and some other infectious diseases have come under control in recent years. But, infantile diarrhea still ranks as a major source of morbidity and mortality in many Navajo communities. From my observations in the Ramah Navajo community and at Zuni Indian Hospital, I would conclude—in agreement with earlier observations of Kluckhohn (1966) around and before 1950—that general morbidity is high among the young and perhaps among the very old. The level of morbidity still follows seasonal and apparent cyclical patterns. The picture of morbidity and mortality in the Ramah Navajo community is remarkably similar to that described for a somewhat larger Navajo community, the Many Farms–Rough Rock community, located near the center of the Navajo reservation (McDermott, Deuschle, and Barnett 1972).

The data presented in Table 39 (crude death rates by five-year periods) combine the effects of deaths that occurred at all ages during a given period. These rates are dependent on the structure of the population, notably the age distribution of the period population. During periods of higher fertility, more infants, relative to other age groups, will be made available for selection via differential mortality. In the Ramah Navajo population, infants and perhaps those children who have yet to reach their fifth year compose the bulk of individuals who are immediately relevant to the operation of this aspect of natural selection. In earlier decades, maternal mortality as a consequence of childbirth was considerable.

If changes in overall mortality pressure and changes in the kinds of factors that cause death differentially affect individuals according to their sex and age, then realistic models of the genetic demography of the present population would seem extremely difficult to construct. Obviously, provided with detailed historical perspective, the Ramah Navajo population—from the mortality analyses alone—cannot be considered a stable population, much less an "untouched" primitive one. Thus, in the empirical study of a small population that still appears to be characterized by a primitive technology and social structure, it is necessary to have comprehensive information available, with regard to both kind and historical depth, in order to properly appreciate the survival of the population over time and its implications for models of the genetic demography of different levels of sociocultural integration.

Crude Birth Rates and Crude Rates of Natural Increase

We have shown that the demographic history of the Ramah Navajo population is characterized by secular changes and sex-differential patterns of mortality. The individuals who composed the Ramah Navajo band during the early years of the founding period were the survivors of presumably severe mortality conditions of captivity at Fort Sumner. In addition, many of these individuals were already engaged in fertile matings or were immediately at risk for mating, with the exception, of course, of young children accompanying a founder parent or couple. The conditions of the later years of the founding period and most of the stabilization period supported high fertility and rapid growth of the population, especially during the first 15 years of the stabilization period. Very high average rates of annual growth of the Ramah Navajo population for 1890–1904 were demonstrated by the values given in Table 33. We expected that most of this growth would be attributable to natural increase, to high crude birth rates, and to relatively low crude death rates. The average annual crude death rates, given in Table 39, were intermediate for most of the stabilization period, except for the high values during the final five-year period (1915–19). We have attempted to explain the subsequent rise, then fall, in crude death rates on the basis of significant historical disease patterns. This latter pattern does not appear to be dissimilar from the historical experience of mortality of newly developing countries (Keyfitz 1964).

Crude birth rates and crude rates of natural increase for the Ramah Navajo population, 1890–1964, are given in Table 40. Estimates of the mid-period populations were given in Table 39, along with the crude death rates. We would caution the acceptance of the very high birth and nat-

TABLE 40
AVERAGE ESTIMATES OF ANNUAL CRUDE BIRTH RATES
AND CRUDE RATES OF NATURAL INCREASE FOR
EACH FIVE-YEAR PERIOD OF THE RAMAH NAVAJO
POPULATION, 1890–1964*

Five-year Period: Interval of Years	Average Annual Crude Vital Rates†		Five-year Period: Interval of Years	Average Annual Crude Vital Rates†	
	Birth Rate‡	Rate of Natural Increase§		Birth Rate‡	Rate of Natural Increase§
1890–94	75.2	61.1	1930–34	45.3	24.8
1895–99	68.6	60.2	1935–39	51.2	31.0
1900–04	61.2	52.5	1940–44	51.5	28.1
1905–09	48.3	32.2	1945–49	45.0	29.7
1910–14	38.4	22.7	1950–54	41.9	29.9
1915–19	59.4	32.3	1955–59	41.1	34.8
1920–24	49.9	23.3	1960–64	40.7	34.2
1925–29	41.1	15.3			

* Periods have been grouped to conform with the format of Table 39, which provides the values for the mid-period populatoin estimates and the average annual crude death rates. The data are based on Table 32.

† The rates are per 1,000 mid-period population. See Table 35 for formula and definitions.

‡ Calculated as follows: $\frac{1}{5} \cdot \frac{(\text{births during the } i\text{th period}) \times 1,000}{(i\text{th mid-period population estimate})}$.

§ The crude rate of natural increase = (crude birth rate) − (crude death rate).

ural increase rates at face value for the first three five-year periods. Although we do believe that these rates were occasioned by the selective conditions of the early history of this population, we have previously mentioned that a number of individuals have been excluded from the founding period population, either because they were judged not to have been stable residents in the community or because they were "pre-founders." Of these individuals, perhaps five of them survived into or through most of the stabilization period. However, none of these individuals was considered to have given birth to or to have fathered any offspring born in the population after 1889. Thus, the rates given in Table

40 for the first three five-year periods may be too high by an average of 5 percent, at most. In any event, the average annual rates of natural increase for the years 1890 to 1904 do demonstrate the effects of historical circumstances on the fertility and mortality of the early years of population growth.

The values in Table 40 have been grouped in the same manner as those of the mid-period population estimates and crude death rates given in Table 39. By comparing the two tables, we note that the high rate of births for 1915–19 more than compensated for the high rate of deaths caused primarily by the influenza pandemic of 1918. Falling birth rates over the next decade—perhaps a result, at least partially, of the loss of reproductive individuals by early mortality of previous cohorts—could not compensate for the sustained high death rates of these years. However, after 1934, it appears that the birth rates, after reaching a new high, exhibit a pattern similar to that of the crude death rates—that is, beginning in the five-year period 1945–49, the most recent 20 years of Ramah Navajo history are characterized by declining mortality and fertility. The relatively low crude death rates for the years 1955–64 would seem to be guaranteed by the continuing efforts of the Public Health Service, Division of Indian Health. On the other hand, it is difficult to predict the future course of crude birth rates for this community, at least for the immediate future. I have noted, however, that the number of births in 1965 and 1966 seem uncharacteristically low. Evidence was also presented to the effect that birth-control devices were accepted by a small proportion of fertile women during 1965 and 1966 (Morgan 1968). During my fieldwork, many of the young multiparous women interviewed expressed interest in birth control. Part of the decline in crude birth rates before 1965 may be attributable to the increased emphasis on continued education, job training, and so forth, which would contribute to a decreased fertility of a small number of females. On the other hand, declining fertility has not proceeded very far, and the crude birth rates for 1960–64 are still very high. In any event, the decline of crude death rates has been faster than that of crude birth rates, resulting in increases of the crude rate of natural increase during the fourth historical period of the Ramah Navajo population.

One of the most rapidly growing populations of this century is the Hutterite sect studied by Eaton and Mayer (1953). Their estimate of the annual crude death rate of the Hutterites for the period 1941–49, based on the mid-period population estimate, was 4.4 per 1,000. This is three to six times smaller than corresponding values for the Ramah Navajo (see Table 39 and Eaton and Mayer). By contrast, Eaton and Mayer found the Hutterite crude birth rate during the five-year period 1946–50 to be 45.9 per 1,000, which is only a little higher than the estimate for the Ramah Navajo population for about the same period (Table 40).

A culturally more relevant comparison with the Ramah Navajo population data of the late 1950s and early 1960s is afforded by the data on the Many Farms–Rough Rock Navajo community located near Chinle (Mc-Dermott, Deuschle, and Barnett 1972). For the five-year period 1957–61, this community grew from a size of 1,963 individuals to 2,299. Infant mortality fluctuated considerably during this period of a health care experiment at Many Farms and averaged 70.0 per 1,000 livebirths. The average crude death rate was 6.2 per 1,000 population, and the average crude birth rate was 45.8 per 1,000 population. Johnston (1966) notes an average crude birth rate for the five-year period 1955–59 in the Many Farms community of 49.5 per 1,000 population. Apparently, then, the crude birth rate has been declining, being 48.4 per 1,000 population in 1957 and 40.0 per 1,000 population in 1961. These average values for births and deaths should be compared with the corresponding period figures for the Ramah Navajo given in Table 37 (for infant death rates), Table 39 (for average crude death rates), and Table 40 (for average crude birth rates). It appears, therefore, that the Ramah population experience of a gradual decline in fertility, along with a dramatic reduction in infant mortality, anticipates the experience of the Many Farms community during the health care experiment.

By way of summarizing the natural increase of the Ramah Navajo population, we note that high crude birth rates have been sustained in this population over a respectably long period of time. In this respect, the community is quite characteristic of the general Navajo experience. His-torical circumstances have, however, contributed to rates of growth that have often exceeded those estimated for the total Navajo population. Appreciation of the natural increase of the Ramah Navajo population can profit from a comparison with ranges of probable rates derived by John-ston (1966) from his exhaustive study of Navajo population data. The values he provides are to be considered "plausible" estimates of average annual rates of natural increase for population totals at selected years and are provided along with some additional comparisons in Table 41.

TABLE 41
RANGES OF AVERAGE ANNUAL RATES OF NATURAL
INCREASE ESTIMATED FROM REPORTED NAVAJO
POPULATION TOTALS FOR SELECTED PERIODS, 1870–1971,
AND COMPARABLE VALUES ESTIMATED FROM THE
DIFFERENCE BETWEEN THE CRUDE BIRTH AND
DEATH RATES FOR THE RAMAH NAVAJO POPULATION,
1890–1971, AND FOR THE CHINLE–MANY FARMS
AREA, 1957–61

Population and Period	Range of Average Annual Rates of Natural Increase (percent)	Source
Navajo Tribe		
1870–1900	1.5 to 2.0	Johnston (1966)
1900–30	1.75 to 2.25	Johnston (1966)
1920–50	2.4 to 2.8	Johnston (1966)
1950–62	2.4 to 3.3	Johnston (1966)
1965–71	2.5	Wise (1972)
Ramah Navajo		
1890–1900	6.0 to 6.1	Table 40
1900–30	1.5 to 5.25	Table 40
1920–50	1.5 to 3.1	Table 40
1940–50	2.8 to 3.0	Table 40
1950–64	3.0 to 3.5	Table 40
1963–71	(4.0)	Growth rate from census figures
Chinle–Many Farms Navajo Area		
1957–61	3.4 to 4.3	McDermott, Deuschle, and Barnett (1972)

Age and Sex Distribution of Navajo Population

The Ramah Navajo population at the end of 1964 was a youthful population. The demographic structure that has resulted from the operation of all factors over 95 years of Ramah Navajo history is shown in Table 42 and that for the total Navajo tribal population in Table 43.

Seventy-five years after the end of the founding period, the Ramah Navajo population contained more females than males. According to Johnston (1966), the total Indian population for the continental United

TABLE 42

DISTRIBUTION OF THE RAMAH NAVAJO POPULATION
BY AGE AND SEX ON 1 JANUARY 1965

Age Group (in years)	Males Number	Males Per-cent	Females Number	Females Per-cent	Both Sexes Number	Both Sexes Per-cent	♂♂/♀♀
Under 5	97	9.03	94	8.75	191	17.78	1.03
Under 1	[23]	—	[22]	—	[45]	4.19	1.05
1 to 4	[74]	—	[72]	—	[146]	13.59	1.03
5 to 9	80	7.45	88	8.19	168	15.64	0.91
10 to 14	63	5.87	73	6.80	136	12.67	0.86
15 to 19	53	4.93	56	5.21	109	10.14	0.95
20 to 24	49	4.56	53	4.93	102	9.49	0.93
25 to 29	38	3.54	45	4.19	83	7.73	0.84
30 to 34	31	2.89	27	2.51	58	5.40	1.15
35 to 39	16	1.49	23	2.14	39	3.63	0.70
40 to 44	18	1.68	30	2.79	48	4.47	0.60
45 to 49	21	1.96	24	2.23	45	4.19	0.88
50 to 54	9	0.84	16	1.49	25	2.33	0.56
55 to 59	10	0.93	7	0.65	17	1.58	1.43
60 to 64	5	0.47	12	1.12	17	1.59	0.42
65 to 69	7	0.65	10	0.93	17	1.58	0.70
70 to 74	6	0.56	5	0.47	11	1.03	1.20
75+	3	0.28	5	0.47	8	0.75	0.60
Total	506	47.13	568	52.87	1,074	100.00	0.89
Median Age	16.50		17.50		—		—

States in 1960 numbered 546,228 individuals of all ages, of whom 50.1 per-cent were males and 49.9 percent were females. He further found that for the Navajo area Indian population of New Mexico in 1960, 35,451 indi-viduals were estimated, of whom 48.9 percent were males and 51.1 percent were females. The total Navajo area population at the beginning of 1971 was estimated at 129,422, with a sex distribution of 49.5 percent males and 50.5 percent females (Table 43). For the Ramah Navajo population at the end of 1964, we note the total deficiency of males among those individuals of age five and older. The total deficiency of males for the Ramah Navajo is in the same direction but greater than that of various Navajo populations in 1960 (Johnston). The sex ratio for ages five and over for the Ramah Navajo at the start of 1965 is 0.863, while that for the

TABLE 43

DISTRIBUTION OF THE NAVAJO AREA POPULATION BY
AGE AND SEX, ESTIMATED FOR 1 JANUARY 1971

Age Group (in years)	Males Number	Females Number	Both Sexes Number	Both Sexes Percent	♂♂/♀♀
Under 5	9,450	8,984	18,434	14.24	1.052
5 to 9	9,944	10,187	20,131	15.55	0.976
10 to 14	8,904	9,461	18,365	14.19	0.941
15 to 19	7,248	7,361	14,609	11.29	0.985
20 to 24	5,806	6,029	11,835	9.14	0.963
25 to 29	4,968	5,315	10,283	7.95	0.935
30 to 34	3,940	4,229	8,169	6.31	0.932
35 to 39	2,997	3,289	6,286	4.86	0.911
40 to 44	2,484	2,555	5,039	3.89	0.972
45 to 49	1,853	1,981	3,834	2.96	0.935
50 to 54	1,582	1,552	3,134	2.42	1.019
55 to 59	1,357	1,393	2,750	2.12	0.974
60 to 64	1,175	1,058	2,233	1.73	1.111
65 to 69	760	722	1,482	1.15	1.053
70 to 74	606	445	1,051	0.81	1.362
75 to 79	491	371	862	0.67	1.323
80 to 84	244	202	446	0.34	1.208
85 to 89	161	125	286	0.22	1.288
90 to 94	73	71	144	0.11	1.028
95+	27	22	49	0.04	1.227
Total	64,070	65,352	129,422	99.99	0.980
Median Age	17	17	—	—	—

SOURCE: Navajo Area Population Register (1970).

total Navajo area population six years later is 0.969. We note that the age-sex distribution for the Navajo Reservation population of 1960 (according to Johnston) for individuals under five years of age is not the same as that for the Ramah population of 1960. Thus, the Ramah population shows slightly more males than females under the age of five (Table 42), while all of the Navajo estimates for 1960 show slightly more females than males for these ages. On the other hand, estimates for the total Indian population of the United States in 1960 show slightly more males than females for the ages under five years and, in addition, show a total proportion of individuals under five years of age of 16.7 percent. As mentioned previously, the Navajo Population Area Register from the time of its inception in 1965 recognized the probable underreporting of individuals under five years of age. Therefore, adjustments for this age group, especially, were carried out in 1965, based on the 1960 census data for the total American Indian population distributed by age and sex. This age adjustment has been continued each year as part of the projection procedure (Wise 1972). Thus, we now find that for the total Navajo area population, the sex ratio is in favor of males for the age category of under five years (see Table 43), but the proportion of the total in this age category is slightly less than at Ramah.

The youthfulness of the Ramah Navajo population in 1964 compares quite favorably with that of one of the youngest populations ever recorded—the Hutterite population of 1950 (Eaton and Mayer 1953). On 31 December 1950, slightly over half of the Hutterite population, 50.6 percent, was under 15 and 2.3 percent over 65. The values for the Ramah Navajo in 1964, after about the same number of years of population growth as that of the ethnic Hutterite population of 1950, were 46.1 percent under 15 and 3.4 percent at age 65 or older. Estimates of Ramah Navajo population in 1971 for these age categories seem not to have changed—49 percent under age 16 years and 3.5 percent of age 65 years and older. Similarly, the Navajo area population at the beginning of 1971 is estimated to be comprised of 44 percent under age 15 and only 3.34 percent of the total who are 65 years of age and older.

Coale (1964) points out that high fertility is the major determinant of youthfulness of a population. Mortality affects the age distribution of a population much less than does fertility. Reduced mortality, in fact, increases the number of young persons as well as the number of old individuals. Under conditions of sustained rates of high fertility, typical of Navajo populations in recent decades, reduced death rates will contribute to the growing youthfulness of the population. Probably typical of the Navajo experience since about 1945 is Coale's (1964:50) observation: "The reason that the reduced death rates, which prolong man's life, make the population younger is that typical improvements in health and medicine produce the greatest increases in survivorship among the young rather than the old."

Eaton and Mayer (1953) point out that the fertility ratio (or child-woman ratio)—the number of children under five years of age per 100 (or per 1,000) women of ages 15 to 49—"is a somewhat more accurate measure of fertility than the crude birth rate." They found that for the

Hutterite population, the 1950 fertility ratio was 963 per 1,000 women and "greater than that of any other human population." Johnston (1966) estimates that the child-woman ratios for various Navajo populations for the period 1920 to 1957 generally fall within a range from 720 to 792, with an unweighted average of 760. However, he points out that on the basis of the 1960 census returns, it may be necessary to adjust the earlier ratios because of deficiencies in the rolls of the Navajo populations of 1920–57. The child-woman ratio calculated from the reported age-sex distribution for non-Whites residing within the boundaries of the Navajo Reservation in 1960 was 942, almost as high as the Hutterite value of 1950. On the basis of the Navajo figure for 1960, an adjustment of the child-woman ratio for the earlier Navajo populations raises the average, according to Johnston, from 760 to 816. However, it appears from the data presented in Table 43 that the child-woman ratio for the Navajo area population is now considerably lower—599 per 1,000 women. Of course, some part of this apparent decrease in the child-woman ratio must be due to under-reporting for the age category of under five years. For the Ramah Navajo at the end of 1964, the child-woman ratio was 740 per 1,000 women. Thus, the Ramah Navajo could be considered a high fertility population in 1964. On the basis of age-sex distributions of the Ramah Navajo population of 1880–1948, which were originally compiled by Spuhler,[2] Johnston obtained synthetic totals for the three periods of the Ramah data and calculated the following Ramah child-woman ratios: (1) Ramah Navajo synthetic totals for 1880–98, 1,076 per 1,000 women; (2) for 1900–18, 1,049 per 1,000 women; and (3) for 1920–48, 792 per 1,000 women. The first two Ramah Navajo child-woman ratios are consistent with our observations on the very high fertility of Ramah Navajo women during the earlier years of population growth before the end of the stabilization period. Although they are estimates for a small population, they represent the highest child-woman ratios on record for comparable populations. The trend toward declining child-woman ratios is also consistent with our demographic-historical analysis of the Ramah Navajo population.

ASPECTS OF GENETIC DEMOGRAPHY *no specific genetics*

The ancestral populations of the Navajo and Apache—the hunting-gathering Athapaskans who migrated from northern territories to the American Southwest—experienced extensive contact with Pueblo peoples.

299

The development of a land-based subsistence economy and a matrilineal clan system permitted larger local populations, some demographic stability, and a network of social relationships that, although weak, could extend beyond the local community. Although the Navajo occupied an extensive area in the Southwest as early as the late seventeenth century, it must be assumed that they were only loosely organized.

Throughout the long period of Spanish control in the Southwest—which spanned almost three centuries, from the early 1600s to the middle of the 1800s—the true character of Navajo social integration was along the lines of widely dispersed band-type local communities based on a common land-use subsistence economy. With the acquisition of the horse and the gun, the Navajo achieved an increased mobility and expanded into new territories. To call this phase of Navajo culture "nomadic," however, is as erroneous as to consider the Navajo to have possessed a strong tribal structure (Kluckhohn and Leighton 1962). Roaming widely, the Navajo did trade and fight with groups as far away as the Pawnee of western Nebraska. But raiding and other warlike activities did not become the way of life for the Navajo as it did for the Ute, Comanche, and Apache. Agriculture continued to be the basis of Navajo subsistence economy and demanded at least one dwelling close to the fields, with some members of the lineage in permanent residence for a large part of the year. Hogans and outlying sheep camps could be supplied by horse from considerable distances, but mobility was primarily restricted to a well-defined territory claimed by a particular cooperating group of individual families. The shifts between fixed abodes within the range followed the winter-summer climatic changes and were dictated by the demands of maintenance of agricultural and pastoral activities and the availability of wood fuel and water. The acquisition of horses also permitted more frequent visiting among widely scattered families and supported substantially larger gatherings at ceremonials and other social functions.

Undoubtedly, there was an appreciable amount of genetic exchange between various Southwest Amerindian populations and those of the Navajo and Apache. Navajo raids and forays made against local Navajo populations by other groups continued the exchange of genetic information via captured individuals. The extent of past genetic exchange between local groups and between neighboring tribes would be difficult to quantitate but probably was significant in the history of the Navajo.[10] The Navajo have been classified as a lineal tribe with a pastoral and simple

Kenneth Morgan

horticultural subsistence economy (Service 1962). However, the Navajo tribe as a true political structure has not yet developed (Hill 1940). The basic political unit, as has been pointed out, was the economically-based local community or, in other words, the natural community. We may presume that the size of the population of any natural community was, in the past, determined primarily by the availability of natural resources in the territory that could support a subsistence economy based on small livestock such as sheep. Hill's estimates of the size of these local Navajo populations range from 10 to 40 families.

The survival and rapid expansion of the total Navajo population must be attributed to the success of the individual communities in adapting to environmental changes. The natural communities were economically and politically independent. They acted without the advice or consent of other such units and often without regard to the repercussions their actions would have for other units. Rarely did two or more units join forces and then, only temporarly. Since 1874–75, the development of Anglo communities, institutions, and various government services near the important Navajo territories has reinforced this separatist situation. As Hill (1940: 24) points out, "there remain only the natural communities whose only common interests are those of a minority fraction. From the administrative point of view, they are so many distinct problems, each varying in needs and type of natural resources."

Changes in Selection Patterns

The index of total selection intensity developed by Crow (1958) provides an estimate of the upper limit of the rate of change in fitness of a population brought about by differential mortality and fertility. The contributions of differential mortality and fertility to the total index obtained by this method are useful for comparing populations that represent different levels of sociocultural integration. The method assumes that fitness is completely heritable, that is, that each offspring has exactly the average of his parents' fitnesses. In addition, it is assumed that the correlations between the productivity measures and fitness do not change.

Irrespective of the difficulties in determining to what extent the genetic assumptions hold for any set of demographic data, an index of potential selection intensity is very useful as a summarizing statistic for genetic demography. The major difficulties in the application of any method reside in the existing data. Available studies are heterogeneous in purpose, in sample sizes, in periods of coverage, in accuracy of age estimation, in completeness of ascertainment of mortality and fertility, and in accounting for losses and additions of information due to migration that occurred before the collection of the sample (see Spuhler 1962 and Neel and Chagnon 1968 for comments on the deficiencies of existing population data).

I have previously discussed in some detail the differential fertility of Ramah Navajo mothers (Morgan 1968). Relative to this, summary information basic to the application of Crow's (1958) method is given in Table 44. It should be noted that the means and square roots of the variances (based on n degrees of freedom) are for total ascertained livebirths of a given group of women; furthermore, they have been[corrected for progeny produced out of the Ramah population—where information was available—by the inclusion of all of a mother's liveborn progeny.] But, in eight cases, information was not available, possibly because of the women's out-migration before age 44, thus making their subsequent reproductive history unknown. This is indicated in Table 44 by the frequencies of the event. However, the measures of the means and variances of progeny number in Table 44 *include* these eight women. Correction for this possible effect on fertility—which actually concerns seven of the eight emigrants—will be presented later.

One immediate problem that arises in the application of Crow's method to the Ramah data concerns the estimation of prereproductive mortality and, thus, the calculation of the component of the index of potential selection due to differential mortality. Since the Ramah population is not closed to in-migration, this phenomenon, especially during the ages 15 to 44, results in an underestimation of early mortality if we use the cohort data as given in Table 44. This is very significant for the oldest three cohorts of women, because only 18 of the 46 females are judged to have been born in the community during the founding period. We have approached the problem in the following way. For females born in 1844–89, we estimate the proportion of livebirths dying before the reproductive period (Crow's p_d) as 2/18, or 0.111. Thus, the estimated proportion surviving to the age of reproduction is $p_s = 1 - p_d$, or 0.889, for the first three cohorts of Ramah Navajo females. Therefore, the mor-

TABLE 44
SUMMARY OF INFORMATION ON THE MORTALITY
AND FERTILITY OF LIVEBORN RAMAH NAVAJO
FEMALES BORN 1844–1924 AS OF 31 DECEMBER 1964

Cohorts of Women: Interval of Birth Years	Total Number of Females	Ages 0–14 (number) Died	Ages 15–44 (number) Died	Emi-grated	Means (and standard deviations) of Total Number of Liveborn Progeny Based on All Females in Cohort	Based on Survivors to Age 15
1844–68	13	—	3	—	6.462 (3.500)	6.462 (3.500)
1869–79	17	1	3	—	8.176 (4.382)	8.688 (3.996)
1880–89	16	1	5	—	4.875 (2.619)	5.200 (2.372)
1844–89	46	2	11	—	6.543 (3.860)	6.841 (3.680)
1890–94	19	6	2	—	3.632 (4.233)	5.308 (4.158)
1895–99	21	2	8	—	4.429 (4.478)	4.895 (4.459)
1900–04	19	3	3	—	4.842 (3.498)	5.750 (3.052)
1905–09	22	2	11	1	3.818 (3.916)	4.200 (3.906)
1890–1909	81	13	24	1	4.173 (4.082)	4.971 (3.985)
1910–14	27	5	5	—	4.148 (3.679)	5.091 (3.437)
1915–19	44	13	5	2	3.591 (3.990)	5.097 (3.864)
1920–24	47	8	4	5	4.638 (4.383)	5.590 (4.223)
1910–24	118	26	14	7	4.136 (4.111)	5.304 (3.934)
1844–1924	245	41	49	8	4.600 (4.161)	5.525 (3.961)

TABLE 45
SURVIVAL OF LIVEBORN RAMAH NAVAJO FEMALES TO
VARIOUS AGES BY GROUPS OF BIRTH COHORTS

Interval of Birth Years	Number of Female Livebirths	Proportion of Livebirths (percent) Surviving to Various Ages (in years)							
		15	20	25	30	35	40	45	50
1890–1909	77	83.1	76.6	68.8	62.3	58.4	54.5	53.2	50.6
1910–24*	97	73.2	71.1	70.1	66.0	62.9	60.8	60.8	—
1925–39*	134	76.9	75.4	73.1	72.4	—	—	—	—
1940–49*	139	74.8	73.4	—	—	—	—	—	—
1945–54*	138	87.0	—	—	—	—	—	—	—

* Where values cannot be computed because of the closing date at the end of 1964, this is indicated by —. In addition, the last survival value for these groups of cohorts may be overestimates, again because of the truncation of events at the end of 1964.

tality component, which can be defined as $I_m = p_d/p_s$, would be 0.125 for females born in 1844–89. The basic values for the calculation of I_m can be extracted from the data given in Table 45 for the remaining cohorts of females grouped according to (1) females born in 1890–1909 and (2) females born in 1910–24. The grouping of females born in 1890–1924 into three larger cohorts was dictated by the patterns of mortality in the history of this population and by consideration of the demographic-historical changes that might be expected to affect the composition of a cohort and the fertility of its women via migration.

The fertility component of the index of total selection intensity[11] is defined as

$$I_f = V_f/\bar{x}_s{}^2,$$

where x_s is the mean number and V_f is the variance in the number of births restricted to women who have reached the reproductive age. These latter two values have been calculated for livebirths for the Ramah population and are provided by the last column in Table 44 where I have tabulated the standard deviation in place of the variance.

The index of total selection intensity that results from the combination of the mortality and fertility components[12] is

$$I = I_m + I_f/p_s$$
$$= V/\bar{x}^2,$$

where V is the variance and $\bar{x}$ is the mean in the number of progeny per female ever born. These values are provided in the next-to-last column of Table 44. For the present study, we will use the first definition of the index of potential selection and attempt to account for the effect of out-migration information loss on V_f.

Another problem raised by the Ramah population data is the significance of females who survived to age 15, but who produced no ascertainable liveborn offspring. For reasons that may be considered far removed from the operation of genic selection, some of these individuals may never have been exposed to the risk of pregnancy. Of course, "social selection" for or against reproduction must extend in varying degrees to all women in the population, and its intensity can also change temporarily and secularly. We have commented on the historical circumstances of the late founding period and most of the stabilization period that supported high effective fertility and the resultant rapid growth of the Ramah Navajo population. The high rates of annual growth and natural increase for the years 1890–1904 (see Tables 33 and 40) are consistent with the high fertility of women of the founding period population born in 1844–79 and their daughters (see Table 44). By contrast, we may suppose that as acculturation proceeds, some proportion of younger females will electively (or otherwise) limit their families or completely remove themselves from the risks of pregnancy. These latter factors most probably have not been very important in the fertility of the women discussed here, that is, for women born before 1925.

Of all females born in 1844–1924, about 28 percent did not produce an ascertainable livebirth as of 31 December 1964 (Morgan 1968). Unproductive females totaled 69 individuals out of 245; 41 individuals died before age 15 (Table 44), and the remaining 28 women survived to age 15 or older. An important factor limiting the fertility of women in the past was mortality before age 40 or so. By the data in Table 45, we have shown that this mortality among women was considerable. Since the mean age at first maternity has remained about 20 years for this population (Morgan), mortality of women around or before age 20 might be expected to be a cause of livebirth unproductivity. According to Morgan, among the 28 nonproductive women who survived to at least age 15, seven died between the ages of 15 and about 21. Although there are a number of factors that limit the productivity of Ramah Navajo females, one of the more interesting ones concerns the frequency of apparent physiological sterility.

sterility 'gene' from one ancestor?

It has been suggested earlier that complete sterility has not been of high incidence in the Ramah population. However, there is some evidence for the operation of genetic factors in sterility in this population (Kluckhohn 1966:351):

> Of those who had reached adulthood by 1950, there is a presumption that seven men and five women are infertile because all of these had married at least two different individuals and failed to have children. Three other men and one woman had a single marriage of three years or more duration without conception resulting. Lack of fertility seems to attach to a limited number of family lines. Four of the men and two of the women who have had two or more marriages, and all three of the men with a single marriage, are closely related, all being descendants of the Chiricahua Apache women who married at Ramah. Three of the other women who are infertile are full sisters.

Although details are not necessary here, it is important to note certain factors that will have to be incorporated in the building of any realistic, genetic-demographic model: the number of clans in a small population where the approach to homozygosity through endogamous mating is slowed by the operation of clan and clan-group exogamic rules; their distribution among the individuals in the population at given points in time; the survival of a clan in the population over time (hence, the concept of the "half-life" of a clan); and "certain preferential tendencies for clans to exchange members in ways not determined by the system of linked clan exogamy" (Spuhler and Kluckhohn 1953). A final point—which may be self-evident by now—is that the differential production and/or survival of the two sexes have important consequences for the survival of a clan in small populations of a lineal tribe.

Measurement of Potential Selection

The results of the application of Crow's (1958) method to the mortality and fertility data of Ramah Navajo females are given in Table 46. Mortality estimates for the first group of females were discussed above; estimates for the second and third groups are derived from the data given in Table 45. The fertility data for the third group and the total series given in Table 44 have been corrected for information losses due to out-migration by excluding the seven women whose reproductive histories could not be followed to age 44.

The values of $\bar{x}$ given in Table 46 place the Ramah Navajo at the upper end of Spuhler's (1962) series of "tribal populations" and near that of the

TABLE 46
POTENTIAL SELECTION IN THE RAMAH NAVAJO
POPULATION, BASED ON THE LIVEBIRTH FERTILITY OF
FEMALES BORN IN 1844–1924 AS OF 31 DECEMBER 1964*

Interval of Birth Years of Women	$\bar{x}$	$\bar{x}_s$	p_d	p_s	I_m	I_f	I_f/p_s	$I = I_m + I_f/p_s$
1844–89	6.543	6.841	0.111	0.889	0.125	0.289	0.325	0.450
1890–1909	4.173	4.971	0.169	0.831	0.203	0.643	0.774	0.977
1910–24	4.234	5.529	0.268	0.732	0.366	0.518	0.707	1.073
1844–1924	4.660	5.629	0.214	0.786	0.271	0.499	0.634	0.905

* Calculations based on total ascertained liveborn progeny as of the end of 1964; seven emigrant women excluded.

series of small "state populations." The values provided by the females who were born in 1844–89 characterize the founding and early stabilization of the Ramah Navajo band. The decade immediately preceding the founding of the Ramah band, 1860–70, "can well be termed the Navaho 'time of troubles'" (Johnston 1966). As a result of American military reprisals before their surrender, the constant harassment of older enemies during the 1860s, and mortality during the "Long Walk" to Fort Sumner, the Navajo suffered severe losses. Johnston (1966:132) concludes that "these losses, together with the severe privations experienced during the 4 years at Fort Sumner itself (1864–1868), appear to have halted, at least temporarily, the increase in the Navajo population"; but, since their return to their former territories in 1869, it appears that Navajo death rates have remained well below their birth rates. Our primary interest here is in the "reality" of mortality estimates provided for the early periods of Ramah Navajo history. According to Johnston (1966:150):

> In his study of early Navaho history, Worcester . . . mentions four factors which are associated with the relative stability of Navaho death rates throughout this period. First, their food supplies were sufficiently stable to permit survival, albeit with much periodic hardship. Secondly, the early cessation of hostilities against the Americans and the effective prohibition of predatory activities both by and against Navahos after 1864 combined to eliminate the heavy male mortality which commonly occurred among Plains Indian tribes. Thirdly, the geographic dispersion of the Navaho effectively insulated them from the worst effects of epidemics which decimated the populations of many densely settled Indian villages and communities. Finally, the profound isolation of most Navahos from outside contacts permitted them to maintain a relatively stable social existence from the time of their return to their homelands in 1869 well into the 20th century.

Thus, I believe that the value of p_d provided for the Ramah Navajo females born in 1844–89 does not greatly underestimate the "true" value. The increase in p_d over the next two groups of females follows the rise in crude death rates that began in 1905–09 and continued, with some fluctuations, through 1944 (see Table 39).

The values of the index of potential selection and its components for the first group of Ramah Navajo females are all much lower than corresponding estimates for two populations representing "Early Man," as provided by Neel and Chagnon (1968). In fact, the value of I for the Ramah Navajo band, that is, females born in 1844–89, is matched only by the slightly smaller value of 0.384 of the Hutterite population provided by Spuhler (1962). In general, all of the values for I_m in the Ramah data are low enough to be compatible with the estimates for primitive populations, but they are too low to be compatible with those of early agricultural populations and too high with respect to modern industrialized nations (Neel and Chagnon 1968, Spuhler 1962, Salzano 1970). On the other hand, it is I_f (or I_f/p_s) that creates the greater problem in interpretation. The average values for the fertility components in this study of the Ramah Navajo are generally larger than those for three South American Indian populations described in the category "agriculturalists, fishers, and tribes somewhat acculturated" (Salzano 1970). However, the average total index falls near the middle of this group average—$I = 0.63$, 0.88,

1.29. We must concur with Neel and Chagnon that contemporary populations of primitive man are characterized by "intermediate *effective* fertility and early mortality." In the case of the Ramah Navajo band, the circumstances surrounding the founding and early stabilization of the band population brought about a decrease in selection intensity attributable to differential mortality and fertility. From the point of reference of the founding period population, we need consider only the early, very rapid growth of the Ramah Navajo with regard to shifts in the intensity of selection. Mayr (1963:238–39) describes this situation and the evolutionary implications:

> A shift in the intensity of selection pressure nearly always accompanies (or results from) a change in population size. Any sudden change in population size will affect genetic variability . . . . Temporary relaxation of selection pressure will permit survival of otherwise inferior genotypes, facilitating rare genetic recombinations that would be impossible during periods of severely adverse selection. Certain of these "improbable" genotypes may represent new adaptive peaks, and may be retained in the population when the period of higher selection intensity is reestablished.

Thus, we may conclude that initial heterogeneity introduced into the Ramah population by some of the founder families (Morgan 1968), the rapid growth of the population, especially during most of the stabilization period when the population was almost "closed" to the influx of new genetic material, the tendency toward multiple mating, clan and clan-group exogamy, and appreciable rates of in-migration, especially after 1929, have contributed to the maintenance of genetic variability in the Ramah Navajo population. The values of the index of potential selection (Table 46) for the Ramah Navajo population suggest that the potential for evolution has not decreased in recent decades. From the mortality analyses for the years since about 1950, however, we would predict that I_m will decrease rapidly in the future. Although there is also some evidence to suggest that fertility may be declining in the population since about 1950 (see Table 40), we cannot conclude that this is a real trend, nor can we predict the future course of I_f in this population. In their study of variously acculturated groups of Aymará-speaking people in the Andean region of Arica, Chile, Cruz-Coke et al. (1966) assert "that the total selective opportunities (measured by Crow's method) decrease in correlation to cultural evolution, but the fertility component increases."

large I_m upon first contact?

309

CONCLUSIONS

This study of the demographic history of the Ramah Navajo has attempted to provide empirical data of intrinsic value for students of population who are attempting to elucidate the structure and evolutionary potentials of small, anthropologically important populations and especially those populations faced with continuing changes in their physical and cultural environments. Furthermore, the data make clear not only the great complexity of factors that enter into the determination of the genetic structure of technologically primitive populations, but also the need for more complex models and procedures for evaluating the significance of any surveyed population for conclusions about early human evolution. With respect to the kinds of data needed to provide an adequate description of the genetic structure of primitive populations, Schull (1966:26–27) asserts:

> At a minimum, therefore, we are interested in a complete enumeration of the population; the best possible assessment of fertility and survival; a careful description of the social, biological, and physiological environments; and, quite possibly, the collection of genetic and/or physiological and/or growth and development data that are not conspicuously related to birth and death.

initial population survey

restrictions of synchronic studies ✳

Some of these kinds of data are available for the Ramah Navajo population of 1948 and 1950 but have not been presented here; other data are simply inadequate with regard to the time periods they cover. Furthermore, the suggestions quoted above with regard to data collection were specifically directed toward the design of genetic surveys of those populations that can reasonably satisfy an assumption of a kind of "biocultural equilibrium." Within the framework of about a hundred years of information, the Ramah Navajo population presents an almost ever-changing picture of genetic-demographic structure. It would not be surprising to find an additional dimension or development in the history of survival of this population if the population were again studied in this decade or during the next one.

With regard to the importance of cultural information in the empirical study of primitive groups, Neel and Salzano (1966:256) have emphasized that we must collect "data on those aspects of the cultural pattern with biological implications. Since without detailed knowledge it is impossible to dismiss any aspect of culture as without biological relevance, the implication is that these genetic studies must be paralleled by equally complete cultural studies." We have noted (Morgan 1968) how certain aspects of Navajo social organization, specifically the matrilineal clan system, have not only influenced the initial genetic composition of the population, but also the character of migration, the genetic contribution of migrants to the population, and the regulation of degree of consanguinity of endogamous matings. The significance of social organization for the determination of the initial genetic composition of reestablished and newly established band populations has been discussed in the case of two South American Indian tribes by Arends et al. (1967), Neel (1967), and Neel and Salzano (1967). The evolutionary implications of this "lineal effect" for intratribal genetic differentiation have been studied by Arends et al. and by Neel and Ward (1970), among others. In the case of the Ramah Navajo population, this effect of social organization on initial composition of the band and the subsequent distribution of genetic information had already been implied in the works of Kluckhohn and Griffith (1951), Kluckhohn (1956), and Spuhler and Kluckhohn (1953).

In the case of the Ramah Navajo, we further note that intertribal, intratribal, and probable European admixture before, during, and after the founding period must have contributed to the store of genetic diversity that we presume exists in the population. Obviously, the breeding unit, with reference to the Ramah Navajo population, has been much larger than the community. This has been pointed out in the case of the Xavante of South America by Salzano, Neel, and Maybury-Lewis (1967: 469), who conclude: "*In general, we believe that recent events have not created but only increased the internal mobility of the Xavantes* [Salzano's italics]. If this is correct, then it is clear that one may derive a very biased picture of the tribal dynamics of this (and presumably any other) Indian tribe during the course of a brief contact." In the present study, we have attempted to link migration patterns with sociohistorical developments. It appears that changes in mobility within and outside of the community after the end of the stabilization period find some explanation in the cyclical nature of Navajo residence and resource-control patterns (Reynolds, Lamphere, and Cook 1967). The residence cycle and the rules for transmitting the control of resources are coherent aspects of Navajo social organization. A growing population and major environmental changes have contributed to the increased dispersion of sibling groups over the entire area and even outside of the community. But, acculturation has *not created* the processes of residence-group formation and fission.

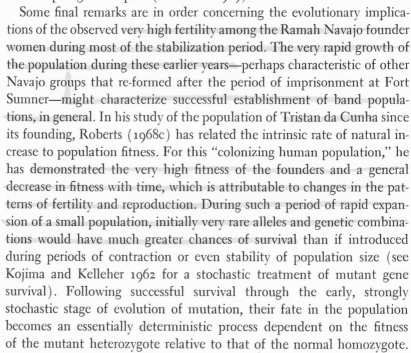

A historical approach to migration between small villages or communities of primitive cultures would seem necessary for adequate assessment of genetic relationships among these population units. This was found to be the case in the study of genetic microdifferentiation among seven villages of Makiritare Indians of southern Venezuela (Ward and Neel 1970b). There is no substitution for histories if we are going to ask questions about the actual paths followed by populations during their evolution. This problem—one of discerning the trajectories—is quite different from that which attempts to model the degree and kind of stability of a set of populations presumed to be in the region of an equilibrium point in a complex genetic space (Lewontin 1969).

Some final remarks are in order concerning the evolutionary implications of the observed very high fertility among the Ramah Navajo founder women during most of the stabilization period. The very rapid growth of the population during these earlier years—perhaps characteristic of other Navajo groups that re-formed after the period of imprisonment at Fort Sumner—might characterize successful establishment of band populations, in general. In his study of the population of Tristan da Cunha since its founding, Roberts (1968c) has related the intrinsic rate of natural increase to population fitness. For this "colonizing human population," he has demonstrated the very high fitness of the founders and a general decrease in fitness with time, which is attributable to changes in the patterns of fertility and reproduction. During such a period of rapid expansion of a small population, initially very rare alleles and genetic combinations would have much greater chances of survival than if introduced during periods of contraction or even stability of population size (see Kojima and Kelleher 1962 for a stochastic treatment of mutant gene survival). Following successful survival through the early, strongly stochastic stage of evolution of mutation, their fate in the population becomes an essentially deterministic process dependent on the fitness of the mutant heterozygote relative to that of the normal homozygote.

The evolution of human populations is greatly influenced by a variable unique to the human species—culture. Viewed as a biological adaption to changing environments, thereby supplementing man's historical evolution (Spuhler 1959), cultural behavior introduces indeterminism into the outcome of human population genetic "experiments."

Kenneth Morgan

N O T E S

1. This work is part of a thesis submitted to the Graduate School of the University of Michigan in partial fulfillment of the requirements for the Ph.D. degree. The support of the U.S. Public Health Service Grant 5–T01–GM–00071–10 and Population Council Grant D67.4 is gratefully acknowledged. Author's present address: Department of Genetics, University of Alberta, Edmonton.

2. The sources of material for this study have been described in detail elsewhere (Morgan 1968). Briefly, census and genealogical materials pertaining to the Ramah Navajo population before about 1950 were made available by J. N. Spuhler, Department of Anthropology, the University of New Mexico. New population data, relevant through the fall of 1966, along with some verification of the older data and collection of other kinds of information, were gathered by me in 1966. Recent census information on selected Navajo populations is also provided in this study.

3. Although the size of the reservation was increased by three times before 1900, and by an additional 50 percent from 1900 to 1933, most of this added area was already occupied by Navajos and was, in general, of the poorest quality for agricultural pursuits.

4. By definition, an "outfit" includes a married couple, their married children, and their married grandchildren.

5. For more detailed information on various aspects of Ramah Navajo history, see Kluckhohn (1956, 1966) and references cited therein.

6. It is important to remember that the present study takes the first generation of the Ramah Navajo genealogy as the origin for various demographic estimates. We have excluded the ancestors of the founders who may have spent some time in the population with their founder offspring. This, however, excludes few individuals who may have survived in the population after 1889. In addition, great effort was expended in attempting to decide whether genealogically relevant individuals were actual residents of the population. Additional comments on the composing of the data will appear when necessary.

7. In the tabulation of the migration data, time spent by certain individuals out of the population on job relocation, in seasonal employment, in military service, and during eventually terminated marriages or affairs is not considered as out-migration, as long as these individuals return to reside in the population for the greater amount of their lives.

Inasmuch as the volume of migration is small in proportion to births and deaths after the founding period, this approach would not appear to invalidate the interpretations of population dynamics. The classification does break down somewhat when applied to the most recent decade of events. Some of the individuals classified as emigrants from the Ramah Navajo community since about 1955 or later might not be considered emigrants according to this classification method, if enough time were permitted for them to return with their families (or without them) to the community. In addition, some young people who continue their education and employment outside the area, and who are currently considered to be members of the population, might be adjudged emigrants from the vantage point of a later period in time.

8. See Kluckhohn (1956) for examples illustrating the character of immigration and emigration in this community during the years 1890 to 1950.

9. The deficiency of male livebirths for the birth cohort 1940–44 is not accounted

313

for by stillborn: of the total of four stillborn ascertained for this cohort, two were female, one was male, and only one was of unknown sex. In addition, only one sex-unknown livebirth is recorded for this same interval of birth years.

10. According to Kluckhohn and Leighton (1962:37), "after the Pueblo Rebellion of 1680, Indians from Jemez and other pueblos took refuge for some years among The People [i.e., the Navajo]. In the eighteenth century numerous Hopi fled from the drought and famine to live with the Navahos, especially in Canyon de Chelly." In addition, captivity at Fort Sumner brought together previously dispersed Navajos and some Apaches. Finally, the Navajos of the Mt. Taylor region and of the Puertecito-Alamo band had some Spanish and Apache ancestry (Kluckhohn 1956).

11. The formulas presented in this section with regard to the index of potential selection—or, as originally termed, the index of total selection intensity—are all those of Crow's (1958) method.

12. For additional definitions and derivations, see Crow (1958) and Spuhler (1962).

Pingelap and Mokil Atolls:
A Problem in Population Structure[1]

N. E. MORTON
J. N. HURD
G. F. LITTLE
Population Genetics Laboratory
University of Hawaii

Pingelap and Mokil atolls lie between the volcanic islands of Ponape and Kusaie in the Eastern Carolines, forming part of Ponape District, U.S. Trust Territory of the Pacific Islands. Despite immigration from considerable distances, they have a high concentration of a recessive gene for achromatopsia and show other evidence of genetic drift. We chose Pingelap and Mokil for intensive study as typical examples of island populations, peculiarly suitable for comparison of different measures of kinship derived from genealogies, bioassay, and demography.

ETHNOHISTORY

In the absence of a definitive ethnology of Pingelap, we relied on three elderly Pingelapese informants. Dison Aia was born in 1882. He held the title of Nanno and was famous for his knowledge of legends and genealogies. (In Pingelap society, titles were hereditary and generally passed from father to son.) About 1960, he went to Kolonia, the District Center, and dictated some of this lore into a disk recorder belonging to the Department of Education. These disks have been lost, but a Ponapean summary by Salo Solomon is kept in the Municipal Office of Pingelap. During our 1969 field trip, this was translated by Elias Robert, representative of Pingelap in the Ponape District Legislature. Typescripts in Ponapean and English are on file in the Bishop Museum, Honolulu, under the title *"Duen Tapida en Wein Pingelap"* ("How Pingelap Began"). Unfortunately, Dison died before our second field trip in 1970; thus, it was not possible to reconcile several inconsistencies and ambiguities in the written account. Among the surviving Pingelapese, the one generally conceded to know the ethnohistory best is Aiel Sikuau, the Nahnkin (one of the higher titles), who was born in 1896. He spent a month with us in Honolulu in 1970, and tape recordings of chants and his review of this material are on file at the library of the University of Hawaii. In the Pingelapese village of Mand on Ponape, the oldest man is Misiel Johnson, born in 1885. A deacon in the church, he holds no secular title. He learned some of the ethnohistory of Pingelap from his mother, a daughter of Okonomwaun, who was, at the time, the Nanmwarki (effectively, the chief of the island). Misiel recorded what he had learned in a notebook, which has been translated by Hurd.

Historical genetic studies require some assessment of the duration of time actually spanned by ethnohistorical events. Reckoning of time, before Western contact, depended on the fishing cycle. The months of March and April are the season for flying fish (Bentzen 1949). Canoes set out when the moon is down. Palm torches bound at intervals with fibers are allowed to smolder until the canoes form a semicircle, whereupon the distal node is shaken off and the torches flare up. In each canoe, one man on the central platform holds a torch high, scattering embers downwind and startling the fish; fore and aft, a man sweeps a large hand net through the air and shallowly into the water in pursuit of single fish. For two months, this is a principal source of protein and an exciting activity for the men, surrounded by taboos: women and the Nanmwarki cannot participate, and food and sexual intercourse are prohibited for the fishermen until they return near dawn. Sometimes in its frightened leap, a needle fish grazes a fisherman, drawing blood. This is offered as the explanation for the taboo on the Nanmwarki. As holder of supernatural power, he is not allowed the human frailty of bleeding, which, in pre-Christian times, could have served as an excuse to depose him.

316

This kind of torch fishing is called *kahlek* ("dancing"), after the graceful motions of the netmen. The same term is applied to the month of March and also means year. Thus, the passage of *n* years is measured by *n* seasons of torch fishing. The year is divided into 12 months, corresponding at the present time to the Gregorian calendar (see Table 47).

TABLE 47
PINGELAPESE MONTHS OF THE YEAR

English	*Pingelapese*
March	kahlek
April	soungpwong in wela
May	palekewar
June	solodan
July	sokosok
August	idid
September	meseneir
October	kepihsukoru
November	pikker
December	ikehwa
January	epwelap
February	memwaleu
year	kahlek

However, a "lunar" calendar of 31 days still exists (Table 48) and is used to regulate fishing and planting and to predict weather for short periods of time. It is constantly readjusted to the lunar cycle, so that in practice, there seems to have been no conflict between the requirements of navigators for a calendar of 365 days and of fishermen for a lunar month of 28 days. Similar compromises were made in other parts of Micronesia (Goodenough 1953).

While the ethnohistorical material summarized in Table 49 should obviously not be taken as literally true, it reveals many aspects of Pingelapese culture. Navigators from other islands have high status. The legendary founders are termed navigators. According to legend, the navigator Waela, who accompanied Mwungesamorou, is dispatched on a confidential mission. The navigator Akakailok, who arrived after Mesou's death, figures more prominently in that legend than the leader Wonlap. The ghost asks for Akakailok by name and has a contest with him. Goodenough (1953) comments on the freemasonry that existed

TABLE 48

PINGELAPESE DAYS OF THE LUNAR MONTH

Day	English	Pingelapese
1	new moon	esukoru
2		eling
3		esehm
4		mesepong
5		mesalim
6		mesawoun
7		meseis
8		mesawel
9		welduadu
10	half moon	medel
11		siepwong
12		arkone
13		sakainpe
14		wolpwu
15		wolmwau
16		mas
17		er
18	full moon	lelidi
19		komwalo
20		edemen komwalo
21		apeleng
22		sengek
23		wesengek
24		dahpas
25		dahpas meing
26		keredakehleng
27		areiso
28		semwenpal
29		ihla
30		esep
31		epei

among navigators in the Central Carolines, who, abroad as well as at home, were served food separately from their crew.

In the centuries after the islands of Ponape District were colonized from the West, there was a marked decline in navigational skill, especially on the high islands of Kusaie and Ponape, where the seagoing outrigger canoe was gradually modified into a shallow-draft vessel suitable for the sheltered waters of the reef. Sarfert (1919) gives evidence that Kusaie once sent canoes as far as Truk and engaged in regular commerce with Gilbertese and other islanders. Loss of navigational skills in the high

TABLE 49
NANMWARKIS OF PINGELAP AND
ETHNOHISTORICAL EVENTS

Number	Name	Events
(1)	Iengir sang Eir	Two navigator brothers from Yap discovered Pingelap. Mwoimok remained, and Palialap continued on to Kusaie. Mwoimok's three children (Riroman, Pikepik en Eir, and Pikepik en Epeng) left Yap to search for him but missed Pingelap. Mwoimok returned to Yap to look for his children. While there, he married Damari and had a daughter Nieri. On their return to Pingelap, Nieri had four children, a son Iengir sang Eir, who became the first Nanmwarki, and three daughters from whom came the people of Pingelap.
(2)	Kaupene	The son of Iengir sang Eir and Langedi, Kaupene made the taro pit. People split into two competing districts, Likinepeng (Lehpeng) and Lepeir, over the quarrel between two men, Luken Epeng and Lapwue. People of Likinepeng won the contest.
(3)	Pakispok	The son of Kaupene and Lienme was Pakispok. People now split into four competing sections, Peruku, Kahkahlia, Sekarakapw, and Mweniap (the richest). Pakispok declared war on Ponape and ordered the women and children to accompany the men. Selepas, one of the fiercest Pingelapese warriors, remained on Ponape when the fleet returned to Pingelap.
(4)	Inenikas	Inenikas was the son of Pakispok and Liekemahu. He and his son were killed in a typhoon called Lenglame, Lenglapalap, or Nohlik. Famine followed.
(5)	Mwungesamorou	Mwungesamorou came from Kusaie with the navigator Waela. Finding Pingelap chiefless, he remained as Nanmwarki and

TABLE 49, cont'd.

Number	Name	Events
		sent Waela to Kusaie to summon Sahu en Welang. Waela returned with Sahu and his 14 children. Mwungesamorou then went back to Kusaie.
(6)	Sahu en Welang	Kusaiean successor to Mwungesamorou was Sahu en Welang.
(7)	Saue	Sahu's son was Saue.
(8)	Naniok	Naniok was the son of Saue. Naniok's son Naweidil declined the nanmwarkiship lest he be a failure.
(9)	Mesou	The son of Naniok's sister was Mesou. He and half the people of Mweniap were eaten by a ghost. Wonlap and navigator Akakailok came from Kusaie.
(10)	Sahu Nadaura	The son of Mesou, Sahu Nadaura went to Ponape with the Kusaiean expedition of Isokehlekel to conquer Nan Madol. He ruled the Pingelapese mercilessly.
(11)	Mwaseudue	Mwaseudue was the son of Sahu Nadaura, according to Dison; according to Aiel, he was the son of Mesou.
(12)	Mwanokasa	The son of Mwaseudue, Mwanokasa was kindly, and the Pingelapese said, "he is not a Delewan."
(13)	Widinenek	Widinenek was the son of Mwanokasa, according to Dison, but according to Aiel, he was the first Delewan Nanmwarki. There was famine during his four-year reign.
(14)	Mwakadue	Mwakadue's relationship to Widinenek is unknown. After 14 years, he resigned.
(15)	Widinenek (again)	Widinenek reigned for 18 years until his death.

Number	Name	Events
(16)	Ikohkepel	Ikohkepel, the son of Widinenek, was cuckolded by Sikimwas, whom he ordered killed. Semenuhwe, Mwahuele, Isimedua, and Manuse, the brothers of Sikimwas, vowed revenge. They were joined by other Pingelapese. After a battle in canoes, the surviving Delewans fled over the horizon.
(17)	Semenuhwe	Before being elected king, Semenuhwe portioned out the land to the men.
(18)	Mwahuele	Mwahuele ("good direction") was the brother of Semenuhwe. When he became Nanmwarki, the typhoon Lengkieki ("rough sky") threw a great block of coral onto the reef. Only about 30 people survived the ensuing famine.
(19)	Mwanenised	The son of Mwahuele and Liwaidak, Mwanenised ruled for 24 years.
(20)	Wadekpene	Wadekpene was the brother of Mwanenised, whose oldest son Saken (Sakelapalap) was considered too young. Wadekpene held a feast at which each of the four sections was to bring only *seuwa* taro. Mweniap won easily. Wadekpene ruled for nine years.
(21)	Okonomwaun	The son of Wadekpene and Liemad, Okonomwaun repulsed a party of Marshallese under Kabua and ruled for 48 years. He called himself Mweikos, "the old-timer," and forbade missionary activity on Pingelap.
(22)	Iengiringer	The adopted son of Okonomwaun, Iengiringer was the true son of Sasang and Losmweniap. He became Nanmwarki in 1870. He had three wives. When the missionaries arrived in 1873, they baptized him Salomon and induced him to divorce one of his two surviving wives. A church was built. Iengiringer ruled until his death in 1881.

TABLE 49, cont'd.

Number	Name	Events
(23)	Sapwenpar	Sapwenpar, the son of Iengiringer and Lieudirong, was a strict Christian who forbade all work or recreation on Sunday. The German governor Doser authorized him to perform weddings. He ruled for 43 years (1871–1924). His formal name was Inapon and, in dealing with Westerners, Napoleon Bishop.
(24)	Dicksalomon	The alleged son of Sapwenpar and Lienwarau, Dicksalomon was rumored to have really been fathered by Sapwenpar's cousin Loawiak. He gained the title of Chief Magistrate from the Japanese administration and visited Japan. He divorced his Pingelapese wife to marry Karlina, a Mokilese. He ruled from 1924–64.
(25)	Dens	Dens was the son of Dicksalomon and Karlina. He went to school in Palau and visited Japan. He became Nanmwarki in 1964 and was elected Chief Magistrate.

islands probably accounts for the infrequent mention of Ponape in the ethnohistory, when all other evidence indicates the closest cultural ties to Pingelap.

The legendary founders were said to have sailed from Yap. This is not to be understood as the high island presently known by this name, since to the natives of the Carolines, Yap is the habitation of the gods in the western ocean.

The expedition of Isokehlekel figures in the legends of both Kusaie and Ponape, where one of the leaders is said to have come from Ngatik; no mention is made of Pingelapese membership in the party of 333 men who allegedly went to Ponape in a single canoe and conquered the palace of Nan Madol, which dates from before the twelfth century (Long 1965). Dison did not refer to this expedition in his narrative; Misiel assigned it to the Nanmwarki Sahu Nadaura, who allegedly accompanied the Kusaieans. Aiel considers that Sahu Nadaura was one of the two Pingelapese participants, but was not a Nanmwarki, and that Isokehlekel's expedition occurred much earlier, perhaps in the reign of Pakispok. Bollig (1927) recounts a presumably derived Truk legend about a chief from Yap called Esoukereker, who, with the help of Trukese, conquered Ponape.

During the reign of Nanmwarki Kaupene, the people of Pingelap split into two competing districts, Lehpeng and Lepeir; this was a common basis for social organization in Micronesia. Then, by the time of Nanmwarki Pakispok, each district had split into four competing sections— Peruku and Kahkahlia comprising Lehpeng, and Sekarakapw and Mweniap being the sections (*pwekil*) of Lepeir. Each section maintained a separate men's house, until the reign of Sapwenpar, when Christian opposition prevented their reinstitution after the 1905 typhoon. Competition between these men's houses included contests of running, jumping, canoe paddling, sailing, wrestling, stick throwing, and kite flying, although in recent years, it appears that only children flew kites. Since the beginning of Christian times, each section has had a chapel, and competition includes the singing of hymns. For many activities, the four sections are more manageable social units than the two districts. At the present time, the sections take turns doing communal work and providing food for guests at the community house. Each section is split into small residential units for certain activities.

The legendary war with Ponape that occurred during the reign of Nanmwarki Pakispok included women and children. This was a frequent pattern in Micronesia, where a warrior who injured a woman or child was shamed. Women could therefore aid their men, not only by ministering to their needs, but also by harassing the enemy in various ways without great physical danger. The story of Selepas, the fierce warrior, is related by Sarfert (1919) as a Kusaiean legend. It agrees with the Pingelapese story in many details.

The disastrous typhoon during the reign of Nanmwarki Inenikas is said to have left only about 30 survivors. Mwungesamorou, leader of an expedition from Kusaie, was able to establish himself as Nanmwarki and be succeeded by a line of Kusaiean kings that, according to Dison, extended until the revolt of Semenuhwe, the seventeenth Nanmwarki. Misiel and Aiel, however, consider that the Kusaiean line terminated after Sahu en Welang and control reverted to the Pingelapese. They believe that Kusaiean women did not accompany Sahu. Misiel's account omits Saue, said by Dison to be the son of Sahu, and inserts a Gilbertese Nanmwarki named Kas between Mesou and Sahu Nadaura. This "reading-frame mutation" preserves the numbering of the Nanmwarkis from 1 to 6 and 10 to 25. No explanation is offered of how a Gilbertese could establish himself as Nanmwarki. Aiel does not recall Kas but considers that the line of Nanmwarkis beginning with Widinenek and called Delewan stems from the Gilbert Islands, perhaps from Tarawa, and arrived on Pingelap in two large canoes. Dison disputed this, believing that Gilbertese have come with women and children from time to time and most recently during the reign of Nanmwarki Okonomwaun, but that they have never succeeded in usurping the nanmwarkiship. He could not explain how the term Delewan came to be applied to the line of Nanmwarkis beginning with Widinenek. Friction between the royal Delewan line and the Pingelapese people led to expulsion of the Delewans after the sixteenth Nanmwarki, Ikohkepel. However, the cause of the friction was not nationalism per se but revenge for the killing of Sikimwas, the Pingelapese lover of Ikohkepel's wife.

The nanmwarkiship was usually transmitted from father to son. Exceptions to patrilineal inheritance of the nanmwarkiship include transmission to a nephew, Mesou, when the son of the former Nanmwarki Naniok declared himself unworthy; conquest, as in the case of Mwungesamorou; and election by the people or their leaders, as with Semenuhwe. By the time of Semenuhwe, property was also patrilineal. According to Aiel, in the reign of Nanmwarki Okonomwaun, women began to inherit land, but in lesser measure than their brothers. The typhoon Lengkieki after Semenuhwe's death caused a famine that killed most of the Pingelapese people and must have required a division of land during Mwahuele's reign. (Aspects of the nanmwarkiship relations may sometimes be inferred from kinship terms that have been provided in Table 50.)

Mwahuele's successor was Mwanenised, during whose time two American ships sighted Pingelap. In 1793, Captain Musgrave, in the ship *Sugar-Cane*, reported some small islands in the approximate location of Pingelap. On 29 October 1809, Captain MacAskill, in the ship *Lady Barlowe* on her passage from Port Jackson to China, rediscovered the atoll and gave its accurate longitude and latitude. It does not appear from Musgrave's account that he landed. Since Captain MacAskill reported the central coordinates for the atoll, he may have gone ashore, but this is not certain. This visit, if it occurred, made little impression on the Pingelapese, who note as the only significant event of Mwanenised's reign

TABLE 50
PINGELAPESE KINSHIP TERMS*

Relation to Ego	Pingelapese Term†
father	semei (addressed as "pahpa")
mother	inei (addressed as "nohno")
son	nei wol, nei pwisak
daughter	nei lih, nei serepein
child	nei seri
husband	wolemen ei pwoud
wife	lihmen ei pwoud
sibling	riei
sibling of opposite sex to ego	peinei
kin (including affines)	peineinei
spouse	pwoudei
uncle	siki semei (addressed as "pahpa")
aunt	sikin inei (addressed as "nohno")
paternal uncle	rien semei wol
paternal aunt	rien semei lih, peinen semei
maternal uncle	rien inei wol, peinen inei
maternal aunt	rien inei lih
father's sibling	rien semei
mother's sibling	rien inei
grandfather	semei mado (addressed as "pahpa")
grandmother	inei mado (addressed as "nohno")
great grandfather	semen semei mado (addressed as "pahpa")
great grandmother	inen inei mado (addressed as "nohno")
maternal grandfather	semen inei
paternal grandfather	semen semei
maternal grandmother	inen inei
paternal grandmother	inen semei
oldest sibling of either sex	meseini
oldest female sibling	meseini lih
oldest male sibling	meseini wol

Relationship	Pingelapese Term†
related, in same generation, even if only by friendship	riari
genetic relationship with male of any older generation or affinal relationship with male of the preceding generation	semasem
genetic relationship with female of any older generation or affinal relationship with female of the preceding generation	inain

TABLE 50, cont'd.

Relationship	Pingelapese Term†
related to a member of opposite sex so closely as to preclude marriage	peinain
to treat as one's father	semanikin
to treat as one's mother	inanikin
to treat as one's child	nainikin
to treat as one's sibling	rianikin
to treat as a sib of opposite sex	peinanikin

* This table uses conventional Ponapean orthography. It is not a phonemic transcription of Pingelapese.

† Any cognate may be prefaced by "udahn" (true) to signify biological kinship.

that he caught a large tuna. During the nineteenth century, Pingelap was commonly known as MacAskill Island, but the captain is now memorialized only in a modern Pingelapese legend that the first name given by Westerners to the atoll was Madagascar Island. (See Table 51 for a brief chronological survey of events in Pingelapese history.)

The ethnohistory of Mokil, although gathered 20 years earlier by Weckler (1949) and Bentzen (1949), is much less detailed than that of Pingelap. From genealogies, Weckler calculated the approximate date of typhoon Lengkieki as 1775. Before the typhoon, a Marshallese invasion is variously said to have been repulsed (Weckler) or to have killed all the men, so that the modern population of Mokil is descended from the children of Marshallese men and a Mokilese woman (Eilers 1934). After the typhoon, there was a redivision of land and a feud among the surviving lineages. Several of the Nanmwarkis were murdered or deposed, with the result that since Lengkieki, Mokil has had twice as many Nanmwarkis as Pingelap. Because of disputes over land rights and copra trading, the Mokilese appointed no successor to Nanmwarki August when he died about 1957.

Contact Within Micronesia

Of the 18 survivors of typhoon Lengkieki on Mokil, one was a woman named Apalaysu, whose parents had come in a canoe from Pingelap. Fourteen other Pingelapese have since migrated to Mokil and had children

TABLE 51

A PINGELAPESE CHRONOLOGY

Year	Event
1000(?)	Settlement of Pingelap
1500(?)	Attack on Nan Madol
1775(?)	Typhoon Lengkieki
1790(?)	Mwahuele dies; Mwanenised becomes Nanmwarki
1793	Pingelap discovered by Capt. Musgrave
1809	Pingelap rediscovered by Capt. MacAskill
1814	Mwanenised dies; Wadekpene becomes Nanmwarki
1822	Wadekpene enfeebled; Okonomwaun becomes Nanmwarki
1824	Visit of Duperry on *La Coquille*
1828	Visit of Lütke on *Le Seniavine*
1833	Capt. MacAuliffe of whaler *Nimrod* killed
1851	Capt. Lewis of whaler *Boy* murdered
1853	Visit of Commander Hammet on *H.M.S. Serpent (Ianowo?)*
1856	Marshallese attack and "Tugulu war"
1858	Visit of Capt. Moore on mission ship *Morning Star*
1870	Okonomwaun dies; Iengiringer becomes Nanmwarki
1872	Bully Hayes holds chief for ransom
1873	Two Pingelapese return from mission school on Ponape
	A school and church are established
1881	Iengiringer dies; Sapwenpar becomes Nanmwarki
1886	Beginning of Spanish period
1895	Visit of Lorenzo Moya on gunboat *Quiros*
1899	Beginning of German period
1905	Typhoon forces emigration of 67 people
1907	First laborers to Nauru
1911	Settlement of Sokehs begins after Germans deport Ponape rebels
1914	Beginning of Japanese period
1924	Sapwenpar dies; Dicksalomon becomes Nanmwarki
1945	Beginning of American period
1954	Homesteading begins in Mand village on Ponape
1957	Typhoon damages crops; famine threatens
1964	Dicksalomon dies; Dens becomes Nanmwarki

there. An old Pingelapese chant (*kepeisik*) recounts how some Pingelapese sailed to Mokil, were received kindly, returned to Pingelap, and then set out again with gifts for Mokil. Missing that island, they arrived on Ponape. Reference to Kolonia in this chant indicates that it was composed in Spanish or German times, but there is no reason to suppose that deliberate canoe voyages were less frequent before foreign contact.

Mokilese legends tell of giants from the northern waves (Eilers 1934). In recent centuries, few Ponapeans have migrated to Pingelap and Mokil.

However, three canoes drifted from Mokil to Ponape in 1840 (Nautical Magazine 1870). Some Ponapeans are said to have put to sea in canoes because of a love affair and landed on Pingelap (American Board of Commissioners for Foreign Missions 1856). Nowadays, Mokilese occasionally go to Ponape in a whaleboat with an outboard motor, rather than waiting for a ship. Coulter (1957:336) noted during his visit to Pingelap that "sometimes when there are strong objections to the marriage, the lovers elope in a canoe and flee to Ponape, as two did about five months before my visit. The journey of 175 miles is not very hazardous in good weather, for the regular trade winds blow in that direction much of the year."

Kusaie, which gave a prehistoric line of Pingelapese Nanmwarkis and the title Dokosa used on Pingelap for the Nanmwarki, has yielded few migrants to the atolls in historic times, the most notable being a man named Kileusa, who traveled to Pingelap in a canoe with two Mortlockese during the reign of Okonomwaun. Kileusa is remembered as the ancestor of many Pingelapese, largely because he had the good sense, when Okonomwaun abducted his wife, to console himself with her younger sister. In the early nineteenth century, two Pingelapese men drifted ashore on Kusaie (Sarfert 1919). The two Mortlockese who came with Kileusa are said by Aiel to have killed a man on Nama Island and fled. They sighted Pingelap but were frightened by kites being flown by the competing men's houses and turned southward to Kusaie. Later, one of them dreamed of Pingelap and persuaded his companion and Kileusa to return.

The extent of prehistoric contact with the Gilbertese is uncertain, as noted in the above discussion of Pingelapese ethnohistory. Aiel believes that Gilbertese men and women often go fishing for sharks far from shore and are carried by wind and current to Pingelap. He considers that the descendants of the Gilbertese who arrived in two canoes became powerful enough to gain the nanmwarkiship until expelled by Semenuhwe. During the time of Okonomwaun, a canoe drifted from the Gilberts. The only survivor was a woman, Tawa. Two other women, Nakedin and Lohra, disembarked from a sailing ship with a man who was killed by the Pingelapese after he murdered the trader John Higgins in a drunken brawl. Tawa and Nakedin married and have many descendants. Lohra, who was childless, is the subject of several drawings in the report of the Hamburg expedition (Eilers 1934) because of her elaborate tattooing. Two Gilbertese men entered the Pingelap genealogies through western contact: Dikerau sailed on a whaling ship to Ponape, and Dongou was transported to Hawaii by blackbirders. While working in the cane fields, Dongou fell in with Kamehlia, the sole survivor of a group of some 30 men who had been shanghaied from Pingelap. They agreed to work on a whaling ship until they got to either Pingelap or the Gilberts. Touching first at Pingelap, they said that the other men had entered a big machine looking for sugar and never returned. With this allegory, they ended their travels and entered the gene pool.

Weckler (1949) notes that about 1880, three Gilbertese who had been fishing drifted to Mokil after six or seven weeks at sea. One died, and the other two returned to the Gilberts with the help of Ponape missionaries. In 1911 or 1912, one of these men returned to Ponape in a whaleboat, staying at Pingelap a month en route. During whaling days, Mokil was a favorite place for recreation, but feuding kept the population small. Several Gilbertese women were abandoned on Mokil by a whaling ship. Tradition disputes whether this act was prompted by boredom, consideration for the limited choice of Mokilese men, or to lighten the load of Mokilese women who went aboard ship for the refreshment of the crew. Missionaries are said to have stopped this practice on Mokil in 1858, but much later, Bully Hayes was still scattering his lights-of-love around the Pacific. At a hearing on Kusaie, witnesses deposed that in March 1872, Bully had held the chief of Pingelap hostage for the delivery of two girls and 7,000 coconuts, but had settled for one girl and 5,000 coconuts; they testified further that in July of that year, he had taken a ten-year-old Pingelapese girl ashore at Providence Island and brutally violated her. These charges were not proven, and Bully was never prosecuted, but his letter of recommendation "to all whom it may concern" was preserved by at least one island beauty who had spent several months on his vessel (Michener and Day 1957).

According to Weckler (1949), the Marshallese made no significant contributions to the Mokilese gene pool before Lengkieki; in fact, Pingelapese legend does not include Marshallese until the nineteenth century. However, Marshallese figure so prominently in later contact that earlier migration must be inferred. King George of Kusaie (1837–54) said that two canoes came from Ebon before his reign and two more since, each carrying five to 20 people, most of whom afterwards returned home (Sarfert 1919). Around 1856, a large fleet of canoes traveling from Ebon to Jaluit was blown off course. Most of them arrived at Kusaie and returned with other Marshallese who had been living there (Simmons et al. 1965a). Two canoes with 30 to 40 people reached Mokil and returned to the Marshalls. The Nanmwarki of Mokil accompanied them to Jabwot. Two other canoes carrying the young Hirohs Kabua (a Marshallese high chief) reached Pingelap and settled on Tugulu (Sukoru) islet. They attacked Pingelap but were driven off by Okonomwaun and returned to Jaluit. Pingelapese legend recounts the friendship of Kabua with a young Pingelapese. When a war party of Marshallese planned to return to Pingelap, he opposed them and at night cut the bindings of the outriggers. Disregarding their chief, the warriors set out, and the entire fleet was lost.

On these bare facts and Pingelapese tradition, a curious tale was built by Louis Becke (1894) in his short story *Ninia*. He begins by an accurate description of Pingelap, followed by an account of a war between Tugulu and Pingelap, in which an American sailor under the Pingelapese chief Sralik massacres the Tugulu people. Eilers (1934) took this for history, but there is no memory on Pingelap of a chief named Sralik, an American sailor with a gun, a civil war, or the names like Ninia and Ruvani used by Becke. Perhaps the story is built on the occupation of Tugulu by the Marshallese. However, since it is obvious that Becke used a few facts about the Pingelapese as the basis for fiction, there is no need for further speculation about the "Tugulu war."

During whaling times and thereafter, a few immigrants came through Ponape to the melting pot of Pingelap and Mokil from other parts of Micronesia, including Ngatik, Truk, Palau, and Guam.

Contacts Outside Micronesia

Gene flow with the whalers began around 1840. On Mokil, a "whaler seaman," a Portuguese sailor (from New Bedford?), a "Captain Wick," and a "Captain Dennis" figure in the genealogies. Two ship captains and a passenger were murdered on Pingelap during the reign of Okonomwaun (*Morning Herald* [Sydney] 1834, *Nautical Magazine* 1854). Several scientific expeditions made visits, including *H.M.S. Serpent* in 1853, which may be the source of the reference to English *lanowo* (man-of-war?) inserted into an older Pingelapese chant, *liamweimwei*. These events and visits of Mokilese women aboard whaling vessels seem to have contributed little, if anything, to the gene pool. Pingelap was more isolated from the whalers, who are not known to have left a child there. Contact with Spain, which owned the islands before 1899, was negligible. One German, called Perman in the genealogies, had a family on Pingelap. The American administration has left a few children on Mokil but not on Pingelap.

During Japanese times, copra traders and a military detachment on Pingelap entered into liaisons that were terminated during the war. Children of these unions are distinctly lighter and more delicately built than the Micronesians. A Filipino variously described as a trader in beche-de-mer and an unsuccessful missionary had a family on Pingelap. When the Germans put down the rebellion in Sokehs, they imported police from New Guinea. Two of these had children with a Pingelapese woman. Even the second generation has Melanesian features.

The most surprising immigration into Mokil and Pingelap is a kindred with a Gm (1, 5, 6) allele, which seems always of African origin. This pedigree stems from Captain Wick, who married the Mokilese woman Moonpwo. According to Weckler (1949), she was half-Caucasian, her father being an Englishman named Sek Semit (Jack Smith); today, however, elderly informants consider that Moonpwo was pure Mokilese. No one living at the time of this study ever saw Moonpwo or Captain Wick, although their daughter, Sera, was described as having curly brown hair (not kinky) and light skin, not much darker than a sunburned Caucasian. Despite her appearance, Sera transmitted a Gm allele of African origin, presumably acquired from a light Mulatto father.

DISCUSSION

We have presented as much ethnohistorical information as we have been able to collect about the composition of the Pingelapese and Mokilese populations. The record leaves no doubt that immigration has been both accidental and deliberate (Riesenberg 1965:156):

Generally the picture is one of almost constant but rather haphazard and random contact, in nearly all directions, with few barriers imposed by prevailing wind or current or other natural phenomena. The number of people making these voyages varied from single survivors to large groups which could significantly change the genetic composition of the island soon upon arrival. Whether in pre-European times those who arrived killed islanders or were killed by them,

331

soon departed alone, or with friends and captives, or were integrated into the island community varied from voyage to voyage. Such fortuitous historical facts were always crucial to understanding the genetic pattern of the populations.

Several features of these populations present interesting problems to the geneticist:

(1) Immigration from all corners of the earth suggests a melting pot, but there is also evidence for genetic drift. Can this paradox be resolved by finding that genealogies, demography, cognate frequencies, polymorphisms, and other evidence from which kinship can be estimated are in quantitative agreement?

(2) The small number of founders after typhoon Lengkieki, the remarkable oral tradition of genealogies in Micronesia, informative kinship terminology (Table 50), and the admirable work of Weckler (1949) and Bentzen (1949) on Mokil a score of years ago make it possible to construct accurate genealogies back to 1775. By using the methods of historical genetics, can we infer the composition of the founder population and the immigrants who contributed additional variability?

(3) What are the genetic effects of division of the population into matrilineal clubs, both at present and in the remote hypothetical time when they were regularly exogamous?

(4) What insight does clan *isonymy* (concordance of clans between pairs of individuals) provide into population structure?

(5) How does the structure of this population compare with other populations in which kinship has been assayed?

(6) Does the history of this population, and especially the small number of founders, explain the high frequency of achromatopsia?

(7) Are there features of this population that facilitate or interfere with methods to reduce the frequency of achromatopsia?

(8) Do inferences from intensive study of this population agree with extensive data on polymorphisms in Micronesia?

Discussion of these questions will be deferred until the data are presented in Chapter 15.

NOTE

1. This work was supported by grant GM 17173 from the U.S. National Institutes of Health.

15

Population Structure of Micronesia[1]

N. E. MORTON

Population Genetics Laboratory
University of Hawaii

An intensive study of Pingelap and Mokil atolls in the Eastern Carolines was recently completed, based on Malécot's theory of kinship. Smaller studies using these and other methods have been carried out on Namu atoll in the Marshalls (Pollock, Lalouel, and Morton 1972) and for all of Micronesia (Hainline 1966, Imaizumi and Morton 1970). Substantial bodies of data on migration and genealogy were collected by social anthropologists on such islands as Yap (Schneider 1962), Truk (Goodenough 1951) and the Gilberts (Goodenough 1955), but never analyzed. Riesenberg (1965) has studied ethnohistorical and historical accounts of Micronesian voyages. Finally, there has been considerable anthropometry and typing of polymorphisms in the Pacific, with a large body of material on the Western Carolines awaiting publication by Gajdusek and his collaborators. What do these sources tell us about the genetic structure of Micronesia?

KINSHIP

To the cultural anthropologist, *kinship* means a set of social relationships, whereas to the geneticist, it is a number measuring genetic similarity and usually defined as a probability of identity by descent. This definition is based on the notion of sampling from a region with frequency Q_k for the kth allele, where

$$Q_k = \sum_i N_i q_{ki} / \sum_i N_i. \tag{1}$$

N_i is the size of the ith population within the region, and q_{ki} is the frequency of the kth allele in that population. Then, if ϕ_{ij} is the probability that a pair of genes, one from i and one from j, be identical by descent, the expected F_1 genotype frequencies, *given the regional gene frequencies*, are

$$\begin{aligned}
P_{k1} &= 2Q_k Q_1 (1 - \phi_{ij}) & (k \neq 1) \\
&= Q_k^2 + Q_k (1 - Q_k) \phi_{ij} & (k = 1)
\end{aligned} \tag{2}$$

Clearly, kinship is defined on a gene pool: if we change the region or the generation in which gene frequencies are determined, we change the value of ϕ_{ij}. A second important point is that kinship is an expectation for a *random* allele (or pair of alleles) at a *random* locus. Therefore, we do not have to be concerned with different values of kinship for different alleles or loci, whether caused by drift or selection, except to estimate their mean. Over a sufficiently small region, migration is a more important systematic pressure than mutation or selection. Then, predictions from genealogy or migration may be reliable, and a small sample of loci will suffice to estimate ϕ_{ij}. Over a vast region such as a continent, mutation and selection may be important, especially diversifying selection for different alleles in different subregions. Then, predictions of kinship from genealogy or migration are unreliable, and a large sample of loci will be required to give a good estimate of ϕ_{ij}.

Definition of kinship as a probability conforms to predictions from genealogy and migration and to Malécot's theory of isolation by distance, both of which are relative to gene frequencies of the regional founders; thus, all values of kinship are positive. However, initial estimates of kinship from phenotype bioassay relate to contemporary regional gene frequencies and therefore tend to be negative for pairs of populations less similar than a random pair of gametes from the region. Also, estimates of kinship from bioassay may be negative through sampling error. To retain our definition of kinship as a probability, we must adjust estimates from phenotype bioassay so that their expectation is positive. Malécot's theory asserts that

$$\emptyset_{ij} \doteq ae^{-bd} \qquad\qquad (a,b > 0), \qquad\qquad (3)$$

where d is the geographic distance between populations i and j. In practice, d is measured in a straight line, which is both easier and more objective than estimation of useful route distance or travel time. If our initial estimate of $\emptyset_{ij}$ from phenotype bioassay is y_{ij}, it is natural to take

$$\emptyset_{ij} = \frac{y_{ij} - L}{1 - L}$$

corresponding to the equation

$$y_{ij} = (1 - L)ae^{-bd} + L, \qquad\qquad (4)$$

where L is the expected value of y_{ij} for the least related populations, since y_{ij} approaches L in the limit for large d. Thus, L is an adjustment for the deviation of contemporary from founder gene frequencies. This is a special case of Wright's hierarchical model, which relates kinship coefficients to successively larger arrays of populations (Malécot 1969). Naturally, L does not include deviations of founders from the larger gene pool (race, species, or higher category) out of which the regional founders were drawn.

Let us denote random kinship as

$$\emptyset_R = \sum_{i,j} N_i N_j \emptyset_{ij} / \sum_{i,j} N_i N_j, \qquad\qquad (5)$$

with

$$y_R = \sum_{i,j} N_i N_j y_{ij} / \sum_{i,j} N_i N_j$$
$$= (1 - L)\emptyset_R + L.$$

If initial estimates are relative to random pairs from the contemporary regional gene pool, then $y_R = 0$ and $\emptyset_R = -L/(1 - L)$. The best estimate of L is by least squares from Equation 4, with a and b estimated simultaneously.

Defining kinship as a probability, the regional gene frequencies in Equation 2 should be understood as relating to the *founders*. Formally, Equation 2 is valid for

$$-Q_k/(1 - Q_k) \leq \emptyset_{ij} \leq 1, \qquad\qquad (6)$$

even though a negative value of $\emptyset_{ij}$ is not a probability but may be a correlation between uniting gametes. If it is desired to estimate F_1 genotype frequencies from the *contemporary* regional gene pool, the $\emptyset_{ij}$ in Equation 2 should be replaced by the contemporary correlation between gametes, which is

$$r_{ij} = (\emptyset_{ij} - \emptyset_R)/(1 - \emptyset_R) = (y_{ij} - y_R)/(1 - y_R). \tag{7}$$

This is such an unusual problem, however, that the definition of kinship as a probability may be retained. Then, if the assumptions underlying prediction of kinship from genealogy and migration are correct, these predictions will be consistent with estimates from bioassay of phenotypes.

There is a function of kinship called *hybridity* that shares with r_{ij} the pleasing property of being invariant under the transformation $\emptyset_{ij} \rightarrow (\emptyset_{ij} - L)/(1 - L)$. More important, hybridity measures the excess of heterozygosity in an F_1 between populations relative to the F_2 and is therefore a positive fraction that increases with genetic differentiation (Morton et al. 1971c). Hybridity between populations i and j is defined as

$$\theta_{ij} = \frac{\emptyset_{ii} + \emptyset_{jj} - 2\emptyset_{ij}}{4 - \emptyset_{ii} - \emptyset_{jj} - 2\emptyset_{ij}}. \tag{8}$$

This is exactly or approximately proportional to measures of genetic distance proposed by Sanghvi and others, but it has a simple biological interpretation and can be predicted, estimated, and averaged for different phenotype systems.

This detailed account of kinship has been presented because it is the basic concept of genetic structure, all the information about which can be summarized in a square, symmetric matrix whose i,jth element is $\emptyset_{ij}$. Any subsequent analysis of genetic structure, such as to measure isolation by distance or construct a dendrogram, is an operation on this matrix.

MIGRATION

Probably many social anthropologists working in Micronesia have collected migration data complete enough to be subjected to genetic analysis, but this has not been attempted, except for the Mokilese material of Weckler and Bentzen (Morton et al. 1971a) and Namu islanders (Pollock, Lalouel, and Morton 1972). Riesenberg (1965) and Gladwin (1970) document voyages in all directions and sometimes over enormous distances, with no possibility of quantifying the impact on recipient populations.

Inferences about kinship from migration depend on three kinds of parameters in successive generations: exchange probabilities, systematic pressures, and effective population sizes (Morton 1969). In practice, these parameters are represented by "typical" values taken as constant over all generations, and it is further assumed that the systematic pressure is dominated by long-range migration, which can be equated to migration from outside the region. Given these simplifying assumptions, we can estimate (1) exchange probabilities and systematic pressures from migration data and (2) effective population sizes from demography or genealogy.

The elementary observation in migration is $C_{jk}^{(i)}$, the number of children in population i whose fathers came from population j and whose mothers came from population k in the preceding generation, where i is within the region, but j and k need not be. Generally, $C_{jk}^{(i)}$ represents the sum over two or more generations. As long as parents and children are enumerated in the same way, there is considerable latitude in interpreting the phrases "in i" and "from j," which in different applications may refer to caste, lineage, clan membership (Morton, Imaizumi, and Harris 1971), place of birth, place of childhood residence, or population of origin as in the patrilineal Swiss sense (Morton and Hussels 1970). The long-range migration rate into population i is defined as

$$m_i = \frac{\sum\limits_{j \& R} C_{jk}^{(i)} + \sum\limits_{k \& R} C_{jk}^{(i)}}{2 \sum\limits_{j} \sum\limits_{k} C_{jk}^{(i)}}, \qquad (9)$$

where the numerator represents the children in i whose fathers came from outside the region, plus the children in i whose mothers came from outside the region, with the children both of whose parents came from the outside counted twice. The denominator is twice the number of children in i, regardless of parentage, the factor of 2 arising because every child is counted once for each parent. The long-range migration rates for n populations within the region form a vector of rank n.

Now we define the exchange probability p_{ji} as the probability that a random gene in i came from j in the preceding generation, where i,j are both within the region. This is the same as the probability that a random parent of a child in i came from j, or

$$p_{ji} = \frac{\sum\limits_{k} C_{jk}{}^{(i)} + \sum\limits_{k} C_{kj}{}^{(i)}}{2 \sum\limits_{j} \sum\limits_{k} C_{jk}{}^{(i)} - \sum\limits_{j\&R} C_{jk}{}^{(i)} - \sum\limits_{k\&R} C_{jk}{}^{(i)}}. \tag{10}$$

The numerator represents the children in i whose fathers are from j, plus the children in i whose mothers are from j, with a child both of whose parents came from j counted twice. The denominator is the difference between the denominator and numerator of m_i and equals the number of children in i whose fathers came from within the region, plus the number of children in i whose mothers came from within the region, every child both of whose parents came from within the region being counted twice. Exchange probabilities for n populations form an $n \times n$ column-stochastic matrix (that is, $\sum\limits_{j} p_{ji} = 1$).

Endogamy (E_i) is the probability, among mating pairs in i, that both are from i. This is different from *endemicity* (p_{ii}), defined as the probability that a random parent of a child in i came from i. If we neglect mating pairs in i, neither of whom is from i, there is a simple relation between endogamy and endemicity, namely,

$$E_i = 1 - 2 \sum_{j \neq i} p_{ji}.$$

But,

$$p_{ii} = 1 - \sum_{j \neq i} p_{ji},$$

and so

$$E_i = 2p_{ii} - 1.$$

The exchange matrix (p_{ji}) is the basic predictor of kinship, while endogamy is only a descriptive statistic. Therefore, it is convenient to take the last equation, although derived on a simplifying assumption, as *defining* endogamy.

There are three problems in the calculation of long-range migration rates and exchange probabilities. First, the observed generations may be atypical, so that some adjustment may seem desirable in predicting kinship, such as guessing a smaller or larger value of long-range migration or endogamy; in the latter case, care must be taken to adjust other elements in the column so as to keep it stochastic.

Secondly, some populations within the region may not have been studied, in which case two estimation principles may be used. If i was studied but j not, we may suppose that the number of migrants from i to j is the same as from j to i, or

$$\sum_k C_{jk}{}^{(i)} + \sum_k C_{kj}{}^{(i)} = \sum_k C_{ik}{}^{(j)} + \sum_k C_{ki}{}^{(j)}. \qquad (11)$$

If neither i nor j was studied, we may suppose that the number of migrants is proportional to the product of populations' sizes and inversely proportional to some power r of the distance between populations. This Pareto distribution is

$$\sum_k C_{jk}{}^{(i)} + \sum_k C_{kj}{}^{(i)} = KN_i N_j / d_{ij}{}^r, \qquad (12)$$

where K and r are constants (usually $r \doteq 2$), d_{ij} is the distance between i and j, and N_i, N_j are the estimated number of children in i and j, respectively, where

$$N_i = \sum_{j,k} C_{jk}{}^{(i)}.$$

By fitting the Pareto distribution in studied populations, the exchange probabilities for other pairs of populations can be estimated (Pollock, Lalouel, and Morton 1972). Alternatively, plausible guesses of numbers of migrants can sometimes be made (Morton et al. 1971a). This is the only solution feasible for long-range migration rates in populations not studied. For example, Morton and Lalouel (1972a) considered Pingelap and Mokil atolls and assumed that other populations in the region had a long-range migration rate that was the average of the values for the two atolls.

The third problem in estimating an exchange matrix is philosophical: should we assume (perhaps incorrectly) that migration is symmetrical, in which case population sizes are expected to remain constant? If we do not impose symmetry, relative population sizes are expected to change and perhaps become far different from their present values, unless we assume some *deus ex machina* that maintains stability. We do not like either alternative under asymmetrical migration and so have preferred to impose symmetry by averaging reciprocal numbers of migrants, which is the transformation

$$\sum_k C_{jk}{}^{(i)} + \sum_k C_{kj}{}^{(i)} \rightarrow \frac{\sum_k C_{jk}{}^{(i)} + \sum_k C_{kj}{}^{(i)} + \sum_k C_{ik}{}^{(j)} + \sum_k C_{ki}{}^{(j)}}{2}.$$

This seems to be mostly a matter of taste, since the predictions of kinship are not appreciably affected. It is convenient to construct the matrix of numbers of migrants and then pass to an exchange matrix by dividing each element by the corresponding column total.

The purpose of discussing migration data in such detail is to make it clear how such material is analyzed and how simplified the assumptions are. Every entry in an exchange matrix or vector of long-range migration rates is subject to error, the contemporary kinship may not be stable, and neither selection nor the kinship of long-range migrants to the region may be negligible. Consequently, predictions of kinship from migration data are subject to appreciable error and should not be accepted uncritically (Bodmer and Cavalli-Sforza 1968).

We come now to the estimation of effective population sizes. One approach estimates the probability of drawing two gametes from the same parent under sampling with replacement and equates this to the reciprocal of the effective size (Wright 1931). If $N_i^{(t)}$ is the number of parents in population i at generation t, and $K_i^{(t)}$, $V_i^{(t)}$ are the mean and variance in the numbers of their offspring that survive to maturity, so that $N_i^{(t+1)} = K_i^{(t)} N_i^{(t)}$, then the effective size in the sense of Wright is estimated by

$$N_{Wi}^{(t)} = \frac{K_i^{(t)} N_i^{(t)} - 1}{\left(\dfrac{N_i^{(t)} - 1}{N_i^{(t)}}\right)\left(\dfrac{V_i^{(t)}}{K_i^{(t)}}\right) + K_i^{(t)} - 1}, \tag{13}$$

and the typical value over T generations is

$$N_{Wi} = T / \sum_{t=1}^{T} \frac{1}{N_{Wi}^{(t)}}. \tag{14}$$

This estimate requires a detailed knowledge of historical demography. It assumes that relatives are uncorrelated in fertility, generations do not overlap, and migration is negligible.

To obtain more accurate estimates of effective population size, some investigators have simulated their populations by Monte Carlo methods, based on the distribution of birth intervals, ages at reproduction, mortality, and other factors (MacCluer and Schull 1970a). Such estimates are certainly more complicated than Wright's: whether they are more or less accurate depends on the reliability of the assumed distributions and the validity of neglecting fertility correlations, migration, and the nonrandomness of the pseudorandom number generator.

Disillusionment with these approaches led us to define effective size in terms of the evolution of kinship (Morton et al. 1971a). We predicted kinship in eastern Micronesia from an exchange matrix and vector of effective long-range migration rates derived from our studies of Pingelap and Mokil atolls, using rough estimates of effective population size. Then we examined the result of multiplying the latter vector by 10 and by 1/10, holding the exchange matrix and long-range migration rates constant. The predicted kinship for successive generations was fitted to the equation

$$\phi^{(t)} = \phi(1 - e^{-t/2N_e\phi}), \tag{15}$$

where

$$\phi = \frac{1}{4N_e m_e + 1}$$

is the kinship as t becomes large, m_e is the *effective systematic pressure*, and N_e is the *evolutionary size*. By estimating N_e, m_e in this way, we were delighted to find that m_e was not appreciably affected by the large differences in assumed size and that N_e/N was constant for each population. This suggested that for the ith population, we could use the values of m_{ei} from migration data to estimate N_{ei} from genealogies and then calculate effective size as

$$N_i = C_i N_{ei}, \tag{16}$$

where C_i is the ratio of effective to evolutionary size from migration data alone. Our results are shown in Table 52. The region was taken to be eastern Micronesia. Because of migration from other populations, evolutionary size exceeds effective size ($C < 1$). Effective size of the two populations is only 6 percent of their current census size, but it is 65 percent of the harmonic mean of their census sizes over the last two hundred years, where the census includes Pingelapese and Mokilese on Ponape. Inbreeding due to small effective size is partly offset by appreciable systematic pressure, mostly due to short-range migration (that is, within eastern Micronesia).

The estimates in Table 52 do not depend on any assumption that the populations are at equilibrium with respect to kinship. They do, of course, depend critically on migration data to estimate m_e and genealogical data for N_e. The material spans the last two hundred years, during which migration has been aided by sailing and motor ships. However, it is by no means certain that migration was less common in prehistoric times. Many of the migrants arrived by canoe, and there is evidence that such voyages

TABLE 52
PARAMETERS DETERMINING KINSHIP IN PINGELAPESE AND MOKILESE

Population	Census Size*		Long-range Migration Rate, m†	Effective Systematic Pressure, m_e†	Ratio of Effective to Evolutionary Size, C†	Evolutionary Size, N_e‡	Effective Size, N*
	1967	Harmonic Mean over 200 Years					
Pingelap	1,600	155	0.00584	0.0267	0.93	87	81
Mokil	900	74	0.01923	0.0763	0.83	82	68

* Morton et al. (1972).
† Morton et al. (1971a).
‡ Morton et al. (1971c).

may have been more frequent in prehistoric times (see Chapter 14). The estimates of Table 52 seem to be as satisfactory as can be obtained by any known method to predict evolution of kinship on these atolls.

GENEALOGY

Pedigrees provide the classical material for prediction of kinship. Recognized limitations of such data are the short time depth, neglect of selection, and the assumption that migrants are unrelated to the local population. Recently, two approaches have been developed to eliminate the first problem. MacCluer and Schull (1970a) introduced Monte Carlo simulation, but in the absence of migration, kinship approaches unity, and in the absence of bioassay, there is no check on predicted kinship. Since the maiden flight of Monte Carlo simulation neglected migrants and was for a population without bioassay, little can be said about the prospects for this approach, which gave poor agreement with predictions from the actual population (Table 53).

The previous section discussed a method for estimating systematic pressure from migration data and evolutionary size from genealogies.

TABLE 53
EVOLUTIONARY SIZE N_e AND SYSTEMATIC
PRESSURE m_e IN DIFFERENT POPULATIONS

Population	m_e Determined from	m_e	N_e	Limiting Kinship φ
Pingelap	migration	0.027	87	0.0938
Mokil	migration	0.076	82	0.0341
Namu*	genealogy	0.045	114	0.0468
Hirado†	genealogy	0.238	195	0.0054
Artificial population†	genealogy	0.000	434	1.0000
Northeastern Brazil‡	genealogy	0.308	124	0.0065
Switzerland§	genealogy	0.203	1499	0.0008

SOURCE: After Morton (1971b) .

* Pollock, Lalouel, and Morton (1972).

† MacCluer and Schull (1970a). In the artificial population, simultaneous estimates give $N_e = 453$ and $m_e = -0.018$; thus, m_e was taken as 0.

‡ Azevêdo et al. (1969).

§ Morton and Hussels (1970).

Kinship may be determined in successive generations, or the distribution of chain lengths of c generations through a common ancestor may be tabulated from a pool of one or more generations. The latter data give monotonically increasing estimates of cumulative kinship, which should be truncated so as to consider only values of c small enough to be reliably ascertained. Then, using the relation between generation and chain length, $t = (c - 1)/2$, and assuming that the distribution of short chain lengths is stable, Equation 15 yields estimates of N_e if m_e is given from migration data, or otherwise of N_e and m_e simultaneously, together with the derived quantity ϕ, the limiting kinship after many generations. The standard error of ϕ is, of course, less if m_e is known from migration.

Table 53 gives such estimates for several populations. The three Micronesian atolls tend to approach much higher levels of kinship than continental populations of peasant or more complex economy. Levels of kinship comparable to atolls have been suggested for slash-and-burn agriculturists in Melanesia (Friedlaender 1971b) and the Amazon (Neel and Salzano 1967). The evolutionary size is small even for so developed a population as Switzerland, but the systematic pressure due to migration increases correspondingly. Therefore, most kinship is due to short chains of relationship in such developed populations, where most kinship in atolls and similar populations is due to multiple long chains of relationship.

The best predictions of kinship require that m_e be determined from migration data and N_e from genealogy. Alternatively, both parameters can be estimated from genealogy, but this is less desirable, because then m_e is not directly based on migration and may be spuriously large due to incomplete ascertainment of remote kinship. The least reliable predictions of kinship are based solely on migration or other purely demographic data (using either deterministic or Monte Carlo simulation), because the assumptions for estimating effective population size may be grossly in error. In any case, predictions of kinship require confirmation from bioassay.

Another use of genealogies is to reveal nonrandom mating. Among first-cousin marriages on Pingelap and Mokil, there is avoidance of descent through two sisters and preference for matrilineal cross cousins. Both deviations from randomness are much reduced in second cousins. Levirate and sororate matings persist as a substantial fraction of polygamous matings, since intimacy with a spouse's siblings outweighs disapproval by the Church. These practices have no important genetic consequences, but

344

they illustrate persistence of patterns of mating, even when they conflict with formalized rules.

HISTORICAL GENETICS

Pedigrees, gene frequencies, historical documents, and legends may be used to interpret contemporary gene frequencies in terms of past events. This constitutes *historical genetics*. In large populations, the deterministic processes of hybridization and selection are ascendant, whereas small numbers of founders and subsequent genetic drift are important in the isolates of Micronesia. One of the objectives of historical genetics is to determine the contribution of principal founders to the current gene pool. If we define as *founders* all members of the population in certain previous generations whose parents came from other groups or are unknown, and if genes of a particular allelic class are derived from a small number of founders, then we may be able to identify these founders.

Estimates of census size since typhoon Lengkieki indicate exponential increase of the population at the rate of nearly 2 percent per year. During this time, Pingelap (with an area of 0.676 mi.²) has maintained a population twice as great as Mokil (with an area of 0.478 mi.²), yet the effective sizes are subequal.?·

This paradox is explained by greater variability of population size among the Pingelapese founders. The principal founder sibship (#1067) contained two polygamous chiefs, who left several of the survivors of Lengkieki. Their successor, Mwanenised, had 10 children. This achievement so impressed his contemporaries that he was given the posthumous name of "Backbone of Pingelap." It was then the custom after the death of an important man for an elder to recount a dream in which the dead man appeared and revealed his new name. Mwanenised's ghost explained that his name did not mean strength or wisdom, but that he had made Sou Serawi (his wife's clan) great on Pingelap. Unmentioned was the fact that he had helped to establish #1067 as the principal founder sibship, with important consequences.

About 5 percent of the Pingelapese and a smaller proportion of Mokilese are affected with congenital achromatopsia, accompanied by high myopia. Segregation analysis shows that inheritance is as an autosomal recessive. Inspection of the complex genealogies, supported by stepwise regression and χ^2 tests, suggests that #1067 was the carrier founder for all cases in both Pingelap and Mokil (Hussels and Morton 1972).

Two brothers in #1067 left survivors of Lengkieki. Semenuhwe had one child, while Mwahuele left seven children by three wives, one of whom married a cousin, the daughter of Semenuhwe. Thus, the most economical hypothesis is that Mwahuele was the only carrier of achromatopsia in his generation. Since the gene is recessive, the selection pressure against it in low frequency is small; thus, it is unlikely that Mwahuele carried a fresh mutation. Most probably, the gene was present but rare before Lengkieki, descending from an earlier mutation, and by chance was transmitted through Mwahuele to several of the few survivors. The ethnohistory of achromatopsia is concerned with three sibships descended from Mwahuele (Figure 37).

Nanmwarki Okonomwaun, who ruled from 1822 to 1870, took the Pingelapese wife of a Kusaiean immigrant (Morton et al. 1972). By this woman Dokas, he had six children, of whom two had achromatopsia. They were explained by the following myth. The god Isoahpahu became enamored of Dokas and instructed Okonomwaun to appropriate her. From time to time, Isoahpahu appeared in the guise of Okonomwaun and had intercourse with Dokas, fathering the affected children, while the normal children came from Okonomwaun. Isoahpahu loved other Pingelapese women and had affected children by them. The "proof" of this is that persons with achromatopsia shun the light but have relatively good night vision, like their ghostly ancestor. Isoahpahu was prominent in the Pingelapese pantheon until overthrown by the missionaries. He is said to have fled in shame when defeated in a test of supernatural power, and his house was destroyed.

Soal was the oldest patient with achromatopsia seen by our most elderly informants. Descended from Nanmwarki Mwanenised by an uncle-niece mating, he married another descendent of Mwanenised and had six children, of whom three were affected. One of the normal daughters went to Mokil and was the ancestress of several sibships with affected children. Imwerou, one of Soal's affected sons, learned witchcraft from other Micronesians in the phosphate mines of Nauru. He was held in some awe by the Pingelapese and Mokilese. George Higgins, the Nahnkin of Mokil, relates how Imwerou prophesied that the first player in a game of stick throwing would have bad luck. George Higgins ignored this warning and threw first. That night, one arm was paralysed by a polio-like disease that

346

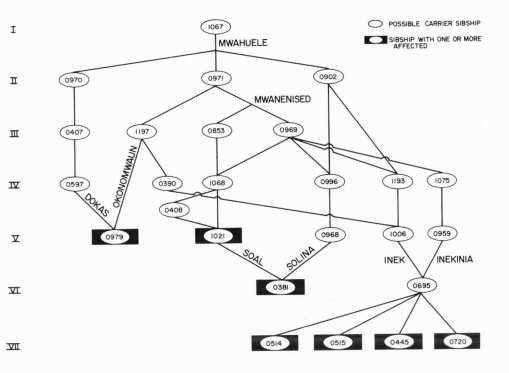

FIGURE 37. Ethnohistory of achromatopsia.

killed or crippled many of the workers on Nauru. When the arm remained weak, Higgins accused Imwerou of witchcraft. Imwerou admitted his responsibility and prepared an herbal potion, which promptly cured his patient-victim. Imwerou did not have children. His stepson is a Christian minister, who seldom displays the mystic arts he is generally believed to have learned from his stepfather.

Married couples baptized by the missionaries often received names like Soal and Solina. One such couple, also descended from Mwanenised, was Inek and Inekinia. Inek was trained in the Christian faith by Mesdon (Mr. Doane) and assigned to Truk, but, because of his large family, he refused to go. According to the Pingelapese legend, Mesdon was angered by this lack of evangelical zeal and cursed the children, four of whom subsequently had affected offspring. In all, seven of Inek's grandchildren had achromatopsia.

These legends reflect prevailing attitudes. The night vision of affected persons excites some awe, but there is a definite stigma attached to the disease. One contemporary couple who had two affected children named their first normal son Aringado (from a Japanese word meaning "thanks"). Achromatopsia interferes with activities that require good vision in bright sunlight, most of which are traditionally men's work, like fishing and picking breadfruit. Bad vision often leads to cuts and bruises. Work in the taro pit and at home is much less impaired, and success in a clerical job is possible. Nevertheless, there is prejudice against marriage to an affected person, because of risk to the children. Affected girls who remain unmarried may have one or more illegitimate children.

The interest of historical genetics is not limited to disease. The *most significant founder* is defined as the one with the largest χ^2 for the 2×2 contingency table of factor x kinship, where factor is a binary variable indicating presence or absence of an attribute and kinship is also binarized (0,1). With the same restriction, the *second most significant founder* then gives the largest χ^2 when sibships with kinship to the most significant founder are excluded. The computer program PHYLON applies this stepwise algorithm to all founders or all migrant founders. An approximate χ^2 test is available to test the null hypothesis that an allele was absent among *autochthonous founders* (here defined as Pingelapese or Mokilese survivors of Lengkieki).

In this way, the ancestor of all known carriers of $Gm^{1,5,6}$ among Pingelapese and Mokilese was identified as Captain Wick, a name assumed by a foreign resident of Mokil. Since this allele is invariably African in origin, we can be sure that the daughter attributed to Captain Wick received the gene from a Mulatto parent. Without this evidence, we would be uncertain whether immigration, mutation, or remote African affinity accounts for this allele in the Ponape district.

The $Gm^{1,2,21}$ allele traces to an American, a Portuguese, and a Japanese (Figure 38). Clearly, this gene was introduced into the Ponape district by recent immigration. Steinberg and Morton (1972) have suggested that only the alleles $Gm^{1,21}$ and $Gm^{1,3,5,13,14}$ are native to eastern Micronesia.

To extend the analysis to other genetic systems, we need to clarify our notions of gene frequency and origin. Alleles in populations are distinguished as *idiomorphs*, *polymorphs*, or *monomorphs*, according as their frequencies are less than 0.01, between 0.01 and 0.99, or greater than 0.99, respectively. Alleles may also be distinguished by their origin as

348

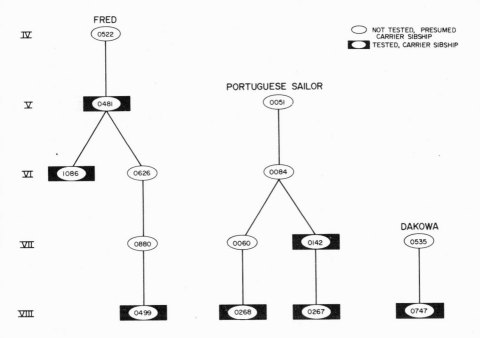

FIGURE 38. The Gm(2) factor in Pingelapese and Mokilese, showing oligophyletic descent.

monophyla, oligophyla, or polyphyla, according as they are identical by descent from the same, a few, or many founder genes. To be specific, we tentatively suggest that *few* means that more than one but less than six founders account for at least 90 percent of known carriers. These concepts do not depend on population size, but distinctions by frequency are more interesting and feasible in large populations, and distinctions by origin in small populations. Classification depends on the founder and reference generations and may change by drift, mutation, or migration. Thus, a single migrant or mutant may convert a monophylon to an oligophylon, which random extinction may again reduce to a monophylon. The number of founder genes in an allelic set often increases with the reference population: an allele may be monophyletic in an isolate but polyphyletic in the region of which the isolate is a part. The apparent number of founder genes may decrease as a genealogy is extended, revealing unsuspected identity by descent. Finally, the apparent number of founders may be increased by parentage errors.

These principles are illustrated by Pingelap and Mokil. Achromatopsia and $Gm^{1,5,6}$ are monophyla. $Gm^{1,2,21}$, $Gm^{1,21}$, and many of the other alleles studied are oligophyla, the majority of carriers coming from a handful of carrier founders. The alleles $Gm^{1,5,6}$, $Gm^{1,2,21}$, B, NS + MS, $R_0 + r$, R_2, PHs^4, $PGM_1{}^2$, PGD^B, and color blindness were apparently absent from the survivors of Lengkieki and are becoming polyphyletic by migration.

Leprosy has a prevalence of 0.0816 among Pingelapese in our master list. Segregation analysis under Falconer's model of quasi-continuity indicated a heritability of 0 ± 0.14, reflecting the lack of any pronounced concentration of cases within particular families. PHYLON fails to identify any founder effect. These two pieces of evidence indicate that genetic susceptibility does not explain the focus of leprosy on Pingelap, which may be due to contacts in the phosphate mines of Nauru at the beginning of this century (Sloan et al. 1972). We see that the methods of historical genetics are capable of excluding as well as elucidating hereditary factors.

CLANS

Genes and clans are transmitted in similar ways, although with quite different rates and modes of mutation. Crow and Mange (1965) showed how clans or surnames give estimates of kinship. Surnames are a foreign introduction to Micronesia and were established as patrinomial during this century. As such, they are not generally useful. Clan names, however, have the stability required for bioassay of kinship. The basic concept is of *isonymy*, or concordance of the clans or surnames of a pair of individuals. Orthographic changes are a problem for surnames: for example, are the pair Smith-Smythe isonymous or not? The corresponding but more difficult problem for clans is homology. Two clans are *homologous* if marriage is discouraged by an exogamy rule on the basis of supposed characteristics, not necessarily including identity by descent. Thus, the convention that two clans are homologous may rest on the belief that they trace to a common ancestor (*true homology*) or be merely a convenient fiction so that members of the society can be confident of their roles in a neighboring population (*fictive homology*). For example, the Pingelapese clan Serawi is popularly identified with the Ponapean clan Dipwinpahnmei, although no informant could say why; we have considered them true homologues. However, clan Kipar stems from one of the sons of the

Nanmwarki Mwahuele. Kipar is said to have created the clan for his sister and himself. On this account, clan Kipar is homologized with the Ponapean clan Dipwilap, the members of which have a reputation for lying. Since there is an established tradition that denies descent from a common ancestor, we consider the pair Kipar-Dipwilap fictive homologues. The rule that homology is accepted in the absence of contrary evidence is consistent with the surname convention that equates cognates: thus, Smith-Smythe are isonymous.

If q_{ki} is the frequency of the kth clan or surname in the ith population, true homologues being pooled but fictive homologues separated, then $\sum_k q_{ki}^2$ is random isonymy in the ith population, and $n_c = 1/\sum_k q_{ki}^2$ is the *effective number of clans*. A population with the distribution q_{ki} of clans behaves genetically, much like a population with n_c clans of equal size. Estimates of n_c are 4, 4, 9, 10 for Pingelap, Mokil, Namu, and Ponape, respectively. Methods to estimate kinship from the q_{ki} were given by Morton (1972), following Crow and Mange (1965).

The rule of clan exogamy was broken by survivors of typhoon Lengkieki, and there is no evidence in the genealogies to support the general belief that clan exogamy was as rigidly enforced in earlier times as it is among contemporary Ponapeans. However, endogamous unions are less than half as frequent on Pingelap as they would be under random mating. Even Mokil, which had greater foreign contact during the nineteenth century, shows in its genealogies some avoidance of intraclan unions. There is strong avoidance of clan isonymy due to known identity by descent (Morton et al. 1971d).

The conjunction of matrilineal clans with predominantly patrilineal inheritance suggests that there might be some tendency to avoid matings in which the father-in-law is of the same clan as ego. On the contrary, the frequency of such clan coincidence is slightly greater than its panmictic expectation on Mokil, and appreciably greater on Pingelap.

The atolls differ in assimilation of new clans. Any Oceanic clan that is regularly matrilineal is accepted on both atolls. Gilbertese clans, which are nonunilineal, become matrilineal on Mokil and as such may be transmitted to Pingelap. However, the Gilbertese women who bore children on Pingelap during the nineteenth century took the clan of their Pingelapese foster mother and/or first husband. With these exceptions, clan affiliation is not altered by adoption or marriage. The uncertainty of young informants about their clan affiliation seems greater among the matrilineal descendents of adopted women. Only by seeking the consensus of older informants can clans be correctly assigned.

In an analysis of regular systems of mating, Morton, Imaizumi, and Harris (1971:1010) concluded that "formal kinship and marriage systems are weak genetic barriers which, except in the most extreme cases of clans separated by generation or geographic distance, can well be ignored by comparison with the effects of population size and migration." This suggests that first, if evolutionary size N_e and systematic pressure m_e are estimated from genealogy and migration, as in the previous section, these parameters will describe evolution of kinship under the given mating system as accurately as under random mating; and second, the effect of the mating system on these parameters will be negligible. The latter point is most easily made by considering different mating systems in populations of constant size and systematic pressure. As expected, the deviation of the actual mating system from panmixia has little effect on kinship (Morton, Imaizumi, and Harris 1971, Pollock, Lalouel, and Morton 1972).

In predicting the genetic effects of clans, one is deeply impressed by the difference between ideal and actual mating practices, which is as profound in other cultures as in America, where marriage with the boss's daughter may be the ideal but is uncommon. There is little evidence that mating in other societies follows the structural rules of kinship theory. To replace an observed exchange matrix by an inflexible rule is to replace the actual population by an artificial one. For example, Lévi-Strauss (1969) tried to infer the mating practice of the Kariera from data so scanty as to be negligible. He produced a kinship diagram, easily represented by an exchange matrix, that has the property of dividing the population into two generation sets, between which mating is formally prohibited. This leads to uncontrolled drift in the sizes and genetic composition of the two sets. Undoubtedly, Maybury-Lewis (1967) was right in suggesting that systems of $2n$ sections are idealized perceptions of age differences in an n-clan system and do not actually function as diagrammed in kinship theory. The next generation of anthropologists can hardly escape the task of replacing idealized kinship systems, erected on inadequate observation, with actual exchange matrices.

Estimates of kinship from clan isonymy in the Eastern Carolines have been found to follow the same parameters for isolation by distance as phenotypes and anthropometrics (Morton and Lalouel 1972a). Apparently, drift and migration play similar roles for clans and genes, suggesting that clans may persist for a long time without fission or extinction.

exchanging genes and words

COGNATE FREQUENCIES

Lexicostatistics has been more concerned with time than distance (Hymes 1960). This is unfortunate, because the estimation of divergence times requires assumptions that often cannot be verified, whereas the effect of distance can be measured directly. As Kroeber (1958:454) remarked, "the greatest danger in lexicostatistics is its involvement with chronology, which is its weakest point, although also the one of widest appeal."

Obviously, words can be disseminated independently of gene flow, but it seems plausible that in general, the systematic pressures will be related as

$$m_L = km_e, \qquad (17)$$

where m_e is the effective systematic pressure for genes, largely due to migration, and m_L is the corresponding pressure on cognates, for which migration is less efficient. Then $0 < k < 1$ is a measure of receptivity to neologism, the probability that the bearer of a new word will transmit it. If the relation between kinship and distance is ae^{-bd}, we expect that the relation of cognate frequency to distance will be $e^{-b\sqrt{(k)}}$ (Morton 1972).

Unfortunately, standard word lists are composed of elements with different retention rates. The effect of this can be approximated by an equation of the type $C = (1 - L)e^{-b'd} + L$, where C is cognate frequency, $b' = b\sqrt{(k)}$ is a parameter of isolation by distance, and $0 < L < 1$ is the fraction of words of high retention rate. Estimates of k in Micronesia are surprisingly close to 1, indicating appreciable receptivity to neologism (Morton and Lalouel 1972a).

ANTHROPOMETRICS

Anthropometrics has the advantage of assaying many gene effects simultaneously but the disadvantage of sensitivity to the environment. The possibility that interpopulational variability is partly due to environmental differences cannot be directly excluded.

353

There are two methods to estimate kinship from anthropometrics. One uses heritability to calculate the genetic covariance between pairs of populations, expressed in terms of hybridity (Morton and Greene 1972). This gave an estimate of about 0.05 for the mean kinship within Pingelap and Mokil. The average anthropometric after covariance adjustment for age and sex had a heritability of 0.565, which is gratifyingly high.

There is another estimate of kinship based on anthropometrics, which does not require an estimate of heritability but which depends on a calculation of the mean kinship within population from phenotypes (Morton and Lalouel 1972a). Applied to a small Micronesian sample (Hasebe 1939), this gave estimates of kinship similar to those derived from phenotypes.

The classical analysis of metrical differentiation is based on Mahalanobis's D^2, which has the disadvantage of increasing with the number of metrics, whereas kinship has the same expectation for each metric or combination of metrics. Thus, samples can be summarized by their means, and missing observations present no problem. Kinship has the further advantage of being a genetic parameter, directly comparable for predictions from genealogy and estimates from polymorphisms, isonymy, and anthropometrics. There is no reason to retain D^2 and other "indices of biological distance," except hybridity (Equation 8), for studies that have as their goal to estimate differentiation.

BIOASSAY

Two methods have been proposed to estimate ϕ_{ij} from phenotype frequencies (Equation 2). One uses phenotype pairs: this gives an unbiased estimate of y_{ii}, but an overestimate of y_{ij} for $i \neq j$ (Equation 4). As a consequence, the Malécot parameter a in Equation 3 is underestimated by one-third, but the estimate of b is unbiased (Harpending 1971a, Morton 1971b).

The other method calculates gene frequencies for each population on the assumption of panmixia and estimates ϕ_{ij} from these (Morton et al. 1971c). By altering the factor-union code to represent codominance, weighted gene frequencies may be used as input. Estimates of ϕ_{ij} are unbiased; thus, this is the preferred method, unless local samples are so small that maximum likelihood estimates of gene frequencies are unreliable, in which case the first method can be used for analysis of isolation by distance, with suitable adjustment of the Malécot parameter *a* and its standard error.

Bioassay of kinship in Micronesia agrees with other evidence that the mean kinship within populations is about 0.05. The greatest differentiation is for Kapingamarangi, the only Polynesian outlier sampled, followed by Pingelap, whose differentiation is undoubtedly due to the small number of survivors of typhoon Lengkieki, conjoined with their variable family size and subsequent low immigration rate.

Hainline (1966) observed a negative correlation between census size and an arbitrary index of genetic differentiation, the difference between largest and smallest gene frequencies at the ABO locus. The same negative correlation is apparent between census size and kinship, as expected from Equation 15, whether kinship is predicted from migration or estimated from phenotypes, metrics, or clan isonymy.

TOPOLOGY

As the number of populations in an array increases, we look for some way to summarize the kinship matrix. Isolation by distance provides the most succinct summary for comparison of different population structures, but it pools different populations. Other methods represent each population by a point in a two-dimensional graph. If the axes represent the first and second eigenvectors of the kinship matrix, this is called *principal component analysis*. Phenotypically similar populations tend to plot close together. If the axes are rotated to maximum congruence with geography, the representation is called *genetic topology*. Migrant populations tend to plot close to their place of origin, rather than residence. This will give a good graph of kinship, whether or not geographic distance is the principal isolating factor. Finally, one axis may represent hybridity (or the complement of cognate frequency), and the other axis may serve merely to space populations equally in a tree diagram, any branch of which may be rotated 180° without changing logical structure: that is, $(AB)\ (C) = (BA)\ (C) = (C)\ (AB) = (C)\ (BA)$. Such a graph is called a *dendrogram*. It portrays actual or expected phenotypic similarity, and no branch need have any phylogenetic validity. On strong assumptions, a dendrogram can be transformed into a *cladogram*, in which the major axis represents time rather than hybridity. Once two populations split, we must assume that there is no subsequent migration between them and that

355

differentiation proceeds at the same rate for all populations. Except in a designed experiment, such assumptions are always false at the subspecific level. The most that can be hoped is that the major branches of a dendrogram have phylogenetic significance.

The above considerations are obvious and are incorporated in numerical taxonomy (Sokal and Sneath 1963). There are several algorithms for constructing a dendrogram. The simplest and most common uses the principle of minimum computer time (Sokal and Sneath 1963, Harpending and Jenkins, Chapter 9), in which the pair of populations with the smallest hybridity is represented by their mean, and one is deleted. The hybridity matrix is reduced stepwise in this way until only one element remains—the mean hybridity between the two major clusters of populations. A vector of weights (which may be unity, sample size, or population size) determines the means at each stage.

Cavalli-Sforza and Edwards (1967) developed the method of minimum evolution, which assumes that a dendrogram is in every detail a cladogram. All possible partitions are considered, with construction of the tree proceeding from the trunk to its finer branches. The amount of computer time increases rapidly with the number of populations, so that it is hardly feasible to consider more than 20 populations at one time. Since the assumptions of the method are implausible, there seems no reason to abandon the techniques of numerical taxonomy with their much lighter computational load. Wishart (1969) has considered some of the disadvantages of minimum variance clustering, the general class to which the method of Cavalli-Sforza and Edwards belongs.

In numerical taxonomy it is often asserted that a dendrogram should be based on at least 100 traits. Genetic studies fall far short of this, and appreciable sampling errors are involved. Kidd and Cavalli-Sforza (1972) showed by Monte Carlo simulation that even in the absence of migration, their algorithm commonly failed to construct the correct cladogram under conditions of high drift. We must therefore reject the method of minimum evolution at the subspecific level and regard a dendrogram from bioassay as a representation of phenotypic similarity, rather than phylogeny.

If the severe limitations of dendrograms are borne in mind, they provide a useful representation of part of the information encoded in a kinship matrix, which may also be portrayed by principal components and genetic topology. Three graphs have been constructed for Micronesia

356

(Morton and Lalouel 1972b). Phenotypes, metrics, and cognates agree in showing a major split between the Polynesian outlier Kapingamarangi and the other populations. Yap, Palau, and the Marianas are differentiated from central and eastern Micronesia, within which Pingelap is most discrepant (Figures 39–41).

ISOLATION BY DISTANCE

Of the many regions studied for isolation by distance, a few pool local populations so severely that the intercept a cannot be interpreted as kinship within a local group. Among the remainder, some were studied by

FIGURE 39. Geography of 14 Micronesian samples. *Source:* After Morton and Lalouel (1972b).

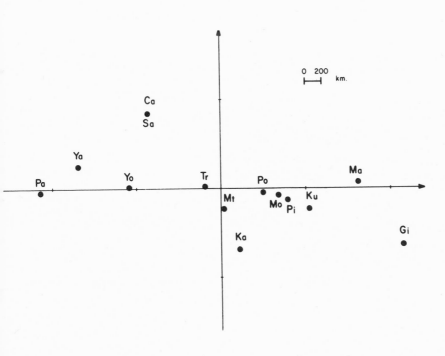

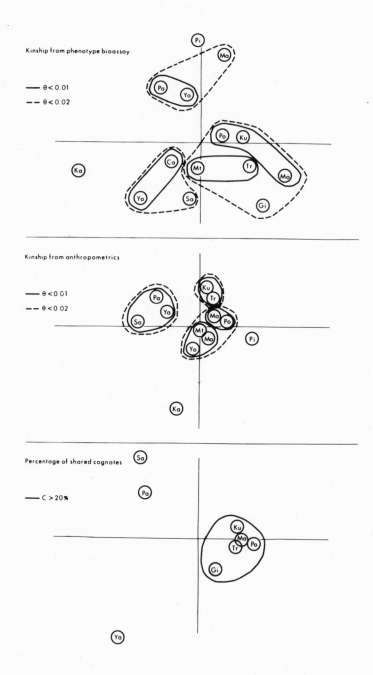

FIGURE 40. Eigenvectorial representations rotated to maximum congruence with geography. *Source:* After Morton and Lalouel (1972b).

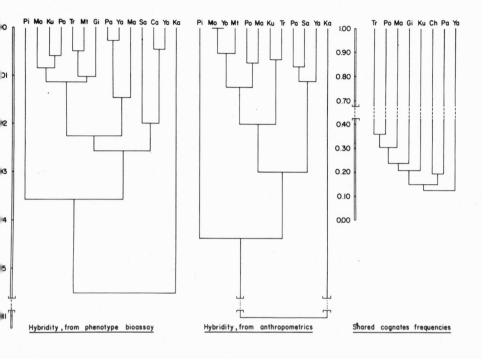

FIGURE 41. Dendrograms of hybridity in Micronesia. *Source:* After Morton and Lalouel (1972b).

the first method of the previous section, so that the estimate of a and its standard error must be multiplied by $3/2$.

When this is done, we obtain the results summarized in Table 54. Oceanic islands have high values of a (about 0.05) and low values of b (about 0.005). Isolates, whether in developed or developing countries, have high values of b, generating the paradox that isolates are more insular than islands! The paradox is easily resolved by noting that a distance of 10 to 20 kilometers, which suffices to reduce kinship greatly for isolates, still includes stepping-stone populations. However, this space is unoccupied for oceanic islands, where migration is necessarily over greater distances. The values of b are more similar when expressed relative to the distance between populations. The samples of South American Indians studied by Roisenberg and Morton (1970) are anomalous in having a

359

TABLE 54
PARAMETERS OF ISOLATION BY DISTANCE, $\varphi = (1 - L)ae^{-bd} + L$

Ecology	Source	L	a	σ_a	b	σ_b
Oceanic islands						
All Micronesia	phenotypes (Morton and Lalouel 1972a)	−0.0081	0.0463	0.0083	0.0023	—
	metrics (Morton and Lalouel 1972a)	−0.0133	0.0569	0.0084	0.0016	0.0006
	cognates (Morton and Lalouel 1972a)	0.1531	1.0000	—	0.0029	0.0005
Pingelap/Mokil with	phenotypes (Imaizumi and Morton 1970)	—	0.0491	0.0086	0.0014	0.0005
others	phenotypes (Morton and Lalouel 1972a)	−0.0103	0.0565	0.0132	0.0069	—
	metrics (Morton and Lalouel 1972a)	−0.0021	0.0884	0.0222	0.0069	0.0041
	cognates (Morton and Lalouel 1972a)	0.3440	1.0000	—	0.0045	0.0014
	migration (Morton and Lalouel 1972a)	0.0000	0.0606	0.0015	0.0120	0.0010
The Marshalls	clans (Morton and Lalouel 1972a)	−0.0121	0.0540	0.0161	0.0111	0.0099
	migration (Pollock, Lalouel, and Morton 1972)	0.0000	0.0431	0.0019	0.0005	0.0001
Isolates						
Bougainville	phenotypes (Friedlaender 1971b)	?	0.0765	?	0.1050	?
	migration (Friedlaender 1971b)	0.0000	0.0588	?	0.0954	?
Papago	phenotypes (Morton et al. 1971c)	−0.0046	0.0182	0.0037	0.0661	0.0395
South American Indians	phenotypes (Roisenberg and Morton 1970)	0.0000	0.0379	0.0096	0.0032	0.0016
New Guinea	phenotypes (Imaizumi and Morton 1970)	−0.0098	0.0444	0.0096	0.0519	0.0164
Makiritare	phenotypes (Lalouel and Morton 1972)	−0.0096	0.0423	0.0065	0.0440	0.0253
Alpine Switzerland	ABO groups (Morton et al. 1968)	−0.0004	0.0088	0.0033	0.1863	0.0783
Oxfordshire villages	migration (Imaizumi, Morton, and Harris 1970)	0.0000	0.0048	0.0000	0.8620	0.0839
Continental regions						
Switzerland	ABO groups (Morton et al. 1968)	−0.0004	0.0029	0.0001	0.0230	0.0010
Belgium	ABO groups (Dodinval 1970)	−0.0001	0.0009	0.0001	0.0247	0.0018
Sweden	phenotypes (Imaizumi and Morton 1970)	−0.0006	0.0033	0.0006	0.0053	0.0014
Northeastern Brazil	phenotypes (Azevêdo et al. 1969)	−0.0010	0.0050	0.0008	0.0021	0.0004

small value of b. This probably reflects preferential sampling of accessible towns, and higher values of b are to be expected for smaller localities. Continental regions have small values of a (0.001–0.01) and small to moderate values of b (0.002–0.02). Indicators as different as phenotypes, metrics, clans, and cognates have comparable parameters (b) of isolation by distance.

Wright (1950) suggested that 0.02 is a plausible upper limit to kinship in human populations. However, these data show that values of 0.05 or more are by no means rare in isolates and oceanic islands. While hunting-gathering societies have not been subjected to detailed analysis of population structure, it is reasonable to conjecture that they resemble oceanic islands, with a large value of a (reflecting small local groups) and a small value of b (reflecting migration over large distances). Presumably, the mean inbreeding coefficient would approach a, as in oceanic islands and isolates. Such a large pressure toward identity by descent probably made inbreeding a more potent force in preindustrial societies than random homozygosity or heterozygosity effects of rare "recessive" genes. It would be interesting to examine kinship in societies practicing preferential consanguineous marriage.

CHRONOLOGY

The first radiocarbon date in the Eastern Carolines is the twelfth century at Nan Madol, the ancient Ponapean temple (Long 1965). Several estimates of atoll occupancy are provided by kinship. Six Nanmwarkis ruled Pingelap from 1790 to 1964, for an average of 29.0 years per reign. This is close to the mean generation time, estimated as 29.1 years. Assuming that the average Nanmwarki ruled for one generation, the first leader, Mwoimok, would have been born in A.D. 1236, and the members of the legendary expedition against Nan Madol (if correctly assigned to six generations before Lengkieki) would have been born in 1557. The reign of a Nanmwarki may well have averaged less than a generation, which would shorten the time span. On the other hand, the legendary first leader may not have been the first inhabitant; the early Nanmwarkis are so surrounded by animistic myths that each may have corresponded to several generations. Thus, genealogies suggest that Pingelap has been occupied for at least 25 generations and perhaps longer than 1,000 years (Morton et al. 1971b).

If ϕ is an estimated kinship matrix, and ϕ^t is a prediction in generation t, we may find the value of t that minimizes the *norm*.

$$\varepsilon_t = \sum_{i,j} (\phi_{ij} - \phi_{ij}^{(t)})^2. \tag{18}$$

Then ϕ and $\phi^{(t)}$ are said to be *congruent*, and t is called the *duration* of the structure. A similar argument applies to θ and $\theta^{(t)}$. For eastern Micronesia, we found $t = 34$ from phenotype bioassay, which is equivalent to 1,000 years (Morton and Lalouel 1972a).

From the frequency of cognates between Pingelap and Ponape (0.708), glottochronology gives

$$t = -2300 \, ln \, 0.708 = 800 \text{ years}$$

as the time since the two languages diverged, based on continental populations. The constant is doubtful, and no allowance is made for borrowing from Ponapean during the last century through missionary endeavors and writings in that language.

Still other estimates of duration can be derived by interpreting dendrograms as cladograms. Assuming 3,000 years as the time since breakup of Malayan-Polynesian, the simple law

$$\phi = ae^{-Bt} \tag{19}$$

gives ridiculously small estimates of divergence time (less than 100 years for minor branches of the tree). However, since increasing time implies increasing distance, with reduced migration and possible exposure to diversifying selection, a more plausible model is

$$\phi = ae^{-Bt^2}, \tag{20}$$

which gives the cladogram of Figure 42. Pingelap and Mokil are estimated to have diverged from the rest of Micronesia about 1,000 years ago for phenotypes and about 850 years ago for metrics. From cognates, the divergence of eastern and western Micronesia is estimated as about 1,050 years ago. It seems impossible to judge the precision of these estimates on present evidence, but they are gratifyingly consistent.

362

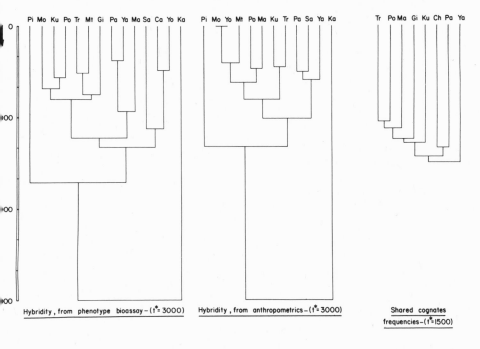

Pi Mo Ku Po Tr Mt Gi Pa Ya Ma Sa Ca Yo Ka   Pi Mo Yo Mt Po Ma Ku Tr Pa Sa Ya Ka   Tr Po Ma Gi Ku Ch Pa Ya

Hybridity, from phenotype bioassay − (t^*= 3000)   Hybridity, from anthropometrics − (t^*= 3000)   Shared cognates frequencies − (t^*= 1500)

Note: t* refers to estimated time since first split.

FIGURE 42. Cladograms of hybridity in Micronesia.

DISCUSSION

The history and ethnohistory of Pingelap and Mokil led to several questions (Chapter 14) that can be answered from a study of population structure:

(1) Genealogies, demography, cognate frequencies, polymorphisms, clan isonymy, and anthropometrics are in quantitative agreement about kinship within and between atolls. The conjunction of high drift and immigration from large distances is no paradox; while long-range migration pressure is appreciable, the evolutionary size is small, partly due to the mortality following typhoon Lengkieki two hundred years ago.

(2) The composition of the founder population and the immigrants who contributed additional variability can be inferred with considerable accuracy by the methods of historical genetics.

(3) The genetic effects of division of the population into matrilineal clans, both at present and in the remote hypothetical time when they were regularly exogamous, are negligible.

(4) Clan isonymy agrees with other evidence about kinship and provides a method to study population structure even in the absence of phenotype data.

(5) These atolls have high values of local kinship (a) and slow decline with distance (b) compared with other populations in which kinship has been assayed.

(6) The history of this population accounts completely for the high frequency of achromatopsia, which was transmitted via a recessive gene from Mwahuele, the genetically most important survivor of typhoon Lengkieki.

(7) Features of these populations that facilitate or interfere with methods to reduce the frequency of achromatopsia have not yet been studied in detail. However, it is clear that endogamy increases the frequency, while the common practice of adoption could be used to reduce the frequency in high-risk sibships.

(8) Inferences from Pingelap and Mokil agree with extensive data on polymorphisms and anthropometrics in Micronesia and with limited data on cognates. Migration pressure is less in the Eastern Carolines than in the Marshalls (and probably the Gilberts and the Western Carolines).

One question that we did not formulate from the ethnohistory is whether prehistoric migrations can be recognized through bioassy of kinship. The numbers of founders and migrants are small, and drift is a more important force than migration pressure from any particular population. Decline of kinship with distance, while relatively slow, is sufficient to make kinship undistinguishable from zero for populations at large distances. The two factors of drift and errors of estimation militate against identification of prehistoric migrations. Table 55 gives estimates of kinship from phenotypes, metrics, and historical migration between the two reference atolls and Kusaie, Ponape, the Mortlocks, the Marshalls, and the Gilberts. There is a suggestion that Pingelap resembles the Marshalls more than the other populations and that Mokil is more like the Gilberts, but these indications could be due to accidents of drift or errors of estimation. There is no evidence that Pingelap is more closely related to the Gilberts, the Mortlocks, or Kusaie than to a random Micronesian population or that Mokil and the Marshalls have

TABLE 55

ESTIMATES OF KINSHIP BETWEEN REFERENCE AND DONOR POPULATIONS

Reference Population	Indicator	Donor Population				
		Kusaie	Ponape	The Mortlocks	The Marshalls	The Gilberts
Pingelap	phenotypes	−0.0012	−0.0163	−0.0158	0.0231	−0.0114
	metrics	−0.0284	0.0443	−0.0080	0.0260	—
	migration	0.0013	0.0008	0.0013	0.0002	0.0004
Mokil	phenotypes	0.0122	0.0110	0.0046	0.0032	0.0356
	metrics	−0.0158	0.0203	0.0165	−0.0046	—
	migration	0.0005	0.0008	0.0007	0.0007	0.0004

any special affinity, despite one tradition. Predictions of kinship from historical migration give no clear discrimination among nonreference populations.

Although prehistoric migration cannot reliably be inferred from present-day observation in so small a region as eastern Micronesia, attempts to infer migrations over large regions from cognates, cultural elements, or biological traits have some chance of success when limited to the major branches of a dendrogram, which is based on resemblance rather than phylogeny. Kinship has been shown to provide quantitative comparison of biological, linguistic, and cultural resemblance.

NOTE

1. This work was supported by grant GM 17173 from the U.S. National Institutes of Health.

16

Some Aspects of Genetic Structure in the Yanomama and Makiritare: Two Tribes of Southern Venezuela[1]

RICHARD H. WARD

Department of Human Genetics
University of Michigan

RATIONALE FOR "ANTHROPOLOGICAL GENETICS"

There appears to be little consensus regarding the proper province of "anthropological genetics," since the rubric has been applied to a variety of studies; these studies range from those that investigate the distribution of genetic markers in "tribal' populations to those that are more sharply focused on the application of genetic theory to the investigation of population parameters (such as mating patterns) that are usually regarded as the province of the anthropologist. Given this diversity of concepts, it seems appropriate to investigate the rationale underlying the current popularity of studies that apply genetic principles to tribal populations. Interestingly enough, attempts to justify the merger of genetics and anthropology invariably result in an acknowledgement of the specific contribution of anthropological data to an evaluation of certain aspects

367

of genetic theory. Rarely has the flow of information been reversed—anthropological theory remains minimally affected by the postulates of genetics, despite the provocative attempts of some geneticists (Morton, Imaizumi, and Harris 1971). In delimiting the field of inquiry then, the perspective of a biologist, rather than the different viewpoint of an anthropologist, will be emphasized. The majority of reasons advanced for the genetic significance of observations of tribal populations (anthropological and otherwise) fall into three somewhat overlapping categories.

The first viewpoint holds that "primitive tribes, especially unacculturated ones, living in intimate association with their environment are more likely to yield information regarding the adaptive value of the diverse nature of the human genome than are urbanized communities separated from their 'natural' environment by complexity of modern technology." This viewpoint presumes that the interplay of genes and environment in unacculturated populations should yield bodies of data in which the action of selection and other evolutionary forces might be readily discerned. Despite the intuitive appeal of such an attitude, no such insights into the operation of selective mechanisms at a specific genetic locus have emerged thus far. Furthermore, with our growing awareness of the intricate population structure of tribes, it now appears exceedingly unlikely that any such insights will ever emerge. This conclusion may seem to run counter to the manner in which the only well-established genome-environment selective interaction in man (that is hemoglobin S and malaria) was discovered; however, it seems clear that with the requirement of very large homogeneous samples to generate conclusive estimates of selection, large urbanized populations, rather than their tribal counterparts, may be the ultimate hope of the "selectionist." Thus, the elucidation of the selective mechanism operating on hemoglobin S may have been more akin to a fortuitous observation than the revelation of a ubiquitous attribute of human populations. It now appears that of the forces traditionally assumed to be important in shaping population gene pools, mating patterns and migration may be the only parameters amenable to detailed analysis in tribal populations.

"The complexity of the human genome can only be understood in a functional sense by adopting a historical perspective that can be achieved by studying tribal populations." This second viewpoint presumes that those few economically primitive tribes still existing as scattered remnants across the globe continue to be characterized by those features that played a predominant role in shaping the major part of human evolution before the establishment of centralized communities some ten thousand years ago. Although this premise will admit certain generalities about the possible effect of demographic parameters and sociopolitical organizations on the genetic structure of an evolving human population, such conclusions are untestable. Despite the inherent interest of this approach, the investigator faces the paradox of constructing models of human evolution, based on populations that, judged from our vantage point at least, have drifted from the mainstream of human progress. While this approach can yield some indication regarding the course evolution may have taken and thereby provide a vantage point from which the present-day condition of mankind may be evaluated, any such conclusions must remain essentially philosophical.

According to the third viewpoint, "human populations can yield biological information that would be difficult, if not impossible, to obtain from natural populations of other organisms (that is, data on migration, family relationships, mating patterns, and so forth). The lack of experimental control can be compensated for by investigating many different populations, each characterized by a variety of contrasting parameters." Tribal populations represent such a diversity, especially with respect to the analysis of many factors of interest to the population geneticist— demography, formation and dissolution of demes, migration between demes, and mating patterns within demes. The fact that tribal populations tend to be categorized on the basis of these features for anthropological purposes forms the nucleus of the anthropological contribution to population studies, while the diversity of such features serves, in large part, to offset the disadvantages of tribal societies for population studies (for example, small size, lack of reliable records, and so on).

Accepting that this last premise gives sufficient rationale for carrying out genetic studies on tribal populations, at least three approaches seem feasible: (1) the selection of a population on the grounds that it displays at least some of the characteristic features of primitive tribalism in unadulterated form and then attempting to analyze as many parameters as is feasible, with the aim of elucidating those that contribute to the discernible genetic structure of the tribe; (2) the selection of a tribal population on the basis of one or more attributes that will allow a rigorous test of hypothesis concerning a specific model of population genetics;

and (3) the analysis of a variety of tribal populations judiciously chosen so that they differ in certain parameters but are concordant in others in order to gauge the effect of changing specified parameters while others are held constant.

While categories (2) and (3) will be more productive in yielding tests of genetic hypotheses, it seems apparent that so far, the majority of genetic studies on tribal populations have fallen into category (1)—which is not to imply that this was the original intent. This is partly the consequence of venturing into a hitherto uncharted field, but it is also due to the fact that all too frequently, the facility with which historical and demographic data can be garnered has ultimately resulted in invalidating a set of apparently innocuous assumptions on which the model for analysis was based. However, when all is said and done, the very general insights into the intimate working of a biological population, gained by the cautious and pragmatic analysis of human data, may do more to advance the theory of population genetics than the uncritical application of the latest mathematical model to populations where the basic assumptions can never be tested.

Concurrent with the increasing acceptance of the cogent nature of genetic studies on tribal populations is an awareness of urgency engendered by the evidence that the majority of tribal societies in today's world are rapidly succumbing to the encroachment of western civilization. With the disappearance and alteration of tribal society as a seemingly inevitable consequence of acculturation, efforts to utilize the special information from tribal societies (whether for genetic or for anthropological purposes) will only be possible for another decade or so—we are likely to be the last generation of scientists able to gather information from unacculturated societies in which the parameters of interest may be presumed to have some historical continuity (Neel and Salzano 1964).

THE TRIBAL POPULATIONS

Given the intrinsic interest of tribal populations, it is perhaps surprising that there have been so few efforts to merge the techniques of genetics and anthropology in this area. Apart from some notable exceptions (Hiernaux 1956, Kraus and White 1956, Oliver and Howells 1957), the first serious attempt to interrelate biological and anthropological concepts in a study of tribal populations in an intensive fashion did not occur until a decade ago. This effort, initiated by Neel and his as-associates as a pilot study of the Xavante of the Brazilian Mato Grosso (Neel et al. 1964), was noteworthy in that it represented the first meticu-lous application of a spectrum of biological disciplines to a tribal popu-lation. The general conclusion of the first report, reinforced by the suc-ceeding series of papers (Neel and Salzano 1967, Salzano, Neel, and Maybury-Lewis 1967), indicated that such intensive studies of an eco-nomically primitive tribal population were not only feasible but would also yield a wealth of biological data. Not only did the findings of these studies provide the background against which the more intensive studies on the Yanomama and Makiritare were formulated, but they also gave the impetus for the initiation of a variety of other studies along similar lines—this text, for example.

To elaborate on these studies, it was deemed necessary to find a some-what larger and even less acculturated tribal population in order to carry out a more intensive analysis. Ultimately, the choice rested on the Yanomama of Southern Venezuela and Northern Brazil. This tribe, which remains one of the largest unacculturated tribal groups in South America, with an estimated population of 10,000 distributed in some 100 to 125 villages, has been extensively described in the ethnographic literature (Becher 1960, Zerries 1964, Chagnon 1968a). The initiation of detailed studies on this tribe, and on an adjacent but much smaller tribe, the Makiritare, began before the last phases of analysis on the Xavante were completed; it soon indicated that the Yanomama would yield a body of data that would have considerable interest to the population geneticist. The remainder of this chapter will be concerned with some of the conclusions arising from a subset of this data. However, it should be remembered that the topics discussed here form but a small portion of a series of very extensive studies, and to attain a proper perspective, the genetic aspects should be evaluated against the full range of the project, which is nothing less than the most complete description of the human biology of a tribal population to date. The wealth of information re-sulting from these studies has been noted in a variety of contexts (Neel et al. 1964, Neel 1967, 1969, 1970, 1971), while the most immediate ethnographic description of the two tribes can be found in Chagnon's study of the Yanomama (1968a) and Arvello-Jimenez's work on the Makiritare (1971).

GENETIC STRUCTURE

Although a multitude of aspects are beginning to emerge as analysis of these tribes proceeds, this chapter will be concerned with but three aspects of the tribes' genetic structure. *Genetic structure* in this instance is broadly defined as the nonuniform distribution of allelic states within a population. Since such a definition encompasses the consequences of a variety of factors, ranging from the existence of spatially discernible demes in a finite population to nonrandom association of uniting gametes as a function of assortative mating, a necessary corollary is that all natural populations will exhibit genetic structure to some extent.

Ideally, analysis of genetic structure would partition out those aspects of structure that are important in determining the evolutionary dynamics of the population (such as the influence of a mutant gene on the rate of fixation); in practice, however, even if the genetic structure of a population can be delimited, determination of those aspects that are most likely to influence the course of evolution remains a problematical exercise at best. The three aspects of genetic structure investigated in this chapter are (1) the extent of genetic microdifferentiation between demes, (2) the pattern of genetic relationship between demes, and (3) the effect of subdividing a population into demes on the distribution of alleles within and between demes. For the purpose of analysis, the somewhat arbitrary distinction is made between a *tribal village* as representing a deme, and a *tribe*, composed of many such demes, as representing a population.

GENETIC MICRODIFFERENTIATION

One of the first observations of the Yanomama studies dealt with the high degree of genetic differentiation among 10 Yanomama villages (Arends et al. 1967), as revealed by nine genetic systems. At that time, inspection of the data indicated that genetic differentiation within the tribe might be an important factor in determining the amount of microevolution at the intertribal level. To investigate this conjecture more rigorously, the investigators used a measure of genetic distance based on the angular transformation of gene frequencies that has been applied to a wide variety of populations since its inception by Cavalli-Sforza and Conterio (1960). This statistic, which, under certain assumptions, can be equated to units of gene substitution (Cavalli-Sforza and Edwards 1967), was initially proposed as a measure of the distance between two populations based on multinomially distributed variables (Bhattacharyya 1946). Other measures of genetic distance (Balakrishnan and Sanghvi 1968, Kurczynski 1970) that are less successful in achieving an equal area transformation (Edwards 1971) will yield slightly different distance values (Krzanowski 1971) but probably without altering any conclusions.

The significance of the observed intratribal microdifferentiation for both the Yanomama and Makiritare was gauged by comparing the magnitude of pairwise genetic distances between villages with the magnitude of a set of intertribal distances already calculated for 12 randomly selected South American tribes (Fitch and Neel 1969). Utilizing the same set of six loci, it was found that the mean intervillage distance based on seven villages from each tribe was on the order of 90 percent of the mean intertribal distance; this indicated that relative to the genetic divergence between tribes, the extent of genetic microdifferentiation within a tribe is considerable (Neel and Ward 1970). However, if one can assume that the "fission-fusion" process (Neel and Salzano 1967) may result in a single village splitting off to found a new tribe, then a more appropriate measure of the contribution to tribal differentiation is to consider the genetic distance of a village from the tribal mean. In this instance, the mean distance of a village from the tribal remainder was 68 percent of the mean intertribal distance, indicating that on the average (if it can be assumed that the gene frequency of the founder village will represent the mean gene frequency of the new tribe), 68 percent of the genetic divergence between tribes arises at the time of inception. Despite the unrealistic assumptions of equal rates of population growth, absence of migration from other tribes, and a homogeneous dispersion of incipient villages from the new tribal nucleus, this first approximation implies that the founding of a new tribe may be of overriding importance in contributing toward intertribal genetic differentiation. While this is not to deny the part played by local selective pressures acting in concert with genetic drift, intertribal differentiation may largely result from the initial "founder event," followed by the partial isolation of the incipient tribe.

Since the single fissioning event that may result in a new tribe appears to have such far-reaching consequences for the extent of intertribal differentiation, it becomes germane to investigate whether the formation of a new village by the fission-fusion process similarly influences the extent of intratribal microdifferentiation. The importance of the initial formative event can be gauged by investigating the amount of dispersion between newly formed villages as compared with the amount of microdifferentiation between well-established villages. In the Yanomama, villages tend to be formed following a fission event, the consequence of which results in the accumulation of people with a higher coefficient of relationship in the new villages than in the original village—the "lineal effect" (Arends et al. 1967). By taking 15 villages whose histories are reasonably well detailed (Chagnon 1966, 1972), it can be established, on the basis of 11 loci, that the genetic divergence between recently separated villages approximates the genetic divergence of villages separated 30 years or more (Ward 1970), as Table 56 indicates.

TABLE 56
RELATIONSHIP BETWEEN GENETIC DISTANCE AND
TIME SINCE SEPARATION

	Time Period of Separation (years)				
	1–10	11–20	21–30	31–40	41–50
Mean intervillage genetic distance	0.328	0.373	0.348	0.328	0.388
N (pairs)	7	2	11	3	10

Despite the short time period involved, results from the Yanomama where village fissions may occur every 10 to 15 years are consistent with a model where the initial splitting causes a high degree of genetic divergence, with subsequent migration between villages slowing down the rate of microdifferentiation. However, genetic divergence can be presumed to increase as a function of genetic drift, since the overall mean genetic distance for 37 Yanomama villages is 0.468, based on the same 11 loci. Such a model implies that for tribal populations and possibly natural populations of other organisms, where the fission-fusion process operates on small, internally structured demes, the initial process of deme foundation by nonrandom sampling may be of overriding importance in determining the extent of genetic microdifferentiation subsequently observed. This, in turn, contrasts with the traditional view in which greater emphasis is placed on the joint operation of local selective pressures and random genetic drift over extensive time periods, following the initial event of isolation.

THE PATTERN OF GENETIC RELATIONSHIPS BETWEEN DEMES

The second aspect of genetic structure to be considered is the pattern of relationships between demes that were previously shown to be genetically distinct. While there are a number of interpretations of "genetic relationship," this analysis used the pairwise genetic distance between villages as the measure on which the analytic structure of genetic relationship was based, in a manner consistent with the preliminary analysis. The primary goal in this instance was to establish an objective representation of the genetic relationships of population subunits for two reasons. First, the objective formation of a structured pattern allows further critical analysis of the effect of population subgroupings. Thus, for example, it is possible to construct models of analysis to investigate the effect of hierarchically defined population units on the distribution of genotypes within the groupings (Heuch 1972). Second, the establishment of an objective measure of the set of genetic relationships existing between villages may be helpful in providing an intuitive assessment as to which factors are most important in determining the observable genetic structure of the tribe.

In this instance, the method of analysis hinges on the construction of a relations graph uniting the villages as a function of the matrix of pairwise genetic distances. While the resulting structure is properly called a tree (Ore 1963), alternate terminology such as "network" may be applied to avoid any inference of phylogenetic descent. Although the specific algorithms employed are derived from those developed by Edwards and Cavalli-Sforza (1964, 1965), the model of analysis is different, since the objective in this case is to describe the nexus of relationships between villages in an objective way rather than infer evolutionary history. The assumptions in the latter instance are less restrictive, though the estimation procedure is correspondingly less ambitious. Thus, the criterion of analysis is that the best representation of the genetic relationships of a set of villages is given by the tree derived from the matrix of genetic distances having the minimal total segment length. While such a criterion has an implicit appeal for models that attempt to evaluate the results of a parsimonious evolutionary process, it is less obvious how well it defines phenetic relationships. The so-called additive tree (Cavalli-Sforza and Edwards 1963, 1967) appears on a priori grounds to be equally suitable, even though application of the two types of criteria to the same set of data can yield different "topologies" (Kidd and Sgaramella-Zonta 1971). While both models have advantages and disadvantages, it seems on balance that for these populations at least, the "minimal string" (spatial) method will yield more informative results than the "additive" model, since the present-day genetic relationships of the villages are largely a consequence of a series of fissioning events in the recent past (that is, an element of evolutionary inference has crept into the analysis).

The first detailed analyses in a tribal population did, in fact, have a historical perspective, since the inquiry attempted to determine whether the historical pattern of migration for seven Makiritare villages yielded a similar pattern of genetic relationships (Ward and Neel 1970b). Figure 43 shows the complex web of relationships revealed by analysis of the migrational history over the past 60 years, while Figure 44 shows the genetic network (tree) for the same seven villages based on the genetic distance matrix derived from 11 polymorphic loci. The tree, or network, is depicted in such a way that the correspondence between the two topologies, historical and genetic, is revealed by visual inspection. The implication of the concordance of the genetic network with the historical pattern is that in tribes such as these, the patterned structure of genetic relationships of demes is largely due to historical processes operating over a relatively short time period. Interestingly enough, this genetic pattern tends to duplicate the nexus of sociopolitical relationships between these villages, whether the latter is measured by the amount of marriages between villages revealed by migration matrices (Ward and Neel 1970b), or whether it is measured by an analysis of the political alliances (Arvello-Jimenez 1971). On the other hand, it should be remembered that the strength of these conclusions is only as good as the ability to measure the degree of concordance of the two types of patterns. Since to date there is no adequate procedure that will evaluate the amount of congruence between a set of topologies, this is usually measured by inspection—a factor that limits the conclusion that can be drawn from such an analysis.

In spite of these limitations, it was possible to carry out a more elaborate analysis on the Yanomama, since the data can be considered

376

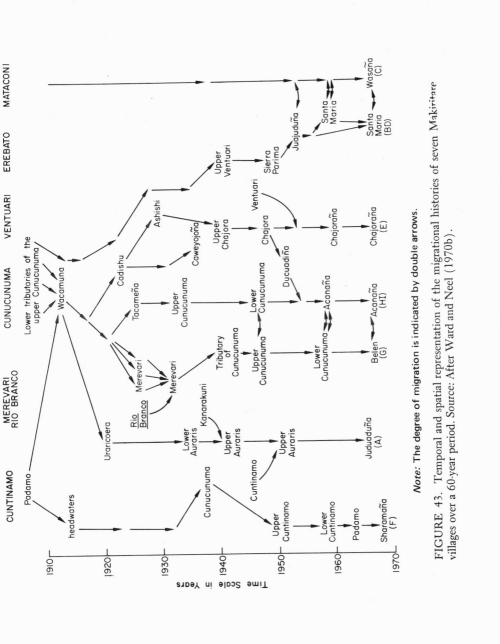

FIGURE 43. Temporal and spatial representation of the migrational histories of seven Makiritare villages over a 60-year period. Source: After Ward and Neel (1970b).

Note: The degree of migration is indicated by double arrows.

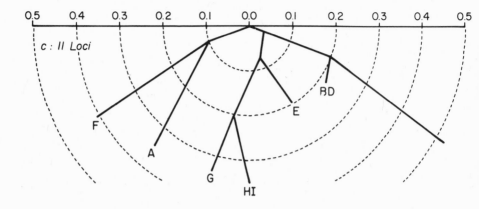

FIGURE 44. The genetic network for the seven Makiritare villages in Figure 43, based on 11 polymorphic loci.

in terms of three hierarchical levels (Ward 1972). At the first level, it is possible to analyze small clusters of closely related villages that have evolved by successive fissionings from an ancestral village in a 70 to 80-year period. In such clusters, recognized on the basis of ethnohistorical information, the genetic divergence between villages appears to result from the unequal distribution of genotypes at the time of splitting, followed by differential fertility and migrations from other villages after the split. At the second level, it is possible to analyze a set of villages that, although not demonstrably descended from a single ancestral village, still participate in a complex web of migrations and fusions. At the final level, there are all the sampled villages whose only common denominator is membership in the same tribe.

The hierarchical analysis can be formulated by first describing five geographical subgroups of the Yanomama defined in terms of the various river basins emanating from the Parima Range, from which the Yanomama appear to have migrated in centrifugal fashion. The groups, with the number of sampled villages in parentheses, are: a central Parima group

378

(four villages) and four peripheral groups; northern, or Sanema (five villages); southern (two villages); eastern (one village); and western (25 villages). Within the more extensively sampled western subgroup, three historically defined village clusters can be recognized: Shamatari cluster (four villages), Namoweitari cluster (four villages), and Wanaboweitari cluster (seven villages). All three clusters originated north of the Orinoco on the western flanks of the Parima Range, having their origins as single villages in the period 1875 to 1900 and all three having had a considerable degree of interaction in the form of trading alliances, warfare, and so forth. While the full complexity of the village interrelationships is glossed over, the main features of the migrations during the past 70 years are depicted in Figure 45. The appropriate genetic networks based on nine polymorphic loci are shown in Figure 46.

The minimum network resulting for the four Shamatari villages has a total net length of 0.96 units, and a comparison with the historical relationships indicates that the initial split is in general agreement with the historical relationships. However, the divergence of villages 11G and 11HI (segment length of 0.46 units), separated barely a year before sampling, is greater than the separation of 03D and 03H (segment length of 0.32 units), which have been separated for seven years. This illustrates once more the extent of the initial genetic divergence due to the lineal founder effect.

In contrast, the Namoweitari network (length of 0.64 units) does not show as good a correspondence with the sequence of village fissions; this may be due to the comparatively recent fragmentation of the Namoweitari village, coupled with dependence on other villages for aid in warfare, which has resulted in a fair degree of gene flow between unrelated villages. The network appropriate to the seven Wanaboweitari villages with a total net length of 1.42 units displays two significant features. First, there is an initial split corresponding to the historical split into the antecedent village of 08S and 08T and the complex 03G, 08N, 03E, 03I, and 03F. Second, the correspondence with the historical relationships for the 08S-08T line is better than the depiction of the other line, since the grouping of 03E with 03G and 03I with 08N and the separation of 03F does not reflect the historical pattern very well. In general, the analysis of the village clusters indicates that while there is a reasonable correspondence between the historical relationships and the genetic networks for the Shamatari and Wanaboweitari clusters, this does not appear as

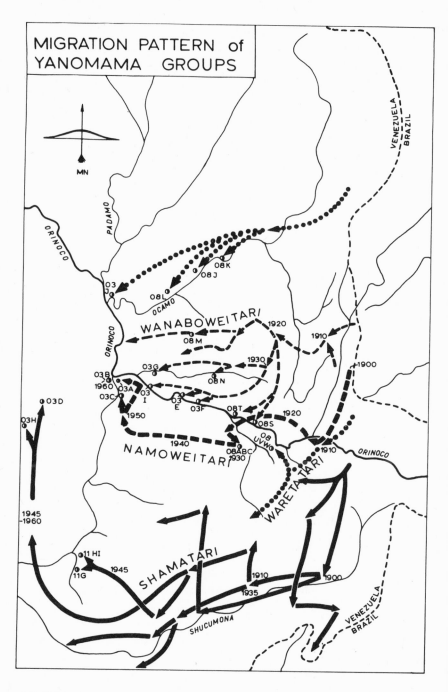

FIGURE 45. Migrational history of three clusters of Yanomama villages, giving the gross patterns of village fissions and subsequent movements over a 70-year period. Source: After Ward (in press).

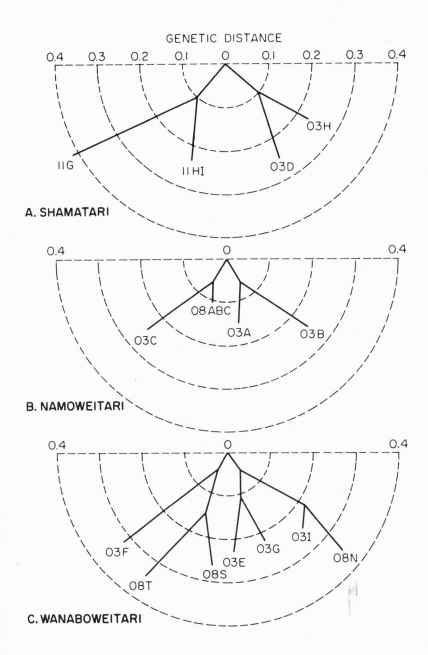

FIGURE 46. The genetic network for three clusters of Yanomama villages, based on nine polymorphic systems. *Source:* After Ward (in press).

impressive as that for the seven Makiritare villages. However, the next level of analysis shows that much of the apparent discrepancy in the genetic networks can be explained by reference to specific historical incidents causing distortion from the historical pattern of village splits.

The second level of analysis deals with 19 villages of the western Yanomama, including all 15 villages previously analyzed, together with the sole representative of a fourth historical cluster (o8UVW) and three villages (presumably interrelated) from the Ocamo River. The analysis at this level tests (1) whether the genetic network adequately represents the historical relationships of the component villages of the subgroup and (2) whether the genetic relationships between villages of a cluster, already shown to be an adequate representation of their historical relationships, are maintained after the incorporation of additional villages. The configuration of the network (length 4.29 units) shown in Figure 47 is in good accord with both the village and cluster histories. Three main groups are distinguished, one branch representing the three Ocamo villages, one branch representing the Shamatari plus village o3C, and the remaining branch representing the Namoweitari and Wanaboweitari combined with village o8UVW. This implies that the Namoweitari and Wanaboweitari are genetically closer to one another (mean distance of 0.14 units) than either is to the Shamatari (0.32 and 0.29 units, respectively), in agreement with the history of the clusters. In addition, the third major group can be interpreted as showing a division between Wanaboweitari villages and Namoweitari villages, with village o8UVW representing the fourth cluster occupying a central position, which tallies with the historical relationships of these clusters.

A finer analysis reveals two important facts. First, the Shamatari cluster is depicted as previously, with village o3C added. This association can be explained by the demonstration that roughly one-half of the sampled population of o3C has Shamatari ancestry. Second, the three remaining Namoweitari villages have now been joined by two Wanaboweitari villages, o3E being associated with o3B, and o3G with o3A and o8ABC. This apparent discrepancy might result from specific historical events, such as lineages in villages being reputed to have the same founder, men of a protector village being granted access to women of a refugee village, and so on (Chagnon 1966).

At the final level of analysis, the pattern of genetic relationships for 37 Yanomama villages showed a reasonably good separation of the five

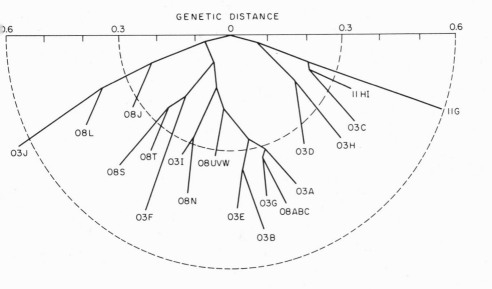

GENETIC DISTANCE

Note: The figure is plotted in polar fashion so that the distance separating two points is the sum of the radii leading to the circle that passes through their common origin.

FIGURE 47. The genetic network for 19 villages of the western Yanomama, including the 15 villages previously analyzed, based on nine polymorphic systems. Source: After Ward (in press).

geographically defined subgroups, while the villages and village clusters of the western subgroup maintained the relationship of the previous analyses with little change (Ward 1972). The fact that clusters maintain their integrity and genetic relationship is a reflection of geographical distribution; apart from this, little can be said about the details of this analysis, since with so many villages, the ability to draw conclusions by visual inspection is considerably lessened. In fact, in the absence of a defined procedure to test for congruence of topologies, the maximum number of populations that can be analyzed in a conclusive fashion is probably no more than 20 (too few populations will, of course, make the analysis trite).

The overall conclusion of these analyses is that the pattern of genetic relationships that can be discerned in these tribal populations is the result of fairly well circumscribed historical events leading up to the formation of new villages by the fission-fusion process. Furthermore, in the Yanomama at least, the pattern of genetic relationships is hierarchically structured, with the small clusters maintaining their integrity even when all villages are analyzed. This implies that fission is more important than fusion and also that intratribal genetic microdifferentiation will tend to be maximized.

THE DISTRIBUTION OF ALLELES
WITHIN AND BETWEEN DEMES

This third section will discuss the effect of population subdivision into demes (villages) on the distribution of alleles within and between villages. The analysis (Neel and Ward 1972) follows the model originally proposed by Wright (1943, 1946, 1951, 1965) for investigating a hierarchically structured population, although other models exist, notably that of Cockerham (1969), designed for similar analyses. Wright's model was used in this instance, not because it is necessarily the most appropriate, but because of reasons of historical precedence and because it appeared to involve the fewest assumptions.

The basic model couched in terms of the correlations existing between gametes may be fairly concisely set out by defining the following three statistics:

F_{IS}: the correlation between uniting gametes within a primary subdivision (that is, a village) relative to the gametes of that subdivision, averaged over all existing subdivisions to give a single measure.

F_{ST}: the correlation between gametes drawn at random from within a subdivision relative to the gametes of the total population.

F_{IT}: the correlation between uniting gametes relative to the gametes of the total population.

In the original model, the correlation of structure due to the hierarchical subdivision is such that these three measures are functionally related as

$$(1 - F_{IT}) = (1 - F_{IS})(1 - F_{ST}).$$

The standard estimates for these parameters in a population subdivided into K demes are given by

$$\hat{F}_{IS} = \sum_{i=1}^{K} \frac{\hat{F}_i}{K},$$

where

$$\hat{F}_i = 1 - \frac{H_i}{2p_i(1 - p_i)},$$

H_i is the proportion of heterozygotes, and p_i is the gene frequency for the ith population.

$$\hat{F}_{ST} = \frac{\sum_{i=1}^{K}(p_i - \bar{p})^2}{K \cdot \bar{p}(1 - \bar{p})},$$

where $\bar{p}$ represents the mean gene frequency averaged over all demes and

$$\hat{F}_{IT} = 1 - \frac{H_T}{2\bar{p}(1 - \bar{p})},$$

where H_T represents the proportion of heterozygotes in the total population.

Even though the validity of these estimators and the relationship between them will only exactly obtain if the population structure of the demes is such that it generates a continuous distribution (a situation that does not apply for tribal villages), these measures do provide a useful tool to evelute certain aspects of population structure. Perhaps the most useful measure is $\hat{F}_{IS}$, since it can be used to estimate how much the overall breeding structure of the tribe deviates from Hardy-Weinberg conditions, as well as to estimate the correlation between uniting gametes. The former was done by correcting for the effects of finite population size (Cannings and Edwards 1969) and estimating $\hat{F}_{ij}$ for the ith village and jth locus. There, $\hat{F}_{ij}$ could then be utilized to derive an estimate of the "average" effect of tribal breeding structure by summing over villages and loci to produce $\hat{F}_{..}$. Similarly, $\hat{F}_{i.}$ will represent the estimate of the effect of breeding structure of the ith village, and $\hat{F}_{\cdot j}$ the effect of the tribal breeding structure on the jth locus. A two-way analysis of variance indicated that there was no significant heterogeneity in the $\hat{F}_{ij}$ values, due to systems effects or village effects; this led to an estimate of the tribal value $\hat{F}_{\cdot \cdot}$ of -0.012 for the Yanomama (significantly less than zero) and -0.023 for the Makiritare (not significantly less than zero).

This analysis may be taken to imply that for the Yanomama and the Makiritare, the sum total of all factors making up the breeding structure of the tribe results in an excess of heterozygotes compared with the proportion expected under Hardy-Weinberg equilibrium. That the breeding structure of primitive tribal populations may be an important factor in retarding drift toward fixation in these small populations seems to add a new dimension to our understanding of the maintenance of genetic variability in the human species. Five of the more important factors have been singled out as contributing toward the total breeding structure.

(1) *Inbreeding and mating patterns.* Inbreeding will contribute to positive values of $\hat{F}_{IS}$ if it exceeds that expected under conditions of random mating. Lacking sufficiently detailed genealogical data to estimate reliable inbreeding coefficients, an estimate of inbreeding coefficients was derived from a simulation of four Yanomama villages, forming a closed population evolving over a 400-year period (MacCluer, Neel, and Chagnon 1971). The results of the simulation indicated that the inbreeding coefficient of a village could well be in the vicinity of 0.05, which would produce a small but positive contribution to $\hat{F}_{IS}$.

(2) *Migration.* Under traditional formulations, this factor should cause $\hat{F}_{IS}$ to tend toward zero, but in these tribal populations, where migration frequently implies the incorporation of discrete groups into a village, a positive contribution to $F_{i\cdot}$ might accrue in a manner analogous to the Wahlund effect (Neel and Ward 1972). At present, the inadequacies of migration data do not enable the magnitude of this positive contribution to $F_{i\cdot}$ to be estimated; by the same token, it is impossible to gauge whether the effects of amalgamation might be outweighed by a more conventional type of migration.

(3) *Differential fertility.* The occurrence of this factor, which will almost always result in an excess of heterozygotes (Purser 1966), has already been documented in these tribal populations (Salzano, Neel, and Maybury-Lewis 1967, Neel and Chagnon 1968). However, further work on this topic will be required before we can give an adequate estimate of

386

the magnitude of the contribution to a negative $\hat{F}_{IS}$ made by differential fertility.

(4) *Inequality in gene frequencies between the sexes.* In small breeding groups such as tribal populations, males and females will almost inevitably have differing gene frequencies at a given locus—a situation leading to an excess of heterozygotes (Robertson 1965). Our first estimates of the magnitude of this effect yielded $\hat{F}_{ij}$ values ranging from 0.0 to -0.06, indicating that this may be an important factor contributing to a negative $\hat{F}_{..}$.

(5) *Selection.* In such small populations, this is a quite unmeasurable factor that traditionally assumes a dominant role in determining the excess of heterozygotes. Lacking an adequate estimate for other factors, the magnitude of selection cannot even be estimated by elimination; if selection is detectable, however, the magnitude will be small, since there was no significant variability of $\hat{F}_{.j}$ values. Of the five deterministic pressures discussed above, only selection is expected to yield different expectations for each system.

Despite the caution that other factors (such as linkage disequilibrium) will undoubtedly contribute either a positive or negative component to $\hat{F}_{..}$ values, it appears that the predominantly negative $\hat{F}_{ij}$ values in the Yanomama and Makiritare result from the overall breeding structures of these small, highly subdivided, tribal populations. That the breeding structure of primitive human populations may operate to preserve genetic variability may be singled out as a provocative conclusion that would be worth further study (Neel and Ward 1972).

The estimation of F_{ST} may be regarded as an adjunct to the previous analyses of genetic microdifferentiation by means of genetic distance. By the demonstration of a high degree of genetic microdifferentiation, the earlier findings were confirmed, though it should be noted that the F_{ST} estimates are uncorrected for the increased variance due to sampling. Despite the lack of comparable estimates from other populations, the magnitude of the average (uncorrected) $\hat{F}_{ST}$ value per locus for the Yanomama, 0.06, remains one of the highest values recorded for human populations (Harpending and Jenkins 1972). An additional use of the $\hat{F}_{ST}$ values attempted to gauge the possible contribution of selection to the observed variability at a locus by considering the ratios of $\hat{F}_{ST}$ values for individual loci within a tribe, with no indication of bimodality in the distribution of $\hat{F}_{ST}$ values. This analysis gave no indication of selection

387

operating to constrain variability at a subset of the loci analyzed in these two tribes. This conclusion corroborates the lack of system effects in the $\hat{F}_{ij}$ analysis and was also independently reached by Lewontin and Krakauer (in press), using a somewhat more sophisticated comparison technique.

Finally, $\hat{F}_{IT}$ values were derived as a summary estimate of the net effects of F_{IS} and F_{ST}. These results indicated that the Yanomama have a slight overall excess of homozygotes in the tribal population, largely as a consequence of the extreme amount of microdifferentiation between Yanomama villages. The Makiritare, on the other hand, with less genetic divergence between villages and with a somewhat higher excess of heterozygotes within villages, had an overall deficiency of homozygotes in the tribal population.

In conclusion, it remains to be seen to what extent these findings with respect to all three aspects of genetic structure can be extended to other tribal populations. At this stage, it seems clear that despite the inherent difficulties of applying any of the three sets of formulations to these tribal populations, the results appear to be internally consistent. It remains to be seen what new insights will be gained by applying other models of analysis to the same body of data. Once this has been done, approach (1), as defined in the introduction (page 369), will have been largely accomplished, and the stage will be set for intertribal comparisons utilizing the same models of analysis. This phase seems likely to be a powerful approach toward the understanding of the extent to which genetic structure is influenced by such population parameters as migration, mating structure, differential fertility, and so on, all of which cannot usually be studied so felicitously in other organisms.

NOTE

1. This chapter represents but a small fraction of the very extensive studies carried out on the Yanomama and Makiritare, which developed from the insight and guidance of James V. Neel—to whom this chapter is respectfully dedicated.

17
Population Analyses in Oceania

EUGENE GILES

Department of Anthropology
University of Illinois

Without doubt, both anthropologists and the peoples they traditionally study have advanced and continue to advance our understanding of genetic mechanisms in human populations. But the other side of the coin also deserves some consideration: in what ways do these genetic studies contribute to anthropology? Such a viewpoint sets this chapter apart and presents no small array of possible approaches. Much to their credit, some geneticists (for example, Morton, Imaizumi, and Harris 1971) are attempting to relate implications of their methodology to social anthropology. A survey emphasizing comparable generalizable consequences of anthropological genetics is not, however, the tack chosen here. Rather, the focus will be on an area—Oceania—and the anthropological consequences of current genetic contributions.

The first section of the chapter will undertake a somewhat personal overview of aspects of Oceanic anthropology that add piquance to investigations there. Following is a sequence of three additional sections taking up types of ongoing studies. The first of these sections covers analyses built around examinations of single-gene traits in living populations. Investigations concerned with polygenic characters form the second section, and the last deals with studies based on examinations of osteological material.

MICROEVOLUTION IN OCEANIA:
THE ANTHROPOLOGICAL BACKGROUND

Is there anything particularly notable about Oceania from the biological anthropologist's point of view? Every region has its interest, but Oceania as an area does have a few special aspects worth brief review. For present purposes, Oceania includes the islands whose inhabitants are commonly denoted as being Polynesian, Micronesian, Melanesian, and Australian (indigenous to that island-continent). What is known, or thought to be known, of the course of human events in this immense and sparsely populated area is largely the result of *anthropological* investigation and interpretation: linguistic, ethnographical, archaeological, and biological. These are the data and the scholars involved; here, written records of any import are very late.

Oceania encompasses considerable human physical variation. The origin and significance of the differences among Australians, Melanesians, Micronesians, and Polynesians impose themselves as concerns of anthropology in the Pacific in a way in which differences among South American Indians, for example, cannot.

If Australia is put, with some justification, in the category of island, then all Oceania here defined consists of island populations, although with Australia and New Guinea, it incorporates the world's largest and third-largest islands. The potential importance of this in terms of genetic mechanisms should be kept in mind. Micronesia exclusively, Polynesia for the most part, and Melanesia to a great extent deploy their populations on small, scattered islands. Australia, and New Guinea within Melanesia, provide large and diverse land masses. In the one case, population size and population intercourse are strongly influenced by physical factors. This is true to a lesser extent for social intercourse, but even here, communication between populations was limited by the achieved seafaring technology at a given point in time, thus limiting also the options for cultural diversity to a greater extent than they would necessarily have been limited on a large land mass. In Oceania, the ramifications of effective population size, population fission and fusion, random genetic effects, and the interaction of cultural factors within these parameters takes place on a stage of greater variation than perhaps anywhere else. The scene ranges from the low-lying islands of Micronesia to the vast expanses of Australia. The question is, does it matter? Hunt (1950) long ago pointed out the isolating potential of the Oceanic islands for human evolution; but Arends and his associates (Arends et al. 1967) have provided evidence of apparently equally great genetic diversification among South American Indian populations where topographical correlates are not nearly as patent.

Oceania is rather late in coming to have well-documented time depth in terms of human occupation. The antiquity of man in the Indonesian islands in the form of *Homo erectus* has long been established. Much more of an open question has been the extent to which Wallace's line, "Oceania's western moat" as Oliver (1961) puts it, served as a barrier to man's migration, as well as to that of many plants and other animals. Sea level fluctuations during the Pleistocene alone exceeded 400 feet in this part of the world (Cotton 1962); obviously, during the Tertiary and Quaternary, a variety of circumstances were available for mammalian immigration. Australia was not completely quarantined, zoologically speaking, for the Cenozoic—witness the excess of placental over marsupial families at European contact—but representation among the mammalian orders evinces a situation of severe selectivity. At what point man's increasing technological capability permitted him to traverse Wallace's quite efficient trough has long been in doubt. On the one hand, Polynesia displays many cultural and linguistic indicia of relatively recent occupation, but the situation in Australia and, to some extent in New Guinea, has been subject to wide disagreement. Abbie (1969) notes a range of "guesstimates" from 150,000 to 6,000 years B.P. There are many reasons for this. Australian and non-Austronesian languages have defied connection-making to other parts of the world and, to a considerable extent, among themselves. This and (from certain points of view) a lack of technological progress among Australians has set these populations apart without really elucidating the time interval involved. From time to time, fossilized human remains have been found, but until recently, there were no clear indications of antiquity other than rather debatable assertions of morphological "primitiveness" or the lack of it. This is not to deny that these specimens were, with total justification, considered to be many thousands of years old; the question was whether the age was demonstrably in excess of, say, 10,000 years. And until recently, the paucity of archaeological excavation and an emphasis on typology, coupled with a distressing and continuing lack of information concerning Paleolithic industries in neighboring areas overseas, provided little substantial evidence for the antiquity of man in Australia.

All this is now changing, and changing fast. Much of the new archaeological information pertains to cultural change and population movements among the Pacific islands in the past few thousand years. But from the biological anthropology point of view, it is the results concerning the early occupation of the area that are of great interest at the moment. This is not the place to sort out these findings, but their cumulative import is great. In the first place, earliest occupation dates for Australia are being pushed back further and further in time, with no end in sight. The Lake Mungo site (Bowler et al. 1970), established at 25,000–32,000 years B.P. by ^{14}C dating, contains stone tools, a hearth, and a human burial, and may not be the oldest yet. It is worth remarking that if the 32,000 B.P. end of the range is prophetic, Australian occupation is thus on the order of twice as ancient as that of the New World. Even the most conservative view would have to yield Australia a 10,000-year age, and such a view is indeed conservative, given the relative amount of post-1948 archaeological activity in the two areas. Outside of Australia, dates of such antiquity have not yet been confirmed, but indications are that the Kosipe site in New Guinea's Highlands is, in part, older than the Mount Lamington ash levels dated at around 18,000 years B.P., with the first occupation in the range of 23,000 to 26,500 years B.P. (White, Crook, and Ruxton 1970).

With the late beginning of scientific excavation in New Guinea in 1959, general conclusions are premature. Although there can be no doubt that Australia and New Guinea were at times joined by a broad land bridge during low sea levels, it is not absolutely certain that Australia's original population passed through New Guinea. Neither New Guinea dates nor aspects of the archaeological complexes in Australia (Jones 1968) support a New Guinea passage, though they are hardly conclusive against what appears to be the most logical port of entry. According to Veeh and Chappell (1970), the last two Pleistocene sea level minima in the New Guinea region were about 55,000 years B.P. and about 15,000–

20,000 years B.P., with a high sea level period extending between 50,000 and 35,000 years B.P. This might lead to the speculation that if occupation of New Guinea and Australia were most easily affected during a period of low sea level, the last minimum may have been too late, according to current archaeological dates, and that even earlier sites may be expected. However, whether the technology required to travel overwater distances on the order of tens of miles in Wallacea during sea level minima differed significantly from that required to cross hundreds of miles during a high sea level period is a moot point.

The archaeological evidence itself in Australia is remarkable in that the so-called "Australian core-tool and scraper tradition" (Bowler et al. 1970) persists, with minor variants, from the oldest sites down to approximately 6,000 years B.P. on the Australian mainland. This may affect the validity of postulated separate migrations to Australia. Conclusions are again premature, particularly in view of some odd features in Australian archaeology, such as the 20,000-year-old ground stone axes in Arnhem Land (White 1967). And finally, the Manton site in the Western Highlands of New Guinea, where an extensive network of water-control ditches has been ^{14}C dated between 4,000 and 2,000 years B.P. (Golson et al. 1967), and the palynological evidence of extensive forest clearing in this region at 5,000–6,000 years B.P. (*Man in New Guinea* [Newsletter] 1970) confirm the existence of systematic horticulture at a remarkably early period in New Guinea.

ANALYTICAL APPROACHES TO SINGLE-GENE TRAITS

Reportage of blood group frequencies began many years ago (in 1924 for Melanesia [Heydon and Murphy 1924]) but picked up tempo only after World War II. It is probably fair to contrast Melanesia with the other main Oceania regions in this regard. In general, the investigator outside Melanesia is faced with an increasing difficulty in discerning "racially" unmixed populations. Thus, in many areas, the focus of investigations turned away, to a considerable degree, from problems in which, so to speak, a present-day simulation of European contact conditions is deemed necessary. This distinction should not be overemphasized, but it has meant that blood group research has increased at a faster pace in

Melanesia than elsewhere and that a greater proportion appears largely descriptive rather than oriented to genetic problems (or rather remotely related, such as the blood group studies spun off from the *kuru* neurological disease investigations).

The initial results of surveys of single-gene traits have been the establishment of certain features relating to distribution. This is not the place to list all the supposed distributional patterns of presumed anthropological interest. Recent discoveries, such as the high frequency of Gerbich negative in parts of New Guinea, await interpretation. Well-established variation, areally consistent—the differences between New Guinea and Australia in ABO and MNSs blood group frequencies come to mind—possibly indicate a period of considerable isolation. (Such an interpretation is not necessarily vitiated by a fuzzing of the distinctions in the Cape York region.) The absence of hemoglobin S from the Pacific (Swindler 1955) is as yet unquestioned; on the other hand, traits of demonstrable relationship to malaria prophylaxis (glucose-6-phosphate dehydrogenase deficiency) and suspected relationship (thalassemia) are present in Oceania with a possible but not at all impressive distributional correlation with malaria endemicity (Giles, Curtain, and Baumgarten 1967).

Transferrin variant D_1 poses an interesting problem (Giles 1970) in that its populational presence appears limited to natives of Australasia and Africa. The Gm and Inv factors hold considerable promise of providing provocative data pertaining to wider connections among Pacific area people, if not the ultimate answer to all problems. Giles, Ogan, and Steinberg (1965) demonstrated a clear-cut correlation between language family and Gm allotype distribution in a region of northeast New Guinea, while Friedlaender and Steinberg (1970) demonstrated just as clearly that the linguistic dichotomy did not obtain on the Melanesian island of Bougainville. Curtain and his associates (1971) have suggested that certain Gm allotypes are markers for Malayo-Polynesian ($Gm^{fa;b}$) and pre-Austronesian ($Gm^{za;b}$) populations on the basis of recently completed work in New Guinea and New Britain. The doctoral dissertation of Schanfield (1971) is based on an evaluation of the most widespread and complete Gm testing yet undertaken for the Pacific area; presumably, this will help clarify the extent to which these allotypes are useful in delimiting historical interrelationships.

Just what gene frequency distributions like those above and many other less striking ones mean has been increasingly complicated by suggestions

394

that one or another manifestation of genetic drift can be held responsible for much of the genetic variation in the Oceanic region. On the surface, it does appear that the island populations of Polynesia and Micronesia, the extreme cultural or at least linguistic fragmentation in New Guinea, and the thinly spread population of Australia maximize the possibilities for such effects. Gajdusek (1964) has promulgated this idea, and a number of studies of gene frequency distributions (Birdsell 1950, Giles et al. 1966, Giles, Wyber, and Walsh 1970) support the proposition.

In the reports by Giles and his associates (1966, 1970), for example, a small New Guinea group, defined by linguistic communality and current marriage patterns in an area in which such entities exist by the hundreds, has been examined to a point approaching complete enumeration. This group, known as the Waffa, number under 1,000 individuals living on the edge of the Eastern Highlands District in five villages. Three of these villages incorporate 88 percent of the Waffa speakers and have been studied to the point that better than 56 percent of *all* extant Waffa speakers as of 1968 had provided blood samples and other biological information. However one wants to regard these data statistically, they do, on the face of it, evince large intervillage frequency differences, particularly in the ABO allele B: 0.02, 0.14, and 0.27.

In the discussion of their results, Giles and his colleagues have been content to argue that random factors must be involved, because other potential differentiating mechanisms (such as selection, mutation pressure, or gene flow) appear, under the circumstances, quite improbable. Cadien (1971) has pointed out that the migration rate between villages and the small size of villages themselves in at least some New Guinea situations may be sufficient as causal factors for observable frequency variation.

Perhaps the most fruitful ongoing types of analysis of single-gene characters are typified by Sinnett et al. (1970) and by Friedlaender (1971). Sinnett and his coworkers have applied the "evolutionary tree" approach popularized by Cavalli-Sforza and Edwards (1967) to five genetic marker systems from seven clans in the Western Highlands of New Guinea. The approach provides a measure of genetic distance between groups that is based on all possible pair-wise comparisons between the populations' adjusted gene frequency differences ordered in a "tree" fashion to reflect the minimum-distance genetic pathway among them. The results of Sinnett's study have shown a pleasing similarity to the oral tradition of the people involved. It is gratifying to see this method applied successfully to regional small-scale populations rather than the much less satisfactory attempts made to relate groups on a continental or even world-wide basis.

Friedlaendar (1971) has applied the operational modifications made by Morton, Imaizumi, and Harris (1971) to a basic theorem of Malécot (1969) concerning the relationship between the coefficient of kinship and the distance between residences of potential mates under appropriate (and simplifying) assumptions. Friedlaender's utilization of this approach to his own data from Bougainville is an important one, and his results are far more convincing than a similar but sweeping use of an enormous amount of heterogeneous published material from New Guinea and Micronesia by Imaizumi and Morton (1970). Friedlaender's work speaks for itself, but it might appear that his main conclusions are that the swidden agriculturists of the South Pacific sustain a higher level of inbreeding than more technologically advanced ones and that shallow pedigrees only hint at the extent of this kinship coefficient. Friedlaender suggests that approaches to interpopulation relationships made along these lines, tied as they are to geography and potentially adaptable to anthropometric and other data sources, will prove more rewarding than analytic techniques like those used by Sinnett et al. (1970), where the genetic data, once grouped, are evaluated without reference to factors possibly acting on them. Harpending's (1971) criticism of the Morton school's assumptions cannot help but undermine such claims.

It is interesting that Friedlaender, following the Malécot-Morton attack, uses simple measures of geographic distances, while Sinnett and his associates, using the Cavalli-Sforza and Edwards approach, adopt a much more anthropological unit, the "clan." Friedlaender's units are essentially geographic, Sinnett's cultural. Morton, Imaizumi, and Harris (1971) have undertaken a mathematical examination of the clan as a genetic barrier and claim it is weak in theory and can be ignored in practice. While this supports Friedlaender's efforts, one can legitimately wonder how well it represents reality. Reid (1971), for example, in an exacting analysis of Indian (Andhra Pradesh) social structures and their demographic effects, finds that they interact to the point that the male generation is 37 percent longer than the female. Such factors obviously have a local genetic effect in Reid's area; at least, it suggests we should not too casually give up the concept that social structure, in practice, has its genetic concomitants, however imperfectly realized.

396

Eugene Giles

ANALYTIC APPROACHES TO
POLYGENIC TRAITS

Many a South Pacific islander has succumbed to the manipulations of the anthropometrist (the Australian army has even produced an anthropometric survey of the New Guinean foot [MacLean n.d.]), but relatively few sophisticated analyses of the resulting data have emerged, and it would appear that the proportional amount of anthropometry vis-à-vis what one might loosely call "serology" has declined precipitously. One reason is, of course, that in recent years, it has been quicker, often easier, and considerably more practical to obtain blood samples than a series of anthropometric measurements, particularly among Pacific islanders. Many who do use blood samples are not primarily anthropologists, and they seek specific nonanthropometric information. But the major problem may lie more in the area of analytic tools for anthropometric data compared with those honed up for treating single-gene traits.

In practice, anthropometric measurements, as well as the demography of preliterate peoples, suffer to a greater or lesser extent from the problem of age determination. In many parts of the Pacific, civil records are such that age is not a problem, but usually the concomitant of such record-keeping is an amount of acculturation sufficient to dampen the enthusiasm of an anthropologist seeking indigenous population variation. As noted previously, Melanesia is least acculturated, and it is here that the art of age gauging still prevails; Giles (1970) has discussed this problem in general terms. Perhaps the least objectionable approach requires the use of mission or other adequate birth records: in New Guinea, Malcolm (1969a, 1969b, 1970) has pioneered this option. Relative dating—using remembered events that can be tied into the Western calendar combined with putative birth order in families—may be all that is available in many regions, but even so, the drawbacks should not be minimized (Epstein and Epstein 1962). In any event, this method requires painstaking effort to reach any level of adequacy. Finally, "guesstimates" based primarily on appearance can only be applied to the grossest categories. Malcolm (*Papua and New Guinea Medical Journal* 1967) has driven home this point. Internal clocks, such as dental development (Friedlaender and Bailit 1969), are most promising but may be affected by environmental factors and so far are limited to the first two decades or so.

Most current analyses of Melanesian anthropometric data concentrate

397

either in aspects of growth and developmental patterns (for example, Malcolm 1969a, 1969b, 1970) or in their utilization in measures of population distance. In these latter studies, genetic aspects of the measurements are usually not overtly considered; rather, the effort is taxonomic with a view toward historical reconstruction by assessing relative affinities among populations. Howells is preeminent among those who have seriously tackled the problem from a multivariate point of view, starting with the Oliver and Howells (1960) paper. Howells (1966a) concentrated his analysis on Bougainville, using various "distances" among 18 groupings (altitudinal, topographic, geographic, linguistic, and so forth) and three measures of biological "distance" (size and shape from eight measurements according to the Penrose [1954] formulation of these categories, and nonmetric characters). The correlation matrix of these distances provided leeway in interpretation while suggesting that the nonmetric traits and measurers of shape are more useful in assessing relationship than they are usually given credit for. It is of interest that the biological distances are more poorly correlated with spatial measures than they are with cultural measures (such as language). In terms of our general perception of Bougainville history, Howells's results confirm a biological base to the linguistic dichotomy (Melanesian—non-Austronesian) on the island; Howells's view on "Negritos" has undergone a reversal (Howells 1970a) since he wrote the Bougainville analysis.

McHenry and Giles (1971) have examined a set of anthropometric data for the New Guinea Waffa villages mentioned earlier. Twenty-six measurements from 115 males and 214 females spread among the three Waffa villages were subjected to multiple discriminant and Mahalanobis's D^2 analyses, and trait differences were examined for their heritability component. Even in this small, circumscribed group, more than a third of the male measurements were significantly heterogeneous among the three villages. It was quite possible to "discriminate" the three villages with only slight overlap. Highly significant F ratios for nearly all traits indicated that variation within sibships is significantly less than that among sibships. When the traits were partitioned into those with high and those with low sibship F ratios, both sets were found capable of distinguishing the three villages, presumably indicating that the morphological heterogeneity among the villages is due to both genetic and environmental factors. Whether the genetic differentiation may be traceable to the fixation of some alleles when the population fissioned, or to the small population size militating against the expression of all combinations of relevant alleles, or to something else again is not directly ascertainable from this sort of analysis.

On a much broader canvas with an even more intricately fashioned brush, Howells (1970a) has attempted a picture of the entire Pacific area. Utilizing multivariate procedures, he has been able to extract from sets of rather heterogeneous data spanning seven decades the outlines of the major population blocks. These he sees as three: Australian, Micronesian-Polynesian (the latter of this pair arising from the more varied former), and a much more variable Melanesian, which affects and is affected to a certain extent by the other two.

In a sense, McHenry and Giles (1971) and Howells (1970a) are looking at polygenic variation in Oceania through different ends of the telescope. Neither study is without blemish. Howell's data, through no fault of his own, leaves much to be desired in terms of variables, coverage, and comparability. McHenry and Giles's technique needs repeating on a larger set of populations displaying a greater range of interrelationships. But what is most intriguing is that both studies, using complicated multivariate statistical procedures, manage to make something of modern interest and sense from material—anthropometric data—that seems a little musty to many.

ANALYTIC APPROACHES TO OSTEOLOGICAL VARIATION

Well-grounded, statistically-sound population oriented studies of osteological material have not always been an anthropological hallmark in the Pacific or elsewhere. There is no intention here to deal with all attempts, however laudable, to extract information from bones but merely to suggest current directions. Typical of early-modern efforts was Wagner's (1937) use of Pearson's Coefficient of Racial Likeness for a rather extensive examination of Pacific crania. The first use of modern multivariate statistic methods on Pacific cranial series was made around 1960 by Marshall and Giles (n.d.). This study, unfortunately never published but occasionally referenced from stray dittoed copies, used Mahalanobis's D^2 analysis of eight measurements from 234 crania to relate nine Polynesian populations, Fiji, and Guam. Since that time, other research has emerged, notably a study centering on Polynesia by Pietrusewsky (1970) involving 600 skulls and one concerned primarily with Australia by Yamaguchi (1967) involving 427 skulls. Both of the latter authors, as well as Kellock and Parsons (1970), who studied 1,336 skulls, have made serious attempts to utilize and compare relationships based on the evidence of nonmetrical characters of the cranium. In addition, the massive investigation of cranial variation on a world basis undertaken by Howells (1970b) incorporates some sample series from Pacific populations.

The analytic techniques for the reports mentioned above are, in general, similar to those used in one or another of the examinations of metric and nonmetric traits in the living recounted earlier. Pietrusewsky, for example, analyzes multivariate-style both metric and nonmetric data, though he considers interpretations based on nonmetric information sounder. He notes a number of parallel results using these two sorts of data. Both show, for instance, an east-west divisioning of the islands, placing Fiji, Tonga, and Samoa in a western set and the Society Islands, Tuamotu, Hawaii, Marquesas, New Zealand, Chatham Island, and Easter Island in an eastern division. Within the latter set, there is a further clustering of central and peripheral islands by both methods. Pietrusewsky believes that these results sit nicely with those of cultural anthropology, both suggesting Fiji-Tonga-Samoa as an interface area with Melanesia, and a source of migrations into the rest of Polynesia.

Osteological studies all seem to look through the wrong end of the aforementioned telescope: none has been concerned with what one might call local populations, though Yamaguchi (1967) and Kellock and Parsons (1970) consider several Australian groups. One particular difficulty facing any examiner of crania in the Pacific region is definition of population. For the most part, the various series are the result of casual collection over a period of time and often over a considerable geographic span as well. Very few have an archaeological context, and some measure of admixture of Europeans or alien Pacific islanders is a possibility in many cases. For Tasmania, the authenticity of almost any skull save Truganini's is open to question. It would appear that the difficulties of the source material in Pacific osteology will for a long time render this category of microevolutionary analysis perplexing.

In concluding, brief note might be taken of Giles's current research on Australian and Melanesian crania. This investigation encompasses a somewhat different approach to the analysis of morphological variation than mentioned before. The substantive problem turns on an analysis of cranial morphology and its patterning among Australian and Melanesian "populations" defined as rigorously as a rather exhaustive search of museum collections indicates is feasible. A part of this research is similar to some previously discussed: a series of 16 measurements on approximately 1,325 crania have been obtained. But in addition, three standardized photographs have been made of each skull. The photographs have been enlarged and each set marked at approximately 120 points representing the major cranial contours and landmarks. With the aid of a digitizing chart reader (OSCAR-F), the coordinates of these points yield a measure of shape variation. Combined with a parallel analysis of the metrics, these data should provide a numerical assessment of cranial variation that even von Török could appreciate.

Genetic Adaptation in Twentieth-Century Man

SOLOMON H. KATZ

Department of Anthropology
and W. M. Krogman Center for Research
in Child Growth and Development
University of Pennsylvania
Eastern Pennsylvania Psychiatric Institute
Philadelphia

INTRODUCTION

A serious investigation of human adaptation and evolution in the twentieth century must take into consideration a complex array of factors. The exponential rate in the growth of human population size throughout much of the world is of evolutionary significance. Linked to this are the changes in world-wide trade that are reordering the patterns of human nutrition, the changes in technology and the associated use of energy sources producing alterations in a number of environmental parameters, and the changes in health and medical technology that are modifying the status of disease through alterations in sanitation and disease control and treatment. Also important and implicit in all of these developments is the level of knowledge man has about the world and himself, and particularly the growing potential for having increasingly direct feedbacks of this knowledge on his own evolution. Thus, for twentieth-century man the world is relatively smaller and more mobile, and perhaps he is more aware of the biology of man and the technology to do something about it.

We have been working for several years on holistic transdisciplinary models that have heuristic value in looking at man's evolution and adaptations in the twentieth century (Katz and Foulks 1970, 1971, Katz 1972). Perhaps following the laws of parsimony, one of the most simple models seems to work best. It is an ecosystems model that operates on the assumption that for purposes of analysis, we can separate man's biological, sociocultural, demographic, and environmental dimensions into four principal variables. From this point, we attempt to look at the multiple interactions of all four primary variables, both synchronically and diachronically, according to the needs and constraints of the particular problem (Figure 48). The idea is to ask our particular question and use the model to make sure that we are covering all aspects of the problem.

In using this model for genetic purposes, we can start with any given genetic problem and trace its interactions with all other variables. This process reveals several important issues, including the fact that for most genetic problems, (1) the phenotypic expression is the unique product of the whole ecosystem as defined by the interacting elements at any given point in time, and (2) the prediction of the microevolutionary course of a particular gene within a population is not only a function of genetic predictions based on classic quantitative estimates but is also a product of a rapidly changing feedback effect of man's ability to alter his "micro"

FIGURE 48. The heuristic biocultural model.

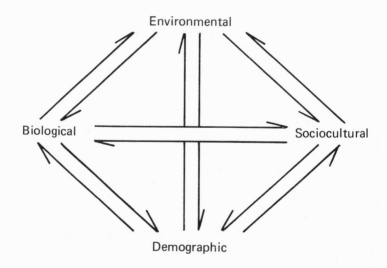

(physiological) and "macro" (habitat) environments. Implicated in such heuristic models are changing levels of technology, economics, and political and social structure, all of which share, directly and indirectly, in affecting both individual and population microenvironment and macroenvironment. Not only should we include the somatic elements of man's microevolution in the twentieth century in our heuristic models, but we must also include the microevolution of his central nervous system and particularly that involving his neocortical functions. In this way, we can begin to include his psychological functions as legitimate issues for microevolutionary research and, at the same time, join new hypotheses generated by these investigations with those of the social and cultural anthropologists interested in explaining variation in human behavior and societies. Thus, by using heuristic models that are holistic, processual, and probabilistic, we may be able to open new perspectives in the investigation and interpretation of the microevolution of contemporary man.

This chapter will attempt to use this model in setting forth some of the interesting ramifications of man's evolution and adaptations in modern populations. Several of the ways in which man is culturally and socially adapting and interacting with his genetic adaptations will be discussed, along with some of the ways in which man's rapid environmental and nutritional changes may be influencing his genetic adaptability. Finally, the chapter will present some examples of the way medical technology in the use of certain drug treatments is interacting with genetic factors, and the way technology, in general, is influencing the evolution of human behavior. The underlying rationale for this approach is twofold: first, to introduce the reader to the phenomenal complexity involved in tracing the multiple courses of human evolution in population subsets of twentieth-century man, and second, to introduce some evidence for the possible genetic significance of certain recent findings in human biology.

SICKLE-CELL ANEMIA—
A MODEL OF COMPLEXITY

Although sickle-cell anemia is well known to all who have any knowledge of genetic phenomena, it is still probably the most useful example to demonstrate the use and complexity of our heuristic ecosystems model. Table 57 shows a broad breakdown of the variables mentioned in Figure 48 and attempts to demonstrate some of the principal specific variables involved in the microevolution of the sickle-cell gene over time, which, as we shall see, is especially complex in the twentieth century.

It is estimated that the sickle cell evolved with the introduction of the yam and slash and burn agriculture some hundred years ago in certain regions of Africa (Livingstone 1958). If we use our model, we can see the interplay of the biological adaptations in the form of the sickle-cell gene that interacted with an environmental factor in the form of falciparum malaria that was transmitted by the Anophales mosquitoes. The breeding places of mosquitoes increased with the new agricultural techniques, which were clearly an advantage from the point of view of nutritional resources. At a demographic level, it is possible to reconstruct some of the effects of changes in migration, population size, density, age, sex, and mortality and morbidity factors on the epidemiology of malaria (Wiesenfeld 1967). When these epidemiological data on malaria are combined with the data on the environmental changes introduced by subsistence patterns dependent on slash and burn agriculture in the presence of the sickle-cell gene, it is possible to predict the direction and probable magnitude of the microevolution of sickle-cell anemia.

However, transposing this model into the twentieth century and to post-World War II, where new measures were introduced to control malaria, we have a somewhat altered, and certainly more complex, pattern. It is said that the postwar eradication of much of the malaria throughout the world by the use of DDT was one of the major factors leading to rapid population increases in many of the technologically "underdeveloped" countries. For example, it has been estimated that the population of Ceylon increased its annual population growth rate by 1.8 percent after the successful introduction of DDT by 1950. This demographic change was presumably based solely on changes in the mortality rates. Thus, the introduction of a new factor in the environment that was specifically designed to cope with this disease problem was highly effective in regulating the malarial vector. Of course, many people now believe that the long-term effects of DDT on the rest of the ecosystem may be more hazardous to man in the long run than were the effects of malaria. Nevertheless, the fact remains that DDT is still used to control malaria in many parts of the world and, as a result, has seriously altered the selective effects on the sickle-cell gene. Essentially, with negligible malaria present as a result of DDT, and inadequate medical technology present to alleviate the phenotypic effects of sickle-cell disease to the point where

MICROEVOLUTION AND SICKLE-CELL ANEMIA

TIME	SOCIOCULTURAL	DEMOGRAPHIC			ENVIRONMENTAL		BIOLOGICAL	
	Subsistence Pattern and Technology	Important Population Factors		Other	Factors Affecting Mosquito Vector	Malaria	Sickle Cell	
		Size	Density				Gene	Phenotype
6,000 years B.P. Pre-agricultural (?)	(Africa)	Small (−)	Lo (−)	———	Tropical rain forest (−) to Anopholes Gambiae slash and burn (+) (produces loss of jungle soil humus and lateralization conducive to puddles and breeding places)	Unknown	?	?
	Malaysian agriculture Slash and burn (Africa)	Large (+)	Hi (+)	———	"	Present	←	←
	Spread of slash and burn	Large (+)	Hi (+)	Migration (+)	"	Present	←	←
Sixteenth century	Continuation of slash and burn (Africa) → Slavery (North America)	Large (+)	Hi (+)	Migration (+) Forced migration (North America) (−)	North American environment (−) (Allison 1955)	Increasing →	← →	← →
Nineteenth century	"Abolition"		Increasing admixture (North America) (−)				→	→
Twentieth century, post-WWII	Public health technology (Africa) (−) → Medical technology (+) Specific treatments	Very large populations (Africa) (+)			DDT control of stagnant water (Africa) (−)	→	↓ (Africa) (Medical technology North America) ↑	↓ (Africa) (Medical technology North America) ↑
1970s	Eugenics (?) and screening (±)						→ (Eugenics)	→ (Eugenics)

(+) Enhances probability of malaria and/or sickle-cell anemia
(−) Lessens probability of malaria and/or sickle-cell anemia
(←→) Increases
(↑↓) Decreases
(→) No effect

individuals can successfully reproduce, the gene undergoes a simple harmonic diminution.

This was basically the case in the United States from the sixteenth-century arrival of the first African slaves, through abolition, until after World War II. Although there was some malaria on the coast of the Carolinas, Georgia, and Louisiana, it was not as significant an environmental problem as it probably was in Africa. Theoretically, it is possible to calculate what the sickle-cell gene frequency was for the slave population as a whole when they left Africa (Allison 1955). However, in order to use the simple formula for harmonic diminution, several assumptions would be required: first, malaria was not a significant problem for the population as a whole; second, there were no disadvantages to having the trait; third, the current frequencies of the gene are known; and finally, an average representative time in this country was used.[1] Making these and other assumptions could give a crude approximation of the HbS gene frequency for the African slave population as a whole. However, one of the problems with this estimate is the real possibility that the conditions which the Negro slaves endured were severe enough to produce expression of the trait. Evidence for this kind of disadvantage was recently reported to be a cause of death in some Negro army recruits with the trait who were undergoing strenuous maneuvers during basic training. On the other hand, the trait may have some yet unknown advantages in resisting diseases other than malaria if the resistance it confers is not just specific for the malarial parasite.

At sociopolitical levels, there is increasing concern for the disadvantaged minority groups in the United States. Finally, for example, the U.S. Congress has very recently appropriated a large sum of money for what some have called the "most serious disease in the Black population." The effects of this economic input could be at least to develop better treatment for those who have sickle-cell anemia, but from the genetic point of view, the most important development by far is the potential effect of genetic counseling. With the development of simple screening methods, several children or adults can be screened for the "trait" in a matter of minutes, and positives confirmed on a single day by elethophoretic methods. For example, the sickle-cell screening program at Children's Hospital of Philadelphia can routinely screen 500 children in one day. Connected with screening is counseling information, which suggests that if one has the trait, one should seriously reconsider having children with a mate also having the trait. Patients thus screened are informed that according to the laws of heredity, the chances of having a child with the incurable disease are one in four, and, although there is only a 25 percent chance that they will have such a child, the fact is that most parents of children with sickle-cell disease openly admit that if they had it to do over again, they would not have had a child.

Having the technical knowledge to be able to recognize the disease, and the biochemical knowledge to realize that it involves a single gene, provides an alternative in our model. Heterozygotes can avoid having children with the trait and the disease "simply" by avoiding mating with someone else who also has the trait. This would effectively eliminate the disease but not the trait. Of course, this does not eliminate the gene but does completely alter one of the basic assumptions in the Hardy-Weinberg equilibrium principle that involves random mating. In other words, a modern society could screen everyone if it so desires, build up a genetic profile of each individual, put this into a data bank, and require that all applicants for marriage at least submit to a profile probability analysis that yields the percent chance for the expression of the various recessive gene combinations that are known to possibly exist between the mates. The technology involved in this kind of information bank concept is probably not far off. Its feedback effects on human evolution could be immense. Basically, it would be eliminating or at least significantly decreasing the random mating with respect to certain genetic loci in modern human populations. Thus, our model of human adaptation and evolution becomes increasingly complex as we add these confounding variables of twentieth-century man. What we must also realize is the fact that we can anticipate some of those changes and begin to develop new models to simulate human evolution operating under different rules in large national and/or international size populations. It may be very useful to follow these kinds of models to their fullest ramifications and give some feedback to the "genetic feedback process"—especially if the adaptive significance of such ramifications falls into the same category as DDT.

HUMAN ADAPTABILITY

In studying twentieth-century man, it becomes increasingly necessary to focus our attention on not only the genetic adaptations within a particular population, but also the phenotypic adaptations that are observed in terms of biochemical, physiological, and psychological responses to the wide range of ecological pressures. This fact is pointed out, for example, by the rapid changes in technology influencing sickle-cell anemia as well as many other aspects of the human ecosystem.

The wide variety of nutritional intake patterns (in terms of substance, quality, and quantity) exhibited by the various human cultures located through an extremely wide range of ecological zones provides a useful example of the problems inherent in these studies. It suggests that either a great deal of inherent plasticity is present at a biological level in the species in order to adapt to these variations, or that, more likely, the phenotypic expression of a particular gene or gene complex is masked by an individual's behavioral ability, alone or with the help of society, to compensate for limitations inherent in his genotype. Analyses of such phenotypic adaptations take on increasing importance if we are interested in differentiating genotypes from various measures of phenotypes in microevolutionary studies of human populations. Since most genetic variations appear to be polygenic, we are left with the choice of using the limited analyses of simple Mendelian traits or attempting to sort out complex genetic variation from studies of human adaptability.

Many human adaptability studies have centered on environments that provide naturally occurring extremes in environmental conditions, such as combinations of high altitude, cold arctic or hot desert climates, and infectious disease. However, the environmental extremes in the twentieth century produced by technological change may provide a more stringent test of human adaptability than any of the naturally occurring econiches that man has occupied to date. Thus, in studying the adaptability and microevolution of twentieth-century man, we should perhaps look at those populations experiencing rapid sociocultural change, heavy environmental pollution (as in some cities of the United States), and advances in drugs and food preservatives, as well as at populations naturally exposed for the first time to certain nutrient distributions and infectious diseases.

FOOD

Another problem for twentieth-century man, closely linked to his exponential increase in population size, is the increased need for nutritional and carbon-based energy resources. The rate of increase in food reserves versus the rate of increase of population size prompts considerations ranging from the current and predicted effects of widespread starvation (Meadows et al.) to the effects of specific diet deficiencies or excesses during a period of rapid world-wide changes in the technology of agriculture and the distribution of food resources (Dubos 1965).

The influence of technological and economic development on diet is illustrated by the United States policy to distribute surplus food to "underdeveloped" nations without taking into account genetic differences in populations. There have been a number of reports that powdered milk and milk additives to cereal grains (milk is added to boost the lysine content of grain) have been widely rejected in Nigeria, Colombia, Guatemala, and Peru (McCracken 1971). According to Huang and Bayless (1967), milk has also been rejected by American Negro children in the Baltimore area. The reason for these rejections was that the milk continually produced diarrheal episodes with some gastroenteric pain. These and other studies revealed considerable evidence that a deficiency of lactase exists that prevents lactose, the disaccharide carbohydrate source in milk, from being digested into the absorbable monosaccharides, glucose and galactose. If the lactase enzyme is absent, the lactose is not digested until it reaches the colon. There, the abundance of lactose induces the rapid proliferation of lactobacillus (a normal bacteria found in the colon). The lactose is broken down and in the anaerobic conditions of the colon, large amounts of lactic acid are produced that, in turn, induce a heavy secretion of water into the colon. The net effect is a diarrhea in which lactose acted as a laxative. (Lactose is still sold in a pure form for this purpose in some older drugstores, and McCracken [1971] reports its use in Bali.) If lactose is continually taken, a chronic effect is ulcerative colitis (Littman, Cady, and Rhodes 1968).

Although all human infants (with the exception of those having the hereditary infantile lactase deficiency, alactasia) are born with the lactase enzyme that is necessary for digestion of the only source of carbohydrate in their mothers' milk, many lose this enzyme ability in later childhood, adolescence, or early adulthood. Whether the failure to synthesize this enzyme is due to the fact that these populations cease to have any source in the diet (unlike the populations that are continuously exposed [Bolin, Crane, and David 1968]), or whether it is the result of some kind of "switch" gene mechanism, absent in these populations, and/or some other factor, is not known. What is known is that lactase deficiency is a population variable and does have some genetic associations (Ferguson

411

and Maxwell 1967). McCracken (1971), in an extensive review, demonstrates an important association between the extensive use of dairy technology and a significant presence of the lactase enzyme in the adult populations of these societies. He favors a genetic hypothesis, suggesting that the adult lactase production is a dominant genetic condition. He further suggests that the gene evolved with the origin of dairying from cows, sheep, goats, and reindeer in Neolithic times. Thus, those populations associated, for example, with Western Europe, who primarily settled in North America, have a low frequency of adult lactase deficiency, as is also the case with many other populations associated with dairying. However, there are dairying populations with a high percentage of lactase deficient adults. McCracken explains this situation by saying that populations such as the Greeks and Cypriots have developed a cultural adaptation to overcome the disability. By making cheese, they utilize lactobacillus bacteria outside of the gastrointestinal tract to digest the lactose without harm to themselves. This enables the population to utilize the dairy products without the side effects of diarrhea, since the lactose is already broken down by the bacteria in the cheese or yogurt. (Any lactic acid is absorbed in the stomach and intestines before reaching the colon.) Thus, the use of cheese may explain how some adult heavy users of dairy products are able to adjust to the lactose load; it also explains the use of cheese in some herding populations where lactase deficiency is fairly frequent.

At a microevolutionary level, it is interesting to examine this problem of lactase deficiency in terms of our heuristic model of the human ecosystem. What becomes a central issue in the twentieth century is the fact that there may be many problems similar to lactose intolerance operating to produce microevolutionary change. For example, McCracken (1971) points out that it is possible that milk supplementation has led to an increase in infant diarrhea. In those populations with the lactase deficiency who receive milk supplementation and also have protein deficiencies, child mortality rates may be raised. In this case, selection would strongly favor those children without the lactase deficiency, since they could digest the milk and avoid the catastrophic effects of early childhood diarrhea in the presence of generalized protein deficiencies. This is but one example of the probable effects of the rapid shifts in nutrition, as world-wide trade, economic assistance, and new technological food treatment patterns (additives and so forth) expose populations to all kinds of subtle, and not so subtle, changes in nutrients. Another example of this kind of problem is favism (Beutler 1966), a hemolytic anemia associated with a red cell deficiency of glucose-6-phosphate dehydrogenase. It can be expressed either as a result of eating fava beans or taking the related antimalarial drug primaquine. Still another similar example recently studied by Greene (1972) is the complex relationship between the inability to taste certain goitrogens, of which PTC is closely related, and the serious side effects of goiter on fertility and mental development. These examples appear to point toward an increasing number of complex problems of microevolution in the twentieth century resulting from the interaction of rapidly changing sociocultural practices, such as taking various medications, eating new foods, or being exposed to new environmental sources of pathology that will require the use of the kind of heuristic model already discussed. Thus, we can anticipate that our studies of microevolution in complex populations will require knowledge of the interaction of not just biological and physical environmental variables, but also a fundamental knowledge of sociocultural processes. Our study of human evolution then becomes not biological evolution but biocultural evolution.

INDUSTRIAL POLLUTION

Air pollution is only one of the complications introduced into the environment of modern man. If we were to enumerate all of the complications and attempt to evaluate the overall selective effects, then we might be able to obtain some overall measure of the impact of modern industrial technology on various populations. There are basically two approaches that could be used in varying combinations. First, we could develop models of the complexity of the interactions of individuals with and without deficiencies of various genetic conditions and then generalize from these models to the problem of the microevolutionary effect of, for example, air pollution. Second, we could use highly sophisticated epidemiological analyses to demonstrate the overall statistical effects of air pollution on mortality and morbidity figures. This section of the chapter will briefly consider both approaches.

In some individuals, an advanced state of air pollution produced by cigarette smoking or serious industrial pollution leads to a sharp decrease in lung compliance (stretchability) that is expressed in a severe shortness of breath. Hypoxia is present, and frequently polycythemia follows in these individuals. This pathophysiological disease is called emphysema. Although it is mostly an old-age disease, it does afflict individuals in their thirties. One hypothesis that attempts to explain some of the incidence of this disease in the younger population is that it is due to a hereditary deficiency of $alpha_1$-antitrypsin (Stevens et al. 1971). This antibody is a fast migrating prealbumin for which there is some evidence suggesting a simple genetic mode of inheritance (Talamo 1971). When particulate matter is inhaled, there is a response by the lungs to dispel the particle by ciliary responses in the epithelial cells lining the bronchioles, and the lungs also secrete trypsin, a potent proteolytic enzyme, to digest any protein in the particulate matter. If the trypsin is released, then it is rapidly deactivated by $alpha_1$-antitrypsin before the proteolytic enzyme starts to break down the local lung tissue. In the individual deficient in this antibody, fraction severe scarification can take place in the lungs, leading to an early degeneration of the lung tissue that results in a decrease in compliance and the development of emphysema.

Although it is not entirely clear, it is quite possible that those individuals with a deficiency of antitrypsin would have a greater risk living in polluted environments versus those with low pollution. The concept here is that with the development of the twentieth-century technology, the energy requirements and demands are such that air pollution by-products may be having some major effects on the genetic adaptability of various human subpopulations.

In terms of our model, it is possible to suggest that migration to regions with low air pollution could begin to skew, for example, the regional gene pool of residents in the southwestern portions of the United States toward higher frequencies of $alpha_1$-antitrypsin deficiency. Taking this line of thought one step further into the prospects of massive screening and early detection of susceptible individuals could alter this regional gene pool as a result of increased migration by these individuals. Once again, it is possible to begin to speculate how a feedback similar to that for sickle-cell trait could be set up that would significantly alter many elements of our interacting model of microevolutionary trends.

Hickey and his associates (1970a, 1970b) have introduced an alternative approach that could prove highly useful in analyses of the micro-evolutionary effects of air pollution. This group is to use standard metropolitan area statistics (SMAS) from 38 major U.S. cities in conjunction with air pollution data to study the effects of various air pollutants on differential mortality in these populations. Along these lines, Boyce, Farhi, and Weischedel (1970) have developed a highly sophisticated optimal regression analysis technique that is particularly designed for this kind of data. Their list of the major pollutants consists of cadmium, chromium, copper, iron, lead, manganese, nickel, tin, titanium, vanadium, zinc, nitrogen dioxide (NO_2), sulfur dioxide (SO_2), sulphate (SO_4), arsenic, and water hardness. Using these statistical techniques in combination with this air pollution and SMAS statistics, Boyce and his associates were able to develop several equations to explain the variance for cancer and heart disease mortality rates. With these methods, they often obtained a multiple correlation coefficient higher than 0.7. These results mean that a considerable portion of the variation found in the patterns of total cancer and heart disease rates were explainable by regression equations developed for these contaminants. For example, using the optimal regression analysis program on 1959 to 1961 mortality data that was unadjusted for age, race, and sex for lung cancer for the total SMAS populations, an equation resulted where M (mortality due to lung cancer) equals $-23.019 + 5.069\ ln$ concentration ($SO_4=$) $-2.448\ ln$ concentration (titanium) $-2.538\ ln$ concentration (copper) $+4.231\ ln$ concentration (NO_2). For this, an R square of 0.695 was obtained with an F statistic of 18.82 for 4, 33° of freedom that was significant at the alpha equals 0.01 level. Likewise, Boyce and his colleagues found that in a number of other similar equations, both sulphur dioxide and nitrogen dioxide were among the predictors that were repeatedly positively correlated with mortality rates for all forms of cancer. It is also interesting to note that some of the metal ions (such as zinc and several others) appeared as correlated predictors in these equations. This suggests the possibility of some protective effects of these particular contaminants in the environment.

While these results are not definitive, they strongly suggest that fruitful approaches to selection in large populations is possible. This means that we may be in a position to use the in-depth experience gained from microevolutionary models of simple genetic models for the interpretation of the complex interaction of factors acting in various combinations on human health patterns that are produced as a result of industrial pollution. Furthermore, this combination of approaches seems to be one of the most promising ways to begin measuring the evolutionary significance of these large-scale technologically produced environmental changes on many modern human populations. There is no question that we need other simple genetic examples such as alpha$_1$-antitrypsin to further develop our basic understanding of the physiological adaptability of individuals and populations to various environments. One promising avenue appears to involve altitude adaptability studies and the occurrence of a compound called 2-3 diphosphoglycerate (2-3 DPG). It is produced in the red blood cell by an enzyme 2-3 DPG mutase from a closely related precursor (1-3 DPG). Recently, it was found that this compound is largely responsible for adaptation of newcomers to high altitudes (Lenfant et al. 1968, 1970) and was also present in high levels for residents. Migration to low lands caused the level of the compound to decrease. Physiologically, the effect of the compound is to shift the hemoglobin saturation curve to the right, which means that O_2 will be released in greater quantities at the tissue level. Large-scale changes in 2-3 DPG indicate that it may be the major rapid adaptation to altitude hypoxia. Although it is speculative, it is entirely possible that genetic variations in the 2-3 DPG mutase enzyme exist. From a theoretical physiological point of view, it may be an ideal candidate for explaining some of the pathophysiological effects of pollution and altitude hypoxia.

By combining possible examples such as 2-3 DPG with the developing statistical models for the interpretation of large-scale population data, it may be possible to develop some reasonably specific explanations of the patterns of variation found in the various studies of the overall effects of industrial pollution. If we are going to begin to develop our models of human microevolution in the twentieth century in any serious manner, such a direction is almost mandatory.

MICROEVOLUTION AND THE CENTRAL NERVOUS SYSTEM

Perhaps the most challenging and, for some obvious and not so obvious reasons, the most controversial modern genetic problem relates to the genetics of central nervous system (CNS) development and function. If we can unravel the genetics of the human CNS, we will be in a new position to better understand the ramifications of man's most important evolutionary adaptation. Looking at twentieth-century man, we cannot help but realize that one of the most significant effects of his modern technology is on the behavioral adaptability of individuals and populations to both the rates of change induced by technology and the kind of abstract and communicative neocortical capacities necessary to produce, operate, and maintain modern levels of technology. It has long been recognized that the ecosystems of hunters and gatherers, for example, may be selecting for entirely different behavioral capacities than those demanded by membership in more complex technological societies. What isn't clear is whether or not these differences in populations that have adapted over millenia to vastly differing environments are significant enough to be measured by any tests of mental abilities. Many tests have been developed, and, of course, those testing "intelligence" have been most widely used to assess heritability of CNS functions (Jensen 1969). However, outside of the well-known examples of single gene characteristics affecting central nervous system functions (such as Huntington's chorea and microcephaly), there is little known about the polygenic characteristics that may underly performance on these tests of mental ability.

The problems of genetic analysis generated by the use of these tests of mental ability are basically twofold. First, these tests represent continuous variables involving, in all probability, many polygenic characteristics that, with the current state of knowledge, make it impossible to calculate gene frequencies. Second, overall interpretations of the role of environment and genetic constitution in the particular phenotypes can be made; but, while "within" population estimates of heritability are common, it is still controversial as to whether "between" population estimates can be made (DeFries 1970). This means that many of the so-called cross-racial and population studies have, in fact, no solid genetic basis for comparison. Scarr-Salapatek (1971) suggests that there are two competing hypotheses to explain differences obtained by social classes and races: one is the environmental deprivation hypothesis, and the other is the genotype distribution hypothesis. Underlying these hypotheses is the evidence for breeding restrictions by race and by social class that result in greater endogamy than exogamy. Scarr-Salapatek has developed two models that spell out the significance of these hypotheses (Figures 49 and 50). She has demonstrated new evidence suggesting that lowered heritabilities were found in White lower-class populations when compared with White upper-class data. Furthermore, she also suggests the impossibility of comparing IQ data of Black children with that of White children when there is evidence for unfavorable environmental conditions in a greater percentage of Black than White children and for the existence of differing Black-White environmental factors. These studies suggest that investigations of the

Model 1: Environmental advantage as the determinant of group differences in IQ.

Assumptions:

1. Genotypic distribution by social class for phenotypic IQ of children (no differences).

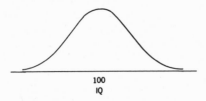

100
IQ

2. Environmental effects on the development of IQ by SES (large effect).

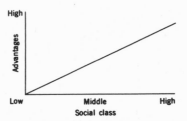

Prediction: Lower h^2 in disadvantaged groups.

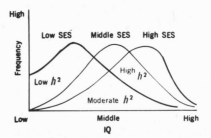

Note: h^2 is heritability for twins; SES is socioeconomic status. Model 1 rests on the assumption that the environment plays a highly important role. It assumes that IQ is distributed normally among social classes and that no differences in genotype exist. Furthermore, it suggests that the greater the environmental enrichment that is directly correlated with social class, the higher will be the heritability estimate of IQ. In other words, the heritability that is best known for studies of upper middle-class White populations increases with class. Lower-class individuals in this case have an unfavorable environment for their phenotypic IQ development. This means lower mean IQ scores, phenotypic variability, expression of individual differences, and genetic variances in phenotypes.

FIGURE 49. Environmental disadvantage, Model 1. *Source:* S. Scarr-Salapatek, "Race, Social Class, and IQ," *Science* 174 (December 1971): 1285–95. Copyright 1971 by the American Association for the Advancement of Science. Reprinted by permission.

Model 2: Genetic differences as the primary determinant of group differences in IQ

Assumptions:

1. Genotypic distribution by social class for phenotypic IQ of children (differences).

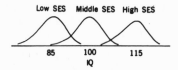

2. Environmental effects on the development of IQ by SES (small effect).

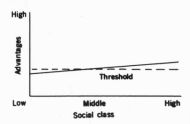

Prediction: Equal h^2 in all groups.

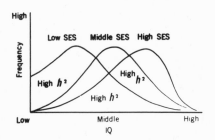

Note: h^2 is heritability for twins; SES is socioeconomic status. Model 2 assumes that genotypic variation among social classes of a population exists and that variation in IQ is largely genetic without being significantly influenced by environment. In this case, it also suggests that there is a small role for environmental effects of social advantages offered by higher social class. Heritability in this case is essentially equal in each social class.

FIGURE 50. Genetic differences, Model 2. *Source:* S. Scarr-Salapatek, "Race, Social Class, and IQ," *Science* 174 (December 1971): 1285–95. Copyright 1971 by the American Association for the Advancement of Science. Reprinted by permission.

effects of class variation in Black populations and standardization of the environmental factors affecting IQ development need to be done before any more comparisons can be made.

Other questions concerning intellectual function also need further examination—for example, the effects of assortative mating in a complex technological society have only recently been examined (Bajema 1971). Another important area may be the relationship between the earlier onset of sexual maturity that is associated with the secular growth trend recorded over the last hundred years (Katz, Rivinus, and Barker 1972). It is entirely possible that the same nutritional, disease, endocrine, and genetic factors that may be operating in the production of the secular growth trend may also have considerable implications for the development of intellectual functioning in the central nervous system. Over the last several months, a group including Scarr-Salapatek, Barker, and Katz has been collaborating at the W. M. Krogman Center for Research in Child Growth and Development in an investigation of the relationship between biological aging as indicated by skeletal aging and various measures of intellectual functioning. One hypothesis that we are testing is concerned with the concept that earlier pubescence may be associated with certain changes in CNS functioning that may be measurable by developmental psychological tests. If the secular growth trend does implicate shifts in the developmental curves of intelligence or behavioral functioning, then the question is: To what extent is selection operating on these changes of behavioral and general biological measures of growth and development? The question could have considerable implications for our understanding of the genetic implications of recent and potentially significant changes in human behavioral variation.

Another important area of behavioral investigation is the effects of rapid social and cultural changes on behavioral adaptability in an emotional sense. Increasingly, various psychotropic drugs are being used to alter brain function and hence individual behavior. Some of these drugs, of course, have unusual side effects, either on central nervous system function or on the organs involved in detoxification and excretion. A now classic example of this kind of problem came as a result of the extensive use of isoniazid to treat tuberculosis in Alaskan Eskimo populations in the 1950s (Armstrong and Peart 1960). The investigators discovered that approximately 10 percent of the population were slow inactivators of the isoniazid, which is a pyridine analogue. Basically, it was found that a

420

genetic polymorphism exists for the lower enzyme involved in acetylation of this and other similar drugs (Lehmann and Liddell 1966). What was also interesting and germane in this context was the fact that the drug also caused a euphoria in some of the individuals to whom it was administered. This stimulated considerable interest in developing antidepressants; in 1951, Fox (Cutting 1964) noted that a closely related analogue to isoniazid, iproniazid, produced a significant euphoria in patients. Later, these drugs were found to be potent monomine oxidose (MAO) inhibitors in the brain. However, to my knowledge, what is not known is whether or not there are genetic polymorphisms regarding the effect of these MAO inhibitors on the central nervous system. In other words, if the deactivation of MAO inhibitors follows a genetic polymorphism and this, in turn, parallels their effectiveness, then we may have evidence for genetic differences either in the response to antidepressants or even in the basic brain mechanisms that are directly involved in the production and development of depression.

Many other intriguing examples of similar kinds of drug side effects are bringing to light a number of interesting problems for genetic analysis. However, from a microevolutionary point of view, it is an unprecedented process to analyze the feedback responses among a rapidly changing society—its effects on the emotional behavioral adaptability of its individuals, its medical technology that attempts to treat the individual behavioral disorders with various drugs, and the discovery of underlying genetic factors possibly regulating central nervous system function by its scientists!

CONCLUSION

If anyone believed that man has ceased to evolve in the twentieth century, as some famous scientists over the years have suggested, then this chapter should give some food for thought. What is also important to point out here is the complexity of the process and the multitude of ways in which the adaptation and evolution can be studied in modern man. We have found that using a heuristically oriented ecosystems model is very helpful in structuring our concepts and turning over new questions in our mind. It becomes clear that this chapter could be rewritten several times, with each one using intriguing examples of similar processes. We need to develop second-order models that begin to structure not only our questions but also the way we treat and retrieve and store data concerning ongoing human evolution. If we are to understand the micro-evolutionary processes in twentieth-century man, we must begin to build these second-order models that can quantitatively deal with genetic adaptability in complex environments. For example, we have been using the stepwise multiple regression analysis as the basis for determining the rank order and statistical significance of various environmental, biological, sociocultural, and demographic factors on health parameters in Eskimo populations. We are also developing the use of a Bayesian Regression model in which we can build in more refined hypotheses as our data base grows. Models of ecosystems in specific populations could be used to test for factors related to genetic conditions. Variables not readily apparent by observation and certainly not quantifiable could be investigated for their interaction with various genetic conditions.

Finally, we must also begin to look at large-scale populations. Previously, the data and methods of collection kept this from the realm of possibility. With computerized data and banks on genetic information on large-scale populations, we as biological anthropologists, human geneticists, and biologists can begin to take a serious look at the effects of such large-scale phenomena as air and water pollution, trace elements in nutrition, the effects of food additives, and the overall effects of drug therapies. We are moving closer and closer to understanding human evolution as it is now going on. I think it would be wise, especially with the humanistic and holistic perspective that anthropology offers, to begin to move more fully into this new arena of man attempting to control his own evolution.

NOTE

1. The basic method of calculating the gene frequency over time with regard to to sickle-cell anemia uses a formula for the complete elimination of recessives: $q_n = \dfrac{q_0}{1 + n q_0}$, where q_n is the gene frequency after n generations and q_0 is the gene frequency at the outset (Li 1968).

19
Anthropological Genetics:
An Overview

JAMES N. SPUHLER

Department of Anthropology
University of New Mexico

When the School of American Research Advanced Seminar "Methods in Anthropological Genetics" assembled in Santa Fe in 1971, this relatively new field in the study of man had just reached its majority. Anthropological genetics is a blend of general genetics and the study of human populations—populations of anthropological interest and, thus, often small and usually non-Western. It is convenient to place the effective beginnings of the new hybrid discipline about 1945 to 1950. Some landmarks include Dunn and Dobzhansky, *Heredity, Race and Society* (1946), Boyd, *Genetics and the Races of Man* (1950), and the Cold Spring Harbor Symposia on Quantitative Biology, *Origin and Evolution of Man*, vol. 15, based on papers read in 1950.

Franz Boas, Ales Hrdlicka, and Earnest Albert Hooton, the great twentieth-century pioneers of anthropological research and instruction in the United States, were opposed to, untutored in, or little influenced by Mendelian genetics or the genetic theory of evolution.

Ever since Blumenbach published *On the Natural Variety of Mankind* in 1775, physical anthropology traditionally has been concerned with three large problems: the comparative biology and (after Darwin 1859) the evolution of man and the primates, especially the higher primates; the growth and development of man, especially after birth; and the classification and origin of the living varieties of man. Thus anthropologists were long interested in inheritance and evolution, but before the beginning of general genetics of 1900, nearly everything written on human inheritance, whether on families or populations, was either wrong or misleading. Paul Topinard's *L'Anthropologie* (1876) is perhaps as representative of notions on inheritance in the period before 1900 as any other single anthropological book. Topinard devoted 18 pages (out of the total 548) to "crossing, inheritance, and consanguineous union," with little integration with the bulk of the text, devoted to the living races of man, or with the final chapter, on the origin of man.

Today most physical anthropologists use change in gene frequency as the master concept to interpret human evolution after the divergence of hominids and pongids as well as the ongoing genetical differentiation of local breeding populations. The concept of gene frequency was first used in Garrod's (1902) analysis of the effects of inbreeding on the incidence of alcaptonuria, a rare recessive trait. The joining of anthropology and genetics dates from 1903, when William C. Farabee, a graduate student at Harvard, wrote his Ph.D. dissertation in anthropology (published in 1905), with Professor William E. Castle as an adviser, on the inheritance of brachydactyly in a kindred of 69 Pennsylvanians, the first demonstration that a morphological variation in man followed a simple Mendelian mode of inheritance. In 1919 L. and H. Hirszfeld, army doctors in the Balkans during World War I, first used blood grouping in the anthropological study of populations; they found significant differences in the distribution of the ABO groups in soldiers from sixteen European races or nationalities.

Anthropological genetics is of course a part of general population genetics, a subject founded by three great theoretical biologists: J. B. S. Haldane (in a series of papers on selection starting in 1924 and summarized in his *Causes of Evolution*, 1932), R. A. Fisher (*Genetic Theory of Natural Selection*, 1930), and Sewall Wright ("Evolution in Mendelian Populations," 1931). Their statistical theory of evolution at the gene level was combined with empirical data from many species into a new synthetic theory of evolution by the pioneering works of Dobzhansky (*Genetics and the Origin of Species*, 1937), Simpson (*Tempo and Mode of Evolution*, drafted in 1938, published in 1944), Rensch (*Neuere Probleme der Abstammungslehre*, 1947), Schmalhausen (1947 in Russian, translated as *Factors of Evolution*, 1949), and Stebbins (*Variation and Evolution of Plants*, 1950). Of these Dobzhansky and Simpson were of special importance in leading physical anthropologists who completed their training after World War II into population genetics.

I will not attempt to summarize each of the individual papers; the authors have done an adequate job in this. Rather I will try to characterize some of them, and to relate all of them to general, contemporary knowledge of human population genetics and of the genetical theory of human evolution. A few points that came up during the discussions in Santa Fe but were not incorporated in the revised papers will be mentioned.

BREEDING POPULATIONS, GENE POOLS, AND GENE FREQUENCIES

The local, more or less isolated breeding population occupies the small end, and the species as a whole the large end, of an intergrading and variable set of structured and hierarchically arranged populations capable of undergoing microevolution. It is now generally agreed that all living hominids belong to a single species, *Homo sapiens*. Problems regarding macroevolution, the origin of species, are not considered in this book.

We identify local breeding populations by making observations on mating and reproduction, by observing or inferring parent-parent and parent-child biological links. The ultimate unit of the breeding population is the mated pair, but more important for the dynamics of human populations is the isolated local, mostly endogamous breeding group, or *deme*, within which the pairing is a close approximation of random mating.

Each of the hierarchic breeding levels within the species (deme, tribe, region, race, continent) may operate as a unit of evolution. The genetic theory of evolution is developed with most precision for the level of the deme, less so for the species at large, and hardly at all for the complex containing all the hierarchic levels of the typical species (Wright 1968, 1969; Cavalli-Sforza and Bodmer, 1971).

On the time scale, recognition of membership in a local human breeding population is complicated because the generations overlap; unlike many species of annual plants and insects, the members of three or more generations of a small human population may be living together at the same time and place. The long generation interval is a handicap in the study of human populations.

On the space scale there are also difficulties. People move in and out of local areas; the parents of babies born in the local population may have been born locally or remotely. But the facts that man has a good memory, keeps records, and communicates make adjustment for these difficulties less serious than for any other species of higher organisms.

All of the papers in this book employ concepts of breeding population, gene pool, and gene frequency, but the first of these three is a primary concern of Benoist (Chapter 4), Lasker (Chapter 7), Johnston and Albers (Chapter 10), Morgan (Chapter 13), and Howell (Chapter 12).

Benoist (Chapter 4) explores the characteristics and research value of several varieties of isolates. It is these populations, especially those of hunters and gatherers, that provide evidence on what human breeding groups were like during much of the past few million years. However, many hunters and gatherers were less reproductively isolated than some modern peasant groups. And some colonial European groups, for example, in the West Indies, are more highly isolated than many "primitives." Benoist makes social behavior and organization the positive factors, and geographical and other barriers the negative factors, in isolate formation and persistence.

Physical anthropology today has fresh interest in the "demographic topics" because births, deaths, mating, migration, and population numbers and composition are of fundamental importance in the study of changes in gene frequency. Sometimes the demographic data are only limiting in value because we do not know the genotypes of the individuals whose vital events are recorded and statistically reduced.

Human biologists are often bored with the seeming preoccupation of professional demographers in making elaborate arithmetical corrections to small numerical discrepancies and deficiencies in the official statistics about man collected by part-time census takers. Yet, as Nancy Howell (Chapter 12) explains, mathematical demographers are justifiably annoyed when anthropologists and geneticists, with perhaps never-to-be-repeated access to small, remote, and "primitive" human populations, return from the field to publish "impossible" demographic results because they fail in the face of problems "that require extremely sophisticated use of Stable Population Theory and other complex aspects of demography."

Roberts's meticulous study (Chapter 1) using the pack method on data from the Tristan da Cunha isolate during the period 1816 to 1961, demonstrates that, [in small populations, events which are completely indeterminate statistically and therefore not covered by available general models can be quantified and shown to have appreciable effect on the genetic constitution of the population.]

Morgan (Chapter 13) presents a detailed study of the population biology of the small but rapidly growing Ramah Navajo community in western New Mexico. This group increased from some 100 individuals around 1875 to 1,074 by January 1965, a recent growth rate of about 4 percent per year. The community is in rapid cultural transition and Morgan traces the importance of cultural-historical variables in the interpretation of observed demographic changes.

The *gene pool* of a breeding population is the collection of genes present at a given locus or at all loci in all members of the population at some given time.

The *gene frequency* at a given locus is easily found where the correspondence of phenotypes and genotypes permits direct identification and counting of genes (as in the MN blood types). When heterozygotes and homozygotes cannot be distinguished by available tests, gene frequencies must be estimated using equilibrium assumptions. Maximum likelihood estimates are now widely used. In some cases correction for biological relationship of the individuals sampled should be used in estimating gene frequencies and their variances.

SYSTEMS OF MATING

A basic problem in anthropological genetics is to study the conditions for stability and the modes of change in population gene and genotype frequencies. The complexity of the genetics of quantitative variation in man is illustrated by the flow diagram presented in Figure 51. Before outlining the major modes of change in gene frequencies, we next consider some conditions for their stability over two or more generations.

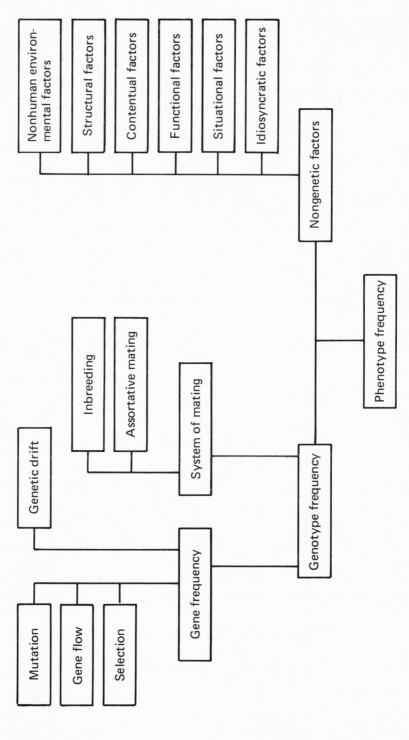

FIGURE 51. A flow diagram showing some determinants of phenotypical variation. Source: Modified from Spuhler (1954).

James N. Spuhler

Random mating and the Hardy-Weinberg Steady State

Hardy and Weinberg independently showed in 1908 that population gene frequencies remain constant from generation to generation under a system of random union of gametes in fertilization when the frequencies of the heterozygotes are equal to twice the product of the square roots of the two homozygotes: $p^2AA + 2pqAa + q^2aa = 1$, where p and q are the frequencies of genes A and a in the population, which is ideally large, with nonoverlapping generations, where there are no changes in gene frequency due to mutation, gene flow, selection, or genetic drift, or where mutation and selection rates are balanced so that there is no net change in gene frequencies.

When multiple alleles are present the steady genotype frequencies are given by the square of the multinomial representing the gene frequencies. In the case of polygenes the equilibrium frequencies of the various genotypes are given by expansion of the products of the squares of the allelic frequencies for each locus in the polygenic set. Alleles at one locus reach equilibrium after a single generation of random mating. Polygenes constantly approach equilibrium (which in theory is never reached) at rates slower for linked than for unlinked loci.

No human population has a strictly random system of mating. However, in many human populations the observed departures from Hardy-Weinberg expectation are sufficiently small as to be negligible, as is shown in this book (especially for the genes controlling the red-blood cellular antigens) in the chapters by Crawford, Livingstone, Harpending and Jenkins, Morton, Hurd and Little, Ward, and Giles.

Inbreeding and assortative mating are two general types of departures from random mating. The parents of inbred individuals are biological relatives. Inbreeding should be distinguished from endogamy, the selection of mates within some social group; if sufficiently large, endogamous groups may have negligible degrees of inbreeding. Inbreeding increases the proportion of homozygotes in the inbred line over that expected in random mating. Continued close inbreeding (brother-sister, single or double first cousins) results in completely homozygous lines.

Assortative mating refers to the concordance or discordance of the phenotypes of mated pairs. When mates in the breeding population have more attributes in common than would be expected by chance, the system is called positive assortative mating; when they have fewer attributes in

429

common than would be expected by chance, the system is called negative assortative mating. Positive assortative mating increases the proportion of some (usually not all) homozygotes, perfect positive assortative mating leading to the fixation of completely homozygous subpopulations. Negative assortative mating has the opposite effect on zygosity, but perfect assortative mating does not lead to a population with complete heterozygosity.

Inbreeding and assortative mating as such are not of evolutionary consequence because they change the distribution of genes into genotypes but not the frequency of genes. However, nonrandom mating in association with selection can change gene frequencies rapidly. Anthropologists have collected much more empirical data on inbred mating than on assortative mating (Spuhler 1968).

Inbreeding

Russell Reid's "Inbreeding in Human Populations" (Chapter 5) considers a first general class of departures from random mating by introducing two different measures of the degree of inbreeding. Wright (1921) defined an inbreeding coefficient (F) as the genetic correlation between gametes uniting at fertilization whether the correlation is caused by biological kinship of the parents, by assortative mating of any cause, or by mating within local races. Malécot (1948) and others define an inbreeding coefficient (f) as the probability that the genes at a given locus in uniting gametes are identical by descent from one or more common biological ancestors.

The Hardy-Weinberg steady state modified in terms of Wright's F to represent the population effects of inbreeding on the distribution of genotypes may be written:

$$(p^2 + pgF)Aa + 2pg(1 - F)Aa + (q^2 + pgF)aa = 1.$$

In some cases Wright's F and Malécot's f may be identical, in others very different. If we start with living individuals and work out their pedigrees for a few generations back (in practice, usually three to about ten), F and f are identical. Or if we consider the theoretical cases of an infinite breeding population where the only departure from random mating is parental consanguinity, F and f are identical.

Reid points to a striking case where the two inbreeding coefficients are

430

highly different. Yasuda (1969) found that Malécot's f calculated from pedigrees in a population in northeastern Brazil of mixed African, European, and American Indian descent was less than one-half of Wright's F calculated from bioassay, that is, using observed departures from Hardy-Weinberg expectation in genotypic proportions for several different genetic systems.

Inbreeding reduces the proportion of heterozygotes expected under random mating $(2pq)$ by a fraction $(1 - F)$. In agricultural practice, where plants and animals are both inbred and artificially selected, gene frequencies may be changed at comparatively fast rates. A regular system of brother-sister mating would reduce an initial frequency of heterozygotes of 0.50 to 0.16 in 5 generations, 0.057 in 10, 0.020 in 15. The reduction after 15 generations in the case of a regular system of single first-cousin mating is to 0.355 and in the case of single second cousins to only 0.491.

Reid finds no record of a human population in which the inbreeding coefficient is greater than 0.05. Most human populations have inbreeding coefficients below 0.005, in which case the proportion of heterozygotes expected under random mating $(F = 0)$ is $2pq = 0.5$ in contrast to the case of $F = 0.005$ where $2\,pq(1 - F) = 0.4975$.

The inbreeding effects are thus sufficiently small in most human breeding populations that some workers ignore them completely in dealing with problems of the genetic dynamics of human populations. Despite the elegance of Wright's and Malécot's approach, Ewens (1969, p. xii) remarked: ". . . . it is unlikely that the mathematical assumptions which are required to obtain a workable theory of inbreeding would apply even approximately in natural populations."

This is not to say that inbreeding is unimportant in anthropological genetics. Since a considerable proportion of all deleterious mutations in human populations are recessive and rare and thus carried in heterozygotes, even small mean levels of inbreeding account for a significant increase in the incidence of deleterious homozygous recessive genotypes. This is the explanation for the well-known observation that the degree of consanguinity is greater among the parents of offspring with rare recessives than in the general population: for example, if $q = 0.001$, and 0.01 of all marriages are between first cousins, then 0.63 of the parents of homozygous recessive children should be first cousins.

The most extensive study of inbreeding in human population was carried out by Schull and Neel (1965) and their associates in Hiroshima and

Nagasaki, Japan. Using a regression analysis, with 1,511 inbred children $(1/64 \leqslant F \leqslant 1/16)$ and 1,608 controls $(0 = F \leqslant 1/256)$, they found that the percentage change with inbreeding varied from 0.9 to 6.7 for the behavioral traits; the change was greater for the psychometric and school performance scores than for neuromuscular scores. The percentage changes due to inbreeding are greater for the behavioral variables in general than for the measurements of body size, which show a small, consistent, and significant inbreeding depression of about 0.5 percent. Compared with the controls, the inbred children as a whole come from families of lower socioeconomic status. The apparent inbreeding depression attributable to socioeconomic variation in neuromuscular tests, psychometrics, and school performance, respectively, is 23, 16, and 25 percent for boys and 26, 21, and 38 percent for girls.

THE ELEMENTARY FACTORS OF EVOLUTION

Change in gene frequency $(\Delta q \neq 0, \delta q \neq 0)$ may be considered the elementary evolutionary process. Many anthropological geneticists follow Wright (1967) in distinguishing three primary modes of change according to the degree of determinancy in the variation they bring about:

(1) *Systematic change.* When Δq is determinate in principle, the following three modes of change in gene frequency are capable of precise mathematical formulation that makes it possible to predict the magnitude and direction of change in gene frequency over specified times if there are no evolutionary processes of an indeterminate nature:

(a) Recurrent mutation
(b) Gene flow
(c) Intragroup selection

(2) *Random change.* When δq is indeterminate in direction (or sign) but determinate in variance, the following four modes of change are capable of mathematical treatment that makes it possible to predict the magnitude but not the direction of changes in gene frequency over specified times:

(d) Genetic drift
(e) Random fluctuations in mutation

   (f) Random fluctuations in gene flow
   (g) Random fluctuations in intragroup selection

(3) *Nonrecurrent change.* The following four modes of change in gene frequency are indeterminate for each locus:

   (h) nonrecurrent mutation
   (i) Nonrecurrent gene flow
   (j) Nonrecurrent selective incidents
   (k) Nonrecurrent extreme reduction in numbers

Although the distinction between (3) and (1), (2) above is arbitrary (for example, is the mutation to "porcupine" skin in man recurrent or nonrecurrent?), it is not only convenient but necessary to consider separately events that are unique or nearly so in the known history of the human species.

All of the above eleven modes of change in gene frequency are considered in this book. Gene flow and genetic drift are given major attention, perhaps because their rates of change are large enough to be relatively easy to detect in anthropological studies. For the species as a whole, here and elsewhere selection is given great theoretical importance, but, because the average selection coefficient is small, we lack accurate estimates of the magnitude of selection for the traits of most anthropological interest.

The work of Livingstone and others on selection for hemoglobins A, S, and C is probably the best documented case for loci in which the rarer allele has a frequency of over 0.05.

Everyone agrees that mutation is the ultimate source of all evolutionary change, but the mutational process is given little attention in this book and in others dealing with observations on differences in gene frequencies between populations, for reasons that will be given in the following more detailed account of the above modes of evolution.

Mutation

Mutation is the source of all new gene variation. A change in the sequence of nucleotide pairs in the DNA macromolecule is the basis of all mutation. In the course of normal human growth and reproduction each gene must, in general, repeatedly duplicate exactly its own nucleotide se-

433

quence. On occasion, however, a gene is not an exact duplicate of its parent gene: a mutant gene comes into being. Mutant genes have a different effect on the development of the organism from that of their parent alleles and they are capable of reproducing their own modified nucleotide sequence. The combination of self-replication and rare mutations followed by replication of the new sequence is the fundamental basis underlying both genetic stability and variability of populations.

The net mutation rate per generation for single alleles is given by

$$\Delta q = dq/dt = v(1 - q) - uq,$$

where u is the mutation rate from a gene with frequency q to its allele with frequency $(1 - q)$, v is the reverse mutation rate, and t is the time in generations. Estimates of spontaneous mutation rates for some 30 loci are known in man (Crow 1961; Spuhler 1956). The estimated rates tend to cluster about 1 in 50,000 although rates as low as 10^{-8} and as high as 10^{-3} are reliably reported. Estimates of reverse mutation rates are not available for man; most workers assume they are about one order of magnitude lower than the forward rates.

Statistical methods for estimating the error of mutation rates have not been devised for the nonexperimental procedures used in human genetics, but in some cases maximum estimates can be made. The rough agreement in the several results for independent estimates of the same character and for estimates of different characters gives some hope that they are of the right order of magnitude.

The human habitat is sufficiently diverse that we should expect differences in mutation rates in some populations. There is considerable geographical variation in the amount of radioactive minerals in the earth's surface. Also, inhabitants of stone, brick, or concrete houses receive more radiation than those living in structures made of plant materials. Sievert (1957) estimates that the irradiation reaching the gonads from natural sources ranges from 2 to 6(8?) rem/30 years, with individuals receiving a minimum of 1 and a maximum of 20(>50?) rem/30 years.

Probably the mutation rate for the marker genes most commonly employed by anthropologists (cellular antigens and serum proteins) is sufficiently low, and the average size of the breeding population sufficiently small, that mutation pressure is not a major determinant of observable local and regional differences in gene frequencies. The effects of mutation on the differences in gene frequencies between populations, while of basic importance, are swamped by those of gene flow, selection, and genetic drift.

Selection

Natural selection may occur when individuals or phenotypes, and always occurs when genotypes or genes, are differentially represented in later generations. Differential fertility and differential mortality, acting singly or together, are the fundamental events of natural selection. Usually, selection is defined to include in an exhaustive way all systematic modes of change in gene frequencies not attributable to mutation, gene flow, or genetic drift. In demographic terms, differences in rates of reaching maturity, mating, fecundity, fertility, mortality, and emigration are the raw materials of selection. Although gene flow could be regarded as a form of intergroup selection, here we restrict selection to its operation between individuals within populations.

demography as best measure of selection?

Natural selection occurs when individuals differ in *genetic fitness*, a notion that is defined *only* in terms of differential survival and fertility, and not in terms of other values or conditions, no matter how desirable or undesirable these may be. It is a tautology that genes which increase genetic fitness increase in number in later generations.

Selection can change gene frequencies only when different genotypes contribute different numbers of progeny to future generations. After the fact, selection is a major guiding force of evolution; present theory does not permit, before the fact, the prediction of the fitness of genes with hypothetical properties that are not correlated with fitness. Much ongoing selection in human populations maintains genetic equilibrium by eliminating deleterious mutants or by keeping up systems of balanced polymorphism. With suitable qualification for the fact that selective events involve entire genomes, the work of selection can be treated as if it were locus specific. Unlike mutation or gene flow, selection is inoperative for gene frequencies at zero or unity. In general, selection is the most important condition for cumulative change in gene frequencies, that is, for evolution, but it works only on variation provided by mutation and gene flow.

Wright (1931, 1969) developed a general formula for selection pressure. The effect of selection on gene frequency depends on the genotype frequencies (g) and their selective values (w). If $\bar{w} = \Sigma wg$ represents the mean selective value of the population and w_i that of A_i (giving hetero-zygotes with A_i a weight of $1/2$ and homozygotes of unity), the fre-quency of A_i, q_i, becomes $q_i \overline{W}_i/\overline{w}$ in the next generation, and

$$\Delta q_i = q_i (\overline{w}_i - \overline{w})/\overline{w}.$$

Under random mating, if the selective values of genotypes A_1A_1, A_1A_2, A_2A_2 are respectively w_{11}, w_{12}, w_{22} and if the frequency of A_i is q and that of A_2 is $(1 - q)$, then

$$\Delta q = q(1 - q) \, [w_{11}q + w_{12} \, (1 - 2q) - w_{22} \, (1 - q)]/\overline{w}$$

$$= q(1 - q) \Sigma w \frac{d\overline{w}}{dq}/2\,\overline{w},$$

which, given that the w's are constant, becomes

$$\Delta q = q(1 - q) \frac{d\overline{w}}{dq}/2w.$$

A case of special interest in anthropological genetics is balanced poly-morphism where two alleles are held at high frequencies by a selective advantage of the heterozygote. If $w_{11} = 1 - s_1$, $w_{12} - 1$, and $w_{22} = s_2$, the equilibrium gene frequency, $\hat{q}$, is independent of gene frequencies being determined completely by the selective values

$$\hat{q} = s_2/(s_1 + s_2)$$

and

$$\Delta q \simeq - q(1 - q) \, (q - q).$$

Selection may be considered to operate at four different levels: total, or individual, selection, phenotypical selection, genotypical selection, and genic selection.

Total or individual selection is measured by the differential survival or fertility (one or both) of individuals without regard to their genotypes. It measures the maximum opportunity for changes in gene frequencies due to selection and not the actual change. Crow (1958) introduced an "Index of Total Selection Intensity," I, which he later (Crow 1966) re-named "Index of Opportunity for Selection." Consider a parental popu-lation with p_i individuals who have w_i children, where $W_i = 0$ for individ-uals who die before maturity or otherwise fail to reproduce. The mean number of offspring to the parental generation is $\overline{w} = \Sigma w_i p_i$. If survival

qualifications to
Crow's Index

and fertility are completely heritable, if an individual on the average has the same viability and fertility as his parents, the mean number in the next generation is

$$\frac{\Sigma(p_i w_i) w_i}{\Sigma p_i w_i} = \frac{\Sigma p_i w_i^2}{\overline{w}}$$

and the index, I, may be defined as the relative increase in fitness in one generation,

$$I = \frac{\Delta w}{\overline{w}} = \frac{p_i w_i^2 - \overline{w}^2}{\overline{w}^2} = \frac{V_w}{\overline{w}^2},$$

that is, the maximum opportunity for selection is given by the ratio of the variance in number of offspring to the square of the mean number. The index may be divided into components due to mortality, I_m, and fertility, I_f, by setting

$$I = I_m + I_f/p_s,$$

where p_s is the probability of survival to the reproductive period, $I_m = (1 - p_s)/p_s = V_m/x^{-2}$, and $I_f = V_f/x_s^{-2}$, $\overline{x}_s$ being the mean number of survivors to the reproductive period. Matsunaga (1966) modified Crow's I to account for certain aspects of contraceptive practice, and Kobayashi (1969) to account for deaths during the reproductive period. Barrai and Fraccaro (1964) give a test of significance based on a truncated negative binomial distribution.

If all females born alive in a breeding population survived the full reproductive period and had exactly the same number of offspring, the maximum opportunity for change in gene frequency due to selection would become zero. As a result of death control in some modern populations, close to 96 percent of live-born females complete the reproductive period. Birth control in some populations or population segments has so reduced the variance in number of live-born children per women that it approaches zero.

Empirical values of I in samples from 64 human populations range from a minimum value of 0.23 to a maximum of 3.69. The values of I_m range from 0.03 to 1.73 and those of I_f from 0.01 to 2.55 (Spuhler 1963, 1973).

A major variety of phenotypical selection involves cases where the fitness of the optimum set of phenotypes (S_o) is greater than overall fitness

(S). Birth weight and survival through the first 28 days after birth and differential marriage (and presumably fertility) tending to exclude the extremes of tall and short stature are two examples of anthropological interest. Birth weight has a moderately low and stature a moderately high heritability. Selection for both characters is stabilizing.

Haldane (1954) introduced an index of phenotypical selection intenisty, I_p, where the mortality due to selection is $S_o - S$:

$$I_p = \ln S_o - \ln S.$$

Of 6,693 English girl babies, Karn and Penrose (1951) found an overall survival to 28 days after birth of 0.959; the survival of babies under 4.5 pounds was 0.414, of those with optimal birth weight of 7.5 to 8.5 pounds 0.985, and those over 8.5 pounds 0.978. If all the babies had belonged to the optimal phenotype, the total survival would have been 0.985. Thus the extra mortality due to selection is $S_o - S = 0.985 - 0.959 = 0.026$. The intensity of phenotypical selection for birth weight in the English sample was $I_p = 0.024 \pm 0.004$.

Selection at the genic and genotypic levels is of greatest theoretical importance in the genetical theory of evolution. Unfortunately selection coefficients for the more useful marker genes are not accurately known. For most such genes the selective differentials are likely to be small and, since the sample size necessary for significant results increases inversely with the square of the selection coefficient, it is difficult to obtain sufficiently large samples from human populations homogeneous for the relevant selective pressures.

The best known selective differential for polymorphs is the selective advantage of about 10 percent for hemoglobin S over hemoglobin A in areas where *falciparum* malaria is holoendemic (see Livingstone, Chapter 3, and Katz, Chapter 18, for additional details). The historical considerations outlined by Katz suggest lactose tolerance in adults may be of the order 2–3 percent. By pooling data, Morton and associates have obtained reasonable estimates of selection coefficients for the ABO blood groups and MN types in European populations as has Livingstone for the ABO groups in West Africa.

The difficulties of studying selection in small human population samples are illustrated by Roberts's (Chapter 1) tracing Rhesus R′ (Cde) and the C_5 serum cholinesterase to their probable common ancestors in the Tristan da Cunha isolate. There was slight loss of R′ and slight loss of C_5

438

James N. Spuhler

frequency due, perhaps, to genetic drift or, perhaps, to selection other than through fertility.

Katz (Chapter 18) reviews some of the complex evidence that natural selection and genetic adaptation are ongoing in twentieth-century industrialized man.

Gene Flow

Gene flow refers to recurrent introduction of genes from the outside into a breeding population. It is sometimes but not always parallel in meaning with migration, immigration, outbreeding, and race mixture. Genes may flow regularly into a human breeding population from the outside without the individuals who introduce the genes (usually males) becoming members of the population. Such casual outbreeding is of only secondary importance in changing gene frequencies. The important type of gene flow is the regular introduction of individuals from neighboring groups that are partially isolated reproductively.

Unlike mutation, gene flow is not locus specific; the gamete with its full genome is the unit of flow. Nonetheless it is possible to study the systematic effect of flow per gene per generation. If m is the rate of gene flow, q_m the gene frequency in the migrants, and q_n that in the natives,

$$\Delta q = mq_m + (1 - m)q_n, \text{ or}$$
$$m = (q - q_n)/(q - q_m).$$

The joint systematic effect of mutation and gene flow may be written

$$\Delta q = (u + mq_m)p - (v + mp_m)q.$$

As Workman (Chapter 6) points out, empirical studies of the effect of recurrent gene flow on genetic variability in human populations have been extremely limited. Workman focuses attention on the larger body of data relating to distinct hybrid populations or to groups of intermixing populations. Some of the more spectacular cases of race mixture, for example the Dunns of Zululand, should be viewed as unique events rather than as examples of gene flow.

Unfortunately, much of the vast literature by demographers on international as well as internal migration, while of great background interest, cannot be applied directly to the study of gene flow because dispersal is classified into "migration" and "no migration" according to movement across political boundaries which may be larger than the average dispersal distances between generations.

Workman and Livingstone make the important observation that certain simple models in human population genetics work well in very simple or in very complex situations. The Hardy-Weinberg steady state gives a reasonable fit to the observed distribution of genotypes in a wide diversity of populations despite the wide range of deviations from idealized conditions. Similarly, the Bernstein model (cf. equations on p. 439) gives important information on gene flow in hybrid populations, despite its static makeup and its neglect of wide variation in the historical patterns of intermixture. The more complex models for gene flow include the dynamic model of Glass and Li, which takes into account the number of generations of admixture, the method of Roberts and Hiorns, which allows estimation of rates of gene flow between any number of populations, and Morton's maximum likelihood method.

The necessity to guess about ancestral frequencies introduces numerous and uncontrollable sources of error in all methods. If an allele is absent or fixed in one of the ancestral populations (for example, the Duffy Fy^a allele in West African ancestors of American Negroes), estimates of gene flow rates are much more reliable.

After the spread of agriculture, gene flow became a major factor in the genetic structure of human breeding populations. Probably no natural and enduring human breeding population has been completely isolated reproductively for more than a few generations during the last 10,000 years, including minority groups that desire a high degree of isolation. A case of gene flow is known from Zulu to Eskimo. Morton (Chapter 15) found that long-range migration pressure is appreciable in Micronesia. In countries like Brazil race mixture between Negroes, Indians, and Whites is common.

Given the raw materials of inherited variability, the genetic structure of the human species depends largely on gene flow between different local areas on the one hand, and local selection intensities on the other. If there is much gene flow, local races do not develop; if there is less, clines may be formed; if still less, local races may differentiate.

A single-locus gene frequency found to be distributed as a cline may be due to gene flow but differences in selection intensity may also account for smooth geographical gradients in gene frequencies. Also genetic drift acting alone can lead to clines in structured populations. For those clines

clines coming before races?

440

actually reflecting gene flow, the frequencies at several loci should show similar clinal distribution when donor and receiver populations differ in those frequencies.

Genetic Drift

Meiosis and fertilization are the biological basis of random drift in gene frequencies. The two genes which occupy each autosomal locus in the fertilized egg are a sample of the four genes at that locus in the two parents. Genetic drift is general for all loci. For two autosomal alleles, the rate of genetic drift is proportional to the variance of a binomial, $\sigma_{\delta_q}^2 = q(1 - q)/2N$, where q and $(1 - q)$ are the gene frequencies and N is the population number. In small populations gene frequencies may fluctuate with high probabilities from generation to generation due to this sampling process. The magnitude, but not the direction, of the change in gene frequencies is determinate.

The action of random drift in gene frequencies may be illustrated by considering a human breeding population of two members maintained by brother-sister mating. If we start with two heterozygotes, $Aa \times Aa$, the gene frequencies are each $1/2$. The next generation could have any of the six following compositions with the probabilities indicated:

Genotypes	Probability	Gene frequencies	
		A	a
AA, Aa	1/16	1	0
AA, Aa	1/4	3/4	1/4
AA, aa	1/8	1/2	1/2
Aa, Aa	1/4	1/2	1/2
Aa, aa	1/4	1/4	3/4
aa, aa	1/16	0	1

In a large number of such populations, random genetic drift would be expected to bring about loss of one allele and fixation of the other in one-eighth, change of the gene frequencies by $\pm 1/4$ in one-half, and no change in three-eighths of the cases.

If the sex ratio in a breeding population is $1:1$, the ultimate rate of decrease of heterozygotes (H) in the proportion is approximately $1/(2N) - 1(4N^2)$ for small N, and $1/(2N + 1) \simeq 1/(2N)$ for moderately large

N. After a number of generations, heterozygotes will decrease at the constant proportion $1/(2N)$ per generation. If we let t equal the number of generations and put

$$dH/dt = -(1/2N)H$$

and let H_o represent the initial proportion of heterozygotes and H_t the proportion after t generations, we obtain

$$H_t = H_o e^{-t/(2N)}.$$

POLYMORPHISMS

The significant beginnings of empirical human population genetics involved an interaction of immunology, genetic theory, and population studies showing that the ABO blood groups differed in frequency between ethnic groups. Unlike observations on body size and shape, both genetics and immunology study numerous, highly specific reacting substances and both use efficient methods for identification and analysis of these substances in individuals.

Today gene frequency data on 40 polymorphic loci, several with multiple alleles, have been identified by immunological methods in two or more human populations. And recent developments in biochemical technology, especially electrophoresis, have made gene frequency data available on 44 serum protein loci in several populations. Considering that a large fraction of all loci are polymorphic and that some 1,000 marker genes are known in *Drosophila*, the prospects are good that the number of polymorphisms useful in anthropological work may increase manyfold in the near future.

Crawford (Chapter 2) reviews the technical and methodological innovations that made available the marker genes used in population studies. A vast amount of data is available. The genetic diversity known today was quite unexpected 20 years ago. Now the building of evolutionary models to account for the gene frequency observations is a preoccupation of anthropological genetics. We know, as Crawford points out, that observed genetic diversity among some relatively small American Indian tribes decreases in the order Yanomama > Papago > Caingang > Xavante, but the evolutionary significance or genetic explanation of the results is not clear. Nor do we know simple and direct explanations why the frequencies of alleles at certain loci vary within a narrow range even

are the genetic markers even pertinent to human evolution?

442

in widespread populations while those of other loci show broad variation even in subdivisions of the same local population.

For a number of anthropological problems the gene frequency data provide immediate answers on the simple assumption that groups showing similar gene frequencies are closely related biologically. The Irish Tinkers ("Gypsies") are more similar to the Irish than to the Asian Indians. Despite their language, the Lapps are distinctly European genetically with no general Mongoloid affinity. And despite their phenotypical similarity in skin color, hair form, nose shape, and stature, the African and Oceanic Negritos are genetically diverse, showing greater affinity to their non-Negrito geographical neighbors than to Negritos elsewhere.

COMPUTER SIMULATION OF GENETIC AND DEMOGRAPHIC PROCESSES

MacCluer (Chapter 11) provides a thorough review of the published works and a preview of several unpublished works on computer simulation in anthropological genetics. Anthropology has long used computers in data analysis and during the last two decades in population model building. With rare exceptions, the source of the data allows little prospect for extensive use of computers in record linkage. And, again with rare exceptions, the resources and manner of anthropological wet-laboratory procedures do not include expensive, production-line methods of analysis.

The objective of simulation is to model a process involving genes, genotypes, phenotypes, or individuals, in cases where the complexity of the situation precludes a simple analytical study. Two general approaches in simulation are often distinguished: analytical models and Monte Carlo models. The former are usually macromodels, where the entire population is treated as a unit, while the latter are usually micromodels, where vital events are followed for each individual member of the population. Simulation in anthropological genetics usually involves a mix in the degree of determinism, starting from the fully deterministic, where probabilities are limited to zero and unity, to the largely stochastic, where several of the events modeled may be random.

Using the genealogical method is expensive. Further, it is often impossible to estimate accurately the contribution of remote relationship to inbreeding levels in human populations. MacCluer found that 15 to 20 percent of total inbreeding may be contributed by the seventh ancestral generation in simulated populations of size 200 to 400.

Johnston and Albers (Chapter 10) report progress on a Monte Carlo simulation of some aspects of the Cashinahua Indian population of the Peruvian rain forest. Their simulation includes cultural factors resulting in nonrandom mating, stochastic factors affecting migration, mortality, and genetic drift, and naturally selective factors working through differential fertility and mortality among genotypes.

It is reassuring that the results of computer simulation are sometimes surprising. For example, Kenneth Morgan did not expect that simulated populations (of size 200 subjected to low age-specific fertility and mortality rates over periods up to 600 years) proscribing consanguinity of degrees where $F \geqslant 1/16$ became extinct less often than those without incest taboos.

Perhaps there is some danger that anthropologists will attempt to simulate the solutions to problems that could better be solved analytically. Simulation is often more expensive than paper-and-pencil work and nearly always less generally satisfactory. Simulation tends to produce unique solutions, and simulation programs to important problems are rarely flexible. Analytical solutions, especially those that include variances or even approximations to variances, are generally preferred. Nonetheless the use of computers has revolutionized population genetics. Statistical methods impractical for desk computation are now commonly and quickly used. And a wide range of theoretical problems that cannot be handled by mathematical techniques are solved routinely by Monte Carlo methods.

There is much need for a computer-operated "World Human Genetic Data Bank" facilitating rapid storage and retrieval of gene and genotype frequencies on nearly 100 polymorphic loci in several thousands of population samples.

GENETIC DISTANCES, TREES, AND MAPS

The use of various distance measures to construct trees and maps is a currently popular application of genetical theory to the interpretation of anthropological data. A wide variety of methods for measuring distance based on gene frequencies are in use (see the chapters by Livingstone,

Lasker, Howells, Harpending and Jenkins, Morton, Hurd, and Little, Ward, and Giles). Since most of the measures are highly intercorrelated, there is little basis for preference among them other than ease of calculation except where the measures are required to be proportional to phylogenetic time.

Measures of genetic distance should be distinguished from measures of kinship: the former are based on the study of the frequencies of the different kinds of genes present in populations, the latter on the identity of genes by descent ascertained through the study of biological relationships in populations.

Lasker (Chapter 7) defines "genetic distance" in the broad sense as the amount of genetic information that two groups or two individuals are able to transmit to their offspring divided by the amount of information held in common. He outlines the quantitative results for several such distances, including those based on deoxyribonucleotide sequences, karyotypes, amino acid sequences, matings, and social classes. Lasker boldly suggests that the time may be ripe to attempt a study of the breeding structure of the whole human species.

Probably a majority of anthropological geneticists consider gene frequency data to be the best data we have for the study of human evolution.

Two different purposes are avowed for the use of trees in the study of human systematics and evolution: (a) to describe evolutionary origin (cladograms), and (b) to describe phenotypical similarity between groups, races, subspecies (dendrograms).

There are many methods used to convert tables of genetic distances into dendrograms or trees. None of them are satisfactory to reconstruct the phyletic history of human populations that exchange genes. Harpending and Jenkins prefer a simple "maximum-linkage" technique that is economical of computer time.

The fundamental postulate in construction of cladograms is that divergence between two groups tends to increase with the time since separation. Distance measures used to make cladograms should be a known function of the time since separation. If drift only is responsible for evolution in populations of equal size, $-\log(1 - f)$ is proportional to time, where f is the Wahlund variance. If selection which is variable over several regions occupied by the species is responsible for evolution, population size is not important, and $\sqrt{f}$ is proportional to time elapsed. If

445

selective drift is acting, a logit transformation of the gene frequencies is correct (Cavalli-Sforza 1973).

Harpending and Jenkins (Chapter 9) point out that there are a number of reasons why two groups should have similar gene frequencies: they share a common ancestor, they exchange genes, their genes have been subjected to similar selection pressure, or (often overlooked) they are large so that little drift has occurred since their separation. The authors continue: "Since drift of mean gene frequencies of a subdivided group is nearly independent of mating patterns within the group (Ewens 1969), consideration of size makes reasonable the finding, for example, that genetic distances between villages within American Indian linguistic groups are as large as distances between linguistic groups" (p. 179).

A number of anthropologists, including Livingstone (Chapter 3) and Howells (Chapter 8) in this book, are skeptical and critical of available phylogenetic trees based on blood-group gene-frequency distances. The criticisms are based both on evolutionary theory and on other anthropological theory and fact. On a wide scale the modes of change in gene frequency are complex; different genes under different environmental conditions may be changed by different evolutionary mechanisms. The neglect of gene flow negates all such cladograms.

The random-drift model produces some results on the grand scale that are not acceptable on anthropological grounds—Koreans are not phyletically close to native Australians! In all of the studies on a world scale, the distance measures were applied in ignorance of real history; they are like surface collections in archaeology.

Oddly enough, some of the trees based on anthropometric or craniometric measurements show better fit to well-documented anthropological and geographical findings. In Europe, Southeast Asia, South Africa, Australia, and native America, regional differences in cranial morphology go well back into the Pleistocene. As Howells indicates, we have no satisfactory explanation of the long, differential persistence over time of these seemingly labile polygenic cranial characters.

Harpending and others consider that a genetic map gives a more satisfactory visual aid for the interpretation of genetic distances than a dendrogram. A genetic map is the result of a principal component analysis of the matrix, in which gene frequencies are transformed into imaginary scaled deviations from the sample mean such that the frequencies of the imaginary genes are uncorrelated. A plot of the populations on axes rep-

446

resenting the two or three most variable genes gives a good picture of the biological relationships among the populations. Principal component analysis should be valuable in identifying clusters of related groups, since relatedness should be the only factor introducing correlations among the groups. Principal component analysis on 15 loci suggest that there is no significant difference between the Bushman and Hottentot peoples of South Africa, and that some of the ascribed differences between the two groups are the results of admixture, diet, and way of life.

POPULATION STRUCTURE

The genetic theory of the elementary factors of evolution was first developed for populations with ideal theoretical properties such as random mating and infinite size. The genetic theory of population structure discards some of the simplifying assumptions in order to build evolutionary models that are more realistic for known human populations.

The raw data of population structure include phenotype frequencies, surname distributions, anthropometric means, pedigrees, birth places of mates, parents, and their children, in-migration and out-migration, births, morbidity, and deaths. The raw observations may be described by census and effective population size, gene frequencies, mating type frequencies, mutation rates, selection coefficients, and coefficients of migration, kinship, and inbreeding. The relation between gene, genotype, and mating type frequencies may be described in terms of genetic loads.

The statistical theory of population structure is difficult and controversial. Monte Carlo simulations are required to supplement available data. The study of population structure is one of the hottest in contemporary anthropological genetics because conflicting claims are put forth by advocates of kinship coefficients, F statistics, and the like.

A breeding population has a structure in time that consists of a network of parent-parent and parent-child links. Fisher, Haldane, and Wright adopted the theory of multiple correlation to deal with such networks. Wright (1931 and later papers) expressed the structure of a population in terms of F, the correlation between uniting gametes: F measures inbreeding relative to some specific foundation population. Letting F_{IT} indicate the F of individuals relative to some total population, F_{IG} that of individuals relative to subgroups within the total, and

447

F_{GT} the correlation between random gametes within the subgroups, the structure of a population may be analyzed by the use of the equation

$$(1 - F_{IT}) = (1 - F_{IG}) (1 - F_{GT}).$$

Wright showed that subdivision of the population into numerous partially isolated groups results in differentiation of gene frequencies between groups with variance $\sigma_q^2 = q_T(1 - q_T)F_{GT}$, where q_T is the gene frequency in the total population.

The "island model" of Wright (1931) is the most simple application of F coefficients to population structure. The total population is assumed to be subdivided into panmictic groups with genes representative of the total population flowing at low rates into each group. A major difficulty in the island model is that in most known human populations gene flow from nearby groups is much more likely than from distant groups. The "neighborhood model" of Wright (1943, 1946) is a closer approximation to real situations. The total population is assumed to be uniformly distributed over a large area, and the locations of parents at a given point in their life cycle are distributed according to a bivariate normal distribution with standard deviation σ for both X and Y coordinates of the parental locations relative to the progeny's locations at the same point in the life cycle. Although this model is improved by giving up the assumptions of random mating and gene flow equally likely from the total population, the assumption of uniform density is violated by most human populations.

Malécot (1948 and later papers) made a probabilistic approach to genetic relationship, covariance, and population structure. Malécot showed Wright's F was identical to the probability that uniting gametes are identical by descent. He introduced a *coefficient de parenté* (sometimes translated as "coefficient of coancestry" but now commonly called "kinship"), ϕ_{ij}, defined as the probability that a gene taken at random from one locus in individual i will be identical by descent with a gene taken at random at the same locus from individual j.

Malécot (1948, 1959, 1966) replaced Wright's three F coefficients (F_{IT}, F_{IG}, F_{GT}) with a single, absolute measure of isolation by distance, d. At greater distance, the local mean kinship decreases according to the relationship

$$\phi = (1 - L) \, ae^{-bd} + L,$$

where d is the linear geographic distance between populations i and j, L is the expected value of ϕ_{ij} for the least related populations, a is the mean coefficient of kinship in local populations, and b varies with the systematic pressures due to mutation, gene flow, selection, and the standard deviation of d in the past. It is assumed that d is large compared with its sigma, mating is random, selection is uniform over local groups, and migration is linear.

Morton and his associates (in Chapters 14 and 15 and several other papers) applied the above kinship model to a wide spectrum of human populations from isolates to industrialized nations. Oceanic islands have high values of a (about 0.05) and low values of b (about 0.005). Isolates have high values of both a and b. Continental regions tend to have small values of a (0.001 − .01) and small to moderate values of b (0.002 − .02). They find that gene flow is a more important systematic pressure than mutation or selection in sufficiently small regions considered over a few generations. Over larger regions up to the size of continents, mutation and selection may be of primary importance, especially diversifying selection for different alleles in different subregions.

Harpending and Jenkins (Chapter 9) point out that it is often impossible to distinguish regional gene frequency variation due to population structure from that due to population history. Similarity of gene frequencies among populations may reflect either common ancestry or mate exchange.

Research on population structure tends to focus on homogeneous areas assumed to be near equilibrium. Variation in gene or genotype frequencies are compared with predictions based on demographic parameters of the population. Each locus yields a measure of the amount of drift which is compared with demographic prediction based on pedigrees, isonymy, the root mean square distance between birth places of parents or parents and offspring, migration matrices measuring gene exchange among areas of villages, or local effective population size.

Evaluation of the results is equivocal because of disputes about what constitutes reasonable agreement or about the interpretation of the predictive models. For example, Harpending and Jenkins found inbreeding statistics from migration matrix models give different results depending on whether they are corrected or not corrected for finite sample size.

Ward (Chapter 16) reports on the extent of genetic microdifferentiation between demes, the patterns of genetic relationship between demes, and the effect of subdividing a population into demes upon the distribution of alleles within and between demes. His chapter presents some major conclusions from the extensive collaborative studies of Neel and his Michigan associates on the Xavante, Yanomama, and Makiritare of South America. The collected results of these studies provide the most complete description and analysis of the human biology and evolutionary processes in tribal populations published to date.

Ward finds that of all the forces which alter population structure, mating patterns and migration may be the only parameters amenable to detailed study in tribal populations.

Based on data from six loci and seven villages from each tribe, the extent of microdifferentiation within tribes is remarkable, reaching as much as 90 percent of mean intertribal distance. The intertribal differentiation may result largely from an initial "founder effect" followed by the partial isolation of the incipient tribe. The genetic divergence between recently separated Yanomama villages approximates that between villages separated 30 years or more. In the Yanomama, new villages are formed both by fission and by fusion, but fission is the more important process and leads to maximum genetic differentiation within the tribe. Among the Yanomama and the Makiritare the net effect of the breeding structure is to increase the proportion of heterozygotes above Hardy-Weinberg expectation. The average (uncorrected) $\hat{F}_{ST}$ of 0.06 for the Yanomama is one of the highest recorded for a human population. The Yanomama show a slight overall excess of homozygotes in the total tribal population, largely due to extreme differentiation between villages. The Makiritare, with less genetic divergence between villages and a higher excess of heterozygotes within villages, have an overall deficiency of homozygotes in the tribal population.

An understanding of population structure is basic to an understanding of the evolutionary processes now at work in *all* human populations, including the consequences of increased mutation, increased gene flow, reduced inbreeding, altered selection, the detection and counseling of genetic carriers, and widespread birth control. Fortunately the study of details of population structure is much easier in man than in other animal populations.

As shown by several chapters in this volume (for example, that of Livingstone), both major aspects of genetic variation in man, that among individuals within a population and that among populations within a

James N. Spuhler

controversy in anthro. genetics

species, are controversial. Within populations there is the mutational load–neutral allele–selective polymorphism argument and between populations there is the race–cline–selection–genetic drift problem.

Nearly all of the authors in this book have views that place them near the pan-neutralist rather than the pan-selectionist extremes of the evolutionary argument. They approach rather than avoid applied mathematics; they think there is much solid to learn about single loci and little to learn about "co-adapted gene complexes" (for example, most would hold that the race mixture studies by Morton and his associates show that human races do not represent "co-adapted gene complexes," although some, like Livingstone, are "a-racial ultrapolymorphists"); they believe that mutant genes should be considered neutral unless otherwise proven and not the reverse; they feel the notion of genetic loads to be useful; and, in general, they accept a view that nature is simple, not so complicated that we can never understand evolution beyond saying that selection alone is important.

References

ABBIE, A. A.
1969 *The Original Australians* (New York: American Elsevier).

ADAMS, M. S. AND J. V. NEEL
1967 "Children of Incest," *Pediatrics* 40(1):55–62.

ALLEN, G.
1965 "Random and Nonrandom Inbreeding," *Eugenics Quarterly* 12(4):181–98.

ALLISON, A. C.
1955 "Aspects of Polymorphism in Man," *Cold Spring Harbor Symposia on Quantitative Biology* 20:239–55.
1964 "Polymorphism and Natural Selection in Human Populations," *Cold Spring Harbor Symposia on Quantitative Biology* 29:137–49.

ALLISON, A. C., B. BROMAN, A. E. MOURANT, AND L. RYTTINGER
1956 "The Blood Groups of the Swedish Lapps," *Journal of the Royal Anthropological Society* 86:87–94.

AMERICAN BOARD OF COMMISSIONERS FOR FOREIGN MISSIONS
1856 Letters and journals for the year 1852 on. Written by missionaries and others from Ponape: Gulick, Sturges, Doane, Roberts, Pierson, and Snow. (Cambridge, Massachusetts: Houghton Library, Harvard University), Anderson to Doane, 13 January 1856.

ANDERSON, W. W. AND C. E. KING
1970 "Age Specific Selection," *Proceedings of the National Academy of Science* 66:780–86.

ARENDS, T., G. BREWER, N. A. CHAGNON, M. L. GALLANGO, H. GERSHOWITZ, M. LAYRISSE, J. V. NEEL, D. SHREFFLER, R. TASHIAN, AND L. R. WEITKAMP
1967 "Intratribal Genetic Differentiation Among the Yanomama Indians of Southern Venezuela," *Proceedings of the National Academy of Science* 57:1252–59.

ARENDS, T., L. R. WEITKAMP, M. L. GALLANGO, J. V. NEEL, AND J. SCHULTZ
1970 "Gene Frequencies and Microdifferentiation Among the Makiritare Indians. II. Seven Serum Protein Systems," *American Journal of Human Genetics* 22:526–32.

ARMSTRONG, A. R. AND H. E. PEART
1960 "A Comparison Between the Behavior of Eskimos and Non-Eskimos to the Administration of Isoniazid," *American Review of Respiratory Diseases* 18:588.

ARVELLO-JIMENEZ, N.
1971 "Political Relations in a Tribal Society: A Study of the Ye'Cuana Indians of Venezuela" (Ph.D. dissertation, Cornell University).

AZEVÊDO, E., N. E. MORTON, C. MIKI, AND S. YEE
1969 "Distance and Kinship in Northeastern Brazil," *American Journal of Human Genetics* 21:1–22.

BAJEMA, C. J.
1971 *Natural Selection in Human Populations* (New York: John Wiley & Sons).

BALAKRISHNAN, V. AND L. D. SANGHVI
1965 "Use of the Digital Computer in the Estimation of the Blood Group Frequencies," *Acta Genetica et Statistica Medica* (Basel) 15:345–57.
1968 "Distance Between Populations on the Basis of Attribute Data," *Biometrics* 24:857–65.

BARNICOT, N. A.
1963 "Anthropology and Population Genetics," in *Genetics Today*, ed. S. J. Geerts, *Proceedings of the Eleventh International Congress of Genetics* 3:953–63.
1964 "Anthropology and Human Genetics," in *Genetics Today*, ed. S. J. Geerts, *Proceedings of the Eleventh International Congress of Genetics* (Elmsford, New York: Pergamon Press).

BARNICOT, N. A., J. P. GARLICK, AND D. F. ROBERTS
1960 "Haptoglobin and Transferrin Inheritance in Northern Nigerians," *Annals of Human Genetics* (London) 24:171–83.

BARRAI, I., L. L. CAVALLI-SFORZA, AND M. MAINARDI
1964 "Testing a Model of Dominant Inheritance for Metric Traits in Man," *Heredity: International Journal of Genetics* 19:651–68.

BARRAI, I., L. L. CAVALLI-SFORZA, AND A. MORONI
1962 "Frequencies of Pedigrees of Consanguineous Marriages and Mating Structure of the Population," *Annals of Human Genetics* (London) 25:347–77.

BARRAI, I. AND M. FRACCARO
1964 "Intensities of Selection in Nomadic and Settled Lapps," *Folia Hered. Pathol.* (Milan) 14:1–6.

BARRETT, J. C.
1967 "A Monte Carlo Simulation of Human Reproduction," in *Symposium on Biological Aspects of Demography*, ed. W. Brass (London: Society for the Study of Human Biology).
1969 "A Monte Carlo Simulation of Human Reproduction," *Genus* 25.
1971 "Use of a Fertility Simulation Model to Refine Measurement Techniques," *Demography* 8:481–90.

BEALE, C. L.
1957 "American Triracial Isolates," *Eugenics Quarterly* 4:187–96.

BEARDSLEY, R. K., J. W. HALL, AND R. E. WARD
1959 *Village Japan* (Chicago: University of Chicago Press).

454

References

BECHER, H.
1960   "Die Surara und Pakidai. Zwei Yanomami-Stamme in Nordwest-brasilien," in *Mitteilungen aus dem Musem fur Volkerkunde in Hamburg 26.*

BECKE, L.
1894   *Ninia in the Ebbing of the Tide* (Philadelphia: J. B. Lippincott).

BECKMAN, L.
1959   "A Contribution to the Physical Anthropology and Population Genetics of Sweden. Variations of the ABO, Rh, MN and P Blood Groups," *Hereditas* 45:5–189.

BECKMAN, L., A. HEIKEN, AND J. HIRSCHFELD
1961   "Frequencies of Haptoglobin Types in the Swedish Population," *Hereditas* (Lund.) 47:599–605.

BECKMAN, L. AND G. HOLMGREN
1961   "Transferrin Variants in Lapps and Swedes," *Acta Genetica et Statistica Medica* (Basel) 11:106–10.

BECKMAN, L. AND E. H. MARTENSSON
1958   "Blood Groups and Anthropology in Dalecarlia (Sweden)," *Acta Genetica et Statistica Medica* (Basel) 8:37–47.

BECKMAN, L. AND T. MELLBIN
1959   "Haptoglobin Types in the Swedish Lapps," *Acta Genetica et Statistica Medica* (Basel).

BECKMAN, L., J. TAKMAN, AND K. E. ARFORS
1965   "Distribution of Blood and Serum Groups in a Swedish Gypsy Population," *Acta Genetica et Statistica Medica* (Basel) 15:134.

BENERECETTI, S. A. S., G. MODIANO, AND M. NEGRI
1969   "Studies on African Pygmies. II. Red Cell Phosphoglucomutase Studies on Babinga Pygmies: A Common PGM_2 Variant Allele," *American Journal of Human Genetics* 21:315–21.

BENERECETTI, S. A. S. AND M. NEGRI
1970   "Studies on African Pygmies. III. Peptidase C Polymorphism in Babinga Pygmies: A Frequent Erythrocytic Enzyme Deficiency," *American Journal of Human Genetics* 22:228–31.

BENOIST, J.
1964   "Saint-Barthélemy: Physical Anthropology of an Isolate," *American Journal of Physical Anthropology* 22:473–87.
1966   "Du Social au Biologique, Étude de Quelques Interactions," *L'Homme* 6:5–26. (English translation in *Yearbook of Physical Anthropology*.)
1968   *Esquisse d'une Biologie de l'Homme Social* (Montreal: Presses de l'Université de Montréal).
1971   "Population Structure in the Caribbean Area," *Ongoing Evolution of Latin American Populations*, ed. F. Salzano (Springfield, Illinois: Charles C Thomas).

BENTZEN, C.
1949   "Land and Livelihood on Mokil. An Atoll in the Eastern Carolines," *Coordinated Investigation of Micronesian Anthropology*, Part II, Final Report No. 11, 59 (Los Angeles: University of Southern California, unpublished).

BERNSTEIN, F.
1931 "Die Geographische Verteilung der Blutgruppen und ihre Anthropologische Bedeutung," Comitato Italiano per lo Studio dei Problemi della Populazione. *Instituto Poligrafico dello Stato, Rome* 227–43.

BERRY, B.
1963 *Almost White* (New York: Macmillan).

BERTALANFFY, L. VON
1968 *General Systems Theory* (New York: George Braziller).

BESHERS, J. M.
1965 "Substantive Issues in Models of Large-Scale Social Systems," in *Computer Methods in the Analysis of Large-Scale Social Systems*, ed. J. M. Beshers (Cambridge, Massachusetts: M.I.T.-Harvard Joint Center for Urban Studies), pp. 85–91.
1967 "Computer Models of Social Processes: The Case of Migration," *Demography* 4:838–42.

BEUTLER, E.
1966 "Glucose 6-Phosphate Dehydrogenase Deficiency," in *The Metabolic Basis of Inherited Diseases*, ed. J. Stanbury, J. Wyngaarden, and D. Frederickson (New York: McGraw-Hill).

BHATTACHARYYA, A.
1946 "On a Measure of Divergence Between Two Multivariate Populations," *Sankhya* 7:401–6.

BIAS, W. B., J. K. LIGHT-ORR, J. R. KREVANS, R. L. HUMPHREY, P. V. V. HAMILL, B. H. COHEN, AND V. A. MCKUSICK
1969 "The Stoltzfus Blood Group, a New Polymorphism in Man," *American Journal of Human Genetics* 21:552–58.

BIELICKI, T.
1962 "Some Possibilities for Estimating Interpopulation Relationships on the Basis of Continuous Traits," *Current Anthropology* 3:3–8.

BILLEWICZ, W. Z., I. A. MCGREGOR, D. F. ROBERTS, AND D. S. ROWE
1970 "Family Studies of Ig Levels," *Proceedings of the Third International Congress on Neurogenetics* (Brussels) (in preparation).

BIRDSELL, J. B.
1950 "Some Implications of the Genetic Concept of Race in Terms of Spatial Analysis," *Cold Spring Harbor Symposia on Quantitative Biology* 15:259–314.
1968 "Some Predictions for the Pleistocene Based on Equilibrium Systems Among Recent Hunter-Gatherers," in *Man the Hunter*, ed. R. Lee and I. Devore (Chicago: Aldine), pp. 229–39.

BLUMBERG, B. S., J. R. MARTIN, F. H. ALLEN, JR., J. L. WEINER, E. M. YITAGLIANO, AND A. COOKE
1964 "Blood Groups of the Naskapi and Montagnais Indians of Schefferville, Québec," *Human Biology* 36:263–72.

BLUMBERG, B. S., P. L. WORKMAN, AND J. HIRSCHFELD
1964 "Gamma Globulin, Group Specific and Lipoprotein Groups in a United States White and Negro Population," *Nature* 202:561–63.

456

References

BODMER, J. G. AND W. F. BODMER
1970   "Studies on African Pygmies. IV. A Comparative Study of the HL-A Poly-morphism in the Babinga Pygmies and Other African and Caucasian Popula-tions," *American Journal of Human Genetics* 22:396–411.

BODMER, W. F. AND L. L. CAVALLI-SFORZA
1968   "A Migration Matrix Model for the Study of Random Genetic Drift," *Genetics* 59:565–92.
1970   "Intelligence and Race," *Scientific American* 223:19–29.

BODMER, W. F. AND A. JACQUARD
1968   "La Variance de la Dimension des Familles Selon Divers Facteurs de la Fécon-dité," *Population* 23:869–78.

BODMER, W. F. AND J. LEDERBERG
1967   "Census Data for Studies of Genetic Demography," in *Proceedings of the Third International Congress of Human Genetics*, ed. J. F. Crow and J. V. Neel (Baltimore: Johns Hopkins Press), pp. 459–71.

BOLIN, T. D., G. G. CRANE, AND A. E. DAVID
1968   "Lactose Intolerance in Various Ethnic Groups in Southeast Asia," *Austra-lasian Annals of Medicine* 17:300–306.

BOLLIG, L.
1927   "Die Bewohner der Truk-Inseln: Leben and Kurze Grammatik eines Mikro-nesienvolkes," *Anthropos Ethnologische Bibliothek*, III, i (Munster: Aschen-dorff).

BONNÉ, B.
1963   "The Samaritans: A Demographic Study," *Human Biology* 35:61–89.

BÖÖK, J. A.
1956   "Genetical Investigations in a North-Swedish Population: Population Struc-ture, Spastic Oligophrenia, Deaf Mutism," *Annals of Human Genetics* (Lon-don) 20:239–50.

BOWLER, J. M., R. JONES, H. ALLEN, AND A. C. THORNE
1970   "Pleistocene Human Remains from Australia: A Living Site and Human Cre-mation from Lake Mungo, Western New South Wales," *World Archaeology* 2:39–60.

BOYCE, D. E., A. FARHI, AND R. WEISCHEDEL
1970   "Using the Optimal Regression Program," Preliminary discussion paper, Re-gional Science Department, Wharton School of Finance and Commerce, Uni-versity of Pennsylvania, Philadelphia.

BOYD, W. C.
1939   "Blood Groups," *Tabular Biology* (Hague) 17:113–240.
1952   *Genetics and the Races of Man* (Boston: Little, Brown).
1963   "Four Achievements of the Genetical Method in Physical Anthropology," *American Anthropologist* 65:243–52.

BRUES, A. M.
1954   "Selection and Polymorphism in the ABO Blood Groups," *American Journal of Physical Anthropology* 12:559–98.
1963   "Stochastic Tests of Selection in the ABO Blood Groups," *American Journal of Physical Anthropology* 21:287–99.

1964 "Genetic Drift in the Differentiation of the American Indigenes: Evidence from the Blood Groups," *Proceedings of the Thirty-fifth Congress of Americanists* (Mexico City, 1962), pp. 115–20.

BURKE, J., G. DE BOCK, AND O. DE WULF
1958 "La Drépanocytemie Simple et l'Anemie Drépanocytaire au Kwango (Congo Belge)," Memoires in -8°, Nouvelle Série, Tome VII, Fasc. 3. Académie Royale des Sciences Coloniales (Bruxelles).

CADIEN, J. D.
1971 "A Note on Genetic Drift in New Guinea," *Human Biology in Oceania* 1:140–43.

CANDELA, P. B.
1942 "The Introduction of Blood Group B into Europe," *Human Biology* 14:413–43.

CANNINGS, C. AND A. W. F. EDWARDS
1969 "Expected Genotypic Frequencies in a Small Sample: Deviations from Hardy-Weinberg Equilibrium," *American Journal of Human Genetics* 21:245–47.

CANNINGS, C. AND M. H. SKOLNICK
1972 "A Study of Human Evolution by Computer Simulation," *Proceedings of the Fourth International Congress of Human Genetics* (Paris) (in press).

CANTRELLE, P. AND M. DUPIRE
1964 "L'Endogamie des Peul's du Fouta-Djallon," *Population* 19(3):529–58.

CASEY, A. E., C. PHILLIPS, K. HALE, B. R. KYNERD, AND E. DOWNEY
1968 "ABO, MN, and Rh Blood Groups Among North Alabama Negroes," *Alabama Journal of Medical Science* 5:209–12.

CAVALLI-SFORZA, L. L.
1963 "Genetic Drift for Blood Groups. The Genetics of Migrant and Isolate Populations," ed. E. Goldschmit (Baltimore: Williams and Wilkins).
1967 "Human Populations," in *Heritage From Mendel*, ed. R. A. Brink (Madison: University of Wisconsin Press), pp. 309–31.
1968 "Recherches Génétiques sur les Pygmées Babinga de la République Centrafricaine," Cahiers de la Maboké 6:19–25.
1969a " 'Genetic Drift' in an Italian Population," *Scientific American* 21(2):30–37.
1969b "Genetics of Human Populations," *Proceedings of the Twelfth International Congress on Genetics* (Tokyo), pp. 405–17.
1973 "Some Current Problems of Human Population Genetics," *American Journal of Human Genetics* 25:82–104.

CAVALLI-SFORZA, L. L., I. BARRAI, AND A. W. F. EDWARDS
1964 "Analysis of Human Evolution Under Random Genetic Drift," *Cold Spring Harbor Symposia on Quantitative Biology* 29:9–20.

CAVALLI-SFORZA, L. L. AND W. F. BODMER
1969 *Genetics* 59:565–92, in C. A. Smith.
1971 *The Genetics of Human Populations* (San Francisco: W. H. Freeman).

CAVALLI-SFORZA, L. L. AND F. CONTERIO
1960 "Analisi Della Fluttuazione de Frequence Geniche Nella Popolazione Della Val Parma," *Atti. Associazione Genetica* (Italy) 5:333–44.

References

CAVALLI-SFORZA, L. L. AND A. W. F. EDWARDS
1963 "Analysis of Human Evolution," in *Genetics Today*, ed. S. J..Geerts, *Proceedings of the Eleventh International Congress of Genetics* (The Hague) 3:923–33.
1967 "Phylogenetic Analysis: Models and Estimation Procedures," *Evolution* 21(3): 550–70, and *American Journal of Human Genetics* 19:233–57.

CAVALLI-SFORZA, L. L., M. KIMURA, AND I. BARRAI
1966 "The Probability of Consanguineous Marriages," *Genetics* 54(1) Part 1:37–60.

CAVALLI-SFORZA, L. L. AND G. ZEI
1967 "Experiments with an Artificial Population," *Proceedings of the Third International Congress of Human Genetics*, ed. J. F. Crow and J. V. Neel (Baltimore: Johns Hopkins Press), pp. 473–78.

CAVALLI-SFORZA, L. L., L. A. ZONTA, F. NUZZO, L. BERNINI, W. W. W. DEJONG, P. MEERA KHAN, A. K. RAY, L. N. WEST, M. SINISCALCO, L. E. NIJENHUIS, E. VAN LOGHEM, AND G. MODIANO
1969 "Studies on African Pygmies. I. A Pilot Investigation of Babinga Pymgies in the Central African Republic (with an Analysis of Genetic Distances)," *American Journal of Human Genetics* 21(3):252–74.

CAZAL, P., R. GRAAFLAND, AND M. MATHIEU
1951 "Les Groupes Sanguins chez les Gitans de France," *Fourth Congress on Blood Transfusions* (Lisbon), pp. 356–64.

CENTERWALL, W. R. AND S. A. CENTERWALL
1966 "Consanguinity and Congenital Anomalies in South India: A Pilot Study," *Indian Journal of Medical Research* 54(12):1160–67.

CENTERWALL, W. R., G. SAVARINATHAN, L. R. MOHAN, V. BOO-SHANAM, AND M. ZACHARIAH
1969 "Inbreeding Patterns in Rural South India," *Social Biology* 16(2):81–91.

CHAGNON, N. A.
1966 "Yanomama Warfare, Social Organization and Marriage Alliances" (Ph.D. dissertation, University of Michigan).
1968 *Yanomama: The Fierce People* (New York: Holt, Rinehart and Winston).
1970 "The Culture-Ecology of Shifting (Pioneering) Cultivation Among the Yanomama Indians," *Proceedings of the Eighth International Congress of Anthropological and Ethnological Sciences* (Tokyo, 1968) 3:249–55.
1972 "Tribal Social Organisation and Genetic Microdifferentiation," in *The Structure of Human Populations*, ed. G. A. Harrison and A. J. Boyce (Oxford: Clarendon Press).

CHAPMAN, A. C. AND A. M. JACQUARD
1971 "Un Isolat d'Amérique Centrale: les Indiens Jicauqes du Honduras," *Génétique et Populations*, Hommage à Jean Sutter, I.N.E.D., Travaux et Documents, No. 60, pp. 163–85.

CHARBONNEAU, H.
1970 Tourouvre-au-Perche, Paris, P.U.F., p. 423.

CHUNG, C. S. AND N. E. MORTON
1961 "Selection at the ABO Locus," *American Journal of Human Genetics* 13:9–27.

CISTERNAS, J. P. AND A. MORONI
1967 "Estudio Sobre la Consanguinidad en España," *Biologica* 40:3–20.

COALE, A. J.
1964 "How a Population Ages or Grows Younger," in *Population: The Vital Revolution*, ed. R. Freedman (Garden City, New York: Doubleday), pp. 47–58.
1972 *The Growth and Structure of Human Populations: A Mathematical Investigation* (Princeton, New Jersey: Princeton University Press).

COALE, A. J. AND P. DEMENY
1966 *Regional Model Life Tables and Stable Populations* (Princeton, New Jersey: Princeton University Press).
1967 *Methods of Estimating Basic Demographic Measures from Incomplete Data*, United Nations, Manual IV.

COCKERHAM, C. C.
1969 "Variance of Gene Frequencies," *Evolution* 23:72–84.

COON, C. S.
1966 "The Taxonomy of Human Variation," *Annals of the New York Academy of Science* 134:516–23.

COOPER, A. J., B. S. BLUMBERG, P. L. WORKMAN, AND J. MCDONOUGH
1963 "Biochemical Polymorphic Traits in a United States White and Negro Population," *American Journal of Human Genetics* 15:420–28.

COTTERMAN, C. W.
1940 "A Calculus for Statistical Genetics" (Thesis, Ohio State University).

COTTON, C. A.
1962 "Low Sea Levels in the Late Pleistocene," Transactions of the Royal Society of New Zealand, *Geology* 1:249–52.

COULTER, J. W.
1957 *The Pacific Dependencies of the United States* (New York: Macmillan), p. 336.

CRAWFORD, M. H. AND W. C. LEYSHON
1971 "Blood Group Frequencies of the Itinerant Populations (Tinkers) of Ireland," unpublished manuscript.

CRAWFORD, M. H., C. MCCLEAN, AND P. WORKMAN
1971 "Hybridization Estimates of a Mestizo Population, Tlaxcala, Mexico," unpublished manuscript.

CROSS, H. E. AND V. A. MCKUSICK
1970 "Amish Demography," *Social Biology* 17:83–101.

CROW, J. F.
1954 "Breeding Structure of Populations. II. Effective Population Number," *Statistics and Mathematics in Biology* (Ames: Iowa State College Press), pp. 543–56.
1958 "Some Possibilities for Measuring Selection Intensities in Man," *Human Biology* 30:1–13.
1961 "Mutation in Man," *Progress in Medical Genetics* 1:1–26.
1966 "The Quality of People: Human Evolutionary Changes," *BioScience* 16:863–67.

CROW, J. F. AND A. P. MANGE
1965 "Measurement of Inbreeding from the Frequency of Marriages Between Persons of the Same Surname," *Eugenics Quarterly* 12:199–203.

References

CROW, J. F. AND M. KIMURA
1970 *An Introduction to Population Genetics Theory* (New York: Harper and Row).

CRUZ-COKE, R., A. P. CRISTOFFANINI, M. ASPILLAGA, AND F. BIANCANI
1966 "Evolutionary Forces in Human Populations in an Environmental Gradient in Arica, Chile," *Human Biology* 38:421–38.

CUISENIER, J., M. SEGALEN, AND M. DE VIRVILLE
1970 "Pour l'Étude de la Parenté dans les Sociétés Européennes: le Programme d'Ordinateur," ARCHIV. *L'Homme* 10:27–74.

CURTAIN, C. C., E. VAN LOGHEM, A. BAUMGARTEN, T. GOLAB, J. GORMAN, C. F. RUTGERS, AND C. KIDSON
1971 "The Ethnological Significance of the Gamma-Globulin (Gm) Factors in Melanesia," *American Journal of Physical Anthropology* 34:257–71.

CUTTING, W. C.
1964 *Handbook of Pharmacology. The Actions and Uses of Drugs*, 2d. ed. (New York: Appleton-Century-Crofts).

DAHLBERG, G.
1929 "Inbreeding in Man," *Genetics* 14:421–54.

DAVIS, K. AND J. BLAKE
1956 "Social Structure and Fertility: An Analytic Framework," in *Economic Development and Cultural Change* 4:211–35.

DE BEAUCORPS, R.
1933 *Les Bayansi Du Bas-Kwilu* (Louvain, Aucam).

DEMPSTER, A. P.
1969 *Elements of Continuous Multivariate Analysis* (Reading, Mass.: Addison-Wesley).

DENIKER, J.
1900 *The Races of Man* (New York: Charles Scribner's Sons).

DESMOND, A.
1965 "How Many People Have Ever Lived on Earth," in *The Population Crisis*, ed. L. K. Y. Ng and S. Mudd (Bloomington: Indiana University Press), pp. 20–38.

DE SOUSBERGHE, R. P. L.
1955 "Structures de Parenté et d'Alliance d'après les Formules Pende (ba-Pende, Congo, Belge)," Memoires in -8°, Nouvelle Série, Tome IV, Fasc. I. Académie Royale des Sciences Coloniales, Classe des Sciences Morales et Politiques (Brussels).

DETTER, J. C., J. E. ANDERSON, AND E. R. GIBLETT
1970 "NADH Diaphorase: An Inherited Variant Associated with Normal Methemoglobin Reduction," *American Journal of Human Genetics* 22:100–104.

DODINVAL, P.
1970 "Population Structure of the A, B, O, AB Blood Groups in Belgium," *Human Heredity* 20:169–77.

DOLINAR, Z.
1965 "A Study of a Geographically Isolated Population," *Annals of Human Genetics* (London), 28:250–60.

DOUGLAS, M.

1963   *The Lele of the Kasai* (London: Oxford University Press).

DRONAMRAJU, K. R.

1964   "Mating Systems of the Andhra Pradesh People,"*Cold Spring Harbor Symposia on Quantitative Biology* 29:81–84.

DUBOS, R.

1965   *Man Adapting* (New Haven, Connecticut: Yale University Press).

DUMONT, L.

1957   "Hierarchy and Marriage Alliance in South Indian Kinship," *Occasional Papers of the Royal Anthropological Institute of Great Britain and Ireland*, No. 12, pp. 3–45.

1968   "Marriage Alliance," *International Encyclopedia of the Social Sciences*, ed. D. L. Sills, 10:19–23.

DUNN, S. P. AND L. C. DUNN

1957   "The Jewish Community of Rome," *Scientific American* 196(3):118–28.

DYKE, B.

1970   "La Population de Northside dans l'île de St.-Thomas : un Isolat Français dans les Antilles," *Population* 25:1197–1204.

1972   "Estimating Effective Population Numbers by Monte Carlo Simulation" (in manuscript).

DYKE, B. AND J. W. MACCLUER

1973   "Estimation of Vital Rates by Means of Monte Carlo Simulation," *Demography* (in press).

EATON, J. W. AND A. J. MAYER

1953   "The Social Biology of Very High Fertility Among the Hutterites; The Demography of a Unique Population," *Human Biology* 25:206–64.

EDMONDSON, M.

1965   "A Measurement of Relative Racial Difference," *Current Anthropology* 6:167–98.

EDWARDS, A. W. F.

1971   "Distances Between Populations on the Basis of Gene Frequencies," *Biometrics* 27:873–81.

EDWARDS, A. W. F. AND L. L. CAVALLI-SFORZA

1964   "Reconstruction of Evolutionary Tree," in *Phenetic and Phylogenetic Classification*, Publication 6, Systematics Association, pp. 67–76.

1965   "A Method for Cluster Analysis," *Biometrics* 21:262–75.

EILERS, A.

1934   "Inseln um Ponape (Kapingamarangi, Nukuor, Ngatik, Mokil, Pingelap)," *Ergebnisse der Sudsse-Expedition* 1908–1910, ed. G. Thilenius (Hamburg: Friederichsen de Gruyter), II, B, 7.

ELSTON, R.

1971   "The Estimation of Admixture in Racial Hybrids," *Annals of Human Genetics* (London) (in press).

EMSHOFF, J. R. AND R. L. SISSON

1970   *Design and Use of Computer Simulation Models* (New York: Macmillan).

References

EPSTEIN, A. L. AND T. S. EPSTEIN
1962 "A Note on Population in Two Tolai Settlements," *Journal of the Polynesian Society* 71:70–82

ERIKSSON, A. W.
1968 "Serologisk Populationsgenetik," *Nordske Medicine* 79:419–24.

EWENS, W. J.
1969 *Population Genetics* (London: Methuen).

FALCONER, D. S.
1961 *Introduction to Quantitative Genetics* (New York: Ronald Press).

FARABEE, W. C.
1905 "Inheritance of Digital Malformations in Man," *Papers of the Peabody Museum of American Archaeology and Ethnology*, Harvard University, 3:69–77.

FERGUSON, A. AND I. D. MAXWELL
1967 "Genetic Aetiology of Lactose Intolerance," *The Lancet* 22:188–91.

FISHER, R. A.
1930 *Genetical Theory of Natural Selection* (Oxford: Clarendon Press).

FITCH, W. M. AND E. MARGOLIASH
1967 "Construction of Phyletic Trees," *Science* 155:279–84.

FITCH, W. M. AND J. V. NEEL
1969 "The Phylogenetic Relationships of Some Indian Tribes of Central and South America," *American Journal of Human Genetics* 21(4):384–97.

FLEISCHER, E. A. AND J. MOHR
1962 "Concerning the Genetics of the Human Haptoglobins: 126 Norwegian Families with 428 Children," *Acta Genetica et Statistica Medica* (Basel) 12:281–91.

FLEISCHER, E. A. AND E. MONN
1970 "Haptoglobin Types and Subtypes in Lappish and Non-Lappish Norwegians," *American Journal of Human Genetics* 22:105–8.

FLEURY, M. AND L. HENRY
1965 "Nouveau Manual de Dépouillement et d'Exploitation de l'État Civil Ancien," Paris, I. N. E. D.

FORTY-SECOND ANZAAS CONGRESS
1970 *Man in New Guinea* (Newsletter) 2(3):11 (Port Moresby, 17–21 August 1970).

FRANKLIN, I. AND R. C. LEWONTIN
1970 "Is the Gene the Unit of Selection?" *Genetics* 65:707–34.

FRASER, A. S.
1957 "Simulation of Genetic Systems by Automatic Digital Computers," *Australian Journal of Biological Science* 10:484–99.

FRASER, A. S. AND D. BURNELL
1970 *Computer Models in Genetics* (New York: McGraw-Hill).

FREIRE-MAIA, N.
1968 "Inbreeding Levels in American and Canadian Populations: A Comparison with Latin America," *Eugenics Quarterly* 15:22–33.

FRIEDENBERG, R. M.

1968 *Pioneering Concepts in Modern Science. I. Unexplored Model Systems in Modern Biology* (New York: Hafner).

FRIEDLAENDER, J. S.

1971a "Isolation by Distance in Bougainville," *Proceedings of the National Academy of Science* 68:704–7.

1971b "The Population Structure of South-Central Bougainville," *American Journal of Physical Anthropology* 35:13–26.

FRIEDLAENDER, J. S. AND H. L. BAILITT

1969 "Eruption Times of the Deciduous and Permanent Teeth of Natives of Bougainville Island, Territory of New Guinea: A Study of Racial Variation," *Human Biology* 41:51–65.

FRIEDLAENDER, J. S., L. A. SGARAMELLA-ZONTA, K. K. KIDD, L. Y. C. LAI, P. CLARK, AND R. J. WALSH

1971 "Biological Divergences in South-Central Bougainville: An Analysis of Blood Polymorphism, Gene Frequencies and Anthropometric Measurements Utilizing Tree Models, and a Comparison of These Variables with Linguistic, Geographic and Migrational 'Distances,'" *American Journal of Human Genetics* 23(5): 253–70.

FRIEDLAENDER, J. S. AND A. G. STEINBERG

1970 "Anthropological Significance of Gamma Globulin (Gm and Inv) Antigens in Bougainville Island, Melanesia," *Nature* 228:59–64.

FROTA-PESSOA, O.

1957 "The Estimation of the Size of Isolates Based on Census Data," *American Journal of Human Genetics* 9:9–16.

FUDENBURG, H.

1963 "Gamma Globulin Levels in Several Populations," *Vox Sanguinous* 8:249–54.

GAJDUSEK, D. C.

1964 "Factors Governing the Genetics of Primitive Human Populations," *Cold Spring Harbor Symposia on Quantitative Biology* 29:121–35.

GAJDUSEK, D. C. AND L. H. REID

1961 "Studies on Kuru. IV. The Kuru Pattern in Moke, a Representative Fore Village," *American Journal of Tropical Medicine and Hygiene* 10:628–38.

GARN, S. M.

1961 *Human Races* (Springfield, Illinois: Charles C Thomas).

GARROD, A. E.

1902 "The Incidence of Alkaptonuria: A Study in Chemical Individuality," *The Lancet* (1902) 2:1616–20.

GERSHOWITZ, H., M. LAYRISSE, Z. LAYRISSE, J. V. NEEL, C. BREWER, N. A. CHAGNON, AND M. AYRES

1970 "Gene Frequencies and Microdifferentiation Among the Makiritare Indians. I. Eleven Blood Group Systems and the ABH-Le Secretor Traits: A Note on Rh Gene Frequency Determinations," *American Journal of Human Genetics* 22:515–25.

GERSHOWITZ, H. AND J. V. NEEL

1965 "The Blood Groups and Secretor Types in Five Potentially Fatal Diseases of Caucasian Children," *Acta Genetica et Statistica Medica* (Basel) 15:261–308.

464

References

GIBLETT, E. R.
1959 "Haptoglobin Types in American Negroes," *Nature* 183:192–93.
1969 *Genetic Markers in Human Blood* (Oxford and Edinburgh: Blackwell Publications).

GIBLETT, E. R. AND L. E. BROOKS
1963 "Haptoglobin Sub-Types in Three Racial Groups," *Nature* 197:576–77.

GIBLETT, E. R. AND A. G. STEINBERG
1960 "The Inheritance of Serum Haptoglobin Types in American Negroes: Evidence for a Third Allele Hp^{2M}," *American Journal of Human Genetics* 12:160–69.

GIESEL, J. T.
1971 "Inbreeding in a Stationary, Stable Population as a Function of Age and Fecundity Distribution," *Genetics* 66:521.

GILBERT, J. P. AND E. A. HAMMEL
1966 "Computer Simulation and Analysis of Problems in Kinship and Social Structure," *American Anthropologist* 68:71–93.

GILBERT, W. H., JR.
1946 "Memorandum Concerning the Characteristics of the Larger Mixed-Blood Racial Islands of the Eastern United States," *Social Forces* 24:438–47.

GILES, E.
1966 "Comment on Howells," *Current Anthropology* 7:538.
1970 "Culture and Genetics," in *Current Directions in Anthropology, Bulletins of the American Anthropological Asscoiation*, ed. A. Fischer, 3(2), Part 2:87–98.

GILES, E., C. C. CURTAIN, AND A. BAUMGARTEN
1967 "Distribution of β-Thalassemia Trait and Erythrocyte Glucose-6-Phosphate Dehydrogenase Deficiency in the Markham River Valley of New Guinea," *American Journal of Physical Anthropology* 27:83–88.

GILES, E., E. OGAN, AND A. G. STEINBERG
1965 "Gamma Globulin Factors (Gm and Inv) in New Guinea: Anthropological Significance," *Science* 150:1158–60.

GILES, E., E. OGAN, R. J. WALSH, AND M. A. BRADLEY
1966 "Blood Group Genetics of Natives of the Morobe District and Bougainville, Territory of New Guinea," *Archaeology and Physical Anthropology in Oceania* 1:135–54.

GILES, E., R. J. WALSH, AND M. A. BRADLEY
1966 "Microevolution in New Guinea: The Role of Genetic Drift," *Annals of the New York Academy of Science* 134:655–65.

GILES, E., S. WYBER, AND R. J. WALSH
1970 "Microevolution in New Guinea: Additional Evidence for Genetic Drift," *Archaeology and Physical Anthropology in Oceania* 5:60–72.

GLADWIN, T.
1970 *East Is a Big Bird* (Cambridge, Massachusetts: Harvard University Press).

GLASS, B.
1955 "On the Unlikelihood of Significant Admixture of Genes from the North American Indians in the Present Composition of the Negroes of the United States," *American Journal of Human Genetics* 7:368–85.

GLASS, B. AND C. C. LI
1953 "The Dynamics of Racial Intermixture–An Analysis of the American Negro," *American Journal of Human Genetics* 5:1–20.

GLASS, B., M. S. SACKS, E. F. JAHN, AND C. HESS
1952 "Genetic Drift in a Religious Isolate: An Analysis of the Causes of Variation in Blood Group and Other Gene Frequencies in a Small Population," *American Naturalist* 86:145–59.

GOMILA, J.
1971 *Les Bedik (Sénégal Oriental): Barrières Culturelles et Hétérogénéité Biologique* (Montréal: Les Presses de l'Université de Montréal).

GOMILA, J. AND L. GUYON
1969 "Etude Comparative de Petites Communautés Rurales. Méthode et Premiers Résultats à Propos de la Consanguinité a Bois-Vert Quebec," *Population* 24: 1127–53.

GOODALL, D. W.
1969 "Simulating the Grazing System," in *Concepts and Models of Biomathematics. Simulation Techniques and Methods*, ed. F. Heinmets (New York: Marcel Dekker), pp. 211–36.

GOODENOUGH, W. H.
1951 "Property, Kin and Community on Truk," *Yale University Publications in Anthropology* 46.
1953 *Native Astronomy in the Central Carolines*, University Museum, University of Pennsylvania (Museum Monographs).
1955 "A Problem in Malayo-Polynesian Social Organization," *American Anthropologist* 57:71–83.

GOODMAN, M., J. BARNABAS, G. MATSUDA, AND G. W. MOORE
1971 "Molecular Evolution in the Descent of Man," *Nature* 233:604–13.

GOODMAN, M., G. W. MOORE, W. FARRIS, AND E. POULIK
1970 "The Evidence from Genetically Informative Macromolecules on the Phylogenetic Relationship of the Chimpanzees," in *The Chimpanzee*, ed. G. H. Bourne (New York: Karger), pp. 318–60.

GRAYDON, J. J., N. M. SEMPLE, R. T. SIMMONS, AND S. FRANKEN
1958 "Blood Groups in Pygmies of the Wissellakes in Netherlands New Guinea," *American Journal of Physical Anthropology* 16:149–71.

GREENE, L.
1972 "Physical Growth and Development, Neurological Maturation, and Behavioral Functioning in Two Ecuadorean Communities in Which Goiter Is Endemic," American Association of Physical Anthropologists Meetings, Kansas.

GULLAHORN, J. T. AND J. E. GULLAHORN
1964 "Computer Simulation of Human Interaction in Small Groups," *1964 Spring Joint Computer Conference Proceedings* 25:103–13.
1965 "The Computer as a Tool for Theory Development," in *The Use of Computers in Anthropology*, ed. D. H. Hymes (The Hague: Mouton), pp. 427–48.

HADDON, A. C.
1925 *The Races of Man* (New York: Macmillan).

466

References

HÄGERSTRAND, T.

1953   *The Propagation of Innovation Waves* (Royal Universities of Lund: Lund Studies in Geography).

HAINLINE, J.

1963   "Genetic Exchange: Model Construction and a Practical Application," *Human Biology* 35:167–91.

1966   "Population and Genetic (Serological) Variability in Micronesia," *Annals of the New York Academy of Science* 134:639–54.

HAJNAL, J.

1963   "Random Mating and the Frequency of Consanguineous Marriages," *Proceedings of the Royal Society, Part B* 159:125–77.

HALBERSTEIN, R. A. AND M. H. CRAWFORD

1971   "Human Biology of Tlaxcala, Mexico. I. Demography," *American Journal of Physical Anthropology* (in press).

HALDANE, J. B. S.

1930   "A Mathematical Theory of Natural and Artificial Selection. VI. Isolation," *Proceedings of the Cambridge Philosophical Society* 26:220–30.

1940a "The Blood Group Frequencies of European Peoples, and Racial Origins," *Human Biology* 12:457–80.

1940b "The Conflict Between Selection and Mutation of Harmful Recessive Genes," *Annals of Eugenics* 10:417–21.

1954   "The Measurement of Natural Selection," *Proceedings of the Ninth International Congress of Genetics, Bellagio (Como.), 24–31 August 1953,* 1:480–87.

1961   "Natural Selection in Man," *Progress in Medical Genetics* 1:27–37.

HALDANE, J. B. S. AND P. MOSHINSKY

1939   "Inbreeding in Mendelian Populations with Special Reference to Human Cousin Marriage," *Annals of Eugenics* 9:321–40.

HALLOWELL, A. I.

1937   "Cross-Cousin Marriage in the Lake Winnipeg Area," *Publications of the Philadelphia Anthropological Society,* ed. D. S. Davidson, 1:95–110.

HAMMEL, E. A.

1964   "Territorial Patterning of Marriage Relationships in a Coastal Peruvian Village," *American Anthropologist* 66:67–74.

HAMMOND, D. T. AND C. E. JACKSON

1957   "Consanguinity in a Midwestern United States Isolate," *American Journal of Human Genetics* 9:61–63.

HANNEMAN, G. J., T. W. CARROLL, E. M. ROGERS, J. D. STANFIELD, AND N. LIN

1969   "Computer Simulation of Innovation Diffusion in a Peasant Village," *American Behavioral Science* 12(6):36–45.

HARDING, T. G.

1960   "Adaptations and Stability," in *Evolution and Culture,* ed. M. D. Sahlins and E. R. Service (Ann Arbor: University of Michigan Press), pp. 45–68.

HARPENDING, H. C.

1971a "Inference in Human Population Structure Studies," *American Journal of Human Genetics* 23:536–38.

1971b "!Kung Hunter-Gatherer Population Structure" (Ph.D. dissertation, Harvard University).

HARPENDING, H. C. AND T. JENKINS

1972 "!Kung Population Structure," in *Genetic Distance*, ed. J. F. Crow (in press).

HARRIS, H.

1966 "Enzyme Polymorphism in Man," *Proceedings of the Royal Society of London* B. 164:298–310.

HARRIS, H., D. A. HOPKINSON, E. B. ROBSON, AND M. WHITTAKER

1963 "Genetical Studies on a New Variant of Serum Cholinesterase Detected by Electrophoresis," *Annals of Human Genetics* (London) 26:359–82.

HARRISON, G. A. AND J. J. T. OWEN

1964 "Studies on the Inheritance of Human Skin Colour," *Annals of Human Genetics* (London) 28:27–38.

HASEBE, K.

1939 "The Natures of the South Sea Archipelago," *Jinruigaku Senshigaku Koza* 1:1–35.

HAYS, D. G.

1965 "Simulation: An Introduction for Anthropologists," in *The Use of Computers in Anthropology*, ed. D. H. Hymes (The Hague: Mouton), pp. 401–26.

HEER, D. M.

1967 "Intermarriage and Racial Amalgamation in the United States," *Eugenics Quarterly* 14:112–20.

HEER, D. M. AND D. O. SMITH

1968 "Mortality Level, Desired Family Size, and Population Increase," *Demography* 5:104–21.

1969 "Mortality Level, Desired Family Size, and Population Increase: Further Variations on a Basic Model," *Demography* 6:141–49.

HEINMETS, F.

1969 *Concepts and Models of Biomathematics. Simulation Techniques and Methods* (New York: Marcel Dekker).

HENRY, L.

1961 "Some Data on Natural Fertility," *Eugenics Quarterly* 8(2):81–91.

HERNDON, C. N. AND E. R. KERLEY

1952 "Cousin Marriage Rates in Western Carolina," paper presented at the 1952 meetings of the American Society of Human Genetics.

HERSKOVITZ, M. J.

1930 *The Anthropometry of the American Negro* (New York: Columbia University Press).

HERTZOG, K. P. AND F. E. JOHNSTON

1968 "Selection and the Rh Polymorphism," *Human Biology* 40:86–97.

HEUCH, I.

1972 "The Effects of a Fusion of Subpopulations on the Total Fixation Index," *Theoretically Applied Genetics* 42:327–30.

HEYDON, G. M. AND T. W. MURPHY

1924 "The 'Biochemical Index' in Natives of the Territory of New Guinea," Supplement to *Medical Journal of Australia* 1:235–36.

References

HICKEY, R. J., D. E. BOYCE, E. B. HARNER, AND R. C. CLELLAND

1970a "Ecological Statistical Studies Concerning Environmental Pollution and Chronic Disease," *I. E. E. E. Transactions on Geoscience Electronics* GE–8, No. 4 (October):186–202.

1970b "Exploratory Ecological Studies of Variables Related to Chronic Disease Mortality Rates," University of Pennsylvania Publication, Philadelphia, Institute for Environmental Studies.

HIERNAUX, J.

1956 "Analyse de la Variation des Caractères Physiques Humains en une Region de l'Afrique Centrale: Ruanda-Urandi et Kivu," *Annales du Musée Royal du Congo Belge* (Series 8, Science de l'Homme) 3:1–131.

1963 "Heredity and Environment: Their Influence on Human Morphology. A Comparison of Two Independent Lines of Study," *American Journal of Physical Anthropology* 21:575–89.

1966 "Human Biological Diversity in Central Africa," *Man* 1:287–306.

HILL, W. W.

1940 "Some Aspects of Navajo Political Structure," *Plateau* 13:23–28.

HIORNS, R. W., G. A. HARRISON, A. J. BOYCE, AND C. F. KUCHEMANN

1969 "A Mathematical Analysis of the Effects of Movement on the Relatedness Between Populations," *Annals of Human Genetics* (London) 32:237–50.

HIRSCHFELD, J. AND L. BECKMAN

1961 "Distribution of the Gc-Serum Groups in Northern and Central Sweden," *Acta Genetica et Statistica Medica* (Basel) 11:185–96.

HIRSZFELD, L. AND H. HIRSZFELD

1919 "Serological Differences between the Blood of Different Races," *The Lancet* 197(2):675–79.

HOLMBERG, I.

1968 *Demographic Models* (Sweden: Demographic Institute, University of Göteborg), Reports 8.

1970 *Fecundity, Fertility, and Family Planning. Application of Demographic Micromodels* (Sweden: Demographic Institute, University of Göteborg), Reports 10.

HOMANS, G. C.

1961 *Social Behavior: Its Elementary Forms* (New York: Harcourt, Brace and World).

HOOTON, E. A.

1931 *Up From the Ape* (New York: Macmillan).

1946 *Up From the Ape*, rev. ed. (New York: Macmillan).

HORVITZ, D. G., F. G. GIESBRECHT, B. V. SHAH, AND P. A. LACHENBRUCH

1971 "POPSIM, a Demographic Microsimulation Program," in Monograph 12, Carolina Population Center, Chapel Hill, University of North Carolina.

HOWARD, J. AND B. L. HOLMAN

1970 "The Effects of Race and Occupation on Hypertension Mortality," *Milbank Memorial Fund Quarterly* 48:263–96.

HOWELL, N.

1973 "The Population of the Dobe Area !Kung Bushmen (zun/wasi)," paper presented at the American Anthropological Association Meetings, New York, November 1971.

HOWELLS, W. W.

1953   "Correlations of Brothers in Factor Scores," *American Journal of Physical Anthropology* 11:121–40.

1959   *Mankind in the Making* (New York: Doubleday).

1966a "Population Distances: Biological, Linguistic, Geographical, and Environmental," *Current Anthropology* 7:531–40.

1966b "Variability in Family Lines vs. Population Variability," *Annals of the New York Academy of Science* 134(2):624–31.

1970a "Anthropometric Grouping Analysis of Pacific Peoples," *Archaeology and Physical Anthropology in Oceania* 5:192–217.

1970b "Multivariate Analysis of Human Crania," *Proceedings of the Eighth International Congress of Anthropological and Ethnological Sciences* 1:1–3.

1973   "Cranial Variation in Man. A Study by Multivariate Analysis of Patterns of Difference Among Recent Human Populations," *Papers*, Peabody Museum, Vol. 67.

HOYER, B. H., B. J. MCCARTHY, AND E. T. BOLTON

1964   "A Molecular Approach to the Systematics of Higher Organisms," *Science* 144:959–67.

HUANG, S. AND T. BAYLESS

1967   "Lactose Intolerance in Healthy Children," *New England Journal of Medicine* 276:1283–87.

HUBINOT, P. O., J. HIERNAUX, J. MASSANT-GUIOT, AND
TH. MASSANT-GUIOT

1953   "Frequence des Genes Conditionnant l'Apparition des Groupes Sanguins ABO, MN, et CDE-cde (Rh) Parmi les Indigenes Batutsi du Ruanda-Urundi," *Comptes Rendus des Seances et Memories de la Societé de Biologie* 146:334.

HUBINOT, P. O. AND J. SNOEK

1949   "Reparition des Genes Rh *(CDEcde)* chez les Pygmees Batswa des Ntomba," *Comptes Rendus de la Societé de Biologie* (Paris) 143:579–81.

HULSE, F. S.

1957   "Exogamie et Hétérosis," *Archives Suisse d'Anthropologie Génetica* 22:103–25.

HUNT, E. E., JR.

1950   "Discussion," *Cold Spring Harbor Symposia on Quantitative Biology* 15:314.

HUNT, E. E., JR. AND C. H. SMEDLEY

1965   "The World History of Smallpox and the Distribution of MN Blood Groups" (abstract), paper presented at meeting of American Society of Human Genetics.

HURTUBISE, R. A.

1969   "Sample Sizes and Confidence Intervals Associated with a Monte Carlo Simulation Model Possessing a Multinomial Output," *Simulation* 1969:71–77.

HUSSELS, I.

1969   "Genetic Structure of Saas, a Swiss Isolate," *Human Biology* 41:469–79.

HUSSELS, I. AND N. E. MORTON

1972   "Pingelap and Mokil Atolls: Achromatopsia," *American Journal of Human Genetics* 24:304–9.

HUSSIEN, F. H.

1971   "Endogamy in Egyptian Nubia," *Journal of Biosocial Sciences* 3:251–57.

References

HYMES, D. H.
1960 "Lexicostatistics So Far," *Current Anthropology* 1:3–44.

HYRENIUS, H.
1965 *New Technique for Studying Demographic-Social Interrelations* (Sweden: Demographic Institute, University of Göteborg), Reports 3.

HYRENIUS, H. AND I. ADOLFSSON
1964 *A Fertility Simulation Model* (Sweden: Demographic Institute, University of Göteborg), Reports 2.

HYRENIUS, H., I. ADOLFSSON, AND I. HOLMBERG
1966 *Demographic Models* (Sweden: Demographic Institute, University of Göteborg), Reports 4.

HYRENIUS, H., I. HOLMBERG, AND M. CARLSSON
1967 *Demographic Models* (Sweden: Demographic Institute, University of Göteborg), Reports 5.

IMAIZUMI, Y. AND N. E. MORTON
1969 "Isolation by Distance in Japan and Sweden Compared with Other Countries," *Human Heredity* 19:433–43.
1970 "Isolation By Distance in New Guinea and Micronesia," *Archaeology and Physical Anthropology in Oceania* 5:218–35.

IMAIZUMI, Y., N. E. MORTON, AND D. E. HARRIS
1970 "Isolation by Distance in Artificial Populations," *Genetics* 66:569–82.

ISKIKUNI, N., H. NEMOTO, J. V. NEEL, A. L. DREW, T. YANASE, AND Y. S. MATSUMOTO
1960 "Hosojima," *American Journal of Human Genetics* 12:67–75.

JACQUARD, A.
1967 "La Reproduction Humaine en Régime Malthusien. Un Modèle de Simulation par la Méthode de Monte-Carlo," *Population* 22:897–920.
1970a "Panmixie et structure des familles," *Population* 25:69–76.
1970b *Structures Génétiques des Populations* (Paris: Masson et Cie), pp. 364–70.

JENKINS, T.
1972 "Genetic Polymorphisms in Southern Africa" (Thesis, University of London).

JENKINS, T. AND V. CORFIELD
1972 "The Red-Cell Acid Phosphatase Polymorphism in Southern Africa," *Annals of Human Genetics* 35:379–91.

JENKINS, T., A. ZOUTENDYK, AND A. G. STEINBERG
1970 "Gamma Globulin Groups (Gm and Inv) of Various Southern African Populations," *American Journal of Physical Anthropology* 32:197–218.
1971 "Red-cell Enzyme Polymorphisms in the Khoisan Peoples of Southern Africa," *American Journal of Human Genetics* 23:513–32.

JENSEN, A. R.
1969 "How Much Can We Boost IQ and Scholastic Achievement?" *Harvard Educational Review* 39:1–123.

JOHNSTON, D. F.
1966 "An Analysis of Sources of Information on the Population of the Navaho," *Smithsonian Institution, Bureau of American Ethnology*, Washington, Bulletin 197.

JOHNSTON, F. E.

1970a "Genetic Anthropology: Some Considerations," in *Current Directions in Anthropology*, ed. A. Fischer, *Bulletin of the American Anthropological Association* 3(1):99–104.

1970b "Phenotypic Assortative Mating Among the Peruvian Cashinahua," *Social Biology* 17:37–42.

JOHNSTON, F. E., B. S. BLUMBERG, K. M. KENSINGER, R. L. JANTZ, AND G. F. WALKER

1969 "Serum Protein Polymorphisms Among the Peruvian Cashinahua," *American Journal of Human Genetics* 21:376–83.

JOHNSTON, F. E., R. L. JANTZ, K. M. KENSINGER, G. F. WALKER, F. H. ALLEN, JR., AND M. E. WALKER

1968 "Red Cell Groups of the Peruvian Cashinahua," *Human Biology* 40:508–16.

JOHNSTON, F. E. AND K. M. KENSINGER

1971 "Fertility and Mortality Differentials and Their Implications for Evolutionary Change Among the Peruvian Cashinahua," *Human Biology* 43:356–64.

JOHNSTON, F. E., K. M. KENSINGER, R. L. JANTZ, AND G. F. WALKER

1969 "The Population Structure of the Peruvian Cashinahua: Demographic, Genetic, and Cultural Relationships," *Human Biology* 41:29–41.

JONES, R.

1968 "The Geographical Background to the Arrival of Man in Australia and Tasmania," *Archaeology and Physical Anthropology in Oceania* 3:186–215.

JUBERG, R. C.

1970 "Blood Group Gene Frequencies in West Virginia," *American Journal of Human Genetics* 22:96–99.

JUBERG, R. C., W. J. SCHULL, H. GERSHOWITZ, AND L. M. DAVIS

1971 "Blood Group Gene Frequencies in an Amish Deme of Northern Indiana: Comparison with Other Amish Demes," *Human Biology* (in press).

KALMUS, H.

1969 "An Effect of Incomplete Population Mixture on Estimates of Frequency of Recessive Genes and of Population Mixture," *Annals of Human Genetics* (London) 32:311–13.

KARN, M. N. AND L. S. PENROSE

1951 "Birth Weight and Gestation Time in Relation to Maternal Age, Parity, and Infant Survival," *Annals of Eugenics* 15:206–33.

KATZ, S. H.

1972 "Biological Factors in Population Control," in *Population Problems and Anthropology*, ed. B. Spooner (in press).

KATZ, S. H. AND E. FOULKS

1970 "Calcium Homeostasis and Behavioral Disorders," Symposium on Human Adaptation, *American Journal of Physical Anthropology* 32:299–304.

1971 "An Ecosystems Approach to Health in the Arctic," abstract, *Second International Symposium on Circumpolar Health*. Paper in press, *Acta Sociomedica Scandinavica*, 1972.

KATZ, S. H., H. RIVINUS, AND W. BARKER

1972 "Physical Anthropology and the Biobehavioral Approach to Child Growth and

Development," American Association of Physical Anthropologists Meetings (Kansas).

KELLOCK, W. L. AND P. A. PARSONS

1970 "A Comparison of the Incidence of Minor Nonmetrical Cranial Variants in Australian Aborigines with Those of Melanesia and Polynesia," *American Journal of Physical Anthropology* 33:235–40.

KEMENY, J. G.

1961 "Mathematics Without Numbers," in *Quantity and Quality*, ed. D. Lerner (Glencoe: Free Press), pp. 35–51.

KERNER, E. H.

1962 "Gibbs Ensemble and Biological Ensemble," *Annals of the New York Academy of Science* 96:975–84.

KEYFITZ, N.

1964 "Population Trends in Newly Developing Countries," in *Population: The Vital Revolution*, ed. R. Freedman (New York: Doubleday), pp. 149–65.

1968 *Introduction to the Mathematics of Population* (Reading, Massachusetts: Addison-Wesley).

KIDD, K. K. AND L. L. CAVALLI-SFORZA

1972 "Error in the Reconstruction of Evolutionary Trees," in *Genetic Distance*, ed. J. F. Crow (New York: Plenum) (in press).

KIDD, K. K. AND L. A. SGARAMELLA-ZONTA

1971 "Phylogenetic Analysis: Concepts and Methods," *American Journal of Human Genetics* 23(3):235–52.

KIMURA, M.

1968 "Evolutionary Rate at the Molecular Level," *Nature* 217:624–26.

1969 "The Rate of Molecular Evolution Considered from the Standpoint of Population Genetics," *Proceedings of the National Academy of Science* 63:1181–88.

KIMURA, M. AND T. OHTA

1969 "The Average Number of Generations Until Fixation of a Mutant Gene in a Finite Population," *Genetics* 61:763–71.

KIMURA, M. AND G. H. WEISS

1964 "The Steppingstone Model of Population Structure and the Decrease of Genetic Correlation with Distance," *Genetics* 49:561–76.

KING, C. E. AND W. W. ANDERSON

1971 "Age-Specific Selection. II. The Interaction Between 'r' and 'K' Selection During Population Growth," *American Naturalist* 105:137–56.

KING, J. L. AND T. H. JUKES

1969 "Non-Darwinian Evolution," *Science* 164:788–98.

KIRKMAN, H. N. AND E. M. HENDERSON

1963 "Sex-Linked Electrophoretic Difference in Glucose-6-Phosphate Dehydrogenase," *American Journal of Human Genetics* 15:241–58.

KLEIN, D. AND F. AMMANN

1964 "Geographical Distribution of Some Isolates with Neuro-Genetical Affections in Switzerland," *Journal of Human Genetics* 13:122–32.

473

KLUCKHOHN, C.

1956 "Aspects of the Demographic History of a Small Population," in *Estudios Anthropológicos*, ed. J. Comas (Mexico City), pp. 359–79.

1966 "The Ramah Navajo," *Smithsonian Institution, Bureau of American Ethnology*, Washington, Anthropological Papers, Bulletin 196, Number 79, pp. 327–77.

KLUCKHOHN, C. AND C. GRIFFITH

1951 "Population Genetics and Social Anthropology," *Cold Spring Harbor Symposia on Quantitative Biology* 15:129–40.

KLUCKHOHN, C. AND D. LEIGHTON

1962 *The Navaho*, rev. ed. (New York: Doubleday).

KOHNE, D. E.

1970 "Evolution of Higher Organisms DNA," *Quarterly Review of Biophysics* 3:327–75.

KOBAYASHI, K.

1969 "Changing Patterns of Differential Fertility in the Population of Japan," *Proceedings of the Eighth International Congress of Anthropological and Ethnological Sciences*, Tokyo, 1:345–47.

KOJIMA, K. I. AND T. M. KELLEHER

1962 "Survival of Mutant Genes," *American Naturalist* 96:329–46.

KRAUS, B. S. AND C. B. WHITE

1956 "Micro-Evolution in a Human Population—A Study of Social Endogamy and Blood Type Distribution in the Western Apache," *American Anthropologist* 58:1017–41.

KRIEGER, H.

1969 "Inbreeding Effects on Metrical Traits in Northeastern Brazil," *American Journal of Human Genetics* 21(6):537–46.

KRIEGER, H., N. E. MORTON, M. P. MI, E. AZEVÊDO, A. FREIRE-MAIA, AND N. YASUDA

1965 "Racial Admixture in Northeastern Brazil," *Annals of Human Genetics* (London) 29:113–25.

KROEBER, A. L.

1958 "Romance History and Glottochronology," *Language* 34:454–57.

KRZANOWSKI, W. J.

1971 "A Comparison of Some Distance Measures Applicable to Multinomial Data, Using a Rotational Fit Technique," *Biometrics* 27:1062–68.

KÜCHEMANN, C. F., A. J. BOYCE, AND G. A. HARRISON

1967 "A Demographic and Genetic Study of a Group of Oxfordshire Villages," *Human Biology* 39:251–76.

KUDO, A.

1962 "A Method for Calculating the Inbreeding Coefficient," *American Journal of Human Genetics* 14:426–32.

KUDO, A. AND K. SAKAGUCHI

1963 "A Method for Calculating the Inbreeding Coefficient. II. Sex-Linked Genes," *American Journal of Human Genetics* 15:476–80.

References

KUNSTADTER, P., R. BUHLER, F. STEPHAN, AND C. F. WESTOFF
1963 "Demographic Variability and Preferential Marriage Patterns," *American Journal of Physical Anthropology* 21:511–19.

KURCZYNSKI, T. W.
1970 "Generalized Distance and Discrete Variables," *Biometrics* 26:525–34.

KURCZYNSKI, T. W. AND A. G. STEINBERG
1967 "A General Program for Maximum Likelihood Estimation of Gene Frequencies," *American Journal of Human Genetics* 19:178–79.

LALOUEL, J. M. AND N. E. MORTON
1972 "Structure of a South American Indian Population" (in preparation).

LANDGRAF, J. L.
1954 "Land-Use in the Ramah Area of New Mexico: An Anthropological Approach to Areal Study," *Peabody Museum American Archaeology and Ethnology Papers* (Cambridge, Massachusetts) Vol. 42, No. 1.

LANGLEY, G. R., F. R. TODD, AND A. J. BISHOP
1969 "Glucose-6-Phosphate Dehydrogenase Deficiency in Canadian Negroes," *Canadian Medical Association Journal* 100:973–77.

LARSON, C. A.
1955 "The Frequency of First Cousin Marriages in a South Swedish Rural Community," *American Journal of Human Genetics* 7:151–53.

LASKER, G. W.
1954 "Human Evolution in Contemporary Communities," *Southwestern Journal of Anthropology* 10:353–65.
1960a "Migration, Isolation and Ongoing Human Evolution," *Human Biology* 32: 80–88.
1960b "Variance of Bodily Measurements in the Offspring of Natives of and Immigrants to Three Peruvian Towns," *American Journal of Physical Anthropology* 18:257–61.
1962 "Differences in Anthropometric Measurements Within and Between Three Communities in Peru," *Human Biology* 34:63–70.
1969 "Isonymy (Recurrence of the Same Surnames in Affinal Relatives): A Comparison of Rates Calculated from Pedigrees, Grave Markers, and Death and Birth Registers," *Human Biology* 41:309–21.
1970 "Physical Anthropology: The Search for General Processes and Principles," *American Anthropologist* 72:1–8.
1973 *Physical Anthropology* (New York: Holt, Rinehart & Winston).

LASKER, G. W. AND B. A. KAPLAN
1964 "The Coefficient of Breeding Isolation: Population Size, Migration Rates, and the Possibilities for Random Genetic Drift in Six Human Communities in Northern Peru," *Human Biology* 36:327–38.

LAUGHLIN, W. S.
1950 "Blood Groups, Morphology, and Population Size of the Eskimos," *Cold Spring Harbor Symposia on Quantitative Biology* 15:165–73.

LAUGHLIN, W. S. AND J. B. JØRGENSEN
1956 "Isolate Variation in Greenlandic Eskimo Crania," *Acta Genetica et Statistica Medica* (Basel) 6:3–12.

LAYRISSE, M., Z. LAYRISSE, AND J. WILBERT
1963 "The Blood Groups of Northern Continental Caribs," *Human Biology* 35: 140–64.

LEACH, E. R.
1961 *Rethinking Anthropology* (University of London: Athlone Press).

LEHMANN, H. AND E. W. IKIN
1954 "Study of Andamanese Negritos," *Transactions of the Royal Society of Tropical Medicine and Hygiene* 48:12–15.

LEHMANN, H. AND J. LIDDELL
1966 "Pseudocholinesterase Deficiency and Some Pharmacogenetic Disorders," in *The Metabolic Basis of Inherited Diseases*, ed. J. Stanbury, D. Fredrickson, and J. Wyngaarden (New York: McGraw-Hill), pp. 1356–69.

LENFANT, C., J. D. TORRANCE, E. ENGLISH, C. A. FINCH, C. REYNA-FARJE, J. RAMOS, AND J. FAURA
1968 "Effect of Altitude on Oxygen Binding by Hemoglobin and on Organic Phosphate Levels," *The Journal of Clinical Investigation* 47:2652–56.

LENFANT, C., J. D. TORRANCE, R. D. WOODSON, P. JACOBS, AND C. A. FINCH
1970 "Role of Organic Phosphates in the Adaptation of Man to Hypoxia," *Proceedings of the Annual Meeting of the Federation of American Societies for Experimental Biology*, Vol. 29, No. 3, May–June.

LEVIN, B. R.
1967 "The Effect of Reproductive Compensation on the Long Term Maintenance of the Rh Polymorphism: The Rh Crossroad Revisited," *American Journal of Human Genetics* 19:288–302.
1969 "Simulation of Genetic Systems," in *Computer Applications in Genetics*, ed. N. E. Morton (Honolulu: University of Hawaii Press), pp. 34–48.

LÉVI-STRAUSS, C.
1969 *The Elementary Structures of Kinship* (Boston: Beacon Press).

LEWIS, W. H. P. AND H. HARRIS
1967 "Human Red Cell Peptidases," *Nature* 215:351–55.
1968 "Pep A 5-1 and Pep A 6-1. Two New Variants of Peptidase A with Features of Special Interest," *Annals of Human Genetics* (London) 32:35–42.
1969 "Peptidase D (Polidase) Variants in Man," *Annals of Human Genetics* (London) 32:317–22.

LEWONTIN, R. C.
1967 "An Estimate of Average Heterozygosity in Man," *American Journal of Human Genetics* 19:681–85.
1969 "The Meaning of Stability," in *Diversity and Stability in Ecological Systems*, Brookhaven Symposia in Biology, 22:13–24.

LEWONTIN, R. C. AND J. KRAKAUER
1972 "Distribution of Gene Frequency as a Test of the Theory of the Selective Neutrality of Polymorphisms," *Genetics* (in press).

LI, C. C.
1955 *Population Genetics* (Chicago: University of Chicago Press).
1958 *Population Genetics*, 2d. ed. (Chicago: University of Chicago Press).

References

LI, C. C. AND D. G. HORVITZ
1953 "Some Methods of Estimating the Inbreeding Coefficient," *American Journal of Human Genetics* 5:107–17.

LITTMAN, A., A. CADY, AND J. RHODES
1968 "Lactase and Other Disaccharidase Deficiencies in a Hospital Population," *Israel Journal of Medical Science* 4:110–16.

LIVINGSTONE, F. B.
1958 "Anthropological Implications of Sickle Cell Gene Distribution in West Virginia," *American Anthropologist* 60:533.
1960 "Natural Selection, Disease, and Ongoing Human Evolution, as Illustrated by the ABO Blood Groups," *Human Biology* 32:17–27.
1964a "Aspects of the Population Dynamics of the Abnormal Hemoglobin and Glucose-6-Phosphate Dehydrogenase Deficiency Genes," *American Journal of Human Genetics* 16:435–50.
1964b "On the Nonexistence of Human Races," in *The Concept of Race*, ed. A. Montagu (London: Collier-Macmillan Ltd.).
1969a "The Founder Effect and Deleterious Genes," *American Journal of Physical Anthropology* 30:55–60.
1969b "Gene Frequency Clines of the β Hemoglobin Locus in Various Human Populations and Their Simulation by Models Involving Differential Selection," *Human Biology* 41:223–36.
1969c "Polygenic Models for the Evolution of Human Skin Color Differences," *Human Biology* 41:480–93.

LONG, A.
1965 Smithsonian Institution Radiocarbon Measurements II. *Radiocarbon* Ponape series samples collected in 1963 by Evans, Meggers, and Riesenberg. Submitted by Evans. *American Journal of Science* 7:253.

MACCLUER, J. W.
1967 "Monte Carlo Methods in Human Population Genetics: A Computer Model Incorporating Age-Specific Birth and Death Rates," *American Journal of Human Genetics* 19:303–12.
1968 "Studies in Genetic Demography by Monte Carlo Simulation" (Ph.D. dissertation, University of Michigan).
1972 "Monte Carlo Simulation: The Effects of Migration on Some Measures of Genetic Distance," in *Volume on Genetic Distance*, ed. J. F. Crow (New York: Plenum Press) (in press).

MACCLUER, J. W., R. GRIFFITH, C. F. SING, AND W. J. SCHULL
1967 "Some Genetic Programs to Supplement Self-Instruction in FORTRAN," *American Journal of Human Genetics* 19:189–221.

MACCLUER, J. W. AND J. V. NEEL
1972 "Genetic Structure of a Primitive Population: A Simulation" (in preparation).

MACCLUER, J. W., J. V. NEEL, AND N. A. CHAGNON
1971 "Demographic Structure of a Primitive Population: A Simulation," *American Journal of Physical Anthropology* 35:193–208.

MACCLUER, J. W. AND W. J. SCHULL
1970a "Estimating the Effective Size of Human Populations," *American Journal of Human Genetics* 22:176–83.

477

1970b "Frequencies of Consanguineous Marriage and Accumulation of Inbreeding in an Artificial Population," *American Journal of Human Genetics* 22:160–75.

MACINTOSH, N. W. G., R. J. WALSH, AND O. KOOPTZOFF
1958   "The Blood Groups of the Native Inhabitants of the Western Highlands, New Guinea," *Oceania* 28:173–98.

MACLEAN, A. J.
n.d.   "Development of Lasts and Footwear for Pacific Islanders from the Foot Survey of Indigenous Soldiers of Papua, New Guinea, 1967," Headquarters Army Inspection Service, Albert Park Barracks, Melbourne.

MACLEAN, C.
1969   "Computer Analysis of Pedigree Data," *Computer Applications in Genetics*, ed. N. E. Morton (Honolulu: University of Hawaii Press), pp. 82–86.

MACLEAN, C. J. AND P. L. WORKMAN
1973a "Genetic Studies on Hybrid Populations. I. Individual Estimates of Ancestry and Their Relation to Observations on Quantitative Traits," *Annals of Human Genetics* (London), in press.
1973b "Genetic Studies on Hybrid Populations. II. Estimation of the Distribution of Ancestry," *Annals of Human Genetics* (London), in press.

MACMAHON, B. AND J. C. FOLUSIAK
1958   "Leukemia and ABO Blood Groups," *American Journal of Human Genetics* 10:287–93.

MAHALANOBIS, P. C., D. N. MAJUMDAR, AND C. R. RAO
1949   "Anthropometric Survey of the United Provinces, 1941," *Sankhya* 9:89–324.

MAKELA, O., A. W. ERIKSSON, AND R. LEHTOVAARA
1959   "On the Inheritance of the Haptoglobin Serum Groups," *Acta Genetica et Statistica Medica* (Basel) 9:149–66.

MALCOLM, L. A.
1969a "Determination of the Growth Curve of the Kukukuku People of New Guinea from Dental Eruption in Children and Adult Height," *Archaeology and Physical Anthropology in Oceania* 4:72–78.
1969b "Growth and Development of the Kaiapit Children of the Markham Valley, New Guinea," *American Journal of Physical Anthropology* 31:39–51.
1970   "Growth and Development of the Bundi Child of the New Guinea Highlands," *Human Biology* 42:293–328.

MALÉCOT, G.
1948   *Les Mathématiques de l'Hérédité* (Paris: Masson et Cie).
1959   "Les Modèles Stochastique en Génétique de Population," *Pub. Inst. Statist. Univ. de Paris* 8:173–210.
1966   *Probabilitié et Hérédité* (Paris: Presse Universitaire de France).
1969a "Consanguinité Panmictique et Consanguinité Systématique," *Annales de Génétiques et de Selection Animale* (France) 1:237–42.
1969b *The Mathematics of Heredity* (San Francisco: W. H. Freeman).

MALINOWSKI, B.
1913   *The Family Among the Australian Aborigines* (London: Hodder). Reprinted with an Introduction by J. A. Barnes (New York: Schocken Books, 1963).

478

References

MANGE, A. P.
1964 "Growth and Inbreeding of a Human Isolate," *Human Biology* 36:104–33.
1969 "Wright's Coefficient of Inbreeding, F, for Human Pedigrees," in *Computer Applications in Genetics*, ed. N. E. Morton (Honolulu: University of Hawaii Press), pp. 72–78.

MARCALLO, F. A., N. FREIRE-MAIA, J. B. C. AZEVÊDO, AND I. A. SIMÕES
1964 "Inbreeding Effect on Mortality and Morbidity in South Brazilian Populations," *Annals of Human Genetics* (London) 27:203–18.

MARSHALL, D. AND E. GILES
n.d. "Polynesian Prehistory: Interpretations from the D^2 Technique in Craniometry, Integrated with Lexico-statistics" (unpublished).

MARTIN, F. F.
1968 *Computer Modeling and Simulation* (New York: Wiley & Sons).

MARTIN, F. G. AND C. C. COCKERHAM
1960 "High-Speed Selection Studies," in *Biometrical Genetics*, ed. O. Kempthorne (Elmsford, New York: Pergamon Press), pp. 35–45.

MARTIN, M. A. AND B. H. HOYER
1967 "Adenine Plus Thymine and Guanine Plus Cytosine Enriched Fractions of Animal DNA's as Indicators of Polynucleotide Homologies," *Journal of Molecular Biology* 27:113–29.

MARUYAMA, M.
1968 "The Second Cybernetics: Deviation-Amplifying Mutual Causal Processes," in *Modern Systems Research for the Behavioral Scientist*, ed. W. Buckley (Chicago: Aldine), pp. 304–13.

MARUYAMA, T.
1970a "Effective Number of Alleles in a Subdivided Population," *Theoretical Population Biology* 1:273–306.
1970b "On the Fixation Probability of Mutant Genes in a Subdivided Population," *Genetical Research* 15:221–25.
1970c "Rate of Decrease of Genetic Variability in a Subdivided Population," *Biometrika* 57:229–311.

MATSUNAGA, E.
1966 "Possible Genetic Consequences of Family Planning," *Journal of the American Medical Association* 198:533–40.

MAYBURY-LEWIS, D.
1967 "The Murngin Moral," *Transactions of the New York Academy of Science* II 29(4):482–94.

MAYR, E.
1963 *Animal Species and Evolution* (Cambridge, Massachusetts: Harvard University Press).

MCCRACKEN, R. D.
1971 "Lactase Deficiency: An Example of Dietary Evolution," *Current Anthropology* 12(4–5):497–517.

MCDERMOTT, W., K. W. DEUSCHLE, AND C. R. BARNETT
1972 "Health Care Experiment at Many Farms," *Science* 175:23–31.

MCHENRY, H. AND E. GILES

1971 "Morphological Variation and Heritability in Three Melanesian Populations: A Multivariate Approach," *American Journal of Physical Anthropology* 35: 241–53.

MCNITT, FRANK

1972 *Navajo Wars: Military Campaigns, Slave Raids, and Reprisals* (Albuquerque: University of New Mexico Press).

MEADOWS, D., D. MEADOWS, J. RANDERS, AND W. BEHRENS

1972 *The Limits to Growth. A Report for the Club of Rome's Project on the Predicament of Mankind* (New York: Universe Books).

MEIER, A.

1949 "A Study of the Racial Ancestry of the Mississippi College Negro," *American Journal of Physical Anthropology* 7:227–39.

MELARTIN, L.

1965 "Studies on the Gc System in Finns and Lapps,"*Acta Genetica et Statistica Medica* (Basel) 15:45–50.

MELARTIN, L. AND E. KAARSALO

1965 "The Distribution of Transferrin Variants in Southwestern Finland and in Finnish Lapland," *Acta Genetica et Statistica Medica* (Basel) 15:63–69.

MICHENER, J. A. AND A. G. DAY

1957 *Rascals in Paradise* (New York: Random House).

MORGAN, K.

1968 "The Genetic Demography of a Small Navajo Community" (Ph.D. dissertation, University of Michigan).

1969 "Monte Carlo Simulation of Artificial Populations: The Survival of Small, Closed Populations," paper presented at the Conference on the Mathematics of Population (California: Berkeley and Asilomar).

MORGAN, L. H.

1871 "Systems of Consanguinity and Affinity of the Human Family," *Smithsonian Contributions to Knowledge* 17:1–590.

MORNING HERALD

1834 May 6. Sydney, Australia.

MORONI, A.

1966 "La Consanguineità Umana in Sardegna," *Ateneo Parmense* 87:3–28.

MORSE, R. M.

1953 "The Negro in São Paulo, Brazil," *Journal of Negro History* 38:290–306.

MORTON, N. E.

1955 "Non-Randomness in Consanguineous Marriage," *Annals of Human Genetics* (London) 20:116–24.

1958 "Empirical Risks in Consanguineous Marriages: Birth Weight, Gestation Time, and Measurements of Infants," *American Journal of Human Genetics* 10(3):344–49.

1968 "Problems and Methods in the Genetics of Primitive Groups," *American Journal of Physical Anthropology* 28:191–202.

1969 "Human Population Structure," *Annual Review of Genetics* 3:53–74.

References

1971a "Kinship and Population Size," in *Génétique et Populations*, Institut National d'Études Démographiques, Travaux et Documents Cahier No. 60 (Paris: Presses Universitaires de France), pp. 103–10.
1971b "Letter to the Editor: Inference in Population Structure Studies," *American Journal of Human Genetics* 23:538–39.
1972 "Pingelap and Mokil Atolls: Clans and Cognate Frequencies," *American Journal of Human Genetics* 24:290–98.

MORTON, N. E. AND D. L. GREENE
1972 "Pingelap and Mokil Atolls: Anthropometrics," *American Journal of Human Genetics* 24:299–303.

MORTON, N. E., D. E. HARRIS, S. YEE, AND R. LEW
1971a "Pingelap and Mokil Atolls: Migration," *American Journal of Human Genetics* 23:339–49.

MORTON, N. E. AND I. HUSSELS
1970 "Demography of Inbreeding in Switzerland," *Human Biology* 42:65–78.

MORTON, N. E., Y. IMAIZUMI, AND D. E. HARRIS
1971 "Clans as Genetic Barriers," *American Anthropologist* 73:1005–10.

MORTON, N. E., H. KRIEGER, AND M. P. MI
1966 "Natural Selection on Polymorphisms in Northeastern Brazil," *American Journal of Human Genetics* 18:153–71.

MORTON, N. E. AND J. M. LALOUEL
1972a "Bioassay of Kinship in Micronesia" (in preparation).
1972b "Topology of Kinship in Micronesia" (in preparation).

MORTON, N. E., R. LEW, I. E. HUSSELS, AND G. F. LITTLE
1972 "Pingelap and Mokil Atolls: Historical Genetics," *American Journal of Human Genetics* 24:277–89.

MORTON, N. E., C. MIKI, AND S. YEE
1968 "Bioassay of Population Structure Under Isolation by Distance," *American Journal of Human Genetics* 20(5):411–19.

MORTON, N. E., I. ROISENBERG, R. LEW, AND S. YEE
1971b "Pingelap and Mokil Atolls: Genealogy," *American Journal of Human Genetics* 23:350–60.

MORTON, N. E. AND N. YASUDA
1962 "The Genetical Structure of Human Populations," in *Human Displacements*, ed. J. Sutter (Monaco), pp. 183–203.

MORTON, N. E., N. YASUDA, C. MIKI, AND S. YEE
1968 "Population Structure of the ABO Blood Groups in Switzerland," *American Journal of Human Genetics* 20:420–29.

MORTON, N. E., S. YEE, D. E. HARRIS, AND R. LEW
1971c "Bioassay of Kinship," *Theoretical Population Biology* 2:507–24.

MOTULSKY, A. G.
1965 "Theoretical and Clinical Problems of Glucose-6-Phosphate Dehydrogenase Deficiency," in *Abnormal Haemoglobins in Africa*, ed. J. H. P. Jonxis (Oxford: Blackwell Scientific Publication), pp. 143–96.

MOTULSKY, A. G. AND J. M. CAMPBELL-KRAUT
1960   "Population Genetics of Glucose-6-Phosphate Dehydrogenase Deficiency of the Red Cell," *Proceedings of the Conference on Genetic Polymorphisms and Geographical Variations in Disease*, ed. B. S. Blumberg (New York: Grune and Stratton).

MOTULSKY, A. G., J. VANDEPITTE, AND G. R. FRASER
1966   "Population Genetic Studies in the Congo. I. Glucose-6-Phosphate Dehydrogenase Deficiency, Hemoglobin S, and Malaria," *American Journal of Human Genetics* 18:514–37.

MOURANT, A. E.
1954   *The Distribution of the Human Blood Groups* (Springfield, Illinois: Charles C Thomas).

MOURANT, A. E., A. C. KOPEC, AND K. DOMANIEWSKA-SOBCZAK
1958   *The ABO Blood Groups* (Springfield, Illinois: Charles C Thomas).

MUGNIER, M., J. SUTTER, AND J. M. COX
1966   "Organigrammes pour l'Étude Mécanographique de la Parenté et de la Fécondité dans une Population," *Population* 21:75–98.

MURPHY, R. F. AND L. KASDAN
1959   "The Structure of Parallel Cousin Marriage," *American Anthropologist* 61:17–29.

NAGEL, R. AND O. SOTO
1964   "Haptoglobin Types in Native Chileans: A Hybrid Population," *American Journal of Physical Anthropology* 22:335–38.

NAUTICAL MAGAZINE
1854   March: 1832–70, London.

NAUTICAL MAGAZINE
1870   London.

NAVAJO AREA POPULATION REGISTER, 1970
1971   *Navajo Area Population Register, Age Group by Sex* (Window Rock, Arizona: Bureau of Indian Affairs, Office of Information and Statistics).

NAYLOR, T. H.
1969   *The Design of Computer Simulation Experiments* (Durham, North Carolina: Duke University Press).

NAYLOR, T. H., J. L. BALINTFY, D. S. BURDICK, AND K. CHU
1966   *Computer Simulation Techniques* (New York: Wiley & Sons).

NEEDHAM, R.
1958   "A Structural Analysis of Purum Society," *American Anthropologist* 60:75–101.

NEEL, J. V.
1967   "The Genetic Structure of Primitive Human Populations," *Japanese Journal of Human Genetics* 12(1):1–16.
1969   "Some Changing Constraints on the Human Evolutionary Process," *Proceedings of the Twelfth International Congress of Genetics* (Tokyo, 1968) 3:389–403.
1970   "Lessons from a 'Primitive' People," *Science* 170:815–22.

References

1971 "Genetic Aspects of the Ecology of Disease in the American Indian," in *The Ongoing Evolution of Latin American Populations*, ed. F. M. Salzano (Springfield, Illinois: Charles C Thomas), p. 561.

NEEL, J. V. AND N. A. CHAGNON
1968 "The Demography of Two Tribes of Primitive Relatively Unacculturated American Indians," *Proceedings of the National Academy of Science* 59:680–89.

NEEL, J. V. AND F. M. SALZANO
1964 "A Prospectus for Genetic Studies of the American Indian," *Cold Spring Symposia on Quantitative Biology* 29:85–98.
1966 "A Prospectus for Genetic Studies on the American Indians," in *The Biology of Human Adaptability*, ed. P. T. Baker and J. S. Weiner (Oxford: Clarendon Press), pp. 245–74.
1967 "Further Studies on the Xavante Indians. X. Some Hypotheses-Generalizations Resulting from These Studies," *American Journal of Human Genetics* 19:554–74.

NEEL, J. V., F. M. SALZANO, P. C. JUNQUEIRA, F. KEITER, AND D. L. MAYBURY-LEWIS
1964 "Studies on the Xavante Indians of the Brazilian Mato Grosso," *American Journal of Human Genetics* 16(1):52–140.

NEEL, J. V. AND W. SCHULL
1962 "The Effect of Inbreeding on Mortality and Morbidity in Two Japanese Cities," *Proceedings of the National Academy of Science* 48(4):573–82.
1968 "On Some Trends in Understanding the Genetics of Man," *Perspectives in Biology and Medicine* 11:565–601.

NEEL, J. V. AND R. H. WARD
1970 "Village and Tribal Genetic Distances Among American Indians and the Possible Implications for Human Evolution," *Proceedings of the National Academy of Science* 65:323–30.
1972 "The Genetic Structure of a Tribal Population, the Yanomama Indians. VI. Analysis by F Statistics (Including a Comparison with the Makiritare and Xavante)," *Genetics* 72:639–66.

NEI, M.
1965 "Variation and Covariation of Gene Frequencies in Subdivided Populations," *Evolution* 19:256–58.

NEI, M. AND Y. IMAIZUMI
1966 "Genetic Structure of Human Populations," *Heredity* 21:9–36, 183–90, 461–72.

NEMESKÉRI, J. AND A. THOMA
1961 "Ivad: An Isolate in Hungary," *Acta Genetica et Statistica Medica* (Basel) 11:230–50.

NEWCOMBE, H. B.
1967 "Record Linking: The Design of Efficient Systems for Linking Records into Individual and Family Histories," *American Journal of Human Genetics* 19:335–59.

NEWCOMBE, H. B., J. M. KENNEDY, S. J. AXFORD, AND A. P. JAMES
1959 "Automatic Linkage of Vital Records," *Science* 130:954–59.

NEWCOMBE, H. B. AND P. O. W. RHYNAS
1962 "Child Spacing Following Stillbirth and Infant Death," *Eugenics Quarterly* 9:25–35.

NISWANDER, J. D. AND C. S. CHUNG
1965 "The Effects of Inbreeding on Tooth Size in Japanese Children," *American Journal of Human Genetics* 17(5):390–98.

OLIVER, D. L.
1961 *The Pacific Islands,* rev. ed. (New York: Doubleday).

OLIVER, D. L. AND W. W. HOWELLS
1957 "Microevolution and Cultural Elements in Physical Variation," *American Anthropologist* 59:965–78.
1960 "Bougainville Populations Studied by Generalized Distance," *Proceedings of the Sixth International Congress of Anthropological and Ethnological Sciences* 1:497–502.

ORCUTT, G. H.
1963 "Views on Simulation and Models of Social Systems," in *Symposium on Simulation Models,* ed. A. C. Hoggatt and F. E. Balderston (Cincinnati: South-Western), pp. 221–36.
1965 "Data Needs for Computer Simulation of Large-Scale Social Systems," in *Computer Methods in the Analysis of Large-Scale Social Systems,* ed. J. M. Beshers (Cambridge, Massachusetts: M.I.T.-Harvard Joint Center for Urban Studies), pp. 230–39.

ORCUTT, G. H., M. GREENBERGER, J. KORBEL, AND A. M. RIVLIN
1961 *Microanalysis of Socioeconomic Systems: A Simulation Study* (New York: Harper & Row).

ORE, O.
1963 *Graphs and Their Uses* (New York: Random House).

OSBORNE, R. H. AND F. V. DE GEORGE
1959 *Genetic Basis of Morphological Variation: An Evaluation and Application of the Twin Study Method* (Cambridge, Massachusetts: Harvard University Press).

OSCHINSKY, L.
1959 "A Reappraisal of Recent Serological, Genetic, and Morphological Research on the Taxonomy of the Races of Africa and Asia," *Anthropologica* 1:1–25.

OTTENSOOSER, F., N. LEON, AND A. B. CUNHA
1961 "Beitrage zur Kenntnis der Gm-Gruppen," *Zeitschrift Fuer Immunitaets Forschung* (Stuttgart: Allergie und Klinische Immunologie) 122:165–78.

OXNARD, C. E.
1967 "The Functional Morphology of the Primate Shoulder as Revealed by Comparative Anatomical, Osteometric and Discriminant Function Techniques," *American Journal of Physical Anthropology* 26:219–40.

PARKER, C. W. AND A. G. BEARN
1961 "Haptoglobin and Transferrin Variation in Humans and Primates: Two New Transferrins in Chinese and Japanese Populations," *Annals of Human Genetics* (London) 25:227–41.

484

References

PARSONS, P. A.
1963 "Migration as a Factor in Natural Selection," *Genetica* 33:184–206.

PAPUA AND NEW GUINEA MEDICAL JOURNAL
1967 "Age Estimate of New Guinea Children," *Papua and New Guinea Medical Journal* 10:122.

PEARL, R.
1913 "A Contribution Towards an Analysis of the Problem of Inbreeding," *American Naturalist* 47:577–614.
1914 "On the Results of Inbreeding in a Mendelian Population: A Correction and Extension of Previous Conclusions," *American Naturalist* 48:57–62.
1917 "Studies on Inbreeding," *American Naturalist* 51:545–49, 636–39.

PEARSON, K.
1926 "On the Coefficient of Racial Likeness," *Biometrika* 17:105–17.

PENROSE, L. S.
1954 "Distance, Size and Shape," *Annals of Eugenics* 18:337–43.

PERRIN, E. B. AND M. C. SHEPS
1963 "A Monte Carlo Investigation of a Human Fertility Model," paper presented at the annual meeting of the American Public Health Association.
1964 "Human Reproduction: A Stochastic Process," *Biometrics* 20:28–45.

PETRAKIS, N. L., K. T. MOLOHON, AND D. J. TEPPER
1967 "Cerumen in American Indians: Genetic Implications of Sticky and Dry Types," *Science* 158:1192–93.

PIETRUSEWSKY, M.
1970 "An Osteological View of Indigenous Populations in Oceania," in *Studies in Oceanic Culture History, Volume 1, Pacific Anthropological Records, No. 11*, ed. R. C. Green and M. Kelly (Honolulu: B. P. Bishop Museum).

POLLARD, J. H.
1969 "A Discrete-Time Two-Sex Age-Specific Stochastic Population Program Incorporating Marriage," *Demography* 6:185–221.

POLLITZER, W. S.
1958 "The Negroes of Charleston (South Carolina): A Study of Hemoglobin Types, Serology and Morphology," *American Journal of Physical Anthropology* 16: 241–63.
1964 "Analysis of a Tri-Racial Isolate," *Human Biology* 36:362–73.

POLLITZER, W. S. AND W. H. BROWN
1969 "Survey of Demography, Anthropometry, and Genetics in the Melungeons of Tennessee: An Isolate of Hybrid Origin in the Process of Dissolution," *Human Biology* 41:388–400.

POLLITZER, W. S., E. BOYLE, JR., J. CORONI, AND K. K. NAMBOODIRI
1970 "Physical Anthropology of the Negroes of Charleston, South Carolina," *Human Biology* 42:265–79.

POLLITZER, W. S., R. C. HARTMANN, H. MOORE, R. E. ROSENFIELD, H. SMITH, S. HAKIM, P. J. SCHMIDT, AND W. C. LEYSHON
1962 "Blood Types of the Cherokee Indians," *American Journal of Physical Anthropology* 20:33–43.

POLLITZER, W. S., R. M. MENEGAZ-BOCK, R. CEPPELLINI, AND L. C. DUNN
1964 "Blood Factors and Morphology of the Negroes of James Island, Charleston, South Carolina," *American Journal of Physical Anthropology* 22:393–98.

POLLITZER, W. S., R. M. MENEGAZ-BOCK, AND J. C. HERRION
1966 "Factors in the Microevolution of a Triracial Isolate," *American Journal of Human Genetics* 18:26–38.

POLLOCK, N., J. M. LALOUEL, AND N. E. MORTON
1972 "Kinship and Inbreeding on Namu Atoll," *Human Biology* 44:459–74.

POLMAN, A.
1951 "Over Consanguine Huwelijken in Nederland," *Onderzoekingen en Madedelingen Uit Het Institut Voor Preventieve Geneeskunde* (Leiden) 7:5–35.

PORTER, I. H., J. SCHULZE, AND V. A. MCKUSICK
1962 "Genetic Linkage Between the Loci for Glucose-6-Phosphate Dehydrogenase Deficiency and Colour Blindness in American Negroes," *Annals of Human Genetics* (London) 26:107–22.

POTTER, R. G. AND J. M. SAKODA
1966 "A Computer Model of Family Building Based on Expected Values," *Demography* 3:450–61.

PRICE, E. T.
1953 "A Geographic Analysis of White-Negro-Indian Racial Mixtures in Eastern United States," *Annals of the Association of American Geographers* 43:138–55.

PRING, M.
1969 "The Analysis of Electron Transport Kinetics in Mitochondria," in *Concepts and Models of Biomathematics. Simulation Techniques and Methods,*" ed. F. Heinmets (New York: Marcel Dekker), pp. 75–104.

PURSER, A. F.
1966 "Increase in Heterozygote Frequency with Differential Fertility," *Heredity* 21:322–27.

RACE, R. R. AND R. SANGER
1962 *Blood Groups in Man,* 4th ed. (Philadelphia: F. A. Davis).

RADCLIFFE-BROWN, A. R.
1913 "Three Tribes of Western Australia," *Journal of the Royal Anthropological Institute* 43:143–94.

RAINIO, K.
1966 "A Study on Sociometric Group Structure: An Application of a Stochastic Theory of Social Interaction," in *Sociological Theories in Progress,* ed. J. Berger, M. Zelditch, Jr., and B. Anderson (New York: Houghton Mifflin), pp. 102–23.

RAMAH NAVAJO TRIBE
1963 Resolution Number 607–63–13. Ramah, New Mexico.

RASER, J. R.
1969 *Simulation and Society. An Exploration of Scientific Gaming* (Boston: Allyn & Bacon).

References

REED, C. A.
1960 "Polyphyletic or Monophyletic Ancestry of Mammals, or: What is a Class?"
Evolution 14:314–22.

REED, T. E.
1968 "Distribution and Tests of Independence of Seven Blood Group Systems in a
Large Multiracial Sample from California," *American Journal of Human Genetics* 20:142–50.
1969a "Caucasian Genes in American Negroes," *Science* 165:762–68.
1969b "A Genetic Experience with a General Maximum Likelihood Estimation Program," in *Computer Applications in Genetics*, ed. N. E. Morton (Honolulu:
University of Hawaii Press).
1969c "Reply to E. N. Anderson's Letter on 'Caucasian Genes in American Negroes,'" *Science* 165:1353.
1971 "Does Reproductive Compensation Exist? An Analysis of Rh Data," *American
Journal of Human Genetics* 23(2):215–24.

REED, T. E. AND W. J. SCHULL
1968 "A General Maximum Likelihood Estimation Program," *American Journal of
Human Genetics* 20:579–80.

REID, R. M.
1971 "Marriage Patterns, Demography, and Population Genetics in a South Indian
Caste: A Study of Inbreeding in a Human Population" (Ph.D. dissertation,
University of Illinois).

REINSKOW, T. AND L. KORNSTAD
1965 "The Gc Types of the Norwegian Lapps," *Acta Genetica et Statistica Medica*
(Basel) 15:126–33.

RESSILER, J. J. C. AND A. LE GROS
1957 "Groupes Sanguins Rhesus dans la Population Noire de Bukavu," *Annales de
la Société Belge. de Medicine Tropicale* (Brussels) 37:285.

REYNOLDS, T. R., L. LAMPHERE, AND C. E. COOK, JR.
1967 "Time, Resources, and Authority in a Navajo Community," *American Anthropologist* 69:188–99.

RIDLEY, J. C.
1972 "The Determinants of Human Fertility," in *Principles and Practice of Family
Planning*, International Federation of Gynecology and Obstetrics (in preparation).

RIDLEY, J. C., J. W. LINGNER, M. C. SHEPS, AND J. A. MENKEN
1967a "Effects of Natality of Alternative Family Planning Programs: Estimation via
Simulation," abstracts of contributed papers, Population Association of America, Cincinnati, Ohio, April 1967.

RIDLEY, J. C. AND M. C. SHEPS
1965 "Marriage Patterns and Natality: Preliminary Investigations with a Simulation
Model," abstracts of contributed papers, Population Association of America,
Chicago, Illinois, April 1965.
1966 "An Analytic Simulation Model of Human Reproduction with Demographic
and Biological Components," *Population Studies* 19:297–310.

RIDLEY, J. C., M. C. SHEPS, J. W. LINGNER, AND J. A. MENKEN
1967b "The Effects of Changing Mortality on Natality: Some Estimates from a Simulation Model," *The Milbank Memorial Fund Quarterly* 45:77–97.

RIESENBERG, S. H.
1965 "Table of Voyages Affecting Micronesian Islands," *Oceania* 36:155–70.

RIVERS, W. H. B.
1907 "The Marriage of Cross Cousins in India," *The Journal of the Royal Asiatic Society*, pp. 611–40.
1914 *Kinship and Social Organization* (London), reprinted in 1968, *London School of Economics Monographs in Social Anthropology*, Monograph No. 34.

ROBERTS, D. F.
1955 "The Dynamics of Racial Intermixture in the American Negro—Some Anthropological Considerations," *American Journal of Human Genetics* 7:361–67.
1956 "A Demographic Study of a Dinka Village," *Human Biology* 28:323–49.
1963 "Remarks Concerning the Communication of J. Sutter," in *The Genetics of Migrant and Isolate Populations*, ed. E. Goldschmidt.
1965 "Assumption and Fact in Anthropological Genetics," *Journal of the Royal Anthropological Institute* 95:87–103.
1967 "The Development of Inbreeding in an Island Population," *Ciência e Cultura* 19:78–84.
1968a "Differential Fertility and the Genetic Constitution of an Isolated Population," *Proceedings of the Eighth International Congress of Anthropological Sciences* 1:350–56.
1968b "Genetic Effects of Population Size Reduction," *Nature* 220:1084–88.
1968c "Genetic Fitness in a Colonizing Human Population," *Human Biology* 40: 494–507.
1969 "Consanguineous Marriages and Calculation of the Genetic Load," *Annals of Human Genetics* (London) 32:407–10.

ROBERTS, D. F. AND R. W. HIORNS
1962 "The Dynamics of Racial Intermixture," *American Journal of Human Genetics* 14:261–77.
1965 "Methods of Analysis of the Genetic Composition of a Hybrid Population," *Human Biology* 37:38–43.

ROBERTSON, A.
1965 "The Interpretation of Genotypic Ratios in Domestic Animal Populations," *Animal Products* 7:319–24.

ROBINSON, J. C., C. LEVENE, B. S. BLUMBERG, AND J. E. PIERCE
1967 "Serum Alkaline Phosphatase Types in North American Indians and Negroes," *Journal of Medical Genetics* 4:96–101.

ROGERS, E. M.
1969 "Computer Simulation of Innovation Diffusion in a Peasant Village," in *Modernization Among Peasants*, ed. E. M. Rogers (New York: Holt, Rinehart & Winston), pp. 343–59.

ROHLF, F. J. AND G. D. SCHNELL
1971 "An Investigation of the Isolation by Distance Model," *American Naturalist* 105:295–324.

References

ROISENBERG, I. AND N. E. MORTON
1970 "Population Structure of Blood Groups in Central and South American Indians," *American Journal of Physical Anthropology* 32:373–76.

ROSE, F. G. G.
1960 *Classification of Kin, Age Structure and Marriage Amongst the Groote Eylandt Aborigines: A Study in Method and a Theory of Australian Kinship* (Berlin: Akademie-Verlag).
1968 "Australian Marriage, Land-owning Groups and Initiations," in *Man the Hunter*, ed. R. Lee and I. Devore (Chicago: Aldine), pp. 200–208.

ROWE, D. S., I. A. MCGREGOR, S. J. SMITH, P. HALL, AND K. WILLIAMS
1968 "Plasma Immunoglobulin Concentrations in a West African (Gambian) Community and in a Group of Healthy British Adults," *Clinical Experimental Immunology* 3:63–79.

SA, N.
1962 "Frequencies of the Genes in the Rh-System in Portugal," *Vox Sanguinous* 7:502–3.

SAHLINS, M. D.
1960 "Evolution: Specific and General," in *Evolution and Culture*, ed. M. D. Sahlins and E. R. Service (Ann Arbor: the University of Michigan Press), pp. 12–44.

SALDANHA, P. H.
1957 "Gene Flow from White into Negro Populations in Brazil," *American Journal of Human Genetics* 9:299–309.
1960 "Frequencies of Consanguineous Marriages in Northeast of São Paulo, Brazil," *Acta Genetica et Statistica Medica* (Basel) 10:71–88.
1962 "Race Mixture Among Northeastern Brazilian Populations," *American Anthropologist* 64:751–59.
1968 "Race Admixture in Chile," *Current Anthropology* 9:455–58.

SALZANO, F. M.
1963 "Blood Groups and Gene Flow in Negroes from Southern Brazil," *Acta Genetica et Statistica Medica* (Basel) 13:9–20.
1968 "Intra- and Inter-Tribal Genetic Variability in South American Indians," *American Journal of Physical Anthropology* 28:183–90.
1970 "Genetic Aspects of the Demography of American Indians and Eskimos," paper, Burg Martenstein Symposium, Number 50, *Demography and Social Structure of Human Populations* (New York: Wenner-Gren).

SALZANO, F. M., F. J. DAROCHA, AND C. V. TONDO
1968 "Hemoglobin Types and Gene Flow in Pôrto Alegre, Brazil," *Acta Genetica et Statistica Medica* (Basel) 18:449–557.

SALZANO, F. M. AND N. FREIRE-MAIA
1970 *Problems in Human Biology. A Study of Brazilian Populations* (Detroit: Wayne State University Press).

SALZANO, F. M. AND J. HIRSCHFELD
1965 "The Dynamics of the Gc Polymorphism in a Brazilian Population," *Acta Genetica et Statistica Medica* (Basel) 15:116–25.

SALZANO, F. M., J. V. NEEL, AND D. MAYBURY-LEWIS
1967 "Further Studies on the Xavante Indians. I. Demographic Data on Two Additional Villages: Genetic Structure of the Tribe," *American Journal of Human Genetics* 19:463–89.

SALZANO, F. M., M. V. SUNE, AND M. FERLAUTO
1967 "New Studies on the Relationship Between Blood Groups and Leprosy," *Acta Genetica et Statistica Medica* (Basel) 17:530–44.

SANGHVI, L. D.
1953 "Comparison of Genetical and Morphological Methods for a Study of Biological Differences," *American Journal of Physical Anthropology* 11:385–404.
1966 "Inbreeding in India," *Eugenics Quarterly* 13:291–301.

SANGHVI, L. D., R. L. KIRK, AND V. BALAKRISHNAN
1971 "Genetic Distances Among Some Populations of Australian Aborigines," *Human Biology* 43:445–58.

SANGHVI, L. D., D. S. VARDE, AND H. R. MASTER
1956 "Frequency of Consanguineous Marriages in Twelve Endogamous Groups in Bombay," *Acta Genetica et Statistica Medica* (Basel) 6:41–49.

SARFERT, E.
1919 *Kusae, Ergebnissen der Sudsee-Expedition, 1908–1910*, ed. G. Thilenius (Hamburg: Friederichsen de Gruyter), II, B, 4:222.

SARICH, V. M. AND A. C. WILSON
1967 "Immunological Time Scale for Hominid Evolution," *Science* 158:1200–1203.

SCARR-SALAPATEK, S.
1971 "Race, Social Class, and IQ," *Science* (December 1971):1223–28.

SCHANFIELD, M. S.
1971 "Population Studies on the Gm and Inv Antigens in Asia and Oceania" (Ph.D. dissertation, University of Michigan).

SCHNEIDER, D. M.
1962 "Double Descent on Yap," *Journal of Polynesian Sociology* 71:1–24.

SCHORK, M. A.
1964 "The Effects of Inbreeding on Growth," *American Journal of Human Genetics* 16(3):292–300.

SCHREIDER, E.
1967 "Body-Height and Inbreeding in France," *American Journal of Physical Anthropology* 26:1–4.

SCHULL, W. J.
1958 "Empirical Risks in Consanguineous Marriages: Sex Ratio, Malformation, and Viability," *American Journal of Human Genetics* 10(3):294–343.
1966 "Some Considerations in the Design of Genetic Surveys," in *The Biology of Human Adaptability*, ed. P. T. Baker and S. J. Weiner (Oxford: Clarendon Press), pp. 25–43.
1969 "Discussion of Monte Carlo Simulation," in *Computer Applications in Genetics*, ed. N. E. Morton (Honolulu: University of Hawaii Press), p. 47.

SCHULL, W. J. AND B. R. LEVIN
1964 "Monte Carlo Simulation: Some Uses in the Genetic Study of Primitive Man," in *Stochastic Models in Medicine and Biology*, ed. J. Gurland (Madison: University of Wisconsin Press), pp. 179–96.

SCHULL, W. J. AND J. W. MACCLUER
1968 "IX. Inbreeding in Human Populations, with Special Reference to Takushima, Japan," *Haldane and Modern Biology*, ed. K. R. Dronamraju (Baltimore: Johns Hopkins Press), pp. 79–98.

References

SCHULL, W. J., H. NAGANO, M. YAMAMOTO, AND I. KOMATSU
1970a "The Effects of Parental Consanguinity and Inbreeding in Hirado, Japan. I. Stillbirths and Prereproductive Mortality," *American Journal of Human Genetics* 22(3):239–62.
1970b "The Effects of Parental Consanguinity and Inbreeding in Hirado, Japan. IV. Fertility and Reproductive Compensation," *Humangenetik* 9:294–315.

SCHULL, W. J. AND J. V. NEEL
1962 "The Effect of Inbreeding on Mortality in Japan," *Acta Genetica Medicae et Gemellologiae* 11(3):292–302.
1963 "Sex Linkage, Inbreeding, and Growth in Childhood," *American Journal of Human Genetics* 15(1):106–14.
1965 *The Effects of Inbreeding on Japanese Children* (New York: Harper & Row).
1966 "Some Further Observations on the Effect of Inbreeding on Mortality in Kure, Japan," *American Journal of Human Genetics* 18(2):144–52.

SCHULL, W. J., T. YANASE, AND H. NEMOTO
1962 "Kuroshima: The Impact on an Island's Genetic Heritage," *Human Biology* 34:271–98.

SCHWARTES, A. R., F. M. SALZANO, I. V. DECASTRO, AND C. V. TONDO
1967 "Haptoglobins and Leprosy," *Acta Genetica et Statistica Medica* (Basel) 17:127–36.

SEEMÁNOVÁ, E.
1971 "A Study of Children of Incestuous Mating," *Human Heredity* 21:108–28.

SERVICE, E. R.
1962 *Primitive Social Organization; An Evolutionary Perspective* (New York: Random House).

SHAPIRO, H. L.
1929 "Descendants of the Mutineers of the Bounty" (Honolulu: Bishop Museum).
1939 *Migration and Environment* (New York: Oxford University Press).

SHEPS, M. C.
1964 "On the Time Required for Conception," *Population Studies* 1:85–97.
1965 "An Analysis of Reproductive Patterns in an American Isolate," *Population Studies* 19(1):65–80.

SHEPS, M. C. AND E. B. PERRIN
1966 "Further Results from a Human Fertility Model with a Variety of Pregnancy Outcomes," *Human Biology* 38:180–93.

SHEPS, M. C. AND J. C. RIDLEY
1965 "Studying Determinants of Natality. Quantitative Estimation Through a Simulation Model," United Nations World Population Conference, Belgrade, Yugoslavia, August–September 1965.

SIEVERT, R. M.
1957 "Exposure of Man to Ionizing Radiations, with Special Reference to Possible Genetic Hazards," in *Effect of Radiation on Human Heredity* (Geneva: World Health Organization), pp. 63–85.

SILBERBAUER, G. B.
1965 *Bushman Survey Report* (Republic of Botswana: Bechuanaland Government Printer, Gaberones).

SIMMONS, R. T., J. J. GRAYDON, P. C. GAJDUSEK, AND P. BROWN
1965a "Blood Group Genetic Variations in Natives of the Caroline Islands and in Other Parts of Micronesia," *Oceania* 36:132–54.

SIMMONS, R. T., J. J. GRAYDON, P. C. GAJDUSEK, F. D. SCHOFIELD, AND A. D. PARKINSON
1965b "Blood Group Genetic Data from the Maprik Area of the Sepik District, New Guinea," *Oceania* 35:218–32.

SIMMONS, R. T., J. J. GRAYDON, AND N. B. TINDALE
1964 "Further Blood Group Genetical Studies of Australian Aborigines of Bentinck, Mornington and Forsyth Islands and the Mainland Gulf of Carpentaria, Together with Frequencies for Natives of the Western Desert, Western Australia," *Oceania* 35:66–80.

SIMMONS, R. T., N. B. TINDALE, AND J. B. BIRDSELL
1962 "A Blood Group Genetical Survey in Australian Aborigines of Bentinck, Mornington and Forsyth Islands, Gulf of Carpentaria," *American Journal of Physical Anthropology* 20:303–20.

SING, C. F. AND D. SHREFFLER
1970 "Evidence for Intergenic Interaction Between Blood and Serum Factors and the ABO System in Man" (abstract), *American Journal of Human Genetics* 22(6):27a–28a.

SINISCALCO, M., L. BERNINI, G. FILIPPI, B. LATTE, P. MEERA KHAN, S. PIOMELLI, AND M. RATTAZZI
1966 "Population Genetics of Haemoglobin Variants, Thalassaemia and Glucose-6-Phosphate Dehydrogenase Deficiency, with Particular Reference to the Malaria Hypothesis," *Bulletin of the World Health Organization* 34:379–93.

SINNETT, P., N. M. BLAKE, R. L. KIRK, L. Y. C. LAI, AND R. J. WALSH
1970 "Blood, Serum Protein and Enzyme Groups Among Enga-Speaking People of the Western Highlands, New Guinea, with an Estimate of Genetic Distances Between Clans," *Archaeology and Physical Anthropology in Oceania* 5(3): 236–52.

SKOLNICK, M. H. AND C. CANNINGS
1972 "The Natural Regulation of Numbers in Primitive Human Populations" (in press).

SLOAN, N. R., R. M. WORTH, B. JANO, P. FASAL, AND C. C. SHEPARD
1972 "Acedapsone in Leprosy Treatment: Trial in 68 Active Cases in Micronesia," *International Journal of Leprosy* 40:48–52.

SMITH, C. A. B.
1969 "Local Fluctuations in Gene Frequencies," *Annals of Human Genetics* (London) 32:251–60.

SMITH, T.
1960 "The Cocos-Keeling Island: A Demographic Laboratory," *Population Studies* 14:94–130.

SMITH, T. L. AND A. MARCHANT
1951 *Brazil—Portrait of Half a Continent* (New York: Dryden Press).

SOKAL, R. R. AND P. H. A. SNEATH
1963 *Principles of Numerical Taxonomy* (San Francisco: W. H. Freeman).

References

SPUHLER, J. N.
1954 "Some Problems in the Physical Anthropology of the American Southwest," *American Anthropologist* 56:604–19.
1956 "Estimation of Mutation Rates in Man," *Clinical Orthopaedics* 8:34–43.
1959 "Somatic Paths to Culture," in *The Evolution of Man's Capacity for Culture*, ed. J. N. Spuhler (Detroit: Wayne State University Press), pp. 1–13.
1962 "Empirical Studies on Quantitative Human Genetics," in *Proceedings of the United Nations/World Health Organization Seminar on the Use of Vital and Health Statistics for Genetic and Radiation Studies*, pp. 241–52.
1963 "The Scope for Natural Selection in Man," in *Genetic Selection in Man*, ed. W. J. Schull (Ann Arbor: University of Michigan Press), pp. 1–111.

SPUHLER, J. N. AND P. J. CLARK
1961 "Migration into the Human Breeding Population of Ann Arbor, Michigan, 1900–1950," *Human Biology* 33:223–36.

SPUHLER, J. N. AND C. KLUCKHOHN
1953 "Inbreeding Coefficients of the Ramah Navajo Population," *Human Biology* 25:295–317.

STEINBERG, A. G., H. K. BLEIBTREU, T. W. KURCZYNSKI, A. O. MARTIN, AND E. M. KURCZYNSKI
1967 "Genetic Studies on an Inbred Human Isolate," ed. J. F. Crow and J. V. Neel, *Proceedings of the Third International Congress of Human Genetics*, pp. 267–89.

STEINBERG, A. G. AND N. E. MORTON
1972 "Immunoglobulins in the Eastern Carolines" (in preparation).

STEVENS, P. M., V. S. HNLICA, P. C. JOHNSON, AND R. L. BELL
1971 "Pathophysiology of Heredity Emphysema," *Annals of Internal Medicine* 74:672–80.

STRONG, W. D.
1929 "Cross-Cousin Marriage and the Culture of the Northeast Algonkian," *American Anthropologist* 31:777–88.

STROUHAL, E.
1971 "Anthropometric and Functional Evidence of Heterosis from Egyptian Nubia," *Human Biology* 43(2):271–87.

SUTTER, J.
1967 "Interprétation Démographique de la Fréquence des Groupes Sanguins chez les Wayana et les Emerillond de la Guyane," *Population* 22:709–34.

SUTTER, J. AND L. TABAH
1955a "L'Evolution des Isolates de deux Départements Français," *Population* 10:227–58.
1955b "L'Evolution des Isolates de deux Départements Français: Loir-et-Cher, Finistere," *Population* 10(4):645–74.
1956 "Méthode Mécanographique pour Établir la Généalogie d'une Population. Application à l'Étude des Esquimaux Polaires," *Population* 11:507–30.

SUTTON, H. E. AND G. W. KARP, JR.
1964 "Variations in Heterozygous Expression at the Haptoglobin Locus," *American Journal of Human Genetics* 16:419–34.

SUTTON, H. E., J. V. NEEL, F. B. LIVINGSTONE, G. BINSON, P. KUN-
STADTER, AND L. E. TROMBLEY
1959   "The Frequencies of Haptoglobin Types in Five Populations," *Annals of Human Genetics* (London) 23:175–83.

SVED, J. A.
1968   "The Stability of Linked Systems of Loci with a Small Population Size," *Genetics* 59:543–63.

SWEDLUND, A. C.
1971   "The Genetical Structure of an Historical Population: A Study of Marriage and Fertility in Old Deerfield, Massachusetts," Research Report No. 7, Department of Anthropology, University of Massachusetts, Amherst.

SWINDLER, D. R.
1955   "The Absence of the Sickle-Cell Gene in Several Melanesian Societies and Its Anthropological Significance," *Human Biology* 27:284–93.

SZALAY, F. S.
1968   "The Beginning of Primates," *Evolution* 22:19–36.

TALAMO, R. C.
1971   "The Apha$_1$-Antitrypsin in Man," *Journal of Allergy and Clinical Immunology* 48(4):240–50.

TAMBIAH, S. J.
1958   "The Structure of Kinship and Its Relationship to Land Possession and Residence in Pata Dumbara, Central Ceylon," *Journal of the Royal Anthropological Institute*, 88, Part I, pp. 21–44.

TATSUOKA, M.
1971   *Multivariate Analysis* (New York: Wiley & Sons).

TEITELBAUM, M. S.
1970   "Factors Affecting the Sex Ratio in Large Populations," *Journal of Biosocial Science*, Supplement 2:61–71.

THODAY, J. M.
1969   "Limitations to Genetic Comparison of Populations," *Journal of Biosocial Science*, Supplement 1:3914.

THOMA, A.
1969   "Analyse de la Différenciation en France des Fréquences Géniques *pA, qB,* et *rO,*" *Biométrie Humaine* 4:1–12.
1970   "Selective Differentiation of the ABO Blood Group Gene Frequencies in Europe," *Human Biology* 42:450–68.

TILDESLEY, M. L.
1921   "A First Study of the Burmese Skull," *Biometrika* 13:176–262.

TONDO, C. V., C. MUNDT, AND F. M. SALZANO
1963   "Haptoglobin Types in Brazilian Negroes," *Annals of Human Genetics* (London) 26:325–31.
1968   "Assortative Mating with Respect to Physical Characteristics," *Eugenics Quarterly* 15:128–40.
1973   "The Maximum Opportunity for Natural Selection in Some Human Populations," paper presented at the School of American Research Advanced Seminar "Demography and Anthropological Research" (Santa Fe).

494

References

TONDO, C. V. AND F. M. SALZANO
1962 "Abnormal Hemoglobins in a Brazilian Negro Population," *American Journal of Human Genetics* 14:401–9.

TORRINHA, J. A. F.
1967 "Haptoglobin Frequencies in the North of Portugal," *Acta Genetica et Statistica Medica* (Basel) 17:74–76.

TREVOR, J. C.
1953 "Race Crossing in Man," *Eugenics Laboratory Memoirs, 36, from the Galton Laboratory, University College, London* (London: Cambridge University Press).

TWISSELMANN, F.
1961 "De l'Evolution du Taux Consanguinité en Belgique entre les Années 1918 et 1959," *Proceedings of the Second International Congress of Human Genetics* (Rome: Instituto G. Mendel) 1:142–50.

TYLER, S. A. (ED.)
1969 *Cognitive Anthropology* (New York: Holt, Rinehart and Winston).

UNITED NATIONS
1955 "Age and Sex Patterns of Mortality, Model Life Tables for Underdeveloped Countries," ST/SOA/Series A, Population Studies No. 22.

VAN DE WALLE, E. AND J. KNODEL
1970 "Teaching Population Dynamics with a Simulation Exercise," *Demography* 7:433–48.

VAN GENNEP
1906 *Mythes et Légendes d'Australie* (Paris).

VEEH, H. H. AND J. CHAPPELL
1970 "Astronomical Theory of Climatic Change: Support from New Guinea," *Science* 167:862–65.

VOGEL, F. AND R. CHAKRAVARTIIM
1966 "ABO Blood Groups and Smallpox in a Rural Population of West Bengal and Bihar, India," *Humangenetik* 3:160–80.

WAGNER, K.
1937 "The Craniology of Oceanic Races," Skrifter Utgitt av det Norske Videnskaps-Akademi i Oslo I. Mat.—Naturv. Klasse, No. 2.

WAHLUND, V. S.
1928 "Zusammensetzung von Populationen und Korrelationserscheinungen vom Standpunkt der Vererbungslehre aus Betrachtet," *Hereditas* 11:65–106.

WALTER, H. AND J. NEMESKÉRI
1967 "Demographical and Sero Genetical Studies on the Population of Bodroghöz (Northeast Hungary)," *Human Biology* 39:224–40.

WANG, A. C., H. E. SUTTON, AND I. D. SCOTT
1967 "Transferrin D_1: Identity in Australian Aborigines and American Negroes," *Science* 156(3777):936, May.

WARD, R. H.
1970 "Microdifferentiation and Genetic Relationships of Yanomama Villages" (Ph.D. dissertation, University of Michigan).

495

1972 "The Genetic Structure of a Tribal Population, the Yanomama Indians. V. Comparison of a Series of Networks," *Annals of Human Genetics* (London) 36:21–44.

WARD, R. H. AND J. V. NEEL

1970a "A Comparison of a Genetic Network with Ethnohistory and Migration Matrices, a New Index of Genetic Isolation," *American Journal of Human Genetics* 22:562–73.

1970b "Gene Frequencies and Microdifferentiation Among the Makiritare Indians. IV. A Comparison of a Genetic Network with Ethnohistory and Migration Matrices; a New Index of Genetic Isolation," *American Journal of Human Genetics* 22(5):538–61.

WARNER, W. L.

1937 *A Black Civilization* (New York: Harper & Row).

WATT, K. E. F.

1968 *Ecology and Resource Management* (New York: McGraw-Hill).

WECKLER, J. E.

1949 "Land and Livelihood on Mokil. An Atoll in the Eastern Carolines," *Coordinated Investigation of Micronesian Anthropology*, Part I, Report No. 25, 69 (Los Angeles: University of Southern California) (unpublished).

WHITE, C.

1967 "Early Stone Axes in Arnhem Land," *Antiquity* 41:149—52.

WHITE, H. C.

1963 *An Anatomy of Kinship: Mathematical Models for Structures of Cumulated Roles* (Englewood Cliffs, New Jersey: Prentice Hall).

WHITE, J. P., K. A. W. CROOK, AND B. P. RUXTON

1970 "Kosipe: A Late Pleistocene Site in the Papuan Highlands," *Proceedings of the Prehistoric Society* 36:152–70.

WIERCINSKI, A.

1962 "The Racial Analysis of Human Populations in Relation to Their Ethnogenesis," *Current Anthropology* 3:9–10.

WIESENFELD, S. L.

1967 "Sickle-Cell Trait in Human Biological and Cultural Evolution," *Science* 157:1134–40.

WILLIAMS, B. J.

1965 "A Model of Hunting-Gathering Society and Some Genetic Consequences" (Ph.D. dissertation, University of Michigan).

WILSON, A. C. AND V. M. SARICH

1969 "A Molecular Time Scale for Human Evolution," *Proceedings of the National Academy of Science* 63:1088–93.

WISHART, D.

1969 "Mode Analysis: A Generalization of Nearest Neighbor Which Reduces Chaining Effects," in *Numerical Taxonomy*, ed. A. J. Coale (London: Academic Press), pp. 282–311.

WITKOP, C. J., JR., C. J. MACLEAN, P. J. SCHMIDT, AND J. L. HENRY

1966 "Medical and Dental Findings in the Brandywine Isolate," *Alabama Journal of Medical Science* 3:382–403.

496

References

WITKOP, C. J., JR., C. H. SHANKLE, J. B. GRAHAM, M. R. MURRAY, D. L. RUCKNAGEL, AND B. H. BYERLY
1960 "Hereditary Benign Intraepithelial Dyskeratosis," *Archaeological Pathology* 70: 696–711.

WOOLF, C. M., F. E. STEPHENS, D. D. MULAIK, AND R. E. GILBERT
1955 "An Investigation of the Frequency of Consanguineous Marriages Among the Mormons and Their Relatives in the United States," *American Journal of Human Genetics* 8(4):236–52.

WORKMAN, P. L.
1968 "Gene Flow and the Search for Natural Selection in Man," *Human Biology* 40:260–79.
1969 "The Analysis of Simple Genetic Polymorphisms," *Human Biology* 41:97–114.

WORKMAN, P. L., B. S. BLUMBERG, AND A. J. COOPER
1963 "Selection, Gene Migration and Polymorphic Stability in a United States White and Negro Population," *American Journal of Human Genetics* 15:429–37.

WORKMAN, P. L. AND J. D. NISWANDER
1970 "Population Studies on Southwestern Indian Tribes. II. Local Genetic Differentiation in the Papago," *American Journal of Human Genetics* 22:24–49.

WRIGHT, S.
1921 "Systems of Mating," *Genetics* 6:111–78.
1922 "Coefficients of Inbreeding and Relationships," *American Naturalist* 56:330–38.
1931 "Evolution in Mendelian Populations," *Genetics* 16:97–159.
1943 "Isolation by Distance," *Genetics* 28:114–38.
1946 "Isolation by Distance Under Diverse Systems of Mating," *Genetics* 31:39–59.
1950 "Discussion on Population Genetics and Radiation," *Journal of Cellular and Comparative Physiology* 35:187–210.
1951 "The Genetic Structure of Populations," *Annals of Eugenics* 15:323–54.
1955 "Classification of the Factors of Evolution," *Cold Spring Harbor Symposia on Quantitative Biology* 20:16–24.
1965 "The Interpretation of Population Structure by F Statistics with Special Regard to Systems of Mating," *Evolution* 19(3):395–420.
1968 *Evolution and the Genetics of Populations. Vol. 1. Genetic and Biometric Foundations* (Chicago: University of Chicago Press).
1969 *Evolution and the Genetics of Populations. Vol. 2. The Theory of Gene Frequencies* (Chicago: University of Chicago Press).

WYBER, S.
1970 "Population Structure in New Guinea" (abstract), *American Journal of Human Genetics* 22(6):29a–30a.

YAMAGUCHI, B.
1967 "A Comparative Osteological Study of the Ainu and the Australian Aborigines," *Australian Institute of Aboriginal Studies, Occasional Papers No. 10, Human Biology Series No. 2*, Canberra.

YAMAGUCHI, M., T. YANASE, H. NAGANO, AND N. NAKAMOTO
1970 "Effects of Inbreeding on Mortality in Fukuoka Population," *American Journal of Human Genetics* 22(2):145–59.

YASUDA, N.

1968a "Estimation of the Inbreeding Coefficient from Phenotype Frequencies by a Method of Maximum Likelihood Scoring," *Biometrics* 24(4):915–35.

1968b "An Extension of Wahlund's Principle to Evaluate Mating Type Frequency," *American Journal of Human Genetics* 20:1–23.

1969a "Estimation of the Inbreeding Coefficient from Mating Type Frequency and Gene Frequency," in *Computer Applications in Genetics*, ed. N. E. Morton (Honolulu: University of Hawaii Press), pp. 87–96.

1969b "The Inbreeding Coefficient in Northeastern Brazil," *Human Heredity* 19: 444–56.

YASUDA, N. AND N. E. MORTON

1967 "Studies on Human Population Structure," *Proceedings of the Third International Congress of Human Genetics*, ed. J. F. Crow and J. V. Neel (Baltimore: Johns Hopkins Press), pp. 249–65.

YELLEN, J.

1971 Paper presented at the Meetings of the American Anthropological Association, New York.

YOUNG, R. W.

1961 *The Navajo Yearbook*, Report No. 8, 1959–1961 (Window Rock, Arizona: Navajo Agency).

1968 "The Role of the Navajo in the Southwestern Drama," *Gallup Independent*, Souvenir Edition, 31 May 1968.

ZAHÁLKOVÁ, M. AND A. PREIS

1970 "Consanguineous Marriages in the Diocesis of Brno, Czechoslovakia. I. Frequency and Coefficient of Inbreeding," *Humangenetik* 8:321–24.

ZELLNER, A.

1965 "Estimation of Parameters in Simulation Models of Social Systems," in *Computer Methods in the Analysis of Large-Scale Social Systems*, ed. J. M. Beshers (Cambridge, Massachusetts: M.I.T.-Harvard Joint Center for Urban Studies), pp. 137–57.

ZERRIES, O.

1964 *Waika. Die Kulturgeschichtliche Stallung der Waika-Indianer des Oberen Orinoco in Rahmen der Völkerkunde Sunamerikas*. Band I. Ergebnisse der Frobenius-Expedition 1954/1955 nach Südost-Venezuela (Munich).

ZUBROW, E. B. W.

1971a "Adequacy Criteria and Prediction in Archaeological Models," paper presented at the Meetings of the American Anthropological Association, New York.

1971b "Carrying Capacity and Dynamic Equilibrium in the Prehistoric Southwest," *American Antiquity* 36:127–38.

1971c "A Southwestern Test of Anthropological Model of Population Dynamics" (Ph.D. dissertation, University of Arizona).

Index

Abbie, A. A., 391
ABO blood grouping, 19, 32, 36, 125,
    166–67, 238, 244, 355, 393–94,
    438, 442
  first use of, in anthropological
    studies, 424
  See also Blood; Blood group varia-
    tion
Aborigines, 47–48
Adams, M. S., 113
Adaptation, genetic, 403–22
Adolfsson, I., 233–34
Age structure, 240–41
Agriculture, effects on gene flow, 440
Albers, M. E., 201, 240, 426, 444
Alcaptonuria, 424
Alleles, plotting of, 188–89
Allen, G., 44, 97
Allison, A. C., 33, 80, 144, 408
Amino acid analysis, 22
American Naturalist, 85
Ammann, F., 75
Anderson, W. W., 241–42
L'Anthropologie (Topinard), 424
Anthropometrics, 173, 353–54, 363,
    364, 397–99
Arends, T., 28, 74, 311, 372, 374, 391
Armstrong, A. R., 420
Arvello-Jimenez, N., 371, 376
Autozygosity, 87, 88, 97, 100
Azevêdo, E., 178, 343, 360

Bailitt, H. L., 397
Bajema, C. J., 420
Balakrishnan, V., 23, 179, 373
Barker, W., 420
Barnett, C. R., 290, 294, 295

Barnicot, N. A., 2, 37, 57, 167
Barrai, I., 38, 57, 79, 102, 108, 112,
    165, 437
Barrett, J. C., 235
Baumgarten, A., 394
Bayless, T., 411
Beale, C. L., 126
Beardsley, R. K., 62
Bearn, A. G., 145
Becher, H., 371
Becke, L., 330
Beckman, L., 34, 60, 65
Benerecetti, S. A. S., 37
Benoist, J., 67, 73, 79, 80, 155, 426
Bentzen, C., 316, 326, 332, 336
Bernstein, F., 32, 120
Berry, B., 126
Bertalanffy, L. Von, 204
Beshers, J. M., 247
Beutler, E., 413
Bhattacharyya, A., 373
Bielicki, T., 31
Billewicz, W. Z., 3
Bioassay, 84, 98, 101, 334–35, 336,
    344, 350, 354–55, 356, 364
Biological distance, 159–60, 398
Biology, 247
Birdsell, J. B., 118, 155, 251, 395
Birth control, 234, 437
Bishop, A. J., 57, 58
Blacks. *See* Negroes
Blake, J., 254
Blood
  in study of evolution, 19–38
  storage of, 22–23
  See also ABO blood grouping
Blood group variation, 44, 65

499

Index

Index

Food, 410–13
Foulks, E., 404
Founder effect, 60
"Four Achievements of the Genetical
   Method in Physical Anthropology"
   (Boyd), 176
Fraccaro, M., 437
Franklin, I., 225
Fraser, A. S., 209, 225
Fraser, G. R., 60
Freire-Maia, N., 98, 99, 128
Friedenberg, R. M., 203, 204
Friedlaender, J. S., 64, 164, 172–73, 175,
   178, 194, 344, 360, 394, 395, 396,
   397
Frota-Pessoa, O., 75
Fudenberg, H., 4
FZD marriages, 230
   See also Cousin marriages

G6PD locus, 49–66, 144–45, 394
Gajdusek, D. C., 62, 117, 333, 395
Garlick, J. P., 2
Garn, S. M., 30
Garrod, A. E., 424
Gene, Mendelian concept of, 42
Gene flow, 117–50, 238, 242–45, 433,
   439, 440, 449
Gene frequency, 2, 3, 7, 11, 12, 16, 29,
   39–66, 108, 156, 241, 345, 348–49,
   355, 387, 394–95, 426, 427, 445,
   446, 449
   as evolutionary process, 432–42
   first use of concept, 424
   hybrid populations and, 117–50
   nonrandom mating and, 430
   effects of selection on, 435–36
   See also Genetic distance
Gene pools, 426
   defined, 427
Genealogy, 343–45, 352, 363
Genetic distance, 132, 151–57, 159–60,
   177–79, 372, 373–74, 375, 376,
   387, 444–47
Genetic drift, 29, 44, 45, 46, 60, 69, 78,
   79–80, 117, 122, 140, 142, 178,
   179, 180, 215, 242–45, 345, 349,
   353, 363, 374, 375, 395, 409, 432,
   433, 440, 441–42, 444
Genetic equilibrium, 104–5
Genetic load, 69
Genetic maps, 444–47
Genetic markers, 19–38

Genetic Theory of Natural Selection
   (Fisher), 424
Genetic topology, 355–57
Genetic trees, 444–47
Genetic variation, 2, 24–29, 39–40, 44,
   45, 57–66
   See also Gene frequency; Hybrid
      populations
Genetics
   demographic, 202–3. *See also*
      Demography
   historical, 345, 350, 363
   Mendelian, 423
Genetics and the Origin of Species
   (Dobzhansky), 425
Genetics and the Races of Man (Boyd),
   423
Genotype frequency, 102–4, 178, 435–36
Geographic distance, 57–66
Gershowitz, H., 23, 24, 28
Giblett, E. R., 25, 145
Giesel, J. T., 244
Gilbert, J. P., 226
Gilbert, W. H., Jr., 126
Giles, E., 64, 65, 72, 79, 155, 164, 166,
   171, 172, 175, 389, 394, 395, 397,
   398, 399, 400, 429, 445
Gladwin, T., 336
Glass, B., 32, 71, 79, 99, 124, 127, 133,
   134, 135, 144, 155, 440
Glycerol, citrated, in blood storage, 23
Gomila, J., 72, 76, 77, 80
Goodall, D. W., 205
Goodenough, W. H., 317, 333
Goodman, M., 152, 153, 154
Graydon, J. J., 36, 155
Greene, D. L., 354
Greene, L., 413
Griffith, C., 311
Gullahorn, J. E., 246
Gullahorn, J. T., 246
Guyon, L., 76, 77
Gypsies, 31, 443

Haddon, A. C., 33
Hägerstrand, T., 245
Hainline, J., 135, 244, 333, 355
Hajnal, J., 102, 230
Halberstein, R. A., 155
Haldane, J. B. S., 42, 46, 85, 118, 424,
   438, 447
Hall, J. W., 62
Hallowell, A. I., 101
Hammel, E. A., 62, 226

502

Index

Murphy, T. W., 393
Mutation, 43, 44, 46, 105, 117, 204, 238, 334, 348, 349, 353, 432, 433–35, 439, 449
MZD marriages, 230
 See also Cousin marriages

Nagel, R., 121, 123
Nahua Indians, 33
Natural selection. See Selection
Navajo Indians. See Ramah Navajo Indians
Naylor, T. H., 222, 247
Needham, R., 62
Neel, J. V., 2, 3, 24, 25, 48, 74, 80, 99, 101, 108, 109, 113, 163–64, 165, 166, 167, 172, 179, 203, 230, 237, 242, 243, 260, 285–86, 302, 308, 309, 310, 311, 312, 344, 370, 371, 373, 376, 384, 386, 387, 388, 431, 450
Negri, M., 37
Negritos, 34–35
Negroes, 121, 123–25, 127–31, 133–34, 142–46, 417–20
Nei, M., 44, 65, 80
Nemeskéri, J., 68, 72, 75, 99
Nemoto, H., 171
Neuere Probleme der Abstammungslehre (Rensch), 425
Newcombe, H. B., 114
Niswander, J. D., 26, 28, 44, 60, 112, 161, 164, 171, 175, 176, 178
Nitrogen, liquid, in blood storage, 22–23
Nuer population, 137–40
Nutrition, 410–13

Oceania, population analysis of, 389–401
Ogan, E., 394
Ohta, T., 43
Oliver, D. L., 370, 391, 398
On the Natural Variety of Mankind (Blumenbach), 424
Orcutt, G. H., 247
Ore, O., 375
Origin and Evolution of Man (Cold Spring Harbor Symposia on Quantitative Biology), 423
Osborne, R. H., 168, 170, 172
Oschinsky, L., 30
Osteological studies, 399–401
Ottensooser, F., 129

Outbreeding, 439
Owen, J. J. T., 2
Oxnard, C. E., 162

Panmictic model, 69
Papago Indians, 26, 44
Papua and New Guinea Medical Journal, 397
Parker, C. W., 145
Parsons, P. A., 118, 400
Partial deterministic/stochastic simulations, 207–8
 See also Simulations
Pathology, 69
Pearl, R., 85
Pearson, K., 161
Pearson's Coefficient of Racial Likeness, 399
Peart, H. E., 420
Pedigree studies, 84, 91–97, 101, 178
Pedigrees, 244, 343, 345
Penrose, L. S., 398, 438
Perrin, E. B., 207, 233, 235
Phenotype frequencies, 447
Phenotypes, 147
 inbreeding and, 105–12
PHYLON, 348
Pietrusewsky, M., 399, 400
Pingelap Atoll, 315–32, 333–66
Pollard, J. H., 228–29
Pollitzer, W. S., 121, 124, 126–27, 131, 132
Pollock, N., 333, 336, 339, 343, 352, 360
Pollution, human adaptation and, 413–16
Polman, A., 98
Polygyny, 5
Polymorphisms, 442–43
Polyploidy, 152–53
Population distance, 159–76
Population genetics, 2–3, 42, 46, 83, 201, 202–7, 369–70, 424–25
Population history, 46, 47–49
 See also Population genetics
Population size, 14, 118
Population structure, 447–51
Populations
 breeding, 42, 44, 45, 425–27
 hybrid, 117–50
 isolate, 67–81
Porter, I. H., 145
Potter, R. G., 235

Index